1966

Joseph Schwartz, Ph.D., University of Wisconsin, is Professor of English and Chairman of the department at Marquette University. He was Chairman of Freshman English at that institution and is a member of the National Council of Teachers of English. Professor Schwartz is co-author with John Rycenga of *Perspectives on Language* published by The Ronald Press Company.

John A. Rycenga, Ph.D., Northwestern University, is Associate Professor of English and Chairman of the department at Sacred Heart University in Connecticut. He previously taught at Wayne State University, Marquette University, and Northwestern University. A specialist in 18th and 19th Century English and Linguistics, Professor Rycenga is co-author with Joseph Schwartz of *Perspectives on Language* published by The Ronald Press Company.

THE PROVINCE
OF
RHETORIC

Edited by

JOSEPH SCHWARTZ

Marquette University

and

JOHN A. RYCENGA

Sacred Heart University

THE RONALD PRESS COMPANY • NEW YORK

Library of Congress Catalog Card Number: 65–12758

INTRODUCTION

The Province of Rhetoric has been edited in order to give substance
to our strong conviction that rhetoric is in and of itself an important
subject for study. If it is true as Allen Tate remarks in "Is Literary
Criticisms Possible?" that man is "by nature, or by the nature of his
language, a rhetorician," then no subject is of greater importance for
study than rhetoric. Tate goes on to say that the "true rationale of
humanistic study is . . . the arts of rhetoric." To many people, however, rhetoric continues to be an unpopular word, and we believe it
deserves to be used pejoratively so long as it is regarded as simply
pragmatic or as "semantically irresponsible." But when it is properly
understood as "the full language of experience" by which men "govern
their relations with one another in the light of truth," rhetoric assumes
an awesome dimension which can be frighteningly sobering. It must
not be allowed to remain "the dreariest and least profitable part of the
waste that the unfortunate travel through in Freshman English" that
I. A. Richards described over 25 years ago. Rhetoric is the most
liberal of the arts, and it deserves our primary, earnest attention.
Along with language itself and logic, it provides the key to everything
else that we learn. Rhetoric may justly be described as "the science of
recognizing the range of the meanings and of the functions of words,
and the art of using and interpreting them in accordance with their
recognition."

What we have said of rhetoric has, we believe, special relevance for
the twentieth century. Given the pluralistic society from which none
of us can escape, effective communication becomes a massively
crucial problem of our time—and the problems of communication
are inescapably the problems of rhetoric. We must understand what
we are talking about, what we are asserting, what we are proposing.
And we must understand, as well, how others are using language
when they talk, assert, and propose. We cannot discover the basic
elements of our own being, or the foundations of our society unless
we use and interpret words in context with care and accuracy.
Without such a skill, truths become ineffective because they remain
unexpressed. In short, without a proper understanding of the im-

portance of communication—which is simply rhetoric extended to its outermost boundaries—we cannot ourselves function effectively, nor can our society. Richard McKeon, philosopher, critic, and rhetorician, provides us with a memorable summation of the value of rhetoric:

> The art of deliberative rhetoric is not a technical or abstruse discipline. On the contrary, it is the instrument of democracy in so far as democracy is based on a conviction that the people are better qualified than any limited or select group to make decisions concerning truth as it affects them, concerning the values presented for contemplation and guidance, concerning their individual destinies, and concerning their common good. Men of one mind can build a society, a nation, and a world community. But to be of one mind is not to be of one opinion. Men are of one mind when they possess reason to judge statements of truth, understanding to appreciate statements of their own values and those of others, desires ordered under freedom, and love of the common good for which men are associated. When men are of one mind in these abilities they can be of different opinions without danger to a society or to each other.

If our first premise in editing this book has been philosophic, our second (and equally important) premise is a practical one. We believe that students will learn most easily and profitably if the basic material in any discipline is usefully organized for them. Hence, we have brought together in a single collection useful and authoritative essays about rhetoric. It should not be assumed, however, that the essays in this volume have been selected merely for the convenience of the casual reader. After a careful survey of the material published on rhetoric, we discovered that certain necessary categories emerged, and that these categories provided a way of organizing the knowledge essential to an intelligent study of rhetoric. After a thorough testing of our organization, we are satisfied that these categories reflect accurately the areas which have been of concern to the best scholars in the field. A detailed explanation of the book's form and content will make its rationale clearer and aid the instructor in the appropriate use of the text; such an explanation follows.

In Section I, "The Nature and Significance of Rhetoric," our principal object has been to define the nature of our subject. The approach by way of definition is appropriate pedagogically for any textbook, and since there may be a good deal of confusion on the user's part not only as to the nature of the subject, but also as to the relationship of rhetoric to the whole spectrum of the communication arts, it seemed especially desirable to begin with essays which described the discipline in large and general terms. Thus, the first essay, Bryant's "Rhetoric: Its Function and Scope," defines rhetoric and places it clearly in the larger context of the communication arts. We believe also that Bryant's article, because of its completeness, its historical content, and its professional competence, is an especially good opening essay for readers beginning a serious study of rhetoric. Duhamel, in "The Function of Rhetoric As Effective Expression," is also concerned with definition, but since rhetoric has a vast and important historical dimension, he goes beyond mere definition by providing, finally, a useful means of understanding the development of the subject. In "The Province of Rhetoric and Poetic," Ong clarifies a distinction essential for the student's thorough understanding of rhetoric; confusion between the terms "rhetoric" and "poetic" has been in some cases harmful even to the scholar. With the background provided by these three essays, the student can now turn profitably to Natanson's "The Limits of Rhetoric." After surveying earlier efforts, Natanson attempts to establish what a philosophy of rhetoric might be and what the relationship between philosophy and rhetoric (an old and much-debated relationship) can be. The difficulty of his task is evident if we remember that the philosophy of rhetoric (with some notable twentieth-century exceptions) has changed little since Aristotle.

Because rhetoric has such a distinguished place in the intellectual tradition of Western culture, Section II of the text, "The Development of Rhetorical Theory," is necessarily extensive. Further, it is in the area of the history of rhetoric that scholars have done their most fundamental and memorable work. Finally, a knowledge of the history of rhetoric is basic to an understanding of the communication process, a point well made by McKeon's remark that "an age usually characterizes itself effectively by the manner in which it poses basic problems and by the means which it employs in seeking solutions to them." Since the history of ancient rhetoric, after the Sophists, can be written in terms of outstanding figures, we have opened our second section with Hunt's survey essay on the Sophists and followed it by essays on Isocrates, Plato, Aristotle, Cicero, and Quintilian, rhetoricians certainly deserving of individual treatment. Though the essays themselves are clear as to the stature of the various classical theorists and practitioners, we call to the reader's attention the central importance of Aristotle, a fact perhaps already apparent from the essays in the first section of the text. Among the Christian rhetoricians, St. Augustine is pre-eminent, and we have included, for that reason, a perceptive essay upon him by C. S. Baldwin, dean of the earlier American writers on rhetoric. Following treatment of the individual figures, we have reprinted complex survey articles by McKeon and Crane, which bring to the reader's attention the major developments in medieval and Renaissance rhetoric. Surveys in both of these cases are adequate, because, with one exception, there was little genuine innovation, though much adaptation, during these periods. The one exception was Ramus; hence, Ong's definitive essay, "Ramist Rhetoric." It should be noted also that, after the Renaissance, British and American rhetoric becomes more prominent; hence, the essays by Crane, Guthrie, and Weaver, on Renaissance, eighteenth century, and nineteenth century rhetoric, reflect what should be the normal concern of the American student with the contributions of the English-speaking theorists. The concluding essay in this section, Howell's "Renaissance Rhetoric and Modern Rhetoric: A Study in Change," was chosen because it not only provides a review of the central intellectual tradition of rhetoric, but also shows how that central tradition has gradually been modified in the period since the Renaissance. The student is also introduced, by Howell's essay, to some of the problems that will be the concern of the third and fourth sections of the text.

In Section III, "Modern Developments in Rhetoric," we seek to bring the student to a realization of two facts: (a) that the vital part of traditional rhetoric still has great meaning for modern users of language, and (b) that new developments in rhetoric—some Aristotelian, some not—are bringing new vigor and excitement to contemporary rhetoric. The opening essay, Weaver's "The *Phaedrus* and the Nature of Rhetoric," attempts to demonstrate the Aristotelian dictum that rhetoric and dialectic should be collaborative, not opposing. Eubanks and Baker, in their "Toward an Axiology of Rhetoric," follow the implications of Weaver's approach by making a strong plea for a return to a concept of rhetoric which is unashamedly value-oriented. The modern developments in rhetoric which seem to reveal significant theoretical differences from the Aristotelian tradition (though not all are *anti*-Aristotelian) are those of I. A. Richards, Kenneth Burke, and the Semanticists. Each is represented by an expository essay, especially chosen for clarity, thoroughness, and appropriateness as an introductory treatment.

In Section IV, "The Uses of Rhetoric," the student is invited to contemplate the practical possibilities of the subject of which he should now have a reasonable theoretical command. This section is divided into two parts: "Some Advice" and "Some Samples." Since rhetoric is a tool, its uses must be carefully examined from a theoretical point of view—hence, the advice. Croft, in "The Functions of Rhetorical Criticism," tells us what this kind of criticism is, what it has been, and what it may be. Although Tuve's discussion is limited to the poetry of a certain period, her analysis is comprehensive enough to remind one that rhetoric is always perhaps involved in poetry. Booth is clear and stimulating in showing that the rhetoric of fiction cannot be ignored. Finally, Hughes and Duhamel discuss the uses of persuasion which result from discoveries and developments peculiar to our own time. The essays by Burke, Beaumont, Ashin, Holloway, and Sloan are easily accounted for. They are "samples" in the sense that each demonstrates how a significant writer (e.g., Donne or Swift) has used rhetorical techniques in moving and persuading his reader.

During the process of editing this book, we have become more and more aware of its unique character. To be sure, the text is not in any absolute sense unique; our bibliography lists a few titles which are collections of essays on specifically rhetorical topics; certainly the teacher of English and the teacher of Speech are besieged with anthologies which have the word "rhetoric" in their titles. But our book, we believe, belongs to neither of these categories; that is, it is not a textbook addressed solely to advanced students in rhetoric. Nor is it a collection of essays, arranged in terms of the rhetorical "modes of discourse," upon which beginners may model their own efforts in "composition." We think, indeed, that the text could be used profitably by classes ranging from beginning to graduate students. But the book should have several other uses as well. It represents, we hope, what Porter Perrin has called "a courageous shift of emphasis"; it is an attempt to bring into proper focus the whole discipline of rhetoric, and the relationship of rhetoric to such seemingly diverse areas of speech, composition, criticism, philosophy, "communication," teacher training, history, and classics. We hope that this book will appeal to scholars and students in each of the areas just named. Certainly, an acquaintance with the general rhetorical tradition has been urged repeatedly by scholars in these fields. Porter Perrin, for example, has written: "With more lore from the main rhetorical tradition there would be less excuse for dodging the central problems of composition; the work would have more inherent interest, could stand more nearly on its own feet, and would be more of college caliber." In his recent book on the teaching of English,

Themes, Theories and Therapy: The Teaching of Writing in College, Albert Kitzhaber recommends that "some provision should be made in these courses for explicit instruction in . . . principles of rhetoric." In the opening section of his authoritative *Art of Persuasion in Greece,* the classical scholar, George Kennedy, reminds us that "rhetoric played the central role in ancient education." Scholars in speech have, of course, always been aware of the importance of rhetoric, and they continue to urge that its systematic and thorough study now be merged with an awareness of new developments in the field; thus, Wayne Thompson has written recently:

> What the writer deplores, to conclude, is the tendency to pass rhetorical doctrine down from one generation of scholars to the next without critical examination. The wisdom of those who created classical rhetoric is one of the marvels of the intellectual history of the world, but to ignore the opportunities which contemporary movements and tools provide for securing new truths and for testing old ones is a folly which warrants the charge of scholarly irresponsibility.

The point does not need more laboring; opinion from many scholars in many fields attests to the need for a book of the sort we have edited. Aware of the cross-disciplinary nature of rhetoric, we have not attempted to produce a book that will serve the need of one discipline only. In the selection of essays, in the aids for analysis, in the practical and extensive bibliography,* we have provided, we hope, a volume that will help readers to understand and appreciate the value of rhetoric. As editors, our greatest gratification will come in the most varied and widest possible use of *The Province of Rhetoric.*

---

* An explanation of the character and rationale of the questions on the selections, and of the bibliography, will be found in the prefatory matter for those sections.

CONTENTS

SECTION I

THE NATURE AND SIGNIFICANCE OF RHETORIC

SECTION II

THE DEVELOPMENT OF RHETORICAL THEORY

SECTION III

MODERN DEVELOPMENTS IN RHETORIC

SECTION IV

THE USES OF RHETORIC

A. Some Advice:

B. Some Samples:

SECTION I

THE NATURE AND
SIGNIFICANCE OF RHETORIC

RHETORIC: ITS FUNCTION AND SCOPE

Donald C. Bryant

When a certain not always ingenuous radio spokesman for one of our large industrial concerns some years ago sought to reassure his audience on the troublesome matter of propaganda, his comfort ran thus: Propaganda, after all, is only a word for anything one says for or against anything. Either everything, therefore, is propaganda, or nothing is propaganda; so why worry?

The more seriously I take this assignment from the Editor to reexplore for the *Quarterly Journal of Speech* (1953), the ground surveyed by Hudson and Wichelns thirty years ago, and since crossed and recrossed by many another, including myself,[1] the nearer I come to a position like our friend's conclusion on propaganda. When I remember Quintilian's *Institutes* at one extreme of time, and lose myself in Kenneth Burke's "new rhetoric" at the other, I am almost forced to the position that whatever we do or say or write, or even think, in explanation of anything, or in support, or in extenuation, or in despite of anything, evinces rhetorical symptoms. Hence, either everything worth mentioning is rhetorical, or nothing is; so let's talk about something encompassable—say logic, or semantics, or persuasion, or linguistics, or scientific method, or poetics, or social psychology, or advertising, or salesmanship, or public relations, or pedagogy, or politics, or psychiatry, or symbolics—or propaganda.

But that is not the assignment. Others have dealt with those subjects, and have given us such illuminating definitive essays as "Speech as a Science" by Clarence Simon,[2] "The Spoken Word and the Great

From *Quarterly Journal of Speech*, December, 1953. Reprinted with the permission of the Speech Association of America, and of the author.

[1] Hoyt H. Hudson, "The Field of Rhetoric," *QJSE*, IX (April 1923), 167–180; Herbert A. Wichelns, "The Literary Criticism of Oratory," *Studies in Rhetoric and Public Speaking in Honor of James Albert Winans* (New York, 1925), pp. 181–216; Donald C. Bryant, "Some Problems of Scope and Method in Rhetorical Scholarship," *QJS*, XXIII (April 1937), 182–188, and "Aspects of the Rhetorical Tradition," *QJS*, XXXVI (April and October 1950), 169–176, 326–332.

[2] *QJS*, XXXVII (October 1951), 281–298.

Unsaid" by Wendell Johnson,[3] "General Semantics [1952]" by Irving Lee,[4] and many other interpretive essays and *apologiae* for the various branches of our curricula and for the multiform captions in our departmental catalogues and organization charts. Among these, "Rhetoric and Public Address" can hardly be thought neglected over the years, at least in the *Quarterly Journal of Speech* and *Speech Monographs*. But perhaps we have assumed too quickly that rhetoric is now at last well understood. On the other hand, Hudson's "The Field of Rhetoric" may be inaccessible or out of date, and Burke's "new rhetoric" too cumbersome or recondite in statement, even after Marie Hochmuth's admirable exposition of it.[5] Even if all this be true, however, one can hardly hope to clarify here what may remain obscure in the work of thirty years—or twenty centuries; but in proper humility, no doubt one can try. At least, common practice seems to presume a restatement of most complex ideas about once in a generation.

I shall not undertake to summarize Hudson's or Wichelns' pioneer essays, relevant as they are to the central problem. They and certain others like Hunt's "Plato and Aristotle on Rhetoric" [6] are by now woven into the fabric of our scholarship. Nor shall I try to duplicate the coverage of my two papers on "Aspects of the Rhetorical Tradition." They can be easily reread by anyone interested.

One further limitation upon the scope of this essay seems necessary: I shall not try to present a digest of rhetoric or even an explanation of the main principles of rhetorical method. Those are also easily available, from Aristotle's *Rhetoric* to the newest textbook in persuasion. Furthermore, I intend to discuss no particular system of rhetoric, but the functions and scope which any system will embrace.

Confusion in Meaning of "Rhetoric"

Very bothersome problems arise as soon as one attempts to define rhetoric, problems that lead so quickly to hair-splitting on the one hand or cosmic inclusiveness on the other, and to ethical or moral controversy, that the attempt usually ends in trifling with logomachies, gloss on Aristotle, or flat frustration. *Rhetoric* is a word in common parlance, as well as in technical use in the SAA and the Chicago school of literary critics. Hence we may presume it to have meanings which must be reckoned with, however vague, various, and disparate; for

[3] *Ibid.* (December 1951), 419–429.
[4] *QJS*, XXXVIII (February, 1952), 1–12.
[5] *Ibid.* (April 1952), 133–144.
[6] *Studies . . . in Honor of James Albert Winans*, pp. 3–60.

a word means what responsible users make it mean. Various as the meanings are, however, one occasionally encounters uses which seem little short of perverse, in persons who ought to know better. Not long since, a doctoral candidate in the classics, who had written as his dissertation a "rhetorical" analysis of one of St. Paul's sermons, was asked how Aristotle had defined rhetoric. Though the question, it would appear, was relevant, the candidate was unable to answer satisfactorily. Whereupon the questioner was taken firmly to task by one of his fellow examiners and was told that after all rhetoric could be adequately defined as a *way of saying something*. Now of course rhetoric may be so defined, as poetic may be defined as a way of making something; but there is little intellectual profit in either definition.

Rhetoric also enjoys several other meanings which, though more common and less perverse, serve to make analysis of it difficult. In general these are the same meanings which Hudson reviewed thirty years ago: bombast; high-sounding words without content; oratorical falsification to hide meaning; sophistry; ornamentation and the study of figures of speech; most commonly among academic folk, Freshman English; and finally, least commonly of all, the whole art of spoken discourse, especially persuasive discourse. This last meaning has gained somewhat in currency in thirty years, especially among scholars in speech and renaissance literature.[7] During the same period the use of the term *rhetoric* (or the combinations *composition and rhetoric* and *grammar and rhetoric*) to label courses and textbooks in Freshman English has somewhat declined, and simultaneously the "rhetorical" content of them has declined also. The tendency now is to prefer just *Composition* or *English Composition*, or to resort to such loaded names as *Basic Writing, Effective Writing, Problems in Writing, Writing with a Purpose*, or *Communication and Analysis*.

In one of his early speeches, President Eisenhower declared that we want action from the Russians, not rhetoric, as evidence of their desire for peaceful settlement. Here is the common use of *rhetoric* to mean empty language, or language used to deceive, without honest intention behind it. Without question this use is in harmony with the current climate of meaning where what our opponents say is rhetoric,

[7] In his *The Ethics of Rhetoric* (Chicago: Henry Regnery, 1953), which has appeared since this article has been in proof, Richard M. Weaver of the College at the University of Chicago makes an interesting and useful effort to restore rhetoric to a central and respectable position among the arts of language and to assign it the function of giving effectiveness to truth.

and what we say is something else. Hence our attempt to define rhetoric leads almost at once into questions of morals and ethics.

Rhetoric as figures of speech or artificial elegance of language is also a healthy perennial, nurtured in literary scholarship and criticism as well as lay comment. Hence the second of the two meanings of *rhetorical* in *Webster's New Collegiate Dictionary* is "emphasizing style, often at the expense of thought." Here we encounter a second obscuring or limiting factor in our attempt at definition. We are to describe rhetoric in terms of those *elements* of a verbal composition for which it is to be held responsible. This mode of procedure has always been attractive. It can produce interesting and plausible conclusions, and it can be defended as schematically satisfying and pedagogically convenient. Thus it proved in the *trivium* of the middle ages and renaissance. If grammar has charge of the correctness of discourse, and if logic has charge of the intellectual content, then it is natural to assign to rhetoric the management of the language of discourse (or the *elocutio*), and if we do not include poetic in our system, the imaginative and emotional content also.

Another definition in the *New Collegiate Dictionary* points to the identification of rhetoric not with the elements of verbal composition but with the *forms* or *genres:* "The art of expressive speech or of discourse, orig. of oratory, now esp. of literary composition; esp., the art of writing well in prose, as disting. from versification and elocution." This approach is promising and on the whole the most popular through the ages. "Originally of oratory, now especially the art of writing well in prose—" this phrase does well enough as a general description of the scope of rhetoric in ancient Greece, as Baldwin has pointed out, when prose itself was virtually defined as oratory and history, and when even history was composed largely in the spirit of oratory. That is, rhetoric could be the art of prose when prose was predominantly concerned with the intentional, directional energizing of truth, of finding in any given situation all the available means of persuasion, and of using as many of them as good sense dictated.

Even then, however, the weakness of genres as the basis for constructing theories or writing handbooks was evident. What is the art of Plato's dialogues, which are in prose? or of Sappho's compositions, which are poems? Neither poetic nor rhetoric is adequate to either. The difficulty multiplies as variety in the kinds of compositions increases in Roman, renaissance, and modern times, and as print supplements—and often supplants—speech as the medium of verbal communication. As *poetic,* the art of imitation in language, became crystallized in Roman and renaissance learning as the theory and practice of the drama (especially tragedy) and the epic, so *rhetoric,* in Quintilian's and Cicero's theory the whole operative philosophy of civil leadership, showed in practice as the art of making winning speeches in the law courts, or later in public exhibitions. The very doctrine in rhetoric of the epideictic or ceremonial speech, as I shall show later, is excellent evidence of the weakness of the types or *genres* as the basis for definition.

All these meanings of rhetoric, in spite of their limitations, contribute something to the exposition of our subject, and the pursuit of each has yielded lucrative insights into the subject, or at least into the problem. Some of them, especially rhetoric as bombast, as excessive ornamentation, and as deceit, are evidence of the falling off of rhetoricians from time to time from the broad philosophy of the art which they inherited from the founders. For a redefinition, therefore, I know no better way of beginning than to return to that broad philosophy.

Working Definition of Rhetoric

First of all and primarily, therefore, I take rhetoric to be the *rationale of informative and suasory discourse.* All its other meanings are partial or morally-colored derivatives from that primary meaning. This rhetoric has been, at least since Aristotle; and at least since Aristotle there has existed a comprehensive, fundamental codification of its principles. It would be idolatrous to suggest that Aristotle uttered the first and last authentic words on rhetoric, or that his system is still adequate, or that it was completely satisfactory even for the Greeks of his day. Like his poetic theory, however, it enjoys unequalled scientific eminence in its field though it has sustained many additions and modifications through the centuries. Its limitations are historical rather than philosophical. Like the limitations of his poetic, the limitations of his rhetoric derive mainly from his failure to consider phenomena which had not yet occurred and to make use of learnings which had not yet been developed.

Now as then, therefore, what Aristotle said of the nature and principles of public address, of the discovery of all the available means of persuasion in any given case, must stand as the broad background for any sensible rhetorical system. Much of Aristotle's formulation, even in detail, survives ungainsaid and can only be rearranged and paraphrased by subsequent writers. Again to cite a parallel with his poetic: though the relative importance of plot in drama has shifted radically since Aristotle, when good plots are made their excellences will still be best discovered by the application of Aristotle's criteria. Similarly, though modern psychology is very different from that of the Greeks, and doubtless more scientific, modern enlightenment has produced no new method of analyzing an audience which can replace Aristotle's.

Aristotle, however, identified rhetoric with persuasion. His chief interests lay in the speaking to popular audiences in the law court and in the legislative assembly, and his system of classification and analysis obviously was framed with those types of speaking as its principal object. Some means of persuasion, however, in spite of Aristotle's comprehensive definition, are not within the scope of rhetoric. Gold and guns, for example, are certainly persuasive, and the basic motives which make them persuasive, profit and self-preservation, may enter the field of rhetoric; but applied directly to the persons to be persuaded, guns and gold belong to commerce or coercion, not to rhetoric.

No more shall we admit the persuasive use of all symbols as belonging to rhetoric. Undoubtedly the persuasive force of pictures, colors, designs, non-language sounds such as fog horns and fire alarms, and all such devices of symbolic significance is great and useful. Traffic lights, however, are not normally agents of rhetorical influence. No more, in themselves, are elephants, donkeys, lions, illuminated bottles of whiskey, or animated packs of cigarettes. Their use has a kinship to rhetoric, and when they are organized in a matrix of verbal discourse, they become what Aristotle called the extrinsic or non-artistic means of persuasion. They are instruments of the wielder of public opinion, and they are staples of two techniques which must be recognized as strongly rhetorical—advertising and propaganda. Unless we are to claim practically all interhuman activity as the field of rhetoric, however, some limits must be admitted, even within the field of persuasion. True, in the "new rhetoric" of Kenneth Burke, where the utmost extension rather than practical limit-setting is the aim, any manifestation of "identification," conscious or unconscious, is within rhetoric. Though the classic limitations of rhetoric are too narrow, others are too broad. Therefore I am assuming the traditional limitation to discourse.

Let us look now at Aristotle's apparent failure to include exposition as well as persuasion within rhetoric. Ancillary to persuasion, of course, exposition is clearly included. The idea of *demonstration*, the characteristic result of the logical mode, implies the most perfect exposition for audiences susceptible of reasoned instruction. Furthermore, another aspect of Aristotle's system admits exposition to independent status. At the expense of a slight venture into heresy (though I believe only a benign heresy) I suggest that any systematic construction of human phenomena, even Aristotle's, will either leave out something important and significant, or will include a category, however named, which is, in effect, "miscellaneous." That I think Aristotle did in discussing the rhetoric of the ceremonial or epideictic speech. The success of his categories, even so, is remarkable. The extension and effective application to the ceremonial speech in general of the principles of the persuasive speech whose end is active decision, provide very plausible coverage of that somewhat anomalous form. The three-fold, tripartite classification of speeches was too nearly perfect to abandon:

Forensic (time, past; ends, justice and injustice; means, accusation and defense.)

Epideictic (time, present; ends, honor and dishonor; means, praise and blame.)

Deliberative (time, future; ends, the expedient and inexpedient; means, exhortation and dehortation.)

When the problems of what to do with time-present in the system, and with Pericles' funeral oration among the observed phenomena had to be solved, the coincidence was too attractive to be resisted. It provided for a piece of practical realism which no system should be allowed to defeat. Through that adjustment Aristotle admitted within the scope of rhetoric the predominantly literary performance on the one hand and gave an opening on the other for the primarily informative and instructional as well as the demonstrative and exhibitionistic. Through this third category rhetoric embraces, in a persuasion-centered system, the *docere* and *delectare*, the teach and delight, of the Roman and renaissance rhetoric-poetic and permits them an independent status outside their strictly ancillary or instrumental functions in persuasion.

Aristotle's system, therefore, and his rationale of effective speaking comprehend with very little violence the art of the good man skilled in speaking of Cicero and Quintilian, or Baldwin's equation of rhetoric to the art of prose whose end is giving effectiveness to truth [8]—effectiveness considered in terms of what happens to an audience, usually a popular or lay audience as distinguished from the specialized or technical audience of the scientific or dialectical demonstration. This distinction, strictly speaking, is a practical rather than a logical limita-

[8] *Ancient Rhetoric and Poetic* (New York, 1924), p. 5.

tion, a limitation of degree rather than kind. No matter what the audience, when the speaker evinces skill in getting into their minds, he evinces rhetorical skill.

If the breadth of scope which I have assigned to rhetoric is implicit in Aristotle's system, the basic delimitation of that scope finds early and explicit statement there. Rhetoric is not confined in application to any specific subjects which are exclusively its own. Rhetoric is method, not subject. But if it has no special subjects, neither are all subjects within its province. In its suasory phase, at least, rhetoric is concerned, said Aristotle, only with those questions about which men dispute, that is, with the contingent—that which is dependent in part upon factors which cannot be known for certain, that which can be otherwise. Men do not dispute about what is known or certainly knowable by them. Hence the characteristic concern of rhetoric is broadly with questions of justice and injustice, of the expedient and the inexpedient (of the desirable and undesirable, of the good and the bad), of praise and blame, or honor and dishonor.

To questions such as these and their almost infinite subsidiary questions, vital and perennial as they are in the practical operation of human society, the best answers can never be certain but only more or less probable. In reasoning about them, men at best must usually proceed from probable premise to probable conclusion, seldom from universal to universal. Hence Aristotle described the basic instrument of rhetoric, the enthymeme, as a kind of syllogism based on probabilities and signs.

Rhetoric, therefore, is distinguished from the other instrumental studies in its preoccupation with informed opinion rather than with scientific demonstration. It is the counterpart, said Aristotle, of dialectic. Strictly speaking, dialectic also may be said to attain only probability, not scientific certainty, like physics (and, perhaps, theology). The methodology, however, is the methodology of formal logic and it deals in universals. Hence it arrives at a very high degree of probability, for it admits the debatable only in the assumption of its premises. Rhetoric, however, because it normally deals with matters of uncertainty for the benefit of popular audiences, must admit probability not only in its premises but in its method also. This is the ground upon which Plato first, and hundreds of critics since, have attacked rhetoric—that it deals with opinion rather than knowledge. This is the ground also from which certain scholars have argued,[9]

[9] For example, Craig La Drière, "Rhetoric as 'Merely Verbal' Art," *English Institute Essays—1948*, ed. by D. A. Robertson, Jr. (New York, 1949), pp. 123–152.

after some of the mediaeval fathers, that rhetoric really deals, characteristically, not with genuine probability but only with adumbration and suggestion. It is, they say, distinguished from dialectic in *degree* of probability—dialectic very high, and rhetoric very low.

The epistemological question is interesting, and in a world of philosophers where only certain knowledge was ever called upon to decide questions of human behavior, it would be the central question. Rhetoric exists, however, because a world of certainty is not the world of human affairs. It exists because the world of human affairs is a world where there must be an alternative to certain knowledge on the one hand and pure chance or whimsey on the other. The alternative is informed opinion, the nearest approach to knowledge which the circumstances of decision in any given case will permit. The art, or science, or method whose realm this is, is rhetoric. Rhetoric, therefore, is the method, the strategy, the organon of the principles for deciding best the undecidable questions, for arriving at solutions of the unsolvable problems, for instituting method in those vital phases of human activity where no method is inherent in the total subject-matter of decision. The resolving of such problems is the province of the "Good man skilled in speaking." It always has been, and it is still. Of that there can be little question. And the comprehensive rationale of the functioning of that good man so far as he is skilled in speaking, so far as he is a wielder of public opinion, is rhetoric.

The Problems of Vocabulary in This Essay

Traditionally *rhetoric* and *oratory* have been the standard terms for the theory and the product. The *rhetor* was the speaker, the addresser of the public, or the teacher of speaking; the *rhetorician*, the teacher of rhetoric or the formulator of the principles of rhetoric. Hence the special bias of the terms as I use them has been and probably still is oral. That is a practical bias and is not carelessly to be thrown away. From the beginning of publication in writing, however, essentially rhetorical performances, whether already spoken or to be spoken, have been committed to paper and circulated to be read rather than heard —from Isocrates' *Panathenaicus* or Christ's *Sermon on the Mount* to Eisenhower's message on the state of the nation. Furthermore, for centuries now, especially since the invention and cheapening of the art of printing, the agitator, the teacher, the preacher, the wielder of public opinion has used the press quite independently of the platform. Hence, obviously, rhetoric must be understood to be the rationale of informative and suasory discourse both spoken and written: of Milton's *Aeropagitica* as well as Cromwell's Address to the Rump Parliament; of John Wilkes' *North Briton* as well as Chatham's speech on the repeal of the Stamp Act; of Tom Paine's *Common Sense* as much as Patrick Henry's Address to the Virginia Assembly; of Swift's pamphlet on the *Conduct of the Allies* as well as Dr. Sacheverell's sermon on Passive Obedience; of George Sokolsky's syndicated columns in the press equally with Edward R. Murrow's radio commentaries or Kenneth McFarland's appearances before conventions of the Chambers of Commerce. I will use *rhetoric* and *rhetorical* with that breadth of scope.

Furthermore, the terms *orator* and *oratory* have taken on, like *rhetoric* itself, rather limited or distorted meanings, not entirely undeserved perhaps, which make them no longer suitable for the designation of even the normal *oral* rhetorical performance. *Practitioner of public address,* or some such hyphenated monstrosity as *speaker-writer,* might be used as a generic term for the product of rhetoric, but the disadvantages of such manipulations of vocabulary are obvious. I am using the terms *speech* and *speaker* for both written and oral performance and written and oral performer, unless the particular circumstances obviously imply one or the other. Likewise, in place of such a formula as *listener-reader,* I shall use *audience,* a usage not uncommon anyway.

One must face still another problem of vocabulary, that of the term *rhetoric* in the three distinguishable senses in which I use it: (1) as the rationale of informative and suasory discourse, a body of principle and precept for the creation and analysis of speeches; (2) as a quality which characterizes that kind of discourse and distinguishes it from other kinds; (3) as a study of the phenomenon of informative and suasory discourse in the social context. Similarly, I fear, the term *rhetorician* will sometimes mean the formulator and philosopher of rhetorical theory; sometimes the teacher of the technique of discourse; sometimes the speaker with rhetorical intention; and finally the student or scholar whose concern is the literary or social or behavioral study of rhetoric. I have been tempted to invent terms to avoid certain of these ambiguities, such as *logology,* or even *rhetoristic* (parallel with *sophistic*), but the game would probably not be worth the candle.

In summary, rhetoric is the rationale of informative and suasory discourse, it operates chiefly in the areas of the contingent, its aim is the attainment of maximum probability as a basis for public decision, it is the organizing and animating principle of all subject-matters which have a relevant bearing on that decision. Now let us turn to the question of the subject-matters in which rhetoric most characteristically functions and of the relations it bears to special subject-matters.

Subjects of Rhetorical Discourse

Wrote Aristotle, "The most important subjects of general deliberation . . . are practically five, viz. finance, war and peace, the defense of the country, imports and exports, and legislation." This is still the basic list, though legislation now would be far more generally inclusive than it was to the Athenian assembly. In addition, within the scope of rhetorical discourse fall the subjects of forensic address—crime and its punishment and all the concerns of justice and injustice. Furthermore, the concerns of teaching, preaching—moral, intellectual, practical, and spiritual instruction and exhortation—and commercial exploitation, wherever the problems of adaptation of ideas and information to the group mind are concerned, depend upon rhetorical skill for their fruition. Thus we are brought again to the position that the rhetorical factor is pervasive in the operative aspects of society.

Does this mean that the speaker must be a specialist in all subjects, as well as in rhetorical method? Cicero seemed willing to carry the demands thus far, at least in establishing his ideal orator; and this implication has been ridiculed from Plato onwards for the purpose of discrediting first the claims of the sophists and then all men "skilled in speaking." Plainly, in practice and in plausible human situations, the suggestion is absurd. Does the public speaker or the columnist or the agitator have to be a military specialist in order rightly to urge peace or war? Does the citizen have to be a dentist and a chemist and a pathologist intelligently to advocate the use of fluorine in the municipal water supply? He does not become a specialist in these fields, of course, any more than the head of an industrial plant is the technical master of the specialties of all the men who serve under him. "He attempts to learn the authorities and sources of information in each, and to develop a method which he can apply to specific problems as they arise. He learns, in any given situation, what questions to ask and to answer. The peculiar contribution of the rhetorician is the discovery and use, to the common good, of those things which move men to [understanding and] action." [10] Looked at another way, the relation of rhetoric to the subject-matters of economics, or public health, or theology, or chemistry, or agriculture is like the relation of hydraulic

[10] Hudson, "Field of Rhetoric," *QJSE*, IX (April 1923), 177.

engineering to water, under the specific circumstances in which the engineer is to construct his dam or his pumping station or his sewage system, and in view of the specific results he is to obtain. He develops a method for determining what questions to ask and answer from all that which can be known about water. If he is a good hydraulics engineer, he will see to it that his relevant knowledge is sound, as the good speaker will see to it that his relevant knowledge of hydraulic engineering is the best obtainable if he is to urge or oppose the building of a dam in the St. Lawrence River. If either is ignorant, or careless, or dishonest, he is culpable as a man and as a rhetorician or hydraulics engineer.

It was not the scientific chronologist, the astronomer Lord Macclesfield, who secured the adoption in England of the Gregorian calendar, thoroughly as he understood the subject in all its mathematical, astronomical, and chronometrical aspects. It was the Earl of Chesterfield, learning from the chronologist all that was essential to the particular situation, and knowing rhetoric and the British Parliament, who was able to impress upon his fellows not necessarily the validity of the calculations but the desirability and the feasibility of making a change. If the truth of scientific knowledge had been left to its own inherent force with Parliament, we would doubtless be many more days out of phase with the sun than England was in 1751. As Aristotle observed in his brief and basic justification of rhetoric, truth itself has a tendency to prevail over error; but in competition with error, where skillful men have an interest in making error prevail, truth needs the help of as attractive and revealing a setting as possible. In the Kingdom of Heaven, truth may be its own sole advocate, but it needs mighty help if it is to survive in health among the nations on earth. As Fielding wrote of prudence in *Tom Jones:* "It is not enough that your designs, nay, that your actions, are intrinsically good; you must take care that they shall appear so. If your inside be never so beautiful, you must preserve a fair outside also. This must be constantly looked to." [11]

In this sense even honest rhetoric is fundamentally concerned with appearances, not to the disregard of realities as Plato and his successors have industriously charged, but to the enforcement of realities. Rhetoric at the command of honest men strives that what is desirable shall appear desirable, that what is vicious shall appear vicious. It intends that the true or probably true shall seem so, that the false or doubtful shall be vividly realized for what it is. A bridge or an automobile or a clothes-line must not only *be* strong but must *appear* to be so. This

[11] Book III, Chapter 7. Modern Library Edn., p. 97.

fact has been an obstacle to the use of many new structural materials. Accustomed to an older kind, we have been reluctant to accept the adequacy of a new, more fragile-seeming substance. Hence one important reason for surrounding steel columns with stone pillars is the necessity of making them seem as strong as their predecessors. Appearances, then, must be the concern of the wielder of public opinion, the rhetorician. Through ignorance or malice, to be sure, skill in establishing appearances may be applied to deceive. This is a grave peril which must be the concern of all men of good will. Knowledge of the devices of sophistry will always be acquired by those whose purposes are bad; ignorance of them will provide no defense for the rest. No great force can be used without hazard, or ignored without hazard. The force understood, rather than the force not understood, is likely to be the force controlled. That understanding is provided by rhetoric, the technique of discourse addressed to the enlightenment and persuasion of the generality of mankind—the basic instrument for the creation of informed public opinion and the consequent expedient public action.

Occasions of Rhetorical Discourse

Whether we will or no, we cannot escape rhetoric, either the doing or the being done to. We require it. As Edmund Burke wrote, "Men want reasons to reconcile their minds to what is done, as well as motives originally to act right." [12] Whether we seek advice or give it, the nature of our talk, as being "addressed," and of the talk of which we are the audience, as being addressed to us, necessitates speaking the language of the audience or we had as well not speak at all. That process is the core of rhetoric. It goes on as genuinely, and is often managed as skillfully, over the frozen-meats counter of the local supermarket as in the halls of Congress; on the benches in front of the Boone County Court House on Saturday afternoon before election as below the benches of the Supreme Court the next Wednesday morning; around the table where a new labor contract is being negotiated as in the pulpit of Sainte-Marie de Chaillot where Bossuet is pronouncing the funeral oration upon Henriette d'Angleterre; in the Petition from Yorkshire to King George III for redress of grievances as in the Communist Manifesto or the Declaration of Independence.

As we are teachers, and as we are taught, we are involved with rhetoric. The success of the venture depends on a deliberate or in-

[12] *Correspondence* (1844), I, 217.

stinctive adjustment of idea-through-speaker-to-audience-in-a-particu-lar-situation. Pedagogy is the rhetoric of teaching, whether formally in the classroom or the book, or informally in the many incidental situations of our days and nights. The psychological principle, for example, that we learn through association becomes a rhetorical principle when we use it to connect one day's lesson with what has gone before. It is the same principle by which Burke attempted to establish in the minds of the House of Commons the rights of American colonists when he identified the colonists with Englishmen, whose rights were known.

As we are readers of newspapers and magazines and all such infor-mation-giving and opinion-forming publications, and as we write for them, we are receiving or initiating rhetorical discourse, bad or good, effective or ineffective. The obligations of the journalists as investigator of the facts, as thinker about the facts, as discoverer of ideas and analyst and critic of ideas, are fundamental. They demand all the knowledge and skill that the political, scientific, and technical studies can provide. The journalist's distinctive job, however, is writing for his audience the highest grade of informative and suasory discourse that the conditions of his medium will permit. Whether editorial writer, commentator, or plain news-writer, reaching into his audience's mind is his problem. If the people who buy the paper miss the import, the paper might as well not be published. Call it *journalism* if you choose; it is the rhetoric of the press: "it is always public opinion that the press seeks to change, one way or another, directly or indirectly." [13] Seldom can the journalist wait for the solution of a problem before getting into the fray, whether the question be a more efficient way of handling municipal finances or independence for India. He must know the right questions to ask and the bases for answering them with greatest prob-ability for his audience now. That is his rhetorical knowledge.

The same is true of the radio and television news reporter, news analyst, and commentator. He must have rhetorical skill to survive in his occupation, and he must have knowledge and integrity if his effect is to be beneficial rather than destructive to informed public opinion. His staple, also, whether good or bad, is rhetoric. His efforts are aimed at the public mind and are significant only as they affect the public mind. If he is an honest rhetorician, he does not imply of most things, "It is so because," but only "I believe so because"; or "I recommend

[13] *The Press and Society: A Book of Readings,* ed. by George L. Bird and Frederic E. Merwin (New York, 1951), preface, p. iv.

so because it seems probable where I cannot be sure." If he is tempted into exploiting the force of extravagant and authoritative assertion, his morals rather than his rhetoric have gone awry. Whether the use be honest or dishonest, the instrument is rhetoric.

It is obvious and commonplace that the agitator, the political speaker, the pamphleteer, the advocate, the preacher, the polemicist and apologist, the adviser of kings and princes, the teacher of statesmen, the reformer and counter-reformer, the fanatic in religion, diet, or economics, the mountebank and messiah, have enhanced the stature of a noble discourse or have exploited a degraded, shallow, and dishonest discourse. It matters not that we resort to exalted names for the one—eloquence, genius, philosophy, logic, discourse of reason; and for the other, labels of reproach and contempt—sophistry, glibness, demagoguery, chicanery, "rhetoric." That naming process itself is one of the most familiar techniques of rhetoric. The fact is that in their characteristic preoccupation with manipulating the public mind, they are one. They must not all be approved or emulated, but they must all be studied as highly significant social phenomena, lest we be ignorant of them, and hence powerless before them, for good or for ill.

Similarly, though perhaps not so easily acceptable into rhetoric, we must recognize most of what we know as advertising, salesmanship, propaganda, "public relations," and commercial, political, and national "information" services. I shall have some special consideration to give to these later. At present I merely cite them as great users of rhetoric. In this day of press, radio, and television perhaps their rhetoric is that most continuously and ubiquitously at work on the public.

Relations of Rhetoric to Other Learnings

These, then, are fundamental rhetorical situations. In them human beings are so organizing language as to effect a change in the knowledge, the understanding, the ideas, the attitudes, or the behavior of other human beings. Furthermore, they are so organizing that language as to make the change as agreeable, as easy, as active, and as secure as possible—as the Roman rhetoric had it, to teach, to delight, and to move (or to bend). What makes a situation rhetorical is the focus upon accomplishing something predetermined and directional with an audience. To that end many knowledges and sciences, concerning both what is external to audiences and what applies to audiences themselves, may be involved, many of which I have discussed in a previous essay.[14] These knowledges, however, have to be organized, managed, given places in strategy and tactics, set into coordinated and harmonious movement towards the listener as the end, towards what happens to him and in him. In short, they have to be *put to use*, for, as Bacon said, studies themselves "teach not their own use; but that is a wisdom without them, and above them, won by observation." "Studies themselves do give forth directions too much at large, except they be bounded in by experience."[15] Rhetoric teaches their use towards a particular end. It is that "observation," that "experience" codified, given a rationale. Other learnings are chiefly concerned with the discovery of ideas and phenomena and of their relations to each other within more or less homogeneous and closed systems. Rhetoric is primarily concerned with the relations of ideas to the thoughts, feelings, motives, and behavior of men. Rhetoric as distinct from the learnings which it uses is dynamic; it is concerned with movement. It *does* rather than *is*. It is method rather than matter. It is chiefly involved with bringing about a condition, rather than discovering or testing a condition. Even psychology, which is more nearly the special province of rhetoric than is any other study, is descriptive of conditions, but not of the uses of those conditions.

So far as it is method, rhetoric is like the established procedures of experimental science and like logic. As the method for solving problems of human action in the areas of the contingent and the probable, however, it does not enjoy a privilege which is at the same time the great virtue and the great limitation of science and logic—it cannot choose its problems in accordance with the current capacities of its method, or defer them until method is equal to the task. Rhetoric will postpone decision as long as feasible; indeed one of its most valuable uses in the hands of good men, is to prevent hasty and premature formulation of lines of conduct and decision. In this it is one with science—and good sense. But in human affairs, where the whole is usually greater than the most complete collection of the parts, decisions —makings up of the mind—cannot always wait until all the contingencies have been removed and solutions to problems have been tested in advance. Rhetoric, therefore, must take undemonstrable problems and do its best with them when decision is required. We must decide when the blockade is imposed whether to withdraw from Berlin or to undertake the air lift, not some time later when perhaps some

[14] "Aspects of the Rhetorical Tradition" (1950), see above, note 1.
[15] "Of Studies."

of the contingencies may have been removed. And the making of the choice forever precludes trying out and testing the other possibilities under the circumstances which would have prevailed had we chosen differently at first. Likewise we must make a choice on the first Tuesday in November, whether we are scientifically sure or not. In each case, rhetoric, good or bad, must be the strategy of enlightening opinion for that choice.

To restate our central idea still another way: rhetoric, or the rhetorical, is the function in human affairs which governs and gives direction to that creative activity, that process of critical analysis, that branch of learning, which address themselves to the whole phenomenon of the designed use of language for the promulgation of information, ideas, and attitudes. Though it is instrumental in the discovery of ideas and information, its characteristic function is the publication, the publicizing, the humanizing, the animating of them for a realized and usually specific audience. At its best it seeks the "energizing of truth," in order to make "reason and the will of God prevail." But except in science, and no doubt theology, the promulgation of *truth*, sure or demonstrable, is out of the question. Normally the rhetorical function serves as high a degree of probability as the combination of subject, audience, speaker, and occasion admits. Rhetoric may or may not be involved (though the speaker-writer must be) in the determination of the validity of the ideas being promulgated. Such determination will be the province in any given situation of philosophy, ethics, physics, economics, politics, eugenics, medicine, hydraulics, or bucolics. To rhetoric, however, and to no other rationale, belongs the efficiency—the validity if you will— of the relations in the idea-audience-speaker situation.

Functioning of Rhetoric

We are ready now, perhaps, if we have not been ready much sooner, to proceed to the question of how rhetoric works, what it accomplishes in an audience. Speaking generally, we may say that the rhetorical function is the *function of adjusting ideas to people and of people to ideas.* This process may be thought of as a continuum from the complete modification or accommodation of ideas to audiences (as is sometimes said, "telling people only what they want to hear") at the one extreme, to complete regeneration at the other (such perfect illumination that the "facts speak for themselves"). This continuum may, therefore, be said to have complete flattery (to use Plato's unflattering epithet) at one end and the Kingdom of Heaven at the other! Good rhetoric usually functions somewhere well in from the extremes. There, difficult and strange ideas have to be modified without being distorted or invalidated; and audiences have to be prepared through the mitigation of their prejudices, ignorance, and irrelvant sets of mind without being dispossessed of their judgments. The adjustment of ideas to people, for example, was being undertaken by the Earl of Chatham in his speech for the repeal of the Stamp Act, when he agreed that Parliament had legislative supremacy over the Colonies but that legislative supremacy did not include the right to tax without representation. And when Booker T. Washington assured the Southern white folk that they and the Negroes could be as separate as the fingers in social affairs and as united as the hand in economic, he was adjusting people to the idea of real freedom for his race.

The moral disturbances which rhetoric and rhetorical activity seem to breed do not usually result from this process of mutual accommodation itself. Most of them arise when the speaker tries so to adjust ideas to people that the ideas are basically falsified, or when he attempts so to adjust people to ideas as to deform or anesthetize the people. Report has it that after Senator Hiram Johnson had campaigned through rural New England charging that England would have three votes to one for the United States in the League of Nations, he was taxed by a critic with misrepresenting the nature of the British Empire. One could not assume, so Johnson's critic declared, that Canada and South Africa would vote with England as a single bloc. "That may be," Johnson is said to have replied, "but New England farmers do not know the nature of the British Empire, and they do know common arithmetic." That is adjusting ideas to people so far as to falsify the basic idea. In the other direction, stimulating the "Red-menace-in-the-air-we-breathe" terror in order to adjust people to the idea of giving up their right of dissent is an effort to dispossess people of their judgments.

In terms of the old, but still convenient, faculty psychology, the terms in which rhetoric is most frequently attacked—reason, imagination, passions (emotions), judgment, will—rhetoric may still be described as the method of applying "reason to imagination for the better moving of the will." To complete our broad idea of the scope of rhetoric we should add "and the better clarification of the understanding." That is Francis Bacon's succinct statement of how rhetoric functions in the audience,[16] and it is still a good one. It establishes

[16] From *The Advancement of Learning*. See Karl R. Wallace, *Francis Bacon on Communication and Rhetoric* (Chapel Hill, 1943), p. 27.

rhetoric squarely as an instrumental learning which manages the creative powers of the whole logical-psychological man toward a single dynamic end.

Rhetoric, therefore, has the greatest possible involvement with the logical and psychological studies. These learnings must be the core of the speaker's equipment. They are the *sine qua non* in the knowledge through which rhetoric must function. In the good rhetoric which Plato described in the *Phaedrus*, after knowledge of the truth, he saw the equipment of the rhetorically skilled man to consist in knowledge of the various possible kinds of arguments, knowledge of the various kinds of souls, and knowledge of which kinds of souls will be affected by which kinds of arguments—that is, knowledge of the mutual adaptation of these processes to audiences. Furthermore, in the great counter-Platonic *Rhetoric* of Aristotle, the first Book is devoted chiefly to the rational processes of rhetoric, and the next Book is the first extant comprehensive treatise on individual and group psychology. Likewise, in one of the best of the recent books on liberal education, which is, therefore, something like a basic statement on rhetoric, Hoyt Hudson sees the fundamental equipment of the liberally educated man to require three parts: the Arm of Information, the Arm of Operative Logic, and the Arm of Imagination.[17] Of these, in practical affairs, rhetoric is based on the second and third, and the first must be the starting place of the speaker in each particular situation.

Where in this pattern, then, does emotion come in, that famous roughneck who is said to spoil the rational life and vitiate the logic of behavior? As Hudson and many others have observed, and as Bacon knew well, emotion is a derivative of both reason and imagination. Love of truth and of the good life must be the results of any genuinely rational functioning, that is, of operative logic; and vivid realization of experience, which is imagination, can hardly occur without those strong emotional accompaniments which, in practice, have given rise to the identifying of emotion with imagination. This point seems hardly to need laboring over again. Hudson's book gives it adequate coverage, and I have summarized the traditional position of rhetoric and rhetoricians on it in the essay already mentioned.[18] The position is that a complete rhetoric, and that is the kind of rhetoric which we are discussing, knows the whole man and seeks to bring to bear the whole man in achieving its ends—what he is and what he thinks he is, what he believes and what he thinks he believes,

---

[17] *Educating Liberally* (Stanford University, 1945), pp. 10 ff.
[18] Above, note 14.

what he wants and what he tells himself he wants. Towards its special ends, rhetoric recognizes the primacy of rational processes, their primacy in time as well as in importance, as Bacon's definition implies—applying reason to the imagination. Just so poetry recognizes the primacy for its purposes of the imagination. But rhetoric has always been akin to poetry—for long periods of history it has in fact annexed poetry—in its recognition of the honest and highly important power of imagination and of that emotion which does not supplant but supports reason, and sometimes even transcends it. Thus Sir Philip Sidney and most literary theorists of the renaissance attributed to poetry the distinctly rhetorical function of using imagination to create what might be called historical fictions to give power and life to ideas. Rhetoric recognizes the strength of the fictions men live by, as well as those they live under; [19] and it aims to fortify the one and explode the other. Rhetoric aims at what is *worth* doing, what is *worth* trying. It is concerned with *values,* and values are established with the aid of imaginative realization, not through rational determination alone; and they gain their force through emotional animation.

We have observed that psychology, human nature, has been a staple of rhetorical learning through the ages. No doubt, therefore, scientific psychology will have more and more to contribute to modern rhetoric. The first notable attempt to ground rhetoric in a systematic modern psychology was made by George Campbell in his *Philosophy of Rhetoric* (1776), in which he stated as his purpose

> to exhibit . . . a tolerable sketch of the human mind; and, aided by the lights which the poet and the orator so amply furnish, to disclose its secret movements, tracing its principal channels of perception and action, as near as possible, to their source: and, on the other hand, from the science of human nature, to ascertain with greater precision, the radical principles of that art, whose object it is, by the use of language, to operate on the soul of the hearer, in the way of informing, convincing, pleasing, moving, or persuading.[20]

That same purpose governs our contemporary writers of treatises and textbooks on public speaking, argumentation, and persuasion, and most of them include as up-to-date a statement as possible of the psychological and the rational bases of rhetoric. It is a commonplace that of the studies recently come to new and promising maturity,

---

[19] See the very relevant analysis of some of the fictions in the ideology of American business in C. Wright Mills, *White Collar* (New York, 1951), Ch. 3, "The Rhetoric of Competition."

[20] 7th edn. (London, 1823), pp. vii–viii.

psychology, especially social psychology, and cultural anthropology have much to teach modern rhetoric and to correct or reinterpret in traditional rhetoric. The same may be said of the various new ventures into the study of meaning, under the general head of semantics. How language *means* is obviously important to the rationale of informative and suasory discourse. Nevertheless, in spite of I. A. Richards' book,[21] the theory of meaning is not *the* philosophy of rhetoric, any more than is the psychology of perception. Rhetoric is the organizer of all such for the wielding of public opinion.

Advertising, Salesmanship, and Propaganda

Now that we have sketched the rhetorical process functioning at its best for the exposition and dissemination of ideas in the wielding of public opinion, with the ethical and pathetic modes of proof in ancillary relation to the logical, with the imagination aiding and reenforcing the rational, let us turn to some of the partial, incomplete, perhaps misused, rhetorics which I have already mentioned briefly.

It is axiomatic that men do not live by reason alone or even predominantly, though reason is such a highly prized commodity and stands in so high a repute even among the unreasoning and unreasonable, that men prefer to tell themselves and to be told that they make up their minds and determine their choices from reason and the facts. Intellectual activity, both learning and thinking, is so difficult that man tends to avoid it wherever possible. Hence education has almost always put its first efforts into cultivating the reasonable portion of the mind rather than the imaginative or emotional. Furthermore, the strength and accessibility of imaginative and emotional responses is so great in spite of education that though men seldom make effective reasonable decisions without the help of emotion, they often make, or appear to make, effective emotional decisions without the help of rational processes or the modification of reasonable consideration. Inevitably, therefore, the available reason in rhetorical situations will vary tremendously, and the assistance which imagination must provide towards the moving of the will must vary accordingly. Except in Swift's unexciting land of the Houyhnhnms, however, imagination will always be there.

Ever since men first began to weave the web of words to charm their fellows, they have known that some men can impose their wills on others through language in despite of reason. Almost as long, other

[21] *The Philosophy of Rhetoric* (New York, 1936).

men have deplored and feared this talent. If the talent were wholly a matter of divine gift and were wholly unexplainable, the only alternative to succumbing to the orator would be to kill him. In time it appeared, however, that this skill could be learned, in part at least, and could be analyzed. Thus if it were good, men could learn to develop it further; and if it were bad, they could be armed in some measure against it. Hence rhetoric, and hence the partial rhetoric of anti-reason and pseudo-reason. And hence the appeal of such rhetorical eruptions as Aldous Huxley's total condemnation of oratory in *The Devils of Loudon.*[22] His indictment of public speakers is indeed skillful, and ought to be taken seriously. If the talent of his golden-voiced Grandiers be indeed magic, then we will have to agree that the fate of man before such wizards is hopeless. Rhetoric teaches, however, that the method and the power of this kind of discourse can be analyzed, at least in large part, and if its subtleties cannot be wholly *learned* by every ambitious speaker, the characteristics of its operation can be understood, and if understood, then controlled, for better or for worse.[23]

The oratory which Huxley would extirpate presents a rewarding approach to the rhetoric of advertising and propaganda, of which it is the historic prototype. In them the techniques of suggestion, reiteration, imaginative substitution, verbal irrelevance and indirection, and emotional and pseudological bullying have been developed beyond, one might hazard a guess, the fondest dreams of the sophists and the historic demagogues. This development does not represent a change in intention from them to our contemporaries, but an advance in knowledge and opportunity and media.

If you have a soap or a cigarette or a social order for quick, profitable sale, you do not neglect any method within your ethical system of making that sale. That is the paramount problem of the advertiser and the propagandist, and their solutions are very much alike. They are rhetorical solutions, at their best very carefully gauged to the mass audience, adapted to special audiences, and varying basically only as the initial sale or the permanent customer is the principal object. What advertising is in commerce, propaganda is in politics, especially international politics. Neither scorns reason or the likeness of reason, the rhetoric of information and logical argument, if the message and the audience seem to make that the best or only means to the sale. Neither, on the other hand, prefers that method to the shorter, quicker ways to

[22] (New York, 1952), pp. 18–19.
[23] Observe the tradition of rhetoric as a systematic study, summarized in my "Aspects of Rhetorical Tradition," *QJS*, XXXVI. (April 1950), 169–172.

unconsidered action. They concentrate—forcibly where possible, rhetorically where necessary—on the exclusion of competing ideas, on the short-circuiting or by-passing of informed judgment. By preference they do not seek to balance or overbalance alternative ideas or courses of action; they seek to obliterate them, to circumvent or subvert the rational processes which tend to make men weigh and consider. As Adlai Stevenson said, slogans, the common staple of advertising and propaganda, "are normally designed to get action without reflection."

That advertising should enjoy a happier reputation than propaganda in a competitive, commercial-industrial nation such as the United States, which is only just now learning the term *psychological warfare*, is not to be wondered at. We do not have a public service institution for the defensive analysis of advertising, like the Institute of Propaganda Analysis, which assumed that propaganda is something from which we must learn to protect ourselves. The ethical superiority of our advertising is no doubt a compliment to our dominant business code—and to our laws. Still, if one wishes to know what the ungoverned rhetoric of advertising can be, he may get a suggestion by listening to some of what is beamed to us from certain radio stations south of the border.

The kinship of advertising and salesmanship, and their somewhat denatured relatives "public relations" and "promotion," to conventional public address, the established vehicle of rhetoric, may be embarrassing at times, but it must be acknowledged. The family resemblance is too strong to be ignored and too important to be denied. The omnipresence of the rhetoric of advertising, as I have suggested, gives it a standing which must be reckoned with, no matter what opinion the student of public address may hold of it. The rhetoric of public address, in this country at least, must function, whether or no, in a public mind which is steeped in the rhetoric of advertising, a rhetoric whose dominating principles must be recognized as adaptations of a portion of the fundamentals of any rhetoric. One need only compare a textbook or handbook of advertising methods with standard, conventional rhetorics—textbooks in public speaking and persuasion— especially in the handling of such topics as interest, suggestion, and motivation, to be convinced of the coincidence of method if not of philosophic outlook. Many times in adult evening classes in public speaking, have I heard speeches on the secrets of successful salesmanship, and as often have I found myself being offered a more or a less competent parody of certain portions of our textbook, which for some reason the student had omitted to read. Not by mere chance, one must confess, does the non-academic public take great interest in the four "miracle" courses to be found among the offerings of many universities—advertising, salesmanship, psychology, and effective speaking. Nor is it remarkable, though one may think it deplorable, that appearances of the officers of our national government before the mass audience of the citizens are characteristic products of the country's leading advertising agencies.

Likewise propaganda and its brother "information" borrow and refine upon certain portions of rhetoric. No doubt it serves a useful purpose to identify propaganda with the vicious forces in the modern world, with the German Government of World War I and with the Nazi and Soviet totalitarianisms of the present time. At the same time, however, it would be the better part of wisdom to recognize that most of the major techniques of this propaganda are long known rhetorical techniques gone wrong, that propaganda is not a new invention which we have no ready equipment for combatting, let alone fumigating and using for our honorable ends. The understanding of propaganda will be founded in the understanding of rhetoric first of all, whatever else may be necessary.[24] Both Ross Scanlan and Kenneth Burke have demonstrated the enlightenment which can come from the application of rhetorical criticism to both the internal and external propanganda of the Nazis; [25] and two articles by Scanlan and Henry C. Youngerman in the first issue of *Today's Speech* (April, 1953) are grounded on the assumption of a close kinship between rhetoric (or its corollary, "public address") and propaganda.[26] In fact, one of Scanlan's concluding statements indirectly makes both the identification and the basic distinction: "Today it is to be hoped that America will find means to match enemy propaganda in effectiveness without sacrificing the standards of morality and intellect that distinguish democracy from the totalitarian order."

Rhetoric as a Method of Inquiry

More than once in the preceding pages I have in passing assigned to rhetoric a secondary function of the discovery of ideas, contributory to its prime function of the popularizing of ideas. That is the con-

[24] See, for example, Everett L. Hunt, "Ancient Rhetoric and Modern Propaganda," *QJS*, XXXVII (April 1951), 157–160.

[25] Burke, *The Philosophy of Literary Form* (1941), pp. 191–220; Scanlan, "The Nazi Party Speaker System, I & II," *SM*, XVI (August 1949), 82–97, XVII (June 1950), 134–148; "The Nazi Rhetorician," *QJS*, XXVII (December 1951), 430–440.

[26] "Two Views of Propaganda," pp. 13–14; "Propaganda and Public Address," pp. 15–17.

sequence of the division of *inventio,* the term applied in Roman rhetoric to the systematic investigative procedures by which rhetoric sought to turn up all the relevant arguments or considerations in any given situation. As part of *inventio,* for example, the elaborate doctrine of *status* was developed, through which by the application of analytical criteria it was possible to determine just what was the core, the central issue in any given case, just what had to be proved as a *sine qua non,* and where the lines of argument for proving it would lie if they were available. In general the division of *inventio* constituted a codification of the *topoi* or *places where arguments are to be found;* for instance, in *fact past, fact future, more and less, etc.* Rhetoric, thus, as we have said, provides scientific assistance to the speaker in discovering what questions to ask and how to go about answering them. It serves the speaker as laboratory procedures for analysis serve the chemist—by systematic inventory it enables him to determine with reasonable completeness what is present and what is absent in any given case.

We need not be surprised, therefore, that so useful a method tended to be incorporated into other arts and sciences where its original provenience was often forgotten. Historically, some of the studies to profit greatly from this borrowing from rhetoric have been the law, theology, logic, and poetic.[27] The Polandizing of rhetoric, one of the characteristic phenomena of its history, accounts in large part for the splinter meanings and the distortions which we have seen as typical of its current and historic significance. It has been the fate of rhetoric, the residual term, to be applied to the less intellectual segments of itself, while its central operating division, *inventio,* has been appropriated by the studies and sciences which rhetoric serves.

The functions of a complete rhetoric, however, have usually been operative under whatever temporary auspices as the whole art of discourse, even as they were in the renaissance tripartite grammar-logic-rhetoric. This splintering may go so far towards specialism, however, that the investigative function of rhetoric, the method of *inventio,* may be diverted from that to which it most properly applies. This diversion may very well be the tendency today, where a complete rhetoric hardly exists as a formal discipline except in those classically oriented courses in public speaking, debate, group discussion, argumentation, and persuasion whose central focus is on *inventio*—the

[27] See Richard McKeon, "Rhetoric in the Middle Ages," *Critics and Criticism, Ancient and Modern,* ed. R. S. Crane (Chicago, 1952), pp. 260–296, reprinted from *Speculum,* January, 1942; and Marvin T. Herrick, "The Place of Rhetoric in Poetic Theory," *QJS,* XXXIV (February 1948), 1–22.

investigation and discovery of lines of argument and basic issues. Mostly rhetoric today survives, as we have seen, under other names and special applications in those specialties which contribute to it or draw upon it or appropriate selectively from its store of method— psychology, advertising, salesmanship, propaganda analysis, public opinion and social control, semantics, and that which is loosely called "research" in common parlance.

May I attempt in summary of this matter to bring rhetoric back to its essential investigative function, its function of discovery, by quoting from Isocrates, the Athenian politico-rhetorical philosopher, and from Edmund Burke, the eighteenth-century British statesman-orator? Wrote Isocrates in the *Antidosis*, "With this faculty we both contend against others on matters that are open to dispute and seek light for ourselves on things which are unknown; for the same arguments which we use in persuading others when we speak in public, we employ when we deliberate in our thoughts." [28] Twenty-two centuries later, the young Burke included in his notebook digest of the topics of rhetoric, which he headed "How to Argue," the following succinct, Baconian statement about the functions of *inventio:*

> To invent Arguments without a thorough knowledge of the Subject is clearly impossible. But the Art of Invention does two things—
> 1. It suggests to us more readily those Parts of our actual knowledge which may help towards illustrating the matter before us, &
> 2. It suggests to us heads of Examination which may lead, if pursued with effect into a knowledge of the Subject.
>
> So that the Art of Invention may properly be considered as the method of calling up what we do know, & investigating that of which we are ignorant.[29]

Rhetoric in Education

If the burden of the preceding pages is not misplaced, the importance of rhetoric in the equipment of the well-educated member of society can hardly be in doubt. I am not inclined, therefore, especially in this journal, to offer to demonstrate the desirability of speech as an academic study. Our conventions and our journals have been full

---

[28] *Isocrates,* trans. George Norlin (Loeb Classical Library, New York, 1929), II, 327.

[29] From an original manuscript among the Wentworth-Fitzwilliam papers in the Sheffield City Library, used with the kind permission of Earl Fitzwilliam and the trustees of the Fitzwilliam settled estates.

of such demonstration for, lo, these thirty years.[30] If enlightened and responsible leaders with rhetorical knowledge and skill are not trained and nurtured, irresponsible demagogues will monopolize the power of rhetoric, will have things to themselves. If talk rather than take is to settle the course of our society, if ballots instead of bullets are to effect our choice of governors, if discourse rather than coercion is to prevail in the conduct of human affairs, it would seem like arrant folly to trust to chance that the right people shall be equipped offensively and defensively with a sound rationale of informative and suasory discourse.

In general education, especially, rhetoric would appear to deserve a place of uncommon importance. That is the burden of a recent article by Dean Hunt of Swarthmore. Rhetoric is the organon of the liberal studies, the formulation of the principles through which the educated man, the possessor of many specialties, attains effectiveness in society.[31] A complete rhetoric is a structure for the wholeness of the effective man, the aim of general education. But, as Dean Hunt concludes, the rhetorician himself must not become a technical specialist:

> He will keep his wholeness if he comes back again and again to Aristotle, but he must supplement those conceptions with what modern scientists have added to the mirror for man; he must illuminate the classical rhetoric with psychology, cultural anthropology, linguistics and semantics, special disciplines, perhaps, but disciplines in which he can lean heavily on interpreters who speak to others than their professional colleagues. Departments of speech which have emphasized training in rhetoric have a new opportunity to establish their place in general education. Their very claim to wholeness has been a source of distrust in an atmosphere of specialism. If now they can relate themselves to newer conceptions in the sciences, social sciences, and humanities, they can show that the ideal of the good man skilled in speaking is like the sea, ever changing and ever the same.[32]

So much for rhetoric in education as a study directed at the creation and at the analysis and criticism of informative and suasory discourse—at the ability, on the one hand, "to summon thought quickly and use it forcibly," [33] and on the other to listen or read critically with the maximum application of analytical judgment.

[30] See, for example, one of the latest, W. N. Brigance, "General Education in an Industrial Free Society," *QJS*, XXXVIII (April, 1952), esp. p. 181.

[31] "Rhetoric and General Education," *QJS*, XXXV (October, 1949), 275, 277.

[32] *Ibid.*, 279.

[33] Herbert A. Wichelns, "Public Speaking and Dramatic Arts," in *On Going to College: A Symposium* (New York, Oxford University Press, 1938), p. 240.

Rhetoric would appear thus to be in certain senses a literary study, or as Wichelns wrote, at least "its tools are those of literature." It is a literary study as it is involved in the creative arts of language, of informing ideas. It is a literary study also as it contributes substantially to literary scholarship. Not only have literature and literary theory been persistently rhetorical for long periods—during much of the renaissance, for example, the seventeenth and eighteenth centuries in England, and for most of the short history of American literature—but writers and readers until fairly recently had been so generally educated in rhetoric that it provided the vocabulary and many of the concepts in terms of which much literature was both written and read. Clark's *Milton at St. Paul's School* may be cited as one conclusive demonstration of the importance of rhetoric in renaissance education and its importance in renaissance literature. This importance is now being recognized by literary scholars, and rhetoric is taking on considerable proportions in their studies, especially among those who are studying the renaissance. Myrick's study of Sir Philip Sidney as a literary craftsman,[34] for example, demonstrates how thoroughly Sidney was schooled in rhetoric and how carefully he constructed his defense of poetry on familiar rhetorical principles. If Myrick has been in error in his construction of the specific genealogy of Sidney's rhetoric, the fact of Sidney's rhetorical system is nevertheless in no doubt.

The plain truth is that whatever the inadequacies in specific cases of the analytical method ingrained in our educated ancestors, they *had* method, the method of formal rhetoric; whereas a general characteristic of our contemporary education is that it inculcates *no* method beyond a rather uncertain grammar and a few rules of paragraphing and bibliography. Rigidity of method is doubtless a grievous obstacle to the greatest fulfillment of genius in either belles lettres or public address; but the widespread impotence and ineptitude even of our best-educated fellows when faced with the problem of constructing or analyzing any but the most rudimentary expository or argumentative discourse, much less a complicated literary work, are surely worse. Rhetoric supplies the equipment for such practical endeavor in the promulgation of ideas, and twenty centuries have learned to use it to supplement and perfect chance and natural instinct.

That such method has at times become sterile or mechanical, that at other times it has been put to uses for which it was least adapted is amusing, perhaps lamentable, but not surprising. The remote uses

[34] Kenneth O. Myrick, *Sir Philip Sidney as a Literary Craftsman* (1935).

to which rhetorical methods of analysis and description have been put, in the absence of a more appropriate method, are well illustrated by the following passage from Sir John Hawkins' *History of Music*, first published in the late eighteenth century:

> The art of invention is made one of the heads among the precepts of rhetoric, to which music in this and sundry instances bears a near resemblance; the end of persuasion, or affecting the passions being common to both. This faculty consists in the enumeration of common places, which are revolved over in the mind, and requires both an ample store of knowledge in the subject upon which it is exercised, and a power of applying that knowledge as occasion may require. It differs from memory in this respect, that whereas memory does but recall to the mind the images or remembrance of things as they were first perceived, the faculty of invention divides complex ideas into those whereof they are composed, and recommends them again after different fashions, thereby creating variety of new objects and conceptions. Now, the greater the fund of knowledge above spoken of is, the greater is the source from whence the invention of the artist or composer is supplied; and the benefits thereof are seen in new combinations and phrases, capable of variety and permutation without end.[35]

From its lapses and wanderings, however, rhetoric when needed has almost always recovered its vitality and comprehensive scope, by reference to its classic sources. But that it should be ignored seems, as Dean Hunt suggests, hardly a compliment to education.

Rhetoric as a serious scholarly study I have treated in my former essay, and I shall not go over the same ground again. That there is a body of philosophy and principle worth scholarly effort in discovery, enlargement, and reinterpretation is beyond question, and fortunately more competent scholars each year are working at it. Rhetorical criticism and the study of rhetoric as a revealing social and cultural phenomenon are also gaining ground. New and interesting directions for research in these areas are being explored, or at least marked out; they are based on newly developed techniques and hitherto neglected kinds of data. One might mention, for example, those new approaches listed by Maloney: [36] the quantitative content analysis as developed by Lasswell; the qualitative content analysis as used by Lowenthal and Guterman; figurative analysis such as applied to Shakespeare by

---

[35] (2 vols., London, 1875), I, xxv.
[36] "Some New Directions in Rhetorical Criticism," *Central States Speech Journal*, IV (February, 1953), 1–5.

Caroline Spurgeon; and intonational analysis. Extensive and provocative suggestions are to be found in quantity in the text and bibliography of Brembeck and Howell's *Persuasion: A Means of Social Control*,[37] especially in Part VI. The section on rhetoric in the annual Haberman bibliography is convincing evidence of the vitality of current enterprise.[38]

Though new avenues, new techniques, new materials such as the foregoing are inviting to the increasing numbers of scholars whose interests and abilities—to say nothing of their necessities—lie in rhetorical research, especially those new directions which lead to rhetoric as a cultural, a sociological, a social-psychiatric phenomenon, the older literary-historical-political studies are still neither too complete nor too good. In any event, each new generation probably needs to interpret afresh much of the relevant history of thought, especially the thought of the people as distinguished from what is commonly considered the history of ideas. For this the scholarship of rhetoric seems particularly adapted. Towards this purpose, I find no need to relocate the field of rhetorical scholarship as envisioned by Hudson and Wichelns, nor to recant from the considerations which I outlined in the *QJS* in 1937.[39] One may find it reassuring to observe, however, that much which was asked for in those essays has since then been undertaken and often accomplished with considerable success. Especially is this true of the study of public address in its bulk and day-to-day manifestations: in the movement studies, the "case" studies, the sectional and regional studies, the studies of "debates" and "campaigns" such as the debates on the League of Nations and the campaigns for conservation.

There remains much to do, nevertheless, and much to re-do in the more familiar and conventional areas of research and interpretation. The editing and translation of rhetorical texts is still far from complete or adequate. The canon of ancient rhetoric is, to be sure, in very good shape, and when Caplan's translation of the *Ad Herennium* is published in the Loeb Library there will hardly be a major deficiency. In post-classical, mediaeval, and renaissance rhetoric the situation is not so good, though it is improving. There are still too few works like Howell's *Rhetoric of Alcuin and Charlemagne* and Sister Therese Sullivan's commentary on and translation of the fourth book of St.

---

[37] (New York, 1952).
[38] "A Bibliography of Rhetoric and Public Address," ed. F. W. Haberman, formerly appearing annually in the *QJS*, latterly in *SM*.
[39] See above, note 1.

Augustine's *De Doctrina.* Halm's *Rhetores Minores,* for example, is substantially unmolested so far.

English and continental rhetoric of the sixteenth, seventeenth, and eighteenth centuries is slowly appearing in modern editions by scholars who know rhetoric as the theory of public address. Our bibliographies show increasing numbers of these as doctoral dissertations, most of which, alas, seem to be abandoned almost as soon as finished. Only a few works of the sort, like Howell's *Fénelon,* represent mature, published work.

In the history and historical analysis of rhetoric, nothing of adequate range and scope yet exists. Thonssen and Baird's *Speech Criticism,* ambitious as it is, is only a beginning. The general history of rhetoric, and even most of the special histories, have yet to be written. Works now under way by Donald L. Clark and Wilbur S. Howell will make substantial contributions, but rhetoric from Corax to Whately needs far fuller and better treatment than it gets in the series of histories of criticism by the late J. W. H. Atkins.

Towards the study of the rhetorical principles and practice of individual speakers and writers the major part of our scholarly effort seems to have been directed. The convenience of this kind of study is beyond question and is hard to resist, either in public address or in literature. And this is as it should be. The tendency to write biographies of speakers, however, rather than rhetorico-critical studies of them, must be kept in check, or at least in proportion. Again for reasons of convenience, if not also of scholarly nationalism, the studies of American speakers are proportionately too numerous. British and foreign public address is still far too scantily noticed by competent rhetorical scholars.

Rhetoric and Poetic

This would not be the place, I think, even if Professor Thonssen's review of rhetorical works were not appearing in this same issue of the *QJS,* for a survey of rhetorical scholarship. The preceding paragraphs are intended only as a token of decent respect to accomplishment and progress in a discrete and important branch of humane scholarship. A further area where rhetorical scholarship may be very profitably pursued, however, perhaps deserves some special consideration.

Even if it were not for the contributions of Kenneth Burke, the study of rhetoric in literature and of the relation of the theory of rhetoric to the theory of poetic would be taking on renewed importance at the present time. The lively revival of rhetorical study in renaissance scholarship which I have mentioned is only one phase of the problem. A renewed or increased interest in satire, deriving in part, perhaps, from the excellent work which of late has been done on Swift, leads directly to rhetoric. The rhetorical mode is obviously at the center of satire, and any fundamental analysis of satire must depend upon the equipment for rhetorical analysis. Likewise, a complete dramatic criticism must draw upon rhetoric, both practically and philosophically. The internal rhetoric of the drama was specifically recognized by Aristotle when he referred readers of the *Poetics* to the *Rhetoric* for coverage of the element of *dianoia*, for the analysis of speeches in which agents try to convince or persuade each other. What, however, is the external rhetoric of the drama? What is the drama intended to do to an audience? Herein lies the question of the province of poetic as opposed to the province of rhetoric. When Antony addresses the Roman citizens in *Julius Caesar*, the existence of an internal rhetoric in the play is clear enough; the relation between Antony and his stage audience is unmistakably rhetorical. But what of the relation between Antony and the audience in the pit, or the Antony-stage-audience combination and the audience in the pit? The more we speculate about the effect of a play or any literary work on an audience, the more we become involved in metaphysical questions in which rhetoric must be involved.

Much contemporary poetry or pseudo-poetry in any generation is rhetorical in the most obvious sense—in the same sense as the epideictic oration. It "pleases" largely by rhetorical means or methods. It "reminds" us of experience instead of "organizing" or "creating" experience. It appeals to our satisfaction with what we are used to; it convinces us that what *was* still may be as it was, that old formulas are pleasantest if not best. It is not so much concerned with pointing up the old elements in the new, even, as establishing the identity of the old and the contemporary. "What oft was thought, but ne'er so well expressed" is a distinctly rhetorical attainment, and it would not have occurred to Pope to suppose that the poetic and the rhetorical were antithetical, if indeed they were separable. Though sporadically the effort of critics and theorists has been to keep *rhetoric* and *poetic* apart, the two rationales have had an irresistible tendency to come together, and their similarities may well be more important than their differences. When the forming of attitude is admitted into the province of rhetoric, then, to Kenneth Burke, rhetoric becomes a method for the analysis of even lyric poetry. Hence a frequent term in certain kinds of literary analysis now is *poetic-rhetoric*, as for example in the first two sentences in Ruth Wallerstein's analysis of two elegies: "I want this paper to consider two poems, John Donne's elegy on Prince Henry and Milton's *Lycidas*, in the light that is shed on them by seventeenth-century rhetoric-poetic as I understand it. Both the significance of that rhetoric and the test of my view of it will reside in its power to illuminate the poems." [40]

Undoubtedly there are basic differences between *poetic* and *rhetoric*, both practical and philosophical, and probably these differences lie both in the kind of method which is the proper concern of each and the kind of effect on audiences to the study of which each is devoted. The purely poetic seeks the creation or organization of imaginative experience, probably providing for reader or audience some kind of satisfying spiritual or emotional therapy. The rhetorical seeks a predetermined channeling of the audience's understanding or attitude. Poetry works by representation; rhetoric by instigation. The poetic is fulfilled in creation, the rhetorical in illumination. "An image," wrote Longinus, "has one purpose with the orators and another with the poets; . . . the design of the poetic image is enthralment, of the rhetorical, vivid description. Both, however, seek to stir the passions and the emotions. . . . In oratorical imagery its best feature is always its reality and truth." [41] Poetry, declared Sir Philip Sidney, cannot lie because it affirms nothing; it merely presents. Rhetoric not only presents but affirms. That is its characteristic. Both poetic and rhetoric attain their effects through language. If the poet's highest skill lies in his power to make language do what it has never done before, to force from words and the conjunction of words meanings which are new and unique, perhaps it is the highest skill of the speaker to use words in their accepted senses in such a way as to make them carry their traditional meanings with a vividness and effectiveness which they have never known before.

Summary

In brief we may assign to rhetoric a four-fold status. So far as it is concerned with the management of discourse in specific situations for practical purposes, it is an instrumental discipline. It is a literary study,

---

[40] "Rhetoric in the English Renaissance: Two Elegies," *English Institute Essays, 1948*, p. 153.

[41] Trans. Rhys Roberts, sec. 15.

involving linguistics, critical theory, and semantics as it touches the art of informing ideas, and the functioning of language. It is a philosophical study so far as it is concerned with a method of investigation or inquiry. And finally, as it is akin to politics, drawing upon psychology and sociology, rhetoric is a social study, the study of a major force in the behavior of men in society.

THE FUNCTION OF RHETORIC AS EFFECTIVE EXPRESSION
P. Albert Duhamel

The recent increase in the critical literature concerned with rhetoric, whether of the Renaissance, Mediaeval, or Classical Periods, calls for a re-examination of the assumptions of past histories of rhetoric and a definition of the fundamental relations existing between rhetoric and other branches of knowledge which future studies must consider. There is a sufficiency of monographs occupied with the determination of the influence of particular rhetoric books on selected authors, or of histories supplying chronological lists of the contents of successive manuals. It is high time that a study of rhetoric, which, even with the limitations of past studies, has long been recognized as fruitful, be established on firm ground. This can come about only through recognizing that rhetoric occupies a peculiar position among the arts, and that it cannot be adequately interpreted apart from the ideological context in which it occurs. Consequently this paper does not attempt to rewrite the history of rhetoric during any period of its history but it does propose to consider some questions of method which must be taken into consideration in any discussion of rhetoric. This purpose can best be accomplished by an evaluation of the methods and assumptions of some past histories of rhetoric and the illustration of the proposed method by reference to the problems to be encountered in some periods of rhetorical history. The rhetoric of Greece and Rome as presented by its better known theorists affords excellent working material for determining the principles which should guide any examination of rhetoric, and, further, the rhetoricians of the Classical Period must be most carefully studied for they established the art and the direction it was to take for a long time afterwards.

Rhetoric is better thought of as an idea, the concept of effective

From *Journal of the History of Ideas*, June, 1949. Reprinted with the permission of the *Journal of the History of Ideas*, and of the author.

expression, than as a set or collection of principles with an abiding purpose. The content and purpose of rhetoric books differ from author to author, and the assumption that techniques and devices in any books are commensurable is unfounded. Terms and purposes are meaningful only within the context of the author's system taken as a whole. All rhetoricians have had one object: the teaching of effective expression. That object can be considered as the "least common denominator" of mental notes which undergo accretion and modification in accordance with an author's conception of what constitutes eloquence. The idea or concept of effective expression is not simple but complex, for it contains more than one element and is invested with several relations. In its simplest form the idea may be said to be undetermined. It is determined by influences external to itself, its relations, which constitute the more basic elements of the rhetoricians's philosophy.

The content of the idea "rhetoric," or of the conception of what constitutes effective expression, is dependent upon the epistemology, psychology, and metaphysic of the system in which it occurs. The rhetorical is determined by the epistemological. The rhetorician's conception of the value of argument, the process of invention by which arguments are to be discovered, the extent to which the devices of elocution are to be employed, is the result of his evaluation of the reliability of the intellect, the nature and availability of truth, and the existence of certitude. Thus Aristotle's idea of rhetoric, or of what constitutes effective expression, differs from Plato's mainly because he conceived of probable truth as valuable *in se* and frequently the best human intelligence can expect. The Middle Ages evidenced some scientific curiosity in their attempt to assimilate Aristotelian science, but had a tendency to eschew systems which sought only the probable, for the conviction that all *necessary* truth was present in revelation underlay most of their thought. Thus Aristotle was preoccupied with the erection of a system of rhetoric which would discover and express probabilities; Plato valued only the Absolute. The arts of probability and practicality occupied a relatively low position in the mediaeval scheme of values. Interest was focussed upon the expression of ideas for which the highest type of certitude was already present, divine testimony. Thus the systems of invention which had been essential in some classical rhetorics for the discovery of arguments disappear as such from the mediaeval rhetorics and are transferred to mediaeval logics where they appear as means of discovering the sense in which terms are to be understood. In place of the traditional *inventio* are extensive considerations of the devices of ornamentation traditionally discussed under elocution. This is easily explained, for the later period merely sought to express more effectively the truth already possessed; Aristotle sought, in his *Rhetoric,* to discover and organize arguments about doubtful matters. Under such differing philosophical circumstances the idea of effective expression undergoes extensive modifications, and *ars bene dicendi* cannot mean the same thing to Aristotle and Hrabanus Maurus.

Further, the content of the idea "rhetoric" when realized in a manual or reduced to practice has an influence upon an orator or stylist. Cicero's style was influenced by his rhetoric. He sought to speak effectively, and his expression mirrors his conception of rhetoric. If he had conceived of effective speech as synonymous with the widespread application of the devices usually considered under *elocutio* to the exclusion of valid arguments, his style would undoubtedly have been more Asiatic. The excessive amount of ornamentation in the expression of an age or author is usually correlated to a rhetorical conception which either lacks, or treats very lightly, a system for the discovery of arguments, because it is either convinced that truth is safely within its grasp or not worth worrying about. The conviction of the Middle Ages and the degeneration of later Stoicism may be taken as ready illustrations. The rhetorical theory may come before or after the expression, as a rationalization *post factum* or as a working hypothesis, but in all instances it aids in the explanation of the manner of expression.

If future histories of rhetoric are to avoid such criticism as that of Mr. Richard P. McKeon, that they are but the "monotonous enumeration of doctrines, or preferably sentences, repeated from Cicero, or commentators on Cicero," they must avoid assumptions such as those made in the past, which have always been implicit determinations or limitations of the idea of effective expression to preconceived or accepted definitions.[1] Such historians of rhetoric have been treating rhetoric in some particular sense, defining a concept which must be kept fluid, if histories of rhetoric are not to be negative or deprecatory.[2] If histories of rhetoric are to be written after first postulating a definition of the concept and then re-examining the history of the assumed concept, the resulting inquiry would be the history not of rhetoric but of one conception of rhetoric. If the definition of the concept postulated be that of Aristotle, the history of rhetoric would reveal a

---

[1] Richard P. McKeon, "Rhetoric in the Middle Ages," *Speculum,* XVII (1942), 1.
[2] *Ibid.,* 2.

tremendous gap between the decline of the Roman Empire and the writings of Francis Bacon.[3] If the definition assumed were that of Martianus Capella or Isidore of Seville, rhetoric would not begin till the Middle Ages, nor would it survive the Renaissance. The varying subject matter attributed to rhetoric by individual theorists, the changing conceptions of the purpose and value of rhetoric, are reflections of more basic changes in the broad spheres of individual ideology. The determination of the concept of effective expression to any complete definition as an assumption of a projected history forestalls the recognition of the relations of the concept and deprives the study, which should be the study of an idea and its inter-relations, of its most fruitful potentialities. A re-evaluation of the conception of rhetoric, therefore, requires a recognition of the relation of effective speech to truth and to style. An adequate study of rhetoric implies a consideration of the assumed content of the rhetoric itself and of the ideas which have determined that content. Such a study may also look to the concrete results, in the styles of various writers or speakers, to evaluate the end product.

Even within the limits of Greek thought it is possible to find changes in the conception of effective expression resulting from alterations in the definition of truth and man. As long as the Greeks defined *areté*, or excellence, in terms of physical prowess and considered it hereditary, democracy was obviously impossible. Democracy became a reality and culture concerned itself with non-physical and non-hereditary elements when political virtues were admitted to some validity.[4] Obviously this change, which can be seen in the overthrow of Achilles as the ideal Greek by Odysseus, represents a change in the conception of man. It represents the development of the concept of justice, and the value of deliberation in arriving at a practical course of action. The articulation of this limited idea of humanity was the work of the Sophists. They continuously thought of man as a social animal and of his nature as adequately fulfilled by assuming a share in the government of the *polis*. Thus their system of education became a preparation for political effectiveness. Since any person might speak in the city state, "eloquence, then, was the point from which any attempt to educate a man for political leadership was bound to start."[5] Rhetoric thus became the chief instrument of their teaching.

[3] On this point see Karl R. Wallace, *Francis Bacon on Communication and Rhetoric* (Chapel Hill, 1943), 172–173 and 76 and 147.
[4] Werner Jaeger, *Paideia* (Oxford, 1939) I, 286–287.
[5] *Ibid.*, 285 and 288.

Sophistic rhetoric is usually criticized because of its preoccupation with devices of ornamentation, its tendency to treat logic lightly, and its emphasis on form.[6] This criticism of the Sophists is based mostly upon indirect evidence, for our knowledge of their techniques and purposes is derived mainly from the dialogues, like the *Gorgias* and the *Phaedrus*, wherein Plato has the Sophists examine their method and content. Essentially, the Sophists were humanists attempting to educate to a limited aim dictated by the pragmatic nature of the society in which they lived and taught. The seriousness with which they took up the challenge of changing conditions and the sincerity with which they tried to perpetuate their ideal could not preserve them from an attack accusing them of not meeting problems which, within the limits of their definition of "humanism," they could not feel as problems. Plato, and later Aristotle, directed their attack against the Sophists on two levels: on a very simple level Plato, in particular, expressed his distaste for what their oratorical style had become and, on a more fundamental level, both Aristotle and Plato criticized their estimate of human nature and man's relation to the universe. As humanists the Sophists failed because they could not answer Socrates' challenging concept of the soul; as rhetoricians they failed because of the degeneration of their style. The stylistic failure was intimately linked to their failure as humanists, for their formalism resulted from an inability to provide substantiating material as the vehicle of their figures. The matter could have been produced by a logical system of investigation, which they lacked, for they lacked the λόγος.

The statement of Protagoras that man is the measure of all things gives a good insight into the basic principles of the Sophists.[7] For Plato, God was much more the measure of things than man.[8] The criterion of educational measure thus changes and the previous anthropocentric nature of Greek thought is temporarily suspended as Plato's orientation becomes completely transcendental. The evaluation of an educational system or of an element in an educational system proceeded on vastly different grounds for Plato than it had for the Sophists. A thing was no longer valuable because it improved the political life

---

[6] See the standard treatment of H. Gomperz, *Sophistik und Rhetorik, das Bildungsideal des* εὖ λέγειν (Berlin, 1912), also E. M. Cope, "On the Sophistical Rhetoric," *Journal of Classical and Sacred Philosophy,* II (1856), 147 ff. and *ibid.,* III (1858), 35–80, 253–288.

[7] Hermann Diels, *Die Fragmente der Vorsokratiker* (Berlin, 1907), Zweite Auflage, zweiter Band, erste Halfte, 536. Protagoras, Frg. 1.

[8] Plato, *Laws,* 716 C. ὁ δὴ θεὸς ἡμιν πάντων χρημάτων μέτρον ἄνείη μάλιστα καί πολὺ μᾶλλον ἢ πού τις ὥς φασιν ἄνθρωπος.

of the individual, but only in so far as it contributed to the knowledge of transcendentals. Truth was no longer to be determined by political expediency; it was something withdrawn and abstract, apart from time and place. Rhetoric could be expected, *a priori*, to fall from its former important position unless it could demonstrate an ability to reach truth, or enable man to acquire the Good.

In the very earliest of his works Plato foreshadowed the aim of his educational activity—"how men can acquire the knowledge of the Idea of the Good." [9] Since rhetoric remains content with emotional persuasion and does not instruct in the matter of right and wrong,[10] it can only be classed with cookery and other skills.[11] The orator thus becomes a mountebank peddling gaudy trifles.[12] Plato, however, like every other theorist, considered some forms of expression better than others. His idea of what constituted effective expression can be inferred from Socrates' second speech in the *Phaedrus*, which is characterized by a plainness of delivery, a following of the natural movements of the mind, and an insistence upon logical definition.[13] In Socrates' opinion, it is the matter and organization of a speech which are worthy of praise; added ornamentation is vain and superfluous.[14] Socrates clearly expected the Sophist, Lysias, to produce finely turned expression, embroidered trivialities, and trite epigrams, for it was against these tendencies of the Sophists that he had been in continual opposition.[15] He criticizes Lysias' speech for its disorderly arrangement of the topics and an absence of logical sequence.[16] Plato's conception of effective speech, or rhetoric, is thus revealed as insistent upon basic wisdom, and a knowledge of the truth. The speech should not be amorphous, but then again not shaped to conform to an artificial pattern. The essentials are the search and discovery of the truth, its expression in unvarnished terms, and the avoidance of all that does not aid in a clearer perception of the ultimate realities which alone are desirable.

The difference between the Platonic and Aristotelian rhetoric is intelligible ultimately only in terms of the profound difference between their two attitudes. Aristotle's view of the world "was essentially pagan

---

[9] W. Jaeger, *Paideia* (New York, 1943), II, 96.
[10] Plato, *Phaedrus*, 260–262 C. Also 272–273 A.
[11] Plato, *Gorgias*, 463.
[12] *Ibid.*, 459 C.
[13] Plato, *Phaedrus*, 244–257 B.
[14] *Ibid.*, 236 A–C.
[15] *Ibid.*, 234 E.
[16] *Ibid.*, 264 B.

because it saw things from the point of view of things themselves," and thus "it is no marvel if Aristotle's philosophy has succeeded in the interpretation of the things of nature: from the first moment it was turned toward the earth and organized for its conquest." Plato's philosophy, on the other hand, "was in the very first intention a philosophy of what is beyond, placing the reason of things outside the things themselves. . . . It was, then, a philosophy of the insufficiency of things and the knowledge we possess of them." [17] Plato constantly sought the Truth, whereas Aristotle was willing to admit the inadequacy of our knowledge of some things and to establish an art with probability as its ultimate goal. Aristotle admitted the certitude of certain basic principles in science, but probability was the very basis and foundation of the Aristotelian system of rhetoric.[18]

Aristotelian rhetoric is to be primarily concerned with the deliberation of things in which two alternatives are possible.[19] Those things which are certain, whether of past, present, or future, do not fall into the province of rhetoric, for no one deliberates about them. As for those things which are metaphysically certain, there is so overwhelmingly obvious evidence present that the mind immediately concedes assent. Aristotle distinguishes himself from the previous compilers of arts of rhetoric who have "provided us with only a small portion of this art, for proofs are the only thing in it that come within the province of the art; everything else is merely an accessory. And yet they say nothing about enthymemes which are the body of proof, but chiefly devoted their attention to matters outside the subject; for the arousing of prejudice, compassion, anger, and similar emotions . . ." [20] Here he is obviously taking the advice of the *Phaedrus* and repudiating the shallow sophistical view which had seen rhetoric as an instrument for the agitation of the passions.[21]

[17] E. Gilson, *The Philosophy of St. Bonaventure* (London, 1938), 96.

[18] E. L. Hunt, "Plato and Aristotle on Rhetoric and Rheoricians," *Studies in Rhetoric and Public Speaking in Honor of James Albert Winans* (New York, 1925), 28 and 49. Also E. M. Cope, *An Introduction to Aristotle's Rhetoric* (London, 1867), 7. See also Thomas De Quincey's remarks in his *Collected Works* edited by D. Masson, X, 90–91.

[19] Aristotle, *Rhetoric*, 1357 A. βουλενόμεθα δὲ περὶ τῶν φαινομένων ἐνδέχεσθαι ἀμφοτέρως ἔχειν.

[20] John Henry Freese, ed. and trs., *Aristotle's "The Art of Rhetoric,"* (New York, 1926), 5.

[21] Cf. G. L. Hendrickson, "Origin and Meaning of the Characters of Style," *American Journal of Philology*, XXXVI (1905), 248–290; also by the same author, "The Peripatetic Mean of Style and the Three Stylistic Characters," *Ibid.*, XXXV (1904), 125–146. Also E. M. Cope, "On Sophistical Rhetoric," 158–159.

After this brief criticism of the Sophists, Aristotle begins to develop his own position and to connect rhetoric with dialectic, which was to remain the distinguishing mark of his system.[22] His arguments for uniting the two are mainly psychological: the true and that which resembles it come under the same faculty, and he who divines well in regard to the truth will divine well in regard to probabilities.[23]

The war between philosophy and rhetoric did not end in Greece; it was continued in Rome. The battle was always joined between those who maintained the relative superiority of philosophy to rhetoric and those who claimed that effective speaking was a question of formal arrangement and that no other substantiation was needed. With the disappearance of the Roman Republic and the advent of the Empire, Roman rhetoric underwent a profound change. Deliberative and forensic oratory assumed a new tone; the previous public interest in the determination of basic issues disappeared and was replaced by a resigned attitude. Justice and law-making had been taken over by the Emperors, and the purpose of oratory was not so much to discover as to approve the Imperial will. Cicero was conscious of this change in its earliest stages but hardly foresaw the complete degeneration of rhetoric. He felt that since the time of Socrates a division, as between soul and body, had been made in the teaching of thought and expression. This separation, really the disjunction of *inventio* and *elocutio,* was the cause of the disreputable state in which rhetoric found itself in Cicero's time.[24] His answer to the situation was simple enough; if you wish to be a great orator, like Demosthenes or Pericles, study Aristotle.[25]

Cicero thereby reveals himself as maintaining a position similar to that of Aristotle. He holds that a philosophical basis, a system of invention to provide matter, is necessary to forestall degeneration into sheer formalism. Through the many Ciceronian works it is possible to trace a conception of rhetoric and the orator which is more fully developed than the short Aristotelian notes. Even a brief review of the first two sections of the first book of Cicero's ethical treatise, *De Officiis,* is sufficient to demonstrate that he was intent upon making man more eloquent about moral ideals. The Ciceronian humanism was based upon a far deeper conception of human nature than the

[22] Cf. Cope, *Introduction to Aristotle's Rhetoric,* 6.
[23] J. H. Freese, *op. cit.,* 11.
[24] Cicero, *De Oratore,* III, xix.
[25] *Loc. cit.*

convenient rhetoricism of sophistry could satisfy. Cicero frequently makes his point that the orator is to be concerned with something else beyond mere form. The orator can employ the voice of a tragedian, the gestures of the greatest actors, but he requires also the acumen of the dialectician and the ethical knowledge of philosophers.[26] Also, the orator works for the good of the state and cannot rest in the flowery excursus of the pedant who acts before his students or a select group of admirers.

Again in the *Brutus,* the thoroughly Ciceronian view, which would not permit a dissociation of thought and expression, or an expression which was unmotivated by questions of truth, serves as a guide in the estimation of the great orators of Roman history. The orators whom he admires were not the formalists, but those who were learned as well as good speakers. Among them Demosthenes was successful because he studied Plato. In two other works, the *Partitiones Oratoriae* and the *Topica,* the relationship of rhetoric to dialectic is examined.[27] The two works are similar to Aristotle's in intention, for they insist upon argument. There is a difference, however, between the two, for Cicero chose "to preserve in a work on rhetoric the emphasis upon the non-logical means of persuasion, and to create in the field where rhetoric assumes the burden of positive demonstration, a system of invention analogous to that used by dialectic." [28] Aristotle, on the contrary, had assumed that the system used by the dialecticians had validity in rhetoric and needed no special interpretation.[29] Aristotle placed his trust in the Organon, while Cicero had his experience with the mobs to require an adjustment of his views.

Quintilian comes at the end. His is the last synthesis within the Classical Period of a fully expressed system of rhetoric which maintains the position suggested by the *Phaedrus* and sketched by Aristotle. He considers the split between rhetoric and philosophy and the subsequent withdrawal of the teachers of each to their own fields as the source of the decay of rhetoric.[30] Here again we find a rhetorician insisting that the end of the speaker is persuasion about matter which must be expressed in a convenient form, and that vain exhibition of self and glittering generalities are not the end of rhetoric. Like Cicero, he

[26] *De Oratore,* I, xxvii.
[27] *Partitiones Oratoriae,* XXXIX, 139.
[28] See the interesting discussion of the relation between rhetoric and dialectic in the introduction of Wilbur Samuel Howell, *The Rhetoric of Alcuin and Charlemagne* (Princeton, 1941), 53.
[29] *Loc. cit.*
[30] Quintilian, *Institutiones Oratoriae,* Bk. I, pr. xiii.

maintains that dialectic is but a concise form of oratory and that the material of the one is the material of the other.[31]

Quintilian tried to prevent what eventually happened to classical thinking about effective expression. Though his emphasis was upon the teaching of rhetoric, he also insisted that effective expression required a union of matter to a form which made the expression more effective. With his failure the Sophists and declaimers won the field. Votiemus Maximus summarizes what happened to oratory in his criticism of Seneca the Elder: "In declamation men speak to please and not to persuade; ornaments are sought for, while argument is dispensed with as being troublesome and uninteresting; it is sufficient to please by means of sententiae and amplifications, the aim being that of personal triumph rather than the triumph of a cause." [32] What had happened can be stated in still other terms: the later rhetoricians, instead of attempting to discover new arguments to persuade about their propositions, sought to express old ideas in epigrammatic form, their sententiae. They did not seek to discover the more probable truth of an issue; they sought to delight their hearers. Preoccupation with form had captured the art of rhetoric and effective expression had become the expression in a well-turned phrase of inconsequential material.

The end of the classical period saw a wholesale turning to epideictic oratory or panegyric.[33] This change in the conception of rhetoric can be explained on different levels. C. S. Baldwin offers this excellent summary on purely historical grounds.[34]

> Of the three fields of oratory distinguished by Aristotle, deliberative, forensic, and occasional, the first was restricted by political changes. It faded with democracy. So later it faded at Rome, and still later in other realms. Deliberative oratory presupposes free discussion and audiences that vote. The steady increase of government from above administered by an appointed official class hastened also the tendency of the second kind of oratory, forensic, to become technical, the special art of legal pleading. Thus the only field left free was the third, the occasional oratory, encomium or panegyric, the commemoration of persons and days, the address of welcome, and the public lecture.

Of late the term "Second Sophistic" has been extended to apply to this period of Roman oratory, though it is more properly applied to the

[31] *Ibid.*, Bk. II, pr. xv.
[32] Quoted by J. W. H. Atkins, *Literary Criticism in Antiquity* (Cambridge, 1934), II, 148.
[33] T. C. Burgess, *Epideictic Literature* (Chicago, 1902).
[34] Charles Sears Baldwin, *Medieval Rhetoric and Poetic* (New York, 1928), 5.

second, third, and fourth Christian centuries of Greek rhetoric.[35] The noticeably widespread distribution of panegyric within this period is fitting in an educational system which was concerned with the forms of things and lacked firmer foundation.[36] Gone were the older days of Roman rhetoric when "on ne parlait pas pour parler, on parlait pour agir." [37] "Rem tene, verba sequuntur," was no longer the guiding principle, as it had been in the days of Cato the orator.[38] More and more Roman education became an education in literary form; but form degenerates when cultivated to the exclusion of substance which should determine it.[39] Subjects were selected "in order to cultivate cleverness of expression," and they did not "bind the writer or speaker to pertinency to the matter in hand." [40] There was no longer any *inventio* or search after truth; there was only an *elocutio* or urge toward ornamentation.

A descriptive statement stops there. It is possible, however, to probe more deeply into the currents of thought at the end of the classical world to discover why these changes in the conception of effective speech radically altered its matter and purpose. What happened to rhetoric is the reflection of deeper, more significant changes in the spheres of thought, and the change in rhetoric can not be said to be thoroughly understood apart from an understanding of those underlying causes.

Plato's question in the *Protagoras*, "About what does the Sophist make man more eloquent?" [41] had been a constant reminder to Greek rhetoricians that there must be a search for truth or the art of rhetoric would degenerate into mere skill. Aristotle's answer to the problem posed by Plato had been formulated within an ideological context which differed radically from that of the Sophists. Aristotle had sought to make man more eloquent for the good of the commonwealth and the ultimate betterment of the people as a whole. The Sophists were without such an aim, for those relationships existing in the individual as a result of his rational relations were entirely foreign to the Sophist assumptions about the nature of man and the end of life. Even Isocrates, who is commonly accused of being a simple stylist, proposed

[35] *Ibid.*, 8.

[36] Gaston Boissier, *La Fin du Paganisme* (Paris, 1898). Cf. particularly Bk. V, Chap. II, Section 3.

[37] M. Boissier, "Les Écoles de Déclamation à Rome," *Review des Deux Mondes*, 11 (1902), 480–502, 482.

[38] *Ibid.*, 484.

[39] Henry Osborn Taylor, *The Classical Heritage of the Middle Ages* (New York, 1929), 37.

[40] *Ibid.*, 35.

[41] Plato, *Protagoras*, 312.

the moral code of the Panhellenic ideal, about which he tried to make man more eloquent.[42] He also suggested a "union of philosophy and the earlier rhetoric . . . for to the acquiring of sound views on life he attached a prime importance." [43] Cicero's conception of eloquent wisdom is too well known to require further delineation. The rhetoric of Plato, Aristotle, Cicero, and Quintilian may be said to be founded upon a belief in the perfectibility of man, the existence of truth, and the possibility of its acquisition by the individual. The knowledge of the truth would then lead to a better and fuller life.

"The Second Sophistic should be taken to heart as a complete historic demonstration of what must become of rhetoric without the urgencies of matter and motive." [44] Greece was kept from that position by the presence of matter and the desire to achieve the ideal life possible in the *polis*. The Roman world did not have the matter or the motive for long. When man came to doubt, when he no longer had any hope of making anything new, then the arts relapsed into a refurbishment of the old. Not only rhetoric but "tragedy, like any other art of mankind, can live and grow only so long as men have hope of making it say something new about the significance of the world." [45] The decline of Greek tragedy seemingly coincides with the decline of Greek philosophy." [46] So also rhetoric degenerated in antiquity when there was a weakening of faith in and a loss of hope in the human intellect. Beginning in the second and developing through the immediately succeeding centuries, the feeling grew that the struggle of the mind with the problems of ethics, government, and life was fruitless. There was no need for man to attempt to find the answer to the contemporary chaos for the Stoics considered this the best of all possible worlds. Stoicism is not unlike Sophism in its tendency to de-emphasize theoretical problems and both seemingly reached a similar position, for they both lapsed into encomium as their standard stock in trade. There was no matter or motive to their expression because there was no reason for the human mind's struggling with greater or less probability.

One of the logical implications of the Stoic position seems to have been a curtailment of the intellectual life.[47] The aim of rhetoric had

[42] Jaeger, *Paideia*, III, Chap. 2.
[43] Atkins, *Literary Criticism in Antiquity*, I, 136.
[44] Baldwin, *Medieval Rhetoric and Poetic*, 12.
[45] Cf. the interesting introductory chapter of Willard Farnham's *Medieval Heritage of Elizabethan Tragedy* (Berkeley, 1936), 11, which correlates the growth and decline of tragedy to more fundamental ideological tendencies.
[46] *Ibid.*, 9.
[47] *Loc. cit.*

been best conceived as the discovery of and the persuasion to right action. The rhetorics of Aristotle and Cicero had as their ultimate aim the erection of a system which made it possible for man to discover truth and then apply it to the people that they might thereby profit and act in a more intelligent manner. With the passing of belief in a validity of reason, there disappeared any hope of finding a firm substance or basis for rhetoric. Thus to say that there was a "Classical Rhetoric" is to compound a gratuitous tag. There were as many conceptions of rhetoric in the period usually called "Classical" as there were philosophies, and the rhetoric can be understood only within the commensurable terms of the philosophy. In every observable instance the rhetoric is dependent for its content and orientation upon the more fundamental concepts which are the burden of epistemological or metaphysical discussion. The complete understanding of a system of rhetoric not only entails a scrutiny of the underlying philosophy but the elucidation of those implications is the task of any future historian of the concept of effective expression.

THE PROVINCE OF RHETORIC AND POETIC
Walter J. Ong

The literature of all ages is inextricably wound up with rhetorical and poetical theory. This is true even of a time like the present, when rhetorical theory often proceeds by a kind of negation of formal rhetoric. The conscious avoidance of certain devices not only is impossible without the substitution of others, but is itself based on a theory. We can avoid certain techniques, but not technique. Though we may have cultivated a horror of naming our tools, which earlier artists did not know, we still retain some knowledge of how to use them. Hence rhetoric and poetic remain with us.

But rhetorical and poetical theory has most often failed to find the location of the boundaries within which each of these two arts operate. Current studies in literary history have not placed the lines of demarcation any more accurately.[1] Although the literary historian's distinc-

From *The Modern Schoolman*, January, 1942. Reprinted with the permission of *The Modern Schoolman*.

[1] Among the studies of rhetoric and poetic should be mentioned Charles Sears Baldwin's *Ancient Rhetoric and Poetic* (New York: The Macmillan Co., 1924), *Medieval Rhetoric and Poetic* (New York: The Macmillan Co., 1928), and *Renaissance Literary Theory and Practice* (New York: Columbia University Press, 1939), as well as Donald Lemen Clark's *Rhetoric and Poetry in the Renaissance* (New

tions between rhetoric and poetic have been more or less sufficient for his immediate purposes, there is still need to settle more definitely how a poetical work differs from a rhetorical one. The investigation of this question falls rather to the lot of the philosopher than to that of the literary historian, and hence the present discussion will be properly philosophical.

I

Those things in the world which are made by man, being artifacts and not as such possessed of any substantial forms of their own, are differentiated from one another in a variety of ways: in terms of a variety of accidents which they possess, as when I speak of square artifacts, or black artifacts; in terms of the material, that is to say, the second matter in which they have their being, as when I speak of works of stone or works of iron; and finally in terms of their final causality—and this is the way in which we most generally speak of them—as when I speak of a table or of a gun or of a fountain pen.

Differentiation of the works of man in terms of final causality will proceed according to the more or less perfect participation of these works in this principle.[2] Thus we have the division into works of non-servile or fine arts and works of servile arts. The former are more perfect in the order of final causality in that they are ordered directly to the speculative intellect, to man's enjoyment as things of beauty, and are therefore destined only indirectly for other use, although their contemplation is of course governed by prudence.

Over against these works of fine arts, we have the works of those arts such as the machinist's or the paint manufacturer's art, which works are not directly for contemplation but means to further ends.

Rhetoric Ordered to Action

Within this division of works of art in terms of final causality the division between works of rhetoric and works of poetic falls.[3] For, if

---

York: Columbia University Press, 1922). A bibliography which includes works on rhetoric and poetic is given by William G. Crane, *Wit and Rhetoric in the Renaissance* (New York: Columbia University Press, 1937), pp. 253–76. There are also bibliographies in Baldwin.

[2] Final causality, form, accident, etc., are of course to be taken analogously when referring to artifacts.

[3] There is no need to quibble over words. Rhetoric has some unpleasant meanings that interfere, but the meaning which is here attached to rhetoric is a traditional and accepted one. All that is asked is that the reader look to what is meant here by rhetoric—call it what he will.

we take rhetoric to signify what Aristotle took it to signify—"the ability to find the available means of persuasion with reference to any subject whatsoever" [4]—works of rhetoric must be ordered to the production of action in another individual and to action in the sense of something other than contemplation. Works of rhetoric have their finality, then, only in terms of that action to which they are ultimately directed. There is another art, which we call poetic, which produces works ordered to contemplation and to no other direct end, that is, works of beauty. Such works are produced simply to be enjoyed by the one contemplating them.

It is to be noted that this rhetoric and this poetic are logical arts directive of the acts of the intellect itself. It is true that there is what we may call a general poetic, an inclusive order of those arts directed to the production of works for contemplation, which has a kind of unity derived from the community of end realized in such works. This order of arts, or general poetic, breaks down into poetic in the ordinary sense, sculpture, music, painting, and so on.

To this general poetic there corresponds another order of arts which we may call a general rhetoric and which includes those arts which may produce action in others not only by intellectual persuasion but by means other than the significative use of words. The sales agent who installs fluorescent lighting to put his customers at ease and thus indirectly persuade them to buy an automobile is practicing this general rhetoric.

However, the rhetoric and poetic which govern the formal use of words (as significative sounds) are both individual arts. They are logical arts, for each is not only a *habitus* of the intellect (all arts are this) but a *habitus* directive of the operations of the intellect itself. And yet they are not of the same species of logic as that according to which science (*scientia*) proceeds; for the connections in the logic of rhetoric and of poetic are not the necessary connections which exist in the logic of demonstration.

It will help to schematize a text from St. Thomas.[5] In the diagram [6] the connection between the members of the syllogism in *logica judicativa* (or *demonstrativa*) is a necessary one. As we proceed

[4] *Rhetoric* i. 2. 1. 1355b.

[5] *In I Anal. Post.*, lect. 1.

[6] There are many points of difference among these arts which a scheme such as the one given here does not bring out. See, for example, Averroes *In Libros Rhetoricorum Aristotelis Paraphrasis*, lib. 1, praef. (ed. Venetiis: apud Iuntas, 1574, p. 65a): "Ars quidam Rhetoricae affinis est artis Topicae: quoniam ambae unum finem intendunt, qui est eloqui cum alio. et quo neutra istarum artium homo secum ipse utitur, sicut est Dispositio artis Demonstrationis: sed utitur eis cum alio."

SCHEMATIZATION OF ST. THOMAS AQUINAS IN I ANAL. POST., LECT. 1.

Ars logica directs the acts of the intellect itself (*actus rationis*).
Ars logica is diversified as are *actus rationis:*

		Treated by Aristotle
I. *Intelligentia indivisibilium*		in: *Praedicamenta Catagoriae*
II. *Compositio vel divisio*		*Perihermenias*
III. *Discursus*		Other logical treatises as follows:

Art, like nature, acts in three ways, and the third act of the intellect has therefore a three-fold diversity, with corresponding arts:

A. *De necessitate* (*cum certitudine*)	*ars logica judicativa*		*ex forma syllogismi: Analytica Priora* *cum forma ex materia syllogismi: Analytica Posteriora*
B. *Frequentius*	*ars logica inventiva*		
1. *In pluribus*			
a. *Cum probabilitate*		*dialectica*	*Topica* (*Dialectica*)
b. *Cum suspicione*		*rhetorica*	*Rhetorica*
c. *Cum existimatione*		*poetica*	*Poetica*
2. *In paucioribus*		*sophistica*	*De Sophisticis Elenchis*

downwards, the connections are seen to become progressively looser. In dialectic (disputation) they require probability. The rhetorical syllogism, or "enthymeme," requires only suspicion—for this degree of certitude is sufficient to induce a man to act. In poetic, the logical connection is merely feigned, for the poet is *making* his connection. Certain and probable connections—more probably ("cum probabilitate") or less probable ("cum suspicione")—exist independently of the poet and hence are not his to make. The sophistical argument, of course, does not really conclude and resists conclusion, so that it is lower on the scale than even the merely assumed argument of poetic.

Rhetoric, then, and poetic both differ from the logic of the sciences in that neither requires certitude for its arguments.[7] Rhetoric must more closely approximate certitude in its conclusions. Poetic contents itself with a logic that is very thin: its argumentation is treated as though it concluded, and this assumption suffices. Furthermore, although rhetoric and poetic are distinct arts directive of the third operation of the intellect, no given work is the product of such an art alone. The works of these arts, as they stand concreted in matter, are erected by other arts as well, arts which are directive of the physical structure

---

[7] Historical works occupy a special place by the side of science. History is not science, though it constantly approaches science, as a calculus to its term.

out of which such things are made, as, for instance, an art which directs the rhythmical use of words, and so on. It is the aggregate of all these arts necessary for the production of a work of rhetoric or poetic which is often meant by "rhetoric" or "poetic," and it is such an aggregate that we have called a "general rhetoric" or a "general poetic." A book professing to teach rhetoric may, then, treat of many things other than the enthymeme and the example, and thus present a composite of several arts. Quintilian's *Institutio Oratoria,* for instance, is a composite of this nature.[8]

II

An important phenomenon in literary history is the persistent confusion of poetic with rhetoric or with demonstrative logic.[9] Poetic and rhetoric are confused when, in an attempt to strengthen its logic, poetic is made to proceed by means of the rhetorical enthymeme and example. Such an attempt can only result in something neither fish nor flesh—a poetic whose works are ordered to the practical intellect. Nevertheless, this sort of monster can be fathered on every age since Plato's. It comes into being when poetry is taken to be a direct means of persuasion, either because the defense of an art which creates objects simply for contemplation is felt to be impossible, or because the common association of certain other arts with both poetic and rhetoric obscures the true position of these latter arts. Since the works of both poetic and rhetoric are concreted in matter which is words, these arts gather around themselves a system of satellitic arts which are often the same for both rhetoric and poetic, arts such as that which governs the production of oral sounds. The fact that these arts are found in connection with both rhetoric and poetic tends to obscure the fact that in each case they are serving a different purpose.

Judicative Logic and Poetic

The confusion which constantly tends to arise between poetic and the logic of demonstration which governs the sciences (including

[8] See, for instance, his treatment of gesture, xi. 3. 65 ff. Quintilian, who was a rhetorician without being a philosopher, defines rhetoric as "bene dicendi scientia." *Op. cit.* ii. 15. 34: "Huic eius substantiae maxime conveniet finitio, rhetoricem esse bene dicendi scientiam." Cf. *ibid.* ii. 15. 38. Not only is Quintilian's rhetoric a composite of many arts, but his "ars" and "scientia" are other things than St. Thomas'.

[9] Baldwin, *Ancient Rhetoric and Poetic,* pp. 100, 229; *Medieval Rhetoric and Poetic,* pp. ix, 24, 39, etc. (see General Index under "poetic merged with rhetoric"). Clark, *op. cit.,* pp. 35–37.

The victory has gone first to one side and then to another. Under the Roman Empire and until the eleventh century the rhetoricians were in the ascendency, but by the thirteenth century philosophy seemed destined to win out, only to receive a sharp set-back when rhetoric triumphed and made the Renaissance.[11]

Meanwhile poetic has had to eke out an existence in occupied territy. Philosophy is eminently speculative. It will do no work. Rhetoric is eminently practical. It will do a work which is itself productive of some work on the part of others. Poetic is practical, but its work is not. It runs shortly to a dead end. Its work is for the speculative intellect here and now, ordered further only indirectly by reason of prudence. Hence, tucked away in its tight little corner, poetical composition has never been accorded the prominence in any curriculum that either rhetoric or philosophy have, and even when rhetoric has fallen on evil days, as it had in the thirteenth century and as it more or less has now, it is still in a position to bestow largess on poetic, which, as an art, is consistently neglected in schools.

Poetry's Results—Indirect

The defense of poetry depends not on what its works do directly, but on what they do indirectly. Because so many well-meaning but unobserving persons insist on defending it for the direct results it produces—a line of defense which is untenable—neglecting the entirely valid argument that the organization which a schooled appreciation of poetry imposes upon the human being is something that cannot be attained independently of words of poetic (or of music, painting, and so on), we are continually having the wrong thing defended or the right thing defended for the wrong reasons. This difficulty is, of course, chronic, and will remain so, for the indirect results which works of poetic bring about in the human being are known only to those who have had experience of them.

It will be seen, then, that the contrast between poetic and scientific writing is a more basic one than that between verse and prose. In the one case the difference arises from final causality, while in the other it is merely of accidental origin, dependent upon and ordered to

[11] For a thorough and enlightening treatment of the conflict between philosophy and rhetoric that runs through the history of Western civilization, I am particularly indebted to some unpublished work of Professor Étienne Gilson made available in a course of lectures delivered recently by Dr. Bernard J. Muller-Thym at St. Louis University. Cf. also Charles Homer Haskins, *The Renaissance of the Twelfth Century* (Cambridge: Harvard University Press, 1927), pp. 93–126.

philosophy) is likewise of some importance. Clearly distinct from a work of rhetoric, a philosophical work, which proceeds according to *logica judicativa* and may be taken as typical of all scientific works, is not so easily distinguished from a poetical work. A philosophical treatise, like a poetical work, is directed to the speculative intellect. But in what way? The philosophical is concerned with the communication of something which has its existence independently of the words used to communicate it, and, while the poetic use of language communicates truth too, it is truth which does not exist in its totality as entirely independent of the language in which it is conveyed. The logical connections are made by the poet. They are fabricated ("cum existimatione"). Consequently, since they do not exist of themselves necessarily, assent to the argument of a poem must be induced by something other than the truths with which the poet deals, so that these truths are apprehended by the intellect with some special kind of cooperation on the part of the senses and emotions that is dependent on the very words in which the truths are presented. Insofar as a work acts independently of the words in which it is presented, it tends toward the scientific treatise.[10]

Now, in the confusion of poetic with rhetoric and with demonstrative logic, it is always poetic which tends to disappear. And the reason for this is not far to seek. The principal domestic struggle of Western culture has been between a philosophically centered and a rhetorically centered regimen. The forces engaged have been the champions of the speculative intellect versus the champions of the practical intellect. On this basis was waged the struggle between Socrates and the sophists, the struggle which led to John of Salisbury's *Metalogicus*, and the struggle which was echoed in Swift's *The Battle of the Books*.

---

[10] Gerard Manley Hopkins, S.J., a poet highly conscious of technique, had an artist's characteristic awareness of this special mode of operation in poetry:

"Poetry is speech framed for contemplation of the mind by way of hearing or speech framed to be heard for its own sake and interest even over and above its interest of meaning. Some matter and meaning is essential to it but only as an element necessary to support and employ the shape which is contemplated for its own sake." *The Note-Books and Papers of Gerard Manley Hopkins*, ed. by Humphrey House (London: Oxford University Press, 1937), p. 249.

It should be noted, however, that what the poet makes is not independent of the truths he makes it of. The truths he employs are not the poetry, and he can use great truths to make poor poetry indeed, but he cannot make great poetry without great truths. Neither stone nor straw is of my making; nevertheless, although I can badly botch a piece of stone construction I attempt, a better house can be made of stone than of straw. For all this, the poet can utilize any material, for he is not making houses but simply things: his art is in a way coextensive with being.

the purpose which the work is to serve.[12] This should be a common-place. It has been said over and over again from Aristotle's time [13] on, even by persons whose discussions are critical rather than philosophical, as, for instance, Coleridge.[14] But it represents a stand which is continually being challenged.

There is, of course, a connection between verse and poetry, as there is between prose and scientific writing. Scientific writing, as has already been said, is concerned with the communication of something which has its existence independently of the words used to communicate it. Hence any configuration of those words lies outside the realm of such writing. If a scientific work is written in verse, the configuration is truly an ornament added to the scientific content of the writing. In poetry, however, the verse functions as an intimate part of the work itself. Apart from what special significative force verse rhythms may themselves exert (as in rhythmic onomatopoeia), they constitute a part of the object to be contemplated. Their relation to the "logical" content is close in a work where the connections in such content are, like the verse itself, of the author's own making.

Poetry in Prose

But this is not to identify verse with poetry, for prose, too, may be written to produce a work for contemplation. Such a work would be poetry in the sense in which this word is used here. No more is it to identify verse with one particular kind of rhythmic patterning (as, for example, with the syllable-counting systems of Homer, Vergil, and most English poets after the Conquest, as against the antithetical patterning of Hebrew poetry or the stress patterning of Old English or modern "free" verse).

Rhetoric, falling between *logica judicativa* and poetic, favors a prose development, for the rhetorician, although he deals with that which is not necessary (or certain), is not the "maker" that the poet is. His logic is not as intimately connected as the poet's is with the words in which it is concreted.

It is seen, then, that poetic is distinguished from rhetoric by the relative tenuousness of its logical connections. The logic of poetic

[12] Cf. Hopkins again, *op. cit.*, pp. 249–51. This short section, headed "Poetry and Verse," is in reality a chapter on poetic, and directly pertinent to the present discussion.

[13] *Poetics* i. 7–12. 1447b.

[14] See *Biographia Literaria*, ed. by J. Shawcross (Oxford: The Clarendon Press, 1907), Ch. XIV (II, 5–13—esp. 10).

and of rhetoric follows the end to which each of these arts is directed—the former to the making of a thing for contemplation, the latter to the production of action in another. Both poetic and rhetoric are distinct from the logic of the sciences in that their arguments do not proceed with necessity, although rhetoric approximates the necessary in a way that poetic does not.

However, as a matter of fact, most writing is a composite, not only in the sense that arts other than those which govern the operations of the intellect are needed in order that a given concrete piece of writing take form, but also in the sense that a given piece of writing will often partake of the nature of many kinds of writing at once. In most of what may be designated as poetry there is a considerable mixture of special pleading which is nothing more or less than dialectic or rhetoric. Again, what we would ordinarily call a poem may *de facto* convey scientific as well as poetic truth, although it is not as a poem that it does so. And a politician who should be practicing rhetoric may introduce a fact for its own sake. Finally, writing ostensibly scientific can and often does become a plea to take this attitude toward the subject, or that. Works of rhetoric, poetic, and science do not exist in the concrete in separate works. We must generally rest satisfied with calling a thing a poem because it is mostly a poem, or a political speech a work of rhetoric because it is nearer to that than it is to anything else.

THE LIMITS OF RHETORIC   *Maurice Natanson*

There are signs of a new excitement in the discipline of contemporary rhetoric; but there are also indications of basic difficulties in the discussions going on to determine the proper province of rhetoric and the possible meaning of a "philosophy of rhetoric." As a philosopher, I think that an effort to show the relationship between rhetoric and philosophy might lead to some clarification of the underlying issues. If the philosopher cannot give the answers, he can perhaps clarify the questions.

But first, what do these "difficulties" in the discussions about rhetoric consist in? Undoubtedly one vast difficulty is generated by the very term "rhetoric." As Bryant points out, rhetoric may mean ". . . bombast; high-sounding words without content; oratorical falsification to hide meanings; sophistry, ornamentation and the study of figures

From *Quarterly Journal of Speech*, April, 1955. Reprinted with the permission of the Speech Association of America, and of the author.

of speech . . . and finally, least commonly of all, the whole art of spoken discourse, especially persuasive discourse." [1] The classical Aristotelian definition of rhetoric is no longer adequate to dispel all these variant connotations, but the inadequacy of defining rhetoric as "the faculty of observing in any given case the available means of persuasion" is to be explained at a different, far deeper level. It will be here that we come to the nucleus of the difficulties regarding rhetoric.

It would appear that what characterizes the Aristotelian as well as recent definitions of rhetoric is a stress on its functional and dynamic character. As Bryant writes:

> Rhetoric is primarily concerned with the relations of ideas to the thoughts, feelings, motives, and behavior of men. Rhetoric as distinct from the learnings which it uses is dynamic; it is concerned with move-ment. It *does* rather than *is*. It is method rather than matter. It is chiefly involved with bringing about a condition, rather than discovering or testing a condition. [2]

Now the emphasis on the directional and pragmatic aspect of rhetoric leads immediately to the question, *Is* rhetoric truly to be characterized as functional, and is the rhetorical function that of "adjusting ideas to people and . . . people to ideas"? [3] The fundamental difficulty, it seems to me, that has confused the discussion is a failure on the part of the analyst to distinguish between the theory of rhetoric and the practice of rhetoric: the former involves ultimately a philosophy of rhetoric; the latter presupposes that philosophy and directs its attention to the structure of rhetorical technique and methodology. But before proceeding to the analysis of these elements, I think it necessary to examine more carefully what is meant by the functional aspect of rhetoric, since my claim is that much confusion is created by assuming this interpretation of the nature of rhetoric.

It is well known that Aristotle begins his *Rhetoric* by asserting that "Rhetoric is the counterpart of Dialectic." If dialectic is the art of logical discussion, then rhetoric is the art of public speaking; but the distinction between rhetoric and dialectic is a more profound one. Dialectic, for Aristotle, has as its object the achievement of knowledge;

---

[1] Donald C. Bryant, "Rhetoric: Its Functions and Its Scope," *QJS*, XXXIX (December 1953), 402.

[2] *Ibid.*, p. 412; cf. Hoyt H. Hudson, "The Field of Rhetoric," *QJSE*, IX (April 1923), 180, where the essence of rhetoric is held to be "adaptation to the end of influencing hearers."

[3] Bryant, *op. cit.*, p. 413.

rhetoric, persuasion. Dialectic strives for and may achieve *epistēmē;* rhetoric, *doxa.* Thus rhetoric is subordinate in the hierarchy of knowledge to dialectic as belief is subordinate to knowledge. Now if we consider the relationship between the Aristotelian rhetoric and the Platonic critique of rhetoric, it becomes evident that Aristotle has articulated a division between rhetoric and dialectic for definite reasons: essentially, for the rescue of "good" rhetoric from "bad," i.e., from sophistic rhetoric. Good rhetoric, as Plato pointed out in *Phaedrus,* presupposes dialectic: persuasion presupposes truth. The division of rhetoric and dialectic warns us against confounding truth with its artful presentation and at the same time shows that they are separate facets of a single universe of discourse: the intelligible world.[4] But what really separates knowledge from belief, dialectic from rhetoric? It is here that we come to the problem of function.

It is certainly the case that Aristotle, after distinguishing between rhetoric and dialectic, proceeds to analyze the applicative uses of rhetoric. His discussions of the modes of persuasion stress the functional character of rhetorical method. Thus the subject matter of rhetoric becomes evidenced in the problems of speaker and audience, political oratory and its devices, etc. And it is precisely here that the subsequent tradition of rhetoric takes its point of departure and so abandons the awareness of the intimate nexus between rhetoric and dialectic; and it is here that confusions begin to germinate.

For Plato, rhetoric—good rhetoric, that is—aspired to be (but was not) *technē,* i.e., art involving knowledge.[5] While dialectic alone could achieve the status of *theōria,* rhetoric nevertheless had a powerful bond which tied it to knowledge. Though Aristotle's division of rhetoric and dialectic preserves the original intention of that bond, his stress on the subject matter of rhetoric (the modes of persuasion) lends itself to a misleading emphasis on rhetorical technique and to a lack of emphasis on the theoretical aspects of rhetoric. In other words, instead of a philosophy of rhetoric, we have drawn from Aristotle a manual of oratorical technique and a debater's guide. The ultimate import of this attitude towards rhetoric is an interpretation of the nature of rhetoric which holds it to be functional in character, directed toward practical problems of convincing and

    [4] Cf. E. M. Cope, *An Introduction to Aristotle's Rhetoric* (London and Cambridge: Macmillan & Co., 1867), p. 6.
    [5] See Werner Jaeger, *Paideia* (New York: Oxford University Press, 1944), Vol. III, Ch. 8.

persuading, and so aimed at a pragmatic, instigative goal: rhetoric is conceived of in terms of men in action.

Now it is the thesis of this paper that this stress on the functional, pragmatic character of rhetoric is the origin of the confusion regarding the role and province of rhetoric today, and further that the confusion consists precisely in the fact that the Platonic and Aristotelian emphasis on the link between dialectic and rhetoric has been ignored in favor of the pragmatic subject matter with the result that the theoretical nature of rhetoric is obscured. It is my contention that a reapproach to the nature of rhetoric is possible through a philosophical examination of its foundations in dialectic.

The need for re-examination of the nature and scope of rhetoric is voiced in many and diverse quarters today, but the stress on the relationship of philosophy to rhetoric is not a recent development. As a matter of fact, it is Bishop Whately who makes the point in connection with a criticism of Cicero as rhetorician:

> Cicero is hardly to be reckoned among the number [of rhetoricians]; for he delighted so much more in the practice than in the theory of his art, that he is perpetually drawn off from the rigid philosophical analysis of its principles, into discursive declamations, always eloquent indeed, and often interesting, but adverse to regularity of system, and frequently as unsatisfactory to the practical student as to the philosopher.[6]

The rhetorician, then, according to Whately, must attend seriously to the philosophical problems which are at the root of his discipline. With regard to logic, Whately writes: "Rhetoric being in truth an offshoot of Logic, that Rhetorician must labor under great disadvantages who is not only ill acquainted with that system, but also utterly unconscious of his deficiency."[7] Unfortunately, as I. A. Richards points out,[8] Whately does not follow his own advice, with the result that instead of taking "a broad philosophical view of the principles of the Art," Whately gives us "a very ably arranged and discussed collection of prudential Rules about the best sorts of things to say in various argumentative situations, the order in which to bring out your propositions and proofs and examples. . . ."[9] Just as Richards correctly points

---

[6] Richard Whately, *Elements of Rhetoric* (New York: Sheldon & Co., 1867), p. 24.
[7] *Ibid.*, p. 26.
[8] I. A. Richards, *The Philosophy of Rhetoric* (New York and London: Oxford University Press, 1936), p. 7.
[9] *Ibid.*, p. 7.

out Whately's failure to carry out his own directive, so we must also add that Richards fails to carry out a sustained inquiry into the philosophy of rhetoric, though he does develop one subsidiary line of approach, that of the analysis of linguistic structure and meaning. The philosophy of rhetoric remains then an unexamined realm; and it is especially interesting that a volume published in 1953 takes as its theme the relationship between philosophy and rhetoric and seeks a radical reapproach to the ancient dualism of rhetoric and dialectic. We shall take Richard Weaver's *The Ethics of Rhetoric* [10] as a point of departure in analyzing the problem before us.

Weaver begins his study of rhetoric by calling us back to the original Aristotelian distinction between rhetoric and dialectic. As we indicated before, rhetoric is concerned with persuasion, dialectic with truth. However, it is necessary to remember that for Aristotle, *both* rhetoric and dialectic are concerned with the world of probability, both begin with the commonsense reality of contingency, not with the realm of apodeictic logic. Aristotle's distinction between scientific knowledge (which includes the organon of deductive logic) and argumentative inquiry (which includes both rhetoric and dialectic) makes clear the difference between the formal deductive syllogism which begins with stipulated premises and arrives then at necessary conclusions and, on the other hand, rhetoric and dialectic, which inquire into the empirical grounds of propositions in an effort to establish the truth and then make clear the available means of its artful presentation.[11] For Aristotle, deductive logic cannot provide any proof of its ultimate premises: such proof is the task of dialectic.[12] The ultimate foundations of science and formal logic, then, rest on dialectic: logic is concerned with validity, dialectic with truth. Thus Weaver writes: "Dialectic is a method of investigation whose object is the establishment of truth about doubtful propositions." [13]

Now it would appear that there are different fields of study dialectic may pursue: the scientific method of induction in the field of botany is quite different from the endeavor to establish the truth in matters of politics or ethics. Which field of dialectic will rhetoric concern itself with? Weaver holds:

[10] (Chicago: Henry Regnery Co., 1953).

[11] Cf. James H. McBurney, "The Place of the Enthymeme in Rhetorical Theory," *SM*, III (1936), 52.

[12] Cf. W. Windelband, *A History of Philosophy* (New York: The Macmillan Company, 1901), p. 137; also P. Albert Duhamel, "The Function of Rhetoric as Effective Expression," *Journal of the History of Ideas*, X (June 1949), 345.

[13] *Op. cit.*, p. 15.

There is a branch of dialectic which contributes to "choice or avoidance" and it is with this that rhetoric is regularly found joined. Generally speaking, this is a rhetoric involving questions of policy, and the dialectic which precedes it will determine not the application of positive terms but that of terms which are subject to the contingency of evaluation.[14]

The dialectic which seeks to establish terms having to do with policy is in an intimate relationship with rhetoric, for rhetoric is meaningful only if dialectic is presupposed. As Weaver says, "there is . . . no true rhetoric without dialectic, for the dialectic provides that basis of 'high speculation about nature' without which rhetoric in the narrower sense has nothing to work upon."[15] It is this internal connection, rooted in the very nature of rhetoric, that provides Weaver with his *rapprochement* between rhetoric and philosophy.

Weaver's original contribution to the problem is expressed in a particular characterization of dialectic. Turning to a more nearly Platonic than Aristotelian conception of dialectic (though the Neo-Aristotelian overtones are obvious), Weaver interprets dialectic as a distinguishable stage in argumentation: "Dialectic is that stage which defines the subject satisfactorily with regard to the *logos,* or the set of propositions making up some coherent universe of discourse; and we can therefore say that a dialectical position is established when its relation to an opposite has been made clear and it is thus rationally rather than empirically sustained."[16] This view of dialectic as purely conceptual leads to a notion of rhetoric as applicative or practical. Thus for Weaver "the urgency of facts is never a dialectical concern;"[17] "what a successful dialectic secures . . . is not actuality but possibility; and what rhetoric thereafter accomplishes is to take any dialectically secured position . . . and show its relationship to the world of prudential conduct."[18] The relationship between dialectic and rhetoric may now be stated as Weaver understands it.

Rhetoric in the wider sense includes dialectic,[19] in so far as dialectic has already functioned in providing the rhetorician with the truth, or in so far as the application of a dialectically secured position is made to the real world. The action that rhetoric professes presupposes in this sense the understanding that good action always involves. This

[14] *Ibid.,* p. 16.
[15] *Ibid.,* p. 17.
[16] *Ibid.,* p. 27.
[17] *Ibid.,* p. 27.
[18] *Ibid.,* pp. 27–28.
[19] *Ibid.,* p. 15.

being so, Weaver's point emerges: the duty of rhetoric in the widest sense is "to bring together action and understanding into a whole that is greater than scientific perception." [20] By itself, then, rhetoric is blind, for it has not truth; concomitantly, an isolated dialectic is empty, for it never engages the issues of the empirical world. Combined, dialectic and rhetoric constitute an instrument for reapproaching the multiple problems of politics, ethics, linguistics, and literary criticism. But in what sense does this union of rhetoric and dialectic provide us with a *rapprochement* between rhetoric and philosophy? At this point we must return to the original problem and see where the argument has led us.

We began, it may be recalled, with the functional stress which is placed on rhetoric today and suggested that much of the confusion regarding the nature and province of rhetoric is due to the divorce between rhetoric and dialectic. Our thesis here converges with that of Weaver, for it is precisely Weaver's point, as we have just seen, that rhetoric must go with dialectic if it is to be meaningful. Now the union of rhetoric with dialectic means, in Weaver's terms, a return of rhetoric to a dialectic understood not as the "art of logical discussion" but in the much broader sense of the conceptual ordering of propositions into coherent structures of an a priori nature. Dialectic in this sense is no longer "argumentative inquiry" but rather, I submit, philosophical inquiry. The unification of rhetoric and dialectic is really the *rapprochement* between philosophy and rhetoric because dialectic is given a unique interpretation: dialectic constitutes the true philosophy of rhetoric.

Understood in this way, the original Platonic and Aristotelian notions of rhetoric and dialectic become clarified: the philosophy of rhetoric achieves the Platonic idea of *technē*, and the Aristotelian idea of dialectic is seen in its most challenging aspect. Rhetoric ceases to be the *technique* of persuasion and truly becomes the *art* it was originally held to be, an art, however, which sustains itself only in and through its involvement with dialectic.

If all this is true, the question naturally arises, What, after all, is the subject matter of the philosophy of rhetoric? Granted the meaningfulness of interpreting rhetoric in this way, what is to be done with the interpretation? Have we invoked Whately's criticism of Cicero, Richards' criticism of Whately, and added our criticism of Richards, only to fall into the same trap ourselves? The unavoidable question is, What problems constitute the subject matter of the philosophy of

[20] *Ibid.*, p. 24.

rhetoric, and how may such a philosophy be articulated? Obviously, we can offer only a fragmentary indication here of the way in which we would approach these problems.

Let us return once again to Aristotle's concept of dialectic. As we noted, dialectic is understood by Aristotle as operating in the realm of probability, not necessity. Dialectic seeks the truth but conducts the search in the midst of the real world of contingency and doubt.[21] Now the new enriched conception of dialectic that we are offering here—dialectic understood as the philosophy of rhetoric—concerns itself not with fact but with the theoretical structure that is logically prior to fact. How is such an a priori system related to the contingent world? The question then is, What is the relationship of dialectical theory to rhetorical fact? Stated in still another way, the question is, What is the relationship of theory to practice? All of these questions are transpositions of our fundamental problem: the true province of rhetoric. The answer to these questions and the exploration of the fundamental problem lead necessarily to the nature of philosophy itself. To answer the question, What is the subject matter of the philosophy of rhetoric, we must investigate the foundational discipline of philosophy, which is the bedrock, the ultimate and absolute ground of all inquiry.

I propose to understand by philosophy the critique of presuppositions. Philosophy in its synthetic aspect seeks to comprehend the nature of reality by inquiring critically into the categories of reality: quantity, quality, relation, and modality, to refer to the Kantian categories. In its analytical aspect philosophy attempts to bring to clarity the meaning of terms which are basic and crucial to the conceptual structure of all special disciplines. So in history, for example, analytic philosophy investigates the meaning of such terms as "fact," "event," "cause," "effect," "consequence," etc. These are the basic terms out of which history constructs its subject matter and builds its schemata. Both the synthetic and analytic aspects of philosophy turn upon a single, though complex, focal point: the systematic and persistent exploration of elements and themes which are taken for granted in both common-sense reality and in the special disciplines. Thus, philosophy is the critique of such presuppositions as the belief in the existence of an external world, of other fellow men in that world, of communication between those fellow men, etc. Philosophy does not deny the existence of these things; rather it seeks to express their

[21] The tremendous philosophical problem of the meaning of "probability" in common-sense reality is necessarily beyond the scope of this paper.

meaningful structure, to bring to complete clarity the conditions which make common-sense experience possible and comprehensible. As a critique of presuppositions, philosophy is a reflexive discipline, i.e., it not only takes for investigation objects and problems external to it, but it also seeks to understand itself. Philosophy is self-problematic: it is the only discipline that begins by inquiring into its own nature and goes on to examine its own instruments of inquiry. The subject matter of philosophy, then, consists of the categories of reality and the basic terms of all particular disciplines; the ultimate goal of the critique of these elements is the reconstruction of the real in perfect self-clarity and illumination.

If this may be taken as the nature of philosophy generally, what is the province of the philosophy of rhetoric? I would suggest that the philosophy of rhetoric directs itself toward the following problems: the relationship between language and what language denotes; the relationship between mind and what mind is aware of; the relationship between knowledge and what knowledge is "of"; the relationship between consciousness and its various contents; etc. Now what differentiates these problems from their generalized setting in the theory of knowledge is the particular kind of context in which these problems arise in rhetoric. Instead of the general problem of meaning, the philosopher of rhetoric is interested in how this problem arises with regard to speaker and listener, poet and reader, playwright and audience. Instead of the epistemology of consciousness, the philosopher of rhetoric directs his attention to those states of consciousness manifest in persuasion. Instead of the generalized problem of knowledge, the philosopher of rhetoric attends to the status of that knowledge which the persuader seeks to persuade us of.

The philosophy of rhetoric, then, has as its subject matter the application of the critique of presuppositions to those presuppositions which characterize the fundamental scope of rhetoric: presuppositions in the relationship of speaker and listener, the persuader and the one persuaded, judger and the thing judged. *The specific object of inquiry here is not the technique of speaking or persuading or judging but the very meaning of these activities.* Thus rhetoric stands in relation to philosophy as science stands in relation to philosophy. In both cases, philosophy investigates what both disciplines presuppose: knowledge, existence, communication, and value. Just as the philosophy of science analyzes the meaning of such elements as "fact," "causation," and "law," so the philosophy of rhetoric studies the elements of "language," "meaning," and "persuasion." This brings us to the question of the relationship of the philosophy of rhetoric to rhetoric in the narrower sense.

The conclusion of our analysis may be expressed in a typology or hierarchical ordering of the different aspects of rhetoric. This will help to make clear precisely what is meant by rhetoric in the broader and narrower sense of the term. Going from the narrower meaning down to the broadest meaning, we have the following aspects of rhetoric: rhetorical intention in speech or writing, the technique of persuasion, the general rationale of persuasion, and finally the philosophy of rhetoric. Rhetoric in the narrower aspect involves rhetorical intention in the sense that a speaker or writer may devote his effort to persuade for some cause or object. Since much of what is commonly called "bad" rhetoric frequently is found in such efforts, the field of rhetoric understood as the technique of persuasion is systematically studied and taught. Here the teacher of rhetoric investigates the devices and modes of argument, the outline for which is to be found in Aristotle's *Rhetoric* or other classical rhetorics. Reflection of a critical order on the significance and nature of the technique of persuasion brings us to rhetoric understood as the general rationale of persuasion. This is what might be termed the "theory" of rhetoric in so far as the central principles of rhetoric are examined and ordered. The emphasis is on the general principles of rhetoric as rhetoric is intimately related to functional, pragmatically directed contexts. Finally, we come to the critique of the rationale of rhetoric which inquires into the underlying assumptions, the philosophical grounds of all the elements of rhetoric.[22] It is here that a philosophy of rhetoric finds its placement. If rhetoric is bound to and founded on dialectic, and dialectic on philosophy, then the limits of rhetoric find their expression in the matrix of philosophical inquiry.

[22] It is interesting to note that Donald C. Bryant approaches a similar typology, though he stops short of the philosophy of rhetoric as we understand it. Speaking of the rhetorician, Bryant writes, *op. cit.*, p. 408: "the term *rhetorician* will sometimes mean the formulator and philosopher of rhetorical theory; sometimes the teacher of the technique of discourse; sometimes the speaker with rhetorical intention; and finally the student or scholar whose concern is the literary or social or behavioral study of rhetoric. I have been tempted to invent terms to avoid certain of these ambiguities such as *logology,* or even *rhetoristic* (parallel with *sophistic*), but the game would probably not be worth the candle." Our point in this paper has been to show that not only is the game worth the candle, but that in a sense without the game no ultimate rhetoric is possible.

SECTION II

THE DEVELOPMENT OF
RHETORICAL THEORY

ON THE SOPHISTS

Everett Lee Hunt

I

The art of rhetoric offered to the Athenian of the fifth century B.C. a method of higher education and, beyond that, a way of life. Plato attacked both. He gave rhetoric a conspicuous place in his dialogues because it represented in Athenian life that which he most disliked. His pictures of the rhetoricians are so broadly satirical that at times they become caricatures; but his literary power and philosophical originality have so impressed themselves upon succeeding ages that the sophists and rhetoricians of Athens have become symbolical of false pretense of knowledge, overweening conceit, fallacious argument, cultivation of style for its own sake, demagoguery, corruption of youth through a scepticism which professed complete indifference to truth, and, in general, a ready substitution of appearance for reality.

We have the more readily accepted Plato's account because these faults have never been absent from civilization. If the sophists and rhetoricians of Plato's dialogues had not existed, it would have been necessary to invent them. The qualities they typify are so universal that certain collective names for them have become a necessity for thought. Even Grote, the great defender of the historical sophists, when he desires to point out the fallacies of the Platonic Socrates, finds it convenient to accuse Plato of "sophistry." [1] These qualities are not only objectively ever present, but we attribute them readily to any persons or arguments when for any reason our approval has not been won. An argument which we do not accept is sophistical, and the person who presents it a sophist. An appeal to the feelings of men which does not happen to warm our own hearts is rhetorical, and its author a rhetorician. It was so in Plato's time, and it was no more safe then than now to take the words "sophistry" and "rhetoric" at their face value.

From "Plato and Aristotle on Rhetoric and Rhetoricians," in *Studies in Rhetoric and Public Speaking in Honor of James A. Winans,* edited by A. M. Drummond. © Russell & Russell, Inc., New York, 1962. Reprinted by permission.
[1] George Grote, *Plato,* London, 1888, III, 63.

When we ask, who were the sophists, what did they teach, and what is the connection between sophistry and rhetoric, we have asked questions involving great historical and philosophical dispute. Generations of historians of philosophy, accepting Plato's account, have made the sophists the scapegoats for all intellectual—and, at times, moral—delinquencies. It is to Hegel that the sophists owe their rehabilitation in modern times.[2] G. H. Lewes, five years before Grote published his famous defense of the sophists, characterized them as professors of rhetoric,[3] and pointed out the bias which had caused their unfair treatment at the hands of Plato. Grote's classic treatment of the sophists in his *History of Greece* [4] was termed by Henry Sidgwick "a historical discovery of the highest order." "Before it was written," says Professor Sidgwick, "the facts were all there, but the learned world could not draw the right inference." In two vigorous essays he defends Grote and makes some significant contributions to the controversy.[5] John Stuart Mill, in an extended review of Grote's *Plato,* defends his interpretation in almost all points, and furnishes many additional arguments in defense of the sophists.[6] E. M. Cope, in his essays on the sophistic rhetoric, rejects many of Grote's conclusions.[7] Zeller is not inclined to look upon the sophists with favor.[8] Chaignet, in his history of rhetoric, accepts the conventional contrast between Plato and the sophists.[9] Jowett, Plato's translator, accepts many of Grote's conclusions, but rejects others.[10] Gomperz, in his *Greek Thinkers,* written fifty years after Grote's history was published, says of his own contemporaries among historians of philosophy:

> They still begin by handsomely acknowledging the ambiguity of the word "sophist," and the injustice done to the bearers of that name in the fifth century B.C. by the ugly sense in which the term came to be used, and they admit that restitution is due. But the debt is forgotten before

[2] G. W. Hegel, *Lectures on Philosophy,* 2d ed., 1840, tr. E. S. Haldane, London, 1892.

[3] G. H. Lewes, *Biographical History of Philosophy,* London, 1857, pp. 87 ff.

[4] Grote, *History of Greece,* London, 1851, VIII, 67.

[5] H. Sidgwick, "The Sophists," *Lectures on the Philosophy of Kant and other Philosophical Lectures and Essays,* London, 1905.

[6] J. S. Mill, "Grote's *Plato,*" *Dissertations and Discussions,* New York, 1874, IV.

[7] E. M. Cope, "The Sophistic Rhetoric," *Journal of Classical and Sacred Philology,* II (1855), 129–69, III (1856), 34–80, 253–88.

[8] E. Zeller, *Pre-Socratic Philosophy,* tr. S. F. Alleyne, London, 1881, II, sect. iii. For still other points of view, see A. W. Benn, *The Greek Philosophers,* London, 1882, ch. 2. Also Sir A. Grant, *The Ethics of Aristotle,* London, 1874, I, 103–54.

[9] A. E. Chaignet, *La Rhétorique et son Histoire,* Paris, 1888, pp. 43, 44.

[10] Introduction to his translation of Plato's *Sophist.*

it is paid; the debtor reverts to the old familiar usage, and speaks of the sophists once more as if they were really mere intellectual acrobats, unscrupulous tormentors of language, or the authors of pernicious teachings. The spirit may be willing, but the reason is helpless against the force of inveterate habits of thought. Verily the sophists were born under an evil star. Their one short hour of triumphant success was paid for by centuries of obloquy. Two invincible foes were banded against them—the caprice of language, and the genius of a great writer, if not the greatest writer of all times.[11]

The itinerant sophists founded no schools, and most of their works have been lost. The evidence in the case is therefore of the kind which makes endless argument possible. A few conclusions may, however, be stated as generally agreed upon. The term sophist originally had no unfavorable connotation, and was applied to any man who was thought to be learned. Thus the seven sages of Greece, universally honored, were at times called sophists.[12] In the time of Plato the word carried with it something of reproach, but it was not a definitely understood term. Rival teachers employed it against each other. Thus Isocrates regarded speculative thinkers (Plato among them) as sophists, because he thought their speculations fruitless. He also attacked as sophists other teachers of rhetoric whose instruction he regarded as unintelligent, and whose promises to their pupils he thought impossible of fulfilment.[13] The general public used the term with almost no discrimination, and Aristophanes seized upon Socrates as the sophist who could be most effectively lampooned.

As to what they taught, it has been established that such terms as a sophistic mind, a sophistic morality, a sophistic scepticism, and others implying a common basis of doctrine, are quite without justification. Their common characteristics were that they were professional teachers, that they accepted fees, and that rhetoric was a large element in the teaching of virtually all of them. The general emphasis upon rhetoric does not mean that, as scholars, all the sophists found their intellectual interests centered in rhetoric. But rhetoric was the one subject with which they could be sure to make a living. The conditions which made rhetorical training a universal

[11] Theodore Gomperz, *Greek Thinkers*, tr. L. Magnus, New York, 1901, I, 422.
[12] For citations illustrating the various uses of the word "sophist" by Greek writers, see Gomperz, *op. cit.*, I, 579.
[13] Isocrates, *Antidosis, Against the Sophists*. For translations of selected passages see Jebb, *Attic Orators*, London, 1893, II, 124–47. See also W. H. Thompson, "On the Philosophy of Isocrates and his Relation to the Socratic Schools," in his edition of Plato's *Phædrus*, London, 1868.

necessity in Athens have been frequently set forth. The sophist who was a master of rhetoric had a number of possibilities before him. He could win power and repute by the delivery of eulogistic orations at public funerals, or deliberative addresses at times of political crises. He could appear at games, or upon occasions of his own making, with what we sometimes call occasional, or literary, addresses, expounding Homer or other works of Greek literature. He could write speeches for clients who were to appear in court. He was not allowed to appear in person as an advocate unless he could show that he had a direct connection with the case, but the profession of logographer was profitable. Finally, he was more certain of pupils in rhetoric than in any other subject.[14] It is not strange, then, that with a wide range of individual interests, the sophists, with varying emphasis, should unite upon rhetoric as the indispensable part of their stock in trade.

The claim to impart virtue has at times been held to be the distinguishing mark of the sophist, and the attempt has been made to divide the sophists from the rhetoricians upon this basis. This cannot be done, for the two activities of making men virtuous and making them eloquent were inextricably intermingled. Hegel has pointed out what he regards as an essential difference between the sophists and modern professors.[15] The professor makes no pretension to making men good or wise; he only presents to students his organized knowledge, realizing that knowledge comes but wisdom lingers. The sophists, on the other hand, laid claim to some actual effect from their teachings; they made men wise. This was at least in part due to the dominance of rhetoric. Aristotle might lecture upon the theoretical aspects of rhetoric—a procedure which seems to have been productive of little eloquence—but the prime purpose of the teaching of rhetoric was practical. Certain sophists made the payment of their fees dependent upon some proof that they had actually given to a pupil the ability to persuade an audience. With such a background, it is natural that the teaching of ethics as abstract knowledge would seem about as futile as the teaching of an abstract rhetoric. A man who taught ethics taught it practically, with injunctions and exhortations, and he expected practical consequences to follow. But one of the consequences always looked for was that the pupil should become such a person as to be persuasive when speaking in a public assembly. Ethics thus was often absorbed in rhetoric.

[14] See O. T. Navarre, *Essai sur la Rhétorique Grecque avant Aristote*, Paris, 1900.
[15] Hegel, *op. cit.*, I, 352.

The failures of many pupils to become either good or persuasive gave rise, then as now, to cynical reflections upon the futility of education, and there were many arguments as to whether virtue or rhetoric could be taught. In these arguments there were two extreme positions. Some inclined to believe that if you teach a man to be virtuous, he will naturally be eloquent, and rhetorical instruction is unnecessary. Other sophists believed it quite impossible to teach virtue, but by constant attention to becoming a persuasive speaker, virtue would be unconsciously acquired. The controversy over the relation of virtue to eloquence runs through the history of rhetoric, and may be viewed as a technical question in that field. The attitude of sophists toward the teaching of virtue, then, cannot distinguish the sophists from the rhetoricians, and for the purposes of our study the two terms may be used almost synonymously—the word sophist, perhaps, being somewhat more inclusive.

II

The way in which the sophists combined their own intellectual interests with the teaching of rhetoric may best be made clear by a brief study of the four principal figures: Prodicus, Hippias, Protagoras, and Gorgias. Since these are the men most often referred to by Plato, it is also desirable to have some historical knowledge of them with which to correct the impressions given by the Platonic pictures.

Protagoras and Gorgias were older than Prodicus and Hippias, but they lived longer and matured later. They were therefore more affected by the movement away from the natural sciences, and as humanists devoted a larger portion of their energies to definitely rhetorical instruction.

Prodicus of Ceos has been called the earliest of the pessimists.[16] He was frail of body, but with a powerful voice he moved his audiences by descriptions of the different ages of man from birth to second childhood and death. He would depict death as "a stony-hearted creditor, wringing pledges one by one from his tardy debtor, first his hearing, then his sight, and next the free movement of his limbs."[17] His pessimism had none of the usual consequences—

[16] For Prodicus, see the following: Philostratus, *Lives of the Sophists*, tr. W. C. Wright, New York, 1922, pp. 37–9; F. Welcker, "Prodikos von Keos, Vorgänger des Sokrates," *Rheinisches Museum für Philologie*, III (1833), 1–39; Gomperz, *op. cit.*, I, 425–30; Benn, *op. cit.*, I, 77–81; Bromley Smith, "Products of Ceos," *Quarterly Journal of Speech Education*, VI, ii (1920), 51.

[17] Pseudo-Platonic *Axiochus*, 360, D. Cited by Gomperz, *op. cit.*, I, 428.

passive resignation, retreat from the world, or a great desire to seek pleasures while they might be found. To face death courageously was a virtue, and he taught his disciples that while we are, death is not; when death is, we are not. Life, while it lasted, was to be lived vigorously. His most famous lecture, *The Choice of Hercules,* has been preserved by Xenophon,[18] who tells us that Socrates quoted it with approval; through many centuries it has had a great effect in exalting the ideals of labor, hardihood, and simplicity. It was not in popular religion that Prodicus found his sustaining faith, for his speculations upon the origin of religion have the point of view of the modern critical historian. He accounted for the divinities of the various nations by pointing out that they deified the objects most useful to them—sun, moon, rivers, fruits of the field, and heroic men.

The more technical instruction of Prodicus was devoted to a study of language. He sought to collect and compare words of similar meaning. He desired to reduce the ambiguities in the arguments of the Greeks, and to aid in the development of literary style. He attempted to clarify ideas by insisting upon accuracy in the use of words, believing, with Hobbes, that "the light of human minds is perspicuous words."

The lectures of Prodicus were well known in all the cities of Greece, and commanded large sums in all places except Sparta, where foreign teachers were discouraged by a law against the payment of fees. Nevertheless he was welcomed there. He served his native island frequently as ambassador, and in the discharge of his civic duties displayed the qualities which in his lectures he urged upon youth.

Prodicus, then, was the rhetor rather than the teacher of rhetoric; and his chief contributions to the thought of his time were made as philosopher and grammarian.

Hippias of Elis, whom Plato especially disliked, is chiefly remembered for his versatility.[19] As an orator he was known throughout Greece. He recited certain well-known compositions of his in which figures of the Iliad are compared upon the basis of their virtues, or old men give advice to aspiring youths. He was rewarded by being made a freeman of many cities, and it is especially significant that his lectures on history and ethics were also acceptable to the conserva-

---

[18] Xenophon's *Memorabilia,* tr. E. C. Marchant, New York, 1923, II, ch. i.

[19] For Hippias, see Philostratus, *op. cit.,* p. 35; Gomperz, *op. cit.,* I, 431–4; Benn, *op. cit.,* I, 81–5.

tive Spartans. He never gave himself to the routine of perfecting his students in rhetoric, but was occupied with innumerable pursuits. He was a mathematician of considerable note; he wrote on theories of sculpture and painting, on phonetics, rhythm, and music; he developed a system that enabled him to perform surprising feats of memory in his old age; he was an ambassador for his native city, Elis; he attempted most of the prevailing forms of literature; and he prided himself upon his facility in mastering all the arts and crafts.

The antithesis between nature and convention seems to have originated with Hippias. He observed the variety and changeability of the laws of the Greek democracies, and felt that only laws possessing the universality and permanence of the laws of nature should be really sacred and binding. To give validity to the laws of men, the laws of all states should be compared, and the universal elements in them selected as the "natural" laws for the governing of nations. In believing that all men were by nature equal, Hippias was perhaps the originator of the doctrine of natural rights. When the distinction between nature and convention has been clearly made, one may, of course, espouse either. Hippias was one of the first preachers of a return to nature. This suggests a reason for his efforts to achieve so wide a versatility. The return to nature is only possible when each person is relatively self-sufficient, and self-sufficiency was a favorite doctrine with Hippias. He doubtless believed, as have men of other ages, that the development of personality gained by the consciousness of being equal to any situation more than offsets the dissipation of energy and efficiency incurred by the performance of all sorts of tasks; but one motive was clearly that of independence, and the development of the sort of ingenuity that enables a Robinson Crusoe to exist. Such a man would live by his work as well as by his wits. Rhetoric would not be the chief means of obtaining what he desired, and it is not surprising that rhetoric should be relatively less important to those who would be governed by nature than to those who saw in convention the power that offers the best government.

Hippias was more than a popular orator preaching to the cities of Greece. In his thought we have the beginnings of the cosmopolitanism of the later Cynics, the self-sufficiency of the Stoics, the belief in natural rights, and the ideal of versatility as a means of developing the whole man.

Protagoras of Abdera accepted the distinction of Hippias between nature and convention; but he had no sympathy for the return to nature.[20] In the variety and changeability of the laws of men lay the great hope of progress. He therefore turned away from the natural sciences and devoted himself to the "humanities." He, too, was a man of great versatility; he invented a porter's pad; as a friend of Pericles, he was given the task of framing the laws for the colony at Thurium. As a teacher, his instruction was chiefly intended to offer a training for public life. He included within his curriculum oratory and its auxiliary arts, educational theory, jurisprudence, politics, and ethics. In his teaching of public speaking he insisted upon the value of practical exercises. He declared that there were two sides to every proposition, and that a speaker should be able to set forth the arguments on either side. His practice of having his students argue upon both sides of certain general themes may have been responsible for the charge against him, recorded by Aristotle, that he made the worse appear the better reason. But as this was a standing reproach against philosophers as well as rhetoricians, and as we have no evidence which impeaches his moral character, we may believe that this charge applied no more to his teaching than to all instruction in the art of reasoning.

In addition to the training in debate. Protagoras practised his pupils in the development of what were called commonplaces. Speeches were made which praised or blamed certain human qualities, such as patriotism, friendship, courage, cupidity. These speeches had no reference to a concrete situation, but they equipped the pupils with a stock of thoughts and phrases for use when a real occasion demanded ready utterance. The debates developed keenness and dexterity; the commonplaces gave the speakers a certain copiousness and elegance.

Grammar was also given attention, and Protagoras is recognized as the first to introduce the subject into his curriculum. It has been remarked that the level attained by Greek literature before Protagoras wrote his book *On Correct Speech* seems to indicate that a mastery of language may be acquired quite independently of conscious rules. But the desire of Protagoras to introduce order and consistency in the tenses of the verb, moods of predication, and genders of substantives, was in harmony with the intellectual tendencies of the

[20] For Protagoras, see the following: Philostratus, *op. cit.,* pp. 33–5; Diogenes Laertius, *Lives of the Philosophers,* tr. C. D. Yonge, London, 1853, bk. ix, ch. 8; Hegel, *op. cit.,* I, 372–8; Gomperz, *op. cit.,* I, 438–75; Benn, *op. cit.,* I, 85–95; E. Barker, *Greek Political Theory,* London, 1918, pp. 60–4; Bromley Smith, "Protagoras of Abdera," *Quarterly Journal of Speech Education,* IV (1918), 196.

times, and shows him to have been by no means totally absorbed in the practical business of advising youth how to get on in the world.

The ethical theory of Protagoras was set forth in the lost work, *On the Incorrect Actions of Mankind.* In his seventieth year he read publicly, at the house of Euripides, his work, *On the Gods.* Only the first sentence has been preserved.

> In respect to the gods, I am unable to know either that they are or that they are not, for there are many obstacles to such knowledge, above all the obscurity of the matter, and the life of man, in that it is so short.[21]

Whether Protagoras meant to assail the belief in the gods, or whether he meant merely to point out that in the nature of the case we could not have *knowledge* of them, we do not know. At any rate, his scepticism so alarmed certain of his contemporaries that his book was publicly burned, and he was exiled.

The philosophical doctrine for which Protagoras is chiefly known, and for which he was vigorously assailed by Plato, is summarized in the dictum that man is the measure of all things. Since we have only the first sentence of the work in which this doctrine was developed, it is not strange that scholars are far apart in their interpretation of the meaning of Protagoras; but they are generally agreed that the Platonic interpretation of it in the *Theætetus* is quite unfair. Few interpreters now consider it to involve the degree of relativity and subjectivism with which Protagoras and the sophists generally have been burdened. Gomperz points out that a man who preached that anything was true which any one believed to be so, would not be the man to suffer for a denial of the possibility of knowledge of the gods. Professor F. C. S. Schiller, in his *Studies in Humanism,* devotes two dialogues to Protagoras; one explaining his humanism, and the other defending his scepticism. In his introduction to the volume Professor Schiller says:

> Our only hope of understanding knowledge, our only chance of keeping philosophy alive by nourishing it with the realities of life, lies in going back from Plato to Protagoras, and ceasing to misunderstand the great teacher who discovered the measure of man's universe.[22]

But this is not the place to discuss the philosophical aspects of the teachings of Protagoras; it is only desired to make it clear that there are grounds for regarding him as did Hegel.

[21] Diogenes Laertius, IX, 51.
[22] Schiller, *Studies in Humanism,* London, 1907, p. xiv.

[He was] not merely a teacher of culture, but likewise a deep and solid thinker, a philosopher who reflected on fundamental questions of an altogether universal kind.[23]

Gorgias of Leontini,[24] who first appeared in Athens as the head of an embassy petitioning for aid against the aggressions of Syracuse upon Sicilian cities, is known as the founder of the art of prose. Chiefly interested in oratory of the epideictic type, he employed what is termed the "grand" style. The resources of the poets, whose works were so successful in holding the attention of Greek audiences, were turned to the purposes of the orator. Gorgias was interested in style for style's sake; his foreign accent and distinguished air delighted the Athenians; and throughout his career he sought to persuade by pleasing. The extravagances and artificialities of his style have often been pointed to as the source of the euphuism of the seventeenth century, and of the stylistic eccentricities of other periods of decadence.

It cannot be said, however, that the oratory of Gorgias was devoid of ideas. In common with other itinerant teachers, he preached Pan-Hellenism in all the cities of Greece. In his Olympian oration he urged the Greeks to cease their internal rivalries, and to turn their spears against the barbarians. In the Athenian funeral oration he warned his hearers that victories over their fellow Greeks called for dirges of lament. As a teacher of oratory, Gorgias was condemned by Aristotle for placing too much emphasis upon memorization and declamation.[25] Little is known concerning his pedagogical method, but there is no reason to suppose that it differed markedly from the custom of having the pupils declaim speeches written by themselves and by the master, drill in topics of amplification and depreciation, and practise upon commonplaces and disputations. Although an epideictic speaker would be constantly praising virtue and censuring vice, and in so doing could hardly avoid entertaining certain ethical theories, Gorgias never announced himself as a teacher of virtue. He agreed with Isocrates that one who tried to become per-

[23] Hegel, op. cit., I, 373.

[24] For Gorgias, see the following: Philostratus, op. cit., pp. 29–33; Diodorus Siculus, bk. xii, ch. 7; The Historical Library of Diodorus the Sicilian, tr. George Booth, London, 1814, I, 465–6; F. Blass, Attische Beredsamkeit, Leipzig, 1864, I, ch. 2; Navarre, op. cit., ch. 3; W. H. Thompson's introduction to his edition of Plato's Gorgias, London, 1871; Hegel, op. cit., I, 378–84; Gomperz, op. cit., I, 476–94; Benn, op. cit., I, 95–100; Bromley Smith, "Gorgias: A Study of Oratorical Style," Quarterly Journal of Speech Education, VII (1921), 335.

[25] Aristotle, Sophistici Elenchi, tr. Edward Poste, London, 1866, ch. 34.

suasive in discoursing about justice and virtue and expediency would probably become as virtuous as mere knowledge could make him.

As a philosopher, Gorgias engaged in controversy with the Eleatic school. All we know of his book *On Nature or Not-Being,* is its threefold thesis that "Being does not exist, if it did exist it would not be cognizable, and if it were cognizable, the cognition would not be communicable." [26] We cannot here enter upon metaphysical questions; but the conventional construction put upon this thesis is that it goes beyond Protagoras, and is the ultimate of sophistical scepticism, that it is a nihilism which makes all knowledge impossible, that it makes immediate plausibility the sole standard of the critical judgment, and that rhetoric was the chief of all subjects for Gorgias because the one certainty of life was that the man who could persuade others to do his will was, temporarily at least, the possessor of great power. This interpretation is not justified either by an examination of the philosophical disputes of the time, or by a study of the life of Gorgias himself. The Eleatic school, following Parmenides and Melissus, was quite willing to doubt all evidence of the senses, and yet to trust implicitly in *a priori* reasoning about Absolute Being. The protest of Gorgias against this was quite in harmony with the growing modesty of the scientific endeavor of the times, which was beginning to see the necessity of increasing knowledge bit by bit, and to question the claim of the philosophers to a higher knowledge. Had Gorgias, in denying the tenets of the Eleatics, meant that he believed scientific truth to be unattainable, it is not likely that he would have written upon physics, nor that a statue would have appeared upon the tomb of Isocrates representing Gorgias as directing the attention of his pupil to a globe. The attack of Gorgias upon the contradictions of his predecessors in philosophy does not show that he abandoned all search for truth. Socrates attacked his philosophical predecessors in a similar manner, he abandoned all inquiry in natural science, and he had as little confidence in the attributes of being as Gorgias; yet he is not accused of denying the validity of established scientific truth, or of abandoning all belief in the possibility of knowledge. The account of Gorgias offered by many historians of philosophy is a *reductio ad absurdum* rather than an interpretation.

Although we think of Gorgias chiefly as an orator and a teacher of oratory, and as a creator of a style which is now looked upon unfavorably, he was too active a participant in the philosophical con-

[26] As translated in Gomperz, *op. cit.,* I, 482.

troversies of his time for us to dismiss him as intellectually insignificant. Since we have lost his philosophical works, we cannot prove that he made a constructive contribution to the thought of his time, but his attack upon an absolutistic philosophy was something, and the evidence certainly does not warrant the supposition that he was guilty of meaningless absurdities, or that his teaching was necessarily immoral in its implications.

Numerous other rhetoricians might be mentioned—Polus and Thrasymachus especially—but our information concerning them is scanty, and the four we have dealt with are the most significant when we consider their prominence as rhetoricians, their contribution to the thought of the time, and the attention they received from Plato.

III

One is inevitably led to ask why such men as these have suffered so greatly in the estimation of posterity. Why has Plato's opinion been accepted uncritically and its perversions further distorted by later commentators? In addition to what has already been suggested —that we need the terminology of the attack upon the Athenian sophists to describe an ever present sophistry—there is the fact that Athenian hostility to the sophists has often been taken as a confirmation of Plato's account. This is to forget that Athenian public opinion distrusted the sophists for reasons similar to those which led it to execute Socrates, and that the disagreement between Plato and the Athenian public was profound. The activities which gave these teachers their influence with the Athenians were just the ones which led Plato to condemn them; while many aspects of their thought which led to popular disfavor were the ones which Plato would have regarded with approval. We may learn much about the sophists by contrasting the typical Athenian criticism of them with that of Plato.

In accounting for the disfavor with which the Athenians looked upon the sophists it must not be forgotten that a complementary picture of their power and influence could quite as easily be drawn, and that both are necessary to a true estimate of their position in Athenian life. The sophists exerted a much greater influence upon their times than Plato, and the element of jealousy should not be entirely overlooked in considering his attitude toward them.[27] But the conservative

---

[27] G. H. Lewes has shown why the relationship between the solitary thinker and the public speaker tends to remain constant. "The Sophists were wealthy; the Sophists were powerful; the Sophists were dazzling, rhetorical, and not pro-

elements of the city, of whom Aristophanes was a prominent representative, charged the sophists with corrupting the youth. Plato dissented from this charge in the case of Socrates, and defended the sophists generally from it, asserting that the real corrupter of youth in Athens was public opinion, which the sophists only reflected.[28] John Stuart Mill, who had reasons for analyzing the motives of those who are overzealous in protecting the young, has stated the case most clearly:

> When the charge of corrupting youth comes to be particularized, it always resolves itself into making them think themselves wiser than the laws, and fail in proper respect to their fathers and seniors. And this is a true charge; only it ought to fall, not on the Sophists, but on intellectual culture generally. Whatever encourages young men to think for themselves, does lead them to criticize the laws of their country—does shake their faith in the infallibility of their fathers and elders, and make them think their own speculations preferable. It is beyond doubt that the teaching of Socrates, and of Plato after him, produced these effects in an extraordinary degree. Accordingly, we learn from Xenophon that the youths of rich families who frequented Socrates, did so, for the most part, against the severe disapprobation of their relatives. In every age and state of society, fathers and elder citizens have been suspicious and jealous of all freedom of thought and all intellectual cultivation (not strictly professional) in their sons and juniors, unless they can get it controlled by some civil or ecclesiastical authority in which they have confidence. But it had not occurred to Athenian legislators to have an established Sophistical Church, or State Universities. The teaching of the Sophists was all on the voluntary principle; and the dislike of it was of the same nature with the outcry against "godless colleges," or the objection of most of our higher and middle classes to any schools but

found. Interrogate human nature—above all, the nature of philosophers—and ask what will be the sentiment entertained respecting the Sophists by their rivals. Ask the solitary thinker what is his opinion of the showy, powerful, but shallow rhetorician who usurps the attention of the world. The man of convictions has at all times a superb contempt for the man of mere oratorical or dialectical display. The thinker knows that the world is ruled by Thought; yet he finds Expression gaining the world's attention. He knows that he has within him thoughts pregnant with human welfare; yet he sees the giddy multitude intoxicated with the enthusiasm excited by some plausible fallacy, clothed in enchanting language. He sees through the fallacy, but cannot make others as clear-sighted. His warning is unheeded; his wisdom is spurned; his ambition is frustrated; the popular Idol is carried onward in triumph. The neglected thinker would not be human if he bore this with equanimity. He does not. He is loud and angry in lamenting the fate of a world that can be so led; loud and angry in his contempt of one who could so lead it. Should he become a critic or historian of his age, what exactness ought we to expect in his account of the popular idol?" *Op. cit.*, p. 88.

[28] *Republic*, VI, 492.

denominational ones. They disapproved of any teaching unless they could be certain that all their own opinions would be taught. It mattered not that the instructors taught no heresy; the mere fact that they accustomed the mind to ask questions, and require other reasons than use and wont, sufficed at Athens, as it does in other places, to make the teaching dangerous in the eyes of self-satisfied respectability. Accordingly, respectability, as Plato himself tells us, looked with at least as evil an eye on Philosophers as on Sophists.[29]

This explanation of Mill's is more applicable to the ethical and philosophical, than to the rhetorical, aspects of the sophists' teaching. To be sure, the rhetoricians professed to be able to speak upon either side of any case, and to impart this ability to their pupils; this was the cause of a certain distrust analogous to that with which lawyers are sometimes viewed today. But when lawyers turn public orators, they are the most vigorous and platitudinous upholders of the *status quo*. So the sophists, as public orators, illustrated and reënforced the received dogmas of Athenian society. Their speeches were acceptable to the most conservative. Even their teaching of the art of speaking upon either side of any case did not rest so much upon a willingness to attack prevalent morality and customs as it did upon the cultivation of an ability to make either side of the case *appear* to be consistent with common standards of right and justice. Rhetoric as the art of persuasion must always appeal to the people upon the basis of whatever beliefs they may happen to have. It is not likely, then, that it was the rhetoric of the sophists which led to the charge that they broke down religion and corrupted youth. It was rather that they concerned themselves enough with philosophy to incur something of the distrust with which speculative thought has always been viewed. In all the disputes between the earlier schools of philosophy there was one point upon which they were agreed; namely, that the popular beliefs and explanations of phenomena were entirely wrong. For them, as for modern philosophers, the incarnation of ignorance was "the man in the street." Their arrogance and their contempt for the public naturally roused resentment. Their lofty pretensions were contrasted with their apparent practical helplessness, and the story of Thales falling into a well while gazing at the stars is typical of the popular attitude toward philosophers. The popular distrust of the sophists was not so much that, as rhetoricians, they were different from Socrates and Plato, but that, as philosophers, they were so much like them.

[29] *Op. cit.*, IV, 262.

There was a certain aspect of the rhetorical teaching which caused a portion of the public to dislike the popular teachers. After the downfall of the Thirty in Athens, it was evident that democracy was the order of the day. Members of the aristocracy could retain their power in the state only by developing their ability to persuade an audience. Teachers of rhetoric, in such a situation, were indispensable. But the fees charged by the sophists placed their instruction beyond the reach of many, who naturally resented what seemed an unfair advantage possessed by those more adequately trained for public life.

The fees of the sophists seem to have been a cause of universal reproach, but the feeling was too complex to be explained simply. There was, of course, the aristocratic bias of Athenian life. Physicians were the only wage-earners who suffered no loss of social standing. Sculptors were artisans rather than artists because their work was a method of gaining a livelihood. Plato, the man of wealth and family, was for once in agreement with the popular prejudice, and he attacked the sophists both for the insignificance of their petty fees, and for the large fortunes that they made.[30] The acceptance of fees marked a certain institutionalizing and mechanizing of higher education, which was disliked. The philosopher whose chief occupation was the pursuit of truth might impart his wisdom to such persons and at such times as suited him, without seriously interrupting his own thinking. He probably found a certain number of disciples a stimulus. But the introduction of fees and the acceptance of responsibility for practical training in public speaking made the teacher seem to be a servant of the pupil. He became a professional educator, and as such insisted disagreeably upon the importance of education. As philosophers, the sophists could probably have retained the measure of freedom and leisure that Plato demanded, even while accepting pay for their work. But as teachers of rhetoric they tended to become submerged in the routine of schoolmastering.

As philosophers, the sophists incurred a different sort of penalty for their fee-taking. Then, as now, certain activities of what may perhaps be termed men's higher natures were especially removed from thoughts of gain. We do not like to think that popular preachers are making money; we deplore the commercialized theatre, and the novel written only to sell. These activities, we believe, should be ends in themselves. It is not difficult to understand why the spectacle of foreign teachers coming to Athens to teach virtue for a price should have

[30] *Apology,* 20; *Cratylus,* 384 and 391.

roused a resentment somewhat distinct from that of those who disliked the teaching of rhetoric.

THE RHETORIC OF ISOCRATES AND ITS CULTURAL IDEAL
Werner Jaeger

Greek literature of the fourth century reflects a widespread struggle
to determine the character of true paideia; and within it Isocrates,
the chief representative of rhetoric, personifies the classical opposition
to Plato and his school. From this point on, the rivalry of philosophy
and rhetoric, each claiming to be the better form of culture, runs like
a leitmotiv throughout the history of ancient civilization. It is impossible to describe every phase of that rivalry: for one thing, it is rather
repetitious, and the leaders of its opposing sides are not always very
interesting personalities.[1] All the more important, therefore, is the
conflict between Plato and Isocrates—the first battle in the centuries of
war between philosophy and rhetoric. Later, that war was sometimes
to degenerate into a mere academic squabble, in which neither side
possessed any genuine vital force; but at its beginning the combatant
parties represented the truly moving forces and needs of the Greek
people. The field on which it was waged lay in the very centre of the
political scene. That is what gives it the vivid colouring of a truly
historical event, and the large sweep which keeps our interest in it
permanently alive. In retrospect, we realize that in this conflict are
symbolized the essential problems of that whole period of Greek
history.

Today as of old, Isocrates has, like Plato, his admirers and exponents; and there is no doubt that since the Renaissance he has
exercised a far greater influence on the educational methods of
humanism than any other Greek or Roman teacher. Historically, it is
perfectly correct to describe him (in the phrase used on the title-page
of several modern books) as the father of 'humanistic culture'—
inasmuch as the sophists cannot really claim that title, and from our
own pedagogic methods and ideals a direct line runs back to him, as

From *Paideia: the Ideals of Greek Culture*, Vol. III, by Werner Jaeger. Translated by Gilbert Highet. © 1943, Oxford University Press, Inc.   Reprinted by
permission.

[1] There is a full account of the history of this conflict in H. von Arnim's *Leben
und Werke des Dion von Prusa* (Berlin 1898) pp. 4–114.

it does to Quintilian and Plutarch.[2] But that point of view, dictated as it is by modern academic humanism, is vastly different from the attitude of this book—for our task here is to examine the whole development of Greek paideia and to study the complexities and antagonisms inherent in its problems and its meaning.[3] It is important to notice that what is often regarded by contemporary educators as the essence of humanism is mainly a continuation of the rhetorical strain in classical culture; while the history of humanism is a far broader and richer thing than that, for it contains all the manifold survivals of Greek paideia—including the world-wide influence exercised by Greek philosophy and science.[4] For this point of view, it is clear that an understanding of the true Greek paideia at once entails a criticism of modern academic humanism.[5] On the other hand, the position and character of philosophy and science within Greek civilization as a whole cannot be properly estimated until they are seen striving against

[2] See, for instance, a work by Drerup's pupil Burk, *Die Pädagogik des Isokrates als Grundlegung des humanistischen Bildungsideals* (Würzburg 1923), and in particular the two sections called *Das Nachleben der Pädagogik des Isokrates* (p. 199 f.) and *Isokrates und der Humanismus* (p. 211 f.). More recently Drerup himself has brought out four lectures entitled *Der Humanismus in seiner Geschichte, seinen Kulturwerten und seiner Vorbereitung im Unterrichtswessen der Griechen* (Paderborn 1934). British scholars like Burnet and Ernest Barker often call Isocrates the father of humanism.

[3] Some critics have laid down that a historian of paideia must begin by giving his own definition of it. That is rather as if they expected a historian of philosophy to start either from Plato's definition of philosophy, or from Epicurus', or from Kant's or Hume's—all four being widely different. A history of paideia should describe as accurately as possible all the different meanings of Greek paideia, the various forms which it took, and the various spiritual levels at which it appeared, and should explain both their individual peculiarities and their historical connexions.

[4] On this see my essay, *Platos Stellung im Aufbau der griechischen Bildung* (Berlin 1928), which first appeared in *Die Antike*, vol. 4 (1928), nos. 1-2.

[5] From this point of view philosophy, and Greek philosophy in particular, has played a decisive role in the development of modern humanism, which would have had no impetus without it, and would not even have been able to expound its own aims. Actually, the study of the philosophical aspects of classical civilization has become more and more important not only in modern philosophy but in modern philology too, and has deeply influenced the purposes and methods of classical scholarship. But, seen from the same point of view, the history of humanism itself takes on a new appearance. Historians usually speak of two sharply contrasting periods—the Middle Ages and the Renaissance, scholasticism and humanism. But this simple pattern is shown to be an over-simplification as soon as we realize that the rebirth of Greek philosophy in the Middle Ages was really another great epoch in the uninterrupted influence of Greek paideia. That influence never died away entirely, but lived on continuously through mediaeval and modern history. *Non datur saltus in historia humanitatis.*

other types of intellectual activity in order to be accepted as the true form of culture. Ultimately, both the rivals, philosophy and rhetoric, spring from poetry, the oldest Greek paideia; and they cannot be understood without reference to their origin in it.[6] But as the old rivalry for the primacy of culture gradually narrows to a dispute about the relative values of philosophy and rhetoric, it becomes clear enough that the ancient Hellenic partnership between gymnastic training and 'musical' culture has at last sunk to a much lower level.

To one who has just read Plato's *Protagoras* and *Gorgias* it seems obvious that the educational system of the sophists and rhetors was fundamentally an outworn ideal; and, if we compare it with the lofty claims advanced by philosophy—the claim that henceforth *all* education and *all* culture must be based on nothing but the knowledge of the highest values—it really was obsolete. And yet (as we have seen from our first glance over the later centuries of Greek history [7]) the older type of education, the method of the sophists and the rhetoricians, remained unconquerably active and alive beside its rival, and in fact continued to hold a leading place as one of the greatest influences on the spiritual life of Greece. Perhaps the savage scorn with which Plato attacks and persecutes it may be party explained by the victor's feeling that he is at war with an enemy who is, as long as he remains within his own frontiers, unconquerable. It is difficult for us to understand the violence of his detestation, if we think of his attacks as directed solely against the great sophists of Socrates' generation, considered as embodiments of the type of culture which he loathed: Protagoras, Gorgias, Hippias, Prodicus. When he wrote his dialogues, these men were dead, and, in that rapid century, half forgotten. It needed all Plato's art to call the strong personalities of the famous sophists out of the shadows to life once more. When he made his caricatures of them (caricatures which in their way are quite as immortal as his idealized portrait of Socrates), a new generation had grown up; and he was attacking them, his contemporaries, as well as his predecessors. We need not go so far as to see, in the opponents whom he describes, mere masks for notable men of his own age; and yet, in his presentment of the sophists, there are many contemporary traits. And there is one absolutely certain fact: Plato never argues with dead men, with historical fossils.

[6] It is impossible to appreciate the part played by philosophy within the organic structure of Greek civilization without being fully alive to its close connexion with the internal and external history of Greece.

[7] See note 1.

Nothing shows how strong and vital sophistry and rhetoric were, at the time when he began his struggle against them, more clearly than the personality of Isocrates, who actually entered on his career after *Protagoras* and *Gorgias* were written.[8] It is particularly interesting that from the very outset he contested the claims of Plato and the Socratic circle, and defended sophistic education against their attacks. This means that he was writing from the firm conviction that such criticisms did not seriously shake his position. He was really a genuine sophist: indeed, it was he who brought the sophistic movement in education to its culminating point. Biographical tradition represents him as the pupil of Protagoras, of Prodicus, and especially of Gorgias; and archaeologists of the Hellenistic age found proof of the third of these connexions in his tombstone, which bore a figure they identified as Gorgias, pointing to a celestial globe.[9] Another tradition asserted that Isocrates had studied with the great rhetor in Thessaly—doubtless during the last phase of the Peloponnesian war.[10] Plato too, in his *Meno*, mentions that some part of Gorgias' career as a teacher was passed in Thessaly [11]: an interesting proof of the fact that the new culture was penetrating even the frontier lands of Greece. Isocrates' first great book, the *Panegyricus*, which brought him fame almost overnight, closely resembles Gorgias' *Olympicus;* and the fact that he deliberately chose to compete with such a celebrated author in treating the same theme—a call to the Greeks to achieve national unity—is, according to Greek usage, a proof that he considered himself Gorgias' pupil. And the chief evidence for the fact is the dominant position he assigns to rhetoric—that is, to the most concrete, the least purely theoretical, type of sophistic culture. Throughout his life he aimed, like Gorgias, at teaching the art or craft of speaking ($\lambda \acute{o} \gamma \omega \nu$ $\tau \acute{e} \chi \nu \eta$); [12]

[8] Plato wrote *Protagoras* and *Gorgias* as early as the first decade of the fourth century. Isocrates cannot have founded his school before 390, because in his extant orations we can trace his work as a hired writer of forensic speeches down to that date at least; perhaps it lasted even into the 'eighties.

[9] The facts of Isocrates' life are thoroughly examined by Blass in the second section of *Die attische Beredsamkeit* (2nd ed., Leipzig 1892); see p. 11 of that book for the traditions about his teachers. On the tombstone, see pseudo-Plutarch, *vit. X orat.* 838d; the author of those biographies took his archaeological and antiquarian data from a work by the Hellenistic epigraphist Diodorus.

[10] It is impossible to set a definite date for Isocrates' stay in Thessaly, but it must have been either just before or just after 410.

[11] Plato, *Meno* 70b; and cf. Isoc. *Antid.* 155.

[12] He calls it $\dot{\eta}$ $\tau \tilde{\omega} \nu$ $\lambda \acute{o} \gamma \omega \nu$ $\mu \epsilon \lambda \acute{e} \tau \eta$, or $\pi \alpha \iota \delta \epsilon \acute{\iota} \alpha$, or $\dot{\epsilon} \pi \iota \mu \acute{e} \lambda \epsilon \iota \alpha$. Blass, on p. 107 of the work cited in note 9, suggests that he avoids calling it a $\tau \acute{e} \chi \nu \eta$: probably to avoid being confused with the writers of technai, or rhetorical handbooks. But passages like *Soph.* 9-10 and *Antid.* 178 are enough to show that he held his $\varphi \iota \lambda o \sigma o \varphi \acute{\iota} \alpha$ to be a $\tau \acute{e} \chi \nu \eta$.

but he preferred to apply the title 'sophist' only to theorists, whatever their special interests might be. He used it, among others, for Socrates and his pupils, who had done so much to discredit the name. His own ideal he called 'philosophy'. Thus, he completely inverted the meanings given by Plato to the two words. Today, when Plato's definition of 'philosophy' has been universally accepted for centuries, Isocrates' procedure appears to have been a mere whim. But really it was not. In his time, those concepts were still developing, and had not yet finally hardened into their ultimate shapes. It was not Plato, but Isocrates, who followed the general idiom in calling Socrates and his pupils 'sophists' quite as much as Protagoras or Hippias; and in using 'philosophy' to mean intellectual culture in general,[13] which is the sense it has in Thucydides, for example. He could well have said (as Pericles says in Thucydides [14]) that the characteristic mark of the whole Athenian state was its interest in things of the mind, φιλοσοφεῖν, and he does actually say something of the kind in the *Panegyricus*. Athens, he writes, invented culture (φιλοσοφία)—and he is obviously thinking of the whole community rather than of the small group of sharp-witted dialecticians gathered round Plato or Socrates.[15] What he was aiming at was universal culture, contrasted with one definite creed or one particular method of attaining knowledge, as preached by the Platonists. Thus, in the opposing claims made by both sides to ownership of the title 'philosophy,' and in the widely different meanings given to the word by the opponents, there is symbolized the rivalry of rhetoric and science for leadership in the realm of education and culture.[16]

Isocrates, then, was the post-war representative of the sophistic and rhetorical culture which had flourished in the Periclean period. But he

[13] It is unnecessary to prove this point by enumerating all the relevant passages. In *Antid.* 270 he claims the title φιλοσοφία for his own work alone, and says that other teachers (e.g. dialecticians, mathematicians, and rhetorical 'technographers') have no right to use it. He is less exclusive in his earlier works, where he speaks freely of the φιλοσοφία of the professional disputers or eristics (*Hel.* 6) and of teachers of rhetoric like Polycrates (*Bus.* 1); and in *Soph.* 1 he uses it as a general description of all the branches of higher education and culture which are characterized in that work.

[14] Thuc. 2.40.1.

[15] *Paneg.* 47. The word καταδείξαι describes the act of the founder of a cult. In this place the word φιλοσοφία does *not* mean 'philosophy.'

[16] Blass (p. 28 of the book quoted in note 9) points out that in Isocrates' time the word 'philosophy' still meant 'culture,' so that there is nothing silly about his claim to 'teach philosophy'; however, he says it is arrogant of Isocrates to pretend to be the only representative of true philosophy—i.e. true culture. Still, Plato and all the other schools and teachers made the same claim: see Plato *ep.* 7. 326a, *Rep.* 490a, etc.

was much more. To think of him as nothing more than that is to ignore the best and most characteristic aspects of his personality. The particular way in which he distributes the emphasis, magnifying the importance of rhetoric and of practical politics, and pushing mere sophistry and theory into the background, shows his fine perception of the Athenian attitude to the new culture. It had, during his boyhood and youth, achieved an astonishing success in his native city of Athens; but it had also been violently opposed. Although he was far from being the first Athenian to declare himself its pupil and its champion, it was not really naturalized in Athens until he gave it a truly Athenian dress. In Plato the rhetors and sophists who argue with Socrates are always at a disadvantage, simply because they are foreigners, and do not understand the real problems of Athens and the Athenians. They always seem to be outsiders, as they enter the close, compact Athenian society, bringing with them their knowledge, 'imported ready-made', as it were.[17] Of course they all speak the same international language, in which they can be understood by every educated man. But it never has the Athenian overtones. They lack the casual grace and the social ease without which they cannot achieve full success in the Athenian world. Their wide culture and their fabulous technical skill are admiringly welcomed, but in a deeper sense they remain ineffectual—at least for the time. Before it could become effective, the new element had to coalesce with the very special way of life which characterized the incomparable state of Athens; and none but an Athenian could bring about the coalition —an Athenian who, like Isocrates, was fully alive to the nature of his city and of the crisis which then confronted it. It was a full generation after its first appearance in Athens that rhetoric was naturalized there, under the influence of the tremendous events of the war and the post-war years—events which wrought a deep change in the very nature of rhetoric. At the same time it was profoundly affected by the moral reformation initiated by Socrates,[18] and by the great social

[17] Plato, *Prot.* 313 c f.

[18] It is difficult to tell how much historical truth there is in that passage of Plato's *Phaedrus* where Socrates is made to prophesy a great future for Isocrates. Perhaps the two had met at some time, and there is no more in it than that. It can hardly mean that Isocrates was Socrates' friend, still less his pupil. And yet his works show many traces of the influence of Socratic ideas. The fullest examination of them is H. Gomperz' *Isokrates und die Sokratik* (*Wiener Studien* 27, 1905, p. 163, and 28, 1906, p. 1). He assumes, correctly, that Isocrates got his knowledge of these ideas from books about Socrates; and this is supported by the fact that he did not begin to talk about them till the years between 390 and 380, when he himself first entered the field of educational theory. Still, I think Gomperz exaggerates the influence of Antisthenes upon Isocrates.

crises which had shaken the Athenian state throughout Isocrates'
youth and early manhood. The new generation, heir to the Periclean
system, found tasks of enormous difficulty confronting it. It was
rhetoric, and not philosophy in the Platonic sense, that seemed to
Isocrates to be the intellectual form which could best express the
political and ethical ideas of his age, and make them part of the
intellectual equipment of all contemporary Athenians. With this
new conception of its purposes, Isocrates' rhetorical teaching emerged
as part of the great post-war educational movement of Athens, into
which all the efforts of his day to reform and rejuvenate the Athenian
state were inevitably destined to flow.

The factors which brought this about were very various. Despite
his mastery of language and of style, Isocrates was not a born orator.
And yet, by its very nature, the Athenian democracy still held that
no man could be an effective political force unless he were a master of
oratory. He says himself that physically he had a weak constitution.
His voice was not nearly powerful enough to reach large audiences;
and he had an invincible fear of making a public appearance. Crowds
terrified him.[19] In speaking without embarrassment of this agoraphobia,
Isocrates was not merely offering an excuse for his complete abstention
from all political activity; besides that, he felt that his strange condition
was a very personal feature of his character, rooted far in its depths. As
with Socrates, his refusal to enter politics was not a sign of lack of
interest, but the result of a profound intellectual and spiritual conflict
—a conflict which both hampered his activity and at the same time
enlarged his understanding of the part he must play in the contemporary political crisis. Like the Platonic Socrates, he was convinced that he must initiate the much-needed reformation in some
other way than by entering an active career as an orator in the
assemblies and the law courts. Thus, he felt that the personal dis-
abilities which made him unfit for normal political life summoned
him to a higher vocation. His weakness was his destiny. But whereas
Socrates, with his incessant questioning and examining, became an
explorer in the sphere of morality, and found himself at last standing
before the closed gates of a new world of knowledge, the more practical
Isocrates, although for the time being he was deeply impressed by the
personality of his great contemporary, and constantly strove to rival

[19] For the facts of Isocrates' life, see Blass (cited in note 9) p. 8 f.; Jebb,
Attic Orators (London 1876) 11, p. 1 f.; and Münscher's exhaustive article in
Pauly-Wissowa's *Realenzyklopädie der klass. Altertumswiss.* 9.2150 f. On his weak
voice and his timidity, see *Phil.* 81, *Panath.* 10.

the lofty standard he set, felt nevertheless that his special gifts and his natural dislike for the mob predestined him to become within a small circle the teacher of a new type of political action.[20]

Even the age in which he lived seemed to make this course inevitable. In the calm and concentration of his retirement, he wished to educate statesmen who could give new direction to the efforts of the misguided masses and to the politics of the Greek states, which had long been revolving hopelessly in a closed circle. He set out to inspire every pupil with a passion for the new aims which occupied his own mind. There was within him a political visionary whose thought moved in the same direction as that of the practical statesmen, and was led like them by such aspirations as Power, Glory, Prosperity, Progress. Gradually his experience led him to modify his aims; but from the very beginning he held that they could not be fulfilled by the outworn methods of the Periclean age—competitive diplomacy and exhausting wars between the separate Greek city-states. In that his thought is wholly a product of the weakness of Athens after the Peloponnesian war. Dreamer that he was, in his visions of the future he overleapt that weakness. He believed that Athens could play a leading part in Greek affairs only in peaceful agreement with Sparta and the other Greek states, with entire equality between victors and vanquished; for then the intellectual superiority of Athens to her coarser rivals would assure that she acquired the balance of power.[21] Only such establishment of equality among the Greek states and their devotion to one great national purpose could arrest the dissolution of Greece, and therewith the total annihilation of the small separate states—which hitherto had striven only to destroy one another, although none of them had ever acquired a real superiority over all the rest, with the supreme power which would impose a lasting peace on the entire nation. To save Greece, a common national purpose must be found. And, after the bitter experiences of the Peloponnesian war, Isocrates considered that the essential duty of true statesmanship was to find it. True, there was an urgent preliminary: the political life of the Greek state had to be purged of its deep corruption, and of the cause of that corruption—the poisonous

---

[20] In *Phil.* 81–82 he admits his physical and psychical weakness, but nevertheless claims to be far ahead of others in phronésis and paideia.

[21] That is the role which he assigns to Athens in the *Panegyricus*. Even after the collapse of the second naval confederacy, he continued to maintain the spiritual leadership of Athens—for instance in the *Antidosis* and the *Panathenaicus*. But he later (as in the *Peace* speech and *Philip*) abandoned the claim that Athens should likewise wield the political hegemony of Greece.

mutual hatreds of the separate states and parties. It was exactly that
selfish hatred of each for his neighbour which, according to Thucydides'
tragic description, had during the Peloponnesian war served as a justification for every kind of monstrous crime, and had destroyed the
foundations of all established moral codes.[22] But Isocrates did not,
like the Platonic Socrates, believe that the sorely needed reformation
could be achieved by the creation of a new moral world, a state as it
were within each man's soul.[23] He held that the *nation*, the idea of
Greece, was the point round which the new elements in the spiritual
renaissance were to crystallize. Plato had accused rhetoric of being
able only to teach men how to convince an audience, without pointing out any ideal to be pursued: and therefore of being only a practical
means to provide intellectual instruments by which to achieve immoral
ends.[24] That weakness in the pretensions of rhetoric was undeniable;
and, at a time when the conscience of the best of the Greeks was constantly becoming more sensitive, it was a real danger for the art. In
the adoption of the Panhellenic ideal, Isocrates saw the way to solve
this problem also. The essential was to find a mean, as it were, between
the moral indifference which had previously characterized rhetorical
education, and the Platonic resolution of all politics into morality,
which from a practical point of view was certain to lead away
from all politics.[25] The new rhetoric had to find an ideal which
could be ethically interpreted and which at the same time could be
translated into practical political action. This ideal was a new moral
code for Greece. It gave rhetoric an inexhaustible theme; in it the
ultimate topic of all higher eloquence seemed to have been discovered
once and for all. In an age when the old beliefs were losing their
binding force and the long-established structure of the city-state was
breaking up (the structure in which, till then, the individual had felt
his own moral foundations securely embodied), the new dream of
national achievement appeared to be a mighty inspiration. It gave
life a new meaning.

In that critical time, therefore, Isocrates was, by his own choice of
rhetoric as a career, driven to formulate the new ideals which we
have described. It is entirely probable that he had been directly impelled towards them by Gorgias, whose *Olympicus* set forth the theme
that was to be the centre of Isocrates' life-work. That happens often

[22] Thuc. 3.82.

[23] Plato, *Rep.* 591e; see *Paideia* 11, 353 f.

[24] See *Paideia* 11, 131 f.

[25] In the speech *Against the sophists*, Isocrates draws a contrast between these
two extreme types of contemporary paideia.

enough: in his last years a great master formulates an ideal, inspires his pupil with admiration for it, and through it shapes and directs his pupil's entire career. If Isocrates wanted to become a politician without being an orator, if he wished to assert himself as an educator and a rhetorical teacher against the competition of Socratic philosophy and of the earlier type of rhetoric, and to make head against their criticisms, he had found the only possible method of doing so in his concentration on the new ideal. That explains the doggedness with which he followed it to the end. His weaknesses make it easy enough to criticize him; but it is hard to find a man who fulfilled his self-imposed task more completely than Isocrates, and who was better suited to his own conception of his mission. That conception gave rhetoric the realistic content which it had long been accused of lacking.[26] Through it the teacher of rhetoric at last achieved the dignity which put him on a level with the philosopher and made him independent of machine politicians—which actually gave him a higher rank than they possessed, inasmuch as he represented a higher interest than that of any separate state. The defects in Isocrates' own nature—not only his physical weakness, but the faults in his intellect and his character—and even the defects of rhetoric itself were, through his programme, almost converted into virtues; or so it seemed. The rhetor, the political pamphleteer and ideologist, has never since found himself in such a favourable situation or commanded such a widespread influence throughout an entire nation; and if his influence lacked something in richness, power, and genius, Isocrates partially compensated for that by an exceptionally long life of determined industry. Of course his determination does not affect the quality of his work; but still it was a vital element in the success of his mission, which, like that of the teacher, depended on his relation to living men.

For centuries past, historians have seen in Isocrates nothing more than a moralist, and have conceived him too exclusively as a writer and publicist, too little as a teacher. They did not fully realize that all his published writings, like those of Plato and Aristotle, were ancillary to the educational programme of his school. But the modern view of his career now does full justice to the political content of his books, and understands all their significance in the history of the fourth century. They were of course intended to produce an effect even outside the circle of his own pupils, and through them he often influenced men who had never heard him teach. But at the same time

[26] Cf. Plato, *Gorg.* 449d, 451a, 453b–e, 455d. Later he repeated the charge in *Phaedrus*.

his political speeches were models of the new type of eloquence which he taught in his school. Later, in the *Antidosis,* he himself exemplified to a wider public the special character of his teaching, in a selection of passages taken from his most celebrated speeches. These speeches were intended to be models not only of content but of form,[27] for in his teaching the two elements were inseparable. Whenever we try to re-create from the orations—which are our only evidence—the real character of the culture which he taught, we must always remember that dual purpose. Fortunately for us, he often expressed his views of his art and of his educational ideals; he often seized an opportunity to break off the thread of his argument, and to explain what he was saying, how he was saying it, and why. Indeed, at the beginning of his career he published several programme-works which clearly defined his position with reference to the other educational authorities of his time. We must start with them, if we are to comprehend the full extent of his activity, the true character of his paideia.

He had been a 'speech-writer', which in many respects corresponded to the profession of a barrister today; but we know nothing of the time when he abandoned that vocation for that of a teacher of rhetoric, or the reasons which led him to do so. Like Lysias, Isaeus, and Demosthenes, he had taken it up in order to make money—for his father's property had been largely destroyed by the war.[28] At a later time he was reluctant to mention that period of his career, although (as Aristotle humorously pointed out) volumes and volumes of the legal speeches he had written lay in the bookshops.[29] Only a few of them survive: his pupils, who had charge of editing his works after his death, had no more interest in preserving them than the master himself.[30] We can trace them no later than 390 or so.[31] Therefore, the foundation of Isocrates' school roughly coincided with that of Plato's.[32]

[27] Isocrates' 'speeches' were never delivered as such. Their oratorical form is a pure fiction.

[28] On his work as a logographer, see Dion. Hal. *de Isocr.* 18, and Cicero, *Brutus* 28 (whose source is Aristotle's συναγωγὴ τεχνῶν). He mentions the destruction of his father's property, in *Antid.* 161.

[29] Cf. Dion. Hal. *de Isocr.* 18.

[30] According to Dion. Hal. *de Isocr.* 18, Isocrates' stepson Aphareus said, in his speech against Megacleides, that his stepfather had *never* written forensic speeches; but that can only mean never since he became the head of a school. His pupil Cephisodorus admitted that there were some such speeches by him in existence, but said only a few were authentic.

[31] The *Trapeziticus* and *Aegineticus* can be dated roughly to 390.

[32] There is no confirmation for the statement of pseudo-Plutarch, *vit. X orat.* 837b that Isocrates first had a school in Chios (σχολῆς δέ ἡγεῖτο ὥς τινές

In his introductory speech *Against the sophists,* it is clear that he has Plato's 'prospectuses', *Gorgias* and *Protagoras,* before him, and is deliberately trying to set up his own ideal of paideia in contrast to theirs.[32a] That takes us back to the same period. The incomparable value of that speech for us lies in the vividness with which it re-creates, blow upon blow, the first battle of the generation-long cultural war between the two great schools of education. And it is no less interesting for us to trace in it the immediate impression which Plato made on many of his contemporaries at his first appearance. Accustomed as we are to estimate his importance by the influence of his philosophy on more than twenty centuries of human history, we naturally imagine that he exercised the same powerful influence on the men of his own time. For that view Isocrates is a useful corrective.

He begins by saying that the representatives of paideia have a bad reputation, and he traces it to the excessive hopes which their self-advertisement excites among the public.[33] Thereby he steps forth to oppose the exaggerated estimates of the power of education that were customary in his day. And, as a matter of fact, there must have been something very bizarre in the revolutionary change from Socrates' loudly expressed doubts whether such a thing as education really

---

φασιν, πεῶτον ἐπὶ Χίου). And ἐπὶ Χίου is an uncommon way to say εν Χίῳ. What we should expect, following ἐπὶ, is the name of the archon in whose time Isocrates began to teach; but if Χίου is a corruption of that name, it is difficult to emend. None of the archons in the 'nineties or early 'eighties has a name like χίου. If it were <Μυστι>χίδου that would take us down to 386–385, which is a very late date for the foundation of Isocrates' school.

[32a] Isocrates himself, in *Antid.* 193, says that the speech *Against the sophists* belongs to the beginning of his teaching career. There is a list of the many works which deal with his relation to Plato, in Münscher's article in Pauly-Wissowa 9.2171. Unfortunately, many of them are obsolete, since the assumption on which they are based is false—the assumption that Plato's chief dialogue on rhetoric, *Phaedrus,* was written in his youth or middle life. Münscher's article, which is otherwise an admirable introduction to the subject, still goes on the same assumption. Modern scholars have revised their views on this point. (About the late date of *Phaedrus,* see p. 330, n. 5 f.) On the other hand, I think it is impossible to follow Wilamowitz (*Platon* 11, 108) and avoid the conclusion that *Against the sophists* attacks Plato just as violently as the other Socratics. It assumes knowledge of Plato's *Protagoras, Gorgias,* and perhaps *Meno* too (see my discussion of the problem on pp. 56 and 66). Münscher's belief, that when Isocrates wrote the speech he still 'felt himself in agreement with Plato' in everything essential, cannot be backed up by anything in the speech, and is actually contradicted by every line of it. The sole basis for that belief is the early dating of *Phaedrus,* in which Plato is clearly more friendly to Isocrates than to rhetors like Lysias. The assumption that it was written before or soon after *Against the sophists* would compel us to make a forced interpretation of that speech as expressing friendship for Plato.

[33] Isocr. *Soph.* 1.

existed, to the passionate educational conviction of Plato's earlier dialogues. Here as elsewhere, Isocrates represents the happy mean. He himself, of course, wants to be a teacher too; but he 'very well understands' the laymen who would rather do nothing about education at all than believe the enormous promises of professing philosophers.[34] How is it possible, he asks, to put any trust in their yearning for truth, when they themselves arouse so many false hopes? Isocrates names no names, but every word of his polemic is aimed straight at the Socratics, whom here and elsewhere he contemptuously calls 'disputers',[35] In *Protagoras* and *Gorgias* Plato had presented dialectic as an art far superior to the long-winded orations of rhetoricians. His opponent makes short work of dialectic: he couples it with eristic—namely, argument for argument's sake. True philosophy always endeavoured to keep itself free from eristic,[36] although the methods of Plato's Socrates often seem to have much in common with it; and in fact there is a good deal of it in the earlier dialogues like *Protagoras* and *Gorgias*.[37] No wonder then that Isocrates does not see dialectic in the same favourable light as the Socratics, who thought it was a perfect panacea for all spiritual ills. The infallible knowledge of values (φρόνησις) which they promise as the result of their teaching must appear to ordinary reasonable people to be something too great for mankind to attain.[38]

[34] Of course the word 'philosopher' is not confined to those representatives of paideia whom we should call philosophers to-day—the Socratic circle. It includes all sorts of professed teachers of culture (see *Soph.* 11 and 18). But it does include philosophers in the strict sense, as we can see from *Soph.* 2, where Isocrates ridicules their claim to teach 'truth'. That is aimed at *all* the Socratics, not merely (as some have held) at Antisthenes' book *Truth*.

[35] *Soph.* 1: οἱ περὶ τὰς ἔριδας διατρίβοντες οἳ προσποιοῦται τὴν ἀλήθειαν ζητεῖν; *Antid.* 261: οἱ ἐν τοῖς ἐριστικῆς λόγοις δυναστεύοντες. In the latter passage the 'disputers' are put in the same class as teachers of geometry and astronomy—both subjects which were taught in Plato's Academy. Münscher's illogical assumption that in the later speech on the Antidosis Isocrates means his readers to think chiefly of Plato when he mentions disputers, but does not in the speech on the sophists, is based on the early dating of *Phaedrus* and the inference that Isocrates and the young Plato were friendly (see note 32a).

[36] Most probably it was because Plato found his dialectic being confused with eristic, as in Isocrates' attacks on it, that he distinguished Socrates so sharply and clearly from the eristics in *Euthydemus*. In *Rep.* 499a he repeats his complaint that no one knows the true philosopher, and he tries to vindicate him from confusion with mere disputers. There he describes him as a man who finds no pleasure in clever but useless arguments, and seeks 'knowledge for its own sake.'

[37] At several points Protagoras refuses to agree with the logical conclusions reached by Socrates, and he obviously thinks his opponent is trying to trap him. Plato describes this in a perfectly objective way, and thereby shows how easy it was for Socrates' dialectic to be called eristic. In the same way Callicles (Plato, *Gorg.* 482 f.) objects to Socrates' trick of giving different meanings to the same concept in the same argument. On this, see *Paideia* 11, 138.

[38] *Soph.* 2.

Homer, who knew so well the frontiers that separate men from gods, claims that only the gods have such unerring insight, and he is right. What mortal man has the audacity to promise to give his disciples infallible knowledge (ἐπιστήμη) of everything they ought to do or leave undone, and to lead them through that knowledge to supreme happiness (εὐδαιμονία)? [39]

In this criticism Isocrates has collected in a small space all the features which make Platonism repulsive to ordinary common sense: the peculiar technique of controversy by question-and-answer, the almost mythical importance which it attributes to phronésis (or knowledge of true values) as a special organ of reason, the apparently exaggerated intellectualism which holds knowledge to be the cure for everything, and the quasi-religious enthusiasm with which 'blessedness' is foretold to the philosopher. Obviously Isocrates is aiming some of his sharpest shafts at the terminological peculiarities of the new philosophical method: he tracks them down with the subtle instinct of the stylist for everything which seems odd or ludicrous to the average educated man; and by contrasting the Universal Virtue (πᾶσα ἀρετή), which is the putative aim of the Socratic knowledge of that which is 'good in itself',[40] with the trifling fees for which the philosophers sell their wisdom, he really makes the man in the street doubt whether what the young student learns from the philosopher is worth very much more than he pays for it.

He adds that the philosophers themselves cannot believe very strongly in the perfect virtue which they say they wish to release in the souls of their pupils, because the regulations of their school betray a far-reaching distrust of its members. They demand that the fees be paid into an Athenian bank in advance, before the pupil can be admitted.[41] They are justified, no doubt, in looking out for their own interests; but how can their attitude be reconciled with their claim to educate men to attain justice and self-mastery? This argument seems to us to be pitched rather too low; but it is not without wit. In Gorgias Plato had argued with just the same malice against the rhetors, who complain about the misuse their pupils make of the art of oratory, without seeing that they are accusing themselves—for if it were true

---

[39] Soph. 2–4.
[40] Plato contrasts 'universal virtue' and 'special virtues' like justice, courage, self-control, etc. Sometimes he calls the former 'virtue in itself' (αὐτὴ ἡ ἀρετή)—a kind of expression new and strange to his contemporaries. In c. 20 also, Isocrates emphasizes the ethical element in the paideia of the 'disputers'; they assert that virtue can be taught (21), which Isocrates and all the sophists violently deny. See Plato's Protagoras.
[41] Soph. 5.

that rhetoric improved its students, it would be impossible for those who had really learnt it to misuse it as they do.[42] Actually, the amoral character of rhetoric was the principal charge against it. In several different contexts, Isocrates supports the view represented by Gorgias in Plato's dialogue: the view that the teacher imparts to his pupil the art of rhetoric in order that he may use it rightly, and is not to blame if the pupil misuses it.[43] That is, he does not accept Plato's criticism, and maintains that Gorgias is wholly in the right. But he goes beyond that, and attacks the philosophers for distrusting their own pupils. That makes it probable that when he was writing the speech *Against the sophists* as an inaugural address, he knew Plato's *Gorgias* and deliberately set out to answer it.[44]

Plato's dialogue must have seemed particularly offensive to him as a pupil of Gorgias, and he must have felt himself arraigned in the person of his master: for as we have shown, it was not only Gorgias himself but rhetoric in all its branches that Plato had impugned. All the typical doctrines of the 'eristics' which Isocrates ridicules in his inaugural speech *Against the sophists* had already been clearly enunciated in *Gorgias*, where they were analyzed with special reference to their significance for the new Platonic system of paideia.[45] (*Paideia* II, 126 f.) Plato and the Socratics are among the foremost of the op-

[42] Cf. Plato, *Gorg.* 456e–457c, 460d–461a.

[43] In *Antid.* 215 f., Isocrates tries to defend teachers of rhetoric against the charge that their pupils learn evil from them. See also *Nic.* 2 f.

[44] This is the most probable view of the dates at which the two works were written. *Gorgias* is now generally believed, on convincing grounds, to have been written between 395 and 390 B.C.; but Isocrates had scarcely opened his school at that time, since we can trace his work as a logographer down to 390. Therefore the speech *Against the sophists*, which gives his programme, was written in the 'eighties. Some scholars have attempted to fix the chronological relationship between *Against the sophists* and Plato's *Gorgias* by what appear to be allusions in Plato's dialogue to Isocrates' speech. But even if Plato speaks of a ψυχή στοχαστική (*Gorg.* 463a) and Isocrates of a ψυχὴ δοξαστική (*Soph.* 17), that does not prove that Plato is imitating Isocrates. Also, δοξαστικὴ is a Platonic phrase. Plato despises mere δόξα, while here as elsewhere Isocrates insists that man's nature does not allow him to engage in more than δόξα and δοξάζειν. The very fact that he is replying to Plato shows that he depends on Plato's formulation of the problem. But the main argument is that given in the text (page 56 f.): the information about Plato's fundamental concepts and their logical interrelation (e.g. πᾶσα ἀρετή :: εὐδαιμονία, ἐπιστήμη :: δόξα, ἀρετή :: ἐπιστήμη) which is contained in *Against the sophists* is so full that it could have been derived from no other early Platonic work but *Gorgias*, the only work of Plato's youth in which he gives a fairly systematic exposition of his thought.

[45] It would anyhow be difficult to name any of Plato's early works which more convincingly and completely expounds all those characteristic features of his philosophy which are referred to by Isocrates, and makes their underlying connexions so clear.

ponents whom Isocrates attacks, and since he attacks them with special violence and completeness, it is clear that he fully understands the danger that threatens his ideal from their teaching. His invective is entirely realistic. He never makes it a theoretical refutation of his opponents' position, for he knows that if he did he would lose his case. The terrain he chooses is that of ordinary common sense. He appeals to the instincts of the man in the street—who, without comprehending the philosophers' technical secrets, sees that those who would lead their followers to wisdom and happiness have nothing themselves and get nothing from their students.[46] Their poverty did not harmonize with the traditional Greek concept of *eudaimonia*, perfect happiness, and other sophists—Antiphon, for instance—had already derided Socrates for exalting it.[46a] The man in the street sees that those who expose the contradictions in people's speeches do not notice the contradictions in their own acts; and that, although they profess to teach their pupils how to make the right decision on every problem of the future, they cannot say anything at all or give any correct advice about the present.[47] And when he further observes that the mob, whose conduct is based on nothing more than Opinion (δόξα), find it easier to agree with one another and to hit the right course of action than those who pretend to be in full possession of Knowledge (ἐπιστήμη), he is bound to end by despising the study of philosophy—concluding it to be empty chatter, mere hair-splitting, and certainly not 'the care of the soul' (Ψυχῆς ἐπιμέλεια).[48]

This last point above all makes it certain that Isocrates is aiming his attacks at Plato and at the rest of the Socratics—Antisthenes in particular. He has deliberately—and in a way justifiably—mixed up their features into a composite portrait of 'the pupil of Socrates' which they all claimed to be.[48a] Nevertheless he knows very well that the pupils of Socrates are bitterly hostile to one another, and he converts their strife into another argument against professional philosophers—the

[46] *Soph.* 6.
[46a] Xen. *Mem.* 1.6.1 f.
[47] *Soph.* 7.
[48] *Soph.* 8.
[48a] Perhaps the charge of asking pupils for contemptibly small fees is more appropriate to Antisthenes than to Plato, who probably took no fees at all. But we know far too little of these matters to judge with certainty. Even in the Academy, pupils probably had to pay a small sum—for instance, their share of the symposium. This was not meant to be the salary of their teacher, but Isocrates may have chosen to describe it as if it were, and to imply that Plato was underbidding his competitors. He attacks Plato and Antisthenes again in *Helen* 1: see note 85. On the fees of the Socratics, see Diog. Laert. 2.62, 65, 80, and 6.14.

favourite argument of common sense in every age. It was Antisthenes in particular who imitated his master's poverty and independence; while the abstract and theoretical aspects of Isocrates' portrait are principally drawn from Plato, and the description of philosophy as hair-splitting is obviously pointed at Plato's elaboration of dialectic into the art of logic.[48b] That was, as Isocrates rightly saw, a step into the sphere of theory and pure form. So he measures this new art of discovering contradictions—the art which attempts to conquer Opinion by Knowledge [49]—against the old Socratic aim of 'caring for the soul,' [50] and throws doubt on its ability to achieve that aim. Thereby he concludes his criticism precisely at the point where (as history shows) the real problem lies. And so, in the argument which we here witness between Plato and Isocrates, there is unfolded part of the long series of conflicts through which the ideal of culture has been developed—a dialectic process which still retains a deep and permanent value, independently of the small personal details of the dispute.

The second group of opponents attacked by Isocrates are described by him as teachers of politics.[51] They do not, like the philosophers, search for the truth. They simply practise their techné—their craft, in the old sense of the word,[52] whereby it implied no trace of moral responsibility. In *Gorgias*, Plato had asserted that true rhetoric ought, like the craft of the doctor, to entail such moral responsibility.[53] Isocrates could not deny Plato's claim; and the moral factor is especially prominent in his treatment of the third group of his opponents, the teachers of forensic oratory. But he did not assert its validity simply in order to exalt Plato. His criticism of those who teach the craft of making political speeches introduces us to a type of education which was the absolute opposite of philosophy—the art of extempore speech-making. As typical of the specialist in this subject we must think of Isocrates' own fellow-student in the school of Gorgias, Alcidamas [54]—

[48b] The charge that dialectic is hair-splitting recurs in *Antid.* 262, where it is admittedly an attack on Plato. Why should it not be an attack on Plato here too?

[49] This description of the art of discovering contradictions, 'elenctic', is aimed at Socrates and Plato. See the parallel in *Helen* 4, where the Socratic technical term ἐλέγχειν is particularly derided.

[50] See *Paideia* 11, 39, which explains how the purpose of all Socrates' educational activity can be described as 'caring for the soul' (ψυχῆς ἐπιμέλεια).

[51] *Soph.* 9: οἱ τοὺς πολιτικοὺς λόγους ὑπισχνούμενοι.

[52] Isocrates' phrasing clearly shows that he is putting the word techné (as used by these teachers of rhetoric) inside quotation-marks, so to speak. The same thing applies to the passages where he parodies the terminology of the Socratics.

[53] See *Paideia* 11, 131, and *passim*.

[54] See J. Vahlen, *Gesammelte Schriften* 1, p. 117 f.; and before him, C. Reinhardt, *De Isocratis aemulis* (Bonn 1873).

who like him published several model speeches, but whose forte was improvisation (αὐτοσχεδιάζειν). One of his speeches, which has been preserved, is significantly aimed against rhetors like Isocrates, who can write well enough but are incapable of seizing the critical moment to say the words demanded by the immediate situation.[55] There can be no doubt that the constant practice of this technique was invaluable training for the student who intended to be an active public speaker, even although the actual teaching often degenerated into mere routine instruction, and grossly neglected the higher claims of art. This class of his opponents Isocrates charges with lack of taste: they have, he affirms, no aesthetic sense.[56] In practice, their type of rhetoric turns out to be nothing more than a collection of formal devices which the pupil gets off by heart and can bring into play at any moment. It enlarges neither his intellect nor his experience, but merely teaches him the patterns of speechmaking as abstract forms to be learnt by rote, as the elementary teacher teaches little children the alphabet.[57] This method is a fine example of the contemporary trend towards mechanizing both education and life itself as far as possible. Isocrates seizes the opportunity to distinguish his own artistry from this empty commercialized technique, and to clear himself from the charge which he might well have incurred through his distaste for the subtleties of philosophical education—the charge of being narrow-mindedly practical. What he is looking for is the middle way between highflown theory and vulgar penny-chasing technical adroitness; and he finds it in artistically disciplined Form.[58] In this he introduces a third principle. Here again we find that he explains himself and his ideal by contrast with another point of view. But by thus waging war on two fronts, he shows that his conflict with philosophical education, important as it is, expresses only half of his own ideal. He is just as far removed in the other direction from rhetoric in the accepted sense. For, in the sphere of rhetoric as well as in that of philosophy, Isocrates' paideia was something perfectly new.

More than any other sphere of life, the art of oratory resists the effort of systematic reason to reduce all individual facts to a number of established *schemata*, basic forms. In the realm of logic Plato calls these basic forms the Ideas. As we have seen, he took this three-dimensional mode of describing them from contemporary medical science,

<hr/>

[55] This speech is best explained as Alcidamas' reply to the attack on him made by Isocrates in the speech *Against the sophists*.

[56] *Soph.* 9.

[57] *Soph.* 10.

[58] *Soph.* 12 f.

and applied it to the analysis of Being. In rhetoric we can see the same process in operation at the same time, though we cannot definitely say that it was directly influenced by Plato's use of the term *idea*. Medicine and rhetoric were by their very nature the spheres in which this conception of basic forms or Ideas could be developed—for medicine reduces a number of apparently different physiological events to a few fundamental types; and rhetoric likewise simplifies what seem to be separate and distinct political or legal situations. The essence of both skills is to analyze the individual case into its general aspects, so as to make it easier to treat in practice. The comparison of these general patterns to the letters of the alphabet (στοιχεῖα)—which we find in Isocrates here, and later in Plato—was obvious enough. The act of reading is just the same as that of political or forensic or medical diagnosis: a large number of variously assembled shapes are reduced to a limited number of basic 'elements', and thus the meaning of each of the apparently manifold shapes is recognized.[59] In science too, the 'elements' which make up physical nature were first called by that name in the same period, and the same analogy, drawn from language and the letters of the alphabet, lies behind it.[60] Isocrates of course does not by any means reject the doctrine of a rhetorical system of Ideas. In fact, his writings show that he largely adopted that doctrine, and that he took as the foundation of his own teaching the mastery of the basic forms of oratory. But oratory which knew no more than these forms would be as sounding brass and a tinkling cymbal. The letters of the alphabet, immovable and unchangeable, are the most complete contrast to the fluid and manifold situations of human life, whose full and rich complexity can be brought under no rigid rule.[61] Perfect eloquence must be the individual expression of a single critical moment, a *kairos*, and its highest law is that it should be wholly appropriate. Only by observing these two rules can it succeed in being new and original.[62]

In a word, oratory is imaginative literary creation. Though it dare not dispense with technical skill, it must not stop short at that.[63] Just as the sophists had believed themselves to be the true successors of the poets, whose special art they had transferred into prose, so Isocrates

[59] Plato compares his 'ideas' to letters of the alphabet in *Cratylus, Theaetetus, The Statesman,* and *The Laws.*

[60] This was first done in Plato's *Timaeus* 48b, 56b, 57c: see H. Diels' *Elementum.*

[61] *Soph.* 12.

[62] Cf. *Soph.* 13, on the καιρός and the πρέπον.

[63] *Soph.* 12.

too feels that he is continuing the poets' work, and taking over the function which until a short time before him they had fulfilled in the life of his nation. His comparison between rhetoric and poetry is far more than a passing epigram. Throughout his speeches the influence of this point of view can be traced. The panegyric on a great man is adapted from the hymn, while the hortative speech follows the model of the protreptic elegy and the didactic epic. And, in these types, Isocrates copies even the order of his ideas from the well-established traditional order which was a rule in each of the corresponding poetic genera. More than that: the position and prestige of the orator are determined by this parallel with the poet. The new vocation must support itself on an old and firmly-established one, and take its standards therefrom. The less Isocrates hopes or wishes to succeed as a practical statesman, the more he needs the prestige of poetry to set off his spiritual aims; and even in the educational spirit by which his rhetoric is inspired, he is deliberately emulating what the Greeks conceived to be the educational function of the poets of old. Later, indeed, he compares his work with that of the sculptor (as Pindar had done) and proudly puts himself on a level with Phidias; [64] but that is more to illustrate the fact that there are still some who, despite the loftiness of his art, consider the rhetor's profession to be something second-rate. The classical Greeks had always tended to depreciate the sculptor's trade a little, as resembling the work of a common artisan—and that although the word *sculptor* could be applied to every worker in stone, from the ordinary mason to the creator of the Parthenon. But later, as the prestige of the plastic arts and their great masters gradually rose in the post-classical centuries, the comparison of oratory to sculpture and painting seems to become commoner. However, the dynastic succession of rhetoric to poetry remained the true image of the spiritual process in which rhetoric arose as a new cultural force: all late Greek poetry is simply the offspring of rhetoric. [65]

Naturally, Isocrates' view of the educational value of rhetoric is defined by this conception of its true character. Being an act of creation, oratory in its highest ranges cannot possibly be taught like a school subject. And yet he holds that it can be employed to educate young men: because of his own peculiar view of the relation between the three factors which, according to the pedagogic theories of the

[64] In *Antid.* 2 Isocrates compares himself to the sculptor Phidias and the painters Zeuxis and Parrhasius—the greatest artists in Greece. So does Plato in *The Republic:* see *Paideia* 11, 258 f.

[65] Plato too, in *Gorg.* 502c, implies that poetry is a kind of rhetoric.

sophists, are the foundation of all education. They are: (1) talent, (2) study, and (3) practice. The current enthusiasm for education and culture had helped to create and disseminate exaggerated views of their powers; [66] but that enthusiasm had been succeeded by a certain disillusionment—due partly to Socrates' far-reaching criticisms of the limitations and pretensions of education,[67] and partly to the discovery that many a young man whom the sophists had educated was no better than those who had never enjoyed such advantages.[68] Isocrates explains the exact value of education with great care. He asserts that natural talent is the principal factor, and admits that great gifts, untrained, often achieve more than mere training without ability—if indeed it is possible to speak of training when there is nothing there to train. The element second in importance is experience, practice.[69] It would appear that until then professional rhetors had theoretically recognized the trinity—talent, study, practice—but had in their own courses pushed study and training into the foreground. Isocrates modestly relegates training (*paideusis*) to the third rank. It can, he says, achieve much if it is helped by talent and experience. It makes speakers more clearly conscious of their art, stimulates their inventive faculty, and saves them much vague and unsuccessful searching. Even a less gifted pupil can be improved and intellectually developed by training, although he can never be made into a distinguished orator or writer.[70]

Rhetorical training, says Isocrates, can teach insight into the 'ideas' or basic patterns out of which every speech is built. He appears to mean that this phase of it, hitherto the only one which had been cultivated, was capable of far profounder development; and we would gladly hear more of his new doctrine of ideas, to be able to compare it with that of the older rhetors. But the real difficulty of the subject does not lie in that aspect of it—all the less so because it is taught so thoroughly. It lies in the right choice, commixture, and placing of the 'ideas' on each subject, in the selection of the correct moment, in the good taste and appropriateness with which the speech is decorated with enthymemes, and in the rhythmic and musical disposition of the words.[71] To do all that correctly needs a powerful and sensitive mind. This, the highest stage of training, assumes in the pupil full knowledge

[66] *Soph.* 1.
[67] See *Paideia* 11, 59 f.
[68] *Soph.* 1 and 8.
[69] *Soph.* 14.
[70] *Soph.* 15.
[71] *Soph.* 16.

of the 'ideas' of speech and skill in their employment; from the teacher it requires the ability to expound everything which can be rationally taught, and beyond that—i.e. in everything which cannot be taught—it demands that he should make himself a model for his pupils: so that those who can form themselves by imitating him may at once achieve a richer and more graceful style than any others.[72]

Plato, in *The Republic*, later declared that the highest culture could be attained only if certain qualities which are rarely found together were to coincide. Similarly, Isocrates asserts that it is impossible for the teacher to succeed unless all the factors which we have mentioned are brought into play at once.[73] Here the general Greek idea, that education is the process by which the whole man is shaped, is enunciated independently of Plato, and variously expounded in such imagery as 'model' or 'pattern' (παράδειγμα), 'stamp' (ἐκτυποῦν), 'imitate' (μιμεῖσθαι).[74] The real problem is how this process of 'shaping' can be converted from a beautiful image into a practical reality—that is, what is to be the *method* of forming the human character, and ultimately what is the *nature* of the human intellect. Plato seeks to form the soul through knowledge of the Ideas as absolute norms of the Good, the Just, the Beautiful, etc., and thus eventually to develop it into an intelligible cosmos which contains all being within itself. No such universe of knowledge exists for Isocrates. For him, rhetorical training is worked out simply by Opinion, not by Knowledge. But he frequently claims that the intellect possesses an aesthetic and practical faculty which, without claiming absolute knowledge, can still choose the right means and the right end.[75] His whole conception of culture is based on that aesthetic power. Plato's dialectic guides the young student step by step towards the Ideas; but that still leaves it to him to employ them in his life and conduct, and the way in which he employs them cannot be rationally explained. In the same way Isocrates can describe only the elements and the separate stages of the educational act. The formative process itself remains a mystery. Nature can neither be wholly banished from it, nor be put wholly in control of it. Therefore, everything in education depends on the proper

---

[72] *Soph.* 17.
[73] *Soph.* 18. Plato also speaks of the 'coincidence' of power and intellect in *Rep.* 473d, and *Laws* 712a. But also, without using the word, he sets up an ideal of many-sided talent (*Rep.* 485b f.)—the φιλόσοφος φύσις, which is a coincidence of qualities that can exist together but seldom do. This way of formulating ideals is characteristic of the literature of paideia.
[74] *Soph.* 18.
[75] Cf. *Soph.* 17, on the ψυχὴ δοξαστική.

cooperation of nature and art. If we once decide that Isocrates' incompleteness (as Plato would call it) and his reliance on mere Opinion (which Plato called the vital force of all rhetoric) were imposed on him by his subject, then we must conclude that his resolute self-limitation, and his deliberate renunciation of everything 'higher', everything which he felt to be obscure and doubtful, were a sort of constitutional weakness converted by him into a strength. This, in the sphere of culture, is the same thing that assured Isocrates' own personal success: he has made a virtue of necessity. He recognizes the empirical character of rhetoric; and, whether or not it is right to call it a true techné or art—Plato in *Gorgias* had claimed that it was not—Isocrates holds fast to its empiricism. Therein he clings to the principle of *imitation* established by his predecessors—the principle which in the future was to play such an enormous part in rhetoric and (as literature came more and more under the influence of rhetoric) in every branch of literature. Here we know more of his method of teaching than we do of his attitude to the rhetorical doctrine of ideas; for all his great speeches were meant to be models in which his pupils could study the precepts of his art.

He spends little time on the third group of educators, the writers of forensic speeches. Obviously he considers them his weakest opponents —although Plato attacked them a good many years later in *Phaedrus*, and therefore thought them fairly important even then. It is clear that Isocrates believes their rivalry far less dangerous than that of the new philosophical culture, in which he recognizes the real threat to his own ideals. The forensic speechmakers were out to make money, and their product was meant for practical use. We know their technique from the sample speeches published by Antiphon, Lysias, Isaeus, Demosthenes, and even Isocrates himself at the outset of his career. This type of literature is one of the most remarkable plants in the garden of Greek literature—and a native Attic vegetable at that. The Athenian mania for litigation, so delightfully satirized by the comedians, is the obverse of the firm legality of the Athenian state: of that foundation in Law of which its citizens were so proud. It produced a universal interest in *agones*—lawsuits and prosecutions. The model speeches written by the logographers served both as advertisements for their authors, as patterns for their pupils to copy, and as interesting reading-matter for the public.[76] Here too Isocrates manifests the more sensitive

[76] Isocrates thinks that, if these model speeches are meant to be specimens of the teaching technique used by their writers, they come under the definition of paideia just as much as his own political rhetoric and its products. After all, that

taste of the younger generation. Ironically he recommends that the logographers should leave it to the enemies of rhetoric (already numerous enough) to display this, its least attractive side, instead of proudly dragging it out into the glare of publicity; and he adds that anything that can be learnt in rhetoric is just as valuable in other spheres as in legal disputes. We need not question the sincerity of this attitude. It explains quite clearly why Isocrates abandoned the profession. He felt that the speechwriter was morally far below the philosopher.[77] Clearly he is thinking not only of the men who write speeches for use in law courts, but of all kinds of rhetors, since he includes them all under the name of 'teachers of political oratory.'[78] Doubtless the subjects investigated in philosophical education are not worth the trouble, and the arguers who 'wallow' in debates would get into serious danger if they applied their conclusions to real facts (here Isocrates is quoting Callicles in Plato's *Gorgias*, and taking his side too), but at least the fact that the rhetors talk about a better subject, politics, must not keep us from recognizing that in practice they generally misuse it and become interfering and ambitious busybodies. Thus Isocrates follows Plato in his criticism of the political orators, though he does not accept his positive conclusions. He does not believe that virtue can be taught, any more than the aesthetic sense. Plato refuses to grant the name of *techné* to any kind of education which does not teach virtue; and Isocrates frankly thinks it impossible to create such education. Nevertheless, he is inclined to concede that education of a political tendency might have some ethical influence if it were practised in the manner he recommends, not in the amoral way represented by earlier rhetoricians.[79]

The striking thing about Isocrates' conception of Plato's paideia, as set forth in his speech *Against the sophists*, is that he entirely overlooks the political content of his opponent's theories. From Plato's early dialogues he must have got the same impression as they made, until a short time ago, on most modern readers—that their author's sole concern was moral reformation, an ideal which is somehow strangely connected with dialectic reasoning. The superiority of rhetoric, as Isocrates conceives it, is that it is entirely political culture. All that it

---

kind of literature represents a formal educational principle which is valuable and interesting in itself. However, since its content has comparatively little importance, it has not been exhaustively treated here. In this, I have accepted the estimate of Plato and Isocrates. General and legal historians will of course take a different view.

[77] *Soph.* 19–20.
[78] *Soph.* 20.
[79] *Soph.* 21.

has to do to attain spiritual leadership in the state is to find a new approach to life and its problems. The older type of rhetoric missed many important opportunities because it was content to serve day-to-day politics as an instrument, instead of rising above it. From this we can see that Isocrates believed he could inspire the political life of his nation with a higher moral creed. Unfortunately only a fragment of the speech on the sophists now survives, without the principal section, which doubtless explained his new ideal. Isocrates must have changed his attitude to Plato's cultural plans as soon as he understood the political aspect of his philosophy. Actually, he had already been warned by Plato's *Gorgias* that Socrates was the only real statesman of his age, because he alone tried to make his fellow-citizens better.[80] That might well be interpreted as pure paradox—especially by Isocrates, who held that the moving impulse of all contemporary writers was to struggle for originality at all costs, hunting out hitherto unheard-of-paradoxes on every subject, and who feared (with justice) that he could not rival Plato and the other philosophers in that exercise. But later, in his *Philip*, he reviews Plato's life-work not long after his death, and treats him as a very great political theorist, whose theories could unfortunately never be put into practice.[81] When did he first change his view of Plato's character and philosophy?

We can find the answer in his *Helen*. *Helen* is a model encomium, addressed to a mythical personage, and paradoxically praising her although she was generally reviled. The exact date of its composition is unknown, but it was obviously written soon after the speech *Against the sophists*—namely, while Isocrates' school was yet new. A lower limit for its date is fixed by the singular form which Isocrates, towards the end, gives to the praise of his heroine: it was she, he says, who first brought about national unity among the Greeks, in the war against Troy that resulted from her abduction.[82] Thus he makes Helen a mythical symbol of the political aspirations which he expressed more fully soon after that, in the *Panegyricus* (380)—of the great struggle to unite the Greek states in a national crusade against the barbarians. In this first decade Isocrates is still moving in the paths beaten out by Gorgias. The relation between his *Panegyricus* and Gorgias' *Olympicus* is the same as that between his *Helen* and Gorgias' *Defence of Helen*. The little speech is (as he says [83]) a first-fruits offering suitable for a

[80] See *Paideia* 11, 150.
[81] *Phil.* 12.
[82] *Hel.* 67.
[83] *Hel.* 66.

man of paideia. It is interesting because of its renewed polemics against the Socratic school and its cultural ideal.[84] Here again, as in the speech on the sophists, he blends the features of Plato and Antisthenes in a composite portrait. His attack is aimed, not at one particular person, but at the entire tendency of the new movement. Isocrates says he cannot interpret their utterances as anything more than attempts at paradoxical wit, when some of them (Antisthenes) teach that it is impossible to make a false statement, or to make two contradictory assertions about the same thing, while others (Plato) try to prove that courage, wisdom and justice are one and the same, and that none of these qualities is implanted in us by nature, but that they are all attained by one and the same knowledge (ἐπιστήμη).[85] Here Isocrates really does distinguish the Socratics from those who are mere arguers, who teach nobody, but only try to make difficulties for others. He objects that all of them try to refute others (ἐλέγχειν), although they themselves have long since been refuted,[86] and that their paradoxes are thrown into the shade by those of their predecessors the sophists: for instance, by Gorgias' statement that no existing thing exists, or Zeno's, that the same thing is both possible and impossible, or Melissus', that the apparently infinite multitude of things is really one.[87]

With this pettifogging, Isocrates contrasts the simple effort to find out what is true: which he conceives to be the effort to get experience of reality and to educate oneself for political action. Philosophers are always chasing the phantom of pure knowledge, but no one can use their results. Is it not better to spend one's time on the things which people really need, even if we cannot achieve exact knowledge, but only approximate opinions about them? He reduces his own attitude towards Plato's ideal of scientific accuracy and thoroughness to the formula that the smallest advance in our knowledge of really important things is better than the greatest intellectual mastery of

---

[84] This attack on the 'disputers' occupies the whole of the introduction to Helen, and has nothing to do with the rest of the speech. It will be enough for our purpose, therefore, to discuss the introduction alone. Aristotle (Rhet. 3.14.1414b26) says that the prooemium need have no connexion with the main part of an epideictic speech, and cites Isocrates' Helen as an example. He compares the introduction to an encomium with the loosely attached prelude (proaulion) to a flute-solo.

[85] Hel. 1. It is easy enough to identify Isocrates' two unnamed opponents. On Antisthenes see Arist. Met. Δ 29.1024b33, with the commentary of Alexander of Aphrodisias on it, and Plato, Soph. 251b.

[86] Hel. 4.

[87] Hel. 2–3.

unimportant trifles which are irrelevant to our life.[88] As a good psychologist, he evidently understands how much young men love dialectical disputation—for at their age, they have no interest in serious private or public problems, and the more futile a game, the more they enjoy it.[89] But those who profess to teach them deserve reproach for allowing them to be charmed by it. They incur thereby the same guilt of which they accuse forensic orators—they corrupt the youth.[90] They do not shrink from preaching the absurd doctrine that the life of beggars and exiles, deprived of all political rights and duties, is happier than that of others—namely, of the full citizens who remain peacefully in their native land. (This is clearly an allusion to the ethical individualism and cosmopolitanism of the radical wing in the Socratic school—Antisthenes, Aristippus, and their followers.[91] He finds the other philosophers to be even more ridiculous: those who think that their moral paradoxes really contribute something to the spiritual upbuilding of the state. This can only be a hit at Plato, who held that Socrates' moral evangel was true political science.[92] If we are right in this identification, it was as early as the 'eighties, soon after he wrote his speech *Against the sophists,* that Isocrates changed his views of Plato's cultural ideal, and recognized that it too had political implications. Only he felt that its concentration on individual morality and on dialectical quibbles—which seemed to him the distinguishing tendency of Plato's educational system—was absolutely irreconcilable with the universally useful purpose which it professed to serve.

Thus, as Isocrates and Plato appear to approach nearer and nearer to each other in the practical aim of their cultural theories, Isocrates' disapproval for Plato's abstract 'roundabout way'[93] becomes more and more pronounced. He knows only the direct route. There is in his system none of the inward tension that exists in the mind of Plato between the urgent will to action and the long philosophical preparation for action. True, he stands far enough away from the politics of his day and the activity of contemporary statesmen to understand Plato's objection to them. But, as a man who keeps to the middle way, he cannot appreciate the bold ethical claims of the Socratic system, which creates a gulf between the state and the individual. He does

[88] *Hel.* 5,
[89] *Hel.* 6.
[90] *Hel.* 7.
[91] *Hel.* 8.
[92] *Hel.* 9.
[93] See *Paideia* 11, 280 and 111, 193.

not look to Utopia for the improvement of political life. He embodies the rooted hatred of the propertied and cultured bourgeoisie both for the mad eccentricities of mob-rule and for the tyranny of individuals, and he has a strong admiration for respectability. But he has none of Plato's uncompromising passion for reformation, no thought of introducing such a terrific intensity into everyday life. Therefore, he does not realize the enormous educational power which lies in Plato's thought: he judges its value exclusively by its immediate utility for the particular political question which interests him. This is the internal condition of Greece, and the future relations of the Greek states to one another, after the great war. The Peloponnesian war had clearly demonstrated that the existing regime could not be permanent, and that the whole Greek world had to be rebuilt. When he wrote *Helen,* Isocrates was already at work on his great manifesto, the *Panegyricus.* Its purpose was to show the world that his school was able to state, in a new language, new ideals—not only for the moral life of the individual, but for the entire nation of the Hellenes.

THE VERBAL MEDIUM: PLATO AND ARISTOTLE
W. K. Wimsatt, Jr., and Cleanth Brooks

I

We have been talking about poetic imitation as if it were a straight copy of its objects, or a vision of them through plate glass; and in so doing we have minimized the possibility of talking about the poem rather than about its objects, about what it may *be* rather than about what it may *say.* In our first three chapters we have heard a debate conducted upon grounds of maximum advantage to the Platonic moral cause. Let us return now to the fact that Aristotle treated plot, character, and thought—the *content* of drama—as only some of its elements. Let us recall that he treated also, by a method of separation which may have seemed to us at first glance rather crude, two elements which he called the *medium*—language and music—and that there was even another element which he called the *manner*—the stage spectacle.

Reprinted from *Literary Criticism: A Short History* by William K. Wimsatt and Cleanth Brooks, by permission of Alfred A. Knopf, Inc. Copyright 1957 by William K. Wimsatt and Cleanth Brooks.

Among these three elements, language stands out as a thing basic to all literature. Language is an inevitable concern of literary criticism. And this fact invites us to canvass a part of ancient critical history which for want of a better name we shall call *Rhetoric*.

It is a commonplace of recent critical history to observe that ancient rhetoric, from its formal beginning near the end of the fifth century B.C. to its second sophistication in the early Christian centuries, was basically a practical art, concerned, that is, with the business of persuading judges in law courts, senators in assemblies, and congregations in churches. The counter facts which we insist on here are that this legal or political art came in Roman times to be practically equivalent to higher education, and that from first to last it dwelt characteristically upon verbal artifice. It was in this art rather than in that of poetics that words were most often deliberately studied, and its examples were drawn indiscriminately from poetry and prose. "The art of contention in speech," says Socrates in the *Phaedrus*,

> is not confined to courts and political gatherings, but apparently, if it is an art at all, it would be one and the same in all kinds of speaking, the art by which a man will be able to produce a resemblance between all things between which it can be produced.—261 [1]

The term *rhetoric* has, and has had from early times, the highly useful secondary sense: *a study of how words work*. It is primarily in this sense that we shall use the term throughout this book.

Corax and Tisias were Sicilian sophists who flourished about fifty years before the birth of Aristotle. They taught legal rhetoric in Syracuse and wrote the earliest recorded treatises on the art, but these have perished. One of their successors was Gorgias of Leontini, who came to Athens on an embassy in 427 and remained to instruct and fascinate the generation of young intellectuals and aesthetes portrayed in the *Clouds* of Aristophanes. A later Sicilian Greek historian has left this account of the matter:

> On arriving at Athens and being allowed to address the people, he [Gorgias] spoke on the theme of federation in a style of such exotic artifice that he cast a spell over his audience, euphuistically inclined as they were and devoted to the ideal of eloquence. He was the first to use the strikingly artificial figures of antithesis, isocolon, parison, homoeoteleuton, and sundry other embellishments of this kind, which came at

[1] With one exception, indicated in a note, quotations from Plato's *Phaedrus* in this chapter are reprinted by permission of the publishers from the translation of H. N. Fowler, *Plato . . . Euthyphro, Apology, Crito, Phaedo, Phaedrus*, 1938, Loeb Classical Library, Cambridge, Mass.: Harvard University Press.

that time as admired novelties, though now they seem rather ridiculously affected and precious.[2]

Gorgias and a fellow rhetorician Polus are the antagonists of Socrates in an early and lengthy Platonic attack on rhetoric, the dialogue entitled *Gorgias;* and the same rhetorical school is the subject of criticism in the mature, highly sophisticated and dramatic *Phaedrus,* a document which is not only the earliest substantial counter-rhetoric now surviving but is still one of the most formidable in all rhetorical history.

II

The *Phaedrus* contains some of the best-known Platonic passages on love and beauty—ones which we have alluded to in an earlier chapter —most notably the illustrative oration by Socrates built on the elaborate allegory of the soul or intellective principle as charioteer, with difficulty driving his two horses, a noble steed of the higher desires and a balky beast of the lower passions, toward the empyreal sphere of divine forms. Classical scholars have disagreed as to whether this main motif of the dialogue shows sufficient relevance to an equally conspicuous second motif—an examination of the art of rhetoric. The relevance between the two motifs (and hence the unity of the whole dialogue) actually seems very close. It is the relevance of ideal illustration to a theory of an art ideally conceived. A main assumption of the whole dialogue is the Socratic principle that virtue is knowledge, and, springing from this, the main argument is that a worthy rhetoric —one aimed at the highest good—will be, not a way of fooling people in law courts, but an approach to knowledge, or an embodiment of it— a kind of inspired philosophy. The theme of love and beauty, which Plato believed to be the only adequate theme of philosophy, was the only one which he could have employed for the full illustration of the thesis.

The argument begins adroitly with an enthusiastic reading by Phaedrus, and a cool analysis by Socrates, of a shoddy speech—either an actual speech of the orator Lysias or a parody—an academic invective against ardent lovers.[3] The objections of Socrates are two: that the speech is wrongheaded (though he ironically professes not to urge this) and that its style is confused. Some sort of connection between these two facts is perhaps a main innuendo.

[2] Diodorus Siculus, *Historical Library* XII, 53.
[3] The homosexual meaning alluded to in our first chapter is to be assumed throughout this discussion.

SOCRATES: How now? Are you and I to praise the speech because the author has said what was called for, or is the sole point whether the expressions, taken singly, are clear, compact, and finely turned? If we must judge it by the substance, I readily give way to your opinion; the substance because of my ineptitude, escaped me. I paid attention to the rhetoric of it only, and this I doubted whether Lysias himself would consider adequate. If you will let me say so, Phaedrus, it seemed to me he said the same things over twice or thrice, perhaps because he wasn't very well supplied with things to say on a given subject, or perhaps he didn't bother about a point like that. And then it seemed to me that he was showing off in youthful fashion how well he could say the same thing over in two different ways.

PHAEDRUS: Nonsense, Socrates! What you call repetition is the peculiar merit of the speech. . . .[4]

The speech of Lysias is in fact a tediously overlapping enumeration of reasons against the eager lover and in favor of the person who is more calculating in his approach, or, as he is called, the "non-lover." At a later point in the argument (264) Socrates likens it to an inscription that was said to appear on the tomb of Midas the Phrygian. Any line of it could be put first or last.

> A bronze maiden am I; and I am placed upon the tomb of Midas.
> So long as water runs and tall trees put forth leaves,
> Remaining in this very spot upon a much lamented tomb,
> I shall declare to passers by that Midas is buried here.

Some of the distortions of style which the basically careless structure of thought has forced upon the writer—the "two different ways" of saying the same thing to which Socrates alluded—may be more apparent in the Greek than in English translations where efforts of translators to tidy up have missed the point.

> For lovers repent (*ekeinois* . . . *metamelei*) of the kindnesses they have done when their passion ceases; but there is no time when non-lovers naturally repent (*metagnōnai prosēkei*).—231

Here the translator's logical repetition of *repent* covers up the pointless "elegant variation" of the Greek. The following example is more faithful to the Greek text.

> And besides, lovers consider the *injury they have done to their own concerns* on account of their love, and the benefits they have con-

---

[4] *Phaedrus* 234–5. We quote the translation by Professor Lane Cooper, *Phaedrus, Ion, Gorgias* (London, 1938), p. 15, by permission of the Oxford University Press, Inc., New York.

ferred, and they add *the trouble they have had,* . . . ; but non-lovers cannot aver *neglect of their own affairs* because of their condition, nor can they take account of the *pains they have been at in the past.*—231

The italicized phrases tease a very simple meaning into coy but drab variations. The gist of the matter is that this is a bad speech, and that it is badly written. And both these things are true, implies Socrates, because the author does not know what he is talking about.

The next step in the dramatically conceived argument is accomplished by a second speech on the same theme—one delivered by Socrates, *ex tempore,* with his head wrapped up for shame, in the character of a crafty lover who tries to gain favors by pretending to be a non-lover. It is a better speech than the first, because it begins with a definition of love (as desire) and proceeds, in a style which is at least orderly, to expound the evil of being ruled by that force. Socrates even makes a pretense of being in a kind of dithyrambic frenzy and winds up his speech with a hexameter.[5] But the whole argument is negative, at the expense of the lover, and stops without saying a word in actual favor of the non-lover—because, of course, nothing can be said in his favor. Whereas the first speech and the critique of it has suggested the union or even identity of bad, ignorant thinking and bad style, the second speech exhibits the severe handicap imposed upon himself by the person who in a sense knows the truth but who pretends not to know it—and leads "his hearers on with sportive words" (262).

Almost immediately Socrates is stricken with remorse at having participated in a blasphemy and, in the manner of a man who not only knows the truth but is inspired to speak in its defence, launches into his palinode, the prolonged and eloquent allegorical discourse upon love, beauty, and immortality to which we have already alluded. Despite its enthusiasm and lavish invention, the speech is well ordered, beginning with a fourfold celebration of *mania* (244–245) or inspired madness and pursuing the theme of the soul's immortality in the figure of the charioteer and his two horses. This figure itself might be taken as a symbol of orderly composition and division.

The rhetorical significance of the three speeches on love becomes unmistakable in the comparison of their merits and the theoretical discussion which follows.

But I do think you will agree to this, that every discourse must be organised, like a living being, with a body of its own, as it were, so as

---

[5] *Phaedrus* 238, 241. Aristotle is apparently thinking of these passages when in his *Rhetoric* (III, 7) he alludes to the ironic use of emotive language in the *Phaedrus.*

not to be headless or footless, but to have a middle and members, composed in fitting relation to each other and to the whole.—264

The second speech of Socrates is described apologetically as figurative, plausible, perhaps expressive of some truth—a "sportive jest."

> . . . but in these chance utterances were involved two principles, the essence of which it would be gratifying to learn, if art could teach it.
> PHAEDRUS: What principles?
> SOCRATES: That of perceiving and bringing together in one idea the scattered particulars, that one may make clear by definition the particular thing which he wishes to explain; just as now, in speaking of love, we said what he is and defined it whether well or ill. Certainly by this means the discourse acquired clearness and consistency.
> PHAEDRUS: And what is the other principle, Socrates?
> SOCRATES: That of dividing things by classes; where the natural joints are, and not trying to break any part, after the manner of a bad carver. —265
> Now I myself, Phaedrus, am a lover of these processes of division and bringing together, as aids to speech and thought; and if I think any other man is able to see things that can naturally be collected into one and divided into many, him I follow after and "walk in his footsteps as if he were a god." And whether the name I give to those who can do this is right or wrong, God knows, but I have called them hitherto dialecticians.—266

In short, rhetoric, so far as it is anything at all but a sham, is philosophy. To be able to define and divide, the rhetorician has to be able to think; he has to know the truth. There would seem to be some hedging on the part of Plato in this dialogue—as to whether the truth to be known is the cognitive content, the doctrine, about which the rhetorician would persuade his hearers, or another kind of truth, the psychological truth about their individual temperaments, which he must know if his discourse is to be a successfully administered persuasion (*Psuchagōgia*).—271

> He must understand the nature of the soul, must find out the class of speech adapted to each nature, and must arrange and adorn his discourse accordingly, offering to the complex soul elaborate and harmonious discourses, and simple tales to the simple soul.—277

But the emphasis of the dialogue is very largely upon the question *what* is to be said, not upon the question *to whom*, and the chief distinction is between the politico-legal rhetorician, who prefers "what seems to be true," or what is probable, to actual truth, and the philosophic rhetorician, who labors "not for the sake of speaking and acting before men, but that he may be able to speak and to do everything, so far as possible, in a manner pleasing to the gods." (273) In short, the main distinction is between professional rhetoricians as they are actually found to be, and the ideal rhetorician as he may be conceived to be. And here the Socratic identification of virtue with knowledge works relentlessly. If he who knows what is right will always do it, then he who does wrong (a sophistical rhetorician who uses his "art" to work evil) cannot know the right—or at least the so-called "art" by which he works evil cannot be a way of knowing it. As in the *Ion* the retreat was ironically from poetry as an art or form of knowledge to poetry as divine insanity (and indeed the same retreat occurs in the *Phaedrus* on several planes of irony and seriousness), so the specific resort imputed to rhetoric (a close relative of poetry) is from artful knowledge to the cheapness of a knack or trick (*tribē*). That is the only way to explain its undoubtedly effective, but subversive, performance.

> I seem, as it were, to hear some arguments approaching and protesting that . . . ["the art of speaking"] is lying and is not an art, but a craft devoid of art (*hoti pseudetai kai ouk esti technē all' atechnos tribē*). A real art of speaking . . . which does not seize hold of truth, does not exist and never will.—260

This explanation had been given a fancier (and no doubt to the rhetoricians an even more exasperating) shape in the earlier *Gorgias,* where the same key concept, *tribē* or knack, is applied in a four-point analogy. As the cheap knack of *cookery* is to the art of *gymnastic* in building health, and as *cosmetic* is to *medicine* in repairing health, so in the field of politics, *sophistic* is the meretricious rival of *legislation,* and *rhetoric* is that of *jurisprudence.*

At one place in the *Phaedrus* (267), Socrates makes a scornful review of contemporary rhetoricians and the niceties of their art (*ta kompsa tēs technēs*): Theodorus of Byzantium, with his introduction, narrative, testimony, proofs, probability, confirmation and further confirmation, refutation and further refutation; the "illustrious Parian" Evenus, with his covert allusion, indirect praises (*parepainoi*), and indirect censures (*parapsogoi*); Gorgias and Tisias, who make small things seem great and great things small, and new things old and old things new, and who invented conciseness (*suntomia logōn*) and measureless length on all subjects (*apeira mēkē peri pantōn*); Prodicus and Hippias of Elis; Polus, with his duplication (*diplasiologia*), sententiousness (*gnōmologia*), and figurativeness (*eikonologia*); Licymnius, with his beautiful diction (*euepeia*); Protagoras, with his correctness of diction (*orthoepiea*); the "mighty Calcedonian" Thrasymachus, with his genius for rousing audiences to wrath and for soothing them again, for devising or for refuting calumnies on any grounds whatsoever. On one piece of technique, that of summarizing a speech at the end, all seem to be agreed, though some call it recapitulation (*epanodos*), others something else. This is a section of the *Phaedrus* which might be transplanted almost verbatim into Benedetto Croce's expressionistic history of *Aesthetic*.

The ground of Plato's objection to rhetoric may be perhaps most deeply understood, near the end of the *Phaedrus,* in a distinction between written and spoken words, a distinction which is the more relevant to the argument because of the fact that Attic oratory made no pretense of being *ex tempore.* The written word, urges Socrates, is a static thing useful only to tell people what they already know, an amusement, a reminder for the forgetfulness of old age. But the spoken word is the true, vital, and dialectic word—it is written in the mind of the hearer and is able to defend itself in the process of question and answer.

> But the man who thinks that in the written word there is necessarily much that is playful, and that no written discourse, whether in metre or in prose, deserves to be treated very seriously (and this applies also to the recitations of the rhapsodes, delivered to sway people's minds, without opportunity for questioning and teaching), but that the best of them really serve only to remind us of what we know; and who thinks that only in words about justice and beauty and goodness spoken by teachers for the sake of instruction and really written in a soul is clearness and perfection and serious value, that such words should be considered the speaker's own legitimate offspring, first the word within himself, if it be found there, and secondly its descendants or brothers which may have sprung up in worthy manner in the souls of others, and who pays no attention to the other words,—that man, Phaedrus, is likely to be such as you and I might pray that we ourselves may become.—277–8 [6]

In this clear confirmation of the anti-mimetic doctrine of the *Republic,* we may see that in theory at least (or at least in this dialogue) Plato prefers the object imitated in his dialogues, the actual conversations as they may be supposed to have taken place, to his own highly artful or poetic embodiment of them in fixed words. And this may remind us

---

[6] Cf. Atkins, I, 148 on the niceties possible in written style and on the "deliberative" oratorical style as shadow-painting (*skiagraphia*).

that poetic quality does indeed reside in fixity, or determinacy, of words. Not only meter and rhyme and all the minute effects of a lyric but the dialogue and succession of scenes in a tragedy, the whole economy and precision of poetic power in words, depend on choice, limitation, and fixation, and hence are opposed to the fluid character of dialectic or of the bull session—though the latter, in virtue of its capacity to shift words, correct, repeat, rephrase, paraphrase, and in general adjust itself to the exigencies of debate, may in a sense fit closer to the truth of the matter which is discussed.

III

It was no less against literary than against oratorical interests that Plato was fighting. The close alliance of rhetoric and poetry as his enemies, seen more than once in the *Phaedrus,* is suggested a final time in a closing allusion to the rhetorician Isocrates.

> I think he has a nature above the speeches of Lysias and possesses a nobler character; so that I should not be surprised if, as he grows older, he should so excel in his present studies that all who have ever treated of rhetoric shall seem less than children; and I suspect that these studies will not satisfy him, but a more divine impulse will lead him to greater things; for my friend, something of philosophy is inborn in his mind.—279

The fictional date of the dialogue is about 410 B.C., when Isocrates, the pupil of Gorgias, was making his first appearance on the scene. But the dialogue was written perhaps as late as 370,[7] at a time when Isocrates was the most eminent and affluent teacher of rhetoric at Athens and hence the chief rhetorical antagonist of the Platonic school. The *Art of Rhetoric* which Isocrates wrote survives only in a few fragments. But from several of his discourses, especially that *Against the Sophists* and the *Antidosis,* which deal with education—and from the style itself of his writing—we get an idea of the kind of campaign which he waged against law-court and assembly rhetoric and the debased form of ethical dialectic which he calls "eristic." Although he discountenanced the academic exercise on mythological topics or on paradoxical themes such as those affected by Gorgias and Protagoras—"that we cannot lie," or "that nothing exists"—or on such anticipations of Swift's broomstick as "humble bees" or "salt," the theory of Isocrates was literary rather than practically oratorical. The form of speech which he chiefly sponsored was the epideictic (the encomiastic or the invective declamation), and this was an oratory that had moved as far as possible away from the

[7] R. Hackforth, *Plato's Phaedrus* (Cambridge, 1952), pp. 3–8.

give and take of dialectic toward the fixity of a set piece or essay—
albeit an essay that would seem by our standards a rather florid one.
The epideictic style, Aristotle would say in his *Rhetoric* (III, 12), is
especially suited to written compositions; it aims at being read. Isocrates hoped that his *Antidosis* would prove a "monument more noble
than statues of bronze." The rhetoric of Isocrates was a scheme of
general education (*paideia*) which aimed at a liberal union of philosophy and persuasion, and understanding of elevated and large political
topics, and withal an artistic verbal style, imaginative (*poiētikos*) and
diverse. The "thoughts" of the graduate rhetorician were to be not
only "dignified and original" but "adorned with a number of striking
figures." What was desired was a kind of poetic prose oratory, or
literary prose, something which would serve not only for statesmen but
for critics of poetry, for historians, for writers of panegyric. Isocrates
entertained a highly integrated view of life and letters; he conceived
the former as greatly in need of the latter. The sum of his teaching
was a genial, flowery, belletristic kind of humanism.[8]

IV

This was one kind of answer both to the Sophists and to Plato. A
rhetorician of later antiquity [9] reports that Aristotle's systematic treatise
on the question, his *Rhetoric* in three books, was the outcome of a feud
with Isocrates. The story says that during his first residence in Athens
(367–347 B.C.) Aristotle sneered at the ideas of Isocrates and the
method of their dissemination in bundles of speeches hawked by the
booksellers. Yet the difference between the two as theorists of rhetoric
is not so profound. Aristotle takes more examples from the orations of
Isocrates than from the works of any other author. The difference between them might be summed up, without great distortion, in the
statement that Aristotle, looking on rhetoric in a far more utilitarian
way than Isocrates, is somewhat closer to being sophistical; as a
philosopher, however, as a teacher of rhetoric in Plato's Academy, he
is at the same time more systematic than Isocrates. The latter virtue
is the one by which Aristotle gains the advantage of having his ideas
preserved not in speeches but in a treatise.[10]

"Do you think we have reproached the art of speaking too harshly?"
asks Socrates in the *Phaedrus*. "Perhaps she might say:

[8] See Atkins, I, 124–8, 148, 154–5.
[9] Dionysius of Halicarnassus, *On Isocrates* 18; Atkins, I, 133.
[10] Aristotle's *Theodectia,* on style, and other works on rhetoric are lost. Atkins,
I, 133, 135, 136.

'Why do you talk such nonsense, you strange men? I do not compel
anyone to learn to speak without knowing the truth, but if my advice is
of any value, he learns that first and then acquires me. So what I claim
is this, that without my help the knowledge of the truth does not give
the art of persuasion.'—260

It would not be unfair to say that Plato has here anticipated the gist of
Aristotle's doctrine. "What makes the sophist," says Aristotle, "is not
skill in argument, but [defect of] moral purpose." [11]

Aristotle's *Rhetoric* opens with the statement: "Rhetoric is a counterpart of dialectic." But the term *dialectic* has for Aristotle a softer
meaning than for Plato—the meaning of a conversationally plausible
inquiry rather than of a metaphysically compelling demonstration.
Dialectic is a comfortable neighbor to rhetoric, on the higher side.
Both dialectic and its practical counterpart, rhetoric, enjoy a kind of
cushioning from the severity of theoretical science (mathematics,
physics, metaphysics). Dialectic is the argumentative technique of the
social, practical deliberative and "alternative" sciences (ethics and
politics). "It is the mark of an educated man" says Aristotle in his
Ethics, "to look for precision in each class of things just so far as the
nature of the subject admits; it is . . . equally foolish to accept
probable reasoning from a mathematician and to demand from a
rhetorician scientific proofs." [12]

Even that much would have been enough to protect rhetoric from
the full brunt of the Platonic inquisition. But Aristotle does more.
There is a moment in the first chapter of Book I when he seems bent
on treating rhetoric rather rigorously within the limits of its probable
arguments (its "examples" and "enthymemes"). [13] "Proofs," he says, "are
the only things in . . . [rhetoric] that come within the province of
art." And he is severe upon the previous compilers of handbooks who
have devoted their attention chiefly to methods of arousing prejudice.

[11] *Ho gar sophistikos ouk en tē dunamei all' en tē proairesei* (*Rhetoric*, I, 1).
[12] *Nicomachean Ethics* I, 3.
[13] The term "enthymeme" was used by Aristotle's successors, as it is by modern
logicians, to refer to the elliptical syllogism. But for Aristotle, in his *Rhetoric* and
in his logical writings, "enthymeme" is the name of the rhetorical syllogism, which
is a *probable* argument for a *particular* conclusion. The enthymeme is thus
distinguishable from two other kinds of syllogism, the dialectic syllogism, which
is a probable argument for a general conclusion, and the apodeictic or scientific
syllogism, which is a certain argument for a universal conclusion. See J. H.
Freese, *Aristotle . . . the "Art" of Rhetoric* (London: Loeb Classical Library,
1939), p. 474, Glossary, s.v. *Dialektikē;* James H. McBurney, "Some Recent
Interpretations of the Aristotelian Enthymeme," *Papers of the Michigan Academy
of Science, Arts and Letters*, XXI (Ann Arbor, 1936), 489–500.

Nevertheless, the argument begins to change even in the same chapter; there is a disposition to talk more about persuasion that about proof. The truth may be the truth, but it may need help before it is accepted. Not all persons are easy to persuade by reason. The orator should be able to prove opposites—like a logician—not for the sake of doing this, but just for understanding. All good things except virtue itself may be abused. The function of rhetoric is not so much to persuade as to find out the existing means of persuasion. Thus runs what would seem to be almost the dialogue of Aristotle with his own conscience, as he moves toward the empirical and anti-Platonic procedure of justifying rhetoric as it is found in fact to be. The second chapter begins by "defining rhetoric anew." "Rhetoric then may be defined as the faculty of discovering the possible means of persuasion in reference to any subject whatever." And we learn in this chapter that there are no fewer than four kinds of "artificial proof" [14] or means of persuasion: (1) the ethical or those depending on the moral character of the orator himself—by which he elicits confidence in himself; (2) the affective or those which appeal to the emotions of the audience (It was only the *exclusive* use of such proofs to which I alluded disparagingly in my first chapter, he explains); (3) valid arguments, which tend to establish the truth of whatever we are maintaining; and (4) apparent arguments, which only seem to establish it. The first two books of Aristotle's *Rhetoric* do in fact proceed in that pattern, the first Book telling about materials, or areas of argumentative probability, the second Book giving us mainly the psychology of good relations between speaker and audience. Aristotle has put a four-layered mattress between rhetoric and the inexorable or scientific truth—two of the layers being psychological, that is, relating to the character and feelings of the speaker and audience, one, the layer of probable cognitive arguments being at least nonscientific, and the fourth, the layer of apparent arguments, being feathered with actual deception. Aristotle thus defends rhetoric on approximately the same grounds as those on which Plato condemns it.

These Aristotelian graduations away from the strictness of scientific demonstration are not the immediate stuff for a rhetoric of verbal surface. But they do provide the underlying contour of such a rhetoric. They enable or make plausible a fifth and a sixth graduation—verbal style (*lexis*) and structure or architecture (*taxis*), the subjects of Aristotle's third book. About Aristotle's conception of *taxis* Plato could not have complained, though he might have related this (the organic order,

---

[14] I.e., artful, as distinguished from the inartificial or ready-made, such as witnesses, tortures, contracts.

beginning, middle, and end named in the *Phaedrus*) more intimately to "dialectic." But *lexis* is the apex and epitome of the difference between Plato and Aristotle as rhetoricians, and not so much the details of what Aristotle said about *lexis* as the very fact that he thought it reasonable to devote twelve chapters to the topic.

"We have therefore next to speak of style; for it is not sufficient to know what one ought to say,—but one must also know how to say it, and this largely contributes to making the speech appear of a certain character" (III, 1). It is almost as if this matter of style should be grouped with the newly acknowledged and even more external art of delivery (a kind of acting, *hupokrisis*), a thing that has to be conceded, not as right but as necessary, owing to the corruption of politicians and judges. Just a little more can be said for style:

> . . . it does make a difference, for the purpose of making a thing clear, to speak in this or that manner; still, the difference is not so very great, . . . all these things are mere outward show for pleasing the hearer; wherefore no one teaches geometry in this way.[15] III, 1

It is a cautiously divided account of style, giving due recognition to clarity and purity (*esti d' archē tēs lexeōs to hellēnizein*—the first principle of style is to use good Greek [16]) and in general to propriety, but at the same time showing considerable respect for the elevated and ornate, for a certain strangeness or departure from the ordinary which (like a foreigner among our fellow citizens) appears more distinguished (III, 2 and 5).

One of the most interesting technical features [17] of the discussion is a marked concern for metaphor. The section of his *Poetics* (Chs. XXI–XXIV) devoted to the element of tragedy which Aristotle calls dic-

---

[15] He continues: ". . . . written speeches owe their effect not so much to the sense as to the style. The poets, as was natural, were the first to give an impulse to style; for words are imitations, and the voice also, which of all our parts is best adapted for imitation, was ready to hand; thus the arts of the rhapsodists, actors, and others, were fashioned. And as the poets, although their utterances were devoid of sense, appeared to have gained their reputation through their style, it was a poetical style that first came into being, as that of Gorgias." In the *Poetics* (XXIV) appears the rather frigid statement: "The diction should be elaborated in the pauses of the action, where there is no expression of character and thought. For . . . character and thought are merely obscured by a diction that is over brilliant."

[16] Under this head comes a censure of ambiguity (*amphiboloi*), III, 5.

[17] The statements in III, 8 that prose should have rhythm but not meter (*rhythmon dei echein tōn logōn, metron de mē*) and that the best rhythm for prose is the paeonic, are Aristotle's attempt to reconcile the Pythagorean and Platonic doctrine that number confers order and limit (see the literary application in *Philebus* 23) with the fact that the "rhythm" or movement of good prose is not really a matter of number or measure.

tion or style, *lexis*, is mentioned four times in the first two chapters of Book III of the *Rhetoric*. If we turn back to the *Poetics*, we find the often-quoted statement that to be a master of metaphor is the greatest poetic gift, because metaphor shows an eye for resemblances, and metaphor cannot be learnt from anyone else.[18] We find also the definition: "Metaphor consists in assigning to a thing the name of something else," and the four classes of metaphoric reference: from genus to species, from species to genus, from species to species, and by proportion.[19] Somewhat more specific, if miscellaneous, remarks on the same subject appear in the *Rhetoric*. "It is metaphor above all that gives perspicuity, pleasure, and a foreign air" (III, 2). "It must be appropriate and not far-fetched," but not too obvious either (III, 11). It can make things look either better or worse—as when a pirate calls himself a "purveyor" or an actor calls himself an artist, or someone else calls the actor a flatterer of Dionysus. A metaphor is like a riddle. Metaphors should mostly be "derived from things that are beautiful." "It does make a difference, for instance, whether one says 'rosy-fingered morn,' rather than 'purple-fingered,' or, what is still worse, 'red-fingered'" (III, 2). A climax to these obiter dicta and to the whole treatment of *lexis* occurs in Chapters 10 and 11, where metaphor is joined with figures of parallel sound and sense and with various verbal deceptions or jokes shading into paronomasia or pun.

> "And he strode on, under his feet—chilblains," whereas the hearer thought he was going to say "sandals."

> The more special qualities the expression possesses, the smarter it appears; for instance, if the words contain a metaphor, and a metaphor of a special kind, antithesis, and equality of clauses, and actuality.

"Actuality" or vividness (*energeia*) [20] is perhaps better taken as a term for summing up the effect of rhetorical figures than as a name for another figure on the same footing. But we may say that Aristotle has here very shrewdly observed a close relation among rhetorical features which are not always or easily seen as so closely related—the logic of parallel and distinction, the apparently alien pun or trick with sounds,

[18] A thought repeated in *Rhetoric* III, 2.

[19] Proportion is defined in *Ethics* V, 3 as "an equality of ratios, implying four terms at least." See *Rhetoric* III, 4: "If the goblet is the shield of Dionysus, then the shield may properly be called the goblet of Ares."

[20] Roman rhetoricains (Dionysius of Halicarnassus, *De Lysia*, VII; Longinus, *Peri Hupsous*, XV; Quintilian, *Institutio Oratoria* VIII, 3, 62) use the term *enargeia* in approximately the same sense. Cf. W. Rhys Roberts, *Longinus on the Sublime* (Cambridge, 1935), pp. 197–8.

and mediating these extremes the imaginative force of metaphor. He has thus come not far from supplying an accurate formula for a long tradition of poetical wit.

> Here Britain's statesmen oft the fall foredoom
> Of foreign Tyrants and of Nymphs at home;
> Here thou, great ANNA! whom three realms obey,
> Dost sometimes counsel take—and sometimes Tea.

V

The important thing about both Aristotle and Isocrates as rhetoricians is, in brief, that they affirm the power of the word—Aristotle the more systematically and analytically, Isocrates the more eloquently. This is the point at which to make a brief return to Isocrates for the sake of introducing some of his enthusiastic conceptions. According to Isocrates eloquence is creative process (*poiētikon pragma*), the source of civilization, of laws and arts, and of most other human blessings, the mark which distinguishes men from the brutes, the instrument and test of wisdom. It is the adorner and transformer of experience, making old things new and new things old, the big little and the little big. It is an expression of intelligence, a reflection of character, an outward image of a true and virtuous soul (*psuchēs agathēs kai pistēs eidōlon*).[21] The rhetorical doctrine made current by Isocrates had been heard before from sophists and much earlier had had a more lyric orientation, as in the myth of Orpheus taming savage men and beasts by his music, and that of Amphion charming stones with his poetry and building the Theban walls.[22] It had been aligned with such verbal and poetic interests as the allegorical interpretation of Homer rejected by Plato in Book III of the *Republic* or the semi-facetious etymological reasoning about the right sense of words, the natural relation between words and things, in Plato's *Cratylus*. The Stoic Zeno's *Homeric Problems* would later establish the school of allegorical criticism for the post-Aristotelian or Hellenistic age;[23] the natural expressiveness of language would be defended by the school of Analogists among the Alexandrian grammarians and critics.[24] A commonplace of antiquity, especially among the Stoic philosophers,[25] was a doctrine which we may call

---

[21] *Against the Sophists* 12; *Nicocles* 5–9; *Antidosis* 254; *Panegyricus* 8; all cited in Atkins, I, 125–6.

[22] Atkins, I, 13, 29, 127.

[23] Atkins, I, 187.

[24] Atkins, I, 184; II, 17.

[25] E. Vernon Arnold, *Roman Stoicism* (Cambridge, 1911), esp. pp. 128–49.

simply that of the *Logos*—the word as the expression and hence the mold and determination of reason and intelligence: in a mathematical sense, as in the logos of Euclid, in grammatical, etymological, symbolic, exegetic, rhetorical and moral senses—in the grand and synthesizing sense that eloquence and wisdom are inseparable. The relation of this doctrine to literary criticism may be hinted by allusion to the earliest extant Greek *Grammar*, the sixteen pages of the second-century Dionysius Thrax, a standard for centuries, in which we ascend through six stages, from accurate reading aloud and interpretation of figures of speech, to the crown of all, the criticism of poetry. The *Grammaticus* of this age was scarcely the figure for a mid-19th-century *Grammarian's Funeral*. He was the professionally qualified *poetarum interpres*.[26] Finally, the doctrine of the *Logos* with all that it implied was a doctrine less dear even to poets and grammarians than to statesmen. It was one of the main theoretical supports of a life devoted to public leadership. "I am grateful to the Stoics," said Cicero, "for this reason: that they alone of all the philosophers have declared eloquence to be virtue and wisdom." [27] The debate about rhetoric which we have been considering is but an early chapter, though an important one, of a controversial history which continues through later antiquity, the Middle Ages, and the Renaissance. The ancient quarrel between the philosophers and the poets to which Plato alludes in the *Republic* was the same in principle as a later and much longer quarrel between dialecticians (in the Platonic sense, philosophers tending toward science) and rhetoricians.[28] On the side of the dialecticians one might align in one consistent team: Plato, Abelard, Occam, Ramus, Descartes. On the side of the rhetoricians, poets and grammarians: Aristotle, Cicero, Quintilian, Augustine,[29] John of Salisbury, Bonaventure, and Richard

[26] Atkins, I, 182–3; J. E. Sandys, *A History of Classical Scholarship* (Cambridge, 1921), I, 6–11; Richard McKeon, "The Philosophic Bases of Criticism," in R. S. Crane, *Critics and Criticism*, p. 507.

[27] "Stoicis hanc habeo gratiam, quod soli ex omnibus eloquentiam virtutem ac sapientiam esse dixerunt" (quoted in Arnold, *Roman Stoicism*, p. 149). Cf. J. S. Watson, *Cicero on Oratory and Orators*, 1890, p. 210; *De Oratore* III, 18.

[28] The Stoic philosopher Zeno made a comparison (recorded in Cicero's *Orator* XXXII, 113) between the concise form of dialectic utterance, a "closed fist," and the expanded expression of rhetoric, an "open palm." The fact that Stoic philosophers promoted the doctrine of the Logos (or verbal power) but at the same time favored a concise and severe dialectic style must be looked on as an anomaly arising characteristically enough out of the complex issue concerning verbal style and content. Cf. *post* Chapter 12, our account of Ramism and 17th-century rhetoric.

[29] The theological aspect is well illustrated in this passage from the *Adversus Praxean* of Tertullian (about A.D. 213): "This reason is His own thought; this is

Hooker.[30] The following retrospective passages in the *De Oratore* of Cicero define the role of Socrates in the long debate and the importance of the whole incident in which Plato, Isocrates, and Aristotle were the other chief participants.

It was Socrates who . . . separated the ability to think wisely from the ability to speak gracefully, though these are naturally united—Socrates! the philosopher whose genius and varied conversation Plato's dialogues have committed to immortality, but who himself has left us nothing in writing. Hence arose that divorce of the tongue from the heart (*discidium illud . . . quasi linguae atque cordis*), that absurd, needless, and deplorable conception, that one set of persons should teach us to think, and another should teach us to speak.—*De Oratore* III, 16

The ancients, till the time of Socrates, used to combine the whole of their study and science pertaining to morality, to the duties of life, to virtue, and to civil government, with the art of speaking; but afterward, the eloquent being separated by Socrates from the philosophic, and the distinction being continued by all the followers of Socrates, the philosophers despised eloquence, and the orators philosophy . . . . the followers of Socrates excluded the pleaders of causes from their own ranks, and from the common title of philosophers—though the ancients had been of the opinion that the faculty of speaking and that of understanding were allied in a marvellous harmony.—*De Oratore* III, 19 [31]

Aristotle . . . said it was disgraceful that he should remain silent and let Isocrates do all the speaking. He therefore undertook to equip that philosophy of his with due illustrations and ornament and to connect the knowledge of things with skill in speaking. This of course came to the notice of that sagacious monarch Philip, who summoned Aristotle as a tutor for his son Alexander. Let the boy get from the same teacher instructions in behavior and in language.

Now, if anybody desires to call that philosopher who instructs us fully in things and words an orator, he may do so without opposition from me; or if he prefers to call that orator whom I describe as having

---

what the Greeks call 'Logos,' which word we translate also by 'speech.' . . . To understand it more easily, take knowledge from yourself, I pray you, as from the image and likeness' of God. . . . See, when you silently meet with yourself in the process of thinking, that this very process goes on within you by reason meeting you along with word at every movement of your thought, at every beat of your understanding. Whatsoever you think is word; whatsoever you understand is speech" (*Tertullian Against Praxeas,* trans. A. Souter, London, 1920, pp. 36–7, Par. 5).

[30] See H. M. McLuhan, "Edgar Poe's Tradition," *Sewanee Review,* LII (January–March, 1944), 24–33.

[31] Adapted from J. S. Watson, *Cicero on Oratory and Orators* (New York, 1890), pp. 209, 212.

wisdom united with eloquence a philosopher, I shall make no objection . . . . If I had to choose one of the two, I should prefer uneloquent good sense to loquacious folly. But if it be inquired which is the more eminent excellence, I give the palm to the learned orator, and if you will admit that this person is also a philosopher, there is an end of controversy; but if you insist on distinguishing the orator from the philosopher, the philosopher will be inferior—for the equipment of a complete orator includes the knowledge of the philosopher, but the knowledge of the philosopher does not necessarily include the eloquence of the orator.—*De Oratore* III, 35 [32]

NOTES ON ARISTOTLE'S RHETORIC   *Friedrich Solmsen*

Rather vaguely we thing of *Rhetoric* and *Poetics* as proceeding along parallel lines or as complementing each other. Depending on the spirit in which they are treated they may or may not show mutual regard. For the generations after him Aristotle was to be an authority in both fields; his name and prestige were to do their part in drawing the two subjects together. One reason for this is that poetry serves Aristotle in the *Rhetoric* as a mine of illustrative material—it is remarkable how many excellent arguments he lifts from the speeches of tragedy. Still his original interest was not in the parallels between oratory and poetry but in those between rhetorical and dialectical argumentation. To set up standards of literary excellence was his intention when he composed the *Poetics;* in the *Rhetoric* he has no such ambition. True, the orations of Lysias and Demosthenes rank, if not with Homer, Sophocles and Plato, yet among the acknowledged masterpieces of Greek literature; they were "read" in Aristotle's day too. True too, the speeches of Burke and of the orators of the French revolution, the eloquence of Cobden and Bright, Webster and Lincoln, Gladstone and Churchill claim a place in the literature of their nations. Yet, apart from the question whether this claim is often honored, it is safe to say that the speaker's own and immediate concern is with his contemporary audience. Aristotle certainly visualizes a speech not as composed for the admiration of literary connoisseurs through all time but as designed for a specific, practical end, as delivered before

From the introduction to *The Rhetoric and the Poetics of Aristotle*, edited by Friedrich Solmsen, copyright, 1954, by Random House, Inc. Reprinted by permission.
[32] Adapted from J. S. Watson, p. 233.

an audience, as calculated to prove and to convince. In the nature of things it could hardly have been otherwise.

Yet it also lies in the nature of things that speech and poetry have some characteristics in common. Sooner or later Aristotle had to become aware of them. In the *Poetics,* when isolating some facets of the finished work, he realizes that they need but little comment since to discuss them fully would mean to duplicate sections of the *Rhetoric* (it is immaterial whether these sections were already written out; in fact the question whether the *Poetics* or the *Rhetoric* is the earlier work is almost meaningless since both grew and developed over the years). Thought is one of the "qualitative parts" of tragedy and it will be in point to remember how "rhetorical" poetic thought had become since the days of Euripides. Everything under the sun is discussed; arguments and counter-arguments abound so freely that the large and small doses of thought that are dispensed in carefully constructed speeches must often have diverted interest from the central idea of the play. By conceding the primacy in this point to rhetoric Aristotle follows poetry's own lead. He goes a step further when he refers to his *Rhetoric* both for the arousing of the emotions (in the speeches) and for their portrayal (in the plot). Yet history has borne him out; for the chapters on the passions in the Second Book of the *Rhetoric* were for centuries regarded as the classical treatment whose authority was recognized alike by orators, poets, philosophers, political thinkers and students of "the nature of man."

Another area of overlapping interests is style, and there is more than a grain of truth in Aristotle's sly observation that early orators affected poetic diction because they realized how much of the poets' success was due to the beauty and elaboration of their language. Aristotle does not in so many words say that the gaps left in his somewhat sketchy discussion of style in the *Poetics* should be filled by referring to the more detailed analysis presented in the *Rhetoric.* Nor does he, when dealing with character in the *Poetics,* remind us of the other work with its sketches—at once sympathetic and detached, sure of touch as well as penetrating—of the distinctive character traits of young and old, rich and poor. Posterity, however, needed no reminder; for many centuries to come the discussion of poetic diction was dominated by the criteria of good and bad style which Aristotle had established in the *Rhetoric;* as for the character sketches, we find them as early as Horace bodily transferred from *Rhetoric* to *Poetics.* Moreover, what happened in these instances happened also in others; later writers on poetry used the *Rhetoric* as a quarry, furnishing many a stone for their edifice which, while standing firm on the foundations of Aristotle's *Poetics,* could yet do with a good deal of filling out in other parts of its structure.

Still it behooves us to distinguish between Aristotle and the Aristotelian tradition and to recognize that he himself organized the two subjects along utterly different lines. If rhetoric and poetry were associated in Aristotle's mind it may have been for a reason on which we have already touched when speaking of poetry's rehabilitation. Here are two forms of human activity whose aims are set high—high enough to compete with philosophy. Rhetoric's need for rehabilitation was if possible even greater than poetry's, and in his treatise Aristotle actually reforms this subject and gives it a philosophically respectable standing. And just as in the *Poetics* Aristotle ignores poetry's claim to reveal the truth about man's place and condition in the scheme of things, so his *Rhetoric* ignores whatever pretenses teachers of rhetoric were making of providing an all-round education and of fashioning the highest type of man. As an alternative to philosophy neither rhetoric nor poetry could any longer be accepted; yet the one as well as the other might fill a modest place and achieve something of value in the measure in which it conformed or submitted to philosophical rules and postulates.

For a time philosophy had refused to have any traffic with rhetoric. Plato had rejected rhetoric—the "artificer of persuasion"—on the ground that its practitioners seek to persuade without having either knowledge of or regard for the truth. The orator who aims at pleasing the crowd, while working for his own ascendancy, is a slave to the desire for power and operates within a scheme of utterly false values. If poetry is banished from the ideal state rhetoric has to share its exile; in fact its case is worse. Yet there are indications from the very beginning— though perhaps less clearly perceptible in the case of rhetoric—that either of them may work its way back on condition of good conduct. This implies reform, and it meant much that philosophy itself would show the way. In order to do so, a cynic might comment, philosophy itself had to reform; in any case it had to broaden, if not its basis, yet certainly its range; it had to relax its inhospitable rigor and find a way downward from the realm of Forms to the realities of this world. Such a development does indeed come to pass in the philosophy of Plato's later years; and the reader who turns from the *Gorgias,* with its wholesale condemnation of rhetoric and all that it stood for, to the *Phaedrus*—a much later dialogue—will be surprised to find, side by side with another condemnation of average rhetorical practices, the blueprint of a truly philosophical rhetoric. The new conception which accounts for this is Plato's recognition of "Forms of souls." In less philosophical language we may call them personality types. In every "form" of soul a different part of the soul prevails, which means that some persons are dominated by one emotion, others by another. Plato's philosophy and dialectic would not stoop to concern themselves with these emotional propensities; they address themselves to man as a rational being. Here then is the point where rhetoric may lend valuable aid by supplementing the work of philosophy. If it studies the different "forms" of soul (and comes to the point of recognizing them in individuals) it will know how to adjust the philosophical argument to different kinds of people. For indeed the argument as such, the method of procedure, and the way toward the truth can only be one—regardless of the audience. In this essential point rhetoric is not permitted to diverge from philosophy.

The kind of rhetoric which Plato here envisages could be supplied only by a member of his own school. It was Aristotle who undertook this task. The ancient evidence at our disposal indicates that his first lectures on rhetoric—embodied in parts of our treatise—were delivered during Plato's lifetime, i.e. while Aristotle still counted himself a member of the Academy. The course was a challenge to the professional teachers of speech; more particularly it was a gauntlet thrown down before the celebrated leader of the Athenian school, Isocrates, who had made the art of rhetoric both more elastic and more elaborate, and in whose eyes rhetorical education was synonymous with liberal education and at the same time a passport to a splendid political career. The opening chapter of Aristotle's *Rhetoric*, in which he soon proceeds to an attack upon the current systems, castigating their failure to provide a doctrine of argument and their concentration on the emotional appeal, must go back to this early course. It breathes the same contempt for the fashionable—and presumably often successful—devices as Plato's own polemic against rhetoric as an art of flattery or as the "artificer of persuasion" at all costs.

Where then lies the superiority of Aristotle's philosophical rhetoric over the art of persuasion and success as taught in the professional schools? What makes his system more philosophical, more scientific, more exact? If we turn to the chapters dealing with the emotions, we can see that, albeit with considerable freedom in the execution, Aristotle has implemented Plato's demand. He does not distinguish Forms of souls (which in his own scheme would make little sense);

instead he starts in the case of each emotion with a precise and carefully worded definition which at once indicates under what conditions
this emotion may be aroused and what kind of people are amenable
to it. The more specific statements concerning the occurrence of these
emotions are derived from this initial definition which serves as a kind
of first principle or basic premise. This is good scientific method, and
a speaker possessed of such knowledge would be able to assess a given
situation and to decide what passion could be aroused (or allayed)
and how this should be done. (Earlier teachers of rhetoric seem
to have told their pupils in effect: "if you wish to move your listeners
to pity, choose or combine some of the ready-made sentences which I
have worked out for this end and herewith sell to you for memorization.")

Even more philosophic is the new doctrine of rhetorical proof. No
one before Aristotle would have dreamt of basing this doctrine on the
syllogism, for the simple reason that the syllogism had not yet been
discovered. Even Aristotle needed time to discover it, that is to say
develop it out of the relationships obtaining between Platonic Forms.
Originally the Greek word "syllogism" was used loosely in a not at all
technical sense ("putting facts together by argument"). With Aristotle
the word gradually becomes highly technical, yet in the *Rhetoric* he
often emphasizes the parallel between the rhetorical argument and
the syllogism without yet knowing the three valid forms of syllogistic
reasoning which he was some day to proclaim. Thus the arguments
drawn from "commonplaces" which bulk so large at the end of Book
II in no way presuppose a knowledge of the syllogistic figures or the
logical insights that guarantee their validity. Take any of the commonplace arguments, for instance, this one: "if not even the gods know
everything, still less do men." Here is neither a major nor a minor
premise, nor is there anything like the orthodox relation between these
terms. To be sure, another illustration which Aristotle gives for the
same commonplace could easily be recast into an orthodox syllogism
by making "whoever beats his father will also beat his neighbor" the
major premise, adding the minor "X beats his father," and combining
both in the conclusion "X beats his neighbor"—but this is not what
Aristotle at this point has in mind. After Aristotle had made his great
discovery of the syllogistic figures some of his pupils got busy "resolving" commonplace arguments into these figures. Their enterprise
may well have had the blessing of the master; yet he evidently never
saw a need for refashioning the commonplace arguments of the
Rhetoric into technically correct syllogisms. It is sufficient that with

the help of these "commonplaces" plausible arguments can be formed, and that by conforming to them the rhetorician's reasoning acquires method and structure. If Aristotle occasionally points out that the "entire system" of an earlier teacher corresponds to one of his commonplaces, he still can claim for himself the credit of having abstracted the underlying idea—the formal principle or whatever one may choose to call it. What his precursors had done was to give their pupils a large number of arguments, all of the same type—so at least Aristotle suggests—without yet being able to abstract or formulate this type. Here lies the difference between a hack-rhetorician unable to rise above the practical details and a man with philosophical training who has learnt in Plato's school to look for the form and principle common to many individual specimens.

Matters are different in other chapters where Aristotle examines certain traditional varieties of "evidence" and judges the validity of each by comparing it with his syllogisms. Here the full-fledged theory of the syllogistic figures is clearly presupposed. "The fact that he has a fever is a sign that he is ill" is a valid argument, since it can be cast in the form of a correct syllogism in the first figure with the major, "whoever has a fever is ill"; the minor, "X has a fever"; and the conclusion "X is ill." On the other hand, to conclude from the two premises, "Socrates is just" and "Socrates is wise," that wise men are just, would not be cogent because the theory of the syllogism shows that two affirmative premises which have the same term (in this instance Socrates) as subject cannot be combined in a correct conclusion.

Still other chapters list first premises about expediency (usefulness, goodness), nobility (or beauty), and justice, the three basic values, each of which dominates in one kind of speech, since the political orator must prove that the course of action he recommends is expedient, the panegyrist must establish the nobility of whatever he wishes to praise, and the forensic speaker the justice (or injustice) of a particular course of action. Thus if the political orator speaks in favor of peace and against war he may start from the premise "good is what is chosen for its own sake" and go on to show that peace is chosen for its own sake (whereas war is at best elected because of things that result from it like power or revenues). In this way he would establish that peace is good. Or, if he prefers to use a more down-to-earth argument, he may choose a premise like "good is that of which the opposite is expedient to the enemy" and labor the point that in the prevailing situation war would be a boon for the other party.

These premises Aristotle compares to the "first principles" of demonstrative science. What he means is that a mathematician starts with say a proposition about the angles of an equilateral triangle and goes on to show that, because the triangle with which he happens to be concerned is equilateral, its angles must be as stated in the proposition. As Aristotle sees it, our speaker who makes his case for peace proceeds basically in the same manner as this mathematician.

But is it really necessary for a speaker in an assembly or before a jury to proceed in such strict and logical fashion? Aristotle would not maintain this. While deeply interested in the logical structure of arguments he yet allows in his *Rhetoric* modes of reasoning which in his treatise on formal logic he would brand as incorrect and inconclusive. Nor does he want the orator to bore his audience by pendantically conforming to the theory, i.e. by enunciating first one premise, then the other, and after that solemnly moving on to the conclusion. The presentation of an argument need not bring out its logical form. Even the chapters in which Aristotle collects premises with such painstaking care may in the end simply serve as an inventory of generally useful ideas that in some way or other can help the orator to shape and organize his facts. This would imply that the original meaning of the premise as a part of a syllogism fades from sight.

In his search for useful premises of this kind Aristotle must have been indefatigable. Besides those connected with the cardinal values—the good, the beautiful, and the just—he provides sets of others by which it may be proved that something is possible, or that it has happened, or will happen, or that of two good and expedient courses of action one is the better, of two crimes one worse than the other. He also draws up a list of particular things, each properly defined, that are good or expedient; he enumerates the major topics on which a political orator should be well informed; he goes into the kinds, the motives, the conditions of crimes. Indeed, when dealing with the province of the forensic orator his zeal for completeness seems to know no bounds. Not only does he take stock of the entire variety of people that are likely either to inflict or to suffer injustice; he also discourses on law and equity and when he comes to the question of motivation he refuses to be satisfied with anything short of a complete survey of the causes of human actions. There are, in all, seven causes, and the list includes items as different as external compulsion, accident, character, habit, calculation, and impulse. Yet perhaps even this list fails to cover the entire subject of revelant motives; perhaps additional factors should be taken into consideration. Would it not help,

Aristotle wonders, to study the differences between youth and old age and the differences of economic status in order to find out how they are reflected in the pattern of human actions? Fortunately however, these subjects are taken care of in another part of treatise (under the heading of "speaker's character"); the section on motives need not get entangled in them. Yet even so it does not come to an end before still another cause of human actions is taken up and treated in the most thoroughgoing fashion. This motivation is pleasure, and Aristotle's account of the causes and objects of pleasure is almost a little treatise in its own right; it goes far beyond what by the widest stretch of the imagination could be considered as relevant to pleadings in the law courts.

Almost everywhere the philosopher is at work, doing his job of defining, distinguishing, proving, generalizing, arguing, and deducing. Yet the philosopher happens to have a shrewd eye for human nature and he knows life—life in general and Greek life in particular. In fact, with regard to the content of these sections as distinct from their methods, the reader will often wonder whether Aristotle speaks as philosopher determined to uphold the true moral values at whatever cost and showing a noble indifference to practical necessities, or whether he has his eye on the practical situation, making concessions, sometimes small but at other times quite large. For the various sections differ considerably in this respect, and as the *Rhetoric* was not a "book" intended for publication but rather something like a professor's lecture notes which Aristotle used not once or twice but a good number of times and kept revising, it stands to reason that these differences in attitude reflect deeper changes in his approach to the subject. In a general way it is true that his sympathy for practical considerations—for "things as they are"—increased in the measure in which he outgrew the speculative and idealistic bent of his youth and the distance between him and Plato became larger; yet the greatest caution is needed in applying this guiding idea to individual sections of the work. Two observations may sharpen the reader's feeling for these differences in attitude and orientation. The goods of life that are set forth in Chapter V of Book I hold a middle position between a philosophical ethics and popular valuations; while consideration is shown for the man in the street (these sections often teach us more about the average Greek's "view of life" than the corresponding ones in the *Ethics*) it is nonetheless obvious that these are not the "goods" the knowledge of which would come in handy for a speaker in the political assembly. Clearly it is the philosopher who speaks here, descending a little, it is true, from the height of his sovereign position, yet still intent on enlightening us about the true goods. The other point to be noted is that in the same part of the work there is a curious wavering between the "good" and the "expedient." Which of the two does Aristotle really mean to set up as the goal towards which the political orator should direct his efforts? If Aristotle were writing as a philosopher the answer could not be in doubt: for the theorist, the ethicist, the Platonist, the "good" is the norm and end of all human action; and where would he find a comparable opportunity for reforming the less exalted outlook of the politicians? For neither can it be doubted that the politicians and the deliberative bodies of Aristotle's day were sufficiently realistic to think in terms of expediency rather than of "the good." Somehow Aristotle shirks the issue; here he deals with the "good," there with the "expedient," while at times he actually treats the concepts as identical—a curious attitude, yet characteristic of more than one section of this work, and not completely unknown to students of his other treatises.

No doubt there are sections in the *Rhetoric* where the touch of philosophy is light—so light indeed that one hardly feels it at all. Any orator with a minimum of experience knew by Aristotle's time that if statements made under torture supported his cause he must stress them to the utmost by insisting that there was no surer way of finding out the truth, while in the opposite case he must harp on the notorious unreliability of such statements, pointing out that unfortunate people will say anything in order to put an end to their agonies (though again on other occasions it must be emphasized that some keep up their lies even under torture). Such are the methods which the practitioners in the last three generations before Aristotle had developed for dealing with what he calls "non-technical proofs," to wit laws, witnesses, contracts, tortures, and oaths. Though these "proofs" are still important they no longer decide a law suit in the rather automatic fashion in which they did before argument and rational proof came into their own. As Aristotle says, these proofs have not to be "invented" but to be "used." And the philosopher, while not entirely abandoning his right to his own opinions and to somewhat wider perspectives, on the whole does little more than endorse the time-honored devices—not to say, tricks of the trade—which the experts "use" to their own advantage.

Another section where the philosopher is almost eclipsed and where the contact with practice is again very close is the second part of Book III. The teachers of rhetoric had for some time taught their pupils what to say in the various "parts of the speech" (proem, narration, proofs, etc.); they had shown them ways and means of securing the favor of their audience at the beginning of their speech, of setting forth the facts of the case convincingly, of meeting the opponent's argument, of counteracting his slander and the like. Aristotle follows in their path, though not without qualms and not without attempts to rise above their level. With his customary shrewdness, his knowledge of human nature, and his irony he identifies—usually in a few brief words—the psychological factors that must be taken into consideration; not seldom he points to the poets with their superb handling of comparable situations as models for the orator. Still he clearly follows where those before him had shown the way and it is hard to resist the conclusion that some passages are taken over, more or less verbatim, from the system of a rhetorician of Isocrates' school (presumably that of Theodectes, to whom Aristotle once in this book refers by name). Any reader may judge for himself how far Aristotle in this part of his *Rhetoric* has traveled from the noble and austere principles laid down in the first chapter of the work where proof—and nothing but proof—is said to be the concern of a genuine teacher of rhetoric.

CICERO AND QUINTILIAN ON RHETORIC
Lester Thonssen and A. Craig Baird

Interrelation of Greek and Roman Thinking

The Greeks gave us the basic principle of rhetoric. But the Romans and Graeco-Romans were highly skilled students whose penchant for organization and refinement of traditional lore asserted itself in their treatment of speechcraft. They may not have added much that was new, but they elaborated upon the previously determined tenets and placed them in patterns of somewhat sharper outline. Furthermore, the practical turn of the Roman mind insured the likelihood of certain departures from the philosophical point of view regarding rhetoric, to a more purely pragmatic, pedagogical development. This is most clearly shown in the treatises of Cicero, the orator speaking on his art, and in the writings of Quintilian, the teacher discoursing on methods of instruction.

Lester Thonssen and A. Craig Baird, *Speech Criticism—The Development of Standards for Rhetorical Appraisal.* Copyright 1948 by The Ronald Press Company.

Despite certain differences in emphasis and point of view between early Greek and Graeco-Roman writings on rhetoric, the latter quite naturally and uninterruptedly grows out of and blends with the former, so that the tradition of the subject is sustained in unbroken continuity. The following sections show how the basic postulates of Greek inquiry served as the substructure of Roman thinking.

The ad Herennium

The *Rhetorica ad Herennium,* sometimes ascribed to Cicero (106–43 B.C.), provides a pattern of the rhetorical system taught at Rome during the early days of Cicero. Perhaps published about 86 B.C., this treatise in four books is, according to Atkins, "the first work of real significance belonging to the first century B.C. . . ."[1]

Book I deals with the kinds of oratory and the parts of rhetoric.[2] Demonstrative, deliberative, and judicial oratory represent the types of causes that a speaker may consider. In order to carry out his assignment, an orator must deal with five aspects or parts of rhetoric: *inventio, dispositio, elocutio, memoria,* and *pronuntiatio.* Each of these five parts can be acquired by an orator through art, imitation, and practice.

An orator's invention is revealed in six sections of an address: *exordium, narratio, divisio, confirmatio, confutatio,* and *conclusio.*

Three kinds of causes, or *constitutio causae,* are mentioned: those of fact (*coniecturalis*), interpretation (*legitima*), and right or wrong (*iuridicialis*). Under the heading of the status, or state, these concepts are discussed in a later section.

Book II treats of invention as it relates to forensic oratory; Book III, as it relates to deliberative and demonstrative speaking. *Dispositio, memoria,* and *pronuntiatio* also receive consideraion.

The last book of the *ad Herennium* is devoted to *elocutio,* or style, and takes up about half of the entire treatise. A. S. Wilkins remarks that this section is of interest, not only because it is the first work on the subject in Latin, but also because it provides an abundance and excellence of illustration.

The author lists three kinds of style—*gravis, mediocris,* and *attenuata.* The general requirements of the speaker's language are elegance, or word choice; composition, or the union of words; and

---

[1] J. W. H. Atkins. *Literary Criticism in Antiquity.* London, 1934. II, 16.
[2] Cf. Augustus S. Wilkins. *M. Tulli Ciceronis De Oratore.* 3rd ed. Oxford, 1895. I, 56–64.

dignity, or adornment. To further the realization of the last requisite, the *ad Herennium* provides a long list of figures (*verborum exornatio* and *sententiarum exornatio*).

The Classical Divisions of Rhetoric

The parts or canons of rhetoric set forth in the *ad Herennium* represent the broad divisions of the whole subject; in many respects, they constitute the basic pattern of all theoretical and critical investigations into the art and practice of speaking.

According to the classical tradition, all rhetoric is divided into five parts: invention, disposition, elocution, memory, and delivery. This fivefold division is fairly standard in all major works after Aristotle until the eighteenth century. Minor changes in the meaning of the terms are developed in various treatises, but the pattern remains the same until the time of George Campbell, when *memory* practically drops out of the analysis.

These parts have distinctive functions. They are not only the concepts with which an orator must deal and which he must master in order to deliver an effective speech; they are also the aspects of the delivered oration which the critic, viewing the finished speech as a creative product, examines and evaluates.

The exact origin of the fivefold plan is in doubt. The first division of speech materials was probably into substance and form; next, into invention and arrangement. But the fivefold division is hard to trace.

The Inventive Aspect.—Invention involves the attempt on the part of the orator, as Cicero says, "to find out what he should say . . . ." It is an investigative undertaking, embracing a survey and forecast of the subject and a search for the arguments suitable to the given rhetorical effort. As Baldwin remarks in his commentary, it refers to "the investigation, analysis, and grasp of the subject matter." [3] Thus certain writers—Aristotle among them—give more attention to invention than to the other parts of rhetoric. This is done on the ground, and perhaps properly, that the content is the most important part of a speech.

Without proposing to categorize the constituents of rhetorical theory, we may say in general that the concept of invention includes the entire investigative undertaking, the idea of the *status,* and the modes of persuasion—logical, emotional, and ethical—in all of their complex interrelations.

[3] Charles Sears Baldwin. *Ancient Rhetoric and Poetic.* New York, 1924. p. 43.

Disposition of Materials.—Disposition covers the concept of arrangement, of orderly planning and movement of the whole idea. Although the treatment of it differs within a narrow range among the several treatises, the general meaning is twofold: the appreciation of a plan for the speech as a whole, and the development of the specific parts of the speech, such as the exordium, narration, proof, peroration, and whatever other divisions the authors specify. Baldwin is correct in saying that what is noticeably missing, not only in Aristotle's treatment of disposition, but in the other works of the classical tradition as well, "is some definite inculcation of consecutiveness." [4]

In some treatises, ancient and modern, invention and disposition are treated under a common head—the assumption being that the orderly arrangement of the materials constitutes an essential part of the inventive process.

The Stylistic Feature.—The third part of rhetoric was originally called *elocutio,* and it referred specifically to style. It embraced the concept of expression in language, resulting, basically, from the choice of words and their arrangement or composition. Among the ancient rhetoricians, the study of words and composition led to an analysis of the distinguishing marks of the kinds of style. Accordingly, in Cicero's *Orator,* to name but one treatise, the plain, the moderate, and the grand style are described and analyzed.

The Memory in Rhetoric.—*Memoria,* the fourth part of rhetoric, does not receive systematic treatment in Aristotle's *Rhetoric.* Cicero, Quintilian, and other rhetoricians give it consideration. However, when we come to the major works of the eighteenth century, we note that this canon has been dropped. In recent volumes it receives only incidental treatment, although Lionel Crocker's *Public Speaking for College Students* devotes a complete chapter to "The Memory in Speech."

In the older sense, memory was a fairly comprehensive concept, embracing the speaker's mastery of all his material in sequential order. "Why should I remark," says Cicero,

> . . . how excellent a thing it is to retain the instructions which you have received with the cause, and the opinion which you have formed upon it? to keep all your thoughts upon it fixed in your mind, all your arrangement of language marked out there? to listen to him from whom you receive any information, or to him to whom you have to reply,

[4] *Ibid.,* p. 34

with such power of retention, that they seem not to have poured their discourse into your ears, but to have engraven it on your mental tablet? [5]

That Cicero regarded memory as an important part of the orator's equipment is further revealed in his criticism of the eminent speakers. He censures Curio for his "extremely treacherous" memory, saying

. . . after he had divided his subject into three general heads, he would sometimes, in the course of speaking, either add a fourth, or omit the third. In a capital trial, in which I had pleaded for Titinia, the daughter of Cotta, when he attempted to reply to me in defense of Servius Naevius, he suddenly forgot every thing he intended to say, and attributed it to the pretended witchcraft and magic artifices of Titinia.[6]

In commenting on Hippias' contribution to rhetoric, and on the subsequent disappearance of the canon of memory, Bromley Smith says:

With the passing of the years . . . the notion that the memory of orators can be trained by systematic devices has almost disappeared. Memory itself remains and is highly esteemed, yet it has lost its ancient importance. Long ago Plato foresaw this when he remarked that the invention of writing by the Egyptian God, Theuth, caused learners to trust external written characters rather than themselves. That he was right may be judged from the number of speakers who read their addresses. Hippias, however, belonged to the old school; he believed he could train the memories of the future statesmen. His labors must have had a measure of success, sufficient indeed to encourage others. Since his days thousands have followed his idea, like a will-o'-the-wisp, through the bogs of discipline. At last sinking below their depth, they have disappeared, leaving only a few bubbles to remind the world that Memory, 'the warder of the mind,' was once a canon of rhetoric.[7]

Delivery.—The last part of rhetoric—*pronuntiatio*—is the art of delivery. Its constituent elements are vocal utterance and bodily action. From Aristotle to the present day all systematic treatises on rhetoric have given some space to this canon.

A Great Orator's Conception of His Art

A Functional Approach to Speechmaking.—"The Romans," said W. S. Teuffel, "were naturally well qualified for oratory by their acute

[5] *De Oratore.* Trans. by J. S. Watson. Philadelphia, 1897. II, lxxxvii.
[6] *Brutus.* LX.
[7] "Hippias and a Lost Canon of Rhetoric." *Quarterly Journal of Speech Education,* 12:144 (June, 1926).

intellect, their love of order and their Italian vivacity, tempered with Roman gravity." [8] They were practical people; so it is natural that their works on speaking should emphasize the functional aspects of the art. Cicero represented this practical inclination at its best. "The most eminent orator of Roman civilization, he wrote more than any other orator has ever written on rhetoric; and historically he has been more than any other an ideal and model." [9]

While discussing the efforts of the philosophers—Aristotle and Theophrastus included—as writers on rhetoric, Cicero inquires whether it would not be advantageous to consider the art of speaking from the point of view of the practicing orator *and* the philosopher. Surely the orator would be able to "set forth with full power and attraction" those same topics of virtue, equity, laws, and the like, with something more than the "tame and bloodless phraseology" of the philosophers. Accordingly, Cicero would interest himself in the development of an orator so "accomplished and complete" that he would be able to "speak on all subjects with variety and copiousness." [10]

Cicero tried, as his works show, to restore rhetoric to something of its earlier scope and vitality. As Atkins indicates,[11] he was "protesting against the narrowing of the province" of the speaking art, hoping to restore rhetoric as a "system of general culture" which would train men to write and speak competently on all possible subjects. In this effort Cicero was influenced and guided by the doctrines of Isocrates whom he regarded as the "father of eloquence."

Cicero was an eclectic. With the possible exception of the *Brutus*, the contents of all his works originate in the contributions of his predecessors and contemporaries. However, he embellished the old, saying it so much better that it took on a character of finality.

The Substance of the *De Oratore*.—*De Oratore* is Cicero's most important book on rhetorical theory. Like many treatises of its kind, it is in dialogue form, with the celebrated orators Crassus and Antonius playing the major roles; and Scaevola, Catulus, Cotta, Sulpicius, Caesar, and Rufus serving in a minor way as interlocutors.

In Book I Crassus comments on the qualifications of the Ideal Orator, while in Book III he develops the Ciceronian conception of oratorical style. Antonius, serving as the protagonist in Book II, discourses on

---

[8] *Teuffel's History of Roman Literature*. Trans. and ed. by George C. W. Warr. London, 1891. I, 64.
[9] Baldwin. *Op. cit.*, p. 37.
[10] *De Oratore*. I, xiii.
[11] Atkins. *Op. cit.*, II, 23.

invention and disposition. Incidental remarks on humor are also introduced by Caesar.

Book I of *De Oratore*.—In the first book we find, reminiscent of
Isocrates and Aristotle, a development of the theme that to be successful the orator must conform to high and exacting qualifications. He
must be a man of great learning.

> A knowledge of a vast number of things is necessary, without which
> volubility of words is empty and ridiculous; speech itself is to be
> formed, not merely by choice, but by careful construction of words;
> and all the emotions of the mind, which nature has given to man, must
> be intimately known; for all the force and art of speaking must be
> employed in allaying or exciting the feelings of those who listen. To
> this must be added a certain portion of grace and wit, learning worthy
> of a well-bred man, and quickness and brevity in replying as well as
> attacking, accompanied with a refined decorum and urbanity. Besides,
> the whole of antiquity and a multitude of examples is to be kept in the
> memory; nor is the knowledge of laws in general, or of the civil law
> in particular, to be neglected. And why need I add any remarks on
> delivery itself, which is to be ordered by action of body, by gesture, by
> look, and by modulation and variation of the voice, the great power of
> which, alone and in itself, the comparatively trivial art of actors and the
> stage proves, on which though all bestow their utmost labor to form
> their look, voice, and gesture, who knows not how few there are, and
> have ever been, to whom we can attend with patience? What can I
> say of that repository for all things, the memory, which, unless it be the
> keeper of the matter and words that are the fruits of thought and in-
> vention, all the talents of the orator, we see, though they be of the
> highest degree of excellence, will be of no avail? Let us then cease
> to wonder what is the cause of the scarcity of good speakers, since
> eloquence results from all those qualifications . . . .[12]

Cicero shortly after sets forth his oft-quoted remark that the "proper
concern of an orator, . . . is language of power and elegance accom-
modated to the feelings and understandings of mankind."[13]

We note, then, that Cicero, through his mouthpiece, Crassus, insists
upon the orator's having virtually universal knowledge and skill. In
the dialogue, Antonius holds that somewhat less learning is necessary,
although he, too, urges broad familiarity with the field of knowledge.
But he insists upon a more *intensive* training leading to the acquisition
of oratorical excellence. Antonius would develop the orator's natural

[12] *De Oratore.* I, v.
[13] *Ibid.,* I, xii.

talents and capacities for oratory, even if his intellectual control over
the field of learning were somewhat more moderate than Crassus
believed essential. Baldwin feels that, in a sense, both Crassus and
Antonius are right. "Normally rhetoric is both extensive and intensive,
both a comprehensive study of life and a specific art, even as the
means of persuasion are both extrinsic and intrinsic." [14]
    In this book Crassus also is made to delineate the five parts of
rhetoric when he announces:

> If, therefore, any one desires to define and comprehend the whole and
> peculiar power of an orator, that man, in my opinion, will be an orator,
> worthy of so great a name, who whatever subject comes before him,
> and requires rhetorical elucidation, can speak on it judiciously, in set
> form, elegantly, and from memory, and with a certain dignity of
> action.[15]

However, the principal reference at this point is to *invention*.

The Second Book.—Book II treats mainly of invention and disposition, and with particular emphasis, of course, upon these concepts in
their relation to forensic oratory. Care is taken to point out that the
orator's painstaking investigation of the facts is indispensable to inventive skill. The accomplished orator will conduct research before taking
the platform, will "take one time for premeditation, and another for
speaking."
    Though not original, Cicero's treatment of the *status*—determination
of the character and issues of the case—is important to the study of
rheorical theory. He remarks:

> There are in all, therefore, three sorts of matters, which may possibly
> fall under doubt and discussion; what is now done, what has been done,
> or what is to be done; what the nature of a thing is, or how it should
> be designated; for as to the question which some Greeks add, whether
> a thing be rightly done, it is wholly included in the inquiry, what the
> nature of the thing is.[16]

These are frequently called states of conjecture, definition, and quality,
respectively. Cicero remarks that these considerations apply to all
types of oratory in which dispute centers—forensic, deliberative, and
panegyric.
    The objects of discourse are said to be: "That we prove what we
maintain to be true; that we conciliate those who hear; that we pro-

[14] *Op. cit.*, p. 46
[15] *De Oratore*. I, xv.
[16] *Ibid.*, II, xxvi.

duce in their minds whatever feeling our cause may require." [17] The whole business of speaking, Cicero allows, rests upon these things for success in persuasion.

Cicero's treatment of pathetic and ethical proof adds little, if anything, that is new. He indicates that "mankind makes far more determinations through hatred, or love, or desire, or anger, or grief, or joy, or hope, or fear, or error, or some other affection of mind, than from regard to truth, or any settled maxim, or principle of right, or judicial form, or adherence to the laws." [18] He therefore comments on the way to make audience analyses, to move people to various emotional states, and to make the speaker's character aid in the persuasive undertaking.

As to arrangement of speech materials, Cicero offers little that is new. He indicates that two methods may be observed: "one, which the nature of causes dictates; the other, which is suggested by the orator's judgment and prudence." [19] The plan of organization he then describes is more detailed than Aristotle's, the difference resulting largely, however, from the fact that he is making an adjustment to forensic speaking.

Memory, as a distinct part of rhetoric, receives attention in Book II. Cicero opens his discourse by recalling the traditional incident which presumably prompted Simonides to "invent" the art of memory:

> For they relate, that when Simonides was at Crannon in Thessaly, at an entertainment given by Scopas, a man of rank and fortune, and had recited a poem which he had composed in his praise, in which, for the sake of embellishment, after the manner of the poets, there were many particulars introduced concerning Castor and Pollux, Scopas told Simonides, with extraordinary meanness, that he would pay him half the sum which he had agreed to give for the poem, and that he might ask the remainder, if he thought proper, from his Tyndaridae, to whom he had given an equal share of praise. A short time after, they say that a message was brought in to Simonides, to desire him to go out, as two youths were waiting at the gate who earnestly wished him to come forth to them; when he arose, went forth, and found nobody. In the meantime the apartment in which Scopas was feasting fell down, and he himself, and his company, were overwhelmed and buried in the ruins; and when their friends were desirous to inter their remains, but could not possibly distinguish one from another, so much crushed were the bodies, Simonides is said, from his recollection of the place

[17] *Ibid.*, II, xxix.
[18] *Ibid.*, II, xlii.
[19] *Ibid.*, II, lxxvi.

in which each had sat, to have given satisfactory direction for their interment. Admonished by this occurrence, he is reported to have discovered, that it is chiefly order that gives distinctness to memory; and that by those, therefore, who would improve this part of the understanding, certain places must be fixed upon, and that of the things which they desire to keep in memory, symbols must be conceived in the mind, and ranged, as it were, in those places; thus the order of places would preserve the order of things, and the symbols of the things would denote the things themselves; so that we should use the places as waxen tablets, and the symbols as letters.[20]

Cicero then observes that those things "are the most strongly fixed in our minds, which are communicated to them, and imprinted upon them, by the senses . . ." And for the orator, the "memory of things is the proper business . . ." "This we may be enabled to impress on our ourselves by the creation of imaginary figures, aptly arranged, to represent particular heads, so that we may recollect thoughts by images, and their order by place." [21]

The Third Book.—In addition to restating the theme on the union of rhetoric and philosophy, the last book of *De Oratore* considers style and delivery.

The section on style deals chiefly with word choice, composition, and the various ornaments of speech. Cicero's point of view is clearly stated in this passage:

> A speech, then, is to be made becoming in its kind, with a sort of complexion and substance of its own; for that it be weighty, agreeable, savoring of erudition and liberal knowledge, worthy of admiration, polished, having feeling and passion in it, as far as is required, are qualities not confined to particular members, but are apparent in the whole body; but that it be, as it were, strewed with flowers of language and thought, is a property which ought not to be equally diffused throughout the whole speech, but at such intervals, that, as in the arrangement of ornaments, there may be certain remarkable and luminous objects disposed here and there.[22]

Baldwin looks upon Cicero's twenty chapters on style as a "brilliant instance of what the ancients meant by amplification. Logically they do little more than iterate the truism that style is inseparable from substance; but actually they make the truism live." [23]

[20] *Ibid.*, II, lxxxvi.
[21] *Ibid.*, II, lxxxviii.
[22] *Ibid.*, III, xxv.
[23] *Op. cit.*, p. 55.

Finally, Book III of the *De Oratore* sets forth a general theory of delivery, that phase of oratory which Cicero said had "the sole and supreme power." Without effective delivery, "a speaker of the highest mental capacity can be held in no esteem, while one of moderate abilities, with this qualification, may surpass even those of the highest talent." [24] Cicero comments on the use of gestures and bodily action, and on the necessity of varying the tones in vocal expression.

It may be said that, while constructing the pattern for the Ideal Orator, Cicero kept constantly in mind the practical requirements of one who proposed to play "the part of a true Roman citizen in the conflicts of the assembly and the law courts."

The *Orator* and a Conception of Style.—Cicero's *Orator* is less comprehensive than the *De Oratore*, being devoted almost wholly to style. John E. Sandys says the purpose of it was to "meet the wishes of Brutus" and "to win over Brutus to his own side in the controversy with the Atticists . . . ." Another purpose, surely, was "to delineate the ideal orator." And it is evident that "the living image of his own oratorical greatness forms the foundation on which he builds his ideal fabric. His own speeches supply him with examples of every variety of oratorical excellence . . . ." [25] Baldwin remarks, apropos of the *Orator*, that few men "writing on style have shown in their own styles so much precision and charm."

The Doctrine of the Three Styles.—In the *Orator*, which Sandys says belongs to the "aesthetics of oratory," Cicero classifies and describes the three kinds of style: the plain, the moderate, and the grand. These types arise from the orator's attempt to prove, to please, and to move; and the skilled orator should be able to do all three.

Regarding the plain style, Cicero says:

> . . . we must give a sketch of the man whom some consider the only orator of the Attic style.
>
> He is a gentle, moderate man, imitating the usual customs, differing from those who are not eloquent in fact rather than in any of his opinions. Therefore those who are his hearers, even though they themselves have no skill in speaking, still feel confident that they could speak in that manner. For the subtlety of his address appears easy of imitation to a person who ventures on an opinion, but nothing is less easy when he comes to try it; for although it is not a style of any

[24] *De Oratore.* III, lv.
[25] John Edwin Sandys. *M. Tulli Ciceronis ad M. Brutum Orator.* Cambridge, 1885. pp. lviii, lxiv.

extraordinary vigour, still it has some juice, so that even though it is
not endowed with the most extreme power, it is still . . . in perfect
health. First of all, then, let us release it from the fetters of rhythm.
For there is, as you know, a certain rhythm to be observed by an orator,
proceeding on a regular system; but though it must be attended to in
another kind of oratory, it must be entirely abandoned in this. This
must be a sort of easy style, and yet not utterly without rules, so that
it may seem to range at freedom, not to wander about licentiously. He
should also guard against appearing to cement his words together; for
the hiatus formed by a concourse of open vowels has something soft
about it, and indicates a not unpleasing negligence, as if the speaker
were anxious more about the matter than the manner of his speech.
But as to other points, he must take care, specially as he is allowed
more license in these two,—I mean the rounding of his periods, and the
combination of his words; for those narrow and minute details are not
to be dealt with carelessly . . . .

The language will be pure and Latin; it will be arranged plainly and
clearly, and great care will be taken to see what is becoming . . . .

There will be a moderate use of what I may call oratorical furniture;
for there is to a certain degree what I may call our furniture, consisting
of ornaments partly of things and partly of words . . . .

He will have besides this, action, not tragic, nor suited to the stage,
but he will move his body in a moderate degree, trusting a great deal
to his countenance; not in such a way as people call making faces, but
in a manner sufficient to show in a gentlemanlike manner in what sense
he means what he is saying to be understood.

Now in this kind of speech sallies of wit are admissible, and they
carry perhaps only too much weight in an oration. Of them there are
two kinds,—facetiousness and raillery,—and the orator will employ
both; but he will use the one in relating anything neatly, and the other
in darting ridicule on his adversaries.[26]

As for the moderate style, it is

> . . . more fertile, and somewhat more forcible than this simple style of
> which we have been speaking; but nevertheless tamer than the highest
> class of oratory . . . In this kind there is but little vigour, but there is
> the greatest possible quantity of sweetness; for it is fuller than the
> plain style, but more plain than that other which is highly ornamented
> and copious.
>
> Every kind of ornament in speaking is suitable to this style; and in
> this kind of oratory there is a great deal of sweetness. It is a style in
> which many men among the Greeks have been eminent; but Demetrius

[26] *Orator.* From *The Orations of Marcus Tullius Cicero.* Trans. by C. D.
Yonge. London, 1852. IV, 403–407, *passim.*

Phalereus, in my opinion, has surpassed all the rest; and while his oratory proceeds in calm and tranquil flow, it receives brilliancy from numerous metaphors and borrowed expressions, like stars. . . .

The same kind of oratory (I am speaking of the moderate and temperate kind) admits of all sorts of figures of expressions, and of many also of ideas. Discussions of wide application and extensive learning are explained in it, and common topics are treated without any impetuosity. In a word, orators of this class usually come from the schools of philosophers, and unless the more vigorous orator, whom I am going to speak of presently, is at hand to be compared with them, the one whom I am now describing will be approved of.[27]

The orator who uses the grand style

. . . is the sublime, copious, dignified, ornate speaker, in whom there is the greatest amount of grace. For he it is, out of admiration for whose ornamented style and copiousness of language nations have allowed eloquence to obtain so much influence in states; but it was only this eloquence, which is borne along in an impetuous course, and with a mighty noise, which all men looked up to, and admired, and had no idea that they themselves could possibly attain to. It belongs to this eloquence to deal with men's minds, and to influence them in every imaginable way. This is the style which sometimes forces its way into and sometimes steals into the senses; which implants new opinions in men, and eradicates others which have been long established. But there is a vast difference between this kind of orator and the preceding ones. A man who has laboured at the subtle and acute style, in order to speak cunningly and cleverly, and who has had no higher aim, if he has entirely attained his object, is a great orator, if not a very great one; he is far from standing on slippery ground, and if he once gets a firm footing, is in no danger of falling. But the middle kind of orator, whom I have called moderate and temperate, if he has only arranged all his own forces to his satisfaction, will have no fear of any doubtful or uncertain chances of oratory; and even if at any time he should not be completely successful, which may often be the case, still he will be in no great danger, for he cannot fall far. But this orator of ours, whom we consider the first of orators, dignified, vehement, and earnest, if this is the only thing for which he appears born, or if this is the only kind of oratory to which he applies himself, and if he does not combine his copiousness of diction with those other two kinds of oratory, is very much to be despised. For the one who speaks simply, inasmuch as he speaks with shrewdness and sense, is a wise man; the one who employs the middle style is agreeable; but this most copious speaker, if he is nothing else, appears scarcely in his senses. For a

[27] *Ibid.,* IV, 407–409, *passim.*

man who can say nothing with calmness, nothing with gentleness; who seems ignorant of all arangement and definition and distinctness, and regardless of wit, especially when some of his causes require to be treated in that manner entirely, and others in a great degree; if he does not prepare the ears of his hearers before he begins to work up the case in an inflammatory style, he seems like a madman among people in their senses, or like a drunken man among sober men.[28]

Baldwin observes that the philosophy of such a classification, whatever its origin, "has been vicious as pedagogy." "Historically, the trail of the three styles has been baneful. For inculcating style perhaps the least fruitful means is classification."[29]

One of Aristotle's pupils, Theophrastus, is usually credited with being the formulator of the threefold classification of style. In Latin literature, the *ad Herennium* furnishes the first statement of the doctrine. That Aristotle recognized a distinction among types of literary expression is evident from several of his remarks in the *Rhetoric*. In the third book, he remarks that "to each kind of rhetoric is adapted a peculiar style," and goes on to show how written and oral style differ in that the former is more "precise" while the latter "partakes more of declamation."[30] Furthermore, he implies throughout that the different types of speaking deliberative, forensic, and epideictic call for different styles. However, he does not classify the styles according to the divisions which we have just discussed. Later theorists, it may be added, sometimes added a fourth kind. Philodemus evidently conceived of a fourfold classification; and Demetrius added the "forcible" type to the original three.

The doctrine of the three styles permeates the literature of rhetoric, either through open statement or through implication. "In the sphere of oratory," J. F. D'Alton remarks,

> . . . the division became important, when it was adapted to the theory of the 'officia oratoris,' according to which it was the orator's duty to instruct, delight, and move his audience. The Plain style, with its predominant qualities of clearness and logical subtlety, was best suited to the purposes of instruction. When the Middle style became identified with the 'genus floridum,' with its characteristics of smoothness and charm, it was naturally assigned the task of giving pleasure to, or winning over an audience. The orator, however, could point to his greatest achievements as effected through the medium of the Grand

[28] *Ibid.*, IV, 409–410.
[29] *Op. cit.*, pp. 56–57.
[30] *Rhetoric.* Trans. by Theodore Buckley. London, 1883. pp. 246–247.

style, which was calculated to play at will upon the feelings of an assembly. Cicero and Quintilian considered this style to be supreme, just as they considered that to stir the emotions was the highest function of the orator.[31]

The necessary qualities of a good style, as Cicero interpreted Theophrastus' teaching, were correctness, clearness, appropriateness, and ornament. Cicero did not, however, ascribe ornamentation to the Plain style, that being reserved in part for the Middle, and wholly for the Grand. Accordingly, we note that the so-called "virtues," or essential qualities, were not necessarily applied to all styles; instead, they were often assigned to particular styles for which they seemed uniquely suitable.

Cicero's Treatment of Rhythm.—Cicero's theory of oratorical rhythm derives largely from Gorgias and Isocrates. Commenting on the nature of his doctrine, he says:

> Let oratory then be, . . . mingled and regulated with regard to rhythm; not prosaic, nor on the other hand sacrificed wholly to rhythm; composed chiefly of the paeon, . . . with many of the other feet which he passes over intermingled with it.
>
> But what feet ought to be mingled with others, like purple, must be now explained; and we must also show to what kind of speech each sort of foot and rhythm is the best adapted. For the iambic is most frequent in those orations which are composed in a humble and lowly style; but the paeon is suited to a more dignified style; and the dactyl to both. Therefore, in a varied and long-continued speech these feet should be mingled together and combined. And in this way the fact of the orator aiming at pleasing the senses, and the careful attempt to round off the speech, will be the less visible, and they will at all times be less apparent if we employ dignified expressions and sentiments. For the hearers observe these two things, and think them agreeable: (I mean, expressions and sentiments.) And while they listen to them with admiring minds, the rhythm escapes their notice; and even if it were wholly wanting they would still be delighted with those other things . . . .
>
> Accordingly, if the question is raised as to what is the rhythm of an oration, it is every sort of rhythm; but one sort is better and more suitable than another. If the question is, what is the place of this rhythm? it is in every portion of the words. If you ask where it has arisen; it has arisen from the pleasure of the ears. If the principle is sought on which the words are to be arranged; that will be explained

[31] J. F. D'Alton. *Roman Literary Theory and Criticism.* London, 1931. pp. 74-75.

in another place, because that relates to practice, . . . If the question is, when; always: if, in what place, it consists in the entire connexion of the words. If we are asked, What is the circumstance which causes pleasure? we reply, that it is the same as in verse; the method of which is determined by art; but the ears themselves define it by their own silent sensations, without any reference to principles of art.[32]

The observations on the preceding pages suggest that, all in all, the *Orator* is to be regarded as one of Cicero's important works. It is, in the opinion of Torsten Petersson, "Cicero's final statement not only of his oratorical idea but also of what he conceived himself to have attained." [33]

Other Rhetorical Treatises.—Among Cicero's other rhetorical works, excluding the *Brutus* and *On the Best Style of Orators* which may more appropriately engage our attention later, are *On Topics, Dialogue Concerning Oratorical Partitions,* and *On Rhetorical Invention.*

On Topics is largely an abstract of Aristotle's treatment of the same subject. Cicero defines a topic as "the seat of an argument, and . . . an argument is a reason which causes men to believe a thing which would otherwise be doubtful.[34] The sources and types of topics receive a fairly full measure of analysis.

A Dialogue Concerning Oratorical Partitions includes a brief and superficial discussion between Cicero and his son on the elements of the speaking situation—orator, speech, and subject—and on the parts of an oration—opening, narration, confirmation, and peroration.

On Rhetorical Invention, written when Cicero was about twenty-one years of age, demonstrates the truth of a remark found in the same work: "of those who are worthy of fame or recollection, there is no one who appears either to have said nothing well, or everything admirably." [35] Indeed, this is no consummate statement of the art of rhetoric, although it does reveal Cicero's early enthusiasm for oratory and, in a juvenile sort of way, his early mastery of many of its details. Only two of the four books remain. In later years, Cicero himself renounced the whole work as being "scarcely worthy of my present standing in life." His treatment of what Wilbur S. Howell calls the

---

[32] *Orator.* IV, 442–445, *passim.*
[33] Torsten Petersson. *Cicero: A Biography.* Berkeley, Calif., 1919. p. 442.
[34] *On Topics.* In *The Orations of Marcus Tullius Cicero.* Trans. by C. D. Yonge. London, 1919. IV, 460.
[35] *On Rhetorical Invention.* In *ibid.* IV, 309.

"Positions of Argument" is, however, important to rhetorical theory. Says Howell:

> Both in *De Inventione* and the *Rhetorica ad Herennium*, analysis and synthesis are specific procedures designed on the one hand to yield, and on the other to employ, arguments and appeals which meet the severest tests of relevance and coherence. Each book is important to us because it gives expression to a precise intellectual method contrived to render purposeful the speaker's search for the natural divisions and the underlying unity of his speech.[36]

Cicero's contributions, in general, are less concise than Aristotle's *Rhetoric;* they are given more fully to the encouragement in the orator of copiousness in language; but they are developed more consistently from the point of view of the orator himself.

Pedagogical Inquiry into Rhetoric

". . . The premier teacher of imperial rhetoric and the greatest Latin authority upon education"—that is J. Wight Duff's [37] estmate of Quintilian who, about 95 A.D., brought out the truly monumental *Institutes of Oratory*, or the Teaching of Rhetoric. Like Cicero, Quintilian was erudite in an eclectic sort of way; in the *Institutes* he reveals a remarkably wide familiarity with and deep appreciation of the Greek and Latin writers. Living during the so-called Silver Age of Latin life, about 14 to 138 A.D., when, as Duff indicates, the "main clue to the literary qualities is to be found in education, and particularly in rhetorical education," Quintilian preserved much of the classical tradition and integrity of rhetoric. He did this at a time when rhetoric was no longer a powerful instrument in public affairs; when it was no longer a severe discipline, devoid of exhibitionism, for training the average man for active citizenship.

The Point of View in the *Institutes*.—On the side of rhetorical theory, there is relatively little in the *Institutes* of an original character. Because most of what Quintilian sets down on the side of systematic rhetoric has been said before, we shall confine our summary to those aspects of the *Institutes* which enlarge the conception of theoretical speechcraft; and we shall omit most of the pedagogical details which, though interesting and significant, are not germane to this inquiry.

[36] Wilbur Samuel Howell. "The Positions of Argument: An Historical Examination." In *Papers in Rhetoric*. Donald C. Bryant, ed. St. Louis, 1940. p. 9.
[37] J. Wright Duff. *A Literary History of Rome in the Silver Age.* New York, 1927. p. 387.

Quintilian sets out to form the Perfect Orator who, in his words, "cannot exist unless as a good man." The orator conforming to his standards is, therefore, the good man speaking well.

> Since an orator, then, is a good man, and a good man cannot be conceived to exist without virtuous inclinations, and virtue, though it receives certain impulses from nature, requires notwithstanding to be brought to maturity by instruction, the orator must above all things study *morality*, and must obtain a thorough knowledge of all that is just and honorourable, without which no one can either be a good man or an able speaker.[38]

Quintilian's conception of the orator as a good man would alone tend to refute the charge of insincerity against the *Institutes* voiced by a critic who called it a treatise on "Lying as a Fine Art for Those Fully Conscious of Their Own Rectitude." [39]

The formation of this perfect orator is not to be left to the philosophers; instead, the orator shall receive the necessary "excellence of mind" through rhetorical education. "I cannot admit," Quintilian observes, "that the principles of moral and honourable conduct are . . . to be left to the philosophers . . . ." Further in the discourse, he remarks:

> As to the objection which some make, that it is the business of *philosophy* to discourse of what is good, useful, and just, it makes nothing against me; for when they say a philosopher, they mean a good man; and why then should I be surprised that an orator, whom I consider also to be a good man, should discourse upon the same subjects? especially when I have shown, . . . that philosophers have taken possession of this province because it was abandoned by the orators, a province which had always belonged to oratory, so that the philosophers are rather trespassing upon our ground.[40]

Hence, he voices what Colson calls "the age-long antithesis between rhetoric and philosophy." Colson also indicates that

> Quintilian's view of the superiority of the 'rhetor' to the philosopher is clearly reflected in two events of the time. The first of these is the endowment of rhetoric by Vespasian. The other is the expulsion of the philosophers from Rome about A.D. 94. The latter, whatever its other causes may have been, was certainly from one point of view a triumph for Quintilian's educational views.[41]

[38] *Institutes of Oratory.* Trans. by J. S. Watson. London, 1856. XII, ii, 1.
[39] F. H. Colson. *M. Fabii Quintiliani Institutionis Oratoriae Liber I.* Cambridge, 1924. p. xxviii.
[40] *Institutes.* II, xxi, 12–13.
[41] *Op. cit.*, p. xxiv–xxv.

The Use of Rules.—While Quintilian respected rules in rhetoric, he did not allow them to interfere with the common-sense principles of speech preparation. He advocated a flexibility of usage, observing that "one great quality in an orator is discretion, because he must turn his thoughts in various directions, according to the different bearings of his subject." [42] A forensic orator, for instance, should, in his pleadings, "keep two things in view, *what is becoming,* and *what is expedient;* but it is frequently *expedient,* and sometimes *becoming,* to make some deviations from the regular and settled order . . . ." [43] Quintilian says "rhetoric would be a very easy and small matter, if it could be included in one short body of rules, but rules must generally be altered to suit the nature of each individual case, the time, the occasion, and necessity itself . . . ." [44]

A Conception of the Status.—The plan of the *Institutes* is based upon Quintilian's acceptance of the fivefold division of the art of rhetoric: invention, disposition, elocution, memory, and delivery; [45] of the threefold classification of the types of oratory: deliberative, forensic, and panegyric; [46] and of the threefold analysis of the speaker's object or purpose: to inform, to move, and to please. [47]

A feature of Quintilian's treatment of invention which differs in scope and detail from that of many of his predecessors is that of the *status,* or *state of a cause.* The concept of the *status,* or the location of a center of argument, finds its first formal embodiment in the *ad Herennium* and in Cicero's *On Invention.* This concept is among the most important contributions of the Latin writers to rhetorical theory. By elevating the study of invention, and by providing the speaker with methods by which to find, evaluate, and use his ideas on a given case, this doctrine exercised a profound influence upon subsequent theory and practice in public speaking and debating.

After examining the views adopted by previous writers on the subject, Quintilian thinks it best "to regard that as the *state of the cause* which is the strongest point in it, and on which the whole matter chiefly turns." [48] "Status," Baldwin comments, "meaning the essential character of the case as it appeared to preliminary survey of all the

---

[42] *Institutes.* II, xiii, 2.
[43] *Ibid.,* II, xiii, 7.
[44] *Ibid.,* II, xiii, 2.
[45] *Ibid.,* III, iii.
[46] *Ibid.,* III, iv.
[47] *Ibid.,* III, v.
[48] *Ibid.,* III, vi, 21.

material and all the bearings, had come to denote a uniform system of determining that essential character by leading questions." [49] Through the medium of the status, therefore, the investigator or orator was able to find out what the body of material in the case meant.

Quintilian discusses two general states—the legal and the ratiocinatory. The former has many species, "as laws are numerous, and have various forms." The latter includes the status of conjecture or fact, the status of definition, and the status of quality.

These general states are, then, of two kinds: those depending upon legality, and those depending upon reasoning. The ratiocinatory states are simpler since they consist "merely in the contemplation of the nature of things . . . ." Briefly, they deal with these possible points in a case: whether a thing is—a matter of fact; what it is—a matter of definition; and of what species it is—a matter of quality. Thus, a case in the courtroom might center about the status of conjecture: Brown was either guilty or innocent of the charge of murder. Or, a case might deal with the status of definition: Brown killed a man but it was in self-defense, and hence was not murder. Or the status might concern quality: "Horatius committed a crime, for he killed his sister; he committed no crime, for he had a right to kill her who mourned at the death of an enemy." [50]

Style Treated Conventionally.—Quintilian recommends that the greatest possible care be given to expression,

> . . . provided we bear in mind that nothing is to be done for the sake of words, as words themselves were invented for the sake of things, and as those words are the most to be commended which express our thoughts best, and produce the impression which we desire on the minds of the judges. Such words undoubtedly must make a speech both worthy of admiration and productive pleasure; but not of that kind of *admiration* with which we wonder at monsters; or of that kind of *pleasure* which is attended with unnatural gratification, but such as is compatible with true merit and worth. [51]

Then follows a long and reasonably conventional discussion of style. The classifications and definitions of the figures and tropes are more systematically handled, however, than in any previous contribution.

Attitude Toward Delivery.—It is of interest to note Quintilian's defense of "extempore" speaking:

[49] *Op. cit.*, p. 74.
[50] *Institutes.* III, vi, 76.
[51] *Ibid.*, VIII, introd., 32–33.

But the richest fruit of all our study, and the most ample recompense for the extent of our labour, is *the faculty of speaking extempore;* and he who has not succeeded in acquiring it, will do well, in my opinion, to renounce the occupations of the forum, and devote his solitary talent of writing to some other employment; for it is scarcely consistent with the character of a man of honour to make a public profession of service to others which may fail in the most pressing emergencies, since it is of no more use than to point out a harbour to a vessel, to which it cannot approach unless it be borne along by the gentlest breezes. There arise indeed innumerable occasions where it is absolutely necessary to speak on the instant, as well before magistrates, as on trials that are brought on before the appointed time; and if any of these shall occur, I do not say to any one of our innocent fellow citizens, but to any of our own friends and relatives, is an advocate to stand dumb, and, while they are begging for a voice to save them, and are likely to be undone if succor be not instantly afforded them, is he to ask time for retirement and silent study, till his speech be formed and committed to memory, and his voice and lungs be put in tune? [52]

Practically, this manner of speaking requires a technique differing from the ordinary mode of address.

Yet if any chance shall give rise to such a sudden necessity for speaking extempore, we shall have need to exert our mind with more than its usual activity; we must fix our whole attention on our matter, and relax, for the time, something of our care about words, if we find it impossible to attend to both. A slower pronunciation, too, and a mode of speaking with suspense and doubt, as it were, gives time for consideration; yet we must manage so that we may seem to deliberate and not to hesitate. [53]

Final Estimate.—Colson has pronounced the *Institutes* "one of the most remarkable and interesting products of Roman common sense." [54] At all points in the twelve books we are impressed by the sanity of the author in refusing to be bound by inflexible rules, and by his insistence upon shaping his doctrine to the varying demands of different speech situations. Eclectic as the treatment is, the contents take on new color and vitality at Quintilian's hands because he weaves his teaching experience and wise counsel into the fabric of the old theory.

[52] *Ibid.*, X, vii, 1–2.
[53] *Ibid.*, X, vii, 22.
[54] *Op. cit.*, p. xxi.

ST. AUGUSTINE ON PREACHING *   *Charles S. Baldwin*

With this elaborate pedagogical tradition [that of the Sophists] a clean break is made by St. Augustine. The fourth book of his *De doctrina christiana* has historical significance in the early years of the fifth century out of all proportion to its size; for it begins rhetoric anew. It not only ignores sophistic; it goes back over centuries of the lore of personal triumph to the ancient idea of moving men to truth; and it gives to the vital counsels of Cicero a new emphasis for the urgent tasks of preaching the word of God.

Abstractly and in retrospect the very character of Christian preaching seems necessarily to reject sophistic. But at the time this seemed anything but inevitable. Sophistic was almost the only lore of public speaking then active. It dominated criticism and education. The Greek fathers Gregory of Nyssa and Gregory Nazianzen might expose its falsity of conception; but they could not escape it. It had brought them up. Its stylistic habits were ingrained in their expression. Augustine too had been brought up on sophistic. Nor could he escape it. Again and again his style rings with its tradition.[1] Not only had he learned it for good; he had taught it. He had been himself, in Plutarch's sense and Strabo's, a sophist. We must hasten to add that the great Christians of the fourth century, if they could not escape sophistic, at least redeemed it by curbing its extravagance and turning it to nobler uses. But Augustine did much more. He set about recovering for the new generation of Christian orators the true ancient rhetoric. He saw that for Christian preaching sophistic must not only be curbed; it must be supplanted. Against the background of his day his quiet, simple book, renouncing the balances and figures of his other works without renouncing their fervor, is seen to be a startling innovation.

Not the least striking trait of the innovation is its reserve. Augustine does not attack sophistic as the Gregorys do; he ignores it. In Chapter xxxi of Book II he had, indeed, mentioned it. Discussing there not style, but matter, he had contrasted the necessary training in argument

---

From *Medieval Rhetoric and Poetic*, The Macmillan Company, New York, 1928. Reprinted by permission of Marshall Baldwin.

° In the present volume, a small portion of material in the original essay has been omitted, as well as some of the original footnotes.

[1] For detailed analysis, see Barry (Sr. Inviolata), *St. Augustine the Orator*, Washington, D.C., 1924.

with sophistic quibbling, and had then added, forecasting Book IV, that superfluous stylistic ornament also is sophistic.

> But training in argument on questions of all such kinds as are to be investigated and resolved in sacred literature is of the highest value; only we must beware of the lust for quarelling, and of the puerile display of skill in disappointing an opponent . . . . This sort of quibbling conclusion Scripture execrates, I think, in the text *Qui sophistice loquitur odibilis est.*[2] Even though not quibbling, a speech seeking verbal ornament beyond the bounds of responsibility to subject matter (*gravitas*) is called sophistic. II. xxxi.

But an uninformed modern reader of Book IV would hardly be aware that sophistic existed. No denunciation could be more scathing than this silence. In Augustine's view of Christian preaching sophistic simply has no place. A good debater, instead of parrying he counters. He spends his time on his own case. A good teacher, he tells his neophytes not what to avoid, but what to do. He has so far renounced sophistic that he has no concern to triumph. He wishes simply to teach sound rhetorical doctrine. He achieves an extraordinary conciseness not so much by compression as by undeviating straightforwardness.

A reader familiar with the times, however, will be reminded of sophistic by many allusions. Single phrases or sentences some of them, a few more extended, they all serve to illuminate by contrast the true rhetoric.

> All these things, when they are taught by rhetors, are thought great, bought at a great price, sold with great boasting. Such boasting, I fear, I may suggest myself in speaking so; but I had to answer those ill-educated men who think that our authors are to be despised, not because they lack the eloquence which such critics love too much, but because they do not use it for display. vii.
>
> [But an audience of Christian sobriety] will not be pleased with that suave style in which though no wrong things are said, right things slight and frail are adorned with foamy circumlocution. xiv.
>
> I think I have accomplished something not when I hear them applauding, but when I see them weeping. xxiv.

Display, inflation, thirst for applause—every reader of Augustine's time would recognize in these allusions a repudiation of sophistic.

[2] Even though the application of the text from *Ecclus.* xxxvii. 20 be questioned, the rebuke of sophistic display, whether in dialectic or in style, is none the less clear.

For Augustine thinks that Christian preaching is to be learned best from Christian preachers. As if in reply to Julian's scornful "Let them elucidate their Matthew and Luke," he recommends not only for doctrine, but for rhetoric, the Epistles, the Prophets, and the Fathers, and proceeds to analyze their style. The analysis, though based on the current Latin version, is generally transferable to the Greek, since it is much simpler than the classification set forth by sophistic. It exhibits sentence movement simply in climax, period, balance—those devices which are most easily appropriated and most useful. The general ancient counsels of aptness and variety are applied specifically to preaching. As to cadence (*clausula*), Augustine dispenses with all subdivisions, and even makes bold to assert that it must sometimes be sacrificed. Similarly omitting all classification of figures, he manages to suggest in a few words what figures are for. In a word, he shows how to learn from the Canon and the Fathers the rhetoric that is vital to homiletic.

This rhetoric, not only simpler than sophistic, but quite different in emphasis, is set forth in the terms of Cicero. Augustine has gone back four and a half centuries to the days before *declamatio*. The instruction that he draws from his analysis of Christian literature is planned upon the "instruct, win, move" (*docere, delectare, movere*) of *De oratore* and upon the corresponding three typical styles (*genus tenue—medium—grande*) of *Orator*. Evidently Augustine had the greater Cicero, not the lesser that sufficed for the Middle Age. He neither quotes nor cites any other rhetorician; and though his doctrine of aptness and of variety is common throughout the older rhetoric, for this too he had no need to go beyond the master's two great works. Nor have any others been more persuasive as to imitation, which is Augustine's controlling idea. This first Ciceronianism, too immediately aware of the perverted imitation of style taught by sophists to fall into the archaism and redundancy of later worship of Cicero, is a penetrative recovery of Cicero's larger meaning. Augustine's application of the three typical styles is more just and more practically distinct than Cicero's own. Would that all Ciceronians had been equally discerning!

The fourth book of the *De doctrina christiana* is specifically linked by its proem to the preceding three as setting forth presentation (*modus proferendi*). Books I–III have dealt with study of the subject matter (*inventio*); Book IV is to deal with expression. Augustine thus makes traditional fivefold division twofold. *Inventio*, which under sophistic had lapsed, he restores to its rightful place and gives it a new

TABULAR VIEW OF ST. AUGUSTINE'S *DE DOCTRINA CHRISTIANA* IV

application to the exegesis of Scripture. Of the remaining four left to his second heading he discusses only style (*elocutio*). Delivery and memory are mentioned incidentally; plan is omitted. The omission is not negligent. The first chapter warns us not to expect a manual of rhetoric. Nevertheless a modern student cannot help wishing that so suggestive a treatise had both applied to preaching the ancient counsels as to plan and exhibited the New Testament in this aspect. Thus to analyze for imitation not only the style of the Pauline epistles, but their cogency of order, would doubtless have made the work unduly extensive. One hopes that seminarians of the fifth century were stimulated, and that seminarians of the twentieth century will be stimulated, by the example of the treatise itself, to study *Romans* not only for appeal, but for cogency. Meantime Augustine's fourth book remains one of the most fruitful of all discussions of style in preaching.

Who dare say that the defenders of truth should be unarmed against falsehood? While the proponents of error know the art of winning an audience to good will, attention, and open mind, shall the proponents of truth remain ignorant? While the [sophist] states facts concisely, clearly, plausibly, shall the preacher state them so that they are tedious to hear, hard to understand, hard to believe? While the one attacks truth and insinuates falsehood by fallacious argument, shall the other have too little skill either to defend the true or to refute the false? Shall the one, stirring his hearers to error, urging them by the force of oratory, move them by terror, by pity, by joy, by encouragement, and the other slowly and coldly drowse for truth? ii.

But to learn such skill from rules, he goes on, is the way rather for boys than for men who have immediately before them the urgent tasks of preaching.

For eloquence will stick to such men, if they have the talent of keenness and ardor, more easily through their reading and hearing of the eloquent than through their following of the rules of eloquence. Nor does the Church lack literature, even outside the Canon established in the citadel of authority, to imbue a capable man with its eloquence, even though his mind be not on the manner but on the matter, provided he add practice in writing, in dictating, finally also in composing orally what he feels according to the rule of piety and faith. Besides, if such talent be lacking, either the rules of rhetoric will not be grasped, or if by great labor some few of them are partially grasped, they will be of no avail . . . . [Young preachers] must beware of letting slip what they have to say while they attend to saying it in good form. iii.

They must, indeed, know the principles of adaptation (iv), and develop their expression as far as they can; but they will do so best by imitation.

Whoever wishes to speak not only with wisdom, but with eloquence . . . . I rather direct to read or hear the eloquent and to imitate them by practise than advise to spend his time on teachers of the art of rhetoric. v.

Expressed in modern terms, Augustine's position is that rhetoric as a classified body of doctrine is properly an undergraduate study. It is not the best approach for seminarians because its method is analytical. The young preacher, needing rather promotion than revision, will advance more rapidly by imitation.

Starting from this principle, that the more fruitful study for learning to preach is imitation of Christian eloquence, Augustine proceeds to show (vi–viii) how distinctive is the eminence of such models and how repaying to analysis. His vindication should be pondered by those who still permit themselves to disparage without distinction the literary value of the New Testament, and by those who, granting poetic to Ambrose, remain unaware of his rhetoric.

At this point the question, perhaps, arises whether our authors, whose divinely inspired writings constitute for us a canon of most salutary authority, are to be called philosophers [3] only, or also orators. To me and to those who agree with what I am saying, the question is very easily answered. For where I comprehend them, nothing can seem to me either more philosophical or more eloquent. And all, I venture to say, who rightly comprehend what they speak, comprehend at the same time that they could not have spoken otherwise. For as there is an eloquence becoming to youth, another to age, nor can that be called eloquence which does not befit the character of the speaker, so there is an eloquence becoming to men most worthy of the highest authority and evidently inspired. Our authors have spoken with such eloquence. No other is becoming to them, nor theirs to others. For it is like themselves; and, the more it rejects display, the more it ranges above others not by inflation, but by cogency. Where on the other hand I do not comprehend them, though their eloquence is less apparent to me, I have no doubt that it is such as I find it where I do comprehend. The very obscurity of inspired and salutary utterances has been tinged with such eloquence that our minds should be stimulated not only in study [of their meaning], but in practise [of their art]. Indeed, if there were leisure, all the virtues and graces of eloquence with which those are inflated who put their style ahead of the style of our authors not by greatness, but by distension, could be exhibited in the sacred literature of those whom divine Providence has sent to instruct us and to draw us from this corrupt world to the world of happiness. But what delights me more than I can say in their eloquence is not what it has in common with pagan orators and poets. What I rather admire, what fills me with amazement, is that the eloquence which we hear around us has so been used, as it were through another eloquence of their own, as to be neither deficient nor conspicuous. For it should be neither condemned nor displayed; and they would have seemed to do the one if they shunned it, the other if it became noticeable. Even in those places where perhaps it is noticeable to experts, such is the message that the words in which it is expressed seem not to be sought by the speaker, but to subserve that message naturally, as if one saw philosophy issuing from her own home in the heart of the philosopher, and eloquence following as an inseparable servant even when not called.[4] vi.

---

[3] Thus I venture to translate *sapientes,* remembering the connotation of the word both for Augustine and for his master Cicero.

[4] So toward the close "The Christian preacher prefers to appeal rather with matter than with manner, and thinks neither that anything is said better which

The vindication of an eloquence distinctly Christian has the more weight because its doctrine of form and substance echoes from Cicero the best ancient tradition. The older tradition had in Augustine's time been so overlaid that he could do no better service to rhetoric than to recall it. In fact, Christian eloquence redeemed public speaking by reviving the true persuasion.

The insistence on the Ciceronian doctrine that style is not separable has a bearing more than historical. Not only for Augustine's time, but for any time, the truism must be reasserted. His iteration is more than preoccupation with Cicero, more than repudiation of sophistic. It springs from the cardinal importance of the truism for homiletic. In the pulpit the sophistic heresy of art for art's sake becomes intolerable.

Augustine's next step (vii) is to support his general claims for Christian eloquence, and to show how it may be studied, by analyzing briefly three typical passages. In the first, *Romans* v. 3–5, he analyzes prose rhythm under the familiar heads of classical sentence movement (*compositio*): phrases and subordinate clauses (*cæsa*), coordinate clauses (*membra*), period (*cırcuitus*), climax (*gradatio*), adding the equivalent Greek terms.

The passage is short enough, and the sentence movement simple enough, to be grasped readily. Its balance is striking without being monotonous, and is reinforced by a linking iteration that leads to a climax.[5] He is a wise teacher who begins with an instance so memorable. It must have seized even more quickly a generation familiar with both the terms and the method.

The next example, 2 *Corinthians* xi. 16–31, shows the same sentence devices carried through a much longer reach, and is therefore used both to reinforce the first and to add the importance of rhythmical variety. The counsel of variety, though a commonplace of the older rhetoric, had especial point by contrast with the sophistic fondness for trimming and prolonging balances. Incidental to the exhibition of variety is a reminder of aptness; and the analysis concludes:

> Finally all this breathless passage is closed with a period of two members . . . . But how after this impetus the brief statement interposed comes to rest, and rests the reader, how apt it is and how charming, can hardly be said. vii.

The analysis of the third example, *Amos* vi. 1–6, leads the study to longer and more sustained rhythmical reaches. Lest it seem the more

---

is not said more truly, nor that the teacher must serve words, but words the teacher." xxviii.

[5] The linking iteration is characteristic of climax as practised by sophistic.

difficult in the more figurative version of the Septuagint, Augustine quotes it "as translated from the Hebrew into Latin style through the interpretation of the priest Jerome, expert in both languages."

Much more urgent, leaping to attack, rising, prolonging, varying, subsiding to a pregnant close, the prophecy widens the conception of rhythmical range. Marking the rhythms briefly, Augustine uses it also to show the oratorical force of figures.[6] Thus a few pages of analysis are made to yield wide and definite suggestion. This, perhaps, is their outstanding merit; while they show the student what to look for, they invite him to go on for himself. But the pedagogical achievement does not stop there. The professor of rhetoric has seen that rhetorical analysis must be simplified, and that it must be made progressive. Where else shall we find so much drawn from three analyses? The first reduces the complicated lore of rhythm to its essentials. The second, reinforcing and extending these, dwells upon aptness as a corrective of rhetorical zeal, and as a constructive principle. The third, quoting rhythms still more urgent with emotion, passes to the emotional value of concrete words. To bring the over-classified lore of sophistic back to the simplicity of Aristotle was a service not only to homiletic, but to all rhetoric. A greater service was to substitute for the static and formalized pedagogy of the day a vital order. Augustine had been doubtless a popular professor; Christianity made him a great teacher.

Pedagogically, therefore, even his incidental definitions are worth noticing. That the function of grammar is traditionally to impart correctness of speech (iii) is used to support the contention that even this elementary skill comes best in fact from imitation. The period (vii) is defined so as to throw the emphasis on delivery. Its "clauses are suspended by the speaker's voice until it is concluded at the end." Therefore it "cannot have fewer than two clauses." So he points out in the passage from *Amos* that the rhythm is available for delivery (*in potestate pronuntiantis*) either as a series of six or as three pairs, and that the latter is more beautiful. So he suggests limiting analysis to give room for oral interpretation.

> This same passage which we have set as an example can be used to show other things relevant to the rules of eloquence. But a good hearer is not so much instructed by discussion in detail as he is kindled by ardent delivery. vii.

[6] Chapter xxix of Book III relegates the study of figures to *grammatica;* but there also Augustine reminds his readers that figures, without regard to books or teaching, are a natural expression of the imaginative impulse.

The next and longest section (ix–xiv) is based on Cicero's "inform, please, move" (*docere, delectare, movere*). Distinguishing each of these tasks clearly, Augustine is at the same time careful to unite them, by progressively iterative transitions, in the single and constant task of persuasion. In exposition (*docere*) clearness may demand the use of popular expressions. What avails correctness in a diction that is not understood?

> He who teaches will rather avoid all words that do not teach. If he can find correct words that are understood, he will choose those; if he cannot, whether because they do not exist or because they do not occur to him at the time, he will use even words that are less correct, provided only the thing itself be taught and learned correctly. ix.

The correctness (*integritas*) of diction boasted by the sophists, and carried by them even to the pedantry of archaism, is here faced squarely. The assertion that it must sometimes be sacrificed, the making of clearness absolutely paramount, is the bolder at a time when Christian preaching was not yet recognized as having secure command of elegance. Unmistakable clearness, Augustine goes on, is so much more important in preaching than in discussions permitting question and answer that the speaker must be quick to help unspoken difficulties.

> For a crowd eager to grasp will show by its movement whether it has understood; and until it has given this signal the subject must be turned over and over by various ways of expressing it—a resource beyond the power of those who deliver speeches written out and memorized. x.

No warrant here, he adds (xi), for dilation beyond the demands of clearness, but good warrant for making instruction pleasant and appealing in order to hold attention. Passing thus to the two other tasks of oratory, he quotes (xii) Cicero's "to instruct is of necessity, to please is for interest, to move is for victory." The three are then both carefully distinguished and shown to be a sort of geometrical progression. The first is first of necessity. It must be mastered; but it is rarely sufficient. To supply the lack, the second demands more rhetoric by demanding further adaptation to the audience; but it too must remain insufficient. So the third task, to move, is not merely the third item in a classification; it is the final stage in a progress. That progress is increasingly emotional. The last stage demands not only all the rhetoric of the preceding, but also the art of vivid imagery and of urgent application. So Augustine arrives at one of those linking summaries which constitute almost a refrain.

> Therefore the eloquence of the Church, when it seeks to have something done, must not only explain to instruct and please to hold, but also move to win. xiii.

The next chapter (xiv) warns against resting in the second stage.[7] To make the pleasing of the audience an end in itself is the typical vice of sophistic. If preaching tolerates it, "the time will come when they will not endure sound doctrine; but after their own lusts shall they heap to themselves teachers, having itching ears." Augustine quotes, not these words of St. Paul, but Jeremiah, and rises to denunciation of mere pleasing. "Far from us be that madness." One of Cyprian's rare descriptive passages is adduced to show how "the wholesomeness of Christian preaching has recalled his diction from [sophistic] redundancy and held it to a graver eloquence of less display." As the ultimate objection to the sophistic ideal is moral, so is the preacher's ultimate resource. Since his strength is derived from a source deeper than human skill, his best preparation is prayer. Augustine is not above enforcing this reminder by playing upon the words *orare, orator, oratio*. Nevertheless human skill is to be cultivated. Prayer itself proves the folly (xvi) of making no other preparation. He who abjures human lore of preaching because God gives us our messages might equally well abjure prayer because God knows us and our needs. The Pauline counsels specify how Timothy should preach. As God heals through doctors and medicines, so he gives the gospel to men by men and through man.

The transition (xvii) to the final task of moving men to action is another full and explicit iteration of all three, and at the same time a preparation for the next section on the corresponding three typical styles. Since the subject matter of preaching is always great, at least in implication (xviii), does it not always demand a great style? No; for a great matter (xix) may at the time rather demand exposition; and this in turn demands a restrained style. Again, a great matter may

---

[7] The warning is repeated where Augustine is gathering the three tasks into the final and constant idea of persuasion: "But that which is handled in the way of charm . . . is not to be made an end in itself (xxv) . . . nor does it seek merely to please." Nothing is more admirable in Augustine's exposition than this expert linking of his chain of progress.

at the time rather demand praise or blame; and here enters the second task of so adapting the style as to win sympathy.

> But when something ought to be done, and we are talking to those who ought to do it and will not, then the great subject is to be expressed greatly and in such wise as to bend their minds . . . . What subject is greater than God? Is it therefore not a subject for instruction? Or how can any one expounding the unity of the Trinity do it except by confining himself to exposition, that so difficult a distinction may as far as is possible be understood? Is ornament demanded here, and not rather argument? Is there here something that the audience is to be moved to do, and not rather something that it is to be taught to learn? Again, when God is praised in himself or in his works, what a vision of beautiful and splendid diction rises before any one praising as well as he can him whom no one praises aright and no one fails to praise in some way or other! But if God be not worshipped, or if idols be worshipped with him or even in his stead, whether dæmons or any other created being, then to meet so great an evil, and from this evil to save men, the preaching too must be great. xix.

Augustine has passed (xvii–xix) from Cicero's three tasks of oratory to his three typical styles by applying to the preacher Cicero's definition of the orator: "He, then, shall be called eloquent who can speak small things quietly, larger things proportionately, great things greatly." [8] Thus the three styles are *genus submissum* (or *tenue*), *genus temperatum* (or *medium*), and *genus grande*. As in Cicero, these correspond to *docere, delectare, movere,* and the second is connected with panegyric.

Augustine now proceeds to exemplify the first style (xx) from *Galatians* as calling for skill in reasoning and for a memory trained to bring in objections and difficulties where they can best be met. This debater's memory is precisely the ancient *memoria,* the fifth of the traditional parts of rhetoric. It seems to have fallen into abeyance under sophistic. What the sophists boasted was verbal memory, which Augustine merely mentions in his appendix as something quite different.

The same chapter (xx) exemplifies the second, or median style from *Timothy* and *Romans* as having the charm of aptness. Here Augustine confronts squarely the sophistic habit of making rhythmical beauty paramount and the pagan disparagement of Christian style. Some one may find the cadence of *Romans* xiii. 14 defective. Certainly it would soothe the ear more rhythmically if the verb came last.

[8] *Orator,* xxix. 101.

But a graver translator has preferred to keep the usual word-order [and, he might have added, the logical emphasis]. How this sounds in the Greek used by the apostle they may see whose expertness in that language goes so far. To me at least, the word-order, which is the same as in our version, does not seem there either to run rhythmically. Indeed, the stylistic beauty (*ornatum*) which consists of rhythmical cadences is defective, we must confess, in our authors. Whether this is due to our versions, or whether, as I incline to think, the authors deliberately avoided these occasions for applause, I do not venture to affirm, since I confess that I do not know. But this I know, that anyone who shall make their cadences regular in the same rhythms—and this is done very easily by shifting certain words that have equal force of meaning in the new order—will recognize that these inspired men lacked none of those things which he learned as great matters in the schools of the grammarians or rhetors. Moreover, he will discover many sorts of diction of so great beauty as to be beautiful even in our customary language, much more in theirs, and never found in the literature with which [the sophists] are inflated. But we must beware lest the addition of rhythm detract from the weight of inspired and grave sentences. Most learned Jerome does not carry over into his translation the musical skill in which rhythm is learned most fully, though our prophets did not lack even that, as he shows in the Hebrew meters of some of them; [and he gave this up] in order to keep truth to their words . . . . As in my own style, so far as I think I may do so modestly, I do not neglect rhythmical cadences,[9] so in our authors they please me the more because I find them there so rarely. xx.

The third, or great style, whether it be elegant or not, has for its distinguishing quality the force of emotional appeal. The instances are from 2 *Corinthians* vi and *Romans* viii. *Romans* is a long epistle, not a sermon. Though it was read aloud, of course, it is essentially a treatise, a philosophy of history. It is largely expository and argumentative. Since it is addressed primarily to reflection and reason, its main artistic reliance is on cogency of order. But even here presentation does not remain purely logical. For persuasion it must rise also emotionally. As we read in *Acts* xvii the outline of the apostle's Areopagus speech, we discern beyond the logical chain of propositions an expanding conception of the Life-giver. Who can doubt that the style too, as in *Romans*, rose to *grande?* The traditional doctrine of the peroration, easily as it may be abused, is only the expression in rhetoric of the audience's final demand and the speaker's final answer. That demand and that answer are emotional.

[9] For his cadences, see Barry, *op. cit.*

Adding *Galatians* iv, Augustine says of it:

> Although the whole epistle, except in the elegant last part, is written
> in the plain style, nevertheless the apostle inserts a certain passage of
> such moving force that it must be called great even though it has no
> such embellishments as those just cited. . . . Is there here either an-
> tithesis, or subordination for climax, or rhythm in phrase, clause, or
> period? None the less for that there is no cooling of the great emotion
> with which we feel the style to glow. xx.

After quoting without further comment examples from Cyprian and
Ambrose, Augustine shows (xxii, xxiii) the need of variety. More
even than other forms of oratory, preaching seems to suffer from a
stylistic level. No one of the three styles, least of all the third, can
effectively be prolonged; the change from style to style gives relief;
and subordination of what might be heightened may enhance the
emotion of what must be. What must be heightened is what is to
rouse the audience to action. So the test of achievement in the third
style is not applause, but tears and change of life (xxiv). So also the
end of all eloquence, in whatever style, is persuasion (xxv).

> In the restrained style the orator persuades of truth. In the great
> style he persuades to action. In the elegant style is he to persuade him-
> self that he is speaking beautifully? With such an end what have we
> to do? Let them seek it who glory in language, who display themselves
> in panegyrics and such exercises, in which the hearer is neither to be
> instructed nor to be moved to any action, but merely to be pleased.
> But let us judge this end by another end. xxv.

Thus Augustine is more explicit than Cicero in showing that the
three typical styles are but three ways (xxvi) of achieving a single
end, even as the three corresponding tasks, though one of them absorbs
attention at a time, are but three aspects of the single task. Nor can
persuasion dispense with a means beyond art, the appeal of the
speaker's life [10] (xxvii). Though the Church speaks not merely through
a man, but through his office, persuasion needs for full effect his whole
influence. Because his life is without shame, the preacher speaks not
shamelessly (xxviii), not only with restraint and charm, but with
power, to win obedience to the truth.

The historical significance of the *De doctrina christiana,* important
as it is, should not obscure its value as a contribution to homiletic.
The first homiletic, though one of the briefest, remains one of the most
suggestive. It omits no essential; while it reminds us of the general

[10] Aristotle, *Rhetoric* I. ii.

principles of rhetoric, it emphasizes those applications to preaching which are distinctive; and it proceeds pedagogically. Though the *doctrina* of the title refers strictly to exposition, and this is amplified and iterated as a constant necessity, Augustine includes specifically and from the start both charm and appeal, and concludes by showing emotional appeal to be the final stage of the comprehensive task of persuasion. Homiletic is an application of rhetoric long established as permanent, consistent, and in both materials and conditions fairly constant. That it is also comprehensive, demanding all three typical styles, including argument in its exposition, winning sympathy in order to urge action, varying its art while holding to its single aim, is most suggestively established here in its first great monument.

Not only does Augustine forbid the arid and the tedious, not only does he insist on emotional appeal; he also vindicates for Christian eloquence the importance of charm. This was the more delicate because charm was both abused by contemporary sophists and still suspected by contemporary preachers. Augustine presents it at once frankly and with just discrimination. To make it an end in itself, he is careful to show, is indeed sophistic; but to ignore it is to forget that preaching is a form of the oratory of occasion.[11] The Areopagus speech of St. Paul, though it is only summarized in *Acts* xvii, is evidently occasional, and has clear indications of that adaptation to win sympathy which is Augustine's interpretation of Cicero's *delectare*. The speech on occasion, favorite form of oratory in Augustine's time, had been conventionalized to the point of recipe. The recipes, though he knew them all, Augustine simply ignores; the field he redeems. He shows Christian preaching how to cultivate it for real harvest. History has shown no other direction of rhetoric to be so peculiarly homiletic.

Already Christian eloquence had reached conspicuous achievement in panegyric and more widely in the field of occasional oratory. The pagan sophist must look to his laurels. But these very triumphs had brought the danger of lapsing into too familiar conventions. What in pagan oratory might be no worse than pretty or merely exciting, in Christian oratory would be meretricious. To hold his difficult course, the preacher, as Augustine reminds him again and again, must at every moment steer for his message. He must never deviate. Though sophistic lost its dominance centuries ago, it has never been quite dead, and it always besets preaching. Therefore a constant concern of homiletic is to exorcise it by a valid rhetoric; and no book has ever

[11] In the passage quoted above from Chapter xix, and in other places there are clear references to occasional oratory.

revealed this more succinctly, more practically, or more suggestively than the *De doctrina christiana.*

RHETORIC IN THE MIDDLE AGES [1]   *Richard McKeon*

Medieval and Renaissance rhetoricians and philosophers, following the example of Cicero, seldom omit from their treatment of rhetoric some consideration of the subject matter, nature, and end of the art. Long before Cicero, rhetoric had become one of the focal points of the differences of philosophic schools, and the practice and application of the art had long wandered from field to field, reflecting and sometimes even affecting the complexities of philosophic discussions. Yet in histories which touch upon it, rhetoric is treated as a simple verbal discipline, as the art of speaking well, applied either as it was in Rome in forensic oratory and associated with the interpretation of laws or, more frequently, as it was in the Renaissance in the interpretation and use of the works of orators and poets and associated with, or even indistinguishable from, poetic and literary criticism. The history of rhetoric as it has been written since the Renaissance is therefore in part the distressing record of the obtuseness of writers who failed to study the classics and to apply rhetoric to literature, and in part the monotonous enumeration of doctrines, or preferably sentences, repeated from Cicero or commentators on Cicero. Scholarly labors have reconstructed only a brief and equivocal history for rhetoric during the Middle Ages. The development consists of slight and original increments of erudition in the compendia composed from the fourth to the ninth century—derived largely from the *De inventione* of Cicero and the *Ad Herennium*—and in later commentaries and treatises to the elaboration of coherent and complex doctrines in the twelfth century based on Quintilian and the later rhetorical works of Cicero, the *Orator*, the *De oratore*, and the *Topica.* The sequence of development is fortuitous and even implausible, for the treatment of rhetoric becomes more perfunctory as erudition in the works of rhetoricians increases, and rhetoric disappears abruptly when knowledge of it is at a maximum, particularly from the works of the authors who acknowledge the influence of Cicero and Quintilian. The translation of the *Rhetoric* of Aristotle, of the pseudo-Aristotelian *Rhetorica ad Alex-*

From *Critics and Criticism, Ancient and Modern,* R. S. Crane, ed., copyright 1952, The University of Chicago Press. Reprinted by permission.
[1] Reprinted with alterations from *Speculum,* January, 1942.

andrum, and of the *De elocutione* of Demetrius in the thirteenth century would seem to have had, by this account, no effect comparable to that of the other translations of the century in stimulating interest in its subject; and the return of rhetoric to prominence during the Renaissance is explained only on the supposition that men's minds were turned once more, after a long interval, to literature and life.[2]

[2] Valla, Vives, Ramus, and other Renaissance rhetoricians who treat the history of rhetoric pass over the intermediate period separating them from antiquity, to criticize, refute, and occasionally approve of the doctrines of Aristotle, Cicero, Quintilian, and Boethius. In early works of erudition and philology the scope of the history of rhetoric is no broader than the scope of contemporary controversy. D. G. Morhof makes the transition from Cicero, Quintilian and their predecessors, who are considered in the first nine of the thirty-two paragraphs headed *De scriptoribus rhetoricis* in his *Polyhistor, literarius, philosophicus et practicus* (vi. 1 [3rd ed.; Lubecae, 1732], I, 941–56), to the Renaissance rhetoricians treated in the last twenty-three paragraphs with the remark, 'Nos vero, missis nunc veteribus, ad recentiores sparsim enumerandos progredimur." J. Clericus carries the *Historia rhetorica* down to the Church Fathers in his *Ars critica* (Pars II, Sectio I, cap. 17 [Leipzig, 1713], I, 336–52). The history of rhetoric has more recently been extended to the Middle Ages, but it is always rhetoric in some particular sense, applied to some particular subject, and the history is usually negative or at least deprecatory. J. B. L. Crevier thus traces the history of rhetoric in education by noting the absence of any provision for rhetoric in the regulations of the University of Paris until the restoration of letters (*Histoire de l'Université de Paris* [Paris, 1761], I, 299, 307, 376, 479; II, 450; IV, 190, 243–44, 249, 330, 349, and *passim*). The pattern of rhetoric had, incidentally, not changed from the Renaissance to the eighteenth century in the important respect that Crevier found little use in his own writings on rhetoric for any authors between the ancients and his contemporaries, and the imperfections of Aristotle, Cicero, and Quintilian are his excuse for writing: "Aristote me paroit trop philosophe, Cicéron trop orateur, Quintilien trop scholastique" (*Rhétorique françoise* [Paris, 1808], I, xix). E. Norden treats rhetoric primarily in terms of style and is able, therefore, to dispose of the entire period from the ninth century to the time of Petrarch briefly in terms of the opposition of the study of authors to the study of the liberal arts, of classicism to scholasticism (*Die antike Kunstprosa vom vi. Jahrhundert v. Chr. bis in die Zeit der Renaissance* [4th ed.; Leipzig, 1923], II, 688–731); cf. the treatment of rhetoric and poetic (*ibid.*, pp. 894–98). According to C. S. Baldwin, the fate of rhetoric is determined by shifts in the interrelations of the arts of the trivium: rhetoric was dominant until the fall of Rome, grammar during the Carolingian period, dialectic during the Middle Ages (*Medieval Rhetoric and Poetic* [New York, 1928], p. 151). Rhetoric was crowded into medieval education between grammar for boys and dialectic for men, and Baldwin is therefore at pains to find reasons which explain "why there was no medieval rhetorician who really advanced the study" (*ibid.*, p. 182). The history of rhetoric during the Middle Ages is consequently the account of its misapplications and extensions: poetic is a misapplication of rhetoric to style (*ibid.*, pp. 185 ff., esp. 191–95); the dictamen is a development of rhetoric, but without need of perversion (*ibid.*, pp. 208 ff., esp. 214–15); and preaching in the absence of political and forensic oratory makes use of epideictic or occasional oratory, the third of Aristotle's genera (*ibid.*, pp. 229 ff.). According to P. Abelson (*The Seven Liberal Arts: A Study in Medieval Culture* [New York, 1906], pp. 52 ff.), rhetoric consisted of a practical training during the Roman period; then of the technical rules of a science; and, finally,

There is little reflection in the histories of rhetoric of the differences concerning the subject matter and purpose of rhetoric by which rhetoricians thought to distinguish and oppose their doctrines; and only occasionally and opaquely do some of the consequences of basic philosophic differences appear in the place given to rhetoric in the enumerations and classifications of the arts and sciences. The theoretic presuppositions which underlie the shifts and alterations of rhetorical doctrines are readily made to seem verbal and arbitrary preferences, for in the course of discussion all the terms are altered in meaning, and the contents and methods of each of the arts are transformed when grammar, rhetoric, poetic, dialectic, and logic change places or are identified one with another, or are distinguished from one another, or are subsumed one under another. Yet the confident readjustments of Renaissance rhetoricians, their redistribution of technical devices among the arts, and their correction of the confusions of the ancients seem no less whimsical and haphazard, if their reasons and criteria are ignored and only the repetition of enumerations of the disciplines and their parts is recorded. Rhetoricians from Cicero to Ramus have in common a persistent care in defining their art, and it seems plausible that a history of rhetoric traced in terms of its matter and function, as specified at each stage, might give significance and lively interest to the altering definitions, the differentiation of various conceptions of rhetoric itself, and the spread of the devices of rhetoric to subject matters far from those ordinarily ascribed to it. Such a history would not treat an art determined to a fixed subject matter (so conceived, rhetoric is usually found to have little or no history, despite much talk about rhetoric and even more use of it, during the Middle Ages), nor, on the other hand, would it treat an art determined arbitrarily and variously by its place in classifications of the sciences (so conceived, the schemes of the sciences would be arbitrary in their alterations and uncontrolled by philosophic principles or material content). The

---

when this theoretical and logical form of rhetoric fell into obsolescence, of the practical rules for writing letters and documents. In the account of N. Valois (*Guillaume d'Auvergne* [Paris, 1880], pp. 224 ff.) rhetoric was taught as a liberal art until the end of the twelfth century and then fell into discredit except as a practical discipline applied to preaching and prayer. The judgment of C. H. Haskins (*The Renaissance of the Twelfth Century* [Cambridge, Mass., 1928], p. 138) is no less concise in statement: "Ancient rhetoric was concerned with oratory, mediaeval rhetoric chiefly with letter-writing," and is illustrated with detailed evidence. More simply, if rhetoric is viewed as a form of literary criticism and associated with poetic, the decline of rhetoric is a symptom of the eclipse of the study of ancient literature (cf. L. J. Paetow, "The Arts Course at Mediaeval Universities with Special Reference to Grammar and Rhetoric," *University of Illinois Studies, III* (January, 1910), esp. 67 ff.; and D. L. Clark, *Rhetoric and Poetry in the Renaissance* (New York, 1922), pp. 43 ff.

history of rhetoric should have as subject an art which, although it has no special subject matter according to most rhetoricians, nonetheless must be discussed in application to some subject matter: rhetoric has been applied to many incommensurate subject matters; it has borrowed devices from other arts, and its technical terms and methods have become, without trace of their origin, parts of other arts and sciences; its own devices have been bent back upon themselves in such a way that any part of rhetoric or any matter incidentally involved in it—words and style, character and passion, reason and imagination, the kinds of orations, civil philosophy, practical action—have been made basic to the definition of all technical terms and distinctions. Moreover, if the succession of subject matters and functions can be used to reduce the welter of changes in rhetoric to a significant historical sequence, the theories implicated in the shifts of its subject matter should emerge, not merely as philosophic or sophistic disputes, but in concrete application, each at least defensible and each a challenge to the conception of intellectual history as the simple record of the development of a body of knowledge by more or less adequate investigations of a constant subject matter.

I

Three distinct lines of intellectual development during the Middle Ages were decisively determined or strongly influenced in their initial stages by rhetoric: first, and most properly, the tradition of rhetoricians themselves, who found their problems assembled and typical answers discussed in the works of Cicero and Quintilian; second, and less obviously, the tradition of philosophers and theologians who found in Augustine a Platonism reconstructed from the Academic and Neo-Platonic philosophies (conscientiously reversing the process by which they were derived from Plato's doctrines) and formulated in terms refurbished and simplified from Cicero's rhetorical distinctions; and, finally, the tradition of logic which passed as "Aristotelian," yet which followed Aristotle only in the treatment of terms and propositions and resorted to Cicero in the treatment of definitions and principles. Whatever the estimate that critics and historians are disposed to make of Cicero's achievement, originality, and consistency, his choices and emphases fixed the influence and oriented the interpretation of ancient thought, Greek as well as Latin, at the beginning of the Middle Ages and again in the Renaissance; and we today are far from having freed ourselves from the consequences of that long tradition in scholarship, criticism, or taste. During the Middle Ages and Renaissance many of the oppositions and agreements of theology and dialectic, no less than problems internal to each, were stated in language borrowed from or influenced by rhetoric and reflected theories by which rhetoricians had in antiquity opposed philosophers and logicians; surprising parallels were disclosed in theology and dialectic as well as in other arts and sciences, and they were expressed in language familiar to the rhetorician; innovations and discoveries were made which seem to follow the dictation of nature if their pattern of statement is ignored; and mere equivocations were pursued into interminable and recurrent verbal disputes.

The rhetoricians of the Middle Ages followed Cicero or suggestions found in his works when they discussed civil philosophy as the subject matter of rhetoric or divided that subject matter according to the three kinds of oratory—deliberative, judicial, demonstrative—or when they sought to determine it more generally by means of the distinction between *propositum* and *causa* (or *thesis* and *hypothesis,* as the Greek terms were Latinized), or by consideration of the characteristics of controversies and the constitutions (or *status*) of questions.[3] Moreover, they could learn, even from the *De inventione,* that there had been controversy on most of these points; and, in particular, the brief history of three views concerning the matter of rhetoric—Gorgias holding that it is all things, Aristotle dividing it into three kinds proper to the three kinds of oratory, and Hermagoras distinguishing "causes," which are specific to persons, and "questions," which are without such specification—supplied the arguments by which to dissent from, as well as those to support, Cicero's version of Aristotle's solution.[4] Major alterations in the contents and doctrines of rhetoric attended these changes in subject matter, and they required for their elaboration only

[3] Cf. Cicero *De inventione* i. 4. 5: "Sed antequam de praeceptis oratoriis dicimus, videtur dicendum de genere ipsius artis, de officio, de fine, de materia, de partibus." After determining that its *genus* is "civilis scientia," its *officium* "dicrere adposite ad persuasionem," and its *finis* "persuadere dictione," Cicero defines the matter of all arts, including the art of rhetoric (*ibid.* 5. 7): "Materiam artis eam dicimus, in qua omnis ars et ea facultas, quae conficitur ex arte, versatur."

[4] *Ibid.* 5. 7–7. 9. Cf. *ibid.* 9. 12 for illustration of the process by which basic terms are altered and the distinctions of rhetoric are bent back on themselves: in this case the dispute is concerning whether deliberation and demonstration are the genera of "causes" or are themselves parts of a particular genus of "cause." Isidore's list of the "inventors" of the art reflects the influence of Cicero's history of the matter of rhetoric, since the inventors are clearly determined by this history, as is the testimony to the elusiveness of the distinctions; cf. *Etymologiae* ii. 2: "Haec autem disciplina a Graecis inventa est, a Gorgia, Aristotele, Hermagora, et translata in Latinum a Tullio videlicet et Quintiliano, sed ita copiose, ita varie, ut eam lectori admirari in promptu sit, comprehendere impossible. Nam membranis retentis quasi adhaerescit memoriae series dictionis, ac mox repositis recordatio omnis elabitur."

a little erudition, such as might be derived from study of the points of difference between the *Ad Herennium* and the *De inventione,* or from the information supplied by Fortunatianus concerning figures and the Greek technical terms of rhetoric, or, finally, from Quintilian's orderly enumerations of divergent views and his statement and rectification of inconsistencies attributed to Cicero.[5] Even apart from the influence of theology and even before the influence of dialectic was felt, the remnants of old and the seeds of new controversies were preserved in rhetoric itself.

Rhetoric influenced Augustine both in his reactions against it and in his assimilation and use of devices borrowed from it; he differentiated two eloquences and two arts, much as Plato had proved rhetoric a pseudo-art in the *Gorgias* and yet had illustrated the method of the true rhetoric based on dialectic in the *Phaedrus.* Augustine was first attracted to philosophy by Cicero's *Hortensius,* which he encountered in the course of his rhetorical studies, and he was put off in his further attempt to combine philosophy with the name of Christ by the contrast of the scriptural and Ciceronian styles.[6] That stumbling block was finally removed in part by the aid of a rhetorical device which Augustine learned from Ambrose' preaching—the analogical method of interpreting Scripture [7]—and, although thereafter he refused to answer questions concerning Cicero's *Orator* and *De oratore,* on the grounds that it was a task unworthy of a bishop distracted with ecclesiastical cares,[8] his statement of Christian doctrine was, in the terms of Cicero, sublimated to new meanings and transformed to new uses. When he wishes to enumerate the questions basic to all inquiry, he resorts to Cicero's three "constitutions of causes"—whether a thing is, that it is, and what sort; and when he enumerates the methods to be used in treating scriptural questions, they turn out to be two of Cicero's five

---

[5] Cf. *Institutio oratoria* iii. 5. 4 ff. for an excellent statement of the problems involved in rhetorical "questions," and the disputes concerning "thesis" and "hypothesis," and esp. 14–15 for the development of Cicero's doctrine. For a brief summary of some of the characteristic statements of the definition and end of rhetoric cf. *ibid.* ii. 15; for disputes concerning its matter, *ibid.* 21. Or again, in illustration of the bending-back of rhetorical distinctions, what one man holds to be the "parts of rhetoric" another treats as the "work of the orator" (*ibid* iii. 3. 11 ff.); the two positions are taken, respectively, by Cicero, *De inventione* i. 7. 9, and Fortunatianus, *Ars rhetorica* i. 1 (Halm, *Rhetores Latini minores* [Leipzig, 1863], p. 81; henceforth cited as "Halm").

[6] *Confessions* iii. 3. 6–5. 9 (*Patrologia Latina,* XXXII, 685–86; henceforth cited as "PL").

[7] *Confessions* v. 13. 23 and vi. 4. 5–6 (*PL,* XXXII, 717 and 721–22). Cf. also the conversion of Victorinus the rhetorician and the effect of *salus* and *fides* on his rhetoric (*Confessions* viii. 2. 5 [*PL,* XXXII, 751]).

[8] *Epistola CXVIII ad Dioscorum* i. 2 and v. 34 (*PL* XXXIII, 432–33 and 448).

parts of rhetoric—discovery and statement; moreover, these two sets of questions seem to him exhaustive, and all problems and doctrines are concerned, as in the manuals of rhetoric, with "things" or with "signs." [9] This rhetorical language has, however, been adapted to the statement of a theology: discovery has been qualified as discovery of "what should be understood" and statement as statement of "what has been understood," with the result that the classification of signs and their uses is dependent, as it had not been in rhetoric, on the classification of things. In the *De doctrina Christiana* the first three books are concerned with discovery, the fourth with statement. The treatment of discovery is based, in the first book, on the distinction of things into those which as final ends are loved or enjoyed (*frui*) and those which as intermediate ends are used (*uti*) for further ends; consideration of the former takes the form of a theological inquiry into the attributes of God and divine things; the treatment of the nature of things is supplemented, in the second book, by a philological inquiry into the nature of words in relation to the Scriptures and the arts and institutions of the pagans; and, finally, in the third book, the inquiry into means of removing verbal ambiguities requires appeal to two sets of rules—grammatical rules applied to the manner of statement and rhetorical rules to determine the circumstances of fact.[10] The treatment of statement in the final book is therefore concerned not so

[9] *Confessions* x. 9. 16–10. 17 (*PL* XXXII, 786). Cf. Cicero *Orator* 14. 45: "Nam quoniam, quicquid est quod in controversia aut in contentione versetur, in eo aut sitne aut quid sit aut quale sit quaeritur: sitne, signis; quid sit, definitionibus; quale sit, recti pravique partibus—quibus ut ute possit orator, non ille volgaris sed hic excellens, a propriis personis et temporibus, si potest, avocat controversiam." The context and application of the questions are rhetorical in the *Confessions*, but cf. *De diversis quaestionibus LXXXIII* 18 (*PL*, XL, 15): "Ideoque etiam cum veritas quaeritur, plus quam tria genera questionum esse non possunt; utrum omnino sit, utrum hoc an aliud sit, utrum approbandum improbandumve sit." The tendency of these questions toward generalization beyond their specifically rhetorical meanings is assisted by some of the names attached to them: the pseudo-Augustine calls them "rational or logical" questions (*De rhetorica* 9 [Halm, p. 142]); Martianus Capella calls them "principal status" (*De rhetorica* 6 [Halm, p. 455]); Clodian names them "rational status" (*Ars rhetorica* [Halm, p. 590]). A fourth question or constitution or status is added by Hermagoras, is rejected by Cicero and Quintilian, and is mentioned by the pseudo-Augustine and Clodian. Concerning the variety and evolution of questions (or "status," as he prefers to call them), cf. Quintilian iii. 6. 29–85; his own decision is presented as one prescribed by nature and coincident with the doctrine of Cicero (*ibid.* 80); "Credendum est igitur his, quorum auctoritatem secutus est Cicero, tria esse, quae in omni disputatione quaerantur, an sit, quid sit, quale sit? quod ipsa nobis etiam natura praescribit." For Augustine's enumeration of scriptural methods and problems cf. *De doctrina Christiana* i. 1–2 (*PL*, XXXIV, 19–20).

[10] *De doctrina Christiana* iii. 4. 8, and 12. 18 (*PL*, XXXIV, 68 and 72–73).

much with the *precepts* of rhetoric, although some precepts can be found from analysis of the fashion in which the three styles of Cicero are applied to their appropriate matters by "ecclesiastical orators," as with an eloquence in which the words are supplied by the things and by wisdom itself and the speaker is unlearnedly wise.[11] The judgment expressed by Cicero at the beginning of the *De inventione,* that wisdom without eloquence is of little benefit to the state and eloquence without wisdom a great danger, is transformed by Augustine's dialectic, and all the terms take on two meanings. The wisdom and eloquence of the world are to be contrasted to eternal wisdom and eloquence; for there are not only two kinds of things, temporal and divine, but two kinds of words, the external words instituted and used by men which have no correspondence to things except by designation and no controllable influence on our thought except by way of the context of other words, and the internal words, by which a master speaking within us teaches the truth.[12] Whether things be treated as signs or signs as things, only the eternal meanings and realities are important; knowledge of temporal things and of the arts is chiefly useful for the interpretation of the language and symbolism of Scripture, and the Sacraments are signs adapted to the mutability of human sensibilities but immutable in their significance of the changeless things of God.[13]

[11] *De doctrina Christiana* iv. 1. 1–7. 11 (*PL,* XXXIV, 89–94).

[12] *De magistro* 3. 5–6 and 11. 36–12. 46 (*PL,* XXXII, 1197–98 and 1215–20). Cf. the excellent statement of the relation of language to thought by E. Gilson, *Introduction à l'étude de Saint Augustin* (Paris, 1929), pp. 87–103. Augustine's conception of rhetoric is developed most fully in the *De doctrina Christiana, De ordine, De catechizandis rudibus,* and *Contra Cresconium.* Cf. also J. Žůrek, "De S. Aurelii praeceptis rhetoricis," *Dissertationes philologae Vindobonenses* (Vienna, 1905), VIII, 69–109; M. Comeau, *La Rhétorique de Saint Augustin d'après le "Tractatus in Iohannem"* (Paris, 1930); G. Combés, *Saint Augustin et la culture classique* (Paris, 1927), esp. pp. 49–56, where true eloquence is distinguished from the oratorical art; H.-I. Marrou, *Saint Augustin et la fin de la culture antique* (Paris, 1938), esp. pp. 507–40 on Christian eloquence. The rhetoric of Cicero was moral and political in its applications, and the influence of rhetoric extended to political doctrine. The differentiation of things according to ends loved and means used had already entered Christian ethics in Ambrose' *De officiis ministrorum,* which was based on the distinctions of Cicero's *De officiis;* and Cicero's rhetorically conceived political theory supplies, by virtue of the same distinction, the terminology for Augustine's discussion of the City of God as well as the elements of the terrestrial city to which it is contrasted.

[13] *Epistola CXXXVIII ad Marcellinum* i. 7 (*PL,* XXXIII, 527): "Nimis autem longum est, convenienter disputare de varietate signorum, quae cum ad res divinas pertinent, Sacramenta appellantur. Sicut autem non ideo mutabilis homo, quia mane aliud, aliud vespere; illud hoc mense, illud alio; non hoc isto anno quod illo: ita non ideo mutabilis Deus, quia universi saeculi priore volumine aliud, aliud posteriore sibi iussit offerri, quo convenienter significationes ad doctrinam religionis saluberrimam pertinentes, per mutabilia tempora sine ulla sui mutatione disponeret."

Once account is taken of the distinction of things and words into those which are temporal and those which are changeless, the influence of rhetoric is discernible in many traits of the Augustinian tradition: in the analogical interpretation of Scripture and in the numerous medieval encyclopedias prepared to facilitate such interpretation (for words are signs which are useful less to designate things than to express truths and persuade minds, and things therefore are useful to interpret signs, rather than signs to interpret things); [14] in the literal interpretation in which apparently contradictory texts were reconciled in canon law and theology by use of the rhetorician's "circumstances" of statement, that is, by consideration of "who" said it, "where, when, why, how, with what assistance"; [15] in the organization of theological problems according to the distinction of things and signs; and in the place of rhetoric after dialectic in the enumeration of the liberal arts (since it supplies the means of stating truths, once they have been discovered) instead of before dialectic, as in the enumeration of an opposed tradition (since it achieves only probability and persuasion but falls short of truth).[16]

The discussion of logic during the Middle Ages may be divided into four periods. During the first period, the elements of logic were learned from simple treatises like the pseudo-Augustine's *Principia dialecticae* and *Categoriae decem* (which Alcuin recommended to Charlemagne as Augustine's translation of Aristotle's *Categories*) or the sections on dialectic in such handbooks as those of Martianus Capella, Cassiodorus, and Isidore of Seville. During the second period, after the curriculum instituted by Gerbert at the end of the tenth century the basis of instruction in dialectic was broadened to include the works and translations of Boethius, among them two of the six books of Aristotle's *Organon*, which together acquired the traditional name of the "Old Logic." During the third period, the translation of the remaining four books in the twelfth century set up the New Logic, constituted of the *Introduction* of Porphyry, the *Organon* of Aristotle, and the *Six Principles* of Gilbert de la Porrée; but the authority of the Old Logic continued strong, since the contemporaries of John of Salisbury found the *Posterior Analytics*, which treats of the principles of scientific demonstration, difficult or even unintelligible [17] (and,

[14] Cf. Gilson, *op. cit.*, pp. 151–53.

[15] *De doctrina Christiana* iii. 12. 18–29. 41 (*PL*, XXXIV, 72–81).

[16] For the fashion in which rhetoric follows and supplements dialectic according to Augustine, cf. *De doctrina Christiana* ii. 35. 53–37. 55 (*PL*, XXXIV, 60–61); *De ordine* ii. 13. 38 (*PL*, XXXII, 1013).

[17] John of Salisbury *Metalogicon* iv. 6, ed. C. C. J. Webb (Oxford, 1929), p. 171: "Deinde hec utentium raritate iam fere in desuetudinem abiit, eo quod

indeed, the first important commentary on that work was written in the thirteenth century by Robert Grosseteste, while as late as the fourteenth century William of Ockham prepared an *Expositio aurea et admodum utilis super artem veterem*). Finally, during the fourth period, the discussion of logic is determined less by Aristotle's *Organon* than by the *Summulae*, written in the thirteenth century by Petrus Hispanus, Lambert of Auxerre, and William of Shyreswood. The extent of the influence of rhetoric on the development of logic may be judged from the fact that—although Aristotle's logic is characterized not merely by the schemata of terms, propositions, and syllogisms set forth in the first three books of the *Organon* but even more by the differentiation of proof, in accordance with the principles on which it depends, into three kinds: scientific or demonstrative, dialectical, and sophistical, which are expounded in the last three books, the *Posterior Analytics*, the *Topics*, and the *De sophisticis elenchis*— only the first three books had much influence until the thirteenth century, while principles were treated by devices which Aristotle used in rhetoric and dialectic, and, even after the thirteenth century, scientific method was in constant danger of being assimilated to dialectic, the *Posterior Analytics* to the *Topics*.

The early treatments of dialectic in the handbooks and encyclopedias run through a familiar sequence of subjects: the predicables of Porphyry; the categories of Aristotle; a brief treatment of propositions, in which the testimony of Aristotle's *De interpretatione* is mixed in small doses with that of the treatise by the same name attributed to Apuleius; and exposition of the categorical syllogism derived from the pseudo-Apuleius and of the hypothetical syllogism derived from the rhetorician Marius Victorinus; and, finally, in place of Aristotle's principles of demonstration, sections on definition and on "topics" or "commonplaces" derived from the Greek rhetoricians by way of Cicero and the lost works of Marius Victorinus. So direct is the descent of the principles of demonstration from rhetoric that Cassiodorus closes his consideration of the art of dialectic, having treated of topics, with "atechnical" arguments (which form part of the *Topics* of Cicero but figure in the *Rhetoric* and not the *Topics* of Aristotle) and memory (which, although one of the traditional five parts of rhetoric, is common, according to Cassiodorus, to orators, dialecticians,

---

demonstrationis usus uix apud solos mathematicos est; et in his fere, apud geometras dumtaxat; sed et huius quoque discipline non est celebris usus apud nos, nisi forte in tractu Hibero uel confinio Affrice." In contrast to his brief and almost flippant treatment of the *Posterior Analytics,* John devotes more than half the third book (iii. 5-10; Webb, pp. 139-64) to praise of the utility of the *Topics.*

poets, and jurists),[18] while Isidore supplements his statement of topics with a section on opposites derived from Cicero.[19] The basic pattern of this logic was not crucially altered by the return in the second period to the more extensive logical works of Boethius. "Dialectic" is not distinct from "logic" in the tradition of the Old Logic; rather, dialectic or logic is divided on the authority of Cicero into two parts, one (called "analytic" by the Greeks, according to Boethius) concerned with judgment, the other (called "topic" by the Greeks) concerned with discovery.[20] Boethius translated and wrote commentaries on Aristotle's *Categories* and *On Interpretation*, but he also translated and wrote two commentaries on the *Isagoge* or *Introduction* of the Neo-Platonist Porphyry, which expounds, as introduction to the *Categories*, the predicables treated by Aristotle in his *Topics;* and this dialectical treatment of "the five words" appeared thereafter, even when the influence of Boethius was slight, in medieval, Renaissance, and early modern treatments of Aristotle's logic and editions of his *Organon*. Instead of Aristotle's treatment of syllogism, medieval philosophers had, until the twelfth century, Boethius' essays *On the Categorical Syllogism* (in which the doctrine of Aristotle is modified by the doctrines of Theophrastus, Eudemus, and Porphyry),[21] *On the Hypothetical Syllogism* (in which the authority of Theophrastus and Eudemus is invoked for seeking necessary premises in the forms of propositions rather than in the nature of things),[22] and *On Division* (which goes back

[18] *Institutiones* ii. 3. 16–17, ed. R. A. B. Mynors (Oxford, 1937), pp. 127–28; cf. Cicero *Topica* 4. 24 and Aristotle *Rhetoric* i. 15. 1375^{a}22–1377^{b}12. Mynors argues from the manuscripts that the *Institutiones* went through two recensions by other hands than Cassiodorus, and in them Boethius was substituted as authority in dialectic for Marius Victorinus (pp. xxviii and xxxvii). The closing sections of the later versions of the treatment of dialectic included, in addition to the rhetorical subjects of the earlier versions, a treatment of rhetorical places, discovery, and circumstances (*PL*, LXX, 1196–1202).

[19] *Etymologiae* ii. 31.

[20] *De differentiis topicis* i (*PL*, LXIV, 1173); *In Porphyrium commentaria* i (*PL*, LXIV, 73).

[21] For references to Theophrastus, Eudemus, and Porphyry cf. *De syllogismo categorico* ii (*PL*, LXIV, 813, 814, 815, and esp. 829): "Haec de Categoricorum Syllogismorum introductione, Aristotelem plurimum sequens, et aliqua de Theophrasto et Porphyrio mutuatus, quantum parcitas introducendi permisit, expressi." The *Introductio ad syllogismos categoricos* (*PL*, LXIV, 761 ff.) seems clearly another recension of Book i of the *De syllogismo categorico*.

[22] *De syllogismo hypothetico* i (*PL*, LXIV, 843): "Necessitas vero hypotheticae propositionis et ratio earum propositionum ex quibus junguntur inter se connexiones, consequentiam quaerit, ut cum dico: Si Socrates sedet et vivit, neque sedere eum, neque vivere necesse est; sed si sedet, necesse est vivere. . . . Necessitas enim propositionis in consequentiae immutabilitate consistit." Cf. *De differentiis topicis* i (*PL*, LXIV, 1176), where such propositions are called *per se nota*. For reference to Theophrastus and Eudemus cf. *De syllogismo hypothetico* 831.

to the "peripatetic" tradition, according to the opening sentence of the essay, but cites explicitly only Andronicus, Plotinus, and Porphyry, for treatment of a "scientia dividendi" in which Aristotle himself places little store).[23] The *De definitione* which went under Boethius' name is by Marius Victorinus, and it supplies one more channel for the influence of Cicero and rhetoric.[24] Finally, instead of a treatment of the differences of demonstrative, dialectical, and sophistical principles and proofs, Boethius left two works which had the effect, during the Middle Ages and increasingly during the Renaissance, of translating the problem of distinguishing principles into the problem of discovering arguments or things: his *Commentary on the Topics of Cicero* and his treatise in four books *On Topical Differences*, in which the topical schemes or commonplaces of Themistius and Cicero are set forth and reduced to a single classification.[25] With the advent of the New Logic in the third period, during the twelfth century, however, logic was distinguished from dialectic; and rhetoric became the counterpart of dialectic, although logic continued to be divided into judgment and discovery. Finally, during the fourth period, in the *Summulae* of the thirteenth century the emphasis is again on the topics, as it is also in the reaction against logic during the Renaissance, when the *Topics* of Cicero and of Boethius were once more used (as John the Scot had used topics) as inspiration for a scientific method of discovering, not arguments, but things, and the scholastic logic was viewed as a verbal discipline inferior in precision and practical effectiveness to these devices of rhetoric.

The effects of this extension of the devices of rhetoric to logic became apparent, in turn, in the treatment of rhetoric, and it became important to contrast rhetoric and dialectic when both rhetoricians and dialecticians made use of "places" for purposes of discovery. Paradoxically, in this tradtion in which the methods of rhetoric were similar to those of dialectic, rhetoric was subordinated to dialectic, while, in the tradition in which rhetoric was criticized and then trans-

[23] *De divisione* (*PL*, LXIV, 875–76); cf. Aristotle *Prior Analytics* i. 31. 46ª31–46ᵇ37.

[24] On the question of the authenticity of the *De definitione*, cf. H. Usener, *Anecdoton Holderi* (Bonn, 1877), pp. 59–66. For the effect of the *De definitione* in introducing rhetorical distinctions into the medieval discussions of logic cf. C. Prantl, *Geschichte der Logik im Abendlande* (Leipzig, 1855), I, 688–90.

[25] Boethius refers to translations he has made of other books of the *Organon*, but no evidence has been found in medieval literature of their influence prior to the twelfth century; cf. C. H. Haskins, "Versions of Aristotle's *Posterior Analytics*," in his *Studies in the History of Mediaeval Science* (Cambridge, Mass., 1924), pp. 231 ff. For the rhetorical character and effects of the *De differentiis topicis* cf. Prantl, *op. cit.*, I, 720–22.

formed to theological uses, dialectic was subordinated to rhetoric. The fourth book of Boethius' *On Topical Differences*, which treats of the differences between dialectical and rhetorical places, was used as a textbook of rhetoric in the twelfth and thirteenth centuries, and two short treatises devoted to rhetorical places passed under his name, the *Speculatio de rhetoricae cognatione* (which is more probably a compilation derived from Book iv of *De differentiis topicis* than an independent work by Boethius) and the *Locorum rhetoricorum distinctio*. Boethius finds the distinction between dialectic and rhetoric in their matter, use, and end: the matter of dialectic is "theses," that of rhetoric "hypotheses," and thesis and hypothesis are related as two kinds of "questions," the one universal, the other particularized to circumstances; dialectic uses interrogation and response, and its arguments are set forth in syllogisms; rhetoric uses continuous speech involving enthymemes; the end of dialectic is to force what one wishes from an adversary, that of rhetoric to persuade a judge.[26] Boethius takes over the early position of Cicero, as expressed in the *De inventione*, concerning the matter of rhetoric; but the whole question of end, function, and matter is raised in the context of a considerably longer list of questions, and in that context the other answers have changed. Boethius asks no fewer than nine questions about rhetoric: its genus, species, matter, parts, instrument, the parts of the instrument, the work and duty of the orator, and his end. The genus of rhetoric is no longer "civil science" (as it was for Cicero) but "faculty" (much as Aristotle had held it to be a δύναμις rather than a science). The matter of the faculty is all things suited to discourse, which, as Boethius puts it, is almost equivalent to the "civil question"; this matter of discourse is indeterminate until it is given specific form by the ends of rhetoric: the "civil question" is made into a judicial "cause" when the end considered is the just; into a deliberative "cause" when the end is the useful or the honorable; into a demonstrative "cause" when the end is the good. It is, as Isidore later observed, an elusive question, in which what one man considered the genus of an art can be transmuted by another into its matter; but that strange difference between the treatment of rhetoric as a faculty and as a social science is one of the slight remnants of the difference between Aristotle's conception of rhetoric and that of Cicero and the rhetoricians; and, from that remnant in Boethius' questions, medieval commentators

[26] *De differentiis topicis* iv (*PL*, LXIV, 1205-6). Cf. also *ibid*. i (*PL*, LXIV, 1177).

were to reconstruct, with slowly increasing erudition, the full specifications of the old opposition.

II

These were not technical questions which were discussed by a few learned men, but distinctions which entered into all parts of medieval culture and life. Christianity had grown up in the environment of a culture which was preponderantly rhetorical: indeed, the chief differences between Greek and Latin Christianity may be related to the differences between the Latin rhetoric of the Republic and early Empire (in which the arts and sciences had been put to the aid of rhetoric and civil philosophy had all but been reduced to the art of *forensic* pleading) and the Greek rhetoric of the Empire (in which philosophy itself had been displaced by display or *epideictic* rhetoric in the guise of sophistic, the rules of oratory had become the canons of literature, and Plato's and Aristotle's comparison of rhetoric and medicine had been made into a scientific method which rhetoric shared with medicine).[27] Since many of the early converts who first wrote on Christian

[27] For Greek doctrinal developments which led to the opposition of civil and sophistic rhetoric and to the advancement now of one, now of the other, as the preferred or unique manner of rhetoric cf. C. Brandstaetter, "De notionum πολιτικὸς et σοφιστὴς usu rhetorico," *Leipziger Studien zur classischen Philologie,* V (1893), 128–274. For the oppositions of sophistic, rhetoric, and philosophy cf. H. von Arnim, *Leben und Werke des Dio von Prusa* (Berlin, 1898), pp. 4–114; H. M. Hubbell, "The Rhetorica of Philodemus," *Transactions of the Connecticut Academy of Arts and Sciences,* XXIII (September, 1920), 276–84; J. F. d'Alton, *Roman Literary Theory and Criticism* (London, 1931), pp. 153 ff. For the interpenetration of rhetoric and dialectic and the transformation of dialectic by rhetoric in Hellenistic and Roman thought cf. Prantl, *op. cit.,* I, Abschnitt VIII, 505 ff. Philostratus includes in his *Lives of the Sophists* some of the ancient philosophers who approximated the rhetorical style of the Sophists, but he distinguished philosophy from sophistic (i. 481), since philosophers merely set snares for knowledge by their questioning but asserted that they had no sure knowledge, whereas Sophists of the old school professed knowledge of that whereof they spoke. Philostratus' enthusiastic account of the Sophists of the Empire is vivid indication of the spread and importance of epideictic rhetoric; its influence is likewise to be remarked in the Eastern church particularly among the Cappadocian fathers: cf. Norden, *op. cit.,* II, 529 ff. and 550 ff.; T. C. Burgess, "Epideictic Literature," *University of Chicago Studies in Classical Philology,* III (1902), 89–251; L. Méridier, *L'Influence de la séconde sophistique sur l'œuvre de Grégoire de Nysse* (Paris, 1906); M. Guignet, *Les Procédés épistolaires de St. Grégoire de Nazianze* (Paris, 1911); T. E. Ameringer, *The Stylistic Influence of the Second Sophistic on the Panegyrical Sermons of St. John Chrysostom* (Washington, 1921); J. M. Campbell, *The Influence of the Second Sophistic on the Style of the Sermons of St. Basil the Great* (Washington, 1922); A. Boulanger, *Aelius Aristide et la so-*

doctrine had been professional rhetoricians before their conversions,[28] the rhetorical distinctions which they used in the statement of their problems and the organization of their works emerged often as doctrinal differences and empirical observations in later speculation on their statements. This emergence of rhetoric in the materials of discussion in all fields brought new questions into the technical disputes of the art. The numerous technical distinctions which had entered the apparatus and discussion of rhetoric took on applications which echo or anticipate many of the positions of philosophers, which vary according to three conceptions of rhetoric distinguishable and in shifting opposition in their treatment of the materials to which rhetoric is applied.

Until the coming of the New Logic in the twelfth century, the pattern of that opposition is relatively simple: the rhetorician who professed to treat of subject matters accessible to the "common notions" of the mind, without need of technical competence, found himself opposed, on the one hand, by theologians who had learned from Augustine to use the distinction between words and things to attack the rhetoric of the schools while practicing a rhetoric devoted to divine eloquence and divine things, and, on the other hand, by rhetoricians who had learned from Boethius to use the distinction between thesis and hypothesis to limit rhetoric to probable reasoning concerning specifically delimited questions subordinate to the general questions of dialectic. To the Augustinian, the excessive use or extension of rhetoric or of dialectic was suspect; to the peripatetic follower of Boethius, limitation or criticism of dialectic, whether from the point of view of theology or of rhetoric, was an attack on the use of reason; and to the rhetori-

---

phistique dans la province d'Asie au ii siècle de notre ère (Paris, 1923). The crossing lines of rhetoric and medicine are apparent in Eunapius' Lives of the Philosophers; cf. particularly his accounts of Zeno of Cyprus, Magnus, Oribasius, and Ionicus (Secs. 497–99). Magnus made a happy combination of rhetoric and medicine by persuading the patients of other doctors that they had not been cured and then restoring them to health, apparently also by talk and questions; Ionicus was master of philosophy and medicine as well as the arts of rhetoric and poetry. Cf. P. H. and E. A. De Lacy, Philodemus: On Methods of Inference (Philadelphia, 1941), pp. 130 ff., where the relations between medicine and rhetoric are discussed in terms of an "empirical" or "conjectural" method.

[28] Cyprian (cf. Jerome De viris illustribus 67 [PL, XXIII, 714]), Arnobius (cf. Jerome Chromicon ad annum 329 [PL, XXVII, 675–76]), Lactantius (Jerome Chromicon ad annum 319 [PL, XXVII, 669–70]), Augustine (Confessions iv. 2. 2 [PL, XXXII, 693–94]). Most of the other early Christian writers in the West, even those who had not been teachers of rhetoric, had studied the art as part of their education.

cian, as such, limitation of rhetoric by the laws of logic or theology was unwarranted restriction of the scope of reason and visionary neglect of the practical exigencies of the problems of law and morals. The simple lines of this opposition appear even in the early discussions of rhetoric, and they are preserved after the appearance of the New Logic, beneath the surface of the more intricate distinctions made necessary by the Aristotelian differentiation of logic from dialectic, poetic, sophistic, and rhetoric. These three main positions with respect to rhetoric may be marked off into four historical periods during the Middle Ages, sharply distinguished by the authorities on which the discussion of the arts was successively based: a first stage extending to about the end of the tenth century, when the chief authorities were the pseudo-Augustine, Martianus Capella, Cassiodorus, and Isidore; a second period extending through the eleventh and the first half of the twelfth century, dominated by Cicero, Boethius, and the Old Logic; a third period comprising the latter part of the twelfth century and the greater part of the thirteenth century, in which the New Logic became to some degree effective and was applied after a manner in the interpretation of the Aristotelian corpus; and, finally, the fourteenth century and the Renaissance, in which Aristotle and the Greek rhetoricians, Cicero, Quintilian, and Boethius all had increasing influence.

During the first period, rhetoric was concerned—on the authority of Hermagoras, Cicero, and Boethius, of Fortunatianus, Augustine, and Victorinus, and of all the even more derivative authorities that depended on them—with civil philosophy.[29] According to Cassiodorus, "The art of rhetoric is, as the masters of secular letters teach, the science of speaking well in civil questions"; and that definition is repeated in almost the same words by Isidore, Alcuin, and Rhabanus

[29] Cf. Cicero De inventione i. 5. 6; Ad Herennium i. 2. 2; Boethius De differentiis topicis iv (PL, LXIV, 1207); Fortunatianus i. 1 (Halm, p. 81); pseudo-Augustine, De rhetorica 3 (Halm, p. 138); Fabius Laurentius Victorinus, Explanationes in rhetoricam M. Tullii Ciceronis i. 5 (Halm, p. 171). The authenticity of the De rhetorica attributed to Augustine was questioned by his Benedictine editors in 1679 (cf. PL, XXXII, 1439) and by most authorities since that time; cf. M. Gibert, Jugemens des savans sur les auteurs qui ont traité de la rhétorique (Paris, 1716), II, 98: "Mais pour peu qu'on connoisse le style du Saint, il est aisé de voir que l'Ouvrage n'est pas de lui"; and G. Saintsbury, A History of Criticism and Literary Taste in Europe (New York, 1900), I, 377. Its authenticity has been defended on philological grounds by W. Crecilinus, S. Aurelii Augustini de dialectica liber (Elberfeld, 1857), and by A. Reuter, "Zu dem Augustinischen Fragment Dè arte rhetorica," in Kirchengeschichtliche Studien Hermann Reuter . . . gewidmet (Leipzig, 1888), pp. 324–41; but the arguments adduced have been answered by J. Žůrek (op. cit.). The pseudo-Augustine attributes the position taken by Fortunatianus to Hermagoras.

Maurus.[30] The occasion of the dialogue with Charlemagne in which Alcuin's doctrine is stated is a request made by the emperor for information concerning the art, since he thinks it ridiculous for one whose daily occupation is with civil questions to be ignorant of the precepts of the art; the dialogue, moreover, is frankly moral not only in its traditional title, *On Rhetoric and the Virtues,* but in purpose, since the transition from rhetoric to the virtues is accomplished by recognition that this "sermocinandi ratio" which is applied to civil cases and secular business must be supplemented by the other virtues. Yet, within this broad agreement among rhetoricians that rhetoric is concerned with civil questions, there are numerous differences of statement, which sometimes lead to changes in the devices thought proper to rhetoric and which seem often to entail major philosophic differences. The chief of these is the difference between the position (which seems to go back to Hermagoras and for which Fortunatianus is sometimes given as authority) which treats civil philosophy in terms of the "common notions" of mankind and therefore undertakes to differentiate the subject matter of rhetoric in terms of the questions treated, that is, the kinds of theses and hypotheses, and the position (which goes back to Cicero) which finds the subject matter of rhetoric in the three genera—deliberative, demonstrative, and judicial. The former has the effect of emphasizing the common bases of rhetoric in human knowledge while turning analyses to the peculiarities of the questions that can be asked, the other the effect of centering on the common qualities of the subject matter and directing inquiry to the peculiarities and virtues of the orator. The problems of rhetoric arise largely in the mixtures of the two traditions. Cassiodorus, citing Fortunatianus, defines civil questions as those which fall within the common conception of the mind, that is, which anyone can understand when it is a question of the equitable and the good; Sulpitius Victor as those which are proper to no art but common to the opinion of all; Alcuin as those learned questions which can be conceived by the natural power of the mind.[31] Victorinus, on the other hand, divides

---

[30] Cassiodorus *Institutiones* ii. 2. 1 (Mynors, p. 97); cf. ii. Praef. 4 (Mynors, p. 91): "secundo de arte rhetorica, quae propter nitorem et copiam eloquentiae suae maxime in civilibus quaestionibus necessaria nimis et honorabilis aestimatur"; Isidore *Etymologiae* ii. 1 (Halm, p. 507); cf. i. 2. 1 and ii. 10, where law is treated as one of the subheads of rhetoric; Alcuin *De rhetorica et de virtutibus* 3 (Halm, p. 526); Rhabanus Maurus *De clericorum institutione* iii. 19 (*PL*, CVII, 396).

[31] *Institutiones* ii. 2. 1 (Mynors, p. 97); cf. Fortunatianus i. 1 (Halm, p. 81) and the pseudo-Augustine (*De rhetorica* 4 [Halm, p. 139]), who supplies the Greek

the possible matter of rhetoric into two kinds: that with which the art operates (*ubi fit*)—namely, deliberative, demonstrative, judicial—and that from which the art is formed (*unde fit*)—namely, the arguments which contribute the matter of those three kinds—then limits the consideration of rhetoric to the former and refutes Hermagoras' doctrine of thesis and hypothesis in favor of the Aristotelian and Ciceronian doctrine of the three genera.[32] Martianus Capella repeats this differentiation of two kinds of matter but goes on to the exposition of theses and hypotheses, confining his disapproval to a remark concerning the extremely subtle reasons of some of the sectaries of rhetoric who hold that all rhetorical questions are general or theses.[33] The difference is between a tendency to make distinctions with reference to a subject matter and arguments suited to that subject matter and a tendency to make distinctions—often, indeed, the same distinctions—wih reference to the orator and his problems of discovering and stating arguments. The former emphasis tends to intellectualize the art and change its orientation to a subject matter and its peculiarities into problems of inquiry and understanding, as when Sulpitius Victor, having limited rhetoric to the civil question and having divided the civil question into two parts, thesis and hypothesis, finds three duties for the orator— understanding, discovery, and disposition (the first of which was neglected by Cicero but was adequately treated by the Greeks)—and then three genera of causes in the place of those long customary—the ethical, pathetic, and judicial. The latter emphasis leads to a series of questions, which were much discussed during the Middle Ages, concerning the relation of morals and eloquence, concerning the relation of art and wisdom, and concerning the definition of rhetoric as a virtue or an art or a discipline.[34] Rhetoric was to come into conflict with dia-

---

term κοινὴ ἔννοια suggestive of Stoic origins. Sulpitius Victor *Institutiones oratoriae* (Halm, p. 314) and Alcuin *De rhetorica et de virtutibus* 3 (Halm, p. 526).

[32] Fabius Laurentius Victorinus 5 (Halm, pp. 174–77).

[33] Martianus Capella 5 (Halm, p. 454).

[34] Sulpitius Victor *Institutiones oratoriae* 4 and 6 (Halm, pp. 315, 316). Cato's definition of the orator as *vir bonus dicendi peritus* (Quintilian xii. 1; Seneca *Controversiarum* i, Praef. 9) was frequently repeated before the Carolingian period—by Fortunatianus, Victorinus, Cassiodorus, Isidore (Halm, pp. 81, 177, 495, 507)—and one of the favorite etymologies of "art" derived it from the Greek word for virtue. In the twelfth century Aristotle's authority (cited from the *Categories*) is used to deny that rhetoric is a virtue (cf. Abailard *Dialogus* [PL, CLXXVIII, 1652]; Hermannus *Epitome theologiae Christianae* [PL, CLXXVIII, 1750]; *Sententie Parisienses*, ed. A. Landgraf, *Écrits théologiques de l'école d'Abélard* [Louvain, 1934], p. 52). In the thirteenth century Aristotle's authority (cited from the *Nichomachean Ethics*) could be quoted to place it, together with the other arts, among the intellectual virtues. In the Renaissance, one of the chief

lectic as a consequence of this tendency, as it was to come into conflict
with theology as a consequence of its tendency to annex the problems
of morals and the interpretation of Scripture. Since its discipline was
gradually limited by the transfer of the commonplaces, definition, and,
finally, proof—even in the rhetorical formulations they had received
from Cicero, Victorinus, and Boethius—to the domain of dialectic and
since its subject matter was limited by the transfer of moral and
political questions to theology, rhetoric developed during its second
period along three separate lines: as a part of logic, or as the art of
stating truths certified by theology, or as a simple art of words.

III

The subordination of rhetoric to logic was based usually on the
greater particularity of its subject matter, that is, its concern with
hypotheses rather than with theses. The terms of the discussion of the
relation of rhetoric to dialectic were borrowed from Boethius. The
doctrine is expressed, however, before the appearance of Boethius in
the curriculum of the schools. According to Isidore of Seville, logic
(Isidore adds that the Greek term λόγος means "rational") has two
parts, dialectic and rhetoric.[35] John the Scot omits grammar and
rhetoric from his treatise *On the Division of Nature*, first, because
many philosophers think they are parts of dialectic; second, from considerations of brevity; and, finally, because, unlike dialectic, grammar
and rhetoric do not treat of the nature of things but either of words
significant by convention or of special causes and persons.[36] The

---

grounds for Ramus' violent criticism of Quintilian is found in his tendency to
identify rhetoric with morals (cf. P. Ramus, *Rhetoricae distinctiones in Quintilianum* [Paris, 1559]).

[35] *De differentiis rerum* 39 (*PL*, LXXXIII, 93–94).

[36] *De divisione naturae* v. 4 (*PL*, CXXII, 869–70): "Primum quidem, quia ipsae
duae artes veluti quaedam membra Dialecticae multis philosophis non incongrue
existimantur. Deinde brevitatis occasione. Postremo, quod non de rerum natura
tractare videntur, sed vel de regulis humanae vocis, quam non secundum naturam,
sed secundum consuetudinem loquentium subsistere Aristotles cum suis sectatoribus
approbat, vel de causis atque personis specialibus, quod longe a natura rerum
distat. Nam dum Rhetorica de communibus locis, qui ad naturam rerum pertinent,
tractare nititur, non suas, sed Dialecticae arripit partes." Rhetoric is limited to
hypotheses or finite questions determined by the seven circumstances, while the
common conceptions of the mind have become the property of dialectic; cf. *De
divisione naturae* i. 27 (*PL*, CXXII, 475): "Rhetorica est finitam causam persona,
materia, occasione, qualitate, loco, tempore, facultate discutiens copiose atque
ornate disciplina; breviterque definiri potest, Rhetorica est finitae causae septem
periochis sagax et copiosa disciplina. Dialectica est communium animi concep-
tionum rationabilium diligens investigatrixque disciplina."

pseudo-Rhabanus Maurus was one of the philosophers who divided logic into three parts: grammar, rhetoric, and dialectic,[37] and Remigius of Auxerre divides philosophers into four kinds: dialecticians, rhetoricians, Sophists who always come to false conclusions, and jurists who dispute concerning the status of law.[38] Gerbert, who used all the dialectical works and translations of Boethius in his teaching at Rheims and Paris (including Cicero's *Topics,* which, like Cassiodorus, he thought Cicero had translated from the Greek, and the *On Definition* of Marius Victorinus), likewise considered dialectic and rhetoric parts of logic and taught rhetoric after dialectic.[39] Fulbert, finally, who restored studies at Chartres in the eleventh century and who knew, in addition to the *De inventione* and the *Ad Herennium,* Victorinus' commentary on Cicero and the two treatises on rhetorical places attributed to Boethius, has left twenty-one verses on the differences between rhetoric and dialectic: they are the three differences that Boethius found between the matters, uses, and ends of the arts.[40]

The transition to the third period in this tradition of rhetoric determined relatively to dialectic is accomplished when the increased influence, or at least the increased repute, of the New Logic led to separation of scientific or demonstrative proof from probable proof and to the location of rhetoric with dialectic under the latter. It is a gradual transition, dependent as much on increase of erudition in logic as in rhetoric. In the comprehensive collection of texts in the liberal arts prepared by Thierry of Chartres under the title *Heptateuchon* about 1141, all of Aristotle's *Organon* except the *Posterior Analytics* and the second book of the *Prior Analytics* appears, while under rhetoric are included (in addition to the traditional sources of rhetoric—the *De inventione,* the *Ad Herennium,* and Martianus Capella—and Cicero's *Topics,* which with Boethius' *De differentiis topicis* is classified under dialectic) only Cicero's *De partitione oratoria* and Julius Severianus'

[37] V. Cousin, *Ouvrages inédits d'Abélard* (Paris, 1836), p. 614.

[38] B. Hauréau, "Commentaire de Jean Scot Erigène sur Martianus Capella," *Notices et extraits des manuscrits de la Bibliothèque Impériale,* XX, No. 2 (1862), 11. Cf. *ibid.,* pp. 20–21, for his difference from the doctrine of John concerning the natural bases of rhetoric in human nature.

[39] The sequence of studies, as directed by Gerbert, were: first, dialectic, which included the *Isagoge* of Porphyry (with Boethius' commentary), the *Categories* and *On Interpretation* of Aristotle, the *Topics* (translated by Cicero and with Boethius' commentary), Boethius' *On Topical Differences, On Categorical Syllogisms, On Hypothetical Syllogisms, On Definitions, On Divisions;* second, as preparation for rhetoric, the poets; third, rhetoric; finally, sophistic. He includes the entire program under the term "logic" (Richter, *Historiae,* III, 44 ff. (ed. G. H. Pertz, *Monumenta Germaniae historica,* Vol. V: *Scriptores,* III, 617).

[40] A. Clerval, *Les Écoles de Chartres au moyen-âge* (Chartres, 1895), p. 115.

Precepts on the Art of Rhetoric.[41] Yet Thierry of Chartres wrote a commentary on the *De inventione* in which a history of rhetoric is reconstructed to explain the opening paragraph of Cicero's work as a refutation of Plato and Aristotle: Plato had argued that rhetoric was no art, Aristotle that it was an art but a bad art, while Cicero contends, against both, that it is a good art.[42] A short Preface and an Introduction precede the fragment of the *Commentary* which has been preserved. The Introduction is devoted to asking ten questions concerning rhetoric—its genus, definition, matter, duty, end, parts, species, instrument, who the orator is, and why the art is so called—to which two specific questions are added—the intention of Tully in this work and the utility of the work. The genus of rhetoric is still civil science, it is not a part of logic, and its matter is hypothesis.[43] Nor is the position of Thierry an anachronistic piece of conservatism, for one of the works which was most influential in preparing the way for the new knowledge of the thirteenth century and which was eagerly consulted as a source of information concerning the Arabic learning, the *De divisione philosophiae* of Gundissalinus, contains a section on rhetoric which not merely asks the same ten questions as Thierry of Chartres but is identical, apart from slight variations, with the Introduction to his

[41] *Ibid.*, pp. 222–23; cf. R. McKeon, "Aristotelianism in Western Christianity," in J. T. McNeill (ed.), *Environmental Factors in Christian History* (Chicago, 1939), pp. 215–19.

[42] *Fragmentum scholastae inediti ad Ciceronem De inventione rhetorica* (W. H. D. Suringar, *Historia critica scholiastrum Latinorum* [Leyden, 1834], I, 213–53), pp. 224–36. Thierry's reading in works of rhetoric was apparently more extensive than the contents of the *Heptateuchon,* since he quotes Quintilian (*ibid.*, p. 219).

[43] *Ibid.*, p. 217: "Genus igitur artis rhetoricae est qualitas ipsius artificii secundum ejus effectum: hoc autem est, quod ipsum artificium est, pars civilis scientiae major. Nam civilis ratio dicitur quidquid civitas aut rationabiliter dicit aut agit; dicimus enim: ratio est hoc vel illud facere vel dicere. Item civilis ratio dicitur, scientia dicendi aliquid rationabiliter et faciendi. Et haec quidem ratio, scientia civilis dicitur, cujus quidem pars integra, vel etiam major, rhetorica est. Nam sapientia i.e. rerum conceptio secundum earum naturam, et rhetorica civilem scientiam componunt. Et enim nisi quis sapiens et eloquens fuerit, civilem scientiam habere non dicitur. Major vero pars civilis scientiae dicitur rhetorica, quoniam magis operatur in civilibus causis quam sapientia, etsi sine sapientia nihil prosit. Maximam enim virtutem habet eloquentia in civitate, si sapientiae juncta sit." Thierry then goes on to compare this solution with Boethius' doctrine that the genus of rhetoric is *facultas* and finds the two doctrines in agreement, since the same science is an *art* in the master who teaches its rules and a *faculty* in the orator. He is explicit in excluding rhetoric from logic: "Non est autem dicendum, rhetoricam aut logicam esse aut ejus partem, idcirco quod logica circa thesin solam i.e. circa genera agendi, tantummodo versatur." Cf. *ibid.*, p. 219 for *materia.* Cf Adelard of Bath, *De eodem et diverso* in *Beiträge zur Geschichte der Philosophie des Mittelalters* (henceforth cited as "*BGPM*"), IV, No. 1, 19 ff.

Commentary.[44] Gundissalinus differs slightly from Thierry in the classifiication of rhetoric; for, whereas Thierry would have it a part of civil science and not a part of logic, Gundissalinus classifies both rhetoric and poetic among the eight parts of logic, but he also classifies rhetoric and poetic as parts of civil science.[45]

Hugh of St. Victor, who was contemporary with Thierry of Chartres, follows the suggestion of the Aristotelian division of the sciences into theoretic, practical, and mechanical (which seems to be Hugh's substitute for Aristotle's productive science): logic is a fourth branch and not a part of politics, which falls under the practical sciences. More-

[44] Dominicus Gundissalinus *De divisione philosophiae*, ed. L. Baur (BGPM, IV, Nos. 2–3 [Münster, 1903], 63–69). For the strange history of scholarly inquiries into the commentary of Thierry cf. M. Grabmann, "Eine lateinische Übersetzung der pseudo-Aristotelischen Rhetorica ad Alexandrum aus dem 13. Jahrhundert," *Sitzungsberichte der Bayerischen Akademie der Wissenschaften, Phil.-hist. Abt.* (1931–32), No. 4, pp. 4–5. In spite of the fact that it was published by Suringar in 1834, the fragmentary *Commentary* was discussed as an unpublished document by Rohde in 1881, by Bücheler in 1883, and by Thomas in 1884; its author was supposed to have been a contemporary of Theodoric the Great until Thomas suggested that the document was medieval (and consequently of very little interest); finally, Manitius identified it as the work of Thierry or Theodoric of Chartres, and Klibansky pointed out its identity with the work published by Suringar. Grabmann does not notice that there is one further coincidence, viz., the identity of one of the three sections (Suringar, *op. cit.*, pp. 216–23) with the section on rhetoric in Gundissalinus. Short of examination of the manuscripts—unfortunately impossible at this time—the question of priority is difficult to decide: some of the sections contained in Thierry but omitted by Gundissalinus seem rather in the nature of additions to, than omissions from, an original text, and the references seem better suited to the *Commentary* than to the *De divisiome philosophiae* (as, e.g., where Thierry says [p. 220]: "Sed quid sit circumstantia, in sequentibus melius dicetur," Gundissalinus says [p. 66]: "Set quid sit circumstancia in Tullio dicetur," although no further reference is made to Cicero on this point); on the other hand, the supposition that the work of Thierry was prior runs into the grave difficulty that all the sciences in the *De divisiome philosophiae* are treated by means of the same ten questions here applied to rhetoric.

[45] This section on the genus of rhetoric in Gundissalinus (p. 64) is the same as the statement quoted above (n. 43) from Thierry, but stops short before the discussion of Boethius and the statement that rhetoric is not a part of logic. In the section on logic, Gundissalinus cites Alfarabi for the eight parts of logic (p. 71): "Secundum Alfarabium octo sunt partes logice: cathegorie, perihermenias, analetica priora, analetica posteriora, thopica, sophistica, rhetorica, poetica." He need not have gone to the Arabs for this doctrine, for the equivalent of the six books of Aristotle's *Organon* plus rhetoric and poetic constituted the logic taught by Gerbert (cf. above, n. 39). Gundissalinus gives as the genus of logic that it is a part and instrument of philosophy (p. 69) and denies that its matter is "thesis," arguing that it is the second intention of the understanding (pp. 70–71). The genus of poetic is the same as rhetoric (p. 54): "Genus huius artis [*sc.* poeticae] est, quod ipsa est pars ciuilis sciencie, que est pars eloquencie. Non enim parum operatur in ciuilibus, quod delectat uel edificat in sciencia uel in moribus."

over, his classification of logic makes an excellent transition from the customary classification according to the trivium of grammar, rhetoric, and dialectic to the "Aristotelian" classification as parts of logic and according to the kinds of proof. Following Isidore of Seville, Hugh points out the double etymology of λόγος, i.e., *sermo* and *ratio,* and argues that logic can be called either a verbal or a rational science (*sermocinalis sive rationalis scientia*); rational logic (which Hugh also calls *dissertiva*) is divided into dialectic and rhetoric, while verbal logic is the genus of grammar, dialectic, and rhetoric, and therefore rational logic is contained under it.[46] This treatment of the traditional trivium is supplemented, however, by another division of logic into grammar and *ratio disserendi* or "dissertive" logic, which is concerned with words as understood (*de vocibus secundum intellectus*). "Dissertive" or rational logic is, in turn, divided into integral parts, i.e., parts shared by its kinds, which turn out to be the Ciceronian distinction into discovery and judgment, and divisive parts, i.e., demonstrative, probable, and sophistic; the two parts of probable proof are dialectic and rhetoric.[47] John of Salisbury, one of the pupils of Thierry of Chartres, who had studied the whole of Aristotle's *Organon* and who was widely read in Cicero and Quintilian, attributes to Plato the division of logic into dialectic and rhetoric; but he prefers, as more philosophic, the division into demonstrative, probable, and sophistic, with the further division of probable into dialectic and rhetoric.[48] William of Conches, on the other hand, whom John calls the finest grammarian after Bernard of Chartres,[49] divides eloquence, which

[46] *Didascalicon* i. 11, ed. C. H. Buttimer (Washington, 1939), pp. 20–21; or i. 12 (*PL,* CLXXVI, 749–50). Cf. Isidore of Seville *Etymologiae* ii. 24. 7.

[47] *Didascalicon* ii. 28–30; Buttimer, pp. 44–47; or ii. 29–31 (*PL,* CLXXVI, 763–66).

[48] *Metalogicon* ii. 3, ed. C. C. J. Webb (Oxford, 1929), pp. 64–65. Baldwin complains (*op. cit.,* p. 157) that rhetoric is barely mentioned in the *Metalogicon* and seems "to have no distinctive composing function"; the few references which he finds indicate that he was looking for rhetoric before the treatment of logic, whereas John treats it under the *Topics.* Cf. *Metalogicon* iii. 5 (Webb, p. 139), and esp. 10 (Webb, pp. 154–55): "Quia ergo exercitatio dialectice ad alterum est; pares, quos producit et quos rationibus muniuit et locis, sua docet arma tractare et sermones potius conserere quam dexteras, et tanta cautela imbuit, ut totius eloquentie precepta hinc tracta principaliter, uelut a primitiuo fonte originis sue, manare perspicuum sit. Indubitanter enim uerum est, quod fatentur Cicero et Quintilianus, quia hinc non modo rethoricorum adiumentum, set et principium rethores et scriptores artium assumpserunt; postmodum tamen propriis dilatata est institutis." The matter of dialectic is still the "question" as distinguished from the "hypothesis," which is the matter of rhetoric (*Metalogicon* ii. 12 [Webb, pp. 83–84]).

[49] *Metalogicon* i. 5 (Webb, pp. 16–17): "Willelmus de Conchis, grammaticus post Bernardum Carnotensem opulentissimus."

the ancients called "logic," into grammar, *ratio disserendi,* and rhetoric.[50]

IV

The translations of Aristotle affected the discussions of theology as well as philosophy, and the changes in rhetoric and in the relations of rhetoric to dialectic are reflected in the methods of theology. "Aristotelian" conceptions of the organization of logic with rhetoric as one of its parts were not, however, intruded into theology, since the opposition was between the Augustinian conception of a single body of theological and philosophic truth possessed of a single method and the conception of a philosophy independent in method and subject matter from theology; and therefore the simple organization of the trivium as three rational or verbal sciences continued in theology and even in philosophy under the influence of Augustine long after it became obsolete in the philosophy influenced by Aristotle. Even as early as the sixth century, when Cassiodorus wrote his *Expositio in Psalterium,* he could appeal, in his introductory chapters, "On the Eloquence of the Whole Divine Law" and "On the Proper Eloquence of the Psalter," to an impressive list of learned Fathers—Augustine, Jerome, Ambrose, Hilary—who had studied both the figures which are common to sacred and secular letters and the proper modes of divine speech which are not touched by grammarians or rhetoricians.[51] Divine eloquence is not formed of human words or involved in human ambiguities, but, since its purpose is to spread divine law to all the corners of the world, it makes many uses of modes of speech, and it is "succinct with definitions, adorned with figures, marked by the propriety of words, expedited by the constructions of syllogisms"; and, while these devices are certain and clear in the Scriptures, they stand in need of the liberal arts when they come into contact with the opinions and disputes of men.[52] His commentary consists largely of

---

[50] C. Ottaviano, *Un Brano inedito della "Philosophia" di Guglielmo di Conches* (Naples, 1935), p. 28.

[51] *Expositio in Psalterium,* Praef. xv (*PL,* CLXX, 21).

[52] *Expositio in Psalterium* 19: "Eloquentia legis divinae humanis non est formata sermonibus, neque confusis incerta fertur ambagibus, ut aut a rebus praeteritis oblivione discedat, aut praesentium confusione turbetur, aut futurorum dubiis casibus eludatur; sed cordi, non corporalibus auribus loquens, magna veritate, magna praescientiae firmitate cuncta dijudicans, auctoris sui veritate consistit . . . Eloquentia siquidem est ad unamquamque rem competens et decora locutio." Cf. *ibid.* 20: "Haec mundanarum artium periti, quos tamen multo posterius ab exordio divinorum librorum extitisse manifestum est, ad collectiones argumentorum, quae Graeci topica dicunt, et ad artem dialecticam et rhetoricam transtul-

such aids to understanding, dotted with identifications of kinds of definition, figures of speech, and forms of arguments.[53] The evolution of this use of rhetoric consists, primarily, in the increasing formalization of the methods of interpreting Scripture and the rules of divine eloquence and, secondarily, in the recurrent application of the secular art to Scripture and the recurrent expressions of concern at the excesses of the liberal arts in such application. In the one line of development, Augustine's simple suggestion that things as well as words are signs was elaborated until the spiritual sense, which balanced the literal sense, was divided into three kinds—the allegorical, the moral, and the anagogic; and this thological development of rhetoric eventually, in turn, influenced mundane or poetic rhetoric.[54] In the other line of

---

erunt; ut cunctis evidenter appareat, prius ad exprimendam veritatem justis mentibus datum, quod postea gentiles humanae sapientiae aptandam esse putaverunt. Haec in lectionibus sacris tanquam clarissima sidera relucent, et significantias rerum utilissimis compendiis decenter illuminant."

[53] Cf. *Expositio in Psalterium* i (*PL*, CLXX, 27), for identification of two kinds of definition according to the technical terms of Victorinus; (*PL*, CLXX, 33), where the figure is explained by means of the mathematical disciplines; vi. 1 (*PL*, CLXX, 61), where the fashion in which the divine eloquence has been enriched by the various arts and disciplines is illustrated by discussion of rhetorical *status;* xliii. 15 (*PL*, CLXX, 314), where the figure of *anaphora* is identified, and so *passim.*

[54] Cf. Augustine *De utilitate credendi* 3, 5 (*PL*, XLII, 68) (historical, etiological, analogical, allegorical, senses); Gregory the Great *Moralia, epistola Missoria* (*PL*, LXXV, 510–15) (historical, allegorical, moral); Peter Abailard *Expositio in Hexaemeron* (*PL*, CLXXVII, 731) (historical, moral, and mystic); Hugh of St. Victor *De sacramentis, Prologus* 4 (*PL*, CLXXVI, 184) (historical, allegorical, tropological); and Peter of Poitier *Allegoriae super Tabernaculum Moysi, Prologus,* ed. P. S. Moore and J. A. Corbett (Notre Dame, 1938), p. 1 (historical, allegorical, moral, anagogic); cf. P. S. Moore, *The Works of Peter of Poitiers* (Notre Dame, 1936), pp. 65–77. Cf. Thomas Aquinas *Summa theologica* i. q. 1, a. 10: "Respondeo dicendum quod auctor sacrae Scripturae est Deus, in cujus potestate est ut non solum voces ad significandum accommodet (quod etiam homo facere potest) sed etiam res ipsas. Et ideo, cum in omnibus scientiis voces significant, hoc habet proprium ista scientia quod ipsae res significate per voces, etiam significant aliquid." The first of these significations is historical or literal, the second (in which things signify other things (spiritual, and the spiritual interpretation is further divided into allegorical, moral, and anagogic. Dante follows the division of Aquinas; cf. *Epistola X Domino Cani Grandi de Scala* vii. 98–116; *Convivio* ii. 1 (cf. *ibid.* 14 for rhetoric). The "four senses" are also used to explain the "form of wisdom" (cf. Bonaventura *In Hexaemeron, Collatio* ii [*Opera omnia,* ed. Quaracchi (1891), V, 336–42], i.e., uniform, multiform [allegorical, anagogic, tropological, each of which has two forms], omniform and nulliform) and to classify the sciences (cf. M. Grabmann, *Die Geschichte der scholastischen Methode* [Freiburg i/Br., 1911], II, 43, n. 1, where a quotation is given from an unpublished manuscript, dated broadly as posterior to Hugh of St. Victor, in which the sciences are divided into theoretic, practical, and logical; practical science, in turn, is divided into actual [ethics, economics, and politics] and inspective, which is divided into *historia* and *spiritualis intelligentia;* history simply states the order of things without any hidden meaning apparent from that conveyed by the words; the spiritual understanding is divided into the tropological, allegorical, and anagogic. Rational logic is divided

development, more suspect of error and more frequently condemned in one form by conservative theologians who practiced it in another form, which they found indispensable to the understanding of Scripture, rhetoric supplied devices to clarify the meanings and remove the ambiguities of scriptural statements. Abailard begins his *Commentary on the Epistle of St. Paul to the Romans* with the statement: "The intention of all divine Scripture is to teach or to move in the manner of a rhetorical speech," and derives his triple division of the Old and New Testaments from these two purposes.[55] The divine pages cannot be read and appreciated without grammar and rhetoric.[56] An anonymous commentary on Romans repeats Abailard's statement of the twofold rhetorical purpose of the Old and New Testament, after having specified that all the arts are servants to divinity: grammar, which teaches constructions; dialectic, which expounds by arguments; and rhetoric, which consists in persuasion.[57] Even theologians who, like Robert of Melun, opposed the excessive use of rhetoric in secular as well as in divine letters, repeated the same judgment of the rhetorical purposes of Scripture.[58]

The method of rhetoric was, moreover, put to another and even more characteristic use in the interpretation of theological doctrine. The "scholastic method," as it came to be called, grew out of the assemblage of "sentences," which derived their name and their initial methods of treatment from rhetoric.[59] The early collections of canon law were collections of authorities—statements from Scripture, de-

---

into dialectic, apodictic [or demonstrative], and sophistic). Bonaventura also uses these distinctions as the fourfold division in the "light of sacred Scripture" (*De reductione artium ad theologiam* 5 [*Opera omnia*, V, 321]).

[55] *Commentaria super S. Pauli Epistolam ad Romanos*, Prologus (*PL*, CLXXVIII, 783–84).

[56] *Introductio ad theologiam* ii. 2 (*PL*, CLXXVIII, 1044): "At jam profecto nec grammaticam a Christiano legi convenit, sine documentis cujus nec divina intelligi pagina, nec scriptura aliqua. Sic nec rhetoricam, quae omnis eloquentiae tradit ornamenta, quibus maxime sacra Scriptura est referta, nec ejus decor nisi his diligenter assignatis elucere poterit."

[57] *Commentarius Cantabrigiensis in Epistolas Pauli e Schola Petri Abaelardi: In Epistolam ad Romanos*, ed. A. Landgraf (Notre Dame, 1937), pp. 1–2.

[58] Grabmann, *Die Geschichte der scholastischen Methode*, II, 349, n. 2. H. Denifle, *Die abendländischen Schriftausleger bis Luther über "Justitia" (Rom. 1. 17) und "Justificatio"* (Mainz, 1905), p. 76: "Ad erudicionem autem ipsius omnes scripture facte sunt, quarum partes sunt tam sacre scripture, quam thnice. In ethnicis enim, id est gentilibus, scripturis et sermonum composicio et rerum proprietas docet. Sermonum composicio in trivio, rerum proprietas in methematicis disciplinis secundum extrinseca et intrinseca. . . . Intencionem vero more rethorice oracionis docere et monere."

[59] Cf. G. Paré, A. Burnet, and P. Tremblay, *La Renaissance du XII⁶ siècle: Les Écoles et l'enseignement* (Ottawa, 1933), pp. 267 ff., for an excellent statement of the rhetorical beginnings of the *sentitiae*.

cisions of councils, decretals, opinions of the Fathers—which, because
of the practical problems involved in direction of action, presented
urgently the problem of bringing discordant or apparently discordant
canons into concordance. When Peter Abailard assembled apparently
contradictory texts in his *Sic et non,* the rules for interpreting them
which he set forth in the Prologue are developments of the rules
elaborated by a long line of canon lawyers—notably Hincmar of
Rheims, Bernold of Constance, Ivo of Chartres—and involve such
directions as careful consideration of context; comparison of texts;
specification of time, place, and person; determination of original
cause of statement; and differentiation of general measures from
particular.[60] Although this method led to a further step in the dialectical resolution of the contradictions, the method at this stage is
rhetorical rather than dialectical. The rules of interpretation of the
Prologue of the *Sic et non,* thus, approximate the performance of
Abailard's *Commentary on Romans,* which is grammatical and rhetorical; but the texts such as those assembled there serve him as a store-
house of quotations for his systematic works, the *Theologia "summi
boni,"* the *Theologia Christiana,* and the *Introductio ad theologiam,* in
which the method which Abailard calls "dialectical" is used to resolve
their differences, not by consideration of contexts and circumstances,
but by reduction to an orderly body of true propositions. The difference, far from being slight, was to grow into one of the marks of
differentiation between the line of Christian theology which adapted
itself to the Aristotelian philosophy and made use of logic and dialectic
and the line of Christian theology and philosophy which continued the
distinction of the trivium and subordinated dialectic to rhetoric. One
of the numerous admirers of Abailard, who tried to remove the taint of
unorthodoxy from his doctrines, made that readjustment by shifting
the functions of the arts, assigning to grammar a concern with meanings, to dialectic the production of conviction, and to rhetoric, finally,
the motivation of the will.[61] This is a doctrine, moreover, which need

---

[60] *Ibid.* 286 ff., where, however, the method is stated as dialectical. Cf. Grabmann, *Die Geschichte der scholastischen Methode,* I, 234 ff., and P. Fournier and
G. Le Bras, *Histoire des collections canoniques en occident* (Paris, 1932), II, 334 ff.
In the more orthodox tradition, theology derived its customary organization, indirectly from rhetoric, in Augustine's division of all doctrine into problems of things
and problems of signs (cf. P. Lombard, *Senteniarum liber* i, dist. 1 cap.). The
other distinction which Augustine makes at the beginning of the *De doctrina
Chritiana,* of all treatment of the Scriptures into the mode of discovery and the
mode of statement, served as basis of organization of treatises on preaching (cf.
Bonaventura *Ars concionandi [Opera omnia,* IX, 8]).

[61] [Anonymous] *Ysagoge in theologiam,* ed. A. Landgraf, *op. cit.,* p. 72: "Eloquentia vero est scientia ad congruam agnitorum prolationem suum formans
artificem. Que, quia triplicem habet efficatiam, tres habet partes, respondentque

suffer no opprobrium because of its connection with Abailard, since
the same domination of the trivium by rhetoric is expressed, partly in
the same words, by Bernard Sylvester, the friend of Thierry of
Chartres, in his commentary on Virgil's *Aeneid,* a context which seems
safe from the danger of heresy.[62]

The two general tendencies which came to their culmination in the
thirteenth century, that by which rhetoric was made part of logic and
that by which rhetoric became an instrument of theology, are determined by the important methodological differences which separate the
Aristotelians and the Augustinians. For Thomas Aquinas rhetoric is
one of the parts of logic concerned with probable argumentation; for
Bonaventura rhetoric is the culmination of the trivium. Thomas wrote

---

efficatie partibus ut effectus causis. Est enim prima grammatica, que pertinent ad
intellectum; secunda dialectica, que ad fidem; tertia rethorica, que ad persuasionem.
Quod enim prima vocum attendit accidentia, ideo fit, ut secundum ea competens
fiat earum contextus ad manifestandum conceptum loquentis vel ad constituendum
consimilem in auditore. Sed quia, si pulsetur de veritate, intellectus, quem indicat
et constituit, nequit fidem facere, succedit dialectica, que acceptis orationibus a
prima componit ex eis argumentationem, qua fidem confert. Sed quia possumus
intelligere et intellectum credere et tamen illud nolle, consummationem dat
rethorica. Hec enim accipiens argumentaciones a logica, ut illa orationes a grammatica, ex eis per orationem [*read* perorationem] facit et, quod prima intelligere,
secunda credere, ipsa facit velle."

[62] *Commentum Bernardi Silvestris super sex libros Eneidos Virgilii* vi, ed. G.
Riedel (Gryphiswaldae, 1924), p. 31: "Eloquentia est scientia formans suum
lectorem ad congruam cognitorum prolationem. Haec autem Trivia dicitur quia [a]
tribus artibus quasi tribus viis ad eam incedimus. Ut autem perfecte habeatur
eloquentia, primo oportet scire loqui absque soloecismo et barbarismo quod per
grammaticam habetur. Deinde sic loquendo oportet scire aliquid probare vel
improbare quod fit per dialecticam. Adhuc necessarium [oportet] persuadere vel
dissuadere: possunt enim auditores grammatica oratione aliquid intelligere, dialectica probatione de eodem certi esse et tamen illud nolle: ideo necessaria rethorica
persuasio. Itaque est grammatica initium eloquentiae, dialectica dicitur provectus,
rethorica perfectio. Atque adeo dicitur eloquentia Trivia." Cf. also *ibid.,* pp. 36,
38, 87–88. It would easily be possible to attach too much significance to the order
in which the arts of the trivium are enumerated; yet many of the enumerations of
the twelfth and thirteenth centuries underline the importance of the order; and even
before that time authors tend to a consistency in their enumerations, which suggests
that some degree of importance was attached to the enumeration. Dialectic appears
third in the lists of Cassiodorus (*Institutiones* ii, Praef.; Mynors, p. 91), Isidore
(*Etymologiae* i. 2), Alcuin (*Grammatica* [*PL,* CI, 853]: "Sunt igitur gradus, quos
quaeritis, et utinam tam ardentes sitis semper ad ascendendum quam curiosi modo
estis ad videndum: grammatica, rhetorica, dialectica . . ."), Rhabanus Maurus (*De
clericorum institutione* iii. 18 [*PL,* CVII, 395]: "Prima ergo liberalium artium est
grammatica, secunda rhetorica, tertia dilectica . . ."). Rhetoric is third in Augustine (*De ordine* ii. 13 [*PL,* XXXII, 1013]), Martianus Capella, and Gerbert. After
the eleventh century the tendency is either to place the trivium, together with
demonstration and sophistic, under logic or to list the three with rhetoric in the
dominant position. The rule is far from being universal; e.g., Adelard of Bath,
who was strongly influenced by the Platonism of Chartres, places dialectic third
in his allegory (*De eodem et diuerso* [*BGPM,* IV, No. 1, 21]).

a commentary on two books of Aristotle's *Organon*, and, since he separated the method and subject of the philosophic from those of the theological truth, he could use the devices of Aristotle in the a posteriori proofs of his systematic theology and those of Augustine in his commentaries on Scripture; Bonaventura wrote no work on logic but did compose an excellent *Art of Preaching*, which is useful for the interpretation of his theological treatises and commentaries as well as his sermons.

The translation of the whole of the *Nicomachean Ethics* (which was called the "New Ethics" in contrast to the truncated earlier translation) brought to further refinement the solution of questions concerning the relation of rhetoric to civil questions: according to Aquinas, the matter with which rhetoric is concerned is civil,[63] but rhetoric must not be confused with politics.[64] In much the same fashion the terminology and conclusions of the earlier rhetorical discusssion enter into Thomas' classification of the parts of logic. The parts of logic or rational science or rational philosophy are determined by the diversity of the acts of reason: they are three of which the first is an act of immediate understanding and the last two are acts of reason. The first is the operation of the mind called (by Averroës) "information of understanding" or "imagination through understanding"; the doctrine which Aristotle treats in the *Categories* is ordered to this act of reason. The second is the operation of composition and division, which results in truth or falsity; the doctrine which Aristotle treats in the *De interpretatione* is concerned with this act of reason. Finally, the third act, which is the proper function of reason, is discursive movement from one thing to another, from something known to the unknown: the remaining four books of the *Organon* are concerned with this operation of reason. It may take any of three forms in conformity to a threefold diversity in nature: in some cases nature acts from necessity without the possibility of divergence; in some cases it operates for the most part in a certain way but with the possibility of deviation from its proper act; and there are therefore, in addition to necessary operations, two additional kinds of natural acts, those which occur for the most part and those in which nature deviates from what

[63] *In decem libros ethicorum Aristotelis ad Nicomachum expositio* i, Lectio 3, ed. A. M. Pirotta (Turin, 1934), p. 12, n. 36. Infallible proof is impossible in human affairs, and therefore the conjectural probability of the rhetorician is adequate; cf. *Summa theologica*, i a, ii ae, q. 105, a. 2, ad 8: "Ad octavum dicendum, quod in negotiis humanis non potest haberi demonstrativa probatio et infallibilis, sed sufficit aliqua conjecturalis probabilitas secundum quam rhetor persuadet."

[64] *In decem libros ethicorum Aristotelis* x, Lectio 16 (Pirotta, p. 689, n. 2173).

is proper to it. Corresponding to these there are three processes of reason: those by which scientific certitude is acquired and in which no deviation from truth is possible; those which come to conclusions true for the most part but not necessary; and those in which reason deviates from the true because of some defect of principle. The part of logic which treats the first of these processes is called "judicative," since its judgment is made with the certitude of science, and this part is treated in the *Analytics:* the *Prior Analytics* is concerned with the certitude of judgment which is based only on the *form* of the syllogism; the *Posterior Analytics* with the demonstrative syllogism, in which the certitude depends on *matter* or on the necessary propositions of which the syllogism is composed. The part of logic which is subject to the second process of reason is called inventive, for discovery is not always with certitude. *Topic* or *Dialectic* treats of this process when it leads to conviction or opinion (*fides vel opinio*); *Rhetoric* treats of it when it leads only to a kind of suspicion without total exclusion of the contrary possibility; *Poetic* treats of it when estimation inclines to one of the two parts of a contradiction only because of the manner of its representation. Finally, the third process of reason is called *sophistic* and is treated by Aristotle in the *De sophisticis elenchis.*[65]

Bonaventura's conception of rhetoric and logic, on the other hand, is quite unaffected by the Aristotelian philosophy: they are ordered in the trivium, dominated by rhetoric, and they are treated, with the other arts, by reduction to theology, or as parts of the first vision of God, which is by natural intelligence, or as part of the gift of science, which is one of the seven gifts of the Holy Spirit. There are four lights by which we are illuminated in knowledge: the exterior light of the mechanical arts, the inferior light of sensitive knowledge, the interior light of philosophic knowledge, and the superior light of grace and Sacred Scripture. The interior light by which we are illuminated to intelligible truths is of three kinds—rational, natural, and moral, corresponding to the traditional division of the philosophic sciences into logic, physics, and ethics. Rational truth or the truth of words is of three kinds—the expression of concepts (treated by grammar), the movement to belief (treated by logic), and the movement to love or hate (treated by rhetoric).[66] The actual reduction of rational phi-

[65] *In libros Posteriorum analyticorum expositio* i, Lectio 1 (Rome, 1882), I, 138–40.
[66] *De reductione artium ad theologiam* 4 (*Opera omnia*, V, 321): "Et quoniam tripliciter potest aliquis per *sermonem* exprimere quod habet apud se, ut scilicet

losophy to theology is accomplished by consideration of the speaker (his expression of the conception of his mind is dependent on the eternal Word), his statement (in the congruity, truth, and adornment of which is seen the order of living, for actions by virtue of these have measure [*modus*], beauty [*species*], and order [*ordo*]), and the hearer (in whom the ends of speech are expressing, teaching, and moving, which are accomplished, as Augustine shows, only by the one true doctor who can impress species, infuse light, and give virtue to the heart of the hearer).[67] Or again, the first vision of God, which is by natural intelligence, is divided into three rays, since the light which is the truth of the soul illuminates the truth of things, of signs, and of morals: the second irradiation of truth is divided into three parts: grammar, logic, and rhetoric.[68] The consideration of general and special forms of argument in necessary matter as well as the consideration of "topical places" (in which induction proceeds by probable rather than necessary arguments) and sophistical places falls within logic, while rhetoric is concerned once more with civil utility and is divided into demonstrative, deliberative, and judicial.[69] Or again, the fifth gift of the Holy Spirit is science, comprising the three philosophic sciences (rational, natural, moral), in all of which, including rational philosophy or verbal science, Solomon was adept.[70]

It is in the platonizing Augustinian tradition, moreover, that music and poetry assume a broad sense and dominant importance: Roger Bacon assigns to music the function which Bonaventura ascribed to rhetoric, and then distinguishes both rhetoric and poetic into two kinds —a theoretic rhetoric and poetic (or *rhetorica docens* and *poetica*

---

notum faciat mentis suae conceptum, vel ut amplius moveat ad credendum, vel ut moveat ad amorem, vel odium: ideo *sermocinalis* sive rationalis philosophia triplicatur, scilicet in *grammaticam, logicam* et *rhetoricam;* quarum prima est ad exprimendum, secunda ad docendum, tertia ad movendum. Prima respicit rationem ut *apprehensivam;* secunda, ut *iudicativam;* tertia, ut *motivam.* Eta quia ratio apprehendit per sermonem *congruum,* iudicat per *verum,* movet per sermonem *ornatum:* hinc est, quod haec triplex scientia has tres passiones circa sermonem considerat."

[67] *Ibid.* 15–18 (*Opera omnia,* V, 323–24).

[68] *In hexaemeron,* Collatio iv. 18–25 (*Opera omnia,* V, 352–53).

[69] *Ibid.* 20–21 (*Opera omnia,* V, 352–53).

[70] *De septem domis Spiritus Sancti,* Collatio iv. 5–12 (*Opera omnia,* V, 474–75); esp. 8: "Impossible est, quod sapientia fiat doctrina nisi per sermonem. Sermo autem non est sufficiens ad docendum, nisi sit sententiosus. Et non loquitur homo sententiose, nisi sermo eius *discussivus, inquisitivus,* et *persuasivus,* scilicet quod habeat sermonem potentem ad loquendum omne illud, quod potest apprehendi vel nosci, vel ad quod affectus potest inclinari. Congrue autem exprimit quod dicit per *grammaticam,* rationaliter investigat per scientiam *logicam* et efficaciter persuadet per *rhetoricam.* Ista igitur est pars philosophiae, scilicet scientia sermocinalis, quae triplex est, ut patet, quam adeptus est Salomon."

docens) which are parts of logic and an applied rhetoric and poetic (or *rhetorica utens* and *poetica utens*) which are parts of moral philosophy.[71] The opposed tendencies which led to the dominance of rhetoric in the Augustinian tradition and to the importance of logical demonstration in the Thomist tradition are integral with the total complexions of the two theologies as evidenced in the conclusion of Bonaventura that theology is neither theoretic nor practical but an affective habit midway between theory and practice, as opposed to the argument of Thomas that theology subsumes both theoretic and practical sciences and is itself more theoretic than practical.[72] It is a distinction which later historians have treated crudely by trying to differentiate "voluntarism" from "rationalism."

V

Separate both from the tradition of the rhetoric assimilated to dialectic and proof and from that of the rhetoric assimilated to theology and edification—and the object of suspicion and attack by both—a third tradition of rhetoric seems to have flourished, at least during the second and third periods of the other two traditions, indifferent alike to the logical differentiation of necessary and probable arguments and to the theological limitation of persuasion to profound or salubrious truths. Since the three traditions were engaged in a three-cornered dispute, there is no single statement of the issue, for to logicians the practitioners of this new art seemed sophists, while theologians lumped them with the heretical dialecticians and garrulous ratiocinators; from the point of view of the new art, which professed an exclusive concern with practical issues and effective applications, that is, with actions or with words, the rules of logic were themselves open to question, and visionary theories and inapplicable generalizations were devoid of moral attraction. For the most part we know about the early members of this tradition from the violence of the attacks upon them and the bitterness of the satire in which they were portrayed, but gradually

---

[71] *Opus tertium,* cap. 75 (*Opera inedita,* ed. J. S. Brewer [London, 1859], pp. 303–8, esp. 306–7): "Nam moralis philosophus scit uti sermone suavi, et gestibus convenientibus orationi delectabili conformandis. Similiter logicus et grammaticus. . . . Grammaticus igitur utitur his peuiliter; sed logicus quantum ad formam arguendi quam constituit, in his procedit viriliter, et causas et rationes assignat. Sed quantum ad decorem et ornatum et suavitatem argumenti, certe non potest logicus, sicut nec grammaticus, causas et rationes assignare, sed musicus; sicut geometer causas linearum, et angulorum, et figurarum, quibus utitur carpentator, habet dare." Cf. *Opus majus* iii and iv. 2, ed. J. H. Bridges (Oxford, 1897), pp. 71 and 99–102.

[72] Bonaventura *Proemium in librum primum sententiarum* q. 3, concl.; i. 13; Thomas Aquinas *Summa theologica* i, q. i, a. 4.

in the course of the twelfth and thirteenth centuries they limited their statements to figures and forms of words, accomplishing their practical objectives by that device in a fashion which met with little effective opposition from logicians or theologians; and, since they were un-hampered by the need to consider things or thoughts, they were prolific in production of the "new" methods—they were fond of calling them-selves *moderni*—which constituted one of the important guises in which rhetoric entered the fourteenth century and the Renaissance.

A few fragments of the works of Anselm the Peripatetic are the only remains of the "Drogonic" sect—followers of the philosopher Drogo—which Anselm would have us believe was numerous and influential. He calls his art rhetoric; he professes allegiance to that art along with Hermagoras, Tully, Servius, Quintilian, Victorinus, Grillius, and Boe-thius and thought to illustrate it in his treatise *De materia artis* (now lost) and in the examples of rhetoric set forth in his *Rhetorimachia;* he specifies that rhetoric demonstrates, not truths, but verisimilitudes disguised as truths.[73] The *Rhetorimachia* is divided into three parts, one devoted to each of the genera—demonstrative, deliberative, and judicial—and each example takes the form of an attempt to turn the arguments of an opponent against him. The bearing of Anselm's per-formance on logic is not far to seek, since his approach permits him to deny the principle of excluded middle,[74] while its relation to theology is no less apparent from the allegory of the dream, related as part of his treatment of deliberative rhetoric, in which the embraces and arguments of three virgins named Dialectic, Rhetoric, and Grammar turn him from communion with the saints in Heaven.[75] A "sophist" named John seems in like fashion to have had a numerous following of whom Roscelin of Compiègne alone is easily identifiable.[76] In the twelfth century John of Salisbury attacks the doctrine of a teacher

---

[73] *Epistola ad Drogonem phylosophum* (*Anselm der Peripatetiker, nebust andern Beiträgen zur Literaturgeschichte Italiens elften Jahrhundert,* ed. E. Dümmler [Halle, 1872], pp. 19–20).

[74] *Rhetorimachia* i. p. 34; cf. *Epistola ad Drogonem magistrum et condiscipulos de logica disputatione in Gallia habita,* pp. 56–58.

[75] *Rhetorimachia* ii, p. 42.

[76] Cf. *Historia Francica* (quoted by J. Reiners, *Der Nominalismus in der Früh-scholastik* [BGPM, VIII, No. 5], p. 33, n. 2): "In dialectica quoque hi potentes exiterunt sophistae: Joannes, qui eandem artem sophisticam vocalem esse disseruit, Rotbertus Parisiacensis, Roscelinus Compendiensis, Arnulfus Laudenensis. Hi Joannis fuerunt sectatores, qui etiam quamplures habuerunt auditores." Cf. J. A. Endres, *Forschungen zur Geschichte der frühmittelalterlichen Philosophie* (BGPM, XVII, Nos. 2–3), and *petrus damiani und die weltliche wissenschaft* (BGPM, VIII, No. 3); also J. de Ghellinck, "Dialectique et dogme aux Xe–XIIe siècles," BGPM, Supplementband I, pp. 79–99.

whom he disguises under the name of "Cornificius" (allying with him-self in the attack the most illustrious masters of the age—among others, Gilbert de la Porrée, Thierry of Chartres, William of Conches, Peter Abailard) who broke that union of wisdom and eloquence which is the foundation of philosophy, of society, and of morals and who made everything new in his teaching, innovating in grammar, modifying dialectic, despising rhetoric; his exclusive reliance on the precepts of eloquence apparently leads Cornificius to exploit the traditional puzzles of the sophists, which turn on the confusion of word and thing or the application of a word or statement to itself.[77]

This tradition of rhetoric took form, for the most part, not in con-troversy or theory but in a vast number of textbooks which grew in three distinct groups, differentiated according to the subject matters once treated by rhetoric but now concerned with verbal forms em-ployed in those three fields in lieu of direct treatment of subject matter. First, rhetoric had contributed to the method of studying law, but the substantive consideration of law had moved into theology and had taken with it most of the appurtenances which might have made the law a learned profession, leaving only the verbal rhetoric of the *dicta-men*.[78] Second, the art of preaching, which had assumed in the

[77] John of Salisbury *Metalogicon* i. 1–6 (Webb, pp. 5–21, esp. 21): "Plane eloquentie precepta sapientiam non conferunt; sed nec amorem eius et sepissime quidem ei obtinende non conferunt. Res enim philosophia (aut finis eius, que est sapientia) querit, non uerba. Ex his itaque liquet quia precepta eloquentie ab operis suis philosophia eliminat." Cf. the confusion of the arts of the trivium reported by Hugh of St. Victor *Didascalicon* iii. 5; Buttimer, pp. 55–57. Cf. P. Mandonnet, *Siger de Brabant et l'Averroïsme latin au XIIIme siècle* (2d ed.; Louvain, 1911), I, 122–23.

[78] For the voluminous literature on the *Ars dictaminis* and *Ars notaria*, cf. L. J. Paetow, *A Guide to the Study of Medieval History* (2d ed.; New York, 1931), pp. 448–52; for the relation of these arts to rhetoric, cf. N. Valois, *De arte scribendi epistolas apud Gallicos medii aevi scriptores rhetoresve* ("Bibliothèque de l'École de Chartres," Vol. XXII [1880]), pp. 161, 257; for the relation of rhetoric to the teaching of law, cf. Abelson, *op. cit.*, pp. 60–66. The manner of the change, no less than the pride in the novelty of it, may be judged from the contents of Bon-compagni's two works, the *Rhetorica antiqua* (arranged in six books according to the character of the letter to be written) and the *Rhetorica novissima* (arranged in thirteen books: "Primus est de origine iuris. Secundus est de rhetoricae partibus et causarum generibus. Tertius est de diffinitionibus. Quartus est de naturis et consuetudinibus oratorum. Quintus de causarum exordiis. Sextus de principiis conuentorum. Septimus de rhetoricis argumentis. Octavus de memoria. Nonus de adornationibus. Decimus de invectivis. Undecimus de consiliis. Duodecimus de colloquiis. Tertius decimus de conditionibus"). Boncompagni professes in the Prologue to the former work not to remember ever having read Cicero, but he adds that he never dissuaded anyone who wanted to read him; and in the latter work he gives three reasons why he undertook to find a new rhetoric after Cicero had compiled a rhetoric from the infinite precepts of rhetoricians: (1) according to

Christian tradition an exhortative function approaching that of ancient deliberative oratory—once due allowance is made for differences between the terrestrial and celestial city—gradually moved to a formalism in which doctrine was left to theology and attention was centered on three problems: propriety of division of the subject stated in the theme of the sermon, brevity of distinction, and utility of expansion.[79] Finally,

---

Boethius, the rhetoric edited by the ancients consists solely of precepts, without doctrine or utility; (2) students in civil and canon law would not get a solid foundation in the liberal arts, and (3) Cicero's rhetoric is rendered void, according to students of law, because it is never read in "ordinary" courses but is run through and taught like a mechanical art by stealth; to these he adds a fourth: that Cicero was mistaken about the origin of the law (cf. L. Rockinger, "Über die Ars dictandi und die Summae dictaminum in Italien," *Sitzungsberichte der Königl. Bayerischen Akademie der Wissenschaften zu München, hist. Kl.,* I [1861], 135–45). For the closely related art of pleading, cf. A. Wilmart, "L' *Ars arengandi* de Jacques de Dinant avec un appendice sur ses ouvrages *De dictamine,"* *Analecta Reginensia* (Vatican City, 1933), pp. 113–51. The relations of rhetoric to law and logic are reflected satirically in the "battle of seven arts"; cf. "*La Bataille des vii ars* of Henri d'Audeli," ed. L. J. Paetow, in *Two Medieval Satires on the University of Paris* (Berkeley, Calif., 1927), pp. 43 and 51. Cf. H. Kantorowicz, *Studies in the Glossators of the Roman Law* (Cambridge, 1938).

[79] Cf. the anonymous *Art of Preaching*, portions of which are edited in the *Opera omnia S. Bonventurae* (IX, 6–7), in which four modes of preaching are distinguished: (1) that which concords really and verbally with the words of Scripture —used by "modern" doctors and expounded in this treatise; (2) that which employs only real concordance with Scripture—appropriate to those newly learned in theology; (3) that limited to verbal concordance; and (4) contrasted to the modern method, the ancient mode "quod observant antiqui Sancti, sicut Augustinus et Bernardus et multi allii, quorum sermones in Ecclesia recitantur, in quibus non proponitur aliquod thema, quod sit materia praedicandi, nec solent divisiones vel distinctiones fieri, quae postmodum concordentur, sed quasi narrative procedit." The modern doctors advise against following the ancient mode, for the curious reason that these Fathers were, in a manner, founders of the church (*quasi ecclesiae fundatores*), and therefore they avoided all curiosity concerning distinctions of themes, subdivisions of members, and concordances of both. Bonaventura likewise divides the problems of preaching into three parts, *divisiones, distinctiones, dilatationes* (cf. *Ars concionandi,* Prooemium, ix. 8). For an excellent exposition of the technique of the medieval sermon and review of the methods expounded in most important medieval handbooks, cf. E. Gilson, "Michel Menot et la technique du sermon mediéval," *Les Idées et les lettres* (Paris, 1932), pp. 93–154. Cf H. Caplan, "Classical Rhetoric and the Mediaeval Theory of Preaching," *Classical Philology,* XXVIII (1933), 73–96; "Rhetorical Invention in Some Mediaeval Tractates on Preaching," *Speculum,* II (1927), 284–95; "Henry of Hesse on the Art of Preaching," *PMLA,* XLVIII (1933), 340–61. The treatises of Robert of Basevorn and Thomas of Wales are published in T. M. Charland, *Artes praedicandi: Contribution à l'histoire de la rhétorique au moyen âge* (Ottawa, 1936), preceded by a survey of writers of *Arts* and the customary form of theory. Cf. the differentiation of the two modes most used by moderns, the French and the English (Robert of Basevorn, *Forma praedicandi* 7, p. 244). Cf. also M. M. Davy, *Les Sermons universitaires parisiens de 1230–1231* (Paris, 1931); G. R. Owst, *Preaching in Mediaeval England: An Introduction to Sermon Manuscripts of the Period c. 1350–1450* (Cambridge, 1926); and C. H. Haskins, *Studies in Mediaeval Culture* (Oxford, 1929), pp. 36–71.

the art of poetry came to be considered, after the twelfth century, not a branch of grammar but alternately a kind of argumentation or persuasion (and, as such, subordinate to logic or morals) and a form of composition (and, as such, to be treated in terms of style, organization, and figures borrowed from rhetoric).[80] In common, these three tendencies continue the terms and some points of the organization of the *Ad Herennium* and of Cicero's *De inventione*, but the commonplaces which have been put to so many uses are no longer devices for discovering arguments of things and their traits but devices for remembering, for amplifying, for describing, and for constructing figures.[81]

VI

Two translations of Aristotle's *Rhetoric* were produced during the thirteenth century, and there are also translations of the *Rhetorica ad Alexandrum*, Averroës' commentary on the *Rhetoric*, and Demetrius' *De elocutione*. The effect of the Aristotelian rhetoric and its variant interpretations (both Demetrius and Averroës passed as "Aristotelian") on philosophy may be judged from the fact that these works on rhetoric are frequently found in manuscripts which contain works on morals, politics, or economics, and, indeed, specific marks of the *Rhetoric* can be seen in Aquinas' analysis of the passions.[82] Yet there are relatively few early commentaries on the work itself: Aegidius Romanus

[80] In early treatments poetry, considered as metric, was a part of grammar, while as a form of argument it was a part of topic or dialectic. Thus Cassiodorus defines grammar (*Institutiones* ii. 1. 1; p. 94): "grammatica vero est peritia pulchre loquendi ex poetis illustribus auctoribusque collecta; officium eius est sine vitio dictionem prosalem metricamque componere," but he includes the poets among the artists to whom topical arguments are supplied by memory (*ibid.* 3. 17, p. 127; cf. *ibid.* 2. 2, p. 98, for the function of memory in discovery). Cf. Isidore of Seville *Etymologiae* i. 39; the Venerable Bede, *De arte metrica* (*PL*, XC, 149). John of Salisbury notes the tendency to make poetic an art by itself or to assimilate it to rhetoric rather than to grammar, but he is explicit in his own resolution of the problem; cf. *Metalogicon* i. 17, p. 43: "Profecto aut poeticam grammatica obtinebit, aut poetica a numero liberalium disciplinarum eliminabitur." Cf. C. Fierville, *Une Grammaire latine inédite du XIIIᵉ siècle* (Paris, 1886), pp. 94–119. The transition is gradual from a consideration merely of the words, their character, and position to the consideration of the general conditions or places relevant to the choice and disposition of words; a further step is needed to carry it, during the Renaissance, from the figures of speech and the figures of doctrine to the rhetorical consideration of the thoughts of the author and the effects on the audience.

[81] Cf. E. Faral, *Les Arts poétiques du XIIᵉ et du XIIIᵉ siècle* (Paris, 1924), esp. pp. 52 ff. and 77 ff.

[82] M. Grabmann, "Eine lateinische Übersetzung der pseudo-aristotelischen Rhetorica ad Alexandrum," pp. 6 ff.; G. Lacombe, A. Birkenmajer, M. Dulong, and A. Franceschini, *Aristotleles Latinus* (Rome, 1939), I, 77–79; B. V. Wall, *A Medieval Latin Version of Demetrius' "De elocutione"* (Washington, 1937).

in the thirteenth century and John of Jandun and John Buridan in the fourteenth century are the only outstanding scholastics to have left such commentaries.[83] The old problem of the genus of rhetoric, whether it is a part of civil philosophy or logic, is resolved by Aegidius into the difference between Aristotle (who placed it under dialectic) and Cicero (who made it a part of politics).[84] The position of this pupil of St. Thomas is indeed almost a parody of Bonaventura's doctrine that theology is midway between the practical and the speculative sciences, for he locates rhetoric midway between the moral and the rational sciences.[85] The readjustment is striking illustration of the fashion in which unchanged analyses may in the context of altered philosophies take on contrary significances, for the effort of rhetoricians from Quintilian through the early Middle Ages was to claim consideration of general or indefinite questions or theses and to resist efforts to restrict rhetoric to determinate questions or hypotheses, lest rhetoric yield its place and importance as a science to philosophy: the difference between politics and ethics, on the one hand, and rhetoric, on the other, according to Aegidius, consists in the fact that a science is determined by its subject matter and that, whereas politics and ethics have a determinate genus, rhetoric is indeterminate, being concerned with knowledge of certain common notions which bear on moral questions. John Buridan divides all sciences into two kinds, the "principal" science, which deals with the proper things of the science, and the "instrumental" science, which is concerned with the mode of statement and teaching. The instrument of the theoretic sciences is logic or dialectic, but in moral science the problem involved concerns not only the doubtful and the true but also the need to stir desire as it bears on understanding, and a special moral logic or dialectic is required which is divided into two parts, rhetoric and poetic.[86] John of Jandun divides philosophy into nonorganic (practical and speculative) and organic, which includes grammar and logic, rhetoric being a subdivision of logic.[87]

---

[83] The commentaries of Jandun and Buridan are unedited; that of Aegidius was published in 1515 in Venice, but I have been unable to consult a copy.

[84] *De differentia rhetoricae, ethicae, et politicae,* ed. G. Bruni in *The New Scholasticism,* VI (1932), 5–8.

[85] *Ibid.* (Bruni, p. 2). Cf. *Expositio in artem veterem* (Venice, 1507), 2v–3r, where speculative science is divided into *principalis* (concerned with things) and *adminiculativa* (the three arts of the trivium).

[86] *Questiones super decem libros ethicorum Aristotelis ad Nicomachum,* Prooemium (Paris, 1518), fol. 4r.

[87] *Quaestiones subtilissimae super tres libros de anima,* Prohemium (Venice, 1519), fol. 2v.

The three main lines in which rhetoric developed during the Middle Ages—as they had grown out of philosophic oppositions in antiquity and as they had been continued by medieval writers under the compulsion of the circumstances and nature of the problems they treated— are extended through the discussions of the Renaissance, notwithstanding revolt against the scholasticism of the Middle Ages, alike by the weight of tradition and by the exigencies of the problems themselves. The tradition of rhetoric as a part of rational philosophy subordinate to logic had a long and honorable continuation, which included Zabarella, Campanella, Varchi, Robertelli, and many others.[88] The tradition in which rhetoric dominated the arts continued into the Renaissance not only in the methods and doctrines of theology but in a secular tradition which took one of two forms: either all philosophy

[88] According to Zabarella, De natura logicae ii. 13–23 (Opera logica [Cologne, 1597], pp. 78–100), rhetoric and poetic are instruments of civil discipline and parts of logic (the arts of demonstration, dialectic, and sophistic are also parts of logic); like logic, they are rational faculties, not verbal, like grammar. Logic is divided into two principal kinds, universal and particular; rhetoric and poetic are instances of particular logic. Campanella divided his Philosophia rationalis into four parts: grammar, dialectic, rhetoric, and poetic. Rhetoric is a part of rational philosophy, deriving its arguments from dialectic and its matter from morals; it does not treat of all questions but is limited to persuasion and dissuasion of good and evil; poetic has the same function, but it differs from rhetoric in its universality, since it presents all goods and all truths to all audiences (Philosophia rationalis, pars tertia, rhetorica 1. 1 [Paris, 1538], pp. 1–7; cf. Pars quarta, poetica 1. 1, pp. 89–93). B. Varchi follows the traditional division of philosophy into real, active, and rational; rhetoric and poetic are subdivisions of rational philosophy, although, strictly speaking, poetic is neither an art nor a science, but a faculty; dialectic, rhetoric, and poetic are essentially the same thing, differing only accidentally, and the dialectician, rhetorician, and poet can be put on the same level of nobility and honor; cf. "Della poetica in generale," Opere di Benedetto Varchi (Trieste, 1859), II, 684: "La filosofia razionale, la quale favellando di parole e non di cose, non è veramente parte della filosofia, ma strumento, comprende sotto sè non solo la loica (intendendo per loica la giudiziale) a la dialettica (intendendo per dialettica non tanto lo topica, quanto eziandio la sofistica e la tentativa) ma ancora la rettorica, la poetica, la storica e la grammatica." Robertelli raises the question not in terms of the form of the art but in terms of its matter and end: poetic shares its matter, oratio, with four other disciplines: demonstration, dialectic, rhetoric, and sophistic; grammar is excluded from the list, since it does not involve the intellectual content of what is said. The five are easily and rapidly distinguished (In librum Aristotelis de Arte poetica [Basel, 1555], p. 1): "Ex his quaelibet facultas unum arripit genus. Demonstratoria verum. Dialectice probabile. Rhetroica suasorium. Sophistice id, quod probabilis, sed verisimilis habet speciem. Poetice falsum, seu fabulosum." The end of poetic (ibid. 2) is the "imitating word," as the end of rhetoric is the "persuading word,"; it is (borrowing from Cicero) the imitation of life, the mirror of custom, the image of truth. Cf. H. Cornacchinus, Indagatio verae et perfectae definitionis logicae, Pars V, cap. 21 (Padua, 1606), p. 247: poetic and rhetoric are parts or offshoots of logic, or rather aggregates composed from logic, grammar, and civil philosophy, and (ibid., Pars IV, cap. 10, pp. 220-21) dialectic, sophistic, and rhetoric are midway between grammar and logic.

and all subjects are assimilated to rhetoric, as in the doctrines of Majoragius and Nizolius,[89] or the method of discovery is refurbished and transferred from rhetoric to revitalize and revolutionize dialectic, as in the doctrines of Rudolph Agricola and Petrus Ramus.[90] The tradition in which rhetoric had become a discipline of words, independent alike of philosophy and dialectic, finally established verbal distinctions which grew into doctrines of things: the long and subtle speculations of fourteenth-century philosophers on *insolubilia, obligatoria,* and sophisms laid the foundations for many of the early theories in physics and mathematics, and symbolic logic, though unconcerned

[89] J. L. Vives (*De causis corruptarum artium,* Liber iv [Lugduni Batavorum, 1586], p. 239) reports the doctrine of philosophers who distinguish two rhetorics, one univeral and applicable to all things, the other particular and suited to civil use; Vives interprets the position as being in opposition to the tendency to make rhetoric part of logic. The position is defended by M. A. Majoragius on the authority of Cicero (*De finibus* ii. 6. 17) against Aristotle (*Aristotelis Stagyritae De arte rhetorica libri tres cum M. Antonii Maioragii commentariis,* Liber i [Venice, 1591], p. 2). M. Nizolius holds, again on the authority of Cicero, that philosophy and oratory are not two separate faculties but one and the same art, composed of two arts which are imperfect when separated (*De veris principiis et vera ratione philosophandi contra pseudophilosophos* iii. 3 [Parma, 1553], p. 211); he quotes Laurentius Valla, with approval, when he argues that dialectic is a part of rhetoric, since it consists of only one of the five parts of rhetoric, namely, discovery (*ibid.* 5, p. 240); and, finally, he holds that rhetoric is a general art and science, under which are subsumed all other arts and sciences (*ibid.* iii. 8, p. 268). The distinction of the two rhetorics—the rhetoric of precepts and the rhetoric in use—is preserved by Riccoboni, who also adds "ecclesiastical" as a fourth genus to the traditional three, "deliberative," "demonstrative," and "judicial" (A. Riccobonus, *De usu artis rhetoricae Aristotelis commentarii vigintiquinque, quibus duplex, rhetorica strictim explicatus, altera, quae praecepta tradit persuidendi, altera, quae re ipsa persuadet,* etc. [Frankfurt, 1595]). The use of rhetoric in refurbishing scriptural interpretation is well illustrated in the *Heptaplus* of Pico della Mirandola (in which Moses emerges as the "Idea" of the writer, the exemplar of the prophet) and John Colet's *Enarrationes in Epistolas S. Pauli.*

[90] Rudolph Agricola undertook to reinstate in dialectic the processes of discovery which had become part of rhetoric because civil philosophy came into prominence in Greece before the maturity of the other arts (*De inventione dialectica* ii. 18 [Cologne, 1538], pp. 538 ff.), and to correct the errors which Aristotle, Cicero, and Boethius had committed in treating and classifying the places. The function of rhetoric was limited to *ratio dicendi.* According to Petrus Ramus, logic or dialectic is a general art, the whole art of reason (*Scholae in liberales artes* [Basel, 1569], *scholae dialecticae* ii. 2, pp. 35–37). The parts of dialectic are discovery and judgment (*ibid.* 8, p. 53); the parts of rhetoric are elocution and action (*Scholae rhetoricae,* i, p. 238). The logic of Aristotle abounded in errors, confusions, vain precepts, and altercations: Ramus professed to have supplied the missing virtues, removed the errors, and made the art usable. The error of Cicero consisted in transferring all the Aristotelian devices of dialectic to rhetoric and of having one art of two; and Quintilian mixed rhetoric with all the other arts; Ramus undertook to correct both errors (*Rhetoricae distinctiones in Quintilianum* [Paris, 1559], pp. 3–8.

with its past, still repeats the elements of this heritage; the analysis of the figures of the poet was made, without undue or violent alteration, into a theory of poetry, which dealt with imagination, passion, truth, and virtue; and political philosophy has never entirely lost the rhetorical turn from which its theories derived their modern concreteness and practicality.

Once the general movements in the arts, of which the variegated history of rhetoric is a symptom, have been set into some intelligible schema, the startling and revolutionary shifts of doctrines and of problems are more easily understood. Since the problems of the sciences and the arts are closely related and are often stated in almost identical language, a slight shift of theory or terminology may at a point bring an unsuspected richness from one art into the threadbare terminology of another. The three customary questions of rhetoric—*whether it is, what it is,* and *what sort*—merged readily with the questions of logic and influenced early modern attempts to formulate the scientific method. The customary rhetorical inquiry into the duty of the artist and into the matter and end of the art took on metaphysical generality when it was merged, in the thirteenth century, with the Aristotelian causes by the simple addition of questions of form to what were already questions concerning the efficient, material, and final causes; and, metaphysics apart, the four questions contributed to the foundations of philology in the inquiries into the four causes of books with which Aquinas and Bonaventura and other medieval writers opened their commentaries. The controversy concerning thesis and hypothesis merged with Plato's dialectical use of hypothesis and Aristotle's differentiation of thesis, hypothesis, and definition and contributed unsuspected commitments and implications in modern discussions of scientific method. Rhetoric is, at most, an unusually clear example among the arts and sciences of a tendency which appears in the history of rhetoric only because it is universal in intellectual disciplines. In application, the art of rhetoric contributed during the period from the fourth to the fourteenth century not only to the methods of speaking and writing well, of composing letters and petitions, sermons and prayers, legal documents and briefs, poetry and prose, but to the canons of interpreting laws and Scripture, to the dialectical devices of discovery and proof, to the establishment of the scholastic method, which was to come into universal use in philosophy and theology, and, finally, to the formulation of scientific inquiry, which was to separate philosophy from theology. In manner of application, the art of rhetoric was the source both of doctrines which have long since become the property of other sciences (such as the passions, which were considered in handbooks of rhetoric until Descartes proposed a "scientific" treatment of them different only in details) and of particular devices which have been applied to a variety of subjects (such as to the "commonplaces" which were sometimes techniques for inventing arguments, sometimes means for dilating statements, sometimes methods for discovering things, or to "definition" or "order," which may be determined entirely by consideration of the verbal conditions of expression, the psychological requirements of persuasion, or the circumstantial probabilities of fact). In theory or application, the art of rhetoric was now identified with, now distinguished from, the whole or part not only of grammar, logic, and dialectic (which were, in turn, distinguished from or identified with each other) but also of sophistic and science, of "civil philosophy," psychology, law, and literature and, finally, of philosophy as such. Yet, if rhetoric is defined in terms of a single subject matter—such as style or literature or discourse—it has no history during the Middle Ages; the many innovations which are recorded during that period in the arts with which it is related suggest that their histories might profitably be considered without unique attachment to the field in which their advances are celebrated.

ENGLISH RHETORICS OF THE 16TH CENTURY
William G. Crane

The English rhetorics of the sixteenth century reflect the emphasis which the Renaissance placed on amplification and ornamentation. Prior to 1500 rhetoric had received only slight mention in *The Courte of Sapyence*, ca. 1480, attributed to Lydgate, and in Caxton's *Myrrour & Descrypcyon of the Worlde*, ca. 1480,[1] a translation of a French version of the *Speculum mundi*. That part of Stephen Hawes's *Pastime of Pleasure*, 1509, which deals with rhetoric places special stress upon the amplification of fables under the heading "invention" and upon certain stylistic devices which Hawes terms "the colouryng of sentences." Hawes has given much attention to the allegorical interpretation of fables, examples, and similitudes by poets. Leonard Cox's *The Arte or Crafte of Rhetoryke*, 1524 (?), the first book in English devoted

From William G. Crane, *Wit and Rhetoric in the Renaissance*, New York, Columbia University Press, 1937, pages 97–112. Reprinted by permission.
[1] F. I. Carpenter has reprinted a section in *University of Chicago Studies*, No. 5, 1899.

exclusively to rhetoric, deals only with the first division of the subject, investigation, and with the closely allied matter of judgment. F. I. Carpenter demonstrated in the reprint which he edited for *University of Chicago Studies*, 1899, that the work was based upon and in part translated from Melanchthon's *Institutiones rhetoricae*, 1521. Some material was added from the rhetorical treatises of Cicero, who is named thirty times, and most of the illustrative matter came from his orations. Cox's interest is centered on the means of providing plenty of matter for the development of themes. The *Pro Milone*, one of the most ornate and copious of Cicero's orations, is cited as an example in which he "dyd brynge out of the placis of Rhetoryke arguments to prove his sayde theme or purpose." This oration was Cox's favorite and he never tired of quoting it. After Cicero, Erasmus is the authority most frequently appealed to by Cox. The *Moriae encomium, De conscribendis epistolis,* and *De copia* are mentioned, and the last furnishes illustrative material for several points. Throughout the work Cox's interest in amplification is evident. The use made of the processes of dialectical investigation by orators is stressed by him in his exposition of simple and compound "logical" themes. Regarding the first branch of rhetoric, investigation, he states,

> Inuencyon is comprehended in certayn placys, as the Rhetoriciens call them, out of whom he that knoweth the facultye may fetche easyly suche thynges as be mete for the mater that he shal skepe of . . . The theme proposed, we must after the rules of Rhetoryke go to oure placys that shal anone shew unto us what shalbe to oure purpose.[2]

The second book on rhetoric to appear in English was the compilation published by Richard Sherry in 1550, *A Treatise of Schemes and Tropes*. Though it professes to deal only with matters of style, it is fairly representative of the rhetorical treatises which appeared in Latin during the Renaissance. The latter half of it is little more than an English version of the more important means of gaining plenty of matter set forth in the second part of Erasmus *De duplici copia verborum ac rerum*. Sherry names most of the sources from which he translated and merely claims for himself that he has given some pains to the selection and arrangement of the definitions and that he has furnished some of the examples. He cites Cicero and Quintilian in support of the opinion that "eloqucion" is the principal part of rhetoric. For his definition of "eloqucion" as "wisdom speaking eloquently" he makes acknowledgment to Cicero's *De partitione oratoria*. The three

---

[2] Leonard Cox, *The Arte or Crafte of Rhetoryke*, Folio Aiiii verso.

kinds of style named by Cicero in the *De oratore*, the high, the low, and the mean are discussed. Sherry is particularly concerned with the first of these;

> for it hathe wyth an ample maiestye verye garnyshed wordes, proper, translated, and graue sentences, whych ar handled in amplificacion and commiseracion, and it hath exornacions bothe of woordes and sentences, whereunro [sic] in oracions they ascribe very great strength and grauitie.[3]

Sherry's book may be considered in three sections corresponding to the sources from which each was particularly drawn. The definitions in the first part (B_5 recto to C_7 verso) of the tropes and figures depending upon diction and upon grammatical construction were translated from Mosellanus's *Tabulae de schematibus et tropis*, 1529, as were many of the examples. The section following (C_8 recto to D_7 recto) headed "The fyrst order of figures Rhetorical," came mainly from the last book of the *Rhetoricorum ad C. Herennium libri quatuor*. The third part of the treatise (D_7 verso to F_8 verso) deals with those devices for expanding a theme and obtaining variety of matter which today are called "figures of thought." In the sixteenth century they were generally known as "figures of sentence" or "figures of amplification." Sherry cites Cicero and Quintilian as authorities for designating them as "ornaments of sentence." He used the term "amplification" in the restricted sense of the exaggeration and extenuation of a matter, but he noted that the word might be used in a broader sense to include all the means of expanding a subject, as was pointed out in the commentary on Erasmus's *De duplici copia verborum ac rerum* by John Doelsch, known also under the names Weltkirch and Velcurio. The final section makes up half of Sherry's treatise and is little more than translation from the second part of the *De copia*, with some additions from Doelsch's commentary and from Erasmus's *Ecclesiastae sive de ratione concionandi libri quatuor*, 1535. Sherry also consulted the *Rhetoricorum ad C. Herennium libri quatuor* and Quintilian's *Institutio oratoria*, which were the main sources from which Erasmus drew in both of the works mentioned here. For instance, the discussion of "proues: a copious heaping of probacions" was extended considerably from what Erasmus had written in the *De copia*, by matter taken from the *Ecclesiastae* and, possibly, by some additions from Quintilian's treatise. Sherry directs the reader's attention to the extended treatment of the means of amplifying an oration set forth in the

[3] Richard Sherry, *A Treatise of Schemes and Tropes*, Folio Biii verso.

Ecclesiastae, where this subject occupies Chapters XXVIII to XLIII of Book III. The means of expanding a theme which Sherry presents are: (1) "particion called also diuision & distribucion rhetoricall,— when a thing that may be generally spoken, is more largely declared and diuided into partes"; (2) "enumeracion," of which there are three kinds; (3) "enargia, euidence or perspicuitie called also description rethoricall," of eleven varieties; (4) "amplificacion," in the restricted sense of exaggeration and extenuation; (5) "the inuencion of many proposicions"; (6) "proues, a copious heaping of probacions," under which the difference between circumstances peculiar to rhetoric and those which belong both to rhetoric and to dialectical investigation is pointed out; (7) "examples"; (8) "parable, which some call similitude, some comparacion"; (9) "icon" (vivid description by means of comparison); (10) "indicatio, or authoritie," of seven kinds, including moral sentences, *chria,* and proverbs; and (11) "exergasia" or "expolicion, when we tarye in one thynge, speakyne the same in diuerse wordes and fashions, as though it were not one matter but diuerse." Having set forth these means of expanding a theme Sherry abruptly closed his treatise with the following apology for omitting the remainder of the *De copia.*

> And here me thynketh I maye ryghte well ende these Rhetoricall precepts, although I be not ignoraunt that much helpeth bothe to persuasions and copye, the proper handlyng of tales taken oute of the nature of beastes, dreames, fayned narracions, sumwhat lyke unto the truth, with allegories much used of diuines. But because they requyre a longer treatise, for this tyme I leaue them of, addynge unto these before written rules of oratory, a declamation bothe profitable and verye eloquente, written by Erasmus unto the moste noble Duke of Cleue, as here appereth after.

The *De copia* concluded with discussion of the topics which Sherry declared would "requyre a longer treatise." The declamation by Erasmus printed at the end of Sherry's work consists of a discourse of three and one-half pages on the education of children and "the selfe same matter enlarged by copye" to one hundred and twenty-nine pages. Both the tract and the epitome were printed at the end of some of the copies of the *De copia.* Leonard Cox stated in a letter to the printer Toye, in 1534, that he was making a translation of them. A better illustration could hardly be desired of the stress which Erasmus, Sherry, Cox, and many others in the sixteenth century placed upon amplification.

The only English rhetoric of the sixteenth century which goes beyond translation or close paraphrase is Thomas Wilson's *The Arte of Rhetorique*, 1553. Even it is in large part a compilation from easily recognized sources, particularly Erasmus's *Ecclesiastae sive de ratione concionandi libri quatuor*, Quintilian's *Institutio oratoria*, the *Rhetoricorum ad C. Herennium libri quatuor*, and various treatises of Cicero. For the time at which it appeared *The Arte of Rhetorique* displays an unusual amount of originality. At most points Wilson's sources are evident; yet he selected his materials with a view to the needs of his day and often restated them in words which bear his own stamp. The purpose for which the work was intended and the spirit in which it was written give it a measure of individuality. By reason of Wilson's own inclinations and the fact that one of his chief sources was Erasmus's *Ecclesiastae*, his treatise reflects the religious temper of mid-sixteenth-century England. In a number of ways it is connected with English wit of the sixteenth century. It appealed not only to those attracted by the ideal of Castiglione's *Courtier*, but also to the young men of the court who wished to be saved the trouble of studying rhetoric in the Latin texts. Of chief significance is the stress placed on amplification throughout the volume. Two years before it appeared Wilson had published a treatise on logic in which the processes of dialectical investigation were treated in full. The usefulness of these means of analysis for obtaining variety of matter is emphasized in the first part of *The Arte of Rhetorique*. In connection with "the finding out of apt matter, called otherwise Inuention," Wilson states, "The places of *Logique*, giue good occasion to finde out plentiful matter. And therefore, they that will proue any cause, and seeke onely to teach thereby the trueth, must search out the places of *Logique*, and no doubt they shall finde much plentie."[4] Some pages beyond this he remarks again on the processes of dialectic as aids to amplification.[5]

Two-thirds of the second book of Wilson's *Arte of Rhetorique* is devoted to the discussion of amplification and the subject which Cicero had subjoined to it, "of delighting the hearers and stirring them to laughter." Wilson was not careful to distinguish between the broad and the narrow senses of the term "amplification." So far as this study is concerned his failure to do this is of no great consequence; all of the devices he considered there served for dilation of a theme. The treatment of amplification in the second book of his treatise came prin-

    [4] Thomas Wilson, *The Arte of Rhetorique*, 1553. Reprint of the edition of 1585 by The Clarendon Press, 1909, p. 6.
    [5] *Ibid.*, p. 23.

cipally from Erasmus's *Ecclesiastae*. The long section on moving laughter, which follows, is nearly all from *The Courtier* of Castiglione, who had taken most of it from Cicero's *De oratore*. In *The Rise of English Literary Prose* Professor Krapp has remarked in connection with Wilson's treatment, "This whole passage on various methods of amplification reads like a description of Euphuism." [6] It does present many, but not all, of the means used for amplification by Lyly and many other writers of his day. Some other devices are described in the last part of Wilson's treatise. Since this is readily accessible in the reprint of The Clarendon Press, only a few general comments need be made here. Translating from Erasmus's *Ecclesiastae* Wilson notes that moral sentences, similitudes, examples, and witty sayings are skillful devices with which to open a sermon or a speech.[7] At the beginning of his consideration of amplification, he remarks that it is of two sorts, "The one resteth in wordes, the other in matter." [8] Regarding the latter he states, "Amplifying of the matter consisteth in heaping and enlarging of those places, which serueth for confirmation of a matter. As the definition, the cause, the consequent, the contrary, the example, and such other." In the course of fifteen pages, translated mainly from Erasmus's *Ecclesiastae*, he presents such means of amplification as comparison, moral sentences, proverbs, examples, comparison of examples, causes, and contraries. The heaping together of these devices receives special stress, and many examples are given. Some of Wilson's comparisons of humans with animals [9] are as fantastic as anything in the writings of John Lyly, who, it may be noted, drew many of his similes from the works of Erasmus, one of Wilson's authorities.

Amplification is mentioned several times in the discussion of the ornaments of style in the last book of *The Arte of Rhetorique*. The figures which Cicero called "Exornation of sentences, or colours of Rhetorike" are, according to Wilson, "amplified by heaping examples, by dilating arguments, by comparing of things together, by similitudes, by contraries, and by diuers others like." [10] Again, he notes in the

---

[6] George Philip Krapp, *The Rise of English Literary Prose*, 1915, p. 331 n.

[7] Thomas Wilson, *The Arte of Rhetorique*, p. 105

[8] *Ibid.*, p. 114.

[9] "Againe, in young Storkes, we may take an example of loue towards their damme, for when she is old, and not able for her crooked bill to picke meate, the yong ones feede her. In yong Vipers there is a contrary example (for as *Plinie* saieth) they eate out their dammes wombe, and so come forth. In Hennes there is a care to bring vp their Chickens; in Egles the contrary, which cast out their Egges, if they haue any moe then three: and all because they would not be troubled with bringing vp many."—*Ibid.*, p. 125.

[10] *Ibid.*, p. 170.

course of his remarks on clear explanation and vivid description as means of developing a topic, "Also similitudes, examples, comparisons, from one thing to another, apt translations, and heaping of Allegories, and all such figures as serue for amplification, doe much commend the lively setting forth of any matter." [11] The bulk of Wilson's treatment of style is taken up by those devices which authorities, such as John Susenbrot and Henry Peacham, classed under the heading "figures of amplification." Of particular interest in connection with amplification and the style of *Euphues* are the sections headed as follows: "Wittie iesting," "Digression," "Asking other and answering our self," "Doubtfulnesse," "Distribution," "A familiar talk or communication used," "Description," "A Similitude," "Example," "Of enlarging examples by copy," "Of Fables," "Contrarietie," "Stomach greefe," "Like ending and like falling," "Egall members," "Like among themselues," "Gradation," "Outcrying," "Reckening," "Reasoning a matter with our selues," "Resembling of things," and "Answering to our selfe." [12] Wilson puts special stress upon various kinds of comparison and upon the heaping together of rhetorical devices. The four topics, "Similitude," "Example," "Of enlarging examples by copy," and "Of Fables" take up more space than all of the others which have been mentioned. Regarding similitudes, Wilson notes, "Therefore, those that delite to proue thinges by Similitudes, must learne to knowe the nature of diuers beastes, of mettales, of stones, and al such as haue any vertue in them, and be applied to mans life." John Heywood is named in connection with the remark that proverbs often involve comparison. An example of a "similitude enlarged" is preceded by the statement, "That if we purpose to dilate our cause hereby with poses & sentences, wee may with ease talke at large." The illustration which Wilson gives is remarkable for the amount of balance and antithesis which it involves. Following it he summarizes his discussion of similitudes as follows,

> Thus similitudes might be enlarged by heaping good sentences, when one thing is compared with an other, and conclusion made thereupon. Among the learned men of the Church, no one vseth this figure more than *Chrisostome,* whose writings the rather seeme more pleasaunt and sweete. For similitudes are not onely vsed to amplifie a matter, but also to beautifie the same, to delite the hearers, to make the matter plaine, and to shewe a certaine maiestie with the report of such resembled things, but because I haue spoken of similitudes heretofore in the booke of *Logique,* I will surcease to talke any further of this matter.[13]

[11] "Illustris explanatio."—*Ibid.,* p. 178.
[12] *Ibid.,* pp. 181–208.
[13] *Ibid.,* p. 190.

Brute beasts furnish most of the illustrations which Wilson gives under "Example." [14] They are all of the "unnatural natural history" type, which some critics have particularly associated with the writings of John Lyly. It may be noted in passing that Wilson not only presents devices of sentence structure, such as antithesis,[15] homoioteleuton,[16] parison,[17] and regression,[18] which some authorities have regarded as distinguishing marks of Lyly's style. He points out also that some of these,[19] particularly alliteration, had already been employed excessively before his day.

Henry Peacham's *The Garden of Eloquence, Conteyning the Figures of Grammer and Rhetorick*, 1577, is evidence of interest among English writers of the time in the rhetorical devices of amplification and ornamentation. The chief source of Peacham's material was John Susenbrot's *Epitome troporum ac schematum*. In 1593 a much revised edition of *The Garden of Eloquence* was published. Comparison of the two volumes reveals certain forces which had meanwhile been acting upon English prose. In the later edition, comments headed "the use" and "the caution" were appended to the discussions of most of the figures, and Peacham made an effort to bedeck his own language with "flowers" and "colours," especially with those ornamental devices which had been popularized by the group of writers of whom John Lyly is the best-known representative. It was Peacham, rather than they, who was the follower.

At the beginning of the earlier edition of *The Garden of Eloquence*, 1577, Peacham reproduced the diagrammatic division [20] of figures given in Susenbrot's *Epitome*. Half the book is taken up by the two sections at the close, "figures of sentences" and "figures of amplification." In the edition of 1593 these two parts have been reshuffled and divided into "figures of affection" and "figures of amplification." Neither classification is entirely consistent. Both serve to illustrate the difficulties which confronted rhetoricians in analyzing the various kinds of figures. In particular they were undecided where to place such devices as exclamation, apostrophe, and prosopopoeia, which depend for their appeal upon arousing the emotions. Although useful for amplification, especially in the romances and sentimental novels, they were not, as were the figures of thought, based upon the processes

---

[14] *Ibid.*, pp. 191–94.
[15] "Contrarietie,"—*Ibid.*, p. 199.
[16] "Like ending, and like falling."—*Ibid.*, p. 202.
[17] "Egall members."—*Ibid.*, p. 204.
[18] "Regression."—*Ibid.*, p. 205.
[19] *Ibid.*, pp. 167–69 and 202–3.
[20] *Cf.* Crane, Appendix VII, 1.

of dialectical investigation. Various authorities grouped all, part, or none of them under the heading "figures of amplification." For the purposes of this study it is proper to consider both the figures of thought and the figures of emotion as devices of amplification. In the edition of 1593 Peacham has dealt with the figures of affection under four subheadings, "exclamation," "moderation," "consultation," and "permission," and he has also broken the figures of amplification up into four groups, "distribution," "description," "comparison," and "collection." A more consistent arrangement might have been to place the figures of "description" under the heading "affection." Whatever may be said of Peacham's classification, his interest in copiousness is evident throughout. He particularly recommends the figures of "distribution" as means of furnishing plenty and variety to a theme. Of the eleven devices named in this group, he states that "division," "partition," and "enumeration" serve most for expanding a subject. "Description" is set forth in glowing terms. The twenty figures considered under "comparison" begin with "comparison as it is usually and specially taken." Immediately after this come "similitudo," "dissimilitudo," and "antithesis." Whereas similes are highly commended, their misuse is not particularly stressed. Peacham justifies his term "collection" by assuming that all the figures under it "either leave the sense to be collected by the hearer, or do tend to the collection of proofes and conclusions." Under this heading "syllogismus," "aetiologia," "paradigma" (example), "gnome" (a moral sentence), and "expolition" are emphasized. The importance which Peacham attached to amplification is revealed by his discussion, by the illustrations he furnishes, by his own style, and by the fact that the larger part of his book is devoted to those two groups of figures which particularly serve for dilation. A list of the figures treated in his book is given in an appendix.[21] Many equivalent Latin, Greek, and English terms are given in his comments. The general remarks on amplification [22] in the later edition of his treatise illustrate both the importance which he attached to the means of expounding a theme and also his own efforts to achieve an ornate, copious style.

Aside from some remarks on delivery, Abraham Fraunce's *The Arcadian Rhetorike*, 1588, deals almost entirely with tropes and with figures of words. The explanatory discussions and some of the illustrations were taken either directly from the recension of Audomarus Talaeus's *Rhetorica* by Petrus Ramus or through the intermediary of *The Artes of Logike and Rhetorike*, 1584, usually attributed to Dudley

[21] *Cf.* Crane Appendix VII, 2.
[22] *Cf.* Crane Appendix VII, 3.

Fenner. Both Talaeus and Ramus insisted that the figures of thought, those based on the processes of dialectical investigation, should be considered as belonging to logic. Hence none of these devices receives notice in Fraunce's treatise. Taking amplification in the broadest sense in which it was applied by sixteenth-century rhetoricians, the only figures in the book which fall under it are ten at the close based on appeal to the emotions—"exclamation," "epanorthosis," "aposiopesis," "apostrophe," "prosopopoeia," "addubitation," "communication," praeoccupation," "sufference," and "graunting." The greater part of the space in Fraunce's volume is given over to illustrative material from the writings of Sir Philip Sidney and the other authors named on the title page. So far as this study is concerned the significance of the work is chiefly in the attention which it directs to Sidney's partiality toward the figures which it treats. *The Arcadia* is profusely ornamented with tropes and with those figures, common to the romances, which attempt to arouse the feelings, whereas there are very few figures of the type upon which John Lyly mainly depended, those derived from the processes of dialectical investigation and directed to the reason.

The Arte of Englishe Poesie, 1589, attributed to George Puttenham, contains an extensive treatment of figures in the third book, entitled "Of Ornament." These pertain, the writer admits, mainly to oratory; yet he proceeds to demonstrate their application in poetry. An avowed intention of Puttenham's is to find English names for the Greek and Latin rhetorical terms which have occasioned so much confusion for over twenty centuries. Much information may be gleaned from his description of more than one hundred figures, from the English names he has invented, and from the poetical illustrations he has given. To the three groups of figures he has distinguished he has given the names "auricular," "sensable," and "sententious," which, he states, are equivalent, respectively, to the terms "orthographicall," "syntactical," and "rhetorical." [23] Justification can hardly be found for all that he includes under these heads. In the first group fall twenty figures, such as zeugma, hysteron-proteron, homoioteleuton, alliteration, and asyndetion. The whole of the section labeled "sensable" is made up of tropes. The last division contains everything which is left. In his analysis Puttenham has described this group as follows,

> your third sort serues as well th'eare as the conceit and may be called
> *sententious figures,* because not only they properly apperteine to full
> sentences, for bewtifying them with a currant and pleasant numerositie,

[23] Puttenham, *The Arte of Englishe Poesie*. Arber's reprint, p. 171.

but also giuing them effacacie, and enlarging the whole matter besides with copious amplifications.[24]

At the beginning of his discussion of this group of figures he has placed considerable stress on amplification. Under "antitheton" [25] he noted that Isocrates and Guevara, as well as some Englishmen, abused this figure. "Merismus, or the Distributer," [26] "Orismus, or the Definer of difference," [27] "Sinathrismus, or the Heaping figure," [28] and "Exargasia" [29] are particularly noted as being valuable for the purposes of dilating a topic.

The English formularies of letter writing in the sixteenth century are, like the other books of rhetoric, based on the principles of ancient oratory.[30] The first to appear was William Fulwood's *The Enimie of Idlenesse*, 1568, which passed through seven editions before the end of the century. At the beginning Fulwood states,

> And to describe the true definition of an Epistle or letter, it is nothing else but an Oration written, conteining the mynde of the Orator or wryter, thereby to guie to understand to him or them that be absent, the same that should be declared if they were present.[31]

Dedicated to the "Maister, Wardens, and Company of the Marchant Tayllors of London," it was intended particularly for the merchant class, of which Fulwood was a member. Fulwood's volume is divided into four books. The first contains instructions with profuse illustrations; the other three consist entirely of model letters. The directions have to do mainly with externals of form and the proper language to use in writing to people in various stations of life. For those who may desire more complete treatment of "whether the matter that we write off bee honest, true or such like or whether it be slanderous, doubtfull, obscure, etc.," Fulwood recommends "the Rhetorike of Master Doctor Wilson, or Master Richard Rainolde." He mentions amplification, but in a way to suggest that his knowledge of it went no further than a casual acquaintance with Wilson's treatment.

Collections of epistles are much older than the formularies; and those who sought to provide instruction in the art depended more

[24] *Ibid.*, pp. 171–72.
[25] *Ibid.*, p. 219.
[26] *Ibid.*, p. 230.
[27] *Ibid.*, p. 239.
[28] *Ibid.*, p. 243.
[29] *Ibid.*, p. 254.
[30] *Cf.* E. N. S. Thompson, "The Familiar Letter," in *Literary Bypaths of the Renaissance*, 1924.
[31] William Fulwood, *The Enimie of Idlenesse*, Folio A. recto.

upon examples than upon precepts. Here, again, Cicero was acknowledged as the master. Yet the letters of Pliny, of Seneca, and of many
Renaissance scholars circulated widely. According to John Donne,
Montaigne mentions having seen four hundred volumes of epistles
during his short tour in Italy. Model letters, as has been noted, make
up the greater part of the first book of *The Enimie of Idlenesse* and
the whole of the remaining three books. Fulwood seems to have been
sincere in his desire to suit his work to the merchant class. Still, out
of fifty examples given in the first book, twelve are letters of Cicero,
five are letters addressed to him or written by his contemporaries, and
some others are translations of letters of state. Even business and
domestic correspondence is exemplified from Cicero. Among the other
illustrations in the first book many are suited rather to the scholar than
to the busy man of affairs. One asks the loan of Cicero's *Paradoxes*,
another for a book of rhetoric; a third accompanies a collection of
moral sentences. In the first edition the second book contains twenty-
three letters, all but one of which are from the popular Renaissance
volume *Illustrium virorum epistolae*, made up principally of the correspondence of Angelo Poliziano. Later editions include three additional letters in this section, two of which are from *Amadis de Gaula*.
Book three is made up of domestic and business correspondence, and
book four of amatory epistles in prose and verse. The first among the
love letters is from Aeneas Sylvius's *De duobus amantibus;* some others
are from *Amadis*.

A *Panoplie of Epistles*, 1576, states on the title page that it is
"Gathered and translated out of Latine into English by Abraham
Flemming." Cicero's letters fill the first third of four hundred and
fifty quarto pages; the second third is made up of epistles of Pliny
and of selections attributed to Isocrates and others; the remainder of
the volume contains correspondence of Renaissance scholars, such as
Mantuan, Erasmus, Haddon, and Ascham. The letters are preceded by
"An Epitome of Precepts," by way of a catechism of a student by his
master. This is a translation of Christopher Hegendorff's *Methodus de
conscribendis epistolis*, which deals mainly with the rhetorical commonplaces that serve to develop various kinds of letter. It was derived
largely from Quintilian's *Institutio oratoria*. To the master's request for
the sundry kinds of epistle, the scholar replies, "Of Epistles, some be
demonstrative, some suasorie, and others some iudiciall." Called upon
to give an example of the first, he delivers a long harangue in praise of
Coriolanus, substituted for the one Hegendorff has on Hannibal. The
master rewards him with the criticism, "I like well of your example,

if it had bene breefer, and I commende your wit and inuention." [32]
Shortly after, the following dialogue takes place.

MAISTER. Give me the common places of proofe and confirmation in this
behalfe (the praise of a fact or deed of a person).

SCHOLER. Places of confirmation are drawen from
that which is

$$\left\{\begin{array}{l} \text{Honest} \\ \text{Profitable} \\ \text{Not combersome} \\ \text{Religious} \\ \text{Just, etc.} \end{array}\right.$$

MAISTER. Of a demonstratiue kinde of epistle, touching the thing, what be
the places?

SCHOLER. These and such like be the places, namely
that which is

$$\left\{\begin{array}{l} \text{Honest} \\ \text{Profitable} \\ \text{Not tedious} \\ \text{Hard and difficult} \\ \text{(Aiii recto)} \end{array}\right.$$

In this manner the catechism proceeds, dwelling principally upon the
places, or topics, of rhetorical investigation. Toward the close, the
master asks, "How is a thing amplified or inlarged?" The scholar
replies:—

By circumstances
$$\left\{\begin{array}{l} \text{Of words} \\ \text{Sentences} \\ \text{Figures} \\ \text{Places} \\ \text{Time} \\ \text{Maner, etc.} \end{array}\right\}$$
Fab. lib 8. & Cic. in his particions.

(Bii recto)

We hardly need the gratuitous references to Quintilian and Cicero.
In his copious marginal comments on the model letters, Flemming
occasionally pointed out the figures of speech. A note on Cicero's
"Epistle to Lucceio" calls attention to "how many wordes he bringeth
together to beautifie his Metaphor or translation." The heading "D.
Erasmus Roterodamus to Ilermo Burbanco" is followed by the con-
spicuous statement, "He beginneth his epistle with a [moral] sentence."
Some space is devoted to explaining that the selection from Joannes
Ravisius Textor on idleness, though addressed as a letter to a friend,
is really a "theame." A letter of Ascham's to Queen Elizabeth is pre-

[32] Abraham Flemming, *A Panoplie of Epistles,* 1576, A ii recto.

ceded by a long argument dwelling upon Ascham's skill in the use of rhetoric. It begins, "Writing to the Queenes maiestie, hee beginneth very Rhetorically, with a comparison of her highness, where-with hee was discouraged, and her goodnesse whereby he was imboldened to write to her maiestie." The letter itself opens, "Most excellent Ladie Elizabeth, I haue laboured long in doubtfulnesse of mind, whether I should be more discouraged in consideration of your highnesse, or more imbouldened in respect of your goodnesse, to present you with an epistle." In the romances and sentimental novels the use of this device at the beginning of letters and speeches was a fixed convention. Flemming also called attention to Ascham's use of examples.

The Forest of Fancy, 1579, by H. C., is merely a collection of letters, nearly all of which are amatory and in verse. From their quality it may be inferred that they are original compositions. Angel Day's *The English Secretorie*, 1587, deserves more attention. In it he discusses the methods of developing some thirty kinds of letter grouped under four main headings, "demonstrative," "deliberative," "judicial," and "familiar." For his explanatory matter Day was indebted in a general way to Erasmus's *De ratione conscribendis epistolas liber*. Most of the examples appear to be of Day's own composition. To the revised edition of 1592 he added a discussion of the duties of a secretary and a treatise of tropes and figures taken mainly from John Susenbrot's *Epitome troporum ac schematum*. In addition, marginal notes call attention, among other things, to all the devices of rhetoric serving for ornament and to the topics of rhetorical proof. Sometimes more than one dozen figures to a page are noted. From Day's statement that by a study of tropes and figures the reader may come to recognize them in his own letters one is inclined to suspect that, like a well-known gentleman who suddenly discovered he had been speaking prose, Day became aware that the letters he had written contained figures of rhetoric.

Thomas Blount's *Academie of Eloquence*, 1654, lies beyond the proper limits of this study. Yet it may serve to illustrate the direction in which rhetoric was proceeding at the close of Elizabeth's reign. It is divided into four sections. "The first part," Blount states, "contains a more exact *English Rhetorique*, then has been hitherto extant, comprehending all the most usefull Figures, exemplifi'd out of the *Arcadia* and other our choicest Authors." About twenty-five figures, roughly those treated in Talaeus's *Rhetorica*, are described. But in addition Blount attempts to give proper weight to amplification, which takes up thirty of the forty-six pages of the first book. Regarding the contents of the second part Blount may again be allowed to speak for himself:

> You have [in this book] *formulae majores* or *Common-places,* upon the most usual subjects for stile and speech; The use and advantage whereof is asserted by my Lord Bacon, who (in his *Advancement of Learning*) sayes thus; "I hold the diligence and pain in collecting Common-places to be of great use and certainty in studying; as, that which aids the memory, sub-ministers copy to invention and contracts the sight of judgment to a strength."

This section occupies seventy pages. The third part consists of twenty pages of choice phrases, the fourth of some model letters, For a work which claims to contain "a more exact *English Rhetorique,* then has hitherto been extant," *The Academie of Eloquence* is in entirety an exceptionally feeble performance. It is evidence, however, of the emphasis placed on the devices of amplification in the first half of the seventeenth century and also an indication of the prevalent tendency to rely upon books of commonplaces and selected phrases as aids to composition.

RAMIST RHETORIC   *Walter J. Ong*

> Hamlet. "Word, words, words . . . .
> Polonius. ". . . Yet there is method in't."
> —Hamlet.

1. The Ramist Rhetoric and Its Author

If the Ramist dialectic is the most central item in the complex of cultural phenomena which make up Ramism, Ramist rhetoric is the most symptomatic item in the same complex. Hence it merits close attention. Dialectic and rhetoric have been intertwined at least from the time of the Greek Sophists till our present day, and when Ramus decrees that they must be disengaged from one another once and for all in theory (but always united in practice), he engages some of the most powerful and obscure forces in intellectual history. The divorce between the two disciplines affects rhetoric the most. Ramist dialectic is constructed in the interests of a "simplification" inspired by the topical logic tradition and the vague but powerful premathematicism

Reprinted by permission of the publishers from Walter J. Ong, S. J., *Ramus—Method, and the Decay of Dialogue.* Cambridge, Mass.: Harvard University Press, Copyright, 1958, by The President and Fellows of Harvard College.

connected with this tradition; Ramist rhetoric is constructed with the precise objective of making it something different from dialectic. To realize this objective, Ramist rhetoric reserves to itself only two of the more or less traditional five parts of rhetoric: elocution and pronunciation. These had never threatened to overlap with dialectic. Of the other three parts, invention and disposition or judgment, which had threatened to overlap, are surrendered completely to dialectic. The fifth part, memory, is simply liquidated by being identified with judgment.

Ramist rhetoric, however, did not spring full-fledged from the head of its author, any more than did Ramist dialectic. Partly because of this, the identity of its real author is still something of a mystery, which will probably never be solved. In his 1543 *Training in Dialectic*, Ramus had announced that Omer Talon was to provide a complementary treatment of rhetoric.[1] The treatment appeared in 1545 as *Omer Talon's Training in Oratory*.[2] Its title matches exactly that of Ramus' 1543 work, and the author was identified, like Ramus, as "of the Vermandois" (*Veromanduus*).

Omer Talon (Audomarus Taleus) was one of the four sons of Arthur (or Artus) Talon, an Irish colonel under Charles IX permanently settled in France. He was born around 1510 and according to the biographical dictionaries (there has never been a full study of the man) seems to have been born at Amiens, although Nancel identifies him as "of Beauvais" (*Bellovacus*).[3] Except for a brief time teaching at the College of Beauvais at Paris,[4] Talon was Ramus' man. He lived at the College of Cardinal Le Moine at the time he was sworn in as a teacher at the University of Paris in 1544.[5] Later the same year he joined Ramus and Bartholomew Alexandre in teaching at the little Collège de l'Ave Maria, and remained closely attached to Ramus the rest of his life. Some time before Talon's death, Ramus had him installed as curé of the Church of St. Nicolas du Chardonnet, which was one of the benefices Ramus held and which was very near Ramus' own Collège de Presles. Talon, now ordained a priest late in life,[6] died here in 1562 from some very painful disease.

---

[1] Ramus, *Dialecticae institutiones* (1543), fols. 50–52.

[2] *Audomari Talaei Varomandui Instiutiones oratoriae, ad celeberrimam et illustrissimam Lutetiae Parisiorum Academiam* (Parisiis: Iacobus Bogardus, 1545).

[3] Nancel, *Vita* (1599), p. 12.

[4] *Ibid.*, p. 15.

[5] "Talaeus," *Grand dictionnaire historique*, ed. Louis, Moréri, Goujet, and Drouet (1759).

[6] Nancel, *Vita* (1599), p. 40.

It is quite likely that Ramus had some hand in *Omer Talon's Training in Oratory*, and even more likely that he had a hand in the *Rhetoric* (*Rhetorica*) which emerged from it in 1548. It is quite certain that the rewriting of the text in the 1567 and 1569 editions after Talon's death is Ramus' own.[7] The Talon *Rhetoric* is the expressly designed complement of Ramus' *Dialectic*, a complement in any and all of its stages as perfect as not only Talon, but Ramus himself, knew how to make it.

2. Stages of Development

The development of the Ramist rhetoric parallels roughly that of the Ramist dialectic. There is a three-phase period represented by the *Training in Oratory* (matching the *Training in Dialectic*), followed by a two-part period represented by the *Rhetoric* of 1548 or *Rhetoric in Two Books* of 1562 (paralleled by the *Dialectic* or *Dialectic in Two Books*).[8] The initial three-phase work treats of a "natural" eloquence, an art or teaching (*doctrina*) of eloquence (this art is what is called precisely *rhetorica*), and the use or exercise of the art. As in the case of dialectic, this initial attempt to include a treatment of "nature" and "practice" with the treatment of the art itself is quickly abandoned; and in 1548 we are presented with the *Rhetorica*, which is the two-part art alone. After Talon's death this is equipped with Ramus' prelections (1567), and still later (1569) it is divided clearly into two books as *Rhetoricae libri duo, Petri Rami praelectionibus illustrati*.

Despite Ramus' coming attacks on Quintilian, the rhetoric of the Ramus and Talon team echoes Quintilian from the start. The *Training in Oratory* opens with an almost verbatim quotation from the Iberian rhetorician: "Eloquentia vis [as against Ramus' 1543 *virtus* for dialectic] est bene dicendi."[9] This may be rendered, "Eloquence is the power of expressing oneself well." *Dicendi* cannot be translated "speaking," since it does not exclude writing to the extent that this English word does.

The three parts—nature, art, and exercise—into which Ramus had divided his dialectic are represented in eloquence not by "parts" but by "steps" (*gradus*). Talon makes the same reduction of the "nature of eloquence" which Ramus has made of the "nature of dialectic." *Natura* is taken in the sense of origin, and the assigning of three "steps"

---

[7] See the introductory note with the editions of the *Rhetorica* listed in Ong, *Ramus and Talon Inventory*.

[8] For the detailed relationships, consult Ong, *Ramus and Talon Inventory*.

[9] Talon, *Institutiones oratoriae* (1545), p. 5. Cf. Quintilian *Institutiones oratoriae* ii. 1. 5: "Rhetorice, cui nomen vis eloquentiae dedit."

to eloquence is thus the equivalent of saying that eloquence has an origin, an art, and an exercise.

Talon now provides us with a brief description of the origin of eloquence in the individual man.[10] God generates in man "motions" which are rich and abundant (*uberes et copiosi*—with obvious reference to the *copia verborum* or "copie of words" which it was the ambition of every humanist teacher to instill into his pupils). These motions produce successively: thought (*cogitatio mentis*); a discretion which unfolds the instinctive cognition contained in reason; and finally, embellishment. Talon explains that these powers become less dark and more tractable by use and example even without written arts, as in the case of Ulysses, Menelaus, Nestor, and many living persons. Further than this, he does not explain these powers. The reason is evident. It would be quite a task to show how the first and second apply to Ramist rhetoric at all. Thought (*cogitatio mentis*) looks remarkably like Ramus' first part of the art of dialectic, invention, whereas discretion is the image of judgment, the second part of the same art. The third natural activity produced by the primitive rhetorical motion in the soul, "embellishment," is indistinguishable from the art of rhetoric. Thus unveiled, the three "dark" powers of natural rhetoric reveal themselves as the two parts of the dichotomized art of dialectic in not very convincing disguise; they are flanked by the art of rhetoric, not yet dichotomized and also in disguise.

The second step in eloquence is that of the art or teaching, which is rhetoric proper. Talon defines it in a cautious adaptation of Quintilian, and states that rhetoric proper is "the artificial teaching of good expression in any matter." [11] A certain diffidence concerning Ramus' and others' assumption that art is identified with teaching is evident here. Talon circumspectly specifies that rhetoric is both a teaching (*doctrina*) and an art (*artificiosa*). By 1548 this circumspection will be deemed superfluous, Ramus would have his way, and rhetoric would be simply "the doctrine of expressing oneself well" (*doctrina bene dicendi*),[12] which, with *scientia* substituted for *doctrina*, is exactly Quintilian's definition again.[13]

Talon goes on to say that rhetoric, like dialectic, applies to all subjects. The two parts of the teaching or art of rhetoric are said to cor-

[10] Talon, *Inst. orat.* (1545), pp. 6–7.
[11] "Rhetorica est . . . artificiosa de qualibet re bene dicendi doctrina"—*ibid.*, p. 8.
[12] Talon, *Rhetorica* (1548), p. 1.
[13] Quintilian *Institutiones oratoriae* v. 10. 54: "Rhetorice est bene dicendi scientia."

respond to the parts of natural eloquence, which turn on the "praise" (*laus*) or—as we might prefer to conceptualize it—the assets of single words, and the "praise" or assets of conjoined words. These two parts are, of course, formed by imposing on rhetoric a division paralleling the unit-cluster partition of dialectic: invention (single arguments) and judgment (conjoined arguments). This partition will be a complete failure in rhetoric. In the 1548 *Rhetoric* and editions derived from it, the parts will be redesigned as *elocutio;* this might be rendered in English "style" or "striking expression," but it was conceived largely as "ornament" or "garnishing," and *pronuntiato* or delivery. Striking expression is divided into tropes and figures; delivery into voice (*vox,* or, as it was sometimes confusingly called, simply *pronuntiato*) and gesture (*gestus* or *actio*).[14]

This new division of rhetoric into striking expression and delivery would prove a kind of failure, too. From Talon through Dudley Fenner and his successors, the insufficiency of the new second part of rhetoric will become all too apparent. Delivery is given rather short shrift by ancient rhetoricians such as Cicero and Quintilian. But they did not consider it one complete part of a two-part art. Talon, who later did so consider it, had forgot to mention it at all in 1545, just as Ramus had forgot to mention enunciations and method in dialectic in 1543. In the *Rhetoric* of 1548, the second part amounts to almost nothing, and Talon avers that it comes to the same thing as the first part.[15] In Ramus' revisions done in 1567 and later, it amounts to even less. Fenner would lament that the second part was "not yet perfect," [16] Piscator's more valid excuse for omitting it would be that it varies from country to country and can be learned only by practice.[17]

All this means, of course, is that the irreducibly vocal and auditory phenomena of actual spoken delivery, which the second part of rhetoric purportedly taught, escape the diagrammatic apparatus somehow intrusive in all explanatory approaches to communication. This apparatus is particularly characteristic of Ramist arts, which were themselves the product of the humanists' outlook, and which, despite real interest and skill in oral delivery, is dominantly and incurably textual (as nothing before the Gutenberg era could be) and controlled by the written rather than the spoken word. Of course, Ramus and Talon and others taught boys to *speak* Latin (Ramus, after all, has

[14] Talon, *Rhetorica* (1550), p. 63.

[15] "Nec alia pronuntiationis est doctrina quam elocutionis"—*ibid.*

[16] Dudley Fenner (adapting Talon), *Art of Rhetorick* in *The Artes of Logike and Rethorike* (1584), fol. E1v.

[17] Piscator's preface to his edition of Talon, *Rhetorica* (1590).

been hailed as the greatest orator since Cicero) but how they did so has not come down to us in writing, or has come down very imperfectly. Oral delivery retains an inalienable connection with the spoken tradition—stronger than any connection with written prescriptions. By the same token, it fitted uneasily into a Ramist art. The Ramist "plain style" is a manner of composition, not of voice and gesture.

On the other hand, the first "part" of rhetoric is organized entirely around two well-established, geometrically grounded conceptualizations. These are tropes ("turnings") and figures ("shapes"). Together they constitute all of *elocutio*, and are developed in straightforward Ramist fashion by definition and division; they move toward neater and neater dichotomization from the beginnings in 1545 through the 1548 and later revisions.[18] The Ramist treatment of individual tropes and figures is uneventful and undistinguished by comparison with other rhetorics of the time. It is not insensitive, as when it gives high marks to metaphor. But, like most rhetorics, it maintains the low theoretical level enforced on the subject (in postclassical times) by its place in the lower reaches of the curriculum, and evinces no real understanding of the semantic importance of metaphorical or of any similar processes.

The Ramist distinction between trope and figure is an attempt at tidiness. In the 1545 *Training in Oratory*, the distinction is not in effect, although the various "ornaments" of speech—neologism (*novum ornamentum*), archaism (*vestustum ornamentum*), transfer or metaphor (*ornamentum translatum*), and the rest—are grouped in terms of the unit-cluster division already described. Only in its final form, does the *Rhetoric* mature fairly neat definitions which enable it to divide all the ornaments between trope and figure. A trope consists in changing a word from its "native signification" to another signification—a definition which, in effect, makes all tropes species of metaphor; where a figure varies the "clothing" of speech (*orationis habitus*) from the straightforward and simple.[19]

It is plain that Ramus and/or Talon want to make figure an "ornamentation" of the sound of speech alone. The first examples they give,

---

[18] See the descriptions of the various editions in Ong, *Ramus and Talon Inventory*.

[19] "Elocutio est exornatio orationis . . . . Elocutio est tropus aut figura. Tropus est elocutio qua verbum a nativa significatione in aliam immutatur."— Talon, *Rhetorica e P. Rami praelectionibus observata* (Lutetiae: A. Wechelus, 1574), p. 6. "Figura est elocutio, qua orationis habitus a recta et simplici consuetudine mutatur" —*ibid.*, p. 24.

number or rhythm, repetition of like sounds, and so on, make this clear. To these they apply the old term "figures of diction" (*figurae dictionis*). But they have also to throw in with figures items such as exclamation, apostrophe, personification—which in traditional fashion, they style "figures of sentence" (*figurae sententiae*)—and thus their notion of figure loses outline. Roughly, although Ramists do not put it quite this way, in the Ramist view trope is always some sort of metaphor, and figure is anything else that strikes one as unusual. The Ramist difficulty here is the difficulty of practically all such rhetoric text books: it may be traced to the attempt to describe and classify the unusual without being able to identify what the usual is.

The last part of the 1545 *Training in Oratory*, concerned with use or exercise,[20] drops out of the later *Rhetoric*. It exactly parallels the section on exercise in the *Training in Dialectic* which dropped out of the later *Dialectic*, and is divided the same way into interpretation, writing, and speaking. Interpretation is rhetorical analysis, or identification of the various ornaments.[21] Writing and speaking are treated solely in terms of imitation, which is explained conventionally and jejunely as the following of classical models. How one or another trope or figure is related to one or another rhetorical effect is not attended to. The ideas on style which Ramus and Talon are expressing are representative of Ramism in general and of the central tradition of post-Renaissance Latin. They are neither rabidly Ciceronian nor rabidly anti-Ciceronian. The "pure and elegant" authors—Terence, Antonius, Crassus, Hortensius, Sulpicius, Cicero, Caesar, Virgil, and Ovid—are to be imitated, and Cato, Ennius, Plautus, Pacuvius, and other *rudes et inculti* to be avoided.[22] Plato, Cicero, and Quintilian are the basic authorities on the subject of rhetoric. The two latter are, of course, among Talon's and Ramus' real sources. Plato, who is not a real, immediate source, is cited for prestige and for what Ramus considered his nuisance value in annoying the Aristotelians.

3. The Five-Part Rhetoric and Renaissance Youth

Talon's and Ramus' redesigning of rhetoric was not a purely whimsical event. It derives from tensions in the educational system which were the product of centuries. The more or less traditional five parts of rhetoric commonly adhered to by non-Ramist Renaissance textbook

[20] Talon, *Inst. orat.* (1545), p. 73–83.
[21] *Ibid.*, pp. 73–75.
[22] *Ibid.*, pp. 82–83.

writers—invention, disposition, memory, striking expression (*elocutio*), and delivery—date from ancient Greek times. They were not five abstract parts of an abstract art then, but five activities in which an aspirant was disciplined so that he might become an orator or public lecturer—the common ideal of all ancient liberal education.[23] In antiquity a boy was given a foundation of general information on all possible subjects (*inventio*). He was taught to use this material in composition (*dispositio*), his mnemonic skill was developed (*memoria*), together with his literary style (*elocutio*) and his oral delivery (*pronuntiatio*). These five activities added up to a rather complete educational program extending over a good number of years. As the training which the normal educated man received, these activities today would be called simply education, or perhaps general education.[24]

The Romans had been able, with little difficulty, to take over these five activities from the Greeks. They, too, had been able to teach "rhetoric," in the sense of a general education framed within native Latin expression. Such is the program which Quintilian proposes. But it was quite different in medieval and Renaissance Europe. Rhetoric, which in ancient times had been general culture purveyed in the vernacular, was now culture set within a foreign tongue; the acquisition of culture became identified with, or subordinate to, acquiring the foreign tongue itself. Rhetoric thus became chiefly a course in Latin—advanced as compared with (Latin) grammar, which was the elementary course (elementary schools today are still "grammar" schools). The pattern, which Ramus himself records, of distinguishing art students into two groups, the grammarians or *grammatici* (studying grammar and rhetoric) and the philosophers or *philosophi* (studying dialectic, physics, and the rest) can be clearly seen in the university practice.[25] Outside the grammar-school and university

[23] See H.-I. Marrou, *Hist. de l'éducation dans l'antiquité*, 2d ed. rev. (Paris, 1950), pp. 272–276. As Marrou makes evident, the objectives of Socrates, Plato, Aristotle, and other "wisdom lovers" or philosophers were exceptional—a fact to which we have been more or less blinded because they have subsequently proved the most valuable. The typical product of Greek education was the sophist, a rhetorician, and the typical Greek regarded the "philosopher" as a sectarian and crank. Socrates' execution was consistent with a large pattern of attitudes.

[24] In one place, Ramus himself says that these five parts of rhetoric, as given by Quintilian, are wrong because they are against the third law of method, that general matters be taught first in a general way (*generale generaliter doceatur*), and that they divide "things," not the art itself.—Ramus, *Sch. rhet.* in *Sch. in lib. art.* (1569), col. 344.

[25] Ramus, *Pro philosophica Parisiensis Academiae disciplina oratio*, in *Scholae in liberales artes* (1569), col. 1022.

framework, rhetoric persisted in Ramus' day sometimes in other forms, but nowhere as a course in general culture in the ancient sense. In the Inns of Court, where the subject was of great importance (Thomas Wilson's English *Arte of Rhetorique* [1533] was probably written for young noblemen at the Inns of Court) rhetoric was a still more specialized discipline; it involved not only a tangle of Latin and technicalities but also declamation in still another language foreign to Englishmen (and to everyone else), Law French.[26]

The simplified Ramist rhetoric represents in great part an adjustment to the changed linguistic situation. But the adjustment was far from complete or satisfactory. Ramus' relegation of intention and disposition (this latter including memory) to dialectic and his limitation of rhetoric to style (*elocutio*) and oral delivery suggested still the order which had prevailed in early Greek education. Common sense would dictate that the invention and disposition of matter be taught before its "ornamentation" and delivery, dialectic before rhetoric. Yet Ramus taught rhetoric as a one-year course before dialectic! [27] Indeed, his labored explanation of "natural dialectic," or the ability to discourse which every normal boy supposedly picked up by himself and which saw him through both rhetoric and life until he came to the formal art of dialectic, seems to be a rationalization of Ramus' own procedure and that of almost everyone else. In the school curriculum practice after antiquity, rhetoric was really supplementary to grammar, not to dialectic. Although the Middle Ages witnessed occasional attempts to teach rhetoric after dialectic,[28] such a program proved hardly viable in Northern Europe.[29] If we except the "rhetoric" of various technical secretarial courses (*dictamen*), which, while highly important in the Middle Ages, was not rhetoric in the classical or ordinary sense, the remark made by Rhabanus Maurus as early as the ninth century remained in force: "It is enough for rhetoric if it be the business of youngsters." [30]

[26] See R. J. Schoeck, "Rhetoric and Law in Sixteenth-Century England," *Studies in Philology*, 50:120 (1953), and *passim*.

[27] Ramus, *Pro phil. disc.* in *Sch. in lib. art.* (1569), cols. 1010–1020.

[28] See Richard McKeon, "Rhetoric in the Middle Ages," *Speculum*, 17:1–32 (1942).

[29] See Louis John Paetow, *The Arts Course in Medieval Universities* (Urbana, Illinois, 1910); Hastings Rashdall, *The Universities of Europe*, new ed. (Oxford, 1936); etc.

[30] "Satis est ut adolescentulorum cura sit," quoted in Emile Durkheim, *L'évolution pédagogique en France* (Paris, 1938), [I], *Des origines à la Renaissance*, 69.

During the Renaissance, especially in England, the Erasmian tradition worked for a while to reverse this medieval pattern. It favored theoretically a curriculum with dialectic or logic placed before rhetoric and subordinated to rhetorical purposes.[31] This theory was at times put into effect, for Ascham writes to Sturm that Cheke was teaching Prince Edward dialectic, ethics, rhetoric, in this order.[32] The *Parnassus* plays as late as 1597–1601 associate rhetoric in the curriculum with poetry and seemingly place it after dialectic—although it is not quite clear that this position represents the curriculum order and not simply the order in which the aspirant to Parnassus' heights considers possible means of ascent.[33] But, insofar as the Erasmian philosophy of education was put into effect, it produced a dialectic or logic so rudimentary that it was little more than an elaboration of rhetoric itself. The precocious dialectic or logic which resulted has well been called rhetoric-logic.[34]

Even in England, however, this rhetoric-logic proved not very viable, and in the curriculum finally fixed on under Edward VI, dialectic or logic followed after rhetoric.[35] This seems to have been the predominant order in most Renaissance universities. Accordingly, the "grammar schools" such as Eton, Winchester, and Westminster, even at a time when they were described as "trivial schools," commonly taught grammar and rhetoric only, and left out the third trivial subject, dialectic or logic, for more advanced work.[36] The alinement was thereby the same as that which Ramus reports for medieval and Renaissance Paris.

Talon is quite representative of the general Renaissance pattern, therefore, when he insists that in rhetoric one must have regard for the "tender" years of the pupils.[37] Rhetoric was practically everywhere a matter for still younger boys than was dialectic, and was comparable to a grade-school or junior-high-school subject in America today. The fact that it was Latin rhetoric taught from Latin textbooks often confuses the twentieth-century mind.

[31] T. W. Baldwin, *William Shakspere's Small Latine and Lesse Greeke* (Urbana, Illinois, 1944), I, 76, 94, etc.; cf. Sir Thomas Wilson as cited by Baldwin, *ibid.*, I, 81.

[32] *Ibid.*, I, 237.

[33] *The Pilgramage to Parnassus*, Acts I, II, and III in *The Pilgramage to Parnassus with the Two Parts of the Return from Parnassus*, ed. W. D. Macray (Oxford, 1886), pp. 5, 9, 11.

[34] Baldwin, *William Shakespere's Small Latine*, I, 82 and *passim*.

[35] *Ibid.*, I, 289.

[36] *Ibid.*, I, 76, quoting F. Watson, *The Beginnings of the Teaching of Modern Subjects in England*, p. xxii.

[37] Talon, *Inst. orat.* (1545), pp. 3–4: "teneros adolescentium animos."

4. Ornamentation Theory: Praises and Honors of Words

When Melanchthon accepted the view that dialectic and rhetoric differed in that the former presented things in a naked state, whereas the latter clothed them with ornament, he also was concerned with the age of his pupils. He defends this old and common view of rhetoric on the grounds that, although many persons objected to it, it was one which little boys could understand.[38] Indeed, the idea that rhetoric adds ornament to speech which is originally or natively "plain" would seem to be the common one of the man in the street and quite assimilable by children. Something like it is present in the association of ornamentation with rhetoric which is found in antiquity, particularly in Cicero and Quintilian, and is recurrent through the Middle Ages in the common doctrine concerning the tropes and figures. But in Ramism this ornamentation theory undergoes a significant change —a change which is symptomatic not only of Ramism but of the age, and which reveals much of the significance of Ramist rhetoric.

In its final stage, Ramist rhetoric relies more on ornamentation theory than perhaps any other rhetoric ever has. The basic reason is its restriction of rhetoric to *elocutio*, which meant the use of tropes and figures, commonly considered the "ornaments." As has been seen, the second half of Ramist rhetoric was, practically speaking, nonexistent as a part of the "art" proper. "Just as wisdom treats of the knowledge of all things," Talon states in 1545, "so rhetoric treats of ornamentation and striking expression." [39] These two terms, *exornatio* and *elocutio*, are not complementary opposites but synonyms, as the 1548 *Rhetoric* shows.

Miss Tuve and others have sought to rehabilitate the Renaissance notion of ornament with some success. They have shown that it does not necessarily mean appliqué work in the way the English term ornament suggests today.[40] Indeed, the first meaning of *ornamentum* in Latin—rhetoric as an art existed almost entirely in Latin—is equipment or accoutrements, which the "naked causes" of dialectic, liked naked persons, would need rather more than pretty clothing to get along in this world. Because it conceives of "ornament" as equipment

---

[38] Melanchthon, *Elementa rhetorica*, Lib. I, in *Opera* (Halle, 1834–1860), XIII, col. 420. Cf. Melanchthon, *Erotemata dialectices*, I (opening words), in *Opera*, XIII, col. 513.

[39] "Ut sapientia rerum omnium cognitionem, ita Rhetorica exornationem praestaret atque elocutionem."—Talon, *Inst. orat.* (1545), p. 8.

[40] Rosemond Tuve, *Elizabethan and Metaphysical Imagery* (Chicago, 1947), pp. 61 ff.

rather than as decoration solely, the fifteenth century can conceive of the hand as "a great help and ornament to the body," and the sixteenth century of tackling as the "ornaments of a ship." [41]

The Renaissance notion of ornament, however, has dimensions of still another sort which seem never to have been explicitly adverted to. The terms *ornamentum* or *ornamentatio* have certain definite synonyms which come from Cicero and Quintilian. An "ornament" of rhetoric is also indifferently styled a "praise" (*laus*) or an "honor" (*honos* or *honor*) or a "light" (*lumen*) of words or of speech.[42] All these concepts, *ornamentum* included, are closely connected with the notion that rhetoric demands a continuous flow of oral sound (*oratio perpetua*), a Ciceronian expression which Ramus makes a shibboleth in his program to re-establish an eloquent and rhetorical, as against a scholastic, philosophy.[43]

[41] John Trevisa, *Bart. de P. R.*, V, xxviii (1495), 137, and Cooper, *Thesaurus amphistre* (*ca.* 1565–1573), both as cited in the *New English Dictionary*.

[42] *Inst. orat.* (1545), pp. 8–9, 21–22, 28. The two parts of the art of rhetoric turn on the *laus* of single words and of conjoined words—p. 8. "Singula per se et separatim quam laudem quodve lumen adferant . . . ."—pp. 8–9. "Quamobrem honos verborum singulorum quatuor maxime existit . . . ."—p. 21. "Verba continuata . . . in quorum laudibus et ornamentis quatuor has res animadvertere oportebit . . . ."—pp. 21–22. The passages which follow these explain that these four terms are all referring to tropes and figures. For instances of Cicero's and Quintilian's similar use of these terms, see any large Latin dictionary. Cf. Cicero, *Orator* xxxixff., where the *lumina singulorum verborum* and the *lumina collocatorum verborum*, which together are grammatical schemes or "figures of language," are opposed to the *sententiarum ornamenta* (figures of sentence, which become by the eighteenth century figures of "sentiment"). It is difficult to draw any consistent or telling theoretical distinction between Cicero's *lumina verborum* (in which he hesitatingly includes metaphor) and his *sententiarum ornamenta*, although the latter tend to be rather large-scale operations, such as rhetorical questions, repetitions, the use of dialect and impersonation, and the like. Miss Tuve has remarked on Renaissance attempts to straighten things out and the resulting further entanglements in her *Elizabethan and Metaphysical Imagery*, pp. 105–106, and Sister Miriam Joseph, in her *Shakespeare's Use of the Arts of Language* (New York, 1947), pp. 31ff., juxtaposes some of the manifold classifications and discusses others in detail. Miss Tuve here makes the statement that insofar as the classifications "reflect the purposes of various figures, I have not observed damaging misunderstandings" as between one Elizabethan author and another. This statement I should regard as quite tenable, charitable, but in that it perhaps implies a deep grasp by Renaissance rhetoricians (often teen-agers) of the inherent nature of one or another figure, certainly optimistic.

[43] Ramus, *Oratio initio suae professionis habita* (1551), pp. 16–17, where Ramus ties his program up with the earlier statutes of the University of Paris which called for philosophy to be taught to students "without quill or pen, in continuous and flowing discourse" (*remotis pennis et calamis . . . perpetua voce raptim*)—such statutes being, of course, attempts to do away with the vicious practice of dictation, whereby young masters simply read to their pupils notes which, in turn, had been read to them.

It is exceedingly difficult for the twentieth-century mind to form concepts of tropes and figures as "honors" or "praises" of words or of speech in the way in which these concepts are formed by Cicero and, with rather more effort, by Talon, Ramus, and their contemporaries. "Lights" of words or of speech comes perhaps somewhat more naturally to us, although even this formulation has its difficulties. But the concepts honor and praise are too personalistic in their implications to apply convincingly to words; they treat words as if they are the normal objects of honor and praise, persons. Even the notion of light, in this complimentary or honorific sense, is normally applied to a person: we should call a writer, rather than the words he pronounces, a literary "light," or the great "light" of his age.

Nevertheless, the personalist cast of these terms is entirely relevant to their earlier association with *ornamentum*. This is clear from the fact that this latter term and its cognates are also used by Renaissance rhetoricians in certain personalized senses which strike the twentieth-century ear as strange. Thus Ramus refers to the regius professors such as himself as "ornamented" (or "equipped") with an annual grant from the crown.[44] Even had these grants been easier to collect than they were (they often lagged three or four years in arrears) their use to "ornament" persons strikes us as strange, although their use to 'honor" persons might not; the latter term exists for us in a context involving persons and personal relations. For the sensibility of the sixteenth century and earlier, the term "ornament" existed in a similar context. The whole field over which *laus, honor, lumen,* and *ornamentum* play is obviously one where the distinctions between persons and objects now made automatically at least by English-speaking persons are more or less blurred.

This is obvious on another score. We think of honor or praise as applied to an object by a person, whereas Ramus and his classical predecessors and Renaissance contemporaries are quite willing to have the object somehow emanate honor and praise, in this way performing a kind of personal role. In the title of the orations by Talon's pupils printed in 1548, *Quinque orationes de laude regiae dignitatis,* it is practically impossible to decide whether this means *Five Orations Giving Praise to the Royal Station* or *Five Orations on the Impressiveness Found in the Royal Station,* since *laus* can either emanate from the orator or from the object he is concerned with. Again—in an example to which the *New English Dictionary* does not quite do justice

[44] "Regiis etiam stipendiis ornatos"—Ramus, *Oratio init. suae prof.* (1551), p. 5; cf. *ibid.,* "liberas, . . . alis, . . . ornas."

—George Puttenham's *Art of English Poesie* (III, i) says, "The chief prayse and cunning of our poet is in the discreet using of his figures." Praise, which in Elizabethan and later texts functions also as the Latin *encomium,* functions here as the Latin *laus* and is almost exactly the equivalent of "accomplishment," a thing which we should think of not as a "praise" but as *evoking* praise. A similar use is found in the *Merchant of Venice* (V, v, 108–109), where the sense might better be rendered as "impressiveness": "How many things by season season'd are/ To their right praise and true perfection." In *The Praise of Hemp-Seed* (1620), the author, John Taylor the Water-Poet, lists the "praises" of hemp on the title page as "cloathing, food, fishing, shipping, pleasure, profit, justice, and whipping." We should again incline to think of praise as *applied* freely to hemp because of its value in making these items possible. For the sixteenth- and seventeenth-century mind, the value in the object and the praise elicited by the object tend to be viewed as one whole. This mind does not feel the exterior, objective world and the interior, personal world as distinct from one another quite to the extent that we do. Objects retain a more personal, or at least animistic, glow.

5. The Visualizing of Ornament

Ramus and Talon, and the rhetorical tradition generally, give no effective and convincing explanation of what, from a semantic point of view, the "ornamentation" of language could be. Insofar as their age refrains from regarding this ornamentation, or "garment of style," as appliqué work, it so refrains because the notion of ornament is tempered in the way just indicated largely through equation with terms such as *laus* and *honor* and through a close association with a mysterious, interiorized person world rather than with an object world of surfaces. Nevertheless, at least from its earliest appearance in the Ramist works, the notion of ornament tends to dominate the other terms and to reduce the auditory element, the resonance, of rhetoric, implied in the notions of praise and honor, to something visually comprehensible, and thereby to the spatial and diagrammatic. In the Ramist rhetorical tradition as compared with the ancient Ciceronian, *laus* and *honor* are minimized, and became peripheral notions which occur in the looser discussion of the early *Training in Oratory* and in Ramus' commentary on rhetoric, but not in the presentation of the art of rhetoric proper. By 1555, Ramus' offhand references to rhetoric show that he thinks of it in uncomplicated visualist terms as serving "pour orner la parole." [45] Little wonder that Ramus' followers, such as Bilsten or Alsted, will define rhetoric quite flatly as "the art of expressing oneself ornately." [46] "Praise" and "honor," and with them much of the reality of sound itself, are gone.

6. The Clear and Distinct: Solon's Law

The Ramist insistence that the arts be kept distinct from one another further encouraged thinking of rhetoric in terms of models conceived of as existing in space and apprehended by sight, rather than in terms of voice and hearing. To a great extent, in the ancient cultures rhetoric was related to dialectic as sound was to sight. This is not to say that rhetoric was not concerned with the clear and distinct, nor that dialectic, as the art of discourse, was not concerned with sound at all. The difference was a polar difference: rhetoric was concerned with what was resonant and closer to the auditory pole; dialectic with what was relatively silent, abstract, and diagrammatic. In this kind of view, the two arts are not the same, but neither are they sharply "distinct" from one another in any readily definable way.

For Ramus, they had to be distinct. The ultimate reason is that Ramus conceives of them—and of their parts—by analogy with extended, and hence quantified surfaces, and that two extended objects cannot occupy the same space, at least in the ordinary experience of men. From the very beginning of his career, Ramus' ambition was to present the proper "shape" (*conformatio*) of dialectic and of the other arts, which he wants to "plot in unbroken lines" (*perpetuis lineamentis adumbrare*). [47] Out of this preoccupation grows the most striking expression of his extensional or quantifying mental habits, which he himself styles "Solon's Law."

This law is one which determines the distinction between the various arts, and, within each art, the distinction of its various parts. As its name indicates, it derives from Ramus' metaphorical interpretation of Solon's building ordinance at Athens, which he and his followers cite over and over again. Solon had prescribed a clear space

[45] Ramus, *Dialectique* (1555), Preface. Earlier, he had explained ornamentation as like the bosses or little raised decorations (*thori*) on a crown, although here he is thinking of examples or analogies in dialectic as "ornamenting" definitions and divisions—*Dial. inst.* (1543), fol. 29.

[46] "Rhetorica est ars ornate dicendi"—Johann Bilsten (Bilstenius), *Syntagma Philippo-Rameum* (1588), p. 261; Johann Heinrich Alsted (Alstedius), *Compendium rhetoricum* (an adaptation of Talon) in his *Compendium philosophicum* (1626), p. 1600.

[47] Ramus, *Dialecticae partitiones* (1543), fol. C2.

of a foot alongside each wall, two feet alongside each house, and so on. Ramus calls on this law when he cries haro at Cicero's and Quintilian's failure to keep dialectic and rhetoric distinct from one another.[48] The quantitative basis of the cult of distinctness is only too evident; Ramus is saying that a "place" is really a "place," and that it cannot be occupied by rhetoric and dialectic jointly.

Within this economy, if rhetoric still has to do with sound more than dialectic does, the way in which one conceives of the art undergoes subtle transformations in spatial terms. Striking expression and delivery are still allotted to rhetoric, but invention and judgment cannot be, since they have been assigned to dialectic. Memory, the fifth part of the traditional rhetoric, is unconvincingly identified by Ramus with judgment on the score that judging properly about things facilitates recall. But the real reason why Ramus can dispense with memory is that his whole scheme of arts, based on a topically conceived logic, is a system of local memory. Memory is everywhere, its "places" or "rooms" being the mental space which Ramus' arts all fill.

Within the two-part rhetoric, the spatial and visual carries the day still further. The second half of rhetoric, *oral* delivery, perishes of neglect, and the first half, *elocutio*, is, by the appearance of the later *Rhetoric*, resolved in terms of tropes ("turnings"—a diagrammatically grounded concept) and figures ("shapes"—another visually based notion). Despite the spatial analogy which they involve, figures have to do largely with the sound of words—among the figures are anaphora and other verbal repetition, rhythmic movement, and the quasi-acoustic effects of exclamation and apostrophe (figures of "sentence"). Hence, shying away instinctively from sound, and thus from figures, Ramist rhetoric will declare in favor of tropes when a choice between tropes and figures has to be made.[49] This is a declaration against sound in favor of (silent) thought; but thought is conceived of in terms of (ornamental) structure, with the aid of a spatial model ("turnings").

Ramus' inclination to explain secret or prudential method or *crypsis* as a kind of reversal of his "one and only method" is due to the fact that in his spatial projection of the notion of method, the only kind of variation possible must be itself spatial. The explanation thus given for method has a further effect in the visualist reduction of rhetoric,

[48] Ramus, *Scholae rhetoricae*, in *Sch. in lib. art.* (1569), fols. 255–256, again in cols. 237–238, 292, etc.

[49] Miller notes the fact that the Puritans favored tropes over figures, but does not assign the reason—*The New England Mind: The Seventeenth Century* (1939), p. 356.

for, since *crypsis* is the method resorted to by the specialists in rhetoric —poets, orators, and historians—Ramus exhibits a strong tendency to think of his now soundless rhetoric simply as dialectic in reverse.[50] What this has to do with the hypertrophy of ornament in Ramist rhetoric becomes clear when one recognizes the hypertrophy as part of a shift toward the visual throughout the whole cognitive field.

7. Poetry

Miss Tuve has said that "in so far as they were arts of thought, poetry and rhetoric had not been divided prior to Ramus." [51] This is true of the general scholastic and humanist tradition as the arts of discourse were practiced in the schoolroom, although it is not true, of course, of the upper reaches of the intellectual tradition which were represented by the Italian humanists or even by certain scholastics. Aristotle in his *Poetry* and *Rhetoric* (which were seldom if ever part of the arts course before the sixteenth century) and a few exceptional commentators such as St. Albert the Great or St. Thomas Aquinas differentiated poetry from rhetoric as an art of thought in a way which was relatively decisive, although their differentiation was sketchy and undeveloped (its sponsors were not teaching poetry, and therefore they had not thought painstakingly about it). According to these commentators, poetry, like rhetoric, dealt with the less-than-certain: rhetoric dealt with probabilities and probable conclusions, poetry with feigned conclusions or the semblance of conclusions or of the truth.[52] Because they were abstruse and not without difficulties, if discerning, such views of poetry, like the sometimes even more carefully nuanced views of humanists, were not very viable in a pedagogical tradition. When poetry finally came to be separated from rhetoric, at least within the perimeter defined by Ramism, there was little enough finesse of thought or of poetic sensibility involved at all.

The Ramist notion of poetry is highly quantitative and diagrammatic; it was built up in terms of "number" or counting. Although Ramus elsewhere expresses the opinion that poetry is a separate art, like medicine,[53] from the earliest editions of Talon's *Rhetoric* poetry, in the Ramist tradition, is really treated as a part of rhetoric. The reasons for this are obvious: like rhetorical speech, it is speech which is out

---

[50] Ramus, *Dialectica A. Talaei praelectionibus illustrata* (Basileae, 1569), Lib. II, cap. xix, pp. 577–578.

[51] Tuve, *Elizabethan and Metaphysical Imagery*, p. 339.

[52] Albertus Magnus, *In Lib. I Post. anal.*, Tract. I, cap. ii, in *Opera omnia* (Paris, 1890–1899), II, 7; Thomas Aquinas, *In Post. anal.* I, i; etc.

[53] Ramus, *Sch. rhet.*, in *Sch. in lib. art.* (1569), col. 246.

of the ordinary in that, as sound, it attracts attention.[54] Poetry is differentiated from the rest of rhetoric in terms of "number" (*numerus*), which of course is the Latin term for rhythm or music count. By the time of later editions of the *Rhetoric*, poetry has migrated to a somewhat different position within the art, and is given an even more frankly quantitative treatment. It is now a part of tonal "dimension" (*tonorum dimensio*), for which *numerus* is only a second-best synonym.[55] Tonal dimension has become dichotomized into poetic and oratorical dimension, and poetic dimension into rhythm (length of lines) and meter (kind of feet). This is the sum and substance of Ramist views on poetry, which echo the most mechanistic "poetic" of the medieval dictamen. As has been seen Ramus' poet and orator follow the same methodical procedure in their disposition of arguments and method, using the "secrets of method." [56] When these "secrets" are unraveled or exposed the poet's argumentations reduce equally to a sum of definitions and/or syllogisms —one is never sure which. The "garnishing" which New England divines or others in the Ramist tradition might permit themselves to apply to truth in the writing of poetry was thus taken to be the same thing as rhetorical garnishing. Indeed, if all Ramist rhetoric was appliqué work, poetry was appliqué work of the worst mechanical sort, for, as Ramus occasionally hints, the rules which govern it belong perhaps less to rhetoric than to arithmetic.[57]

Thus later Ramists who split off poetry from rhetoric had at least some of Ramus' earlier positions to go on. But even the definitions of those who made the most of poetry did little to refine the Ramist view of what poetry was. "Poetry," they say dryly and uninspiringly, "is the art of versifying well." [58]

Others in the Ramist milieu, of course, often had more adequate views of poetry than the Ramists. Riolan thought of poetry as "philosophy wrapped up in fable." [59] But, apart from the fact that even Riolan's view could be given a Ramist reading by taking the fable as "ornament," Riolan was a physician, not a master of arts teaching poetry to little boys. He did not register so accurately as the Ramists the arts-curriculum pattern. This pattern moved from words and

---

[54] Talon, *Rhetorica,* 4th ed. (1550), pp. 55–63.

[55] Talon, *Rhetorica e P. Rami praelectionibus observata, postrema editio* (Lutetiae: A. Wechelus, 1574), pp. 25–36.

[56] Ramus, *Dialectique* (1555), pp. 129–135; etc.

[57] Ramus, *Sch, rhet.,* in *Sch. in lib. art.* (1569), col. 251.

[58] "Quid est poetica? Est facultas bene scribendi versus."—Johann Thomas Freigius (Freige), *Paedagogus* (1582), p. 131. "Poetica est ars bene versificandi" —Bilsten, *Syntagma Philippo-Ramaeum* (1596), p. 271.

[59] Jean Riolan the elder, "Disputatio altera," in *Disputationes duae* (1569), fol. 9v.

sounds (grammar and rhetoric) to abstractions and silence (logic, physics, and the rest). The inference was inviting; what was taught in the lower reaches of the curriculum was elementary and childish. These pedagogical perspectives are obviously what determine Ramus' view: poetry belongs to words and sounds and thus to elementary classes. Little boys must be accustomed gradually to the strong meat of logic, first in the thin gruel of poets and orators, then in mathematics, where dialectic is more solid (*solidior*), and finally in physics, medicine, jurisprudence, and theology, that is, in all the rest of life (Ramus takes a curricular measure of life itself), where dialectic is fuller and richer (*copiosior et uberior*).[60] This Renaissance view, at least as typical as Erasmus', is noteworthy for the fact that it orders not only poetic, but all linguistic training to strictly practical ends within the upper nonliterary curriculum. Until it disintegrated, virtually the whole linguistic fabric of the Latin world was controlled by this educational pattern. Little wonder that, when Latin poetry finally perishes, we find ranking high among its last major productions such things as the five-thousand-line poem by the Jesuit scientist Boscovich entitled *The Eclipses of the Sun and Moon,* which explained Newtonian physics, or the three-thousand-line paraphrase of Newton's *Opticks* by Paolo Lucini.[61]

In this climate regulated by the classroom tradition, poetry was not commonly distinguished from rhetoric for the practical reason that it really coincided with rhetoric as a means of inculcating a more than elementary knowledge of Latin. When it was finally differentiated as as elementary subject, it was differentiated in elementary terms—by its measure. As Melanchthon had noted about his differentiation of dialectic and rhetoric, the basis of the distinction might be open to objection, but it meant something to young boys.

8. The Plain Style

There is little evidence from Ramus' contemporaries that anything very new and distinctive resulted immediately from Ramus' or Talon's prescriptions regarding actual style, in writing or in oral delivery. The plain style, about which so much has been written lately, emerges as

---

[60] Ramus, *Oratio init. suae prof.* (1551), p. 31. Cf.: "Poetica, inquam, sunt ista miracula [quae fingis tibi proponendo hunc oratorem perfectum—qui fieri non potest] plena quidem puerilis admirationis, prudentiae vero ac veritatis inania"— Ramus, *Sch. rhet.,* in *Sch. in lib. art.* (1569), col. 246.

[61] See James R. Naiden, "Newton Demands the Latin Muse," *Symposium,* 6:111–120 (1952).

ideal and actuality among their followers, particularly the Puritan or other "enthusiastic" or "methodist" preachers whose formal education was controlled by a Ramist dialectic and rhetoric evolved to the limit of its original implications.

Plainness or simplicity of expression had figured as an occasional or possible rhetorical objective from the period of antiquity. The special urgency which plainness ultimately acquired in the Ramist milieu has been described recently in various ways, particularly in connection with the early New Englander's notion of what a sermon, or composition in general, ought to be.[62] The ideal was "plaine delivery of the Word without painted eloquence" (which is close to saying without "colors"), or, in William Ames' words, expression marked by the "simplicity of the Gospell." The "methodical manner" [63] was to be cultivated, together with "plainness, perspicacity, gravity." Baroque Anglican style, full of sound, was to be put aside for a straightforward technique of "opening" a text by analysis. In place of Donne's way of preaching, "topical" in that it used the topics or places as if they were resonant with sentences or sayings, the advocates of plain style wanted preaching with method and certainty, giving "doctrine" and "reasons" from "axioms."

Axioms are a part of dialectic, of course, whether detached or not, so that what is being recommended is a retreat from rhetoric back into a pure dialectic—in effect, a nonrhetorical style. If this recommendation accords ill with Ramus' injunctions to mingle dialectic and rhetoric, philosophy and eloquence, in practice or use, it accords very well with his view that rhetoric, like prudential method, is, in the last analysis, dissimulation, to be resorted to only when the audience is recalcitrant. Plain style, which is really nonrhetorical style, alone is acceptable to reasonable man. Significantly, one of the earliest Ramist proposals to speak "plainly" occurs in Talon's preface to his *Dialectical Explanations of Porphyry,* a dialectical commentary on a dialectical work, where we are told that Talon will put Porphyry's Greek text into Latin in words which are "proper" (that is, nonrhetorical) and which "signify the matter simply and plainly." [64] Talon's preface is

---

[62] The quotations immediately following here are from Perry Miller, *The New England Mind: The Seventeenth Century* (New York, 1939), Chapter XI, esp. pp. 331ff. and 349ff.

[63] Cf. Ong, "Peter Ramus and the Naming of Methodism," *Journal of the History of Ideas,* 14:235–248 (1953).

[64] ". . . verba pene verbis, propiis tamen, et rem pure planeque significantibus redderem"—Talon, *Praelectiones in Porphyrium* (1547), Preface, in *Opera Socraticae methodicaeque philosophiae studiosis pernecessaria* (1584), pp. 476–477.

overfull here with talk about the "needs of youth" and "popular use" (*ad usum popularem*). In the name of simplification to serve these ends he rejects not only rhetoric, but the old logical refinements.

Of course, the Puritans, who will bring out the fuller implications of the plain style, use rhetoric, as everyone must. Moreover, their preaching bears a strong sense of kerygma. They preach the "word." And yet their favorite explanations of discourse and communication readily generate such things as William Ames' denunciation of "itching ears" and militate against affection for words as such. Words will languish, finally, in this linguistic climate, suspect of failing to "let through" the meaning of the Scripture intended by God as well as method and diagrams could. It is to be noted that the stylistic recommendations related to plainness, such as "perspicuity" in the sense of translucency, are formulated basically by analogy with visual apprehension and represent an attempt to reduce the process of communication in terms of such apprehension. The medium by which light is transmitted seems to act as though it were not there, whereas the medium of sound is felt rather as though it were acting to sustain and to give resonance to sound.

9. Effects of Ramist Rhetoric

Ramist rhetoric and Ramism as a whole are interesting for what they become when the concepts in which Ramism specializes take possession of human sensibilities. There gradually they help to transform man's conceptual life. Ramist rhetoric is perhaps less interesting and less significant when we ask what was its immediate effect on the writing of those who first studied it, not because it had no effects, but because in the beginning the effects deriving from its prescriptions were often not appreciably different from those of other rhetorics. As has been seen, the distinctive plain style emerged later, especially toward the opening of the seventeenth century, but it was not prescribed by Ramist rhetoric, although it was made inevitable by the whole mental setting which constitues Ramism.

Applied in the individual classroom to the formation of (Latin) style, the Ramist rhetoric undoubtedly had variable effects depending on the way different teachers exploited it. As an approach to a text, it had most of the advantages and disadvantages of the other standard rhetorics of the time, such as Melanchthon's, Susenbrotus', Soarez's, and the rest, for the apocopated Ramist rhetoric was always to be used with

Ramist dialectic, which supplied all excised parts. But even when supplemented this way by Ramist dialectic, Ramist rhetoric still had certain lacunae—notably sentence, amplification, and decorum—and these lacunae would give it from the first a characteristic torque. Types of discourse like the fourteen taught in Aphthonius' *Progymnasmata* and other elementary rhetoric exercise books or "formulary rhetorics" —retelling of fable, the *chria* or theme on a known person, the *sententia* or theme on an apothegm or proverb, and so on—were no longer points of reference for Ramist rhetorical organization. They were not points of reference because all organization or structuring was purportedly dialectical or logical by its very nature, and where not ruled by syllogism was ruled by method, which by definition was always one and the same.

Analysis, such as Ramists practiced, was practiced by other rhetoricians, too, and had been from the time the humanists had focused attention on literary texts, although the others did not practice it with such ardor as the Ramists nor make such an issue of it. Although it often meant mere naming of the "ornaments" of tropes and figures, such rhetorical analysis, particularly when abetted by dialectical analysis, demanded that the pupil get into the text, struggle with it, and, in general, involve himself in the linguistic situation.

The exact relevance of what the pupil *thought* he was doing, and the adequacy of his tools or definitions to the linguistic richness of the texts he may have been working on, as well as to the composition or "genesis" with which he was to follow his analysis, may well be questioned, and, indeed, have been.[65] Certainly Ramus and most others never explained with any acumen what the relevance was. Little matter; the boys to whom this and other rhetorics were directed could not have mastered the explanation anyhow. These rhetorics did give them something to do with a text, made them beat back and forth over it till the Latin phrases rang in their ears. In the long run they did this forcefully enough to fertilize their English or other vernacular imaginations, producing not only Latin stylists but, more important, Marlowes and Shakespeares and Lope de Vegas and Montaignes.

Miss Tuve has devoted a chapter and more to the relationship between Ramism, particularly Ramist logic, and Elizabethan literary

[65] I. A. Richards, "The Places and the Figures," *Kenyon Review*, 11:17–30 (1949), where he discusses Baldwin's *William Shakspere's Small Latine and Lesse Greeke*, Sister Miriam Joseph's *Shakespeare's Use of the Arts of Language*, and Donald Lemen Clark's *John Milton at St. Paul's School* (New York, 1948).

imagery.[66] She suggests that the appropriation of all the loci by logic or dialectic strengthens the hold of logic on the poetry and literature of the period in a way which twentieth-century critics have minimized. In particular, Ramism stressed the use of "specials" or individual examples to prove "generals" or universal propositions, and it emphasized the use of disjunction. In these and related ways it seems curiously of a piece with the metaphysical poetry which flowers at the same time Ramism does in the last two decades of the sixteenth century.

These suggestions seem, as a whole, to be well made. At this point, however, some supplementary relationships between Ramism and metaphysical poetry can be indicated. The transfer of all the loci to dialectic or logic and the concomitant development of a logic of places or topical logic, as has been seen, represents a major movement of thought and sensibility. It has at its roots the peculiarly medieval logical developments found in Peter of Spain as well as the pedagogical drives of the humanists; it bears fruit in the mechanism which in Newton's age and later gives the modern mind some of its characteristic outlooks. Within this movement the Ramist interest in "specials" and its emphasis on disjunction come to much the same thing. "Specials" are thought of largely as "generals" cut up into more or less quantitative pieces, and thus as a product of disjunction, effected in concepts more or less openly devised according to visual, spatial analogies.

Therefore, one can, I believe, restate Miss Tuve's contention in even larger perspectives such as these: Ramism assimilated logic to imagery and imagery to logic by reducing intelligence itself, more or less unconsciously, in terms of rather exclusively visual, spatial analogies. The brusque, spatial maneuvers, not to say spastic postures, which conceptualization of the Ramist sort favors (that is, Ramus' ultimate reduction of the "secrets" of method to simple reversal of local motion and his constant invocation of "Solon's Law") obviously have some affinity with the harsh contrasts and grotesquerie of metaphysical poetry as well as of the baroque poetry which grew with or out of the metaphysical.

But Ramists did not write metaphysical poetry, or, indeed, much poetry at all. The lampoons against Ramus on the Paris stage in his own lifetime, the remarks in the *Parnassus* plays at Cambridge, Mar-

[66] Rosemond Tuve, *Elizabethan and Metaphysical Imagery*, Chapter XII, "Ramist Logic: Certain General Conceptions Affecting Imagery," pp. 331–353, and *passim*.

lowe's and Johnson's lines, all show Ramus and Ramism as something the poets perennially regarded as fair game. The apparent collusion between Ramist dialectic and rhetoric and the habits of thought and imagination of Elizabethan poets testifies to common background rather than to any conscious sympathy. Indeed, back of the points of agreement there was a divergence extremely profound.

Most of the best Elizabethan and Jacobean poetry is dialogue at root. This is true not only of the stage, but of the lyric as well (although here only one side of the dialogue is commonly set down), and so true as to be a commonplace. We may wonder to whom Shakespeare's sonnets are addressed, but there is no mistaking that in them he is talking to someone, real or imaginary. He does not muse, as Wordsworth does at his less than best, or as John Stuart Mill believed all poets should. The overtones of "real" or colloquial speech, that is, of *dialogue* between persons, which sixteenth- and seventeenth-century poetry specializes in, give it its characteristic excellence. Ramist rhetoric, on the other hand, is not a dialogue rhetoric at all, and Ramist dialectic has lost all sense of Socratic dialogue and even most sense of scholastic dispute. The Ramist arts of discourse are monologue arts. They develop the didactic, schoolroom outlook which descends from scholasticism even more than do non-Ramist versions of the same arts, and tend finally even to lose the sense of monologue in pure diagrammatics. This orientation is very profound and of a piece with the orientation of Ramism toward an object world (associated with visual perception) rather than toward a person world (associated with voice and auditory perception). In rhetoric, obviously someone had to speak, but in the characteristic outlook fostered by the Ramist rhetoric, the speaking is directed to a world where even persons respond only as objects—that is, say nothing back.

In this orientation, several phenomena, otherwise apparently isolated from one another, exhibit surprising relationships. Combined with Ramus' own lack of interest in dialogue, as evinced by his silence in company,[67] and his way of lashing out to annihilate his opponents or texts he was commenting on, is his and his followers' marked hostility to drama. His educational "reform" included the abolishing of plays by the students at the Collège de Presles.[68] He decreed this despite his own decidedly florid personal eloquence, for, it must be remembered, such eloquence was, in theory, really an evil, made

[67] Nancel, *Vita,* p. 62.
[68] *Ibid.,* p. 15.

necessary by a recalcitrant audience. The Calvinists who were to find Ramus congenial—more for the tone of his teaching than for any assignable doctrinal position—exhibit the same combination as Ramus himself: a "methodical" theory of speech, which their performance seldom fits, and a curiously ingrained dislike of drama. These are people somehow deeply distrustful of words, save perhaps in the homiletic monologue. This, ·of course, is not all such people are, for they exhibit many other tendencies, some of them quite opposed to this, which will develop quite different outlooks and institutions in the course of history. But meanwhile, they do not like metaphysical or other poetry which echoes dialogue, and they do not like the stage, favoring a form of speech which argues from "axioms" with at least a pseudocertainty. Edward Taylor, the one New England Puritan who wrote poetry derivative from the Elizabethan dramatic experience, is the least Puritan and least Ramist of all New England writers.[69] When the Puritan mentality, which is here the Ramist mentality, produces poetry, it is at first blatantly didactic, but shades gradually into reflective poetry which does not talk to anyone in particular but meditates on objects, such as the moon. There is a curious connection here between the plain-style mentality and some later romantic developments.

10. The Meaning of Ramist Rhetoric

The deepest meaning of Ramist rhetoric is to be found in the general framework of man's changing attitudes toward communication, with which rhetoric is so inextricably involved. The history of the arts of discourse is still commonly treated as though, since grammar, rhetoric, and dialectic were and are well-known names, they were transmitted in little packets from generation to generation. Actually, man's approach to speech is too tied up with his attitudes toward himself and toward other persons and toward the universe to admit of such tidy transmission. From the beginning, the arts of communication grow slowly, tortuously, and mysteriously in a curiously strategic position within the human psyche, prolific on the one hand of theories concerning the nature of thought and things, so that they prove to be the seedbed of philosophy itself, and on the other hand deeply involved in action because they are directly concerned with the business of communication, upon which man's other actions so unmistakably depend.

[69] See Kenneth B. Murdock, *Literature and Theology in Colonial New England* (Cambridge, Mass., 1949).

It can be argued that the most distinguishing feature of Western culture is its development of a scientifically managed dialectic and of related formal logics, together with those rhetorics which are the counterparts of such logics. Other civilizations develop no mature formal logic any more than they develop modern science, and the developments in the *artes sermocinales* are more original, more time-consuming, and more fundamental than the scientific developments. Ramist rhetoric belongs to a critical period in the history of these Western *artes sermocinales*, and suggests interrelationships between developments in these arts and the development of letterpress printing, the perfecting of the textbook, the burgeoning of a potentially infinite number of "courses" or "subjects" in the curriculum, and finally the emergence of modern science itself.

Like all rhetoric, Ramist rhetoric is concerned with expression, with communication, with speaking, with not only a subject matter but also an auditor. But it is a rhetoric which has renounced any possibility of invention within this speaker-auditor framework; it protests in principle if not in actuality, that invention is restricted to a dialectical world where there is no voice but only a kind of vision. By its very structure, Ramist rhetoric asserts to all who are able to sense its implications that there is no way to discovery or to understanding through voice, and ultimately seems to deny that the processes of person-to-person communication play any necessary role in intellectual life. It thus throws before us the larger, more generalized perspectives in which exists the Renaissance movement often interpreted as a "revolt against authority." The revolt is not quite against authority, as every-one knows, because, with almost the sole exception of the unfortunate Galileo case, there are few instances of authorities penalizing intel-lectual enterprise and discovery. What there is, is a deep-felt protest against the obtrusion of voices and persons in scientific issues.

In Ramist rhetoric, dialogue and conversation themselves become by implication mere nuisances. When Ramus first laid hold of the topics (that is, what he styles "arguments"), these were associated with real dialogue or discussion, if only because they existed in both dialectic and rhetoric conjointly and thus kept dialectic in touch with the field of communication and thought-in-a-vocal setting which had been in historical actuality the matrix of logic itself. But by the application of "Solon's Law," which severed rhetoric from dialectic with savage rigor and without any profound understanding of the interrelationship of these two disciplines, the topics, relegated by Ramus to dialectic (or logic) exclusively, were in principle denied any oral or aural connections at all. To the Ramist, Dryden's admission that he was often helped to an idea by a rhyme was an admission of weakness if not of outright intellectual perversion.

Furthermore, Ramist rhetoric is a rhetoric which has not only no invention but also no judgment or arrangement of its own. The field of activity covered by the terms judgment or arrangement (*dispositio*) has likewise been dissociated from voice by being isolated from rhetoric and committed to Ramist dialectic or logic. In the process, judgment—which necessarily bespeaks utterance, an assent or a dissent, a *saying* of yes or no—simply disappears, and with it all rational interest in the psychological activities which such a term covers. Arrangement or "positioning" (*dispositio*) secures exclusive rights as the only other phenomenon besides invention which occurs in intellectual activity, and as the sole principle governing the organization of speech. Unlike judgment, which cannot be conceived of independently of some reference to saying, to utterance, and thus to the oral and aural world of personalities, "arrangement" can be conceived of simply by analogy with visually perceived spatial patterns. With all rhetorical organization governed from outside rhetoric by this "arrangement" (syllogism and method), the role of voice and person-to-person relationships in communication is reduced to a new minimum. When, finally, in this development memory also goes insofar as it is aural, and is replaced—again, at least in theory—by the "natural" order in things, which means, as has been seen, almost any order, however arbitrary, picturable in a dichotomized diagram for the visual imagination, all that is left to this rhetoric is style and delivery. Of these the more vocal, delivery, is regularly underdeveloped or totally neglected, proving in effect uncongenial to Ramist theory, and style itself, as has been seen, is reduced further in terms which can be somehow visually conceived.

To be sure, rhetoric is still called rhetoric and is thought of as committed to a world of voice; it does, as a matter of fact, handle expression. And Ramist dialectic remains, in effect, a rhetorical instrument, since the principles of organization it proposes can in the large be given no really formal logical structure. But in the Ramist account of rhetoric, and of the world of voice in which it reportedly operated, the art has been made over by analogy with the silent world of vision. Ideologically, the world of sound has yielded, unwittingly but quite effectively, to the world of space.

This development which is so typical of Ramism is likewise, however, typical in the large of the whole logical and rhetorical development of the West out of which Ramism emerges, so that in his *Logic and Rhetoric in England, 1500–1700,* Wilbur Samuel Howell, with reason sees Ramism not as something incidental but as a pivotal phenomenon. Professor Howell makes it clear that a distinctive mark of the post-Ramist dialectic or logic is that it is a logic of individual inquiry into issues thought of as existing outside a framework of discourse or dialectic rather than a logic of discourse.[70]

Such a logic of inquiry is implicitly conceived of as operating outside the aural world. But the complexity of the forces here at work can be gauged by the fact that when Ramism moved to make dialectic or logic less aural it did so initially by making it seemingly more rhetorical, so that Prantl and others have described Ramist logic as a rhetoric-logic. Here one must distinguish between actuality and theory. In actuality, Ramist logic was rhetorical by the standards of medieval terminists or of modern formal logicians. That is, in reality it was only loosely or "probably" conclusive. It had sacrificed scientific certainty by basing itself on the dialectico-rhetorical topics. Nevertheless, the absorption of these dialectico-rhetorical topics gave it no rhetorical flair. On the contrary, the topics, rechristened "arguments," themselves were superficially transformed into scientific instruments by their insertion within a structural economy thought of as being even more rigid than that dominated by the categories.

In the post-Ramist developments discussed by Professor Howell one can observe this process actually repeating itself. For the new Port-Royal logic which succeeded Ramism in France, and to some extent in England, moves determinedly away from rhetoric, then ambiguously toward it, only to move finally and still more ambiguously away from it again. That is to say, the Port-Royal logicians begin by discarding not only the categories but the Ramist rhetorically nurtured topics or arguments, too—at least they begin by determining to discard all these, for, after denouncing the topics, they bring them in again by the back door, finding that it is not so easy as one might today suppose to construct an art of pure, solitary thinking.[71] But having determined to discard these rhetorical accoutrements, the Port-Royal logicians took over from the rhetorical field something else, a concern with the passions (in this, like Ramus they go back to Rudolph Agricola and his way of being different from Peter of Spain). But, just as the topics were derhetoricized, that is, de-vocalized or mechanized, by

[70] Wilbur Samuel Howell, *Logic and Rhetoric in England, 1500–1700* (Princeton, New Jersey, 1956), pp. 361, 350–360.
[71] Howell, *Logic and Rhetoric,* pp. 350–361.

the Ramists because they were subjugated in dialectic to a diagrammatic economy, so the passions would be de-rhetoricized or mechanized (processed for diagrammatic or visile thinking) by succeeding generations of post-Ramist associationist philosophers and literary critics.[72]

In this economy where everything having to do with speech tends to be in one way or another metamorphosed in terms of structure and vision, the rhetorical approach to life—the way of Isocrates and Cicero and Quintilian and Erasmus, and of the Old and New Testaments—is sealed off into a cul-de-sac. The attitude toward speech has changed. Speech is no longer a medium in which the human mind and sensibility lives. It is resented, rather, as an accretion to thought, hereupon imagined as ranging noiseless concepts or "ideas" in a silent field of mental space. Here the perfect rhetoric would be to have no rhetoric at all. Thought becomes a private, or even an antisocial enterprise. The sequels of Ramism—method and its epiphenomena, which identify Ramism as an important symptom of man's changing relationship to the universe—connect with Ramist dialectic directly but with rhetoric only negatively or not at all. To be sure, techniques of expression will still be taught (although for a while, at least in Puritan lands, the stage, where speech is at its maximum as speech, will go), but all the while a curious subconscious hostility to speech in all its forms will eat away at the post-Ramist age, bringing Thomas Sprat to fear for the members of the Royal Academy that "the whole spirit and vigour of their *Design* [note this visualist concept], had been soon eaten out, by the luxury and redundance of *speech*" and to denounce roundly all use of tropes and figures.[73] Only after the Hegelian rehabilitation of the notion of dialogue and the later discrediting of the Newtonian universe would this hostility begin effectively to wane.

The effectiveness of the obscure forces at work here can be appreciated only if one remains aware of the obscure and mysterious nature of rhetoric itself. It was never a self-possessed art or science in the way in which Euclidean geometry, or even grammar, might be. As at its beginning, when "rhetoric" constituted the ancient Greek plan of general intellectual education, "rhetoric" in Ramus' day is a complex and somewhat protean product of educational needs and theory, working at its center toward a philosophy of expression, but derivative in fact less from such a philosophy than from a complicated pedagogical

[72] Walter J. Ong, "Psyche and the Geometers: Aspects of Associationist Critical Theory," *Modern Philology*, 49:16–27 (1951).
[73] Howell, *Logic and Rhetoric*, p. 389.

situation never entirely under control. Renaissance rhetoric, and Ramist rhetoric in particular, registers the practical pressures of an educational milieu where "rhetoric" is conceived of in actuality as the next language course after grammar, taught only to youngsters, concerned directly with a language foreign to even its most voluable and skilled users, and controlled by silent written and printed documents more than by the spoken word. Within this milieu, Ramist rhetoric registers the further drive toward curriculum simplification and orderliness generated first by the teacher-centered scholasticism of the universities and intensified in other ways by the pupil-centered pedagogy of the humanist schools. These conditions help explain its theoretical deficiencies. Theoretical problems which were involved in the rhetoric-logic dyad or which today would be considered within dialectic, which was more abstract and manageable and which for centuries had commonly existed in a more mature pedagogical context. Ramist rhetorical theory, even abetted by Ramist dialectic theory, is thus understandably thin. But this very fact is meaningful, and, as a gauge of some of the central pressures shaping the evolution of human thought, this rhetoric is one of the most informative there is.

THE ELOCUTION MOVEMENT—ENGLAND
Warren Guthrie

The Elocution Movement

One of the most prominent and in many respects amazing developments in early American rhetoric is the elocution movement. The writers in this area were concerned almost exclusively with delivery, voice and bodily action, in their application to speaking and reading.

Although rhetorical instruction from the beginning had given attention to delivery, there is nothing in the classical tradition to presage the factitious elaborations which appear in many of these volumes. Classical treatments are brief and the emphasis is clearly toward a natural manner in speech. As Quintilian puts it, "What is becoming is the main consideration in delivery, different methods will often suit different speakers." And no orator should attempt to ape the elegancies

From *Speech Monographs*, March, 1951. Reprinted with the permission of the Speech Association of America, and of the author.

of the stage, lest he "lose the authority which should characterize the man of dignity and virtue." [1]

In some respects the closest parallel to the elocution movement of the eighteenth and nineteenth centuries is the absorption with *declamatio* in the decadent rhetoric following Quintilian. Deprived of any real functional significance, rhetoric reverted to a new "sophistic," a rhetoric of display which found its chief outlet in the declamations of the schools. The effect was strikingly similar to that achieved centuries later. As Baldwin puts it, there was one "ideal of orator and audience alike: behold a great speaker!" [2]

We have already seen, in this series of studies, that the first rhetorical tradition to influence England and America was a medieval rhetoric of style. The full impact of Aristotle's *Rhetoric* was not felt in England until the middle of the seventeenth century, and in America the delay was even longer. But even as this classical tradition was beginning to exert its influence, first evidences of a specialized attention to delivery appear. This specialized treatment, known as Elocution, emerges as a separate discipline, and constitutes a peculiar development of rhetorical theory of great significance in attempting to interpret early American rhetoric and speech training.

Beginnings of Elocution in England [3]

Although there is no certain evidence as to the reason for the first interest taken in delivery as a specialized art in England, if Thomas Wilson is to be believed, it was because there was definite need of such interest. Almost half a century before the first work devoted exclusively to delivery appeared he has this to say in regard to the speakers he has heard:

> Some there bee that either naturally, or through folly haue such euill voyces, and such lacke of vutteraunce, and such euill iesture, that it much defaceth all their doinges. One pipes out his wordes so small, through default of his winde pipe, that ye would thinke he whistled . . . . An other speakes, as though he had Plumes in his mouth. An

---

[1] Quintilian *Institutio Oratoria*, translated by H. E. Butler (London, 1922), IV, 349.

[2] Baldwin, C. S., *Medieval Rhetoric and Poetic* (New York, 1928), 17.

[3] Haberman, F. W., "The Elocution Movement in England, 1750-1850" (unpublished Ph.D. dissertation, Department of Speech, Cornell University, 1947), treats the development of the elocution movement in England in full detail. For a more complete discussion of the genesis of this movement see Chapters I, II, III of this work.

other speakes in his throte, as though a good Ale crumme stucke fast. An other rattles his wordes . . . . This man barkes out his English Northernilke, with I say, and thou lad. An other speakes so finely, as though he were brought vp in a Ladies Chamber . . . . Some grunts like a Hogge. Some cackles like a Henne, or a Iacke Dawe. . . . Some suppes their wordes vp, as a poore man doth his Porrage . . . . There are a thousand such faultes among men, both for their speech, and also for their iesture, the which if in their young yeares they bee not remedied, they will hardly bee forgot when they come to mans state.[4]

Whatever the cause, in 1617 there appeared Robert Robinson's *Art of Pronunciation*,[5] which was probably the first book written in English devoted exclusively to the study of delivery. A few years later there is published an even more specialized work, devoted solely to the *actio* phase of delivery. The book carries the following title:

> *Chironomia: or the Art of Manuall Rhetorique. With the Cannons, Laws, Rites, Ordinances, and Institutes of Rhetoricians. Both Antient and Modern, touching the artificiall managing of the Hand in Speaking. Whereby the natural Gestures of the Hand, are made the Regulated Accessories of faire-spoken Adjuncts of Rhetorical Utterance. With Typis, or Chirograms: A New Illustration of the Argument. By J. B. Philochirosophus.*[6]

This work is a thorough study of the gesture of the hands and fingers, tabulating the types of gesture, and discussing and illustrating them in detail. More than a hundred and fifty separate gestures are listed, ranging from "Supplice Gestus I," through "Applaude Gestus V— To clasp the raised hands one against another," to "Dactylogia, or the Dialects of the Fingers."[7] All discussions are complete, and all copiously illustrated so that the prospective orator might easily practice each gesture. Certain cautions, e.g., "Joyne not Esau's *Hands*, with

---

[4] Thomas Wilson, *Arte of Rhetorique*, edited by C. H. Mair (Oxford, 1909), pp. 219–220.

[5] The work is reported by Harding, H. F., "English Rhetorical Theory, 1750–1800," (unpublished Ph.D dissertation, Department of Speech, Cornell University, 1928), p. 87, although he does not indicate having seen the work, and refers to it in the most general of language. Similarly, Haberman makes general reference to it on page 82 of his study. No copy of the book has been located in the course of this author's research, nor has other reference been found to it.

[6] (London, 1644). The preface and dedication was signed "Io Bulvver." This title page reads differently from that recorded by Harding, *op. cit.*, p. 89, but it is taken verbatim from the microfilm copy of the work in the Harvard Library.

[7] Bulwer, *op. cit.*, pp. 11–187.

Jacob's Voyce," [8] are given, but notwithstanding, one might expect such practice to produce a rather mechanical, if showy, delivery.

Of more interest to us, since it indicates a contemporary controversy over delivery in England,[9] and since it was read in America as early as 1755,[10] is the anonymous *Art of Speaking in Public* [11] which appeared a generation later. This is a treatment of delivery for which the author feels there is a real need, and the work is highly recommended by the editor to grammar schools, academies, and universities.[12] It is certainly one of the earliest works in English to present a detailed treatment of all of the phases of delivery, and to be designed for classroom use.

The work begins with a justification for the study of action, using Cicero's "eloquence of the body" as the first excuse, and follows with scores of other citations. Since Aristotle gave little consideration to delivery, as did Cicero, and since Quintilian's treatment is most useful only to the young lawyer, it is argued that this work fills a definite need. Nature cannot shape the orator, and thus it is necessary "to assist nature by art." This is true not only in logic, in moral philosophy, in grammar, or in style, but also in action.[13]

In the discussion which follows the student is told to form good habits early, and to imitate only the good observed in other speakers. The voice is to be trained by practice to a just variety of pitch and force. There is general discussion of the kind of voice to use to represent the various passions, the kind of voice to use in the different parts of a discourse, and the kind of voice best suited to the figures of rhetoric.

Gesture is treated with more specific detail. After some discussion of its value, and of the virtue of naturalness, the following rules are given:

> Use little gesture at the opening of a speech.
> Don't clap your hands, beat your breast, etc.
> Use the right hand only for gestures.
> Don't strike your breast, but place your hand gently upon it.
> Move all gesture from left to right.

[8] *Ibid.,* p. 134.

[9] The editor's preface justifies the publication of the edition on the grounds that a quarrel over standards of delivery between the "Reverend and ingenious Mr. Henley" and a Mr. Wood makes some standard necessary and useful.

[10] By Samuel Johnson, *Career and Writings,* Appendix.

[11] Second edition (London, 1727).

[12] *Ibid.,* p. xxiii.

[13] *Ibid.,* pp. 9–37.

Never lift the hands higher than the eyes.

Don't gesture all the time.

Don't mimic in gesture, and especially do not mimic anything lewd or indecent.[14]

A concluding chapter attempts to set up a way of making all of the preceding advice practical. Each actor should,

> . . . understand these precepts of action, try them on his own person, practice them before a master and in private, and endeavor to get a good habit and the knack of speaking by care and continual exercise.[15]

The work never seems to have had wide circulation in America, but it is indicative of the early English treatment of delivery, and prepares the way for the more detailed books on delivery which are to follow.

English Criticism of Oratory and Education

By 1750 many factors tended to create a critical atmosphere in England in regard to orators and oratory. With the increase of the power of the spoken word in an increasingly democratic society it was only natural that more attention should be paid to the manner of that speech. Education was undergoing a process of change, and it became an open question as to whether instruction should continue in Latin or be turned into the vernacular. Reform movements in the church were rampant, and the tremendous followings acquired by the fiery speaking of Henley and Wesley and others, gave rise to criticism of the speaking habits of the more conservative clergymen. Englishmen traveling on the continent observed the more active oratory of the French clergymen, and they were impressed with its greater success in winning piety and numbers. The rhetoric of Latin and Greek, directed at the few, was being replaced by the rhetoric of English, allied with persuasion, and seeking a response from an increasingly critical lay audience.

Criticisms of British oratory were almost as sweeping as that given by Wilson in an earlier day. Addison has it that,

> Nothing could be more ridiculous than the gestures of most of our English speakers. You see some of them running their hands into their pockets as far as ever they can thrust them, and others looking with great attention on a piece of paper that has nothing written on it; you may see many a smart rhetorician turning his hat in his hands, moulding it into several different cocks, examining sometimes the lining of it, and

[14] *Ibid.*, Chapter 13.
[15] *Ibid.*, p. 212.

sometimes the button, during the whole of his harangue. A deaf man would think he was cheapening a beaver; when perhaps he was talking of the fate of the British nation.[16]

Swift is scarcely less severe in his *Letter to a Young Clergyman:*

> You will observe some clergymen with their heads held down from the beginning to the end within an inch of the cushion to read what is hardly legible; which, beside the untoward manner, hinders them from making the best advantage of their voice: others again have a trick of popping up and down every moment from their paper to the audience, like an idle school boy on a repetition day.[17]

Chesterfield's *Letters to his Son* show the emphasis he places on effective delivery in oratory. In 1748 he devotes an entire letter to a detailed criticism of his son's bad enunciation and delivery, and to methods by which he may be led to a more effective and persuasive delivery. His language is most definite as he advises frequent reading with criticism which requires him to observe the proper stops, emphasis, and rate.[18]

All of these comments would seem to indicate that correctness and gracefulness in delivery were coming to be significant criteria in oratory. Classical rhetorical training was providing sound study of invention and arrangement, but its lack of detail on delivery, and the corresponding lack of emphasis in training in delivery, were opening the door for the elocutionists.

Although strong in their criticism of English oratory, Addison, Swift, and Chesterfield had offered little plan for improvement.[19] Thomas Sheridan was to do this with vehemence. Opening his first discussion in writing on this subject, an essay *On British Education,*[20] Sheridan makes the point that the liberal arts never flourished, or arrived at perfection in any country where the study and practice of oratory was

---

[16] Joseph Addison, *The Spectator*, No. 907.

[17] Jonathan Swift, *Works,* edited by Thomas Sheridan (London, 1803), VIII, 15.

[18] Lord Chesterfield, *Letters to his Son,* edited by C. S. Cary (London, 1912), p. 208.

[19] Addison does note that we must bear with bad delivery of speeches "till they cease at Oxford and Cambridge to grow dumb in the study of eloquence." Quoted by Thomas Sheridan, *A Discourse Being Introductory to His Course of Lectures on Elocution* (London, 1759), p. 38.

[20] The full title is as follows: *British Education: Or, the Source of the Disorders of Great Britain. Being an Essay towards proving, that the Immorality, Ignorance, and False Taste, which so generally prevail, are the natural and necessary Consequences of the present defective System of Education. With an Attempt to show, that a revival of the Art of Speaking, and the Study of Our Own Language, might contribute in a great measure, to the Cure of these Evils* (London, 1756).

neglected. He carries this even to the point of asserting that "it is much more probable that oratory raised and supported the liberal arts, than that the liberal arts raised and supported oratory." [21] The theme of the whole essay is a plea for the teaching of the English language in preference to the classical tongues. When he later sets up his own plan of education, its basic objective is to develop effective speakers in English. Says he, "The sole end proposed at present is to make good Latin and Greek scholars; whereas the true ends of education in all Christian countries, ought to be to make good men, and good citizens." [22]

Other writers take up the refrain. James Buchanan makes his plea for the teaching of English and eloquence on the basic assumption that the Greeks achieved their eminence in part from their attention to their own tongue, for "it is manifest, that they had no language to acquire but their own, nor any books to peruse but what were written in it." [23] Neither of the great English universities suits him, for Cambridge specializes in speculative knowledge, and Oxford in classical correction with no foundation in reasoning, so there are "dry, unaffecting compositions in the one, superficial taste and puerile elegance in the other; ungracious or affected speech in both since the art of speaking agreeably is so far from being taught that it is scarcely talked or thought of." [24] Samuel Whyte [25] and Richard Shepherd [26] present similar points of view.

The Rise of English Elocution

Simultaneously with the appearance of these criticisms of British oratory and teaching, the great English works on elocution began to appear. Since each of these exerted direct or indirect influence on the growth and emphasis of the elocution movement in America, they are reviewed in later paragraphs. The following chronological list will suffice here to show the sequence of the appearance of these works:

1748—John Mason, *Essay on Elocution*.
1759—Thomas Sheridan, *Lectures on Elocution* (This is the date of their delivery, not of their publication.)
1761—James Burgh, *The Art of Speaking*.

[21] *Ibid.*, p. 398.
[22] Thomas Sheridan, *A Plan of Education* (London, 1769), p. 42.
[23] James Buchanan, *Plan of an English Grammar School Education* (London, 1770), p. 10.
[24] *Ibid.*, pp. 103–104.
[25] *Modern Education* (Dublin, 1775).
[26] *Essay on Education* (Holburn, 1782).

1765—John Rice, *An Introduction to the Art of Reading with Energy and Propriety.*
1774—William Enfield, *The Speaker.*
1775—Joshua Steele, *Prosodia Rationalis.*
1775—William Cockin, *The Art of Delivering Written Language.*
1779—William Scott, *Lessons in Elocution.*
1781—John Walker, *Elements of Elocution.*
1789—Anselm Bayly, *The Alliance of Music, Poetry, and Oratory.*
1806—Gilbert Austin, *Chironomia.*

Most of these works went through several editions, and Sheridan
and Walker, for example, produced many other volumes in addition
to those listed above. These were also circulated in America and will
be studied in relationship to their effect on American rhetorical theory
and practice.

Background of the Elocution Movement in America

Growth of interest in the colleges.—In America during the eighteenth
century, as in England, the increased interest in study in English, and
the increased prominence given speaking in daily life, produced more
and more interest in how a speech was presented as well as in how to
construct a speech. Rhetroic had become closely allied with oratory,
and was clearly conceived of as an active art. Rhetoric and oratory
were complementary studies.

Special emphasis on elocution as such can also be found. Sheridan,
Enfield and Burgh are among the most popular books in the college
and society libraries at Brown from 1788 through 1800.[27] Minutes of
the Trustees of the University of Pennsylvania show that in 1773 they
felt that the loss of an elocution teacher was a serious blow to the
prestige of the institution.[28] The Harvard Overseers note with regularity their pleasure or displeasure with the exhibitions.[29] Other similar
indications are legion.[30]

Rhetorical Theses.—Although the practice of publishing theses to be
defended at commencement was not continued throughout the period
under consideration, they also show the emphasis given delivery in
the colleges during the years before their discontinuance. Each year's

[27] The college library withdrawals of 1788 list 10 withdrawals of Enfield, 6
of Sheridan, and 4 of Burgh in a little less than a year. Blair was the only other
speech work to approach this number. In one of the society libraries at Brown,
the Philendian Society, there were four copies of Sheridan's *Lectures.*

[28] Montgomery, T. H., *A History of the University of Pennsylvania*, (Philadelphia, 1900), p. 251, quotes from the minutes of February 2, 1773.

[29] For example, from *Reports to Overseers*, I, October 22, 1816, "On attending
the publick exercises of the students, they were highly gratified with the . . .
correct elocution."

[30] In almost every college catalogue until 1850, and in some on through to 1900,
in addition to the usual requirement of "disputations and declamation" there is
comment on the stress placed on the value of "a good elocution."

listing of theses included many dealing with delivery, until this becomes one of the largest groups. Half of the theses at Yale in 1789
were on delivery. A fourth or more of the theses were concerned with
delivery at Yale in 1754, 1756, 1757, 1760, 1763, 1765, 1766, 1767, 1770,
1783, 1788, 1789, 1790, 1792, and in 1797, when they were discontinued.
At Brown seven out of twelve theses were concerned with delivery in
1788, five out of eight in 1790, and four out of seven in 1813. In almost
every year they made up from one fourth to one half of the total number of theses until the close of their publication in 1817. At Harvard
the trend is not quite so strong, although there are only fifteen years
between 1750 and 1819 when one or more theses on delivery are not
included in the list of those to be defended.

Some of these theses also illustrate the sort of delivery stressed, and
the place given to delivery in the whole doctrine of rhetoric. The first
Brown thesis of 1770, 1772, 1774, 1776, 1778, and 1790 is that "Rhetoric
is the art of making clear with evidence and persuasive force through
words and gestures of the body." A Yale thesis of 1771 has it that
"The face is often more eloquent than words," and another opening
the *Theses Rhetoricae* for 1781 states: "Elocution is the beautifully
measured use in speaking of the countenance, the voice, and gesture."

Even more specific rules are sometimes included in the theses. A
Yale thesis of 1792 tells us: "In oratorical gesture, the left [Hand]
ought not to be used alone, except in despairing." Brown's list, in
1798, includes: "It always happens, in our language, wherever an
accent is added to a consonant, the preceding vowel is short; and also
that, in the unaccented syllables, no vowel has a long sound." 'Admiration lifts the mind and the voice; even so contempt contracts and
diminishes them," says a Harvard thesis of 1785. The growing emphasis
on delivery above all else is indicated by another Harvard thesis,
1788, "The first quality and, as it were, the basic requirement for an
orator is a well-modulated voice."

Americans were critical of the English oratory of the period as well.
For example there is the Harvard theses of 1808:

> In England, sacred eloquence flowers but feebly. There, trusting too
> much in matter, they have almost entirely neglected manner. Among
> the French, however, Bossuet, Bourdaloue, Saurin and Massillon have
> inculcated the sacred truth not only because of their elegant speech,
> but also because of their fervid and sincere delivery.[31]

[31] This might just be national pride, and gratitude to the French, for only a few
years earlier, in 1751, when England was comparatively well-loved, a Yale thesis
holds that "the English orators excel present day speakers of all other nationalities
in eloquence, force of reasoning, clarity of thought, and eloquence of style."

Clearly, American speakers, as those of England, were awakening more and more sharply to the necessity for study of the delivery of materials, as well as of their preparation and composition.[32]

English Influence on American Elocution

From the beginning, the development of interest in delivery in America closely parallels that in Great Britain. We have already seen that one of the earliest works devoted to delivery, the *Art of Speaking in Public*, was read by Samuel Johnson in 1755. Later works were also to be accepted in America almost as quickly as in England.

It should be observed that in the development of elocutionary theory two schools of thought were evident from the very beginning. One group of authors feels that the soundest training in elocution is that which is to be gained from nature herself. Their writings on elocution are designed primarily to free the orator from inhibitions and misconceptions, and thus to enable him to achieve a natural manner. In accord with this design, they offer broad precepts and stress the need for understanding and appreciation of the matter to be read or spoken. This attitude toward elocution was termed variously "natural," "naturalistic," or the "nature school."

Another group of writers, while paying lip-service to the ideal of the natural orator, feel that true naturalness is to be attained through a study of didactic principles on which nature herself is built. They find order in nature and attempt to reduce this to inflexible rule. Accordingly, they offer this same order and arbitrary rule to the study of elocution, framing elaborate systems built with careful attention to minute specifications for every sort of material and situation. This point of view has been termed "mechanical," or "mechanistic." [33]

---

[32] A study of the theses defended in American colleges in more detail might prove most fruitful. Although there seems no place for more detailed discussion in this study, it is interesting to note such theses as the following, which may indicate that such a study would provide a wealth of material for the student of this period in many fields.

Yale, 1783—"Indian tongues and dialects, lacking belles-lettres and any art of speaking, nevertheless lend to speech the beauty of accuracy and terseness."

Pennsylvania, 1761—"He seems to do greater wrong who corrupts another with speech, than he who corrupts through bribes; for one who is impervious to bribery may be corrupted by a speech."

[33] For a detailed discussion of the accuracy of this sort of labelling, see Haberman, *op. cit.*, 48–64 and Robb, Mary Margaret, *Oral Interpretation of Literature in American Colleges and Universities*, (New York, 1941), pp. 19–69, *passim*. The labels are used here in a descriptive sense with no attempt to judge or evaluate the differences of opinion expressed above.

Mason.—John Mason first published his *Essay on Elocution* [34] in 1748. The work was offered for sale in New York as early as 1755,[35] and was in the Harvard Library in 1762.[36] It was included among the first list of books ordered by Brown University in 1783.[37]

Mason's theory of delivery is derived largely from Quintilian, to whom frequent reference is made, and is in the "nature" school. He believes that good pronunciation may be acquired by rule, by imitation, and by practice, but his great canon for delivery is to follow nature and to avoid affectation. The work is a practical manual for training the beginning speaker.

In addition to the use of Mason noted earlier, he seems to have been one of the chief victims of "borrowing" during the whole period. Dodsley uses Mason's *Essay* in most editions of the *Precentor,* and thus all of the circulation of that work was also circulation of Mason. The anonymous *Directions concerning Pronunciation and Gesture* which was published in London in 1793 [38] is nothing more nor less than a paraphrase of Mason without any acknowledgment whatsoever. Harding notes similarities between the *Directions* and Mason's *Essay on Elocution.*[39] One might note more accurately that there are some differences between the two works, but many more points of similarity than of difference.

Sheridan.—Thomas Sheridan is best remembered for his many other interests, yet between 1757 and 1780 he was easily the best known non-academic teacher of speaking, and the author of some fifteen

[34] (London, 1748). Other editions were published in 1748, 1751, and 1761. No American edition has been found. It is of interest to note that Mason seems to have been the first writer to justify the use of the term "elocution" in the sense of delivery. He adds this footnote to the first page of the work: "I use the term elocution here in its common or vulgar sense, to signify Utterance, Delivery, or pronunciation, in which sense we frequently use it in the English language, and which its Latin etymology very well justifies; though I know some good writers apply to it a different idea, in conformity to the sense in which the Latin orators used the term *Elocutio.* But it is no uncommon thing for derivative words in one language to be taken in a different sense from that, in which the words they are derived from are taken from another." For further discussion of the changes in the meanings of "elocution," "pronunciation," etc., see Haberman, *op. cit.,* Ch. III.

[35] By Garratt Noel, bookseller.

[36] *Harvard library charging catalogue* (MS.). Two copies were listed in the Harvard catalogue in 1765, and the work was also listed in the *Selected Catalogue* of 1773.

[37] Manuscript record of books ordered by Brown University from England in the Brown University archives.

[38] The work is included in The Works of the Reverend John Wesley, A.M., fourth edition (London 1840–1842), XIII, 488 ff.

[39] Harding, *op. cit.,* p. 253.

books or essays on the reading, speaking, and teaching of English. When he first delivered the famous lectures on elocution some three hundred gentlemen attended, and in all the lectures were given three times to seventeen hundred subscribers who paid a guinea each for the privilege. Boswell was a student of Sheridan's and considered himself an apt pupil when Johnson said to him, "Sir, your pronunciation is not offensive." [40]

Sheridan's works were circulated widely in America. The Harvard library catalogue of 1765 lists Sheridan "on Elocution" [41] and "on British Education." The Harvard charging catalogue shows that Sheridan's *Lectures* were charged three times during 1767, more frequently than any other rhetorical work. The *Lectures* were also in the 1775 catalogue of the Philadelphia Library Company. When Brown sent its first order of books to England in 1783 four of Sheridan's works were included, the "Oratorical Lectures," [42] the *Lectures on Reading,* the *Plan of Education* [43] and the essay on *British Education.* The *Lectures on Elocution* were included in the Brown course of study in 1783, and still listed for freshmen as late as 1823. [44] The same work was used in classes at the University of South Carolina in 1806. [45] American editions of Sheridan's works are as follows: *A Rhetorical Grammar of the English Language* (Philadelphia, 1783): [46] *Lectures on Elocution* (Providence, 1796): *Lessons in Elocution* arranged by J. P. Henshaw from Sheridan (Baltimore, 1834).

Sheridan defines elocution as "the just and graceful management of the voice, countenance, and gesture in speaking." [47] His treatment of these factors is characterized by a relative moderate and seemingly practical approach. He refuses to set down a complicated system of rules, but sets the standards and manner of good conversation as most suited to platform speaking. Later editions stress this natural manner and make strong attacks on the so-called "mechanical school."

[40] Boswell's *Life of Samuel Johnson,* II, 159.

[41] Undoubtedly the *Lectures on Elocution* (London, 1763).

[42] This is probably the *Lectures on Elocution* since the *Lectures on Reading* (Dublin, 1775) is also listed.

[43] *A Plan of Education* (London, 1769).

[44] Bronson, W. C. *The History of Brown University* (Providence, 1914), pp. 103, 167.

[45] E. L. Green, *A History of the University of South Carolina* (Columbia, S. C., 1916), p. 182.

[46] This is probably the second speech work to be published in America, and it was brought out under the supervision of Archibald Gamble, Professor of English and Oratory in the University of Pennsylvania.

[47] *Lectures on Elocution,* p. 19.

In his various works, Sheridan, in addition to his repeated emphasis of the importance of speech, divides his teaching of delivery into discussion of Articulation, Pronunciation, Accent, Emphasis, Pauses or Stops, Pitch and Management of the Voice, Tones, and Gestures. In each of these a just variety, together with a combination of force and grace is desired. Specific rules are not given, for he holds that they are useless if they are too exact. Even so, he moves much further toward mechanical rules than does Mason. Observing that action is of great value in speaking, he offers general descriptions that were to become rules for later writers.[48] For example, "Mirth opens the mouth towards the ear, crisps the noise, half-shuts the eyes, and sometimes fills them with tears."[49] Again, "A correct speaker does not make a movement of limb or feature for which he has not a reason . . . . He does not start back, unless he wants to express horror or aversion . . . ."[50] The way is opened for the more detailed rules to be considered by later writers.

Burgh.—The first of the mechanical works was that of James Burgh, *The Art of Speaking.*[51] First published in 1761, that edition was in the Harvard library in 1767,[52] and the interest in the work was great enough that an American edition was published in 1775[53]—the first speech work to be published in America.

The Art of Speaking, in the manner of its construction at least, is a more representative work than Sheridan's. Where Sheridan devotes his entire volume to a consideration of the theory of elocution, Burgh presents a relatively short "Essay" on elocution which is followed by a much larger section containing lessons and materials for practice. This plan is followed by most of the later writers on elocution. The

---

[48] Discussions and summaries of Sheridan's theories are to be found in Harding, *op. cit.,* and Haberman, *op. cit.,* pp. 46–100. Sheridan's various works are also readily available in American libraries.

[49] *Rhetorical Grammar,* p. 168.

[50] *Ibid.,* p. 190. This sentence is repeated in literally dozens of later elocution texts, many of which were extremely mechanical in their approach and point of view.

[51] (London, 1761).

[52] The copy now in the Harvard Library is so marked on the title page.

[53] Published by Robert Aitken, in Philadelphia. Other American editions include Newburyport, 1782, Philadelphia, 1786, and 1800, Boston, 1793, 1795, Danbury, 1795 and Baltimore, 1804. The work was not listed in any college course of study, but it seems to have had a wide popular reception from the very beginning. Goodhue lists it among the works read by the members of the Harvard speaking club between 1770 and 1781. (Goodhue, Albert, "The Reading of Harvard Students, 1770–1781, as shown by the Records of the Speaking Club" *Essex Institute, Historical Collections,* lxxiii, 107–129).

following excerpt from the title page of the book explains the plan of organization:

I. AN ESSAY: in which are given Rules for expressing properly the principal Passions and Humours, which occur in Reading or Public Speaking; and

II. LESSONS: taken from the Ancients and Moderns (with Additions and Alterations where thought useful) exhibiting a Variety of Matter for Practice; the emphatical words printed in Italics; with Notes of Direction referring to the Essay; to which are added, A Table of Lessons; and an Index of the various Passions and Humours in the Essay and Lesson.

The essay comprises only forty-six of three hundred seventy-two pages, but it is an amazingly detailed catalogue of the various meanings and passions which gesture and voice are capable of portraying. Almost three hundred "passions or humours" are mentioned in reference to the selections in Part IX and about a third of these are described in the essay. For example, in Lesson XLVIII one line of the selection offered for reading practice is annotated marginally as a line requiring the emotion of joy. The reader is thus referred back to the essay where joy is described as follows:

> Joy, when sudden and violent, expresses itself by *clapping of hands,* and exultation or leaping. The eyes are opened wide; perhaps filled with *tears;* often raised to *heaven,* especially by devout persons. The countenance is smiling, not composedly, but with features *aggravated.* The voice rises, from time to time, to very *high* notes.[54]

Much of the material on action is quoted directly from Sheridan's *Rhetorical Grammar,* although no acknowledgment is made. The "Lessons" are made up of selections from writers such as Pope, Milton, and Dryden and each selection is interpreted in detail as suggested above. Elaborate as was Burgh's attempt to indicate precisely the attitudes of speaking and acting on the printed page, much more detailed attempts were soon to follow.

Rice.—Burgh's book was followed by John Rice's *An Introduction to the Art of Reading with Energy and Propriety,*[55] a work in the natural school. Unlike the earlier books on elocution, however, it deals only with voice.

Rice's work was given to the Harvard library in 1827, but there are not further evidences of use in America.

[54] Note the increase in detail and instruction over Sheridan, whose description of Joy has been quoted on an earlier page.
[55] (London, 1765).

Enfield.—*The Speaker* of William Enfield [56] is also largely natural in its approach, and thus somewhat under the influence of Sheridan. Like Burgh's *Art of Speaking* it is made up of a short essay on speaking, and many selections for practice. Best organized of the works on elocution since Mason, Enfield sets down eight rules by which his principles may be made clear. "Follow nature is certainly the fundamental law of oratory, without a regard to which, all other rules will only produce affected declamation, not just elocution," is an early precept. The general principles are given since, "the acquisition of the art of speaking, like all other practical arts, may be facilitated by rules."[57] The rules follow:

I. Let your articulation be distinct and deliberate.
II. Let your pronunciation be bold and forcible.
III. Acquire a compass and variety in the height of your voice.
IV. Pronounce your words with propriety and elegance.
V. Pronounce every word consisting of more than one syllable with its proper accent.
VI. In every sentence, distinguish the more significant words by a natural, forcible, and varied emphasis.
VII. Acquire a just variety of pause and cadence.
VIII. Accompany the emotions and passions which your words express by correspondent tones, looks, and gestures.[58]

The stress is always communication, and the final advice given indicates the author's point of view:

Avail yourself, then, of your skill in the Art of Speaking, but always employ your powers of elocution with caution and modesty; remembering, that though it be desirable to be admired as an eminent Orator, it is of much more importance to be respected, as a wise statesman, an able lawyer, or a useful preacher.[59]

The book seems to have had some college circulation as well as popular sale, for it was ordered by Brown in 1783, and a special edition published by William Woodward in Philadelphia in 1789 prints a list of subscribers which includes, "William Thomson, Professor of Languages, Dickinson College, Carlisle, 2 copies, and 16 Dickinson students."

[56] (London, 1774). The first American edition was published in Boston, 1795, and other American editions appeared in 1798, 1799, 1803, 1805, 1808, 1814, and 1817. The work was also the source of much of the explanatory material, along with Burgh, of Noah Webster's *Grammatical Institute of the English Language,* Part III (Hartford, 1785), the first elocution and collection of pieces to be compiled by an American. These notes are from the Enfield's Boston edition of 1795.
[57] Enfield, *op. cit.,* p. iv.
[58] *Ibid.,* pp. v–xiv.
[59] *Ibid.,* p. xvii.

Steele.—One portion of the mechanistic approach to elocution was presented in its most extreme form in Joshua Steele's *Prosodia Rationalis.*[60] One of the most remarkable books on prosody ever written, it presents a most unusual effort to systematize the speech of an orator so that it might become as set as a musical composition. Concerned solely with reading, it seeks to bring out the fact that there are many variations of the voice possible, and that these variations may form patterns. The author asserts:

> Had some of the celebrated speeches from Shakespeare been noted and accented as they spoke them, we should be able now to judge, whether the oratory of our stage is improved or debased. If the method here essayed can be brought into familiar use, the types of modern elocution may be transmitted to posterity as accurately as we have received the musical compositions of Corelli.[61]

Regardless of Steele's real worth—and even the most sympathetic of critics describe his system as utterly wild [62]—he does appear to provide the elocution teacher with the answer to many of his perplexing problems. If we are to believe the author, here are rules with uniformity and universality in their application, and a method of recording with mechanistic perfection. This possibility of making "Garrick live as long as Shakespeare," intrigued a multitude of imitators and critics from Walker, Bayly, and Thelwall in English, to Rush and his followers in America. The mystic signs recorded in Steele are to "linger long" in American elocution.

Cockin.—Sheridan's essential precepts are further summarized by Cockin.[63] The stress of his entire work is toward a conversational, natural manner, as is the theory of Sheridan. Cockin feels that he has one original contribution to make, however, and takes strong exception to Sheridan's effort to make reading appear as nearly as possible speaking. Cockin sets up different standards for reading and speaking. In reading, the "chief business being to repeat what he reads with accuracy, one discovers only a faint imitation of these signs of the emotions, which we suppose agitated him from whom the

[60] (London, 1775). No early evidence of the work in America has been found, but its indirect influence was great, and it may well have been in private libraries soon after its publication.

[61] Steele, *op. cit.,* p. 14.

[62] For example, see T. S. Omond, *English Metrists in the 18th and 19th centuries* (London, 1907), p. 92.

[63] Cockin, William, *The Art of Delivering Written Language* (London, 1775).

words were first borrowed." [64] Thus the reader is truly seeking only to communicate.

> If we are directed by nature and propriety, the manner of our delivery in reading ought to be inferior in warmth and energy to what we would use, were the language before us the spontaneous effusions of our own hearts in the circumstances of those out of whose mouths it is supposed to proceed.[65]

Walker.—In the many works of John Walker the "mechanics" school of elocution receives its most detailed and influential treatment up to this time.[66] He develops rules to fit every conceivable sort of sentence structure, every inflection, pause and gesture, and seems to feel that careful study of these, together with faithful practice, will produce the perfect orator.

In the first of these works, *The Elements of Elocution,* this predilection for rules is clearly shown. After the usual discussion of the value of the field of elocution and the work to be presented, the section on Rhetorical punctuation takes some seventy pages to present and explain sixteen rules for pauses. More than a hundred pages are given over to a myriad of rules on inflections, and then some thirty more rules are added for the use of inflection in the pronunciation of sentences. The rules given for modulation of the voice are repeated so often in later works, and become such a standard for American elocution, that they may well be repeated here: (1) At the end of each sentence the voice should be dropped to a lower key, so as to commence the next sentence in the same low key; (2) Words on which the voice is to be lowered should be begun with a monotone; (3) The ranges of the voice may be improved by practice; (4) The high tones may be practiced in selections requiring their use; (5) The middle tones are best practiced by declaiming very passionate speeches

---

[64] *Ibid.,* p. 203.

[65] *Ibid.,* p. 7.

[66] The following works were written by Walker; *Elements of Elocution,* 1781, (notes taken from the Boston edition of 1810); *Hints for Improvement in the Art of Reading,* 1785; *Rhetorical Grammar,* 1785 (notes for this study are from the first American edition, Boston, 1814); *Melody of Speaking Delineated, or, Elocution Taught Like Music,* 1787; *The Academic Speaker,* 1801 (notes from the first American edition, New York, 1808); and *The Teacher's Assistant,* 1787 (notes from the Boston edition of 1810). An addition to a digest of Walker's rules was published in Boston in 1896 under the title of *The Art of Reading.* Each of these passed through many editions, both in England and America. Walker's various works were used at Dartmouth, 1822–1827; Vermont, 1826–1841; and Williams, 1824–1860; for example.

in a low tone, while keeping the voice on a middle pitch; (6) Relief from speaking in a high pitch may be achieved by bringing the voice to a lower tone; and (7) This may be accomplished by adopting some passion which requires a lower key.[67]

Most of the discussion of gesture is concerned with what not to do. The left hand must not be used; the hand is not to be raised above the shoulders; all gestures are to move from left to right; arms akimbo is taboo; gestures must not cross the mid-line of the body; the rhythm and timing of gesture is to be as described in reference to the whole problem of posture and delivery:

> The first plate represents the attitude in which a boy should always place himself when he begins to speak. He should rest the whole of his body on one leg, the right; the other just touching the ground at the distance at which it would naturally fall if lifted up to show that the body does not bear upon it. The knees should be straight and braced; and the body, though perfectly straight, not perpendicular, but inclining as far to the right as firm position on the right leg will permit. The right arm must then be held out with the palm open, the fingers straight and close, the thumb almost as distant from them as it will go; and the flat of the hand neither horizontal nor vertical, but exactly between both.
>
> When the pupil has pronounced one sentence in the position thus described, the hand as if lifeless, must drop down to the side the very moment the last accented word is pronounced; and the body without altering the place of the feet, poise itself on the left leg, while the left hand raises itself into exactly the same position as the right was before, and continues in this position until the end of the next sentence, when it drops down on the side as if dead; and the body, poising itself on the right leg as before, continues with the right arm extended; and so on, from right to left, and from left to right, alternately, till the speech is ended . . . .
>
> If the pupil's knees are not well formed, or incline inwards, he must be taught to keep his legs at as great a distance as possible, and to incline his body so much to that side, on which the arm is extended, as to oblige him to rest the opposite leg upon the toe; and this will, in a great measure, hide the defect of his make.[68]

The work concludes with an analysis of the passions which is based on Burgh, and which is copied from Burgh with only minor changes in phrasing.

[67] Walker, *Elements of Elocution*, pp. 286–301.
[68] *Ibid.*, p. 305, quoting material from the *Academic Speaker*, pp. 10–11.

The Rhetorical Grammar which Walker feels is his greatest work, and in which he introduces his concept of the circumflex, or wave of the voice, was published in 1785. Here, Walker feels, is his prime contribution, for with the discovery of the circumflex one can acquire "more permanent *data* on which to found a system of rhetorical punctuation." [69]

The work sets out to be a complete rhetoric, and opens with these lines:

> The part of Rhetoric which relates to composition has been so elaborately treated both by the ancients and moderns, that I shall in some measure invert the common order, and at first chiefly confine myself to that branch of it which relates to pronunciation and delivery.[70]

Following the discussion, which is very similar to that in the *Elements of Elocution,* he presents the figures of rhetoric and gives rules on how to pronounce them. This is followed by a discussion of composition and style which is nothing more nor less than a series of excerpts from Blair, and a discussion of invention which is excerpted from Priestley and Ward. So does Walker construct his "perfect work" on which he lays his claim to elocutionary [71] fame!

The Melody of Speaking Delineated seems little more than a pirating of Steele's *Prosodia.* Marks set up for the recording of sounds are very similar to Steele's, and Walker's much vaunted "discovery," the circumflex, was already in Steele.

The Academic Speaker combines Walker's basic rules with many selections for practice. The rules are divided into three sections, one dealing with the elements of gesture, another with the acting of plays at schools, and a third presenting some of the rules given by Enfield, although no acknowledgment is made.

The rules dealing with gesture we have already quoted in some detail. Those concerned with the acting of plays are just as detailed, until one fears that the actors must have been rendered almost as rigid as the gentlemen portrayed in Walker's illustrative plates.

The Teacher's Assistant is devoted to composition, developing the plan that students may be best taught to write by giving them a synopsis of a theme and letting them expand this. Again nonchalant

[69] Walker, *Rhetorical Grammar,* p. xv.
[70] *Ibid.,* p. 17.
[71] Walker was, of course, more solidly famous as a lexicographer. His *Critical Pronouncing Dictionary and Expositor of the English Language* (London, 1791) is referred to in the *Dictionary of National Biograph* as "the statute book of English orthoepy."

about his sources, Walker seems not to suspect that such an arrangement has ever been in use before, and he offers it as a "discovery."

Walker's various works illustrate the new elocution. Departing rapidly from the natural standards which Sheridan and his followers had attempted to set up, the tendency toward mechanical rules is in full swing. Sheridan attempted to gain care and practice from the speaker with his advice: "A correct speaker does not make a movement of limb or feature for which he has not a reason," [72] now Walker uses the same sentence to preface the most complex description of emotional portrayal.[73] Walker had set a standard that was to become a fashion; minute analysis of gesture, vocal qualities, and facial expression, together with a multitude of rules purporting to come from nature, and systems of notation which were thought to record for posterity every quaver of the voice. This was the new elocution!

Scott.—These *Lessons on Elocution*, extremely popular in America,[74] were copies of earlier writings. The section on gesture was abstracted from Walker, as was the section on the acting of plays at schools. The treatment of the emotions was from Burgh. General rules on voice, which Walker had borrowed from Sheridan were in turn taken by Scott from Walker. To these he added "choice Selections."

Austin.—The last of the English works which exerted a large influence in America is that of Gilbert Austin.[75]

The book is most frequently thought of as a manual of action alone, but although these sections were most quoted and most influential, the work presents a complete elocutionary doctrine. As a matter of fact, it is much more thorough on the justification of the study of delivery than any of the other works, presenting an imposing list of testimonies, ancient and modern, as to the value of delivery.[76]

The discussion of gesture appears to be as comprehensive as the most ardent elocutionist might desire. Some of the chapter headings will serve to indicate the elaboration with which the entire treatment is characterized. One chapter treats of the position of the feet and lower limbs; another of the positions, motions and elevations of the arms; another of the positions, motions and elevations of the hands; another of the head, eyes, shoulders; another of the stroke and time

---

[72] Sheridan, *Rhetorical Grammar*, p. 190.

[73] Walker, *Elements of Elocution*, p. 307.

[74] The first American edition was published at Hartford in 1795, a fourth appeared in 1796, a fifteenth by 1806, and others came out yearly until 1820.

[75] *Chironomia; or a Treatise on Rhetorical Delivery* (London, 1806).

[76] These include Isocrates, Demosthenes, Cicero, Quintilian, Dionysius, Pliny, Aristotle, Victor, Rollin, Maury, Burke, Alcuin, Isidore of Sevile, and many others.

of gesture; there is one chapter on the preparation, transition, and accompaniment of gesture; one on the frequency, moderation, and intermission of gesture; and a final set of chapters on the significance of gesture.

More than a hundred plates are given at the close of the work to illustrate the various gestures. These greatly intrigued later elocutionists, and were reprinted in part in many other works. More important, however, to many of the elocutionists, was Austin's development of a method of marking gesture with the same accuracy and completeness Steele had given to the markings of sounds. This system provided a symbol in the form of a letter to be written down for each position of the hands, arms, head, eyes, and feet. Symbols were also provided for placing of the different parts of the body and for expressions of the countenance, as well as for the force and rapidity of the voice in delivery. Thus the complete orator can be diagrammed. This whole system is illustrated with a poem, "The Miser and Plautus." [77]

While it is unlikely that Austin's work had wide popular use in America, its indirect influence was tremendous. The system of notation developed was used by most of the later writers on elocution, in England and America, and even the single illustration cited above was reprinted in dozens of texts. From 1806 through 1860 *Chironomia* remained the definitive work on gesture.

As in the whole of rhetorical theory, the patterns for American elocutionary training were largely set in England. There, mounting criticism of the delivery of contemporary speakers, had, by 1806, matured into a specialized art of elocution.

As the elocution movement gathered momentum in England, two schools of thought formed themselves in sharp conflict; one holding that the best delivery was to be gained from "nature," the other, that a mechanical system was the best way to acquire a "natural" delivery. Through the writings of Sheridan and Walker, Steele and Austin, these disciplines were carried to America.

THE SPACIOUSNESS OF OLD RHETORIC
Richard Weaver

Few species of composition seem so antiquated, so little available for any practical purpose today, as the oratory in which the genera-

From *The Ethics of Rhetoric*, by Richard M. Weaver. Copyright © by Henry Regnery Company, Chicago, 1953. Reprinted by permission.
[77] Austin, *op. cit.*, pp. 360–370.

tion of our grandparents delighted. The type of discourse which they would ride miles in wagons to hear, or would regard as the special treat of some festive occasion, fills most people today with an acute sense of discomfort. Somehow, it makes them embarrassed. They become conscious of themselves, conscious of pretensions in it, and they think it well consigned to the museum. But its very ability to inspire antipathy, as distinguished from indifference, suggests the presence of something interesting.

The student of rhetoric should accordingly sense here the chance for a discovery, and as he begins to listen for its revealing quality, the first thing he becomes aware of is a "spaciousness." This is, of course, a broad impression, which requires its own analysis. As we listen more carefully, then, it seems that between the speech itself and the things it is meant to signify, something stands—perhaps it is only an empty space—but something is there to prevent immediate realizations and references. For an experience of the sensation, let us for a moment go back to 1850 and attune our ears to an address by Representative Andrew Ewing, on the subject of the sale of the public lands.

> We have afforded a refuge to the down-trodden nations of the Old World, and organized systems of internal improvement and public education, which have no parallel in the history of mankind. Why should we not continue and enlarge the system which has so much contributed to these results? If our Pacific Coast should be lined with its hundred cities, extending from the northern boundary of Oregon down to San Diego; if the vast interior hills and valleys could be filled with lowing herds and fruitful fields of a thriving and industrious people; and if the busy hum of ten thousand workshops could be daily heard over the placid waters of the Pacific, would our government be poorer or our country less able to meet her obligations than at present? [1]

Despite the allusions to geographical localities, does not the speaker seem to be speaking *in vacuo?* His words do not impinge upon a circumambient reality; his concepts seem not to have definite correspondences, but to be general, and as it were, mobile. "Spread-eagle" and "high-flown" are two modifiers with which people have sought to catch the quality of such speech.

In this work we are interested both in causes and the moral quality of causes, and when an orator appears to speak of subjects without an

---

[1] *The Congressional Globe,* Thirty-first Congress, First Session (June 21, 1850), p. 1250.

immediate apperception of them, we become curious about the kind of world he is living in. Was this type of orator sick, as some have inferred? Was he suffering from some kind of auto-intoxication which produces insulation from reality? Charles Egbert Craddock in her novel *Where the Battle Was Fought* has left a satirical picture of the type. Its personification is General Vayne, who holds everything up to a "moral magnifying glass." "Through this unique lens life loomed up as a rather large affair. In the rickety courthouse in the village of Chattalla, five miles out there to the south, General Vayne beheld a temple of justice. He translated an officeholder as the sworn servant of the people. The State was this great commonwealth, and its seal a proud escutcheon. A fall in cotton struck him as a blow to the commerce of the world. From an adverse political fortune he augured the swift ruin of the country" [2] There is the possibility that this type was sick with a kind of vanity and egocentricity, and that has frequently been offered as a diagnosis. But on the other hand, there is the possibility that such men were larger than we, with our petty and contentious style, and because larger more exposed in those limitations which they had. The heroes in tragedies also talk bigger than life. Perhaps the source of our discomfort is that this kind of speech comes to us as an admonition that there were giants in the earth before us, mighty men, men of renown. But before we are ready for any conclusion, we must isolate the cause of our intimation.

As we scan the old oratory for the chief offender against modern sensibility, we are certain to rank in high position, if not first, *the uncontested term*. By this we mean the term which seems to invite a contest, but which apparently is not so regarded in its own context. Most of these are terms which scandalize the modern reader with their generality, so that he wonders how the speaker ever took the risk of using them. No experienced speaker interlards his discourse with terms which are themselves controversial. He may build his case on one or two such terms, after giving them *ad hoc* definitions, but to multiply them is to create a force of resistance which almost no speech can overcome. Yet in this period we have speeches which seem made up almost from beginning to end of phrases loose in scope and but weakly defensible. Yet the old orator who employed these terms of sweeping generality knew something of his audience's state of mind and was confident of his effect. And the public generally responded by putting him in the genus "great man." This brings us to the rhetorical situation, which must be described in some detail.

[2] *Where the Battle Was Fought* (Boston and New York, 1900), p. 4.

We have said that this orator of the old-fashioned mold, who is using the uncontested term, passes on his collection of generalities in full expectation that they will be received as legal tender. He is taking a very advanced position, which could be undermined easily, were the will to do so present. But the will was not present, and this is the most significant fact in our explanation. The orator had, in any typical audience, not only a previously indoctrinated group, but a group of quite similar indoctrination. Of course, we are using such phrases for purposes of comparison with today. It is now a truism that the homogeneity of belief which obtained three generations ago has largely disappeared. Such belief was, in a manner of conceiving it, the old orator's capital. And it was, if we may trust the figure further, an initial asset which made further operations possible.

If we knew how this capital is accumulated, we would possess one of the secrets of civilization. All we know is that whatever spells the essential unity of a people in belief and attachment contains the answer. The best we can do at this stage is look into the mechanism of relationship between this level of generality and the effectiveness of a speech.

We must keep in mind that "general" is itself a relative modifier, and that the degree of generality with which one may express one's thoughts is very wide. One may refer, for example, to a certain event as a *murder*, a *crime*, an *act*, or an *occurrence*. We assume that none of these terms is inherently falsifying, because none of them is in any prior sense required. Levels of generality do not contradict one another; they supplement one another by bringing out different foci of interest. Every level of generality has its uses: the Bible can tell the story of creation in a few hundred words, and it is doubtless well that it should be told there in that way. Let us therefore take a guarded position here and claim only that one's level of generality tells something of one's approach to a subject. We shall find certain refinements of application possible as we go on.

With this as a starting point, we should be prepared for a more intensive look at the diction of the old school. For purposes of this analysis I shall choose something that is historically obscure. Great occasions sometimes deflect our judgment by their special circumstances. The passage below is from a speech made by the Honorable Charles J. Faulkner at an agricultural fair in Virginia in 1858. Both speaker and event have passed into relative oblivion, and we can therefore view this as a fairly stock specimen of the oratory in vogue a hundred years ago to grace local celebrations. Let us attend to it carefully for its references.

If we look to the past or to the present we shall find that the permanent power of any nation has always been in proportion to its cultivation of the soil—those republics which during the earlier and middle ages, were indebted for their growth mainly to commerce, did for a moment, indeed, cast a dazzling splendor across the pathway of time; but they soon passed from among the powers of the earth, leaving behind them not a memorial of their proud and ephemeral destiny whilst other nations, which looked to the products of the soil for the elements of their strength, found in each successive year the unfailing sources of national aggrandizement and power. Of all the nations of antiquity, the Romans were most persistently devoted to agriculture, and many of the maxims taught by their experience, and transmitted to us by their distinguished writers, are not unworthy, even at this time, of the notice of the intelligent farmers of this valley. It was in their schools of country life—a *vita rustica*—as their own great orator informs us, that they imbibed those noble sentiments which rendered the Roman name more illustrious than all their famous victories, and there, that they acquired those habits of labor, frugality, justice and that high standard of moral virtue which made them the easy masters of their race.[3]

A modern mind trained in the habit of analysis will be horrified by the number of large and unexamined phrases passing by in even this brief excerpt. "Permanent power of any nation"; "earlier and middle ages"; "cast a dazzling splendor across the pathway of time"; "proud and ephemeral destiny"; "noble sentiments which rendered the Roman name more illustrious"; and "high standards of moral virtue" are but a selection. Comparatively speaking, the tone of this oration is fairly subdued, but it is in the grand style, and these phrases are the medium. With this passage before us for reference, I wish to discuss one matter of effect, and one of cause or enabling condition.

It will be quickly perceived that the phrases in question have resonances, both historical and literary, and that this resonance is what we have been calling spaciousness. Instead of the single note (prized for purposes of analysis) they are widths of sound and meaning; they tend to echo over broad areas and to call up generalized associations. This resonance is the interstice between what is said and the thing signified. In this way then the generality of the phrase may be definitely linked with an effect.

But the second question is our principal interest: how was the orator able to use them with full public consent when he cannot do so today?

[3] *Address Delivered by Hon. Charles J. Faulkner before the Valley Agricultural Society of Virginia, at their Fair Grounds near Winchester, October 21, 1858* (Washington, 1858), pp. 3–4.

I am going to suggest that the orator then enjoyed a privilege which can be compared to the lawyer's "right of assumption." This is the right to assume that precedents are valid, that forms will persist, and that in general one may build today on what was created yesterday. What mankind has sanctified with usage has a presumption in its favor. Such presumption, it was felt, instead of being an obstacle to progress, furnishes the ground for progress. More simply, yesterday's achievements are also contributions to progress. It is he who insists upon beginning every day *de novo* who denies the reality of progress. Accordingly, consider the American orator in the intellectual climate of this time. He was comfortably circumstanced with reference to things he could "know" and presume everyone else to know in the same way. Freedom and morality were constants; the Constitution was the codification of all that was politically feasible; Christianity of all that was morally authorized. Rome stood as an exemplum of what may happen to nations; the American and French Revolutions had taught rulers their necessary limitations. Civilization has thought over its thousands of years of history and has made some generalizations which are the premises of other arguments but which are not issues themselves. When one asserts that the Romans had a "high standard of moral virtue which made them the easy masters of their race," one is affirming a doctrine of causality in a sweeping way. If one had to stop and "prove" that moral virtue makes one master, one obviously would have to start farther down the ladder of assumption. But these things were not in the area of argument because progress was positive and that meant that some things have to be assimilated as truths. Men were not condemned to repeat history, because they remembered its lessons. To the extent that the mind had made its summations, it was free to go forward, and forward meant in the direction of more inclusive conceptions. The orator who pauses along the way to argue a point which no one challenges only demeans the occasion. Therefore the orator of the period we have defined did not feel that he had to argue the significance of everything to which he attached significance. Some things were fixed by universal enlightened consensus; and they could be used as steps for getting at matters which were less settled and hence were proper subjects for deliberation. Deliberation is good only because it decreases the number of things it is necessary to deliberate about.

Consequently when we wonder how he could use such expressions without trace of compunction, we forget that the expressions did not need apology. The speaker of the present who used like terms would, on the contrary, meet a contest at every step of the way. His audience would not swallow such clusters of related meanings. But at that time a number of unities, including the unity of past and present, the unity of moral sets and of causal sets, furnished the ground for discourse in "uncontested terms." Only such substratum of agreement makes possible the panoramic treatment.

We can infer important conclusions about a civilization when we know that its debates and controversies occur at outpost positions rather than within the citadel itself. If these occur at a very elementary level, we suspect that the culture has not defined itself, or that it is decayed and threatened with dissolution. Where the chief subject of debate is the relative validity of Homoiousianism and Homoousianism, or the conventions of courtly love, we feel confident that a great deal has been cached away in the form of settled conclusions, and that such shaking as proceeds from controversies of this kind, although they may agitate the superstructure, will hardly be felt as far down as the foundations. I would say the same is suggested by the great American debate over whether the Constitution was a "constitution" or a "compact," despite its unfortunate sequel.

At this stage of cultural development the commonplaces of opinion and conduct form a sort of *textus receptus,* and the emendations are confined to minor matters. Conversely, when the disagreement is over extremely elementary matters, survival itself may be at stake. It seems to me that modern debates over the validity of the law of contradiction may be a disagreement of this kind. The soundness of a culture may well be measured by this ability to recognize what is extraneous. One knows what to do with the extraneous, even if one decides upon a policy of temporary accommodation. It is when the line dividing us from the extraneous begins to fade that we are assailed with destructive doubts. Disagreements over the most fundamental subjects leave us puzzled as to "where we are" if not as to "what we are." The speaker whom we have been characterizing felt sure of the demarcation. That gave him his freedom, and was the source of his simplicity.

When we reflect further that the old oratory had a certain judicial flavor about it, we are prompted to ask whether thinking as then conceived did not have a different status from today's thinking. One is led to make this query by the suggestion that when the most fundamental propositions of a culture are under attack, then it becomes a duty to "think for one's self." Not that it is a bad thing to think; yet when the whole emphasis is upon "thinking for one's self," it is hard to avoid a feeling that certain postulates have broken down, and the most courage we can muster is to ask people, not to "think in a certain direction," but to "think for themselves." Where the primary directive of thinking is known, the object of thinking will not be mere cerebral motion (as some exponents of the policy of thinking for one's self leave us to infer), but rather the object of such thinking, or knowledge. This is a very rudimentary proposition, but it deserves attention because the modern tendency has reversed a previous order. From the position that only propositions are interesting because they alone make judgments, we are passing to a position in which only evidence is interesting because it alone is uncontaminated by propositions. In brief, interest has shifted from inference to reportage, and this has had a demonstrable effect upon the tone of oratory. The large resonant phrase is itself a kind of condensed proposition; as propositions begin to sink with the general sagging of the substructure, the phrases must do the same. Obviously we are pointing here to a profound cultural change, and the same shifts can be seen in literature; the poet or novelist may feel that the content of his consciousness is more valid (and this will be true even of those who have not formulated the belief) than the formal arrangement which would be produced by selection, abstraction, and arrangement. Or viewed in another respect, experiential order has taken precedence over logical order.

The object of an oration made on the conditions obtained a hundred years ago was not so much to "make people think" as to remind them of what they already thought (and again we are speaking comparatively). The oratorical rostrum, like the church, was less of a place for fresh instruction than for steady inculcation. And the orator, like the minister, was one who spoke from an eminent degree of conviction. Paradoxically, the speaker of this vanished period had more freedom to maneuver than has his emancipated successor. Man is free in proportion as his surroundings have a determinate nature, and he can plan his course with perfect reliance upon that determinateness. It is an admitted axiom that we have rules in one place so that we can have liberty in another; we put certain things in charge of habit so as to be free in areas where we prize freedom. Manifestly one is not "free" when one has to battle for one's position at every moment of time. This interrelationship of freedom and organization is one of the permanent conditions of existence, so that it has been said even that perfect freedom is perfect compliance ("one commands nature by obeying her").

In the province we are considering, man is free to the extent that he knows that nature is, what God expects, what he himself is capable of. Freedom moves on a set of presuppositions just as a machine moves on a set of ball bearings which themselves preserve definite locus. It is when these presuppositions are tampered with that men begin to grow concerned about their freedom. One can well imagine that the tremendous self-consciousness about freedom today, which we note in almost every utterance of public men, is evidence that this crucial general belief is threatened. It is no mere paradox to say that when they cry liberty, they mean belief—the belief that sets one free from prior concerns. A corroborating evidence is that fact that nearly all large pleas for liberty heard today conclude with more or less direct appeals for unity.

We may now return to our more direct concern with rhetoric. Since according to this demonstration oratory speaks from an eminence and has a freedom of purview, its syllogism is the "rhetorical syllogism" mentioned by Demetrius—the enthymeme.[4] It may not hurt to state that this is the syllogism with one of the three propositions missing. Such a syllogism can be used only when the audience is willing to supply the missing proposition. The missing proposition will be "in their hearts," as it were; it will be their agreement upon some fundamental aspect of the issue being discussed. If it is there, the orator does not have to supply it; if it is not there, he may not be able to get it in any way—at least not as orator. Therefore the use of the rhetorical syllogism is good concrete evidence that the old orator relied upon the existence of uncontested terms or fixations of belief in the minds of his hearers. The orator was logical, but he could dispense with being a pure logician because that third proposition had been established for him.

These two related considerations, the accepted term and the conception of oratory as a body of judicious conclusions upon common evidence, go far toward explaining the quality of spaciousness. Indeed, to say that oratory has "spaciousness" is to risk redundancy once the nature of oratory is understood. Oratory is "spacious" in the same way that liberal education is liberal; and a correlation can be shown between the decline of liberal education (the education of a freeman) and the decline of oratory. It was one of Cicero's observations that the orator performs at "the focal point at which all human activity is ultimately reviewed"; and Cicero is, for connected reasons, a chief source of our theory of liberal education.[5]

---

[4] *On Style* (Cambridge: Harvard University Press, 1946), p. 321.

[5] See Norma J. DeWitt, "The Humanist Should Look to the Law," *Journal of General Education*, IV (January, 1950), 149. Although it is not our concern here, it probably could be shown that the essential requirements of oratory themselves depend upon a certain organization of society, such as an aristocratic republicanism. When Burke declares that a true natural aristocracy "is formed out of a

Thus far we have rested our explanation on the utility of the generalized style, but this is probably much too narrow an account. There is also an aesthetic of the generalization, which we must now proceed to explore. Let us pause here momentarily to re-define our impression upon hearing the old orator. The feature which we have been describing as spaciousness may be translated, with perhaps a slight shift of viewpoint, as opacity. The passages we have inspected, to recur to our examples, are opaque in that we cannot see through them with any sharpness. And it was no doubt the intention of the orator that we should not see through them in this way. The "moral magnifying glass" of Craddock's General Vayne made objects larger, but it did not make them clearer. It rather had the effect of blurring lines and obscuring details.

We are now in position to suggest that another factor in the choice of the generalized phrase was aesthetic distance. There is an aesthetic, as well as a moral, limit to how close one may approach an object; and the forensic artists of the epoch we describe seem to have been guided by this principle of artistic decorum. Aesthetic distance is, of course, an essential of aesthetic treatment. If one sees an object from too close, one sees only its irregularities and protuberances. To see an object rightly or to see it as a whole, one has to have a proportioned distance from it. Then the parts fall into a meaningful pattern, the dominant effect emerges, and one sees it "as it really is." A prurient interest in closeness and a great remoteness will both spoil the view. To recall a famous example in literature, neither Lilliputian nor Brobdingnagian is man as we think we know him.

Thus it can be a sign not only of philosophical ignorance but also of artistic bad taste to treat an object familiarly or from a near proximity. At the risk of appearing fanciful we shall say that objects have not only their natures but their rights, which the orator is bound to respect, since he is in large measure the ethical teacher of society. By maintaining this distance with regard to objects, art manages to "idealize" them in a very special sense. One does not mean by this that it necessarily elevates them or transfigures them, but it certainly does keep out a kind of officious detail which would only lower the general effect. What the artistic procedure tends to do, then, is to give us a "generic" picture, and much the same can be said about

---

class of legitimate presumptions, which, taken as generalities, must be admitted for actual truths" (*Works* [London, 1853–64], III, 85–86) my impression is that he has in mind something resembling our "uncontested term." The "legitimate presumptions" are the settled things which afford the plane of maneuver.

oratory. The true orator has little concern with singularity—or, to recall again a famous instance, with the wart on Cromwell's face—because the singular is the impertinent. Only the generic belongs, and by obvious connection the language of the generic is a general language. In the old style, presentation kept distances which had, as one of their purposes, the obscuring of details. It would then have appeared the extreme of bad taste to particularize in the manner which has since, especially in certain areas of journalism, become a literary vogue. It would have been beyond the pale to refer, in anything intended for the public view, to a certain cabinet minister's false teeth or a certain congressman's shiny dome. Aesthetically, this was not the angle of vision from which one takes in the man, and there is even the question of epistemological truthfulness. Portrait painters know that still, and journalists knew it a hundred years ago.

It will be best to illustrate the effect of aesthetic distance. I have chosen a passage from the address delivered by John C. Breckinridge, Vice-President of the United States, on the occasion of the removal of the Senate from the Old to the New Chamber, January 4, 1859. The moment was regarded as solemn, and the speaker expressed himself as follows:

> And now the strifes and uncertainties of the past are finished. We see around us on every side the proofs of stability and improvement. This Capitol is worthy of the Republic. Noble public buildings meet the view on every hand. Treasures of science and the arts begin to accumulate. As this flourishing city enlarges, it testifies to the wisdom and forecast that dictated the plan of it. Future generations will not be disturbed with questions concerning the center of population or of territory, since the steamboat, the railroad and the telegraph have made communication almost instantaneous. The spot is sacred by a thousand memories, which are so many pledges that the city of Washington, founded by him and bearing his revered name, with its beautiful site, bounded by picturesque eminences, and the broad Potomac, and lying within view of his home and his tomb, shall remain forever the political capital of the United States.

At the close of the address, he said:

> And now, Senators, we leave this memorable chamber, bearing with us, unimpaired, the Constitution received from our forefathers. Let us cherish it with grateful acknowledgements of the Divine Power who controls the destinies of empires and whose goodness we adore. The structures reared by man yield to the corroding tooth of time. These marble walls must molder into ruin; but the principles of constitutional

liberty, guarded by wisdom and virtue, unlike material elements, do not decay. Let us devoutly trust that another Senate in another age shall bear to a new and larger Chamber, the Constitution vigorous and inviolate, and that the last generations of posterity shall witness the deliberations of the Representatives of American States still united, prosperous, and free.[6]

We shall hardly help noting the prominence of "opaque" phrases. "Proofs of stability and improvement"; "noble public buildings"; "treasures of science and the arts"; "this flourishing city"; "a thousand memories"; "this beautiful site"; and "structures reared by man" seem outstanding examples. These all express objects which can be seen only at a distance of time or space. In three instances, it is true, the speaker mentions things of which his hearers might have been immediately and physically conscious, but they receive an appropriately generalized reference. The passage admits not a single intrusive detail, nor is anything there supposed to have a superior validity or probativeness because it is present visibly or tangibly. The speech is addressed to the mind, and correspondingly to the memory.[7] The fact that the inclusiveness was temporal as well as spatial has perhaps special significance for us. This "continuity of the past with the present" gave a dimension which our world seems largely to have lost and this dimension made possible a different pattern of selection. It is not experiential data which creates a sense of the oneness of experience. It is rather an act of mind; and the practice of periodically bringing the past into a meditative relationship with the present betokens an attitude toward history. In the chapter on Lincoln we have shown that an even greater degree of remoteness is discernible in the First and Second Inaugural Addresses, delivered at a time when war was an ugly present reality. And furthermore, at Gettysburg, Lincoln spoke in terms so "generic" that it is almost impossible to show that the speech is not a eulogy of the men in gray as well as the men in blue, inasmuch as both made up "those who struggled here." Lincoln's faculty of transcending an occasion is in fact only this ability to view it from the right distance, or to be wisely generic about it.

We are talking here about things capable of extremes, and there is a degree of abstraction which results in imperception; but barring

---

[6] *Address Preceding the Removal of the Senate from the Old to the New Chamber: Delivered in the Senate of the United States, January 4, 1859* (Washington, 1859), (Printed at the Office of the Congressional Globe), pp. 5, 7.

[7] There is commentary in the fact that the long commemorative address, with its assembled memories, was a distinctive institution of nineteenth-century America. Generalizations and "distance" were on such occasions the main resources.

those cases which everyone recognizes as beyond bounds, we should reconsider the idea that such generalization is a sign of impotence. The distinction does not lie between those who are near life and those who are remote from it, but between pertinence and impertinence. The intrusive detail so prized by modern realists does not belong in a picture which is a picture of something. One of the senses of "seeing" is metaphorical, and if one gets too close to the object, one can no longer in this sense "see." It is the *theoria* of the mind as well as the work of the senses which creates the final picture.

One can show this through an instructive contrast with modern journalism, particularly that of the *Time* magazine variety. A considerable part of its material, and nearly all of its captions, are made up of what we have defined as "impertinences." What our forensic artist of a century ago would have regarded as lacking significance is in these media presented as the pertinent because it is very near the physical manifestation of the event. And the reversal has been complete, because what for this artist would have been pertinent is there treated as impertinent since it involves matter which the average man does not care to reflect upon, especially under the conditions of newspaper reading. Thus even the epistemology which made the old oratory possible is being relegated.

We must take notice in this connection that the lavish use of detail is sometimes defended on the ground that it is illustration. The argument runs that illustration is a visual aid to education, and therefore an increased use of illustration contributes to that informing of the public which journals acknowledge as their duty. But a little reflection about the nature of illustration will show where this idea is treacherous. Illustration, as already indicated, implies that something is being illustrated, so that in the true illustration we will have a conjunction of mind and pictorial manifestation. But now, with brilliant technological means, the tendency is for manifestation to outrun the idea, so that the illustrations are vivid rather than meaningful or communicative. Thus, whereas today the illustration is looking for an idea to express, formerly the idea was the original; and it was looking, often rather fastidiously, for some palpable means of representation. The idea condescended, one might say, from an empyrean, to suffer illustrative embodiment.

To make this difference more real, let us study an example of the older method of illustration. The passage below examined is from an address by Rufus Choate on "The Position and Function of the American Bar as an Element of Conservatism in the State," delivered before the Law School in Cambridge, July 3, 1845.

But with us the age of this mode and degree of reform is over; its work is done. The passage of the sea; the occupation and culture of a new world, the conquest of independence—these were our eras, these our agency of reform. In our jurisprudence of liberty, which guards our person from violence and our goods from plunder, and which forbids the whole power of the state itself to take the ewe lamb, or to trample on a blade of grass of the humblest citizen without adequate remuneration: which makes every dwelling large enough to shelter a human life its owner's castle which winds and rain may enter, but which the government cannot,—in our written constitution, whereby the people, exercising an act of sublime self-restraint, have intended to put it out of their power forever to be passionate, tumultuous, unwise, unjust, whereby they have intended, by means of a system of representation, by means of the distribution of government into departments independent, coordinate for checks and balances; by a double chamber of legislation, by the establishment of a fundamental and permanent organic law; by the organization of a judiciary whose function, whose loftiest function it is to test the legislation of the day by the standard of all time,—constitutions, whereby all these means they have intended to secure a government of laws, not of men, of reason, not of will; of justice, not of fraud,—in that grand dogma of equality,— equality of right, of burthens, of duty, of privileges, and of chances, which is the very mystery of our social being—to the Jews a stumbling block; to the Greeks foolishness,—our strength, our glory,—in that liberty which we value not solely because it is a natural right of man; not solely because it is a principle of individual energy and a guaranty of national renown; not at all because it attracts a procession and lights a bonfire, but because, when blended with order, attended by law, tempered by virtue, graced by culture, it is a great practical good; because in her right hand are riches and honor and peace, because she has come down from her golden and purple cloud to walk in brightness by the weary ploughman's side, and whisper in his ear as he casts his seed with tears, that the harvest which frost and mildew and cankerworm shall spare, the government shall spare also; in our distribution into separate and kindred states, not wholly independent, not quite identical, in "the wide arch of ranged empire" above—these are they in which the fruits of our age and our agency of reform are embodied; and these are they by which, if we are wise,—if we understand the things that belong to our peace—they may be perpetuated.[8]

We note in passing the now familiar panorama. One must view matters from a height to speak without pause of such things as "occupation

[8] *The Position and Function of the American Bar, as an Element of Conservatism in the State: An Address Delivered before the Law School in Cambridge,* July 3, 1845. From *Addresses and Orations of Rufus Choate* (Boston: Little, Brown, 1891), pp. 141–43.

and culture of a new world," "conquest of independence," and "fundamental and permanent organic law." Then we note that when the
orator feels that he must illustrate, the illustration is not through the
impertinent concrete case, but through the poeticized figment. At
the close of the passage, where the personification of liberty is encountered, we see in clearest form the conventionalized image which is
the traditional illustration. Liberty, sitting up in her golden and
purple cloud, descends "to walk in brightness by the weary ploughman's side." In this flatulent utterance there is something so typical
of method (as well as indicative of the philosophy of the method)
that one can scarcely avoid recalling that this is how the gods of
classical mythology came down to hold discourse with mortals; it is
how the god of the Christian religion came into the world for the
redemption of mankind; it is how the *logos* is made incarnate. In
other words, this kind of manifestation from above is, in our Western
tradition, an archetypal process, which the orators of that tradition
are likely to follow implicitly. The idea is supernal; it may be brought
down for representation; but casual, fortuitous, individual representations are an affront to it. Consequently the representations are conventionalized images, and work with general efficacy.

This thought carries us back to our original point, which is that
standards of pertinence and impertinence have very deep foundations,
and that one may reveal one's whole system of philosophy by the stand
one takes on what is pertinent. We have observed that a powerful
trend today is toward the unique detail and the illustration of photo-
graphic realism, and this tendency claims to be more knowledgeable
about reality. In the older tradition which we set out to examine, the
abstracted truth and the illustration which is essentially a construct
held a like favor. It was not said, because there was no contrary style
to make the saying necessary, but it was certainly felt that these
came as near the truth as one gets, if one admits the existence of non-
factual kinds of truth. The two sides do not speak to one another
very well across the gulf, but it is certainly possible to find, and it
would seem to be incumbent upon scholars to find, a conception broad
enough to define the difference.

One further clue we have as to how the orator thought and how he
saw himself. There will be observed in most speeches of this era a
stylization of utterance. It is this stylization which largely produces
their declamatory quality. At the same time, as we begin to infer
causes, we discover the source of its propriety; the orator felt that he
was speaking for corporate humanity. He had a sense of stewardship
which would today appear one of the presumptions earlier referred to.

The individual orator was not, except perhaps in certain postures, offering an individual testimonal. He was the mouthpiece for a collective brand of wisdom which was not to be delivered in individual accents. We may suppose that the people did not resent the stylizations of the orator any more than now they resent the stylizations of the Bible. "That is the way God talks." The deity should be above mere novelties of expression, transparent devices of rhetoric, or importunate appeals for attention. It is enough for him to be earnest and truthful; we will rise to whatever patterns of expression it has pleased him to use. Stylization indicates an attitude which will not concede too much, or certainly will not concede weakly or complacently. As in point of historical sequence the language of political discourse succeeded that of the sermon, some of the latter's dignity and self-confidence persisted in the way of formalization. Thus when the orator made gestures toward the occasion, they were likely to be ceremonious rather than personal or spontaneous, the oration itself being an occasion of "style." The modern listener is very quick to detect a pattern of locution, but he is prone to ascribe it to situations of weakness rather than of strength.

Of course oratory of the broadly ruminative kind is acceptable only when we accredit someone with the ability to review our conduct, our destiny, and the causes of things in general. If we reach a condition in which no man is believed to have this power, we will accordingly be impatient with that kind of discourse. It should not be overlooked that although the masses in any society are comparatively ill-trained and ignorant, they are very quick to sense attitudes, through their native capacity as human beings. When attitudes change at the top of society, they are able to see that change long before they are able to describe it in any language of their own, and in fact they can see it without ever doing that. The masses thus follow intellectual styles, and more quickly than is often supposed, so that, in this particular case, when a general skepticism of predication sets in among the leaders of thought, the lower ranks are soon infected with the same thing (though one must make allowance here for certain barriers to cultural transmission constituted by geography and language). This principle will explain why there is no more appetite for the broadly reflective discourse among the general public of today than among the *élite*. The stewardship of man has been hurt rather than helped by the attacks upon natural right, and at present nobody knows who the custodians (in the old sense of "watchers") are. Consequently it is not easy for a man to assume the ground requisite for such a discourse.

Speeches today either are made for entertainment, or they are political speeches for political ends. And the chief characteristic of the speech for political ends is that it is made for immediate effect, with the smallest regard for what is politically true. Whereas formerly its burden was what the people believed or had experienced, the burden now tends to be what they wish to hear. The increased reliance upon slogans and catchwords, and the increased use of the argument from contraries (*e.g.*, "the thing my opponent is doing will be welcomed by the Russians") are prominent evidences of the trend.[9]

Lastly, the old style may be called, in comparison with what has succeeded, a polite style. Its very diffuseness conceals a respect for the powers and limitations of the audience. Bishop Whatley has observed that highly concentrated expression may be ill suited to persuasion because the majority of the people are not capable of assimilating concentrated thought. The principle can be shown through an analogy with nutrition. It is known that diet must contain a certain amount of roughage. This roughage is not food in the sense of nutriment; its function is to dilute or distend the real food in such a way that it can be most readily assimilated. A concentrate of food is, therefore, not enough, for there has to be a certain amount of inert matter to furnish bulk. Something of a very similar nature operates in discourse. When a piece of oratory intended for a public occasion impresses us as distended, which is to say, filled up with repetition, periphrasis, long grammatical forms, and other impediments to directness, we should recall that the diffuseness all this produces may have a purpose. The orator may have made a close calculation of the receptive powers of his audience and have ordered his style to meet that, while continuing to "sound good" at every point. This represents a form of consideration for the audience. There exists quite commonly today, at the opposite pole, a syncopated style. This style, with its suppression of beats and its consequent effect of hurrying over things, does not show that type of consideration. It does not give the listener the roughage of verbiage to chew on while meditating the progress of the thought. Here again "spaciousness" has a quite rational function in enforcing a measure, so that the mind and the sentiments too can keep up with the orator in his course.

Perhaps this is as far as we can go in explaining the one age to another. We are now in position to realize that the archaic formalism

---

[9] A distinction must be made between "uncontested terms" and slogans. The former are parts of the general mosaic of belief; the latter are uncritical aspirations, or at the worst, shibboleths.

of the old orator was a structure imparted to his speech by a logic, an aesthetic, and an epistemology. As a logician he believed in the deduced term, or the term whose empirical support is not at the moment visible. As an aesthetician he believed in distance, and that not merely to soften outline but also to evoke the true picture, which could be obscured by an injudicious and prying nearness. As an epistemologist he believed, in addition to the foregoing, that true knowledge somehow had its source in the mind of minds, for which we are on occasion permitted to speak a part. All this gave him a peculiar sense of stature. He always talked like a big man. Our resentment comes from a feeling that with all his air of confidence he could not have known half as much as we know. But everything depends on what we mean by knowing; and the age or the man who has the true conception of that will have, as the terms of the case make apparent, the key to every other question.

RENAISSANCE RHETORIC AND MODERN RHETORIC: A STUDY IN CHANGE [1]   *Wilbur Samuel Howell*

I

The Renaissance is a most convenient period with which to begin a discussion of the modern concept of rhetoric. That period, which may be roughly dated from 1450 to 1700, witnessed the last years of medieval civilization in Western Europe and the first years of modern civilization. Thus if we take our stand in the early Renaissance and examine the theory of communication which prevailed at that time, we are face to face with arrangements that counted almost two thousand years of history behind them and had changed only in detail in that double millennium. At the same time, as we look around in the Renaissance, we begin to see that things are changing in the theory of communication as in politics and theology and science, and that those changes have a familiar look, as if they would not be out of place among the similar arrangements of our twentieth-century world. In other words, the Renaissance is the one point in the history of Western Europe where the communication theory of ancient Greece

From *The Rhetorical Idiom*, edited by Donald Bryant. © 1961 Cornell University, by permission of Cornell University Press.

[1] This paper represents a development of the final chapter, and a restatement of certain ideas from earlier chapters, of my book, *Logic and Rhetoric in England: 1500–1700* (Princeton: Princeton University Press, 1956).

and Rome and that of modern Europe and America are ranged side by side, the older one still alive but losing ground, the younger one still immature but growing. What better place could be found for the beginnings of a study of what rhetoric has lost and gained in the transition from medieval to modern times?

The ancient theory of communication was interpreted in the Renaissance as a kind of knowledge made up of grammar, rhetoric, and dialectic or logic. These three liberal disciplines, which had been the trivium or lower group of liberal arts in the medieval universities, assumed the entire responsibility for training Renaissance students to speak and write. Latin was the language which those students were asked in grammar school and university to master as the universal basis for all kinds of communication, although as the seventeenth century drew to a close the emphasis upon vernacular languages became more and more pronounced.[2] That the trivium was actually regarded in the Renaissance as a group of studies expressly dedicated to the theory of communication is shown in Francis Bacon's great treatise, the *Advancement of Learning*, where Bacon, speaking of "the fourth kind of Rational Knowledge," proceeds not only to describe this knowledge as "transitive, concerning the expressing or transferring our knowledge to others," but also to term it "by the general name of Tradition or Delivery" and later to analyze it as made up in large part of grammar, logic, and rhetoric.[3]

Bacon's discussion of these three basic liberal arts as three branches of the great science of transmitting knowledge from man to man, from place to place, and from age to age involves a more rational plan, a more fully developed overview, than one finds in the usual Renaissance treatise on education. But this does not mean that Bacon's ideas on the trivium were different from those of his time. On the contrary, although the precise content of any one member of the trivium was defined in different ways by different schools of thought during the

---

[2] In 1660 Charles Hoole, a writer on education, reflected the classical orientation of the grammar school education of his century when he said that "*speaking Latine is the main end of Grammar.*" See "The Usher's Duty," in his *A New Discovery of the Old Art of Teaching Schoole*, ed. E. T. Campagnac (Liverpool and London, 1913), p. 50. The italics are Hoole's. Some years later an educational reformer named John Newton in the Dedicatory Epistle and Preface to his *Introduction to the Art of Logick* (London, 1678) reflected the newer tendencies of the century in asserting that young people should be taught all the sciences in their own tongue and that Latin should be reserved only for those who wished to enter a learned profession.

[3] *The Works of Francis Bacon*, ed. James Spedding, Robert Leslie Ellis, and Douglas Denon Heath (Boston, 1860–1864), VI, 282–303. Cited below as *Works of Bacon*.

Renaissance, Bacon's *Advancement of Learning* is in harmony with his era in treating the three liberal arts as offshoots of the theory of delivery or communication.[4] In all sectors of Renaissance opinion grammar was regarded as the study of the medium of communication, whether the medium was Latin for learned discourse or English for popular address. Similarly, dialectic or logic was for the most part regarded as the study of the means and methods of reaching the learned audience, whether in scholastic Latin sermons, lectures, and disputations, or in vernacular treatises like the *Advancement of Learning* itself. As for rhetoric, most segments of Renaissance opinion accepted it as the study of some or all of the means of making a discourse palatable and persuasive to the popular audience.

To be sure, the Ramists, whose system of dialectic and rhetoric became very popular in England between 1574 and 1620, did not divide dialectic from rhetoric by orienting the one predominantly toward the learned audience and the other predominantly toward the people.[5] But even they, in making rhetoric consist exclusively of style and delivery while dialectic assumed absolute control over invention and arrangement, tended in fact to relegate rhetoric to those crafts which popular discourse needs in more generous measure than does learned discourse. And it should be observed that dialectic and rhetoric were parts of the theory of communication in Ramus' scheme, as in the medieval synthesis, although Ramus explained the relation of these parts to each other in a different way from that used by scholastic logic or Ciceronian rhetoric.

Five changes in the ancient theory of communication began to appear during the Renaissance, and by and large these changes help to explain why modern rhetoric is as it is. I should like to mention these changes here and to indicate what seems to explain them. Then I should like to suggest some of the benefits or disadvantages they have brought to the modern academic study of communication.

II

Perhaps the most significant change that has come over the theory of communication during the last four hundred years is that logic has dissolved its alliance with the communication arts and has aligned itself instead with the theory of scientific investigation. Descartes in his famous *Discours de la méthode* indicated the need for a logic of

[4] See my *Logic and Rhetoric in England,* chs. 2–5.
[5] *Ibid.,* ch. 4.

inquiry to replace the older logic of communication.[6] By and large, his summons proved to be prophetic. Logic has become the interpreter of scientific and philosophical method, whereas it had been the interpreter of the method of transmitting knowledge from expert to expert. In an academic sense, this means that logic has affiliated itself with the department of philosophy and has ceased to have any primary connection with the department of rhetoric. Of course, certain fragments of logic have continued to appear regularly in all treatises devoted by rhetoricians to argumentation and persuasion; but those fragments, which usually concern the forms of reasoning and fallacies, have not represented the full emphasis of the new logic and usually, indeed, have been conspicuous for their perfunctory character, their lack of originality, and their seeming dedication to the appearances rather than the essentials of the tradition they reflect. Meanwhile, logic has studied the sciences and mathematics, has formulated the canons of induction, has denied the priority of the syllogism, and has sought politely to disavow those who wanted to use the study of logic as a practical means of making themselves logical writers and speakers.

There can be little doubt that, since the Renaissance, the major intellectual energies in Western Europe have been devoted to the discovery of new truth, and the greatest reputations in the world of learning have been made by the scientists. At the same time, emphasis upon the communication of new truths across the barriers between persons, specialties, nations, language groups, and generations has been a diminishing study within the universities, although not a diminishing need in the practical world. Thus logic shifted her allegiance from communication to inquiry at an advantageous time. Higher academic rewards lay in the direction of an association with science, while communication could offer her academic devotees little more than a servant's wage. It may seem strange that rhetoric, contemptuously associated with the arts of promotion and self-aggrandizement, should have remained loyal to the unpopular and unprosperous cause of communication, while logic, the aristocratic disdainer of profitable enterprises, should have chosen to go where the academic profits were greatest. But so it was, at least within English and American universities of the late nineteenth and early twentieth centuries.

I do not mean to argue seriously that a shrewd self-interest was the real motive behind the attachment of logic to science. Instead, the

[6] René Descartes, *Discours de la méthode,* ed. Etienne Gilson (Paris, 1935), pp. 62–63.

attachment was a natural consequence of man's success in studying his physical environment. It has been more important since the Renaissance to devote oneself to the search for new knowledge than to the exposition of that knowledge to others, and logic has accepted this value as her guide. A few modern authors like Whately and Bain have continued to write on both logic and rhetoric after the example of Aristotle, Cicero, Thomas Wilson, Ramus, and others. But in the main the two disciplines have parted company, and the logicians have outclassed the rhetoricians in the eyes of the learned community, the favorable verdict for logic being decisive if not always founded upon an impartial examination of the evidence on both sides.

The renunciation by logic of her alliance with the theory of communication has been a serious blow to modern rhetoric. As I mentioned a moment ago, it has led to an obvious and fatal superficiality whenever rhetoricians have affixed to their own works an abbreviated version of traditional logical theory. It has also led to a counterrenunciation of logic by rhetoric, as in the elocutionary movement of the nineteenth century, where rhetoric became completely absorbed in delivery, not in the Baconian sense of the full act of communication but as the vocal and physical components of that act. Perhaps as philosophers and rhetoricians develop their present interest in semantics, a way will be found to create a new logic for the process of communication and to bring logic and rhetoric together in a more significant companionship than any they have enjoyed since the days of Thomas Wilson. Until this happens, however, rhetoric will be detached from some of the impulses that have accounted for her greatest past glories. When Aristotle began his *Rhetoric* by defining his subject as the counterpart of dialectic, he meant to ally his logical treatises, and in particular his *Topics*, with the work he was about to write. We might say that, until modern rhetoric helps to create a modern equivalent of Aristotelian dialectic and contributes vitally to its development, she will continue to lack what the best ancient rhetoric had—a sense of indissoluble kinship with the philosophical aspects of the enterprise of communication.

III

Another significant change that has occurred in the theory of communication since the Renaissance is that rhetoric has attempted to expand her interests so as to become the theory of learned discourse while remaining the theory of popular discourse. As I indicated above, logic had jurisdiction over the former theory in the ancient scheme as interpreted by the Renaissance. Indeed, Renaissance logicians and rhetoricians had a favorite image to describe the relation of logic to rhetoric, and that image associated logic with the closed fist, rhetoric with the open hand. According to Cicero and Quintilian, this image originated with Zeno the Stoic, and if you had asked a learned man of the Renaissance to explain it, he probably would have given you Cicero's interpretation as set forth in these words of the *Orator:*

> The man of perfect eloquence should, then, in my opinion possess not only the faculty of fluent and copious speech which is his proper province, but should also acquire that neighbouring borderland science of logic; although a speech is one thing and a debate another, and disputing is not the same as speaking, and yet both are concerned with discourse—debate and dispute are the function of the logicians; the orator's function is to speak ornately. Zeno, the founder of the Stoic school, used to give an object lesson of the difference between the two arts; clenching his fist he said logic was like that; relaxing and extending his hand, he said eloquence was like the open palm.[7]

Debate and disputation, as used in this passage, stand for all the types of philosophical or scholastic discourses that one finds in the world of learning; eloquence stands for the open, popular speech to political meetings, juries, and gatherings at public ceremonies and celebrations. As logic in the ancient scheme taught the young expert to communicate with his peers while rhetoric taught him to communicate with the populace, so in the modern scheme has rhetoric attempted to teach both functions, inasmuch as logic is no longer available for the purpose it once served.

The advantage of the ancient scheme was that it kept everybody reminded of the two worlds in which communication takes place, of the two types of discourses flowing from speaker to audience, and of the broad differences between the scholar and the popularizer. By his studies in logic and rhetoric a student would get an impression of the differences between dialectical and rhetorical invention, dialectical and rhetorical arrangement. He would also get a sense of the similarities between these procedures as dialectical and as rhetorical operations. Even the duplication between his classroom assignments in dialectic and those in rhetoric would have some value in reminding him of the essential unity of his various subjects. The same lessons studied from two points of view is often better than two lessons studied without

---

[7] *Orator*, 113, trans. H. M. Hubbell (Loeb Classical Library; Cambridge, Mass., and London, 1939), p. 389. See also Quintilian, *Institutio Oratoria*, 2. 20. 7.

reference to each other. And when the same lesson is studied under two teachers, one a rhetorician and the other a logician, the prestige of each increases that of the other, and the student feels a comfortable reassurance in the very fact that his teachers differ only in approach, not in aim.

Of course, when two subjects are adjusted to as narrow a distinction as that between the learned audience and the populace, there is danger that the distinction will seem relatively empty and that one of the two subjects will begin to appear nonessential. This danger was not acute in ancient Greece and Rome, where democratic political institutions and unhampered philosophical debate made rhetoric and logic necessary disciplines in the educational system. But later societies in Western Europe went through a long period of empire and monarchy, during which rhetoric and logic flourished as instruments inherited from the past, although the actual need for the functions discharged by rhetoric was not as pressing as was the need for ability in disputation and learned controversy.[8] Thus rhetoric occupied a somewhat uneasy position in the trivium during the Middle Ages, as grammar and logic were successively the dominant study.[9] It was partly to guarantee rhetoric a firmer standing in education and partly to prevent rhetoric and logic from repeating each other's doctrine that Ramus, as I said before, assigned the entire theory of invention and arrangement to logic and made rhetoric consist wholly of style and delivery. This reform tended to abandon the open emphasis upon the distinction between the learned and the popular audience and to substitute for it a more tangible means of differentiating logic and rhetoric. But neat and practical as it was, Ramism proves that rhetoric becomes a meaningless study unless it is sustained by its ancient concern for the popular audience, even as the Middle Ages show that rhetoric becomes the inferior discipline of communication in any society where the popular audience has no economic and political power.

Modern democratic society would appear to offer rhetoric a greater opportunity than she has had since ancient times; for the popular audience in a democracy is the true source of authority, and the learned community has great need for the technique of learned communication. Rhetoric has grasped that opportunity, so far as her concern for the

8 For a discussion of the effect of absolutism upon Roman eloquence of the early Empire, see Harry Caplan, "The Decay of Eloquence at Rome in the First Century," in *Studies in Speech and Drama in Honor of Alexander M. Drummond*, ed. Herbert A. Wichelns *et al.* (Ithaca, 1944), pp. 295–325.

9 See Charles Sears Baldwin, *Medieval Rhetoric and Poetic* (New York, 1928), p. 151.

popular audience goes. Departments of rhetoric and speech are the focus of study of the ways and means by which the modern speaker reaches the people. But rhetoric has not made much of a show in supplying a theory of learned communication that can compare with Renaissance dialectic. Where, for example, is there an attempt in modern rhetoric to provide a common vocabulary in which the learned men in one field can communicate with the learned men in another? Renaissance dialectic fashioned such a vocabulary from the ten categories of Aristotle and from the ten places of Ramus. Perhaps those vocabularies have completely lost their power to serve modern science. Still, a study of the circle of modern learning might reveal that the barriers between one specialized knowledge and another could be broken down by the use of certain common learned concepts. It would require great scholarship to develop those concepts, and great scholarship is one of the challenges that modern rhetoric has not met. Inspiration might come from the reflection that Aristotle developed his categories from a study of the circle of learning of his time and that a similar enterprise might be undertaken today, perhaps not by one individual scholar, but certainly by an interested group of specialists. Added inspiration might also come from our modern conviction that, unless our learned men can be taught to speak to each other and to the people, we shall create on the one hand a set of Balkanized knowledges and on the other a schism between the people and the intellectual classes. That sort of schism will make the demagogue our master, even as a Balkanized learning will destroy the unity of our culture and the meaning of our spiritual life.

IV

A third great change in the theory of communication since the Renaissance concerns what I have been calling invention. To people untrained in the history of rhetoric, invention means either a mechanical device for the saving of labor or the act of discovering something new. In a contemptuous view of rhetoric, invention often means a falsehood, a deceit, an irresponsible utterance, a cynical departure from the truth for purposes of fraud. But invention to the rhetorical scholar means the devising of subject matter for a particular speech and, by extension, the providing of content in discourse. Lest this definition sound as if subject matter comes only from the speaker's mind, and not from the external realities of his environment, it should be emphasized that subject matter comes from external realities as seen and interpreted by the speaker and thus is not on the one hand the result of his fancy nor on the other the mere equivalent of bare facts. Inventional theory conceived in these terms has greatly changed since the Renaissance.

Perhaps the best way to describe this change is to say that nowadays rhetoric in the quest for a theory of subject matter emphasizes external realities somewhat more than mental interpretation, whereas in the Renaissance, and for a thousand years before, mental interpretation was emphasized somewhat more, at times considerably more, than external realities.

Mental interpretation in the ancient scheme consisted in taking the basic facts in a given case and subjecting them to an armchair examination that had three main phases. The first phase supplied large elements of the speaker's actual arguments, and while in this phase he classified his case in relation to its standing or position in the world of cases. The world of cases was made up of positions of fact, of definition, of quality, and of procedure, according to the youthful Cicero's *De Inventione;* and these four positions were supplemented by five others that applied only to disputes involving written documents.[10] The second main phase of invention supplied materials for the ethical aspects of a discourse. These were found when the speaker classified his common speech in relation to its kind in the world of speeches, there being three kinds, the deliberative, the forensic, and the epideictic, to which were respectively attached the ethical considerations of advantage, justice, and honor.[11] The third main phase of invention supplied materials for the structural parts of discourse, so far as these parts had not been stocked by the two other phases. Cicero listed these parts as six in number: the exordium, the narration, the division, proof, refutation, conclusion. These six parts required various kinds of content, which Cicero describes at length.[12]

A similar explanation of the three main phases of rhetorical invention appeared in Thomas Wilson's *The Arte of Rhetrique* in 1553. In fact, Wilson used Cicero's *De Inventione* as one source of his treatment of invention, although the anonymous *Rhetorica ad Herennium,* which is almost as ancient as *De Inventione* and had for centuries been attributed to Cicero, was Wilson's more important source.[13] Now it must be

[10] *De Inventione,* 1. 8. 10–18; 2. 4–51.
[11] *Ibid.,* 1. 5. 7; 2. 4. 12; 2. 51–59.
[12] *Ibid.,* 1. 14–56.
[13] Russell Halderman Wagner, "Wilson and his Sources," *QJS,* XV (1929), 530–532. For an excellent discussion of the date, authorship, sources, and organization of the *Rhetorica ad Herennium* and its relation to *De Inventione,* see Harry Caplan, trans., *Ad C. Herennium de Ratione Dicendi* (Loeb Classical Library; Cambridge, Mass., and London, 1954), pp. vii–xxxiv.

conceded that *De Inventione* and the *Rhetorica ad Herennium* do not treat all details of inventional theory in the same way, but the differences between them are less significant historically than the similarities, and thus Wilson's special dependence upon the *Rhetorica ad Herennium* does not mean that he departs in any major way from the three phases just outlined.

Since Wilson's day, thanks to the influence of Bacon and Descartes, man has tended more and more to believe that his most important deliberations must be conducted in the light of all the particular facts that bear upon them. No longer does he feel that he can draw predominantly from common sense, general reason, or the wisdom that rests largely upon deductions from analogous past experience. When Descartes abandoned his belief in tradition and custom and decided to reconstitute his knowledge in terms of the direct observation of the great book of the world,[14] he not only took a decisive step toward the creation of modern science, but he also represented in his own personal life the change that was coming over the whole intellectual life of Europe. And that change was too vast to leave rhetoric unaffected.

The modern speaker may be said to approach the problem of content by undertaking to study as many of the facts as he can possibly locate. "The really difficult problem in the preparation of the case," says a distinguished twentieth-century advocate, "is to learn what the facts are, and no matter how long or conscientiously you work, you will never know them all." He adds:

> The law seldom decides the issue, the facts do; and as contrasted with the ascertainment of the facts, the law is relatively easy to discover. There are a hundred good researchers of the law to one who has a genius, I may say a nose, for the discovery of the true facts.[15]

Later, when this same advocate is discussing the modern lawyer's closing speech to the jury, he likens the preparation of that speech to the preparation of a learned book:

> The trial, for the lawyer, is what research is for the author. Histories and biographies, letters, memoirs, diaries, and the archives of great libraries are the material from which a book is made. The evidence, documents, and the demeanor of the witnesses are the stuff from which the advocate's summation must be constructed.[16]

[14] Gilson's ed., p. 51.
[15] Lloyd Paul Stryker, *The Art of Advocacy* (New York, 1954), p. 11.
[16] *Ibid.*, pp. 113–114.

These views emphasize that the modern speaker, whether in the law court or on the political platform, speaks less from the old method of armchair analysis than from the method of research into the realities of his case. Like Burke advocating conciliation with America, the modern speaker allows his speech to refer extensively and minutely to such concrete realities as population figures, trade statistics, and the amount of income from agriculture and fisheries. Like Webster answering Hayne, the modern speaker feels called upon to deal with such complex matters as the history of the federal land question, the tariff, consolidation of powers, internal improvements, and the issue of nullification. Like Lincoln at Cooper Union, he analyzes minutely such biographical and historical considerations as those relating to the individual attitudes of the constitutional Fathers toward slavery in the federal territories. Like Churchill in 1940, he discusses such facts as present military losses and gains on land, on the sea, and in the air. Today we consider such realities the building blocks of any serious and important speech, the grounds of any dependable induction; and our speakers, despite their frequent addiction to the trash and nonsense that clutter oratory no less than literature, adhere at their best to the principle that realities cannot be mastered except as speakers participate in the disciplines of the scholar and scientist.

In changing its predominant emphasis from mental interpretation to external realities, rhetorical invention has in our time simultaneously abandoned the historic distinction between artistic and nonartistic arguments. This distinction stemmed from Aristotle's *Rhetoric,* and upon it was based the concept of proof supplied by the classical system of invention as opposed to proof supplied by other means. Says Aristotle:

> Of the modes of persuasion some belong strictly to the art of rhetoric and some do not. By the latter I mean such things as are not supplied by the speaker but are there at the outset—witnesses, evidence given under torture, written contracts, and so on. By the former I mean such as we can ourselves construct by means of the principles of rhetoric. The one kind has merely to be used, the other has to be invented.[17]

It is doubtful that Aristotle meant this distinction to be as heavy a commitment to mental interpretation, and as light a commitment to external realities, as later classical rhetoricians assumed. In one of the most

[17] *Rhetorica,* 1355[b] 36 ff., trans. W. Rhys Roberts, in *The Works of Aristotle,* ed. W. D. Ross (Oxford, 1924), vol. XI.

important chapters of the second book of his *Rhetoric* he lays great emphasis upon facts as the starting point for the construction of arguments on any subject.[18] But, even so, the passage just quoted seemed to identify external realities with nonartistic arguments and to put them both beyond the pale of the principles of rhetoric. Today the emphasis is almost exactly the reverse. The same external realities that have become the focus of scientific investigation claim the center of interest in the modern concept of rhetorical invention, while mental interpretation is accepted as the means of making those realities humanly important and of deciding how best to present and use them.

V

Still another change in the theory of communication since the Renaissance concerns the method of arranging ideas for public presentation. In this field, the change has been one in which complicated structures have been abandoned and simpler structures adopted.

If we were to wake up tomorrow in the England of 1625 and were interested in studying what that period thought of the problem of organizing discourses, we would find that two distinct practices were then in evidence.

One practice, which was applied to what I have been calling learned discourses, required such communications to be organized either in an ascending or a descending order of generality. The ascending order, called the compositive, required an author to proceed from the smallest units of a subject to the whole, as when a treatise on logic would treat first of words, then of propositions, and finally of syllogisms and arguments. The descending order, called the resolutive, required an author to proceed from the whole to smaller and smaller parts, until at length the indivisible units of the subject were reached.

The theory of learned presentation was not always treated in these two divisions by the logicians of the early seventeenth century. The Ramists, for example, believed that only the descending order was legitimate in the field of learned writing.[19] The Systematics believed in the ascending as well as the descending order, and occasionally one of them added a third method to these standard two.[20] Bacon, who did not belong to either of these schools, adhered to the theory that

---

[18] *Ibid.*, 1396^a–1396^b.
[19] For a discussion of this matter, see my *Logic and Rhetoric in England*, ch. 4.
[20] *Ibid.*, ch. 5.

learned discourse had two other major divisions, "whereof the one may be termed Magistral, and the other of Probation." [21] Bacon means his divisions to represent the difference between elementary, dogmatic exposition and something more inquiring and philosophical; and it must be admitted that this distinction, and his subsequent treatment of it, have greater range and caliber than did the standard distinction, although the latter was the more popular in its time.

The other practice of organizing discourses in the England of 1625 was applied to popular address, and it consisted in following the theory of the classical oration. Thus speakers were taught to arrange their ideas so that there was first an introduction, then a narration, and then a division or preview, these parts being forerunners of the proof, refutation, and conclusion. Cicero was, of course, the great authority behind this theory, although sixteenth-century England knew it also from Thomas Wilson's *The Arte of Rhetorique* and by 1625 from Thomas Vicar's *Manuductio ad Artem Rhetoricam* and Thomas Farnaby's popular *Index Rhetoricus*.

It is obvious that modern rhetoric advocates a simpler and more natural organization than that represented by Renaissance theory. Our learned discourses rarely adhere with regularity to an ascending or a descending pattern. Scholarship, history, biography, scientific exposition, organize themselves unobtrusively into sequences suggested by the relations of their units in space, time, logic, or causality. On many occasions serious arrangement appears to be in the class of things that an author must avoid, at least in outward apperance, as if the learned reader would be insulted by clarity of form, and the layman's delicate interest would not survive in the atmosphere of system and order.

As for our oratory, we organize it theoretically into fewer parts than did Cicero, and we strive in practice for the simplest possible structure. In fact, when Aristotle, long before Cicero, said that a speech needed to have only two parts, the statement and argument, to which on occasion the speaker might want to add an introduction and an epilogue, but no other divisions,[22] he was closer to our current practice than the Roman or medieval rhetoricians are. And why? Perhaps because his times were much like ours in preferring subject matter to form, inquiry to communication, individuality to convention, and democratic procedures to authoritarian rituals. At any rate, it cannot be denied that we have moved away from the ceremonial organization advocated by Cicero toward the simpler theory of Aristotle.

[21] *Works of Bacon*, VI, 289.
[22] *Rhetorica*, 1414^a–1414^b.

VI

The fifth, and for my present purposes the final, change that has come over rhetoric since the Renaissance concerns the theory of style. Style is often conceived as the dress our thoughts wear when they have been made ready to appear in good society. "Elocution," said Thomas Wilson, "getteth words to set forth inuention, and with such beautie commendeth the matter, that reason semeth to be clad in Purple, walking afore both bare and naked." [23] We may elaborate this image a bit and say that the great change in the theory of rhetorical style since Wilson's day has been a change from the convention of imperial dress to the convention of the business suit.

In the sixteenth century rhetorical style was largely, sometimes exclusively, taught in terms of tropes and schemes.[24] Tropes were what we call today figures of speech, including such devices as metaphor, synecdoche, metonymy, irony, and allegory. Schemes were unusual arrangements of language. Thus language arranged in rhymed verses was one sort of scheme, called in Latin *similiter desinens* and in English *like-ending*. Other typical schemes involved saying the same thing in many different ways (*expolitio*), dividing a whole into parts (*partitio*), and changing suddenly from the third person to the second in order to speak as if directly to a person or thing (apostrophe). The list of schemes and tropes was long in sixteenth-century textbooks, as English schoolboys knew to their dismay.[25]

The theory behind tropes and schemes was that men have one language for ordinary intercourse and another for formal communication, and that the latter differs from the former by employing tropes and schemes throughout. Englishmen of the Renaissance did not believe the language of ordinary life to be suitable for formal discourse. They believed instead that formal discourse must be deliberately contrived to appear systematically unlike the language of ordinary life. The contrivances by which ordinary speech was transformed into proper oratorical or poetical speech were what the Renaissance understood tropes and schemes to be.

We all know that in present-day American education students no longer memorize tropes and schemes, nor do they use them as the

[23] George Herbert Mair, ed., *Wilson's Arte of Rhetorique 1560* ([Oxford], 1909), p. 160.
[24] See my *Logic and Rhetoric in England*, ch. 3.
[25] Henry Peacham's *The Garden of Eloquence* (London, 1577, 1593) is one of the most complete of these lists. For a recent edition of this work, see William G. Crane's facsimile reproduction (Gainesville, Fla., 1954).

official public language. Students are taught instead to speak a public language that corresponds to the best elements of the language of ordinary intercourse. Such public language is not unlike the poetic idiom identified by Wordworth as "a selection of language really used by men." [26] Incidentally, Wordsworth's great contribution to English poetry has often been described as that in which poetry abandoned the stylistic conventions of the eighteenth century and learned to express itself the speech of ordinary life. What could also be emphasized, however, is that Wordsworth's reforms in poetry were part of a great trend, begun in the Renaissance and constantly in evidence since, away from a contrived literary language and toward the idioms of everyday speech.

The tendency of modern rhetoric to recommend the speech of ordinary life as opposed to the artful and elaborate speech of the courtier reflects the change that has occurred since the Renaissance as political power and economic influence have been transferred from the aristocrat to the commoner. When the aristocrat was the final source of both of these forms of authority, ordinary language did not serve a decisive political or economic purpose, and tropes and schemes, as the antitheses of that language, were the preferred means of communication. But when the commoner became politically powerful, and wealth began to center in his commercial enterprises rather than as before in the aristocrats' estates, the tropes and the schemes passed into history, except as a way of expressing emotional overtones of meaning, while the idiom of ordinary life, purified of its ordinary defects, assumed a new and growing importance. In support of this same trend, the new science found the fashions of aristocratic speech unsuited to the expression of scientific subject matter and unresponsive to the expectations of those seeking intellectual, humanitarian, or commercial profit from the publication of experiments and discoveries. Small wonder, then, that the scientists of the seventeenth century evolved their new vocabulary from "the language of Artizans, Countrymen, and Merchants, before that, of Wits, or Scholars." [27] Thus did the scientific, the economic, and the political forces in the pattern of Western European culture conspire to produce for the twentieth century a

[26] In his celebrated "Preface to the Second Edition of Several of the Foregoing Poems, Published, with an Additional Volume, under the title of 'Lyrical Ballads.'" See *The Complete Poetical Works of William Wordsworth*, ed. Andrew J. George (Boston and New York, [1904]), p. 791.

[27] See Thomas Sprat, *The History of the Royal-Society of London* (London, 1667), p. 113.

theory of rhetorical style quite different from that in vogue in the early Renaissance.

We should not say, however, that the rise of ordinary speech to a position of prominence in rhetorical style represents a gain for rhetoric, nor that the decline in the importance of tropes and figures represents a loss. What we should say is that ordinary speech as a medium of communication better reflects the needs of a businessman's culture and that the tropes and figures were better for a culture of landed aristocrats. It is the business of rhetoric to react to the situation in which it is used and to reflect in its theory the needs that it serves. Rhetoric does not deserve praise for evolving its present theory of rhetorical style, for that is not praiseworthy which is done as a matter of normal obligation. But rhetoric would deserve blame if it still sought to elevate tropes and figures into the exclusive language of public discourse. That sort of attitude would be in effect a declaration that a given set of means is of greater value than its presumed end—that the way in which a communication is phrased counts more heavily than does the possibility that it will not reach its audience.

VII

Other changes have taken place in the theory of rhetoric during the past four centuries. Some of them have come with the development of mass media of communication, some with the application of the concept of propaganda to the fields of commerce, public relations, and statecraft. Some have come as rhetoric has stated her problems in terms of the principles of modern psychology, some as means have been developed to explore the state of public opinion and to measure the effect of communications upon the audience. These changes are of course vitally important in the growth of modern rhetoric. I have not treated them here because the impulses which produced them have originated within the past half-century and thus cannot be said to have deep roots in the ancient world as well as in our own.

What I have tried to do here is to discuss five problems which rhetoric has faced in antiquity and in the period since the Renaissance; I have tried to indicate that the solutions of those problems have changed as needs have dictated. The emphasis upon the theory of communication during the Middle Ages gave rhetoric and her allied arts a central position in the academic curriculum. As a result of that emphasis, grammar, rhetoric, and logic shared the responsibility for teaching communication and intelligently divided that responsibility among them. Grammar became the study of the medium of communication, rhetoric and logic the study of the means of reaching the two types of audience. As emphasis has shifted from the theory of communication to the theory of inquiry, rhetoric has lost in certain directions but has held her own in others. She has lost her central position in the curriculum; she has lost her productive association with logic; and although she has extended her scope to include a concern for the learned audience, she has failed to develop for modern learning what ancient logic developed in its time—a vocabulary by which specialists in one field can communicate with specialists in other fields. Meanwhile, however, she has developed a theory of invention that fits modern requirements, and she has adapted herself to new conditions in respect to the theory of arrangement and style. Certainly her future will mean further change; and perhaps she can recover some of the ground she has lost in the last four hundred years, if she endeavors always to see her present problems in the light of her long and illustrious history.

SECTION III

MODERN DEVELOPMENTS IN RHETORIC

THE *PHAEDRUS* AND THE NATURE
OF RHETORIC
Richard M. Weaver

Our subject begins with the threshold difficulty of defining the question which Plato's *Phaedrus* was meant to answer. Students of this justly celebrated dialogue have felt uncertain of its unity of theme, and the tendency has been to designate it broadly as a discussion of the ethical and the beautiful. The explicit topics of the dialogue are, in order: love, the soul, speechmaking, and the spoken and written word, or what is generally termed by us "composition." The development looks random, and some of the most interesting passages appear *jeux d'esprit*. The richness of the literary art diverts attention from the substance of the argument.

But a work of art which touches on many profound problems justifies more than one kind of reading. Our difficulty with the *Phaedrus* may be that our interpretation has been too literal and too topical. If we will bring to the reading of it even a portion of that imagination which Plato habitually exercised, we should perceive surely enough that it is consistently, and from beginning to end, about one thing, which is the nature of rhetoric.[1] Again, that point may have been missed because most readers conceive rhetoric to be a system of artifice rather than an idea,[2] and the *Phaedrus*, for all its apparent divagation, keeps very close to a single idea. A study of its rhetorical structure, especially, may give us the insight which has been withheld, while making us feel anew that Plato possessed the deepest divining rod among the ancients.

For the imaginative interpretation which we shall now undertake, we have both general and specific warrant. First, it scarcely needs pointing out that a Socratic dialogue is in itself an example of transcendence. Beginning with something simple and topical, it passes to more general levels of application; and not infrequently, it must make

From *The Ethics of Rhetoric*, by Richard M. Weaver. Copyright © by Henry Regnery Company, Chicago, 1953. Reprinted by permission.
[1] Cf. A. E. Taylor, *Plato: the Man and his Work* (New York, 1936), p. 300.
[2] Cf. P. Albert Duhamel, "The Function of Rhetoric as Effective Expression," *Journal of the History of Ideas*, X, No. 3 (June, 1949), 344–56 *passim*.

the leap into allegory for the final utterance. This means, of course, that a Socratic dialogue may be about its subject implicity as well as explicitly. The implicit rendering is usually through some kind of figuration because it is the nature of this meaning to be ineffable in any other way. It is necessary, therefore, to be alert for what takes place through the analogical mode.

Second, it is a matter of curious interest that a warning against literal reading occurs at an early stage of the *Phaedrus*. Here in the opening pages, appearing as if to set the key of the theme, comes an allusion to the myth of Boreas and Oreithyia. On the very spot where the dialogue begins, Boreas is said to have carried off the maiden. Does Socrates believe that this tale is really true? Or is he in favor of a scientific explanation of what the myth alleges? Athens had scientific experts, and the scientific explanation was that the north wind had pushed her off some rocks where she was playing with a companion. In this way the poetical story is provided with a factual basis. The answer of Socrates is that many tales are open to this kind of rationalization, but that the result is tedious and actually irrelevant. It is irrelevant because our chief concern is with the nature of the man, and it is beside the point to probe into such matters while we are yet ignorant of ourselves. The scientific criticism of Greek mythology, which may be likened to the scientific criticism of the myths of the Bible in our own day, produces at best "a boorish sort of wisdom (ἀγροίκῳ τινὶ οοφίᾳ)." It is a limitation to suppose that the truth of the story lies in its historicity. The "boorish sort of wisdom" seeks to supplant poetic allegation with fact, just as an archaeologist might look for the foundations of the Garden of Eden. But while this sort of search goes on the truth flies off, on wings of imagination, and is not recoverable until the searcher attains a higher level of pursuit. Socrates is satisfied with the parable, and we infer from numerous other passages that he believed that some things are best told by parable and some perhaps discoverable only by parable. Real investigation goes forward with the help of analogy. "Freud without Sophocles is unthinkable," a modern writer has said.[3]

With these precepts in mind, we turn to that part of the *Phaedrus* which has proved most puzzling: why is so much said about the absurd relationship of the lover and the non-lover? Socrates encounters Phaedrus outside the city wall. The latter has just come from hearing a discourse by Lysias which enchanted him with its

---

[3] James Blish, "Rituals on Ezra Pound," *Sewanee Review*, LVIII (Spring, 1950), 223.

eloquence. He is prevailed upon to repeat this discourse, and the two seek out a shady spot on the banks of the Ilissus. Now the discourse is remarkable because although it was "in a way, a love speech," its argument was that people should grant favors to non-lovers rather than to lovers. "This is just the clever thing about it," Phaedrus remarks. People are in the habit of preferring their lovers, but it is much more intelligent, as the argument of Lysias runs, to prefer a non-lover. Accordingly, the first major topic of the dialogue is a eulogy of the non-lover. The speech provides good subject matter for jesting on the part of Socrates, and looks like another exhibition of the childlike ingeniousness which gives the Greeks their charm. Is it merely a piece of literary trifling? Rather, it is Plato's dramatistic presentation of a major thesis. Beneath the surface of repartee and mock seriousness, he is asking whether we ought to prefer a neuter form of speech to the kind which is ever getting us aroused over things and provoking an expense of spirit.

Sophistications of theory cannot obscure the truth that there are but three ways for language to affect us. It can move us toward what is good; it can move us toward what is evil; or it can, in hypothetical third place, fail to move us at all.[4] Of course there are numberless degrees of effect under the first two heads, and the third, as will be shown, is an approximate rather than an absolute zero of effect. But any utterance is a major assumption of responsibility, and the assumption that one can avoid that responsibility by doing something to language itself is one of the chief considerations of the *Phaedrus*, just as it is of contemporary semantic theory. What Plato has succeeded in doing in this dialogue, whether by a remarkably effaced design, or unconsciously through the formal pressure of his conception, is to give us embodiments of the three types of discourse. These are respectively the non-lover, the evil lover, and the noble lover. We shall take up these figures in their sequence and show their relevance to the problem of language.

The eulogy of the non-lover in the speech of Lysias, as we hear it repeated to Socrates, stresses the fact that the non-lover follows a policy of enlightened self-interest. First of all, the non-lover does not neglect his affairs or commit extreme acts under the influence of passion. Since he acts from calculation, he never has occasion for remorse. No one ever says of him that he is not in his right mind, because all of his acts are within prudential bounds. The first point

---

[4] The various aesthetic approaches to language offer refinements of perception, but all of them can be finally subsumed under the first head above.

is, in sum, that the non-lover never sacrifices himself and therefore never feels the vexation which overtakes lovers when they recover from their passion and try to balance their pains with their profit. And the non-lover is constant whereas the lover is inconstant. The first argument then is that the non-lover demonstrates his superiority through prudence and objectivity. The second point of superiority found in non-lovers is that there are many more of them. If one is limited in one's choice to one's lovers, the range is small; but as there are always more non-lovers than lovers, one has a better chance in choosing among many of finding something worthy of one's affection. A third point of superiority is that association with the non-lover does not excite public comment. If one is seen going about with the object of one's love, one is likely to provoke gossip; but when one is seen conversing with the non-lover, people merely realize that "everybody must converse with somebody." Therefore this kind of relationship does not affect one's public standing, and one is not disturbed by what the neighbors are saying. Finally, non-lovers are not jealous of one's associates. Accordingly they do not try to keep one from companions of intellect or wealth for fear that they may be outshone themselves. The lover, by contrast, tries to draw his beloved away from such companionship and so deprives him of improving associations. The argument is concluded with a generalization that one ought to grant favors not to the needy or the importunate, but to those who are able to repay. Such is the favorable account of the non-lover given by Lysias.

We must now observe how these points of superiority correspond to those of "semantically purified" speech. By "semantically purified speech" we mean the kind of speech approaching pure notation in the respect that it communicates abstract intelligence without impulsion. It is a simple instrumentality, showing no affection for the object of its symbolizing and incapable of inducing bias in the hearer. In its ideal conception, it would have less power to move than $2 + 2 = 4$, since it is generally admitted that mathematical equations may have the beauty of elegance, and hence are not above suspicion where beauty is suspect. But this neuter language will be an unqualified medium of transmission of meanings from mind to mind, and by virtue of its neutrality minds can remain in an unprejudiced relationship to the world and also to other minds.

Since the characteristic of this language is absence of anything like affection, it exhibits toward the thing being represented merely a sober fidelity, like that of the non-lover toward his companion. Instead of passion, it offers the serviceability of objectivity. Its "enlightened self-interest" takes the form of an unvarying accuracy and regularity in its symbolic references, most, if not all of which will be to verifiable data in the extramental world. Like a thrifty burgher, it has no romanticism about it; and it distrusts any departure from the literal and prosaic. The burgher has his feet on the ground; and similarly the language of pure notation has its point-by-point contact with objective reality. As Stuart Chase, one of its modern proponents, says in *The Tyranny of Words*: "*If we wish to understand the world and ourselves, it follows that we should use a language whose structure corresponds to physical structure*"[5] (italics his). So this language is married to the world, and its marital fidelity contrasts with the extravagances of other languages.

In second place, this language is far more "available." Whereas rhetorical language, or language which would persuade, must always be particularized to suit the occasion, drawing its effectiveness from many small nuances, a "utility" language is very general and one has no difficulty putting his meaning into it if he is satisfied with a paraphrase of that meaning. The 850 words recommended for Basic English, for example, are highly available in the sense that all native users of English have them instantly ready and learners of English can quickly acquire them. It soon becomes apparent, however, that the availability is a heavy tax upon all other qualities. Most of what we admire as energy and fullness tends to disappear when mere verbal counters are used. The conventional or public aspect of language can encroach upon the suggestive or symbolical aspect, until the naming is vague or blurred. In proportion as the medium is conventional in the widest sense and avoids all individualizing, personalizing, and heightening terms, it is common, and the commonness constitutes the negative virtue ascribed to the non-lover.

Finally, with reference to the third qualification of the non-lover, it is true that neuter language does not excite public opinion. This

---

[5] *The Tyranny of Words* (New York, 1938), p. 80. T. H. Huxley in *Lay Sermons* (New York, 1883), p. 112, outlined a noticeably similar ideal of scientific communication: "Therefore, the great business of the scientific teacher is, to imprint the fundamental, irrefragable facts of his science, not only by words upon the mind, but by sensible impressions upon the eye, and ear, and touch of the student in so complete a manner, that every term used, or law enunciated should afterwards call up vivid images of the particular structural, or other, facts which furnished the demonstration of the law, or illustration of the term."

fact follows from its character outlined above. Rhetorical language on
the other hand, for whatever purpose used, excites interest and with
it either pleasure or alarm. People listen instinctively to the man whose
speech betrays inclination. It does not matter what the inclination is
toward, but we may say that the greater the degree of inclination, the
greater the curiosity or response. Hence a "style" in speech always
causes one to be a marked man, and the public may not be so much
impressed—at least initially—by what the man is for or against as by
the fact that he has a style. The way therefore to avoid public comment is to avoid the speech of affection and to use that of business,
since, to echo the original proposition of Lysias, everybody knows
that one must do business with others. From another standpoint,
then, this is the language of prudence. These are the features which
give neuter discourse an appeal to those who expect a scientific solution of human problems.

In summing up the trend of meaning, we note that Lysias has been
praising a disinterested kind of relationship which avoids all excesses
and irrationalities, all the dementia of love. It is a circumspect kind
of relationship, which is preferred by all men who wish to do well in
the world and avoid tempestuous courses. We have compared its
detachment with the kind of abstraction to be found in scientific
notation. But as an earnest of what is to come let us note, in taking
leave of this part, that Phaedrus expresses admiration for the eloquence, especially of diction, with which the suit of the non-lover has
been urged. This is our warning of the dilemma of the non-lover.

Now we turn to the second major speech of the dialogue, which is
made by Socrates. Notwithstanding Phaedrus' enthusiastic praise,
Socrates is dissatisfied with the speech of the non-lover. He remembers
having heard wiser things on the subject and feels that he can make
a speech on the same theme "different from this and quite as good."
After some playful exchange, Socrates launches upon his own abuse of
love, which centers on the point that the lover is an exploiter. Love
($\xi \varrho \omega \varsigma$) is defined as the kind of desire which overcomes rational opinion and moves toward the enjoyment of personal or bodily beauty.
The lover wishes to make the object of his passion as pleasing to himself as possible; but to those possessed by this frenzy, only that which
is subject to their will is pleasant. Accordingly, everything which is
opposed, or is equal or better, the lover views with hostility. He
naturally therefore tries to make the beloved inferior to himself in
every respect. He is pleased if the beloved has intellectual limitations

because they have the effect of making him manageable. For a similar reason he tries to keep him away from all influences which might "make a man of him," and of course the greatest of these is divine philosophy. While he is working to keep him intellectually immature, he works also to keep him weak and effeminate, with such harmful result that the beloved is unable to play a man's part in crises. The lover is, moreover, jealous of the possession of property because this gives the beloved an independence which he does not wish him to have. Thus the lover in exercising an unremitting compulsion over the beloved deprives him of all praiseworthy qualities, and this is the price the beloved pays for accepting a lover who is "necessarily without reason." In brief, the lover is not motivated by benevolence toward the beloved, but by selfish appetite; and Socrates can aptly close with the quotation: "As wolves love lambs, so lovers love their loves." The speech is on the single theme of exploitation. It is important for us to keep in mind the object of love as here described, because another kind of love with a different object is later introduced into the dialogue, and we shall discuss the counterpart of each.

As we look now for the parallel in language, we find ourselves confronting the second of the three alternatives: speech which influences us in the direction of what is evil. This we shall call base rhetoric because its end is the exploitation which Socrates has been condemning. We find that base rhetoric hates that which is opposed, or is equal or better because all such things are impediments to its will, and in the last analysis it knows only its will. Truth is the stubborn, objective restraint which this will endeavors to overcome. Base rhetoric is therefore always trying to keep its objects from the support which personal courage, noble associations, and divine philosophy provide a man.

The base rhetorician, we may say, is a man who has yielded to the wrong aspects of existence. He has allowed himself to succumb to the sights and shows, to the physical pleasures which conspire against noble life. He knows that the only way he can get a following in his pursuits (and a following seems necessary to maximum enjoyment of the pursuits) is to work against the true understanding of his followers. Consequently the things which would elevate he keeps out of sight, and the things with which he surrounds his "beloved" are those which minister immediately to desire. The beloved is thus emasculated in understanding in order that the lover may have his way. Or as Socrates expresses it, the selfish lover contrives things so that the beloved will be "most agreeable to him and most harmful to himself."

Examples of this kind of contrivance occur on every hand in the impassioned language of journalism and political pleading. In the world of affairs which these seek to influence, the many are kept in a state of pupillage so that they will be most docile to their "lovers." The techniques of the base lover, especially as exemplified in modern journalism, would make a long catalogue, but in general it is accurate to say that he seeks to keep the understanding in a passive state by never permitting an honest examination of alternatives. Nothing is more feared by him than a true dialectic, for this not only endangers his favored alternative, but also gives the "beloved"—how clearly here are these the "lambs" of Socrates' figure—some training in intellectual independence. What he does therefore is dress up one alternative in all the cheap finery of immediate hopes and fears, knowing that if he can thus prevent a masculine exercise of imagination and will, he can have his way. By discussing only one side of an issue, by mentioning cause without consequence or consequence without cause, acts without agents or agents without agency,[6] he often successfully blocks definition and cause-and-effect reasoning. In this way his choices are arrayed in such meretricious images that one can quickly infer the juvenile mind which they would attract. Of course the base rhetorician today, with his vastly augmented power of propagation, has means of deluding which no ancient rhetor in forum or market place could have imagined.

Because Socrates has now made a speech against love, representing it as an evil, the non-lover seems to survive in estimation. We observe, however, that the non-lover, instead of being celebrated, is disposed of dialectically. "So, in a word, I say that the non-lover possesses all the advantages that are opposed to the disadvantages we found in the lover." This is not without bearing upon the subject matter of the important third speech, to which we now turn.

At this point in the dialogue, Socrates is warned by his monitory spirit that he has been engaging in a defamation of love despite the fact that love is a divinity. "If love is, as indeed he is, a god or something divine, he can be nothing evil; but the two speeches just now said that he was evil." These discourses were then an impiety—one representing non-love as admirable and the other attacking love as base. Socrates resolves to make amends, and the recantation which

[6] That is, by mentioning only parts of the total situation.

follows is one of the most elaborate developments in the Platonic system. The account of love which emerges from this new position may be summarized as follows.

Love is often censured as a form of madness, yet not all madness is evil. There is a madness which is simple degeneracy, but on the other hand there are kinds of madness which are really forms of inspiration, from which come the greatest gifts conferred on man. Prophecy is a kind of madness, and so too is poetry. "The poetry of the sane man vanishes into nothingness before that of the inspired madman." Mere sanity, which is of human origin, is inferior to that madness which is inspired by the gods and which is a condition for the highest kind of achievement. In this category goes the madness of the true lover. His is a generous state which confers blessings to the ignoring of self, whereas the conduct of the non-lover displays all the selfishness of business: "the affection of the non-lover, which is alloyed with mortal prudence and follows mortal and parsimonious rules of conduct will beget in the beloved soul the narrowness which common folk praise as virtue; it will cause the soul to be a wanderer upon the earth for nine thousand years and a fool below the earth at last." It is the vulgar who do not realize that the madness of the noble lover is an inspired madness because he has his thoughts turned toward a beauty of divine origin.

Now the attitude of the noble lover toward the beloved is in direct contrast with that of the evil lover, who, as we have seen, strives to possess and victimize the object of his affections. For once the noble lover has mastered the conflict within his own soul by conquering appetite, and fixing his attention upon the intelligible and the divine, he conceives an exalted attitude toward the beloved. The noble lover now "follows the beloved in reverence and awe." So those who are filled with this kind of love "exhibit no jealousy or meanness toward the loved one, but endeavor by every means in their power to lead him to the likeness of the god whom they honor." Such is the conversion by which love turns from the exploitative to the creative.

Here it becomes necessary to bring our concepts together and to think of all speech having persuasive power as a kind of "love." [7] Thus, rhetorical speech is madness to the extent that it departs from the line which mere sanity lays down. There is always in its statement a kind of excess or deficiency which is immediately discernible when the

---

[7] It is worth recalling that in the Christian New Testament, with its heavy Platonic influence, God is identified both with *logos*, "word, speech" (*John* 1:1); and with *agape*, "love" (2 *John* 4:8).

test of simple realism is applied. Simple realism operates on a principle of equation or correspondence; one thing must match another, or, representation must tally with thing represented, like items in a tradesman's account. Any excess or deficiency on the part of the representation invokes the existence of the world of symbolism, which simple realism must deny. This explains why there is an immortal feud between men of business and the users of metaphor and metonymy, the poets and the rhetoricians.[8] The man of business, the narrow and parsimonious soul in the allusion of Socrates, desires a world which is a reliable materiality. But this the poet and rhetorician will never let him have, for each, with his own purpose, is trying to advance the borders of the imaginative world. A primrose by the river's brim will not remain that in the poet's account, but is promptly turned into something very much larger and something highly implicative. He who is accustomed to record the world with an abacus cannot follow these transfigurations; and indeed the very occurrence of them subtly undermines the premise of his business. It is the historic tendency of the tradesman, therefore, to confine passion to quite narrow channels so that it will not upset the decent business arrangements of the world. But if the poet, as the chief transformer of our picture of the world, is the peculiar enemy of this mentality, the rhetorician is also hostile when practicing the kind of love proper to him. The "passion" in his speech is revolutionary, and it has a practical end.

We have now indicated the significance of the three types of lovers; but the remainder of the *Phaedrus* has much more to say about the the nature of rhetoric, and we must return to one or more points to place our subject in a wider context. The problem of rhetoric which occupied Plato persistently, not only in the *Phaedrus* but also in other dialogues where this art is reviewed, may be best stated as a question: if truth alone is not sufficient to persuade men, what else remains that can be legitimately added? In one of the exchanges with Phaedrus, Socrates puts the question in the mouth of a personified Rhetoric: "I do not compel anyone to learn to speak without knowing the truth, but if my advice is of any value, he learns that first and then acquires me. So what I claim is this, that without my help the knowledge of the truth does not give the art of persuasion."

Now rhetoric as we have discussed it in relation to the lovers consists of truth plus its artful presentation, and for this reason it becomes necessary to say something more about the natural order of dialectic

---

[8] The users of metaphor and metonymy who are in the hire of businessmen of course constitute a special case.

and rhetoric. In any general characterization rhetoric will include dialectic,[9] but for the study of method it is necessary to separate the two. Dialectic is a method of investigation whose object is the establishment of truth about doubtful propositions. Aristotle in the *Topics* gives a concise statement of its nature. "A dialectical problem is a subject of inquiry that contributes either to choice or avoidance, or to truth and knowledge, and that either by itself, or as a help to the solution of some other such problem. It must, moreover, be something on which either people hold no opinion either way, or the masses hold a contrary opinion to the philosophers, or the philosophers to the masses, or each of them among themselves." [10] Plato is not perfectly clear about the distinction between positive and dialectical terms. In one passage [11] he contrasts the "positive" terms "iron" and "silver" with the "dialectical" terms "justice" and goodness"; yet in other passages his "dialectical" terms seem to include categorizations of the external world. Thus Socrates indicates that distinguishing the horse from the ass is a dialectical operation; [12] and he tells us later that a good dialectician is able to divide things by classes "where the natural joints are" and will avoid breaking any part "after the manner of a bad carver." [13] Such, perhaps, is Aristotle's dialectic which contributes to truth and knowledge.

But there is a branch of dialectic which contributes to "choice or avoidance," and it is with this that rhetoric is regularly found joined. Generally speaking, this is a rhetoric involving questions of policy, and the dialectic which precedes it will determine not the application of positive terms but that of terms which are subject to the contingency of evaluation. Here dialectical inquiry will concern itself not with what is "iron" but with what is "good." It seeks to establish what belongs in the category of the "just" rather than what belongs in the genus *Canis*. As a general rule, simple object words such as "iron" and "house" have no connotations of policy, although it is frequently possible to give them these through speech situations in which there is

---

[9] Cf. 277 b: "A man must know the truth about all the particular things of which he speaks or writes, and must be able to define everything separately; then when he has defined them, he must know how to divide them by classes until further division is impossible; and in the same way he must understand the nature of the soul, must find out the class of speech adapted to each nature, and must arrange and adorn his discourse accordingly, offering to the complex soul elaborate and harmonious discourses, and simple talks to the simple soul."
[10] 104 b.
[11] 263 a.
[12] 260 b.
[13] 265 a.

added to their referential function a kind of impulse. We should have
to interpret in this way "Fire!" or "Gold!" because these terms acquire
something through intonation and relationship which places them in
the class of evaluative expressions.

Any piece of persuasion, therefore, will contain as its first process
a dialectic establishing terms which have to do with policy. Now a
term of policy is essentially a term of motion, and here begins the
congruence of rhetoric with the soul which underlies the speculation
of the *Phaedrus*. In his myth of the charioteer, Socrates declares that
every soul is immortal because "that which is ever moving is immortal."
Motion, it would appear from this definition, is part of the soul's
essence. And just because the soul is ever tending, positive or indifferent terms cannot partake of this congruence. But terms of tendency—
goodness, justice, divinity, and the like—are terms of motion and therefore may be said to comport with the soul's essence. The soul's perception of goodness, justice, and divinity will depend upon its proper
tendency, while at the same time contacts with these in discourse confirm and direct that tendency. The education of the soul is not a process
of bringing it into correspondence with a physical structure like the
external world, but rather a process of rightly affecting its motion.
By this conception, a soul which is rightly affected calls that good
which is good; but a soul which is wrongly turned calls that good
which is evil. What Plato has prepared us to see is that the virtuous
rhetorician, who is a lover of truth, has a soul of such movement
that its dialectical perceptions are consonant with those of a divine
mind. Or, in the language of more technical philosophy, this soul is
aware of axiological systems which have ontic status. The good soul,
consequently, will not urge a perversion of justice as justice in order
to impose upon the commonwealth. Insofar as the soul has its impulse
in the right direction, its definitions will agree with the true nature of
intelligible things.

There is, then, no true rhetoric without dialectic, for the dialectic
provides that basis of "high speculation about nature" without which
rhetoric in the narrower sense has nothing to work upon. Yet, when
the disputed terms have been established, we are at the limit of
dialectic. How does the noble rhetorician proceed from this point on?
That the clearest demonstration in terms of logical inclusion and exclusion often fails to win assent we hardly need state; therefore, to
what does the rhetorician resort at this critical passage? It is the
stage at which he passes from the logical to the analogical, or it is
where figuration comes into rhetoric.

To look at this for a moment through a practical illustration, let us suppose that a speaker has convinced his listeners that his position is "true" as far as dialectical inquiry may be pushed. Now he sets about moving the listeners toward that position, but there is no way to move them except through the operation of analogy. The analogy proceeds by showing that the position being urged resembles or partakes of something greater and finer. It will be represented, in sum, as one of the steps leading toward ultimate good. Let us further suppose our speaker to be arguing for the payment of a just debt. The payment of the just debt is not itself justice, but the payment of this particular debt is one of the many things which would have to be done before this could be a completely just world. It is just, then, because it partakes of the ideal justice, or it is a small analogue of all justice (in practice it will be found that the rhetorician makes extensive use of synecdoche, whereby the small part is used as a vivid suggestion of the grandeur of the whole). It is by bringing out these resemblances that the good rhetorician leads those who listen in the direction of what is good. In effect, he performs a cure of souls by giving impulse, chiefly through figuration, toward an ideal good.

We now see the true rhetorician as a noble lover of the good, who works through dialectic and through poetic or analogical association. However he is compelled to modulate by the peculiar features of an occasion, this is his method.

It may not be superfluous to draw attention to the fact that what we have here outlined is the method of the *Phaedrus* itself. The dialectic appears in the dispute about love. The current thesis that love is praiseworthy is countered by the antithesis that love is blameworthy. This position is fully developed in the speech of Lysias and in the first speech of Socrates. But this position is countered by a new thesis that after all love is praiseworthy because it is a divine thing. Of course, this is love on a higher level, or love re-defined. This is the regular process of transcendence which we have noted before. Now, having rescued love from the imputation of evil by excluding certain things from its definition, what does Socrates do? Quite in accordance with our analysis, he turns rhetorician. He tries to make this love as attractive as possible by bringing in the splendid figure of the charioteer.[14] In the narrower conception of this art, the allegory is the rhetoric, for it excites and fills us with desire for this kind of love, depicted with many terms having tendency toward the good. But in the broader conception the art must include also the dialectic,

[14] In the passage extending from 246 a to 256 d.

which succeeded in placing love in the category of divine things before filling our imaginations with attributes of divinity.[15] It is so regularly the method of Plato to follow a subtle analysis with a striking myth that it is not unreasonable to call him the master rhetorician. This goes far to explain why those who reject his philosophy sometimes remark his literary art with mingled admiration and annoyance.

The objection sometimes made that rhetoric cannot be used by a lover of truth because it indulges in "exaggerations" can be answered as follows. There is an exaggeration which is mere wantonness, and with this the true rhetorician has nothing to do. Such exaggeration is purely impressionistic in aim. Like caricature, whose only object is to amuse, it seizes upon any trait or aspect which could produce titillation and exploits this without conscience. If all rhetoric were like this, we should have to grant that rhetoricians are persons of very low responsibility and their art a disreputable one. But the rhetorician we have now defined is not interested in sensationalism.

The exaggeration which this rhetorician employs is not caricature but prophecy; and it would be a fair formulation to say that true rhetoric is concerned with the potency of things. The literalist, like the anti-poet described earlier, is troubled by its failure to conform to a present reality. What he fails to appreciate is that potentiality is a mode of existence, and that all prophecy is about the tendency of things. The discourse of the noble rhetorician, accordingly, will be about real potentiality or possible actuality, whereas that of the mere exaggerator is about unreal potentiality. Naturally this distinction rests upon a supposal that the rhetorician has insight, and we could not defend him in the absence of that condition. But given insight, he has the duty to represent to us the as yet unactualized future. It would be, for example, a misrepresentation of current facts but not of potential ones to talk about the joys of peace in a time of war. During the Second World War, at the depth of Britain's political and military disaster, Winston Churchill likened the future of Europe to "broad sunlit uplands." Now if one had regard only for the hour, this was a piece of mendacity such as the worst charlatans are found committing; but if one took Churchill's premises and then considered the potentiality, the picture was within bounds of actualization. His "exaggeration" was that the defeat of the enemy would place Europe in a position for long and peaceful progress. At the time the surface trends ran the other way; the actuality was a valley of humiliation. Yet the

[15] Cf. 263 d ff.

hope which transfigured this to "broad sunlit uplands" was not irresponsible, and we conclude by saying that the rhetorician talks about both what exists simply and what exists by favor of human imagination and effort.[16]

This interest in actualization is a further distinction between pure dialectic and rhetoric. With its forecast of the actual possibility, rhetoric passes from mere scientific demonstration of an idea to its relation to prudential conduct. A dialectic must take place *in vacuo,* and the fact alone that it contains contraries leaves it an intellectual thing. Rhetoric, on the other hand, always espouses one of the contraries. This espousal is followed by some attempt at impingement upon actuality. That is why rhetoric, with its passion for the actual, is more complete than mere dialectic with its dry understanding. It is more complete on the premise than man is a creature of passion who must live out that passion in the world. Pure contemplation does not suffice for this end. As Jacques Maritain has expressed it: "love . . . is not directed at possibilities or pure essences; it is directed at what exists; one does not love possibilities, one loves that which exists or is destined to exist." [17] The complete man, then, is the "lover" added to the scientist; the rhetorician to the dialectician. Understanding followed by actualization seems to be the order of creation, and there is no need for the role of rhetoric to be misconceived.

The pure dialectician is left in the theoretical position of the non-lover, who can attain understanding but who cannot add impulse to truth. We are compelled to say "theoretical position" because it is by no means certain that in the world of actual speech the non-lover has more than a putative existence. We have seen previously that his speech would consist of strictly referential words which would serve only as designata. Now the question arises: at what point is motive to

---

[16] Indeed, in this particular rhetorical duel we see the two types of lovers opposed as clearly as illustration could desire. More than this, we see the third type, the non-lover, committing his ignominious failure. Britain and France had come to prefer as leaders the rhetoricless businessman type. And while they had thus emasculated themselves, there appeared an evil lover to whom Europe all but succumbed before the mistake was seen and rectified. For while the world must move, evil rhetoric is of more force than no rhetoric at all; and Herr Hitler, employing images which rested on no true dialectic, had persuaded multitudes that his order was the "new order," *i.e.*, the true potentiality. Britain was losing and could only lose until, reaching back in her traditional past she found a voice which could match his accents with a truer grasp of the potentiality of things. Thus two men conspicuous for passion fought a contest for souls, which the nobler won. But the contest could have been lost by default.

[17] "Action: the Perfection of Human Life," *Sewanee Review,* LVI (Winter, 1948), 3.

come into such language? Kenneth Burke in *A Grammar of Motives* has pointed to "the pattern of embarrassment behind the contemporary ideal of a language that will best promote good action by entirely eliminating the element of exhortation or command. Insofar as such a project succeeded, its terms would involve a narrowing of circumference to a point where the principle of personal action is eliminated from language, so that an act would follow from it only as a non-sequitur, a kind of humanitarian after-thought." [18]

The fault of this conception of language is that scientific intention turns out to be enclosed in artistic intention and not *vice versa*. Let us test this by taking as an example one of those "fact-finding committees" so favored by modern representative governments. A language in which all else is suppressed in favor of nuclear meanings would be an ideal instrumentality for the report of such a committee. But this committee, if it lived up to the ideal of its conception, would have to be followed by an "attitude-finding committee" to tell us what its explorations really mean. In real practice the fact-finding committee understands well enough that it is also an attitude-finding committee, and where it cannot show inclination through language of tendency, it usually manages to do so through selection and arrangement of the otherwise inarticulate facts. To recur here to the original situation in the dialogue, we recall that the eloquent Lysias, posing as a non-lover, had concealed designs upon Phaedrus, so that his fine speech was really a sheep's clothing. Socrates discerned in him a "peculiar craftiness." One must suspect the same today of many who ask us to place our faith in the neutrality of their discourse. We cannot deny that there are degrees of objectivity in the reference of speech. But this is not the same as an assurance that a vocabulary of reduced meanings will solve the problems of mankind. Many of those problems will have to be handled, as Socrates well knew, by the student of souls, who must primarily make use of the language of tendency. The soul is impulse, not simply cognition; and finally one's interest in rhetoric depends on how much poignancy one senses in existence.[19]

[18] *A Grammar of Motives* (New York, 1945), p. 90.

[19] Without rhetoric there seems no possibility of tragedy, and in turn, without the sense of tragedy, no possibility of taking an elevated view of life. The role of tragedy is to keep the human lot from being rendered as history. The cultivation of tragedy and a deep interest in the value-conferring power of language always occur together. The *Phaedrus*, the *Gorgias*, and the *Cratylus*, not to mention the works of many teachers of rhetoric, appear at the close of the great age of Greek tragedy. The Elizabethan age teemed with treatises on the use of language.

Rhetoric moves the soul with a movement which cannot finally be justified logically. It can only be valued analogically with reference to some supreme image. Therefore when the rhetorician encounters some soul "sinking beneath the double load of forgetfulness and vice" he seeks to re-animate it by holding up to its sight the order of presumptive goods. This order is necessarily a hierarchy leading up to the ultimate good. All of the terms in a rhetorical vocabulary are like links in a chain stretching up to some master link which transmits its influence down through the linkages. It is impossible to talk about rhetoric as effective expression without having as a term giving intelligibility to the whole discourse, the Good. Of course, inferior concepts of the Good may be and often are placed in this ultimate position; and there is nothing to keep a base lover from inverting the proper order and saying, "Evil, be thou my good." Yet the fact remains that in any piece of rhetorical discourse, one rhetorical term overcomes another rhetorical term only by being nearer to the term which stands ultimate. There is some ground for calling a rhetorical education necessarily an aristocratic education in that the rhetorician has to deal with an aristocracy of notions, to say nothing of supplementing his logical and pathetic proofs with an ethical proof.

All things considered, rhetoric, noble or base, is a great power in the world; and we note accordingly that at the center of the public life of every people there is a fierce struggle over who shall control the means of rhetorical propagation. Today we set up "offices of information," which like the sly lover in the dialogue, pose as non-lovers while pushing their suits. But there is no reason to despair over the fact that men will never give up seeking to influence one another. We would not desire it to be otherwise; neuter discourse is a false idol, to worship which is to commit the very offense for which Socrates made expiation in his second speech.

Since we want not emancipation from impulse but clarification of impulse, the duty of rhetoric is to bring together action and understanding into a whole that is greater than scientific perception.[20] The

---

The essentially tragic Christian view of life begins the long tradition of homiletics. Tragedy and the practice of rhetoric seem to find common sustenance in preoccupation with value, and then rhetoric follows as an analyzed art.

[20] Cf. Maritain, *op. cit.*, pp. 3–4: "The truth of practical intellect is understood not as conformity to an extramental being but as conformity to a right desire; the end is no longer to know what is, but to bring into existence that which is not yet; further, the fact of moral choice is so individualized, both by the singularity of the person from which it proceeds and the context of the contingent circumstances in which it takes place, that the practical judgment in which it is

realization that just as no action is really indifferent, so no utterance is without its responsibility introduces, it is true, a certain strenuousity into life, produced by a consciousness that "nothing is lost." Yet this is preferable to that desolation which proceeds from an infinite dispersion or feeling of unaccountability. Even so, the choice between them is hardly ours to make; we did not create the order of things, but being accountable for our impulses, we wish these to be just.

Thus when we finally divest rhetoric of all the notions of artifice which have grown up around it, we are left with something very much like Spinoza's "intellectual love of God." This is its essence and the *fons et oigo* of its power. It is "intellectual" because, as we have previously seen, there is no honest rhetoric without a preceding dialectic. The kind of rhetoric which is justly condemned is utterance in support of a position before that position has been adjudicated with reference to the whole universe of discourse [21]—and of such the world always produces more than enough. It is "love" because it is something in addition to bare theoretical truth. That element in addition is a desire to bring truth into a kind of existence, or to give it an actuality to which theory is indifferent. Now what is to be said about our last expression, "of God"? Echoes of theological warfare will cause many to desire a substitute for this, and we should not object. As long as we have in ultimate place the highest good man can intuit, the relationship is made perfect. We shall be content with "intellectual love of the Good." It is still the intellectual love of good which causes the noble lover to desire not to devour his beloved but to shape him according to the gods as far as mortal power allows. So rhetoric at its truest seeks to perfect men by showing them better versions of themselves, links in that chain extending up toward the ideal, which only the intellect can apprehend and only the soul have affection for. This is the justified affection of which no one can be ashamed, and he who feels no influence of it is truly outside the communion of minds. Rhetoric appears, finally, as a means by which the impulse of the soul to be ever moving is redeemed.

It may be granted that in this essay we have gone some distance

---

expressed and by which I declare to myself: this is what I must do, can be right only if, *hic et nunc*, the dynamism of my will is right, and tends towards the true goods of human life.

That is why practical wisdom, *prudentia*, is a virtue indivisibly moral and intellectual at the same time, and why, like the judgment of the conscience itself, it cannot be replaced by any sort of theoretical knowledge or science."

[21] Socrates' criticism of the speech of Lysias (263 d ff.) is that the latter defended a position without having submitted it to the discipline of dialectic.

from the banks of the Ilissus. What began as a simple account of passion becomes by transcendence an allegory of all speech. No one would think of suggesting that Plato had in mind every application which has here been made, but that need not arise as an issue. The structure of the dialogue, the way in which the judgments about speech concentre, and especially the close association of the true, the beautiful, and the good, constitute a unity of implication. The central idea is that all speech, which is the means the gods have given man to express his soul, is a form of eros, in the proper interpretation of the word. With that truth the rhetorician will always be brought face to face as soon as he ventures beyond the consideration of mere artifice and device.

TOWARD AN AXIOLOGY OF RHETORIC
Ralph T. Eubanks and Virgil L. Baker

"What I relate," Nietzsche wrote near the close of the nineteenth century, "is the history of the next two centuries. I describe what is coming, what can no longer come differently: the advent of nihilism." [1] This passage is prescient when considered in the light of the deepening moral crisis of modern man, who finds it increasingly hard to accept his world as one of history and action and to distinguish and choose between better and worse. One of the most poignant truths of the present human situation is its axiological impotence. Introducing a recent symposium on human values, Abraham Maslow wrote: "The ultimate disease of our time is valuelessness." [2] More than a decade ago in a study of the moral decay of the West, Richard M. Weaver warned: "We approach a condition in which we shall be amoral without the capacity to perceive it and degraded without means to measure our descent." [3] Modern man's present state of anhedonia is, without question, "more crucially dangerous than ever before in history." [4] It

From *Quarterly Journal of Speech*, April, 1962. Reprinted with the permission of the Speech Association of America, and of the authors.
[1] Friedrich Nietzsche, *The Will to Power*, Preface.
[2] Abraham Maslow (ed.), *New Knowledge in Human Values* (New York, 1959), p. vii.
[3] Richard M. Weaver, *Ideas Have Consequences* (Chicago, 1948), p. 10.
[4] Maslow, p. vii.

may be his finest fortune not to have lost completely his power to perceive the extent of his moral affliction.

Multiplying signs show his deepening concern. New lines of research have been recently opened in the field of value theory; hopeful minds from diverse academic disciplines are searching for ways of helping twentieth-century man regain his axiological health.[5] We are inspired to believe that modern man may yet make—to use Arnold J. Toynbee's terms of cultural rise and fall—a corporate "response" to the "challenge" that faces him.

This epochal challenge holds special pertinence to liberal education in general and to rhetorical education in particular. Each derives its *raison d'etre* from its potential for helping man with the related questions of whether he shall be free of the forces that work to brutalize him and, if so, how he shall use his "burden of freedom." Both are thus centrally and persistently concerned with human values, here taken to mean universal concepts basic to civil decision and action. Human values are therefore the ultimate ground of human action; they are also a concomitant of human freedom. Since man can "transcend" through consciousness and objective situation of which he is a part, he can have a hand in shaping his destiny by the "exercise of choice based on values."[6] In a nutshell, man can have freedom only because he has a scheme of values; he is—as Joseph Wood Krutch called him— "The Animal Which Can Prefer."[7]

The tradition of liberal education has been one of deep involvement with the issue of how man may best use his freedom. Historically its mission has been to develop the whole man, to prepare men, in Milton's words, "to perform justly, skilfully, and magnanimously, all the offices, both private and public, of peace and war."[8] Yet ironically, when the "great society" most needs the help of liberal education in solving its problems of value, the liberal arts colleges are found to be in disintegration. They are boldly charged with having forsaken their mission. Writes one critic: "They have to a large extent abandoned their ancient and honorable task of training young people to live informed, intelli-

---

[5] In addition to Maslow, the following studies illustrate some of the new lines of investigation in value theory: Clyde Kluckhohn, *et al.*, "Values and Value-Orientations in the Theory of Action," in *Toward a General Theory of Action*, ed. Talcott Parsons and Edward A. Shils (Cambridge, Mass., 1951), pp. 388–433; Charles Morris, *Varieties of Human Value* (Chicago, 1956); Dewitt H. Parker, *The Philosophy of Value* (Ann Arbor, 1957); Otto von Mering, *A Grammar of Human Values* (Pittsburgh, 1961); and P. Sorokin (ed.), *Symposium: Forms and Techniques of Altruistic and Spiritual Growth* (Boston, 1954).

[6] Walter A. Weisskopf, "Existence and Values," in Maslow, pp. 108–109.

[7] Joseph Wood Krutch, *The Measure of Man* (New York, 1954), p. 172.

[8] John Milton, "Of Education."

gent, and integrated lives. They seem to have forgotten the admonition
of Montaigne that "the object of education is to make, not a scholar,
but a man.'" [9] Ironically too, the ideal teacher of the times appears
to be one whose work is animated by the spirit of determinism and
amorality. "For a half century," observes the president of Boston College, Michael Walsh, "educators have been avoiding the problems of
teaching values and *teachers have been priding themselves in their
ability to employ a rhetoric of non-commitment.*" [10] American liberal
education has thus neglected its crucial responsibility for transmitting
knowledge about and faith in abiding human values—for helping man
with the problem of what he will do with his freedom. "At this moment," declares Walsh, "when civilization seems faced with a choice
between survival and suicide, [the] responsibility to choose and to
declare the values upon which choice is to be based has never been
more terrifying or more immediate." [11]

Rhetoric has a vital relevance to the value illnesses of twentieth-
century man. Rhetoric is a dynamic force in the nurture of human
values, and that looks toward the amelioration of man's present state
of anhedonia. The basic meaning of rhetoric in the Western tradition,
as Duhamel notes, is "the discovery of and persuasion to right action." [12] And "right action" is central in man's value-world, for it places
before him the crucial question of how he shall use his freedom.
Behind the proposals and theses of public utterance are value propositions. In a sense, human values are fundamental in rhetoric. "It is
impossible," observes Richard M. Weaver in his analysis of Plato's
Phaedrus, "to talk about rhetoric as effective expression without having
as a term giving intelligibility to the whole discourse, the Good . . . . [13]
Rhetoric's essential preoccupation, then, is with abiding human values.
Richard Murphy declares pointedly: "The art of rhetoric is used to
express and activate principles we believe in, the substance of things
for which we live." [14] In a word, the central function of rhetoric is to
crystallize and transmit human values, the "what-fors" of a culture.

[9] Earl J. McGrath, *The Graduate School and the Decline of Liberal Education*
(New York, 1959), p. vi.
[10] Michael P. Walsh, S.J., "Values in Education," *Vital Speeches,* XXVI (June
15, 1960), 529. Italics supplied. Cf. discussion of the "modern abdication of
direct, responsible judgment" in Jacques Barzun, *The House of Intellect* (New
York, 1959), pp. 245 ff.
[11] Walsh, p. 529.
[12] P. Albert Duhamel, "The Function of Rhetoric as Effective Expression,"
Journal of the History of Ideas, X (June 1949), 356.
[13] Richard M. Weaver, *The Ethics of Rhetoric* (Chicago, 1953), p. 25.
[14] Richard Murphy, "Preface to an Ethic of Rhetoric," *The Rhetorical Idiom,*
ed. Donald C. Bryant (Ithaca, New York, 1958), p. 141.

Put another way, rhetoric is purposive speech about the human condition.

Yet contemporary rhetorical education, like liberal education, cannot be said to be discharging fully its responsibility in the realm of human values. We are painfully aware that teachers of public address do not always practice a rhetoric of commitment. Indeed, as Murphy suggests, some of them maintain the amorality of rhetoric, taking the ground that to discriminate among values may lead to their being labeled "propagandizers." [15] Similarly, rhetorical critics occasionally run out on their duty to examine and to pass judgment on a speaker's dialectical and axiological bearings. Barnet Baskerville, noting this slackness, has pointed out that such a critic offers "the excuse that truth is relative, that everyone is entitled to his own opinion, and that the rhetorical critic's task is to describe and evaluate the orator's skill in his craft and not to become entangled in complex ethical considerations." [16] What Baskerville describes is pseudo-criticism, which not only contributes to the dehumanization of rhetoric but also aggravates mankind's present condition of "valuelessness."

To make rhetoric a more potent power in generating "right action" it must be related *directly* to important human values. Rhetoric must become boldly axiological, seeking out and committing itself to a sound system of civilizing values. Only then can it move out of the world of "dis-value" and become a positive force for the amelioration of man's present condition of anhedonia. Only then can it become, in the fullest meaning of the term, a "rhetoric of commitment." Such a rhetoric will attain the humanizing function assigned to it in Bacon's analysis, of "applying reason to the imagination for the better moving of the will." [17]

Let us try to sketch the broad outlines for an axiological approach to rhetoric. First are presented the critical determinants, the rationale, for such an approach. Second is described a value analysis which may serve as a guide for the planning and conduct of rhetorical discourse. Finally, a set of empirical guides for the teaching of a rhetoric of values is described. Five terms are crucial and therefore need definition. The term *axiology* (from the Greek *axios*, meaning valuable) is used in its usual sense as the study of value phenomena. *Values*, generically defined, are conceptions of the desirable which shape human

[15] *Ibid.*, p. 129.
[16] Barnet Baskerville, "Emerson as a Critic of Oratory," *The Southern Speech Journal*, XVIII (December 1953), 404.
[17] *The Advancement of Learning*, Bk. 2, Sec. XVIII.

"action commitments." [18] *Rhetoric* means, comprehensively, "the rationale of informative and suasory discourse." [19] Abstracted from its functional phase, rhetoric also means tendentious speech having to do with man's symbolic universe of value. The term *Justice* is used to mean a social condition of equity fashioned from the commitment of individual persons to the classic ideals of liberty, equality, and fraternity under "a rule of law." *Democracy* refers to any social order which creates and fosters the values and institutions necessary for the fullest development of the individual human being.[20] Democracy is interpreted to mean the common instrumentality of Justice.

1.

What, let us first ask, are to be our rational guides in maintaining the essential validity of a rhetoric of values? No attempt is made here to offer an exhaustive analysis; rather, only those propositions which appear most obvious and cogent are presented.

The conception of the central function of rhetoric as enhancement of human values bears the sanction of classical tradition. Analysis of the theory and practice of rhetoric in the ancient Western civilizations clearly shows the basically axiological mission of rhetoric. In Plato's ideal system of rhetoric, the speaker was to have "such a high moral purpose in all his work that he will ever be concerned about saying that which is 'acceptable to God.' " [21] Quite to the point here is Plato's use of the twin themes of love (*eros*) and beauty (*kalos*) in the *Phaedrus* to illuminate the rhetorical motif. In this dialogue, as Richard M. Weaver observes, the "noble rhetorician" is "aware of axiological systems that have ontic status." [22]

Aristotle was also sensitive to the connections between the art of rhetoric and men's conceptions of the preferable. His efforts to locate rhetoric in man's universe of knowledge show, for example, his awareness of the axiological character of his topic. In the early pages of

[18] The definition is based upon the discussions of the meaning of values found in Kluckhohn, pp. 394–396, and Parker, pp. 3–29.

[19] Donald C. Bryant, "Rhetoric: Its Functions and Its Scope," *QJS*, XXXIX (December 1953), 404.

[20] Conceived as polity, *democracy* refers to "a form of government by which the ultimate control of the machinery of government is committed to a numerical majority of the community." John Morley, *Oracles on Man and Government* (London, 1923), p. 29.

[21] Everett Lee Hunt, "Plato and Aristotle on Rhetoric and Rhetoricians," *Studies in Rhetoric and Public Speaking in Honor of James A. Winans* (Ithaca, New York, 1925), p. 38.

[22] Weaver, *Ethics of Rhetoric*, p. 17.

The Rhetoric, he affirms that "Rhetoric is a kind of offshoot, on the one hand, of Dialectic, and, on the other, of that study of Ethics which may properly be called 'political.'"[23] From this generalization and the exposition immediately following, Aristotle's meaning emerges: rhetoric conjoins argumentative method with ethical theory. Insofar as the popular and probable axioms employed by rhetoric constitute the bases of wise civil decision and action, rhetoric is first, last and always, an axiological pursuit.[24] Aristotle also expresses the aims of each kind of rhetoric in value terms. The ends of deliberative speaking are *expediency* and *inexpediency*, of forensic speaking, *justice* and *injustice*, of epideictic speaking, *honor* and *dishonor*.[25] Still more impressive evidence of Aristotle's realization of the axiological nature of his topic is his preoccupation with the desired and the desirable in his lengthy analysis of the premises from which a speaker must argue in the various kinds of rhetoric.[26]

Especially relevant to our thesis is the pedagogy of Isocrates, who postulated the highest cultural function for the "art of discourse." In the Isocratic system of general education (*paideia*), the axiological motif is evident. Not only must the rhetor concern himself with those causes which are "great and honourable, devoted to the welfare of man and the common good," he should choose from "all the actions of men which bear upn his subject those examples which are most illustrious and most edifying."[27] The Isocratic orator was to be, above all, a student of moral values and duties, of the estimable in human conduct.

Under the strong influence of his Greek predecessors, Cicero kept rhetoric in the established tradition. To him the study of rhetoric was the pursuit of humane wisdom. Rhetoric had led men from the brutish to the civilized state.[28] His ideal speaker, the *doctus orator*,

[23] *The Rhetoric of Aristotle*, trans. Lane Cooper (New York, 1932), p. 5. Cooper's interpolation is worthy of note: "With Aristotle, Ethics, the science dealing with individual conduct, shades off into Politics (a broader subject), which deals with the conduct and activities of men in groups—the State."
[24] In this connection it might be noted that while Aristotle insists that as a "faculty" (distinguished from a "science") rhetoric has no subject matter of its own, yet he does devote the bulk of Book I to an anlysis of "Goods" as related to public affairs.
[25] Cooper (trans.), pp. 16–18.
[26] Positing *happiness* as the "end which determines what [men] choose and what they avoid," he analyzes the "internal" and "external" Goods (conceptions of the preferable) which lead to happiness. See *Rhetoric* 1360^b et *passim*.
[27] Isocrates *Nicocles* 10–13. Cf. Prodicus in Bromley Smith, "Prodicus of Ceos: The Sire of Synonomy," *QJS*, VI (April 1920), 51.
[28] *De Inventione* i. 2–3; *De Oratore* i. 33.

was dedicated to the nurture of moral ideals.[29] The "eloquent wisdom" of which Cicero speaks rests upon a study of "virtues" (character values). Advising his son in *De Officiis,* he asserts that a study of the cardinal virtues is essential so that "the relations of man to man in human society may be conserved, and . . . largeness and nobility of soul may be revealed." [30]

The view of rhetoric as a force of social cohesion whose ultimate business is the nurture of moral and political values was continued in Quintilian with his elaboration of a system of rhetorical education for the "good man." In attempting a synthesis of the Classical view, Tacitus wrote: "For them [the ancients] the one thing needful [to the practice of rhetoric] was to stock the mind with those accomplishments which deal with good and evil, virtue and vice, justice and injustice." [31] In the Classical analysis, then, rhetoric and *axios* were intimately associated. On this point perhaps the final word should go to J. H. Randall, who, in appraising the influence of Aristotle's *Rhetoric,* has written: "It is hardly too much to trace back through Cicero to Aristotle the central conviction running through the whole tradition of literary humanism in medieval and modern times . . . that the study of good writing and good speaking must be indissolubly wedded to the study of good living." [32]

The very logic of rhetorical discourse suggests another determinant for developing an axiological approach to the teaching and practice of rhetoric. The logical function of rhetoric in man's sociocultural universe is the realization of the highest goals of human life, expressible through the concepts of Justice and Order. The concept of Justice synthesizes the classic trinity of democratic ideals, liberty, equality, and fraternity, whose central premise is the essential worthfulness and profound potentialities of the individual human being. Rhetoric, as the method of compulsive address about the human situation, thus joins the instrumentality of democracy toward the realization of a Society of Justice and Order. The broader logic of rhetoric, then, is the maintenance of the conditions necessary to a Society of Justice. But the democratic approach to Justice is the ideal of liberty which opens the door to the realization of latent human possibilities. In a less comprehensive sense, the basic and sweaty burden of rhetoric is the

---

[29] *De Oratore* i. 32; ii. 35; iii. 142–143.
[30] *De Officiis* i. 5.
[31] Tacitus *Dialogue on Oratory* 31.
[32] John H. Randall, Jr., *Aristotle* (New York, 1960), pp. 286–287.

maintenance of freedom. The ultimate sanction of freedom, as T. V. Smith has observed, lies in "the very constitutionality of all living forms." [33] Thonssen and Baird have written: "The inviolable logic of [rhetorical] discourse is to secure, safeguard, and preserve liberty." [34] But rhetoric can only achieve its logical end insofar as it is joined effectively to *axios*. Similarly, from the theory of preferential conduct rhetoric draws its potential for helping man decide wisely how he will use the freedom he owns.

We are now in position to affirm our second premise: *The conception of the logical end of rhetoric as the realization of Justice suggests the wisdom of making more direct the association between rhetorical method and axiology.* From such a union a genuinely effective "rhetoric of commitment" can be wrought. For its part, rhetoric supplies the methodology by which man may both discover sound alternatives and urge their adoption. It operates *in* freedom and *for* freedom. "Persuasion involves choice, will," explains Kenneth Burke; "it is directed to man only insofar as he is *free*." [35] If rhetoric has any sort of *special* subject matter province, that substance is constituted in the popular and probable value axioms related to the civil decision making of a free society. Rhetoric and the study of "choice" behavior share a common rootage in the essential nature of being; their common fruit, ideally termed, is the *summum bonum*. "Axiology," observes R. S. Hartman, "puts the spine into democratic ideology. It shows with crystal clarity the infinite and unique value of the human person." [36] Rhetoric, as the great energizer of judgment decisions in public affairs, draws its potency from axiology. Together, axiology and rhetoric may offer some genuine hope for restoration of vitality to man's moral life. Perhaps these are the twin levers with which man, once again, can move his world.

2.

With these determinants for a rhetoric of values in mind, let us now (a) consider an instance of a sound, usable value typology, and (b) offer some suggestions for translating the theory into classroom practice.

[33] T. V. Smith and Eduard C. Lindeman, *The Democratic Way of Life* (New York, 1955), p. 46.

[34] Lester Thonssen and A. Craig Baird, *Speech Criticism* (New York, 1948), p. 472.

[35] Kenneth Burke, *A Rhetoric of Motives* (New York, 1950), p. 50.

[36] R. S. Hartman, "The Science of Value," in Maslow, p. 32.

Since the establishment of a rhetoric of values rests ultimately upon an understanding of values as one of the "available means of persuasion," an accounting of the role of values in human conduct should first be given. Values were earlier defined as "conceptions of the desirable" which shape human "action commitments." In the rhetorical sense, *human values* have been described as logical constructs of the good which provide the bases of civil decision and action. Both definitions will help provide access to a rhetoric of values.

The literature of axiology contains a wealth of knowledge useful to the rhetorician. First of all, values are generally perceived as concepts by which "preferential" conduct is governed. Most discussions of values, regardless of the special field of interest, rest upon a view of the good as not that which is merely desired but rather as that which "ought" to be desired (i.e., the "desirable"). Distinguishing sharply between morally justifiable preference and preference determined by impulse or expediency Kluckhohn and associates write: "Value is more than mere preference; it is limited to those types of preferential behavior based upon conceptions of the desirable." [37] Again, these conceptions are described generally as sociocultural creations. Human values are indeed—to borrow L. von Bertalanffy's phrase—"symbolic universes" of speech and thought that have been shaped and verified in human history.[38] The concept "culture" is therefore roughly equivalent to the concept "human values." Yet these logical constructs of the preferable are presumed to have a physiological origin. Man's unique symbol-making power enables him to convert the "ergs" of psychobiological "drive" into conceptions of the desirable. Leslie White, the anthropologist, has characterized symbolism itself as "that modification of the human organism which allows it to transform physiological drive into cultural values." [39] Further, man's conceptions of the culturally preferable are normative ("ought") conceptions which come to have great suasive power and regulative strength. In ontological terms, "Value is Man's essential being, put as an imperative against him." [40] In whatever verbal form they may be expressed, value statements are hortative in character: they function as "commands." In rhetoric, as

---

[37] Kluckhohn, p. 422. John Dewey, one of the most influential American exponents of the "right" theory of values, perceived genuine good as the resolution of conflict among "incompatible impulses and habits," leading to "an orderly release of action." See his *Human Nature and Conduct* (New York, 1922), p. 211.

[38] Ludwig von Bertalanffy, "Human Values in A Changing World," in Maslow, p. 68.

[39] Cited in Kluckhohn, p. 401.

[40] Paul Tillich, "Is a Science of Human Values Possible?" in Maslow, p. 195.

Marie Hochmuth Nichols has observed, cultural values are presented as "symbols of authority designed to evoke response." [41] For example, when an American president-elect implores the nation in his Inaugural Address to "ask not what your country can do for you—ask what you can do for your country," [42] he is exhorting them to honor their *commitment* to the traditional American values, "self-reliance" and "patriotism"—cultural values that are subsumed in still higher goods, *power* and *rectitude*.

Insofar as human values represent in part desirable states to be striven for, some of their suasive force may be accounted for through the highest, or more human, order of motivation. This level of motivation, called by Allport "propriate striving," refers to the goal-seeking, tension-producing level of human behavior as opposed to the lower, or *homeostatic* level, which is characterized by drive-reduction, "opportunistic adjustment," and the maintaining of "steady states" within the organism. [43] Just as ideals contribute immeasurably to the "go" of adult human life, so also do human values. The realm of ideals and the realm of values are, in fact, almost co-extensive. Values are also regulative, functioning to dissuade as well as to persuade. Any culture abounds in symbols of command which serve to "restrain or canalize impulses in terms of wider and more perduring goals." [44]

The suasive potential of human values has not been extensively investigated. One recent study in the field of public address is suggestive, however. Russel Windes, in a rhetorical analysis of Adlai E. Stevenson's 1956 campaign speaking, sought to isolate the rhetorical factors associated with Stevenson's "effective" and "ineffective" efforts. One of the characteristics of the typical "effective" speech—as opposed to the typical "ineffective" speech—was emphasis on "appeals to values rather than needs." [45] To sum up: Human values are doubly important in the highest order of human motivation. Not only do they supply the *criteria* for choosing among alternative courses of conduct, they may also serve as desirable (and possible) *goals* or states that are

[41] Marie K. Hochmuth, "The Criticism of Rhetoric," in Marie K. Hochmuth (ed.), *A History and Criticism of American Public Address* (New York, 1955), III, 17.

[42] John F. Kennedy, "Inaugural Address," *The New York Times*, January 20, 1961.

[43] See Gordon F. Allport, *Becoming: Basic Considerations for a Psychology of Personality* (Yale Paperbound, 1960), pp. 65–68.

[44] Kluckhohn, p. 399.

[45] Russel R. Windes, Jr., "A Study of Effective and Ineffective Presidential Campaign Speaking," *SM*, XXVIII (March, 1961), 48.

critical in human transactions beyond the homeostatic level of drive-reduction.

One of the most promising value analyses for making rhetorical education more directly a function of democratic ideology is that formulated by Lasswell. Fashioned around the concept of "power relationships in the social process," this analysis is in the ethico-political tradition. "In the social process," explains Lasswell, "*Man* pursues *Values* through *Institutions* or *Resources*." [46] Lasswell's analysis embraces eight "representative" goal-values which he relates as follows to the "institutions usually specialized to each in our civilization":

VALUE	INSTITUTION
Power	Government
Respect	Social class distinction
Affection	Family, friendship
Rectitude	Church, home
Well-being	Hospital, clinic
Wealth	Business
Enlightenment	Research, education
Skill	Occupations [47]

Lasswell and Kaplan have classified these values into two groups: "welfare" values (*well-being, wealth, skill,* and *enlightenment*), and "deference" values (*power, respect, rectitude,* and *affection*). Welfare values are described as "those whose possession to a certain degree is a necessary condition for the maintenance of the physical activity of the person." Deference values, on the other hand, are those that "consist in being taken into consideration in the acts of others and of the self." [48]

Both "welfare" and "deference" values are manifestly important in the life of democratic man. *Well-being* refers to "physical and psychic integrity"; *wealth* means "services of goods and persons accruing to the individual in any way whatever"; *skill* means "proficiency in any practice whatever, whether in arts or crafts, trade or profession"; and *enlightenment* refers to "knowledge, insight, and information concerning personal and cultural relations." [49] Profoundly critical to the good health of a democratic commonwealth are the "deference" values. *Power,* or "participation in the making of decisions," is one of the

[46] Harold D. Lasswell, *Power and Personality* (New York, 1948), p. 17.
[47] *Ibid.*
[48] Harold D. Lasswell and Abraham Kaplan, *Power and Society: A Framework for Political Inquiry* (New Haven, Conn., 1950), pp. 55–56.
[49] *Ibid.;* Lasswell, pp. 16–17.

so-called "democratic variables." Of this goal-value, Lasswell and Kaplan have written: "The concept of power is perhaps the most fundamental in political science: the political process is the shaping, distribution, and exercise of power (in a wider sense, of all the deference values, or of influence in general)." [50] *Affection,* or love, which includes both a reproductive and a productive aspect is the great leavening value of the human enterprise. Writes Maslow: "Love is union with somebody, or something, outside oneself, *under the condition of retaining the separateness and integrity of one's own self.*" [51] The centrality of human love in the life of democratic man is self-evident. Another cardinal democratic goal-value is *rectitude,* or uprightness, which makes possible a just commonwealth built upon a "rule of law." A human—as distinguished from an inhuman— society is only possible insofar as its members give allegiance to morality. Another important "deference" value in Lasswell's analysis is *respect,* or "the value of status, of honor, recognition." [52]

Lasswell's value typology consists of human values deemed fundamental for a rhetoric of values keyed to the concept of human dignity and to the power relations of a democratic polity. From these eight "master" conceptions of the desirable should flow most of the volitional statements of popular discourse: "We must educate our youth" (*enlightenment*); "Let us seek full employment" (*wealth*), et cetera. The Lasswell typology may thus be viewed as a framework of "demand" symbols from which are drawn the innumerable value-axioms rhetoricians invoke in the shaping and promulgation of policy. This value typology, or a close approximation of it, would seem inevitable for a rhetoric of democratic commitment. It can supply rhetoric with a sound axiology, and also furnishes a motivational analysis adequate to the planning and conduct of rhetorical discourse.

The Lasswell typology—consisting as it does of those large conceptions of the desirable in a democratic commonwealth—may indeed serve as a substitute for existing motives typologies in a thoroughgoing rhetoric of commitment. Inevitably, the Lasswell formulation would replace those "wants" typologies based on a homeostatic drive-reduction view of human behavior. As demonstrated earlier, values themselves are suasive, functioning as compelling "demand" symbols. But their compulsive quality must also be ultimately associated with a psychobiological origin. As a "needs" typology for a rhetoric of values the Lasswell list combines the "desired" and the "desirable,"

---

[50] Lasswell and Kaplan, p. 75.
[51] Maslow, "Values, Psychology, and Human Existence," p. 153.
[52] Lasswell and Kaplan, p. 56.

conjoins "wish" and "ought." Thus, it provides rhetorical motivation with both a cognitive and an affective dimension. And, finally, it offers a motivational formula for rhetorical practice and instruction that combines homeostasis and "propriate striving," tension-reduction and tension-creating.

Adoption of a rhetoric of values alters in a limited, though significant way, the motivational data of contemporary rhetoric. An axiology furnishes another major "means of persuasion," analyzable and usable, to enrich the already abundant literature on attitudes, sentiments, opinion, stereotypes, and attention. It may be made even more effective if wedded to Walter's typology of "motivational situations." Based upon a view of the rhetorical situation as a "problem" situation, the Walter analysis includes five basic motivational situations labeled as the *"Difficulty Situation"* the *"Goal-Oriented Situation,"* the *"Barrier Situation,"* the *"Threat Situation,"* and the *"Identification Situation."* For each of these "situations" are offered typical "lines of argument" a speaker may use with his audience. The *"topoi"* of Walter's analysis are related to *pathos*.[53] Since these *topoi* concern the choice of alternative paths of conduct, their effectiveness might be enhanced by relating them also to a set of master conceptions of the good.

Manifestly, a rhetoric wedded to axiology must become a more potent force of cultural cohesion. Aberle and associates define a society as "a group of human beings sharing a self-sufficient system of action which is capable of existing longer than the life-span of an individual, the group being recruited at least in part by the sexual reproduction of its members."[54] Preservation of a "self-sufficient system of action" rests in large measure on a society's ability to keep alive those master symbols of demand which inform its decision-making and shape its power relations. Such a rhetoric, preoccupied with humane substance, would bear little resemblance to the hedonistic rhetoric of Plato's *Gorgias*, described by Socrates as a "knack" for "procuring a certain gratification and pleasure."[55] Nor would it resemble the rhetoric of conditioned reflex and cultural regression practiced by the "hidden persuaders" of mid-twentieth-century America.

3.

No attempt is made here to draft a full set of empirical guides to the teaching of a rhetoric of democratic values; rather some key sug-

[53] Otis M. Walter, "Toward an Analysis of Motivation," *QJS*, XLI (October 1955), 271–278.

[54] D. F. Aberle, *et al.*, "The Functional Prerequisites of a Society," *Ethics*, LX (January 1950), 101.

[55] *Gorgias* 462.

gestations are given for translating the theory into classroom practice.

The teacher of public address must seek first, of course, to reflect in his own classroom conduct the human values for which he contends. Quite obviously, to do so would be to abandon forever the nerveless contention that to become a critic of ideas and values (content) in the classroom is to become a "propagandizer." Other implications are also quite clear. The teacher of a rhetoric of values will find himself immersed in humanistic studies, from which he may learn that the world of human experience must be examined, interpreted, and communicated in terms of some coherent system of human values. In his private life as well as in his public life, he will become vigorously involved in the great Moral Discussion which for three millennia has been carried on continuously in Western civilization. No longer shall he permit himself to be deceived by the facile doctrine of "cultural relativism" which claims that "what is" must be the valid measure of "what ought to be." In fine, he shall find himself practicing wisely and proudly—in the grand Western tradition—a "rhetoric of commitment."

In the management of the units of instruction in public address courses, the most obvious opportunities for refashioning lie in the realm of subject and purpose. As a first step, the relationship between the basic general ends of rhetoric and the values of the axiology can be developed. Thus, for example, in the axiology outlined here, the values of *well-being, affection,* and *rectitude* are typically nurtured by the speech to *inspire;* those of *respect* and *power* by the speech to *convince;* those of *wealth* and *skill* by the speech to *activate;* and the value of *enlightenment* by the speech to *inform.* The public address teacher may also sensitize his students to the axiological implications of topic and thesis selection, providing them with an abundance of topics and issues which involve them in questions of value. Such topics and issues may be found ready at hand, of course, in the traditional disciplines of art, literature, political science, ethics, religion, and history, and in the realm of contemporary public affairs. If the general aim is to put rhetorical education into the business of helping students make wise choices in the realm of human values with the ultimate goal that of creating human excellence, both public and private, students of rhetoric may also be required to make speeches on the Great Ideas of Western Man. In this connection, we can draw upon the 102 recurring themes of the "Great Conversation," making accessible to our students at least the well-known two-volume *Synopti-*

con, if not the whole set, *Great Books of the Western World.* We can also deepen the axiological color of our public address courses by including speaking assignments which may be called "Studies in Greatness." In such assignments, students would be asked to prepare and deliver speeches on great persons in various areas of human endeavor of both the past and the present. In these assignments lies a bright opportunity to teach a genuinely human rhetoric. As Gerald W. Johnson has written: "We are equal to all that we can understand; and to the extent that we can understand true greatness as it appears in men, and how and why it appears, we have the radiant hope of employing that force to carry us forward, not into a new world, but a new universe of power, beauty, and truth." [56]

If the public address teacher aspires to the development of expositors and persuaders who can speak sanely to the so-called "unsolvable problems" of their own generation, he will miss no opportunity to acquaint them with the substance of the past. He shall remember that rhetorical truth is probable truth which becomes the more trustworthy as it is informed by and developed from the accumulated wisdom of mankind. To help the student know and appreciate the wisdom of Western culture is to go a long way toward the establishment of a thoroughly axiological rhetoric. But no headway can be made until the student perceives that "The human being must live in a present that is enriched and sustained by a past; it is his experience stored up in the form of memory which enables him to be something more than an automaton responding to sensory impingements." [57] In a word, the student must come to realize that the men of each new generation are—as Bernard of Chartes put it—like dwarfs seated upon the shoulders of a giant: they can judge more discerningly between better and worse if they have the eyes of human history to help them see. [58]

Two procedures may be suggested for linking rhetorical education more closely with the substance of the past. First of all, the public address teacher can insist that his students know the *background* as well as the foreground of any public issue they undertake to examine, whether in an extemporaneous speech, a debate, or a discussion. He can demand, unapologetically, the quality of research that Lincoln

[56] Gerald W. Johnson, "Emerson's Scholar: A New Chapter in His Biography," *The Key Reporter*, XXIII (July 1958), 3.

[57] Richard M. Weaver, "Individuality and Modernity," *Essays on Individuality,* ed. Felix Morley (Philadelphia, 1958), p. 67.

[58] Cited by Walter Lippmann, "Education vs. Western Civilization," *The American Scholar*, X (Winter 1940–1941), 184.

exacted of himself in the building of his famous "Cooper Union Address." And he shall discover in this procedure the best antidote to the ill-devised proposal, the surest means of infusing soberness into his students' counsels on public questions.

The road to a "rhetoric of commitment" should perhaps prove shorter were we also to revive in our classrooms one of the older customs of the great universities—the custom of requiring the propounding of a philosophical thesis which, as Cotton Mather phrased it, the student had to "defend manfully." [59] In this manner we could bring our students face to face with grave philosophical questions calculated both to tax their mentality and to deepen the humanity that lies within them.[60] Yet to do this would first require on our part the conviction that such universal issues as man's destiny are neither too profound nor too disturbing to take up. Beyond this would be wholehearted acceptance of the view that rhetoric is tendentious utterance about the human condition, and that rhetorical education is justifiable, not as it merely advances a student's career, but as it helps to make of him a fully civilized human being.

Relevant also to the problem of making rhetorical education more richly axiological is the question of language instruction. If the teacher of public address is serious in his democratic and humane allegiances, then he cannot in good conscience propagate any theory of language which seeks to undermine the symbolistic operations of language. Rather, he shall stoutly uphold what Richard M. Weaver has termed "the philosophical quality of language." He shall perceive that he who seeks for "some neutral [linguistic] means which will be a nonconductor of the current called 'emotion' and its concomitant of evaluation," is not only worshipping a false idol but is also contributing to mankind's present state of amorality and emptiness.[61] He shall seek to prevent the isolation of language from the noumenal world, upholding the integrity not only of the process of *definition* but also of rhetorical *figuration*. If indeed he genuinely wishes to put axiological virility into his language instruction, he must begin with a conception of language which affirms the constitutive powers of the human mind and recognizes the reality of man's subjective universe of emotion and value. Such a conception would see rhetoric as being "rooted in an essential function of language itself . . . the use of language as a

[59] *Ibid.*, p. 192.

[60] For an example of a recent effort to link American rhetorical education to "persistent and unresolved questions," see Lester Thonssen and William L. Finkel, *Ideas That Matter: A Sourcebook for Speakers* (New York, 1961).

[61] Weaver, *Ideas Have Consequences*, p. 152.

symbolic means of inducing cooperation in beings that by nature respond to symbols." [62] With such a conception of language he would
also understand the scope of word reference to be "determined by
forces within the psychic constitution and not outside it." [63] The
teaching practices that should emanate from this view of language, or
style, are at once obvious and far-reaching. As students of language,
teachers of rhetoric will go for guidance not to Korzybski, but to
Plato and Longinus and Emerson; not to S. I. Hayakawa or Benjamin
Lee Whorf, but to Richard M. Weaver and Donald C. Bryant. And
if the teacher should need heart, he might recall Barzun's wise dictum:
"The state of the mother tongue is the index of our control over
destiny." [64]

4.

In this essay an attempt has been made to develop a rationale for
rhetorical education which offers some promise of helping twentieth-
century man in the solution of the cataclysmic problems of value which
beset him. The rhetoric described has been called an axiological rhetoric, or a "rhetoric of commitment." Keyed to master conceptions of
the "desirable" in a democratic commonwealth rather than to the
merely "desired," this rhetoric would stress the axiological more than
the purely psychological, the cultural more than the merely personal,
the moral more than the manipulative. Such a rhetoric, the authors
believe, would vitally involve both its teachers and its students in the
pursuit of human wisdom without which modern man may hardly
hope to stay the engines of nihilism. And under the aegis of such a
rhetoric, the ancient art itself can be brought closer to the Platonic
ideal echoed in one of Socrates' replies to Gorgias—the ideal of a
rhetoric whose "propositions are always about justice." [65]

I. A. RICHARDS' THEORY   *Daniel Fogarty*

The work of professor I. A. Richards presents a substantial departure
from the traditional theory of rhetoric. He does not start his inquiry

From *Roots for A New Rhetoric*, New York, Columbia University Press, 1959.
Reprinted with the permission of the author.
[62] Kenneth Burke, p. 43.
[63] Richard M. Weaver, "Relativism and the Use of Language" (Paper read at
Emory University, 1959), p. 6.
[64] Barzun, p. 27.
[65] *Gorgias* 460.

into rhetoric with a metaphysical methodology, as did Aristotle. He starts with the psychobiological origins of man's drive to express himself in linguistic and other symbols. His method of inquiry, too, as he has explained it to the writer, is Platonic and dialectical, rather than Aristotelian and organizational. Plato's idea structure shows also in Richards' near-nominalistic relations between thoughts and things. There are three major additional differences that mark Richards' rhetoric as new. (1) He uses the findings of modern biology and psychology to help him explain the functions of rhetorical language. (2) He regards metaphor as a central aspect of rhetoric. (3) He deals with rhetoric not only as speech but as part of the communication process, whether a person is speaking, listening, writing, or reading to achieve efficient comprehension. These characteristics will, it is hoped, become clear in the delineation of Richards' theory that follows.

The treatment of Richards' theory is divided into six sections: his background and approach to rhetoric; his theory of abstraction; his approach to metaphor; his conception of thought–word–thing relationships; his theory of definition; and his theory of comprehending.

The Background and Approach to Rhetoric

Education at Cambridge University and five subsequent years there as a colleague of C. K. Ogden led to Richards' co-authorship with Ogden in his first important work connected with rhetorical theory, *The Meaning of Meaning* (1923). His research and reading since that time make him a recognized scholar in many relevant fields. Following *The Meaning of Meaning*, he published *Principles of Literary Criticism* (1924) and *Science and Poetry* (1925). Then, still at Cambridge, he published the results of his experiments with comprehension in *Practical Criticism* (1929). These works, all leaning toward a theory of interpretation, were written while Richards worked with Ogden on a basic English vocabulary that would simplify the problems of the translator and the beginner learning the English language. The next year, spent as visiting professor at Tsing Hua University in Peking, not only gave Richards experience with problems of interpretation, but seems to have confirmed his early theory. On his return from the East and while visiting Harvard, he published the results of his Peking studies in *Mencius on the Mind* (1931). The next four years saw three works into print. *Basic Rules of Reason* (1933) and *Coleridge on Imagination* (1934) testify to his persevering interest in the functions of the mind, relative to language. *The Philos-*

ophy of Rhetoric (1936) is a series of lectures on Richards' new conception of rhetoric.

A second visit to Peking, from 1936 to 1938, as Director of the Orthological Institute of China, gave him time to get into publication the results of another set of experiments in interpretation. *Interpretation in Teaching* (1938), prepared for teachers, attempted to apply his theory of interpretation to the classroom. Subsequently he returned to Harvard University and served as Director of the Harvard Commission on English Language Studies, from 1939 to 1944, and from 1944 to the present as Director of Language Research. All this experience in the meaning aspects of language must have had a bearing on the final cast of his theory of rhetoric so directly aimed, as it is, at comprehension of meaning. These later years have provided educators and teachers with the most recent and mature formulation of Richards' work. In a letter commenting on the present analysis of his theory, he says:

> I feel that my later work—with the deep indebtedness to Coleridge and Plato—is likely to be of far more permanent interest than the earlier (with its echoes, via Ogden mainly, of Bentham).[1]

Among other works, the most pertinent to rhetoric in these later years are *How to Read a Page* (1942) and *Speculative Instruments* (1955). The first makes much clearer the function of reason in the abstractive process. The latter contains one chapter that concisely explains what all the other works have been leading up to—his theory of comprehending.

In the wide range of his scholarly publications, the depth of his research in the many fields related to rhetoric stands out. He seems as familiar with Socrates as with Russell, as well read in logic and the mathematics of communication as in linguistics and psychology. Stanley Hyman says:

> His learning in almost every area of knowledge is so tremendous, his significance so great in half a dozen fields besides criticism, and the brilliance and subtlety of at least his earlier books so overpowering, that any hit-and-run treatment of him in a few thousand words is bound to be laughably superficial.[2]

In conversation with the writer, Richards has revealed his deep roots in Plato and Coleridge, and the influence of other philosophers

[1] Letter from I. A. Richards, Boston, December 7, 1956.
[2] Stanley E. Hyman, *The Armed Vision* (New York: Vintage Books, Inc., 1955), p. 278. c1947, 1948, 1955, by Alfred Knopf, Inc.

which is probably more prominent in his later works. He feels that whatever influence Kant and Bentham had on his work must have come through Ogden, and that a lot of his theory about thought–word–thing relationships might have come from the latter part of the "Analytica Posteriora" of Aristotle. Otherwise he acknowledges the help of G. F. Stout's psychology, Piaget's studies of children's language habits, and, for his first notions on primordial abstraction, William James's *Psychology*.[3] There are, however, strong Gestalt leanings [4] throughout his theory supplanting an admitted beginning in Associationism.[5] The preface of the first edition of *The Meaning of Meaning* testifies to the influence of Malinowski,[6] at least upon the contents of that early work.

It is important, for those interested in a practical teaching rhetoric, to remember that Richards is himself a teacher. Much of the research for his books was done in the classroom.[7] Whatever he may offer toward the improvement of courses in composition, speech, writing, and communication will be practical suggestions for a practicing teacher.

Richards' definition of rhetoric is borrowed from George Campbell's *The Philosophy of Rhetoric* (1835). For Campbell, rhetoric was the art of adapting discourse to its end.[8] The approach that brought Richards to this conception of a teaching rhetoric is Platonic rather than Aristotelian, as we have said. Richards does not build upon a foundation with logical blocks, from the ground up. His schematic idea of methodology is to start with whatever sticks up as the most urgent and pertinent element of a problem, and then work in any direction at all that has the scent of truth. The important thing, seemingly, to Richards, is to be free to seek in any direction at any time.[9] As he narrates the progressive steps in his early studies in

---

[3] Interview with I. A. Richards, Boston, October 5, 1956.

[4] Richards' theory of context is clearly Gestaltist, as is his conception of comparison fields in his most recent theory of comprehending.

[5] I. A. Richards, *The Philosophy of Rhetoric* (New York: Oxford University Press, c1936), p. 15.

[6] C. K. Ogden and I. A. Richards, *The Meaning of Meaning* (London: Routledge and Kegan Paul, Ltd., 1923), Preface to 1st ed., p. lx. Originally published by Harcourt, Brace & Co., Inc., New York.

[7] Two of Richards' books are the direct result of classroom experiments: *Practical Criticism* (New York: Harcourt, Brace & Co., Inc., c1929) and *Interpretation in Teaching* (New York: Harcourt, Brace & Co., Inc., c1938).

[8] George Campbell, *The Philosophy of Rhetoric* (Boston: J. H. Wilkins and Co., Hilliard, Gray, and Co., and Gould, Lincoln, and Kendall, 1835), p. 11.

[9] Richards quotes from Plato's "Republic" to illustrate this dialectic seeking of the truth. He illustrates it himself in his inquiry steps from elemental biological

rhetoric, this organismic rather than architectural method of inquiry becomes clear.

His point of departure was the most urgent and obvious question about man. What is the symbol-using power that is uniquely characteristic of him? Beginning with what was observable, Richards turned to the findings of biology and psychology. He could see that man shared with the most elemental types of animal the stimulus and response patterns of the merely nutritive and sense life. The response of an amoeba to prodding or the directional growing of a vine is not essentially different from the blinking of a man's eyes in a sudden strong light or the thrusting out of his hands as he begins to fall. Viewing such phenomena of response in the light of modern biology and psychology, Richards could describe them as fundamental sorting of the things they experienced.[10] Responses of organisms could be classified into two rough categories: acceptance and rejection. Repeated and multiplied experience conditioned the sortings into the habits of growth and feeding we observe.[11]

But man, besides the responses he shares with these elemental animals, has a unique kind of response to stimuli of all kinds, elemental or otherwise. He can use language symbols to express his feelings and needs. He even has a special way of assimilating and integrating with exterior stimuli.[12] He experiences what we call thoughts about these stimuli. Somehow, within his own organism, he can know what he is sorting from what, and make comparisons. Furthermore, he can store away residual traces of his sorting experiences in such a way that he can call them up again and again at will, without the original stimulus being there at all. So man is constantly comparing new experiences with old ones, in search of similarity.[13] At this point Richards seems to have seen that classifying with this conceptual sorting facility means distinguishing things from one another by abstract characteristics. Thus, out of primordial abstraction, or elementary animal sorting, he came to conceptual abstraction. As Richards explains:

> A sensation would be something that was just *so*, on its own, a datum; as such we have none. Instead we have perceptions, responses whose

---

abstraction to conceptual abstraction, to epistemology. For dialectic inquiry method, see *How to Read a Page* (New York: W. W. Norton & Company, Inc., 1942), pp. 215–222.

[10] Ogden and Richards, *op. cit.*, p. 8; also Richards, *The Philosophy of Rhetoric*, pp. 29–31.

[11] Richards, *The Philosophy of Rhetoric*, p. 30.

[12] *Ibid.*

[13] Ogden and Richards, *op. cit.*, p. 52.

character comes to them from the past as well as the present occasion. A perception is never just of an *it;* perception takes whatever it perceives as a thing of a certain sort. All thinking from the lowest to the highest—whatever else it may be—is sorting.[14]

It will help to remember, as we proceed with the discussion of abstraction and metaphor, thought–word–thing relationships and definition, that these four philosophical elements are probably equally basic and quite inseparable except for the purpose of discussion. Abstraction and epistemology and definition elements certainly do imply and include one another. Here we separate them only mentally, and we begin with abstraction only because it follows so naturally from Richards' starting point in primordial sorting.

The Theory of Abstraction

In general, an abstraction is for Richards what it has been to philosophers for centuries: the selection of a characteristic attributable to many real objects, its segregation in the mind as an abstract idea, and its expression in symbols as an abstract word.[15]

But biology and psychology gave Richards insights into the process of abstracting. One of these insights involves his concept of the ἀρχή (reason). The other involves his notion of context.

The ἀρχή notion follows from primordial sorting. Since man possesses the characteristic abilities of each of the animal forms from the simplest to the most complex, he can put all these abilities to work in reaction to a given stimulus. His response can be, at one and the same time, biological, emotional, and conceptual.[16] When he does conceptualize a response, he can express it in language symbols. There is a complexity here, because the biological, emotional, and conceptual elements in the response fight for dominance at one another's expense.[17] There is a risk, then, of loss of real meaning in the expression of the real happening in language symbols. The organism sorts and compares the experience with other similar past experiences. When it conceptualizes the experience, when it abstracts the characteristic it selects (as it must do to classify it), it may be abstracting an emotional

---

[14] Richards, *The Philosophy of Rhetoric*, p. 30.

[15] Ogden and Richards, *op. cit.*, pp. 213–214; and Richards, *The Philosophy of Rhetoric*, p. 31.

[16] Ogden and Richards, *op. cit.*, pp. 223–225; Richards, *The Philosophy of Rhetoric*, pp. 40–41; and *How to Read a Page*, pp. 98–99.

[17] Richards, *How to Read a Page*, p. 75.

aspect and neglecting a very important conceptual meaning.[18] For example, catching a quick glimpse of a large red glow at the stage end of a theatre might call up past similar experiences of glowing red. One could recall the flame that once burned his finger, or a harrowing experience in a flaming building. He might, in instinctive panic, shout, "Fire!" If he did, he would have selected the emotionally frightening element of his own experience to interpret what might, on further examination, be only a red stage light for dramatic effect.

Richards' answer to this complexity of choice in the abstractive process is the ἀρχή (reason) whose function it is to control both the emotional and the conceptual elements in the process in a way that ensures the proper, realistic, and balanced whole meaning of the event. It is under the guidance and control of the reason that the process of abstraction can produce true and realistic abstract symbols.[19]

Richards' other important insight into the abstraction process is as closely connected with meaning as the first. He refers to the term "context" in a special sense. It includes not only all the concomitant but the whole complex of similar thoughts and events that might be compared with it in the mind's sortings. In short, a context embraces the whole field of experience that can be connected with an experienced event, or with the thought of that event.[20]

When we abstract, of course, we select some element from a very intricate maze of contexts, all classified under multiple aspects of past abstractions, like a complicated cross-reference index system.[21] When we abstract the characteristic "red" and apply it to the stage of a theatre, we have selected "red" from thousands of contexts, ranging through fire engines to the flush that accompanies embarrassment. The ἀρχή may have managed to control and balance the emotional elements in these contexts with the conceptual elements, and prevented our jumping to the untrue abstractive judgment that the stage is on fire. But there is another complexity here. The abstraction in any given event to be expressed has its own context, made up of the concomitant external and internal, real and remembered elements that connect with the thought and symbol "red" in this theatre, for this person, at this time.[22] Now the term "red" selects only the color characteristic and leaves out all the rest of the richness of the context.

[18] Ogden and Richards, op. cit., pp. 124–125.
[19] Richards, How to Read a Page, pp. 74–75 and 101–102.
[20] Ogden and Richards, op. cit., pp. 56–58; and Richards, The Philosophy of Rhetoric, pp. 34–37.
[21] Ibid., p. 35.
[22] Ogden and Richards, op. cit., p. 56.

For the full meaning of "red," we have to look to the whole context of the symbol. From the concept of abstraction, Richards has come to the nature of meaning. In this connection he says:

> In these contexts one item—typically a word—takes over the duties of parts which can then be omitted from the recurrence. There is thus an abridgement of the context only shown in the behavior of living things, and most extensively and drastically shown by man. When this abridgement happens, what the sign or word—the item with these delegated powers—means is the missing parts of the context.[23]

Richards' final admonition about abstraction is that we should remember it as a mental activity, and valid only in that sense.[24] In the discussion of parts of context and the conflict between emotion and intellect, we tend to think of these elements as really separate and distinct. This is one of the liabilities of abstraction. The parts of the context are one, and the desiring of the emotions is never quite separable from the thinking of the intellect. As Richards puts it, "We cannot, in fact, wholly leave off wanting. No thinking can be motiveless." [25]

We can proceed now, quite naturally, from Richards' general theory of abstraction to his most important application of it in the theory of metaphor.

An Approach to Metaphor

The analysis that Richards makes of metaphor harks back to his theory of abstraction. All metaphor does, after all, is abstract from one reference (thought) and attribute the abstracted quality of another reference for the purpose of clarifying or livening up its meaning.[26] Take, for example, the metaphor in the utterance "He was a lion in battle." Here are two symbols, "lion" and "man," and two references (thoughts), one for the lion and one for the man. The "lion" reference has been selected by the communicator as suitable to clarify or enliven his communicated reference of the man as a courageous fighter. Abstraction is the process used to select from the "lion" reference the characteristic of courage as being the most appropriate one among all the elements and characteristics in all the "lion" contexts usually known to people. Having eliminated all the other characteristics of "lion" and all the rest of their contexts, the communicator welded the

[23] Richards, *The Philosophy of Rhetoric*, p. 34.
[24] Richards, *How to Read a Page*, pp. 98–99.
[25] *Ibid.*, p. 99.
[26] Ogden and Richards, *op. cit.*, p. 213.

abstracted quality of courage to the other reference, "man." It is this welding, this borrowing of a characteristic from one reference to attach it to another, that is essential to metaphor-making and distinguishes it from ordinary abstraction.[27] Richards sums up this theory in *The Philosophy of Rhetoric:*

> In the simplest formulation, when we use a metaphor we have two thoughts of different things active together and supported by a single word, or phrase, whose meaning is a resultant of the interaction.[28]

For use in the discussion of metaphor, Richards has introduced two new terms, which, for him, avoid the ambiguity of the traditional terminology of metaphor. The term "tenor" he applies to the "underlying idea or principal subject which the vehicle or figure means." [29] This is the man in the example, "He was a lion in battle." The term "vehicle" is attached to the other reference—"lion"—that lends its selected characteristics to make the tenor clearer or more vivid.[30] For the basis of relationship between the two references or parts of the metaphor, he uses the traditional term "ground." [31]

Richards' most emphatic contention about metaphor, thus explained, is that language is naturally metaphoric. Since metaphor is just abstraction for the purpose of clearer and more vivid communication,[32] since it seems to be the nature of our thinking to be perpetually busy with sorting and classifying references and comparing contexts and their parts, and since our language symbolizes this thinking, it seems to Richards that our language must be highly, habitually, and even naturally metaphoric. He takes issue with Aristotle on this point in the early part of his treatment of metaphor in *The Philosophy of Rhetoric*.[33] Aristotle's contention seems to be that ability to use metaphor cannot be taught to another and that it is a sign of genius, inasmuch as it indicates an eye for resemblances. Richards' counter contention is, of course, that metaphor-making ability comes naturally to ordinary people. He remarks, in fact, that:

> We cannot get through three sentences of ordinary fluid discourse without it . . . . Even in the rigid language of the settled sciences we do not eliminate or prevent it without great difficulty.[34]

[27] *Ibid.*, pp. 213–214.
[28] Richards, *The Philosophy of Rhetoric*, p. 93.
[29] *Ibid.*, p. 97.
[30] *Ibid.*, pp. 79 and 100.
[31] *Ibid.*, p. 117.
[32] Ogden and Richards, *op. cit.*, pp. 213–214.
[33] Richards, *The Philosophy of Rhetoric*, pp. 89–93.
[34] *Ibid.*, p. 92.

Richards' theories of abstraction and metaphor have involved three elements of the thought process that need special examination. The next section will deal with Richards' concept of the relationships between thoughts, words, and things.

Thought–Word–Thing Relationships

Richards' epistomological theory concerns itself a good deal more with the operations of thoughts (references), words (symbols), and things (referents) than with their nature. As he states his aim, it is to find out "how words work." [35] The foregoing account of abstraction has shown how the thought process takes place, but has said nothing of the relationships between the three elements involved. The epistemological inquiry is, of course, not a distinct and different inquiry, but rather the same one viewed from a different angle.

At the outset there is need for a definition of Richards' terms. And possibly the best way to answer that need will be to cite his own description of the "match scrape" example of a mental operation and then cite his own definitions of all the elements in that exemplary operation:

> The effects upon the organism due to any sign, which may be any stimulus from without, or any process taking place within, depend upon the past history of the organism, both generally and in more precise fashion. In a sense, no doubt, the whole past history is relevant; but there will be some among the past events in that history which will more directly determine the nature of the present agitation than others. Thus when we strike a match, the movements we make and the sound of the scrape are present stimuli. But the excitation which results is different from what it would be had we never struck matches before. Past strikings have left, in our organization, engrams, residual traces, which help to determine what the mental process will be. For instance the mental process is among other things an awareness that we are striking a *match*. Apart from the effects of similar previous situations we should have no such awareness. Suppose further that the awareness is accompanied by an expectation of a flame. The expectation again will be due to the effects of situations in which the striking of a match has been followed by a flame. The expectation is the excitation of part of an engram complex, which is called up by the stimulus (the scrape) similar to a part only of the original stimulus-situation.[36]

[35] *Ibid.*, pp. 8 and 23.
[36] Ogden and Richards, *op. cit.*, p. 52. Originally published by Harcourt, Brace & Co., Inc., New York, and quoted with their permission.

Here is a sign situation, a reference–symbol–referent unit—that is, a thought–word–thing unit—in which can be found all the elements for which Richards has specific terms. The *reference* is the thought about the scraping match and all its concomitant elements, together with similar groups of elements remembered as past similar experiences.[37] The *symbol* would of course be any language unit used to express what has gone on in the example. "Match scrape," for instance, might express it in a given circumstance.[38] The *referent* is the actual event of the scraping of the match and the real concomitant motions, noises, sights, and so on, that happen independently of the subject's thought.[39] The *sign* is that one stimulus in the whole complex event which has the effect of reminding the subject of the rest of the details of the event as well as remembrances of past associable events—in this case, the scraping itself.[40] The *context* is the whole event with all its associations from the subject's past experience. Richards calls it a *psychological* context when referring to the event in thought process and linked with other, remembered, similar thought processes. He calls it an *external* context when referring to the actual event as happening outside the mind.[41] The movement of the fingers, the flash of light, and all the other concomitant real happenings of the match-scrape event are parts of the external context. The last important element in the sign situation is the *engram.* The term refers to the residual trace of some past excitation, either in the nerve tissue or in some other physiological function of a part of the organism.[42]

Richards' own definitions of these terms will serve to clarify the example and its explanation:

> . . . for words, arrangements of words, images, gestures, and such representations as drawings or mimetic sounds we use the term symbols.[43]

> . . . a reference . . . is a set of external and psychological contexts linking a mental process to a referent.[44]

> . . . a referent . . . thing . . . object.[45]

[37] *Ibid.,* p. 90.
[38] *Ibid.,* pp. 9 and 23.
[39] *Ibid.,* p. 9, footnote.
[40] *Ibid.,* p. 53.
[41] *Ibid.,* pp. 58, 56–57, and 263–265.
[42] *Ibid.,* p. 53.
[43] *Ibid.,* p. 23.
[44] *Ibid.,* p. 90.
[45] *Ibid.,* p. 9, footnote.

A sign is always a stimulus similar to some part of an original stimulus and sufficient to call up the engram formed by that stimulus.[46]

A context is a set of entities (things or events) related in a certain way; these entities have each a character such that other sets of entities occur having the same characters and related by the same relation; and these occur "nearly uniformly." [47]

An engram is the residual trace of an adaption made by the organism to a stimulus.[48]

With the match-scrape example and a definition of terms, it becomes easier to understand Richards' diagram [49] of the relationships between thought, word, and thing; between reference, symbol, and referent:

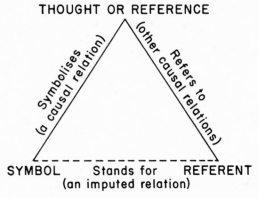

FIGURE 1—From *The Meaning of Meaning*, by C. K. Ogden and I. A. Richards (Routledge and Kegan Paul, Ltd., 1923), p. 11. Used by permission.

As can be seen in Richards' diagram, there is a causal relationship between the reference and the symbol. In other words, the communicator using a certain word or expression can cause his hearers to form a thought somewhat similar to his own. And, conversely, the thought or reference can cause, at least in part, the use of a certain symbol to express it.

The second relationship, between the reference and the referent, is also causal, inasmuch as the thing, or referent, which is or has been seen, felt, heard, and so on, has stimulated the organism and caused

[46] *Ibid.*, p. 53.
[47] *Ibid.*, p. 58.
[48] *Ibid.*, p. 53.
[49] *Ibid.*, p. 11.

it to think about the source of the stimulation or have a reference about it. This causation can be directly from the present stimulation or indirectly from past stimulations or the memory of such stimulations.

But the last relationship—and this is the important one for Richards —is not directly causal, nor is the relationship a real one in the sense of the other two. This "imputed" relationship points to the key principle from which stems Richards' theory of propositional truth, his value norms, his theory of definition, and the validity of his criteria for accurate interpretation. It is the principle stating that there is no referential relation between the symbol and the referent, between the word and the thing. To phrase it differently, the symbol, or word, does not really "refer to" the thing or referent except indirectly through the thought or reference. The symbol merely "stands for" the thing referred to by the reference. Whereas it symbolizes the reference, it does not symbolize the thing.[50]

This key contention about the indirectness of the relationship between the symbol and the referent is of major importance to Richards, because a failure to understand and apply it is, for him, at the root of most of the problems of conceptual meaning.[51] The confusions of ambiguity and word shifts, multiple meaning, and out-of-place definitions are, in his theory, at least partly ascribable to the making of direct relationships between symbols and referents.[52] Such a mistaken, direct, relationship would assume that the communicated content of a symbol is the same, or nearly the same, as the content of the thing it stands for, which is not usually or necessarily so.[53] It is easy to see a wide range of opportunity for ambiguity and inadequate definition in the atmosphere of such an assumption. But with this assumption denied, a word can mean many things to many people, can even mean different things to the same person at different times. It becomes necessary to check back to the referent if one is to understand the symbol. When a communicator uses a word he has so checked against the thing it stands for, he is much more likely to be clearly understood. It is for this reason that Richards so deplores any absolute doctrine of proper meaning [54] which assumes a direct, stable, and real relation between word and thing. Such a doctrine fails to take into account that the word stands for a host of different contexts, patterns, and associations for a different person or at a different time. If the reference

[50] *Ibid.*, pp. 10–12.
[51] *Ibid.*, p. 12.
[52] *Ibid.*, p. 2.
[53] *Ibid.*, pp. 12 and 14–15.
[54] Richards, *The Philosophy of Rhetoric*, p. 11.

is the pivot of the relation between symbol and referent, and if this pivotal reference is continually changing, enlarging, and enriching its contexts,[55] it is no wonder that the meaning of a symbol also undergoes change.

The psychological context of this pivotal reference is important, too. It explains the variability and ever-expanding breadth of the reference that goes with the symbol. For one word or symbol there can be as many references or thoughts as there are persons to think them. The communicator faces as many interpretations of his symbols as he has hearers, and even each of these is momentarily changing.[56] The hearer may be sure, when he hears a symbol, that it can mean something at least slightly different from any meaning it may have had at any other time in his hearing.

The contextual theory of signs clearly allows inferences that could be formulated as rules or laws, the obeying of which might prevent mistakes of comprehension. Richards does draw these inferences and does formulate six laws, which he calls the "Canons of Symbolism." [57] They simply state Richards' logic in the form of precepts, as based upon the principles of contradiction and identity.

The Theory of Definition

The concept of defining here proposed owes its simplicity and directness to the fact that its groundwork has just been laid in the immediately preceding theory of thought–word–thing relationships.

Richards begins by clearing away what he calls "the barren subtleties of Genus and Differentia" [58] in the traditional theory of definition. For him, they lead to four difficulties which a practical theory must avoid:

1. Confusion between real and merely verbal definition, the defining of words and of things.

2. Confusion of symbol and referent in casual conversation; that is, "saying '*chien* means "dog"' when we ought to say 'the word *chien* and the word "dog" both mean the same animal.'"

3. Forgetting that definitions are essentially "*ad hoc*"; in other words, "relevant to some purpose or situation and consequently are

[55] Evidently, contexts must continually change, since fresh stimuli and responses are constantly being added to them as consciously remembered experience.

[56] The "protocol" experiments, to be explained later in this chapter, and embodied in *Practical Criticism* and *Interpretation in Teaching*, will illustrate the varieties of interpretation.

[57] Ogden and Richards, *op. cit.*, pp. 87–108.

[58] *Ibid.*, p. 109.

applicable only over a restricted field or 'universe of discourse.' " . . .
"Whenever a term is thus taken outside the universe of discourse for
which it has been defined, it becomes a metaphor, and may be in
need of fresh definition."

4. Confusing intensive with extensive definitions. According to
Richards an intensive definition calls for no change in the sign situation
that is common to the person defining (or his reference) and the
thing defined. No change is required because the definer prefers to
stick to this one sign situation and analyze it alone and more in-
tensively. In the case of the extensive definition, the definer seeks
outside this sign situation and its context so as to compare it with
other signs and contexts and to distinguish it clearly.[59]

Richards' answer to these four problems is the principle of indirect
relationship between the symbol and the referent. Whenever there is
a difficulty about what a symbol means, when there is a question of
definition, look for the referent.[60] A referent common to all concerned,
in a discussion for instance, must be found. If agreement cannot be
reached this way, then other referents must be found upon which
there is agreement, and from these the required referent can be
evolved through its connections with the other referents.[61] These
relations between the referents known and the referents to be found
are classified by Richards under ten heads that seem to define very
well the range of the communicator's interest:

1. Symbolization
2. Similarity
3. Spatial relations
4. Temporal relations
5. Causal relations of the physical kinds
6. Causal relations of the psychological kinds
7. Causal relations of the psychophysical kinds
8. Referent-reference relations (being the object of a mental state)
9. Common complex relations
10. Legal relations [62]

Clearly, one of the ways to find the referent for the term "cold war"
would be to look for the well-known referents of the term "cold" and
"war." Then, by Richards' similarity relation, a new symbol, "a kind
of war with no firing," is found. And this, after all, is really a beginning
definition of "cold war" which was found by seeking the known
referents behind the unknown one.

[59] Ibid., pp. 111–112.
[60] Ibid., p. 113.
[61] Ibid.
[62] Ibid., pp. 114–120.

Richards then proceeds to describe the range of definition. He regrets that this range is sometimes falsely limited because of the persistent tendency to think of words as having proper and unalterable meanings.[63] He explains how kinds of defining may grow out of purposes in their immediate use. A definition for speculative discussion may be quite different from a definition of the same referent with a view to a practical operation. The subterfuges, by which speakers and writers sometimes suggest unchangeable definition where there really is no such thing, are listed by Richards. The phonetic subterfuge groups a hazy or emotive word, like "discrimination," with others similar in sound but clear in meaning like "dirt" and "death." [64] The hypostatic subterfuge uses the most overloaded and confusing universal or abstract terms, like "liberty" and "glory." [65] The ultraquistic subterfuge uses words that have two meanings, such as the functional meaning of "knowledge" (knowing something), and the objective meaning (what is known).[66]

Up to this point Richards has been involved in highly speculative inquiry. While he has offered several practical rules of thumb, they were guides to efficient mental processes behind our rhetoric and communication rather than guides for immediate use in communicating.[67] At this point, however, he can take all this philosophy of rhetoric and apply it to what he feels is the most important single concern in an improved rhetoric or communication. He proposes that what needs thorough analysis, what needs to be adapted and applied to our symbol-using situation today, is comprehension, efficient interpretation.[68] Consequently, all his speculative inquiries culminate in his still speculative, but nonetheless practical, instruments of comprehending.

Toward a Theory of Comprehending

Although the clearest and most recent formulation of Richards' theory of comprehending is expressed in his latest book, *Speculative Instruments* (1955), the special research technique he uses to compile evidence for the theory is available only in *Practical Criticism* (1929) and *Interpretation in Teaching* (1938).

[63] *Ibid.*, p. 123.
[64] *Ibid.*, p. 133.
[65] *Ibid.*, pp. 133–134.
[66] *Ibid.*, p. 134.
[67] Richards, *The Philosophy of Rhetoric*, p. 23.
[68] *Ibid.*, p. 3.

Faced with the emotive as well as the strictly referential content of language, Richards worked out a system which enabled him to give his students exercises in practical problems of interpretation and to gather evidence from these exercises about the roots of misunderstanding. The students, presented with identified passages of poetry and prose, voluntarily wrote protocols, or interpretations of the passages.[69] Richards' examination of these protocols revealed common patterns of frequently recurring kinds of mistakes, misinterpretations, meaning blocks, prejudices, preconceptions, and stock responses. From this information Richards developed a list of the ten difficulties readers generally have with poetry, and which also apply to prose:

1. Making out the plain sense
2. Sensuous apprehension
3. Imagery visualizing
4. Mnemonic irrelevances
5. Stock responses
6. Sentimentality
7. Inhibition
8. Doctrinal adhesions
9. Technical presuppositions
10. General critical preconceptions.[70]

Such is the material used to substantiate Richards' contentions with regard to the dangerously slippery subject of emotion and value.[71]

It was with these experimental finds that he approached the most recent form of his theory of comprehending. We will need to summarize what Richards intends by the terms "comprehending," "meaning," and 'interpreting." A comprehending is, of course, an accurate and true understanding, but is described by Richards as the nexus or context, or the network of contexts, that connect a whole series of past occurrences of partially similar utterances in partially similar situations.[72] This comprehension is the seizing of a meaning. It is the birth in the comprehending organism of a reference or a feeling or a tendency or a purpose. The meaning itself, which is seized, is first described by Richards as "the missing parts of its context." [73] He means, of course, the missing parts of the psychological and external contexts referred to in his contextual theory of signs. He means the reference with its contexts. Interpretation is the process of seizing this meaning and having this comprehension.

[69] Richards, *Practical Criticism*, pp. 3–4.
[70] *Ibid.*, pp. 12–15.
[71] Richards, *Interpretation in Teaching*, pp. 23–25.
[72] Richards, *Speculative Instruments* (Chicago: University of Chicago Press, 1955), pp. 23–24.
[73] Richards, *The Philosophy of Rhetoric*, p. 37.

By "instruments," in *Speculative Instruments,* Richards means the norms used to compare alternative meanings so as to arrive at accurate and true comprehension. These instruments are the elements common to all utterances and also the elements about which questions must be asked by the interpreter, lest he run the risk of misunderstanding the utterance. It is these instruments that Richards hopes will be at the center of the organization of a new rhetoric.[74] He was aiming at these instruments all along through what, in earlier stages, he called "tasks of rhetoric," "aims of discourse," "language function," and "kinds of meaning." [75]

The seven instruments in question are listed here with Richards' own diagram to show that, even though they are interdependent, purpose has a special place in any instance of comprehending.[76]

1. **Indicating**
2. **Characterizing**
3. **Realizing**
4. **Valuing**
5. **Influencing**
6. **Controlling**
7. **Purposing**

FIGURE 2—From *Speculative Instruments,* by I. A. Richards
(University of Chicago Press, 1955), p. 26.
Used by permission.

He labels this diagram "Comprehending," since these are the sorts of work the communication utterance does to make itself comprehensible. They are the functions of the message working to be understood, as well as the functions of the interpreting mind trying to understand.[77]

Indicating is simply pointing out the referent of the symbol situation. *Characterizing* goes further. It says something about the referent (or thing); sorts it out, to some extent, from other things; attaches characteristics to it; finds a context for it that has been put together by a nexus of other contexts of previously experienced, similar situations.

---

[74] If, as we have seen, the theory of comprehension is the heart of Richards' new rhetoric, then his instruments of comprehending must also be central to it. See *Speculative Instruments,* p. 18, and *The Philosophy of Rhetoric,* p. 3.

[75] Richards, *Interpretation in Teaching,* pp. 12 and 15; *Principles of Literary Criticism,* p. 2; and *Practical Criticism,* pp. 75–76.

[76] Richards, *Speculative Instruments,* pp. 21 and 26.

[77] *Ibid.,* pp. 26–27.

In the utterance to be comprehended, indicating and characterizing merely point out and segregate the referent.[78]

Realizing is not meant in the allowable sense of accomplishing something or bringing something to fruition, but in the sense of understanding, "having before the mind more fully, more consciously, more vividly than on occasions of less realization." [79] It can overlap with characterizing, but it does not need to do so. In fact, as Richards says: "All my seven components can vary independently, though they usually don't." [80]

Valuing is the assessing of the utterance from the vantage point of worth, obligation, or justice. But the assessing must be as philosophically neutral as it can be without losing its truly evaluative function. To exercise this valuing properly, according to Richards' plan, the interpreter need not—and, of course, in this connection, cannot—be detached. But he must be as neutral as possible.[81]

Influencing marks the state of wanting to "change or preserve unchanged" [82] whatever the utterance in question concerns. It is the throwing of the interpreter's weight to the side of keeping the uttered situation as it is or changing it.

Controlling or administering is the instrument that measures interpretations inasmuch as they are making the decisions of stability or change mentioned in the paragraph on influencing. Here the claims of the other instruments of the utterance are objectively balanced and organized by the interpreting mind.[83]

Purposing is the measuring of the intention, the motive, the end, of the utterance. Richards puts this instrument in the central position in the diagram, not because purpose has a higher importance in any hierarchical sense, but because purpose is connected with that original drive of the organism to express itself. The purpose of the utterance is connected with that twofold cause of the use of language in all situations: the inner needs of the organism and the stimulations it receives from outside.[84]

While the first two of these instruments are usually primary, there is no need that they be so. The measuring and comparing that go

[78] *Ibid.*, pp. 28–31.
[79] From Richards' notes commenting on the first draft of the present study, Boston, December 7, 1956.
[80] *Ibid.*
[81] Richards, *Speculative Instruments,* pp. 34–35.
[82] *Ibid.*, p. 35.
[83] *Ibid.*, pp. 36–38.
[84] *Ibid.*, pp. 19–22.

on in each succeeding application of the seven instruments to the comprehending situation will be modified by the applications of the instruments that have been applied to it earlier.[85] Thus characterizing may be fuller and more detailed because it happens after realizing than if it were to happen before realizing. The seven instruments have no special order of application, no distinct sequence, no separation necessarily in time. But "they are all of them coactive together inextricably all the time." [86]

There is no necessary or set hierarchy in the interrelationships of these new instruments:

> There is thus at the heart of any theory of meaning a principle of the instrument. The exploration of comprehension is the task of devising a system of instruments for comparing meanings. But these systems, these instruments, are themselves comparable. They belong with what they compare and are subject in the end to one another. Indeed this mutual subjection and control seems to be the ἀρχή for a doctrine of comprehension—that upon which all else depends.[87]

Thus the mutual control these instruments exercise over one another is the ἀρχή or first principle of the theory. The instruments are the yardsticks or calipers according to which the comparisons of meanings are to be made.[88] Nor does this system of instruments concern only the reader-hearer end of the communication unit. The writer–speaker can use these instruments too, to purify, clarify, and objectivize his communication.[89] But most important of all is the consideration that the education of efficient comprehenders amounts to the preparation of efficiently comprehending audiences which, presumably, would not long put up with the pervading and flagrant ambiguities and distortions of meaning to be found in so much of current spoken and printed material. Presumably, also, an exacting demand would be created for the type of communicator who has been educated to this kind of efficient comprehension, and has become accustomed to subjecting his utterances to a like efficient scrutiny with similar normative principles and instruments.[90] He would, in other words, be behaving as his own first audience to pretest the offering of his own communication.

---

[85] *Ibid.*, pp. 27–28.

[86] From Richards' notes commenting on the first draft of the present study, Boston, December 7, 1956.

[87] Richards, *Speculative Instruments*, pp. 18–19.

[88] *Ibid.*, pp. 19 and 26.

[89] Clearly, both the instruments and the parallel questions Richards derives from them (pages 52 and 53) are as workable for the communicator preparing his communication as for the interpreter comprehending a communication.

[90] Richards, *The Philosophy of Rhetoric*, pp. 3, 8–11, 23–24, and 37.

The sense of these seven instruments and their applicability becomes much clearer when Richards translates them into questions the interpreter may ask himself about different comparable interpretations he may see in any utterances. These questions correspond in number and order to the instruments themselves. Referring to such comparable interpretations, he asks:

1. How far do they pick out the same (or at least analogous) things to talk about?
2. How far do they say the same (or at least analogous) things about them?
3. How far do they present with equal vividness and/or actuality, weak or strong?
4. How far do they value in the same ways?
5. How far would they keep or change in the same ways?
6. How far are the dependencies and interplay between 1, 2, 3, 4, 5, and 6 itself the same in them both?
7. How widely would they serve the same purposes, playing the same parts, within the varying activities they might occur in? [91]

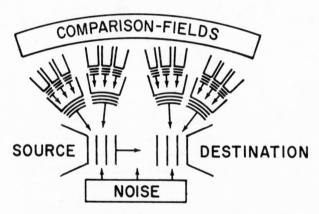

Figure 3—From *Speculative Instruments*, by I. A. Richards
(University of Chicago Press, 1955), p. 23.
Used by permission.

Richards also goes about the business of connecting his instruments with the sociology and psychology of communication. Taking the Shannon and Weaver diagram [92] of communication and making some small changes to suit his purposes better, he first inserts the fields of comparison [93] so that the relation can be seen between the operation of the principles of communication and the operating fields of the

[91] Richards, *Speculative Instruments*, p. 27.
[92] Claude E. Shannon and Warren Weaver, *The Mathematical Theory of Communication* (Urbana, Ill.: University of Illinois Press, 1949), p. 5.
[93] Richards, *Speculative Instruments*, p. 23.

instruments (Fig. 3). Then, turning the diagram out ninety degrees
and looking down it as one might aim down the length of a pole, he
shows the relational position of the instruments themselves (Fig. 4).
The instrument diagram has now been fitted on to the pole of the
communication diagram, much like a wheel upon an axle. The fields
of comparison in Figure 3 are, of course, represented as containing
many different and comparable readings or meanings or interpretations
of the communicated utterance. Consequently they are comparison
fields in the sense that it is here that the interpreting mind will be
making its measurings and sortings according to the seven instruments
on the wheel that encircles the fields at an angle of ninety degrees in
Figure 4.[94]

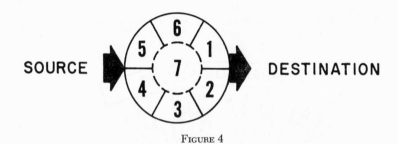

FIGURE 4

These instruments as components of his system of comprehension
are the heart and the head of Richards' proposed new rhetoric, the
core of a discipline that will take the place of the old rhetoric among
the liberal arts.[95] A grasp of such things and much practice and
exercising in them is Richards' tentative answer to the rhetoric problem. As we saw in the early pages of this analysis of Richards' theory,
he is dissatisfied with the way current rhetoric concentrates upon the
mere devices of persuasive composition and speech. He wants a whole
treatment of man's symbol-using power in prose, its philosophy as well
as its practical application. He proposes that this wholeness should be
reflected in a new teaching rhetoric for classroom use.[96]

[94] *Ibid.*, pp. 25–26.
[95] Richards, *The Philosophy of Rhetoric*, p. 3.
[96] *Ibid.*, p. 9.

KENNETH BURKE AND THE
"NEW RHETORIC"

Marie Hochmuth Nichols

I

"We do not flatter ourselves that any one book can contribute much to counteract the torrents of ill will into which so many of our contemporaries have so avidly and sanctimoniously plunged," observes Kenneth Burke in introducing his latest book, A Rhetoric of Motives, but "the more strident our journalists, politicians, and alas! even many of our churchmen become, the more convinced we are that books should be written for tolerance and contemplation." [1] Burke has offered all his writings to these ends.

Burke's first work, Counter-Statement, published in 1931, was hailed as a work of "revolutionary importance," presenting "in essence, a new view of rhetoric." [2] Since that time, he has written a succession of books either centrally or peripherally concerned with rhetoric: Permanence and Change, 1935; Attitudes toward History, 1937; The Philosophy of Literary Form, 1941; A Grammar of Motives, 1945; and his latest, A Rhetoric of Motives, 1950. An unfinished work entitled A Symbolic of Motives further indicates his concern with the problem of language.

Sometimes thought to be "one of the few truly speculative thinkers of our time," [3] and "unquestionably the most brilliant and suggestive critic now writing in America," [4] Burke deserves to be related to the great tradition of rhetoric.

Although we propose to examine particularly A Rhetoric of Motives we shall range freely over all his works in order to discover his principles. We propose to find first the point of departure and orientation from which he approaches rhetoric; next to examine his general concept of rhetoric; then to seek his method for the analysis of motivation;

From Quarterly Journal of Speech, April, 1952. Reprinted with the permission of the Speech Association of America, and of the author.
[1] Kenneth Burke, A Rhetoric of Motives (New York: Prentice-Hall, Inc., 1950), p. xv. Reprinted by permission.
[2] Isidor Schneider, "A New View of Rhetoric," New York Herald Tribune Books, VIII (December 13, 1931), 4.
[3] Malcolm Cowley, "Prolegomena to Kenneth Burke," The New Republic, CXXII (June 5, 1950), 18, 19.
[4] W. H. Auden, "A Grammar of Assent," The New Republic, CV (July 14, 1941), 59.

and finally, to discover his application of principles to specific literary works.

In 1931, in *Counter-Statement*, Burke noted, "The reader of modern prose is ever on guard against 'rhetoric,' yet the word, by lexicographer's definition, refers but to 'the use of language in such a way as to produce a desired impression upon the reader or hearer.'" [5] Hence, accepting the lexicographer's definition, he concluded that "effective literature could be nothing else but rhetoric." [6] In truth, "Eloquence is simply the end of art, and is thus its essence." [7]

As a literary critic, representing a minority view, Burke has persisted in his concern with rhetoric, believing that "rhetorical analysis throws light on literary texts and human relations generally." [8] Although Burke is primarily concerned with literature "as art," [9] he gives no narrow interpretation to the conception of literature. He means simply works "designed for the express purpose of arousing emotions," [10] going so far as to say, "But sometimes literature so designed fails to arouse emotions—and words said purely by way of explanation may have an unintended emotional effect of considerable magnitude." [11] Thus a discussion of "effectiveness" in literature "should be able to include unintended effects as well as intended ones." [12] "By literature we mean written or spoken words." [13]

As has been observed, the breadth of Burke's concepts results "in a similar embracing of trash of every description. . . . For purposes of analysis or illustration Burke draws as readily on a popular movie, a radio quiz program, a *Herald Tribune* news item about the National Association of Manufacturers, or a Carter Glass speech on gold as on Sophocles or Shakespeare. Those things are a kind of poetry too, full of symbolic and rhetorical ingredients, and if they are bad poetry, it is a bad poetry of vital significance in our lives." [14]

Sometimes calling himself a pragmatist, sometimes a sociological critic, Burke believes that literature is designed to "do something" [15] for the writer and the reader or hearer. "Art is a means of communi-

---

[5] *Counter-Statement* (New York, 1931), p. 265.
[6] *Ibid.*, p. 265.
[7] *Ibid.*, p. 53.
[8] *A Rhetoric of Motives*, pp. xiv, xv.
[9] *Counter-Statement*, p. 156.
[10] *Ibid.*
[11] *Ibid.*
[12] *Ibid.*
[13] *Ibid.*
[14] Stanley Edgar Hyman, *The Armed Vision* (New York, 1948), pp. 386, 387.
[15] *The Philosophy of Literary Form* (Louisiana, 1941), p. 89.

cation. As such it is certainly designed to elicit a 'response' of some sort." [16] The most relevant observations are to be made about literature when it is considered as the embodiment of an "act," [17] or as "symbolic action." [18] Words must be thought of as "acts upon a scene," [19] and a "symbolic act" is the *"dancing of an attitude,"* [20] or incipient action. Critical and imaginative works are "answers to questions posed by the situation in which they arose." Not merely "answers," they are *"strategic* answers," or *"stylized* answers." [21] Hence, a literary work is essentially a *"strategy for encompassing a situation."* [22] And, as Burke observes, another name for strategies might be *"attitudes."* [23] The United States Constitution, e.g., must be thought of as the *"answer"* or *"rejoinder"* to "assertions current in the situation in which it arose." [24]

Although Burke distinguishes between literature "for the express purpose of arousing emotions" and "literature for use," the distinction is flexible enough to permit him to see even in such a poem as Milton's *Samson Agonistes,* "moralistic prophecy" and thus to class it as "also a kind of 'literature for use,' use at one remove . . . ." [25]

In further support of his comprehensive notion of art is his conception that since "pure art makes for acceptance," it tends to "become a social menace in so far as it assists us in tolerating the intolerable." [26] Therefore, "under conditions of competitive capitalism there must necessarily be a large *corrective* or *propaganda* element in art." [27] Art must have a "hortatory function, an element of suasion or inducement of the educational variety; it must be partially *forensic."* [28]

Burke thus approaches the subject of rhetoric through a comprehensive view of art in general. And it is this indirect approach that enables him to present what he believes to be a "New Rhetoric." [29] In part, he has as his object only to "rediscover rhetorical elements that had become obscured when rhetoric as a term fell into disuse, and

[16] *Ibid.,* pp. 235, 236.
[17] *Ibid.,* p. 89.
[18] *Ibid.,* p. 8.
[19] *Ibid.,* p. vii.
[20] *Ibid.,* p. 9.
[21] *Ibid.,* p. 1.
[22] *Ibid.,* p. 109.
[23] *Ibid.,* p. 297.
[24] *Ibid.,* p. 109.
[25] *A Rhetoric of Motives,* p. 5.
[26] *The Philosophy of Literary Form,* p. 321.
[27] *Ibid.*
[28] *Ibid.*
[29] *A Rhetoric of Motives,* p. 40.

other specialized disciplines such as esthetics, anthropology, psycho-analysis, and sociology came to the fore (so that esthetics sought to outlaw rhetoric, while the other sciences . . . took over, each in its own terms, the rich rhetorical elements that esthetics would ban)." [30]

II

Sometimes thought to be "intuitive" and "idiosyncratic" [31] in his general theories, Burke might be expected to be so in his theory of rhetoric. "Strongly influenced by anthropological inquiries," [32] and finding Freud "suggestive almost to the point of bewilderment," [33] Burke, essentially a classicist in his theory of rhetoric, has given the subject its most searching analysis in modern times.

According to Burke, "Rhetoric [comprises] both the *use* of per-suasive resources (*rhetorica utens,* as with the philippics of Demos-thenes) and the *study* of them (*rhetorica docens,* as with Aristotle's treatise on the 'art' of Rhetoric)." [34] The "basic function of rhetoric" is the "use of words by human agents to form attitudes or to induce actions in other human agents . . . ." [35] It is *"rooted in an essential function of language itself, a function that is wholly realistic, and is continually born anew; the use of language as a symbolic means of inducing cooperation in beings that by nature respond to symbols."* [36] The basis of rhetoric lies in "generic divisiveness which, being common to all men, is a universal fact about them, prior to any divisiveness caused by social classes." "Out of this emerge the motives for linguistic persuasion. Then, *secondarily,* we get the motives peculiar to particular economic situations. In parturition begins the centrality of the nervous system. The different nervous systems, through language and the ways of production, erect various communities of interests and insights, social communities varying in nature and scope. And out of the division and the community arises the 'universal' rhetorical situation." [37]

Burke devotes 131 pages to a discussion of traditional principles of rhetoric, reviewing Aristotle, Cicero, Quintilian, St. Augustine, the Mediaevalists, and such more recent writers as De Quincey, De

[30] *Ibid.,* pp. xiii, 40.
[31] *The Philosophy of Literary Form,* p. 68.
[32] *A Rhetoric of Motives,* p. 40.
[33] *The Philosophy of Literary Form,* p. 258.
[34] *A Rhetoric of Motives,* p. 36.
[35] *Ibid.,* p. 41.
[36] *Ibid.,* p. 43.
[37] *Ibid.,* p. 146.

Gourmont, Bentham, Marx, Veblen, Freud, Mannheim, Mead, Richards, and others,[38] noting the "wide range of meanings already associated with rhetoric, in ancient texts . . . ."[39] Thus he comes upon the concept of rhetoric as persuasion"; the nature of rhetoric as "addressed" to an audience for a particular purpose; rhetoric as the art of "proving opposites"; rhetoric as an "appeal to emotions and prejudices"; rhetoric as "agonistic"; rhetoric as an art of gaining "advantage"; rhetoric as "demonstration"; rhetoric as the verbal "counterpart" of dialectic; rhetoric, in the Stoic usage, as opposed to dialectic; rhetoric in the Marxist sense of persuasion "grounded in dialectic." Whereas he finds that these meanings are "often not consistent with one another, or even flatly at odds,"[40] he believes that they can all be derived from "persuasion" as the "Edenic" term, from which they have all "Babylonically" split, while persuasion, in turn "involves communication by the signs of consubstantiality, the appeal of *identification*."[41] As the "simplest case of persuasion," he notes that "You persuade a man only insofar as you can talk his language by speech, gesture, tonality, order, image, attitude, idea, *identifying* your ways with his."[42]

In using *identification* as his key term, Burke notes, "Traditionally, the key term for rhetoric is not 'identification,' but 'persuasion.' . . . Our treatment, in terms of identification, is decidedly not meant as a substitute for the sound traditional approach. Rather, . . . it is but an accessory to the standard lore."[43] He had noted that "when we come upon such aspects of persuasion as are found in 'mystification,' courtship, and the 'magic' of class relationships, the reader will see why the classical notion of clear persuasive intent is not an accurate fit, for describing the ways in which the members of a group promote social cohesion by acting rhetorically upon themselves and one another."[44] Burke is completely aware that he is not introducing a totally new concept, observing that Aristotle had long ago commented, "It is not hard . . . to praise Athenians among Athenians,"[45] and that one persuades by "identifying" one's ways with those of his audience.[46] In an observation of W. C. Blum, Burke found additional support for his emphasis on *identification* as a key concept. "In identification lies

[38] *Ibid.*, pp. 49–180.
[39] *Ibid.*, p. 61.
[40] *Ibid.*, pp. 61, 62.
[41] *Ibid.*, p. 62.
[42] *Ibid.*, p. 55.
[43] *Ibid.*, p. xiv.
[44] *Ibid.*
[45] *Ibid.*, p. 55.
[46] *Ibid.*

the source of dedications and enslavements, in fact of cooperation." [47] As for the precise relationship between identification and persuasion as ends of rhetoric, Burke concludes, "we might well keep it in mind that a speaker persuades an audience by the use of stylistic identifications; his act of persuasion may be for the purpose of causing the audience to identify itself with the speaker's interest; and the speaker draws on identification of interests to establish rapport between himself and his audience. So, there is no chance of our keeping apart the meanings of persuasion, identification ('consubstantiality') and communication (the nature of rhetoric as 'addressed'). But, in given instances, one or another of these elements may serve best for extending a line of analysis in some particular direction." [48] "All told, persuasion ranges from the bluntest quest of advantage, as in sales promotion or propaganda, through courtship, social etiquette, education, and the sermon, to a 'pure' form that delights in the process of appeal for itself alone, without ulterior purpose. And identification ranges from the politician who, addressing an audience of farmers, says, 'I was a farm boy myself,' through the mysteries of social status, to the mystic's devout identification with the source of all being." [49] The difference between the "old" rhetoric and the "new" rhetoric may be summed up in this manner: whereas the key term for the "old" rhetoric was *persuasion* and its stress was upon deliberate design, the key term for the "new" rhetoric is *identification* and this may include partially "unconscious" factors in its appeal. Identification, at its simplest level, may be a deliberate device, or a means, as when a speaker identifies his interests with those of his audience. But *identification* can also be an "end," as "when people earnestly yearn to identify themselves with some group or other." They are thus not necessarily acted upon by a conscious external agent, but may act upon themselves to this end. Identification "includes the realm of transcendence." [50]

Burke affirms the significance of *identification* as a key concept because men are at odds with one another, or because there is "division." "Identification is compensatory to division. If men were not apart from one another, there would be no need for the rhetorician to proclaim their unity. If men were wholly and truly of one substance,

[47] *Ibid.*, p. xiv.
[48] *Ibid.*, p. 46.
[49] *Ibid.*, p. xiv.
[50] Kenneth Burke, "Rhetoric—Old and New," *The Journal of General Education,* V (April 1951), 203.

absolute communication would be of man's very essence." [51] In pure identification there would be no strife. Likewise, there would be no strife in absolute separateness, since opponents can join battle only through a mediatory ground that makes their communication possible, thus providing the first condition necessary for their interchange of blows. But put identification and division ambiguously together . . . and you have the characteristic invitation to rhetoric. Here is a major reason why rhetoric, according to Aristotle, 'proves opposites.' " [52]

As a philosopher and metaphysician Burke is impelled to give a philosophic treatment to the concept of unity or identity by an analysis of the nature of *substance* in general. In this respect he makes his most basic contribution to a philosophy of rhetoric. "Metaphysically, a thing is identified by its *properties*," [53] he observes. "To call a man a friend or brother is to proclaim him consubstantial with oneself, one's values or purposes. To call a man a bastard is to attack him by attacking his whole line, his 'authorship,' his 'principle' or 'motive' (as expressed in terms of the familial). An epithet assigns substance doubly, for in stating the character of the object it . . . contains an implicit program of action with regard to the object, thus serving as motive." [54]

According to Burke, language of all things "is most public, most collective, in its substance." [55] Aware that modern thinkers have been skeptical about the utility of a doctrine of substance,[56] he nevertheless recalls that "substance, in the old philosophies, was an *act;* and a way of life is an *acting-together;* and in acting together, men have common sensations, concepts, images, ideas, attitudes that make them *consubstantial.*" [57] "A doctrine of *consubstantiality* . . . may be necessary to any way of life." [58] Like Kant, Burke regards substance as a "necessary form of the mind." Instead of trying to exclude a doctrine of substance, he restores it to a central position and throws critical light upon it.

[51] *A Rhetoric of Motives*, p. 22.
[52] *Ibid.*, p. 25.
[53] *Ibid.*, p. 23.
[54] *A Grammar of Motives* (New York, 1945), p. 57. For discussion of *substance* as a concept, see, *Ibid.*, pp. 21–58; Aristotle, *Categoriae*, tr. by E. M. Edghill, *The Works of Aristotle*, ed. by W. D. Ross, I, Ch. 5; Aristotle, *Metaphysics*, tr. by W. D. Ross, Book △, 8, 1017b, 10; Spinoza, *The Ethics*, in *The Chief Works of Benedict De Spinoza*, tr. by R. H. M. Elwes (London 1901), Rev. ed., II, 45 ff; John Locke, *An Essay Concerning Human Understanding* (London, 1760), 15th ed., I,, Bk. II, Chs. XXIII, XXIV.
[55] *The Philosophy of Literary Form*, p. 44.
[56] *A Rhetoric of Motives*, p. 21.
[57] *Ibid.*
[58] *Ibid.*

In so far as rhetoric is concerned, the "ambiguity of substance" affords a major resource. "What handier linguistic resource could a rhetorician want than an ambiguity whereby he can say 'The state of affairs is substantially such-and-such,' instead of having to say 'The state of affairs *is* and/or *is not* such-and-such'?" [59]

The "commonplaces" or "topics" of Aristotle's *Rhetoric* are a "quick survey of opinion" of "things that people generally consider persuasive." As such, they are means of proclaiming *substantial* unity with an audience and are clearly instances of identification.[60] In truth, *identification* is "hardly other than a name for the function of sociality." [61] "Likewise, the many tropes and figures, and rhetorical form in the large as treated by the ancients are to be considered as modes of identification." [62] They are the "signs" by which the speaker identifies himself with the reader or hearer. "In its simplest manifestation, style is ingratiation." [63] It is an attempt to "gain favor by the hypnotic or suggestive process of 'saying the right thing.'" [64] Burke discusses form in general as "the psychology of the *audience*," [65] the "arousing and fulfillment of desires." [66] The exordium of a Greek oration is an instance of "conventional" [67] form, a form which is expected by the audience and therefore satisfies it. Other recognizable types of form are "syllogistic progression," "repetitive" form, and "minor or incidental" forms which include such devices as the metaphor, apostrophe, series, reversal, etc.[68] The proliferation and the variety of formal devices make a work eloquent.[69]

Reviewing *A Rhetoric of Motives*, Thomas W. Copeland observed, "It gradually appears that there is no form of action of men upon each other (or of individuals on themselves) which is really outside of rhetoric. But if so, we should certainly ask whether rhetoric *as a term* has any defining value." [70] The observation is probably not fair, for Burke does give rhetoric a defining value in terms of persuasion, iden-

---

[59] *A Grammar of Motives*, pp. 51, 52.
[60] *A Rhetoric of Motives*, pp. 56, 57.
[61] *Attitudes toward History* (New York, 1937), II. 144.
[62] *A Rhetoric of Motives*, p. 59.
[63] *Permanence and Change* (New York, 1935), p. 71.
[64] *Ibid.*
[65] *Counter-Statement*, pp. 38–57.
[66] *Ibid.*, p. 157.
[67] *Ibid.*, p. 159.
[68] *Ibid.*, pp. 157–161.
[69] *Ibid.*, pp. 209–211.
[70] Thomas W. Copeland, "Critics at Work," *The Yale Review*, XL (Autumn, 1950), 167–169.

tification, and address or communication to an audience of some sort, despite his observation, "Wherever there is persuasion, there is rhetoric. And wherever there is 'meaning' there is 'persuasion.'" [71]

It is true that in his effort to show "how a rhetorical motive is often present where it is not usually recognized, or thought to belong," [72] Burke either points out linkages which have not been commonly stressed, or widens the scope of rhetoric. A twentieth-century orientation in social-psychological theory thus enables him to note that we may with "more accuracy speak of persuasion 'to attitude,' rather than persuasion to out-and-out action." For persuasion "involves choice, will; it is directed to a man only insofar as he is *free.*" In so far as men "*must* do something, rhetoric is unnecessary, its work being done by the nature of things, though often these necessities are not of natural origin, but come from necessities imposed by man-made conditions," [73] such as dictatorships or near-dictatorships. His notion of persuasion to "attitude" does not alter his generally classical view of rhetoric, for as he points out, in "Cicero and Augustine there is a shift between the words 'move' (*movere*) and 'bend' (*flectere*) to name the ultimate function of rhetoric." And he merely finds that this shift "corresponds to a distinction between act and attitude (attitude being an incipient act, a leaning or inclination)." [74] His notion of persuasion to "attitude" enables him to point out a linkage with poetry; "Thus the notion of persuasion to *attitude* would permit the application of rhetorical terms to purely *poetic* structures; the study of lyrical devices might be classed under the head of rhetoric, when these devices are considered for their power to induce or communicate states of mind to readers, even though the kinds of assent evoked have no overt, practical outcome." [75]

In his reading of classical texts, he had noted a stress "upon *teaching* as an 'office' of rhetoric." Such an observation enables him to link the fields of rhetoric and semantics. He concludes that "once you treat instruction as an aim of rhetoric you introduce a principle that can widen the scope of rhetoric beyond persuasion. It is on the way to include also works on the theory and practice of exposition, description, *communication* in general. Thus, finally, out of this principle, you can derive contemporary 'semantics' as an aspect of rhetoric." [76]

[71] *A Rhetoric of Motives*, p. 172.
[72] *Ibid.*, p. xiii.
[73] *Ibid.*, p. 50.
[74] *Ibid.*
[75] *Ibid.*
[76] *Ibid.*, p. 77.

As he persists in "tracking down" the function of the term *rhetoric,* Burke notes an ingredient of rhetoric "lurking in such anthropologist's terms as 'magic' and 'witchcraft,'[77] and concludes that one "comes closer to the true state of affairs if one treats the socializing aspects of magic as a 'primitive rhetoric' than if one sees modern rhetoric simply as a 'survival of primitive magic.'"[78] Whereas he does not believe that the term *rhetoric* is a "substitute" for such terms as *magic, witchcraft, socializaton,* or *communication,* the term *rhetoric* "designates a *function . . .* present in the areas variously covered by those other terms."[79] Thus, one can place within the scope of rhetoric "all those statements by anthropologists, ethnologists, individual and social psychologists, and the like, that bear upon the *persuasive* aspects of language, the function of language as *addressed,* as direct or round-about appeal to real or ideal audiences, without or within."[80] All these disciplines have made "good contributions to the New Rhetoric."[81]

In "individual psychology," particularly the Freudian concern with the neuroses of individual patients, "there is a strongly rhetorical ingredient."[82] Burke asks the question, "Indeed, what could be more profoundly rhetorical than Freud's notion of a dream that attains expression by stylistic subterfuges designed to evade the inhibitions of a moralistic censor? What is this but the exact analogue of the rhetorical devices of literature under political or theocratic censorship? The *ego* with its *id* confronts the *super-ego* much as an orator would confront a somewhat alien audience, whose susceptibilities he must flatter as a necessary step towards persuasion. The Freudian psyche is quite a parliament, with conflicting interests expressed in ways variously designed to take the claims of rival factions into account."[83]

By considering the individual self as "audience" Burke brings morals and ethics into the realm of rhetoric. He notes that "a modern 'post-Christian' rhetoric must also concern itself with the thought that, under the heading of appeal to audiences, would also be included any ideas or images privately addressed to the individual self for moralistic or incantatory purposes. For you become your own audience, in some respects a very lax one, in some respects very exacting, when you become involved in psychologically stylistic subterfuges for presenting

[77] *Ibid.,* p. 44.
[78] *Ibid.,* p. 43.
[79] *Ibid.,* p. 44.
[80] *Ibid.,* pp. 43–44.
[81] *Ibid.,* p. 40.
[82] *Ibid.,* p. 37.
[83] *Ibid.,* pp. 37, 38.

your own case to yourself in sympathetic terms (and even terms that seem harsh can often be found on closer scrutiny to be flattering, as with neurotics who visit sufferings upon themselves in the name of very high-powered motives which, whatever their discomfiture, feed pride." Therefore, the "individual person, striving to form himself in accordance with the communicative norms that match the cooperative ways of his society, is by the same token concerned with the rhetoric of identification." [84]

By considering style as essentially a mode of "ingratiation" or as a technique by which one gives the signs of identification and consubstantiality, Burke finds a rhetorical motive in clothes, pastoral, courtship, and the like. [85]

Burke links dialectics with rhetoric through a definition of dialectics in "its most general sense" as "linguistic transformation" [86] and through an analysis of three different levels of language, or linguistic terminology. [87] Grammatically, he discusses the subject from the point of view of linguistic merger and division, polarity, and transcendence, being aware that there are "other definitions of dialectics": [88] "reasoning from opinion"; "the discovery of truth by the give and take of converse and redefinition"; "the art of disputation"; "the processes of 'interaction' between the verbal and the non-verbal"; "the competition of coöperation or the coöperation of competition"; "the spinning of terms out of terms"; "the internal dialogue of thought"; "any development . . . got by the interplay of various factors that mutually modify one another, and may be thought of as voices in a dialogue or roles in a play, with each voice or role in its partiality contributing to the development of the whole"; "the placement of one thought or thing in terms of its opposite"; "the progressive or successive development and reconciliation of opposites"; and "so putting questions to nature that nature can give unequivocal answer." [89] He considers all of these definitions as "variants or special applications of the functions" [90] of linguistic transformation conceived in terms of "Merger and division," "The three Major Pairs: action-passion, mind-body, being-nothing," and "Transcendence." [91]

[84] Ibid., pp. 38, 39.
[85] Ibid., pp. 115–127; see, also, p. xiv.
[86] A Grammar of Motives, p. 402.
[87] A Rhetoric of Motives, p. 183.
[88] A Grammar of Motives, p. 402, 403.
[89] Ibid., p. 403.
[90] Ibid.
[91] Ibid., p. 402.

Burke devotes 150 pages to the treatment of the dialectics of persuasion in the *Rhetoric*,[92] in addition to extensive treatment of it on the grammatical level.[93] Linguistic terminology is considered variously persuasive in its Positive, Dialectical, and Ultimate levels or orders.[94] "A positive term is most unambiguously itself when it names a visible and tangible thing which can be located in time and place."[95] Dialectical terms "have no such strict location."[96] Thus terms like "Elizabethanism" or "capitalism" having no positive referent may be called "dialectical."[97] Often called "polar" terms,[98] they require an "opposite"[99] to define them and are on the level of "action," "principles," "ideas."[100] In an "ultimate order" of terminology, there is a "guiding idea" or "unitary principle."[101]

From the point of view of rhetoric, Burke believes that the "difference between a merely 'dialectical' confronting of parliamentary conflict and an 'ultimate' treatment of it would reside in this: The 'dialectical' order would leave the competing voices in a jangling relation with one another (a conflict solved *faute de mieux* by 'horse-trading'); but the 'ultimate' order would place these competing voices themselves in a *hierarchy*, or *sequence*, or *evaluative series*, so that, in some way, we went by a fixed and reasoned progression from one of these to another, the members of the entire group being arranged *developmentally* with relation to one another."[102] To Burke "much of the *rhetorical* strength in the Marxist dialectic comes from the fact that it is 'ultimate' in its order,"[103] for a "spokesman for the proletariat can think of himself as representing not only the interests of that class alone, but the grand design of the entire historical sequence . . . ."[104]

In his concept of a "pure persuasion," Burke seems to be extending the area of rhetoric beyond its usual scope. As a metaphysician he attempts to carry the process of rhetorical appeal to its ultimate limits. He admits that what he means by "pure persuasion" in the "absolute

---

[92] *A Rhetoric of Motives*, pp. 183–333.
[93] *A Grammar of Motives*, pp. 323–443.
[94] *A Rhetoric of Motives*, p. 183.
[95] *Ibid.*
[96] *Ibid.*, p. 184.
[97] *Ibid.*
[98] *Ibid.*
[99] *The Philosophy of Literary Form*, n. 26, p. 109.
[100] *A Rhetoric of Motives*, p. 184.
[101] *Ibid.*, p. 187.
[102] *Ibid.*
[103] *Ibid.*, p. 190.
[104] *Ibid.*, pp. 190, 191.

sense" exists nowhere, but believes that it can be present as a motivational ingredient in any rhetoric, no matter how "advantage-seeking such a rhetoric may be." [105] "Pure persuasion involves the saying of something, not for an extraverbal advantage to be got by the saying, but because of a satisfaction intrinsic to the saying. It summons because it likes the feel of a summons. It would be nonplused if the summons were answered. It attacks because it revels in the sheer syllables of vituperation. It would be horrified if, each time it finds a way of saying, 'Be damned,' it really did send a soul to rot in hell. It intuitively says, 'This is so,' purely and simply because this is so." [106] With such a concept Burke finds himself at the "borders of metaphysics, or perhaps better 'meta-rhetoric'. . . ." [107]

III

Of great significance to the rhetorician is Burke's consideration of the general problem of motivation. Concerned with the problem of motivation in literary strategy,[108] he nevertheless intends that his observations be considered pertinent to the social sphere in general.[109] He had observed that people's conduct has been explained by an "endless variety of theories: ethnological, geographical, sociological, physiological, historical, endocrinological, economic, anatomical, mystical, pathological, and so on." [110] The assigning of motives, he concludes, is a "matter of *appeal*," [111] and this depends upon one's general orientation. "A motive is not some fixed thing, like a table, which one can go to and look at. It is a term of interpretation, and being such it will naturally take its place within the framework of our *Weltanschauung* as a whole." [112] "To explain one's conduct by the vocabulary of motives current among one's group is about as self-deceptive as giving the area of a field in the accepted terms of measurement. One is simply interpreting with the only vocabulary he knows. One is stating his orientation, which involves a vocabulary of ought and ought-not, with attendant vocabulary of praiseworthy and blame-

[105] *Ibid.*, p. 269.
[106] *Ibid.*
[107] *Ibid.*, p. 267.
[108] *The Philosophy of Literary Form*, p. 78.
[109] *Ibid.*, p. 105.
[110] *Permanence and Change*, p. 47.
[111] *Ibid.*, p. 38.
[112] *Ibid.*

worthy." [113] "We discern situational patterns by means of the particular vocabulary of the cultural group into which we are born." [114] Motives are "distinctly linguistic products." [115]

To Burke, the subject of motivation is a "philosophic one, not ultimately to be solved in terms of empirical science." [116] A motive is a "shorthand" term for "situation." [117] One may discuss motives on three levels, rhetorical, symbolic, and grammatical.[118] One is on the "grammatical" level when he concerns himself with the problem of the "intrinsic," or the problem of "substance." [119] "Men's conception of motive . . . is integrally related to their conception of substance. Hence, to deal with problems of motive is to deal with problems of substance." [120]

On the "grammatical" level Burke gives his most profound treatment of the problem of motivation. Strongly allied with the classicists throughout all his works in both his ideas and his methodology, Burke shows indebtedness to Aristotle for his treatment of motivation. Taking a clue from Aristotle's consideration of the "circumstances" of an action,[121] Burke concludes that "In a rounded statement about motives, you must have some word that names the *act* (names what took place, in thought or deed), and another that names the *scene* (the background of the act, the situation in which it occurred); also, you must indicate what person or kind of person (*agent*) performed the act, what means or instruments he used (*agency*), and the *purpose*." [122] Act, Scene, Agent, Agency, Purpose become the "pentad" for pondering the problem of human motivation.[123] Among these various terms grammatical "ratios" prevail which have rhetorical implications. One might illustrate by saying that, for instance, between *scene* and *act* a logic prevails which indicates that a certain quality of scene calls for an analogous quality of act. Hence, if a situation is said to be of a certain nature, a corresponding attitude toward it is implied. Burke explains by pointing to such an instance as that employed by a speaker who,

[113] *Ibid.*, p. 33.
[114] *Ibid.*, p. 52.
[115] *Ibid.*
[116] *A Grammar of Motives*, p. xxiii.
[117] *Permanence and Change*, p. 44.
[118] *A Grammar of Motives*, p. 465.
[119] *Ibid.*
[120] *Ibid.*, p. 337.
[121] *Ethica Nicomachea*, tr. by W. D. Ross, III, i, 16.
[122] *A Grammar of Motives*, p. xv.
[123] *Ibid.*

in discussing Roosevelt's war-time power exhorted that Roosevelt should be granted "unusual powers" because the country was in an "unusual international situation." The scene-act "ratio" may be applied in two ways. "It can be applied deterministically in statements that a certain policy *had* to be adopted in a certain situation, or it may be applied in hortatory statements to the effect that a certain policy *should be* adopted in conformity with the situation." [124] These ratios are "principles of determination." [125] The pentad would allow for ten such ratios: scene-act, scene-agent, scene-agency, scene-purpose, act-purpose, act-agent, act-agency, agent-purpose, agent-agency, and agency-purpose.[126] Political commentators now generally use *situation* as their synonym for *scene*, "though often without any clear concept of its function as a statement about motives." [127]

Burke draws his key terms for the study of motivation from the analysis of drama. Being developed from the analysis of drama, his pentad "treats language and thought primarily as modes of action." [128] His method for handling motivation is designed to contrast with the methodology of the physical sciences which considers the subject of motivation in mechanistic terms of "flat cause-and-effect or stimulus-and-response." [129] Physicalist terminologies are proper to non-verbalizing entities, but man as a species should be approached through his specific trait, his use of symbols. Burke opposes the reduction of the human realm to terms that lack sufficient "coordinates"; he does not, however, question the fitness of physicalist terminologies for treating the physical realm. According to Burke, "Philosophy, like common sense, must think of human motivation dramatistically, in terms of action and its ends." [130] "Language being essentially human, we should view human relations in terms of the linguistic instrument." [131] His "vocabulary" or "set of coordinates" serves "for the integration of all phenomena studied by the *social* sciences." [132] It also serves as a "perspective for the analysis of history which is a 'dramatic' process . . . ." [133]

[124] *Ibid.*, p. 13.
[125] *Ibid.*, p. 15.
[126] *Ibid.*
[127] *Ibid.*, p. 13.
[128] *Ibid.*, p. xxii.
[129] *The Philosophy of Literary Form*, pp. 103, 106.
[130] *A Grammar of Motives*, pp. 55, 56.
[131] *Ibid.*, p. 317.
[132] *The Philosophy of Literary Form*, p. 105.
[133] *Ibid.*, p. 317.

One may wonder with Charles Morris whether "an analysis of man through his language provides us with a full account of human motives." [134] One strongly feels the absence of insights into motivation deriving from the psychologists and scientists.

IV

Burke is not only philosopher and theorist; he has applied his critical principles practically to a great number of literary works. Of these, three are of particular interest to the rhetorician. In two instances, Burke attempts to explain the communicative relationship between the writer and his audience. Taking the speech of Antony from Shakespeare's *Julius Caesar*,[135] Burke examines the speech from "the standpoint of the rhetorician, who is concerned with a work's processes of appeal." [136] A similar operation is performed on a scene from *Twelfth Night*." [137]

Undoubtedly one of his most straightforward attempts at analysis of a work of "literature for use," occurs in an essay on "The Rhetoric of Hitler's 'Battle.'" [138] "The main ideal of criticism, as I conceive it," Burke has observed, "is to use all that there is to use." [139] "If there is any slogan that should reign among critical precepts, it is that 'circumstances alter occasions.'" [140] Considering *Mein Kampf* as "the well of Nazi magic," [141] Burke brings his knowledge of sociology and anthropology to bear in order to "discover what kind of 'medicine' this medicine-man has concocted, that we may know, with greater accuracy, exactly what to guard against, if we are to forestall the concocting of similar medicine in America." [142] He considers Hitler's "centralizing hub of *ideas*" [143] and his selection of Munich as a "mecca geographically located" [144] as methods of recruiting followers "from among many discordant and divergent bands . . . ." [145] He examines

---

[134] Charles Morris, "The Strategy of Kenneth Burke," *The Nation,* CLXIII (July 27, 1946), 106.
[135] "Antony in Behalf of the Play," *Philosophy of Literary Form*, pp. 329–343.
[136] *Ibid.*, p. 330.
[137] "Trial Translation (from *Twelfth Night*)," *Ibid.*, pp. 344–349.
[138] *Ibid.*, pp. 191–220.
[139] *Ibid.*, p. 23.
[140] *Ibid.*
[141] *Ibid.*, p. 192.
[142] *Ibid.*, p. 191.
[143] *Ibid.*, p. 192.
[144] *Ibid.*
[145] *Ibid.*

the symbol of the "international Jew"[146] as that "of a *common enemy*,"[147] the "'medicinal' appeal of the Jew as scapegoat . . . ."[148]

His knowledge of psychoanalysis is useful in the analysis of the "sexual symbolism" that runs through the book: "Germany in dispersion is the 'dehorned Siegfried.' The masses are 'feminine.' As such, they desire to be led by a dominating male. This male, as orator, woos them—and, when he has won them, he commands them. The rival male, the villainous Jew, would on the contrary 'seduce' them. If he succeeds, he poisons their blood by intermingling with them. Whereupon, by purely associative connections of ideas, we are moved into attacks upon syphilis, prostitution, incest, and other similar misfortunes, which are introduced as a kind of 'musical' argument when he is on the subject of 'blood poisoning' by intermarriage or, in its 'spiritual' equivalent, by the infection of 'Jewish' ideas . . . ."[149]

His knowledge of history and religion is employed to show that the "*materialization* of a religious pattern" is "one terrifically effective weapon . . . in a period where religion has been progressively weakened by many centuries of capitalist materialsm."[150]

Conventional rhetorical knowledge leads him to call attention to the "power of endless repetition";[151] the appeal of a sense of "community";[152] the appeal of security resulting from "a world view" for a people who had previously seen the world only "piecemeal";[153] and the appeal of Hitler's "inner voice"[154] which served as a technique of leader-people "identification."[155]

Burke's analysis is comprehensive and penetrating. It stands as a superb example of the fruitfulness of a method of comprehensive rhetorical analysis which goes far beyond conventional patterns.

Conclusion

Burke is difficult and often confusing. He cannot be understood by casual reading of his various volumes. In part the difficulty arises from the numerous vocabularies he employs. His words in isolation are

[146] *Ibid.*, p. 194.
[147] *Ibid.*, p. 193.
[148] *Ibid.*, p. 195.
[149] *Ibid.*
[150] *Ibid.*, p. 194.
[151] *Ibid.*, p. 217.
[152] *Ibid.*
[153] *Ibid.*, p. 218.
[154] *Ibid.*, p. 207.
[155] *Ibid.*

usually simple enough, but he often uses them in new contexts. To read one of his volumes independently, without regard to the chronology of publication, makes the problem of comprehension even more difficult because of the specialized meanings attaching to various words and phrases.

Burke is often criticized for "obscurity" in his writings. The charge may be justified. However, some of the difficulty of comprehension arises from the compactness of his writing, the uniqueness of his organizational patterns, the penetration of his thought, and the breadth of his endeavor. "In books like the *Grammar* and the *Rhetoric*," observed Malcolm Cowley, "we begin to see the outlines of a philosophical system on the grand scale . . . . Already it has its own methodolgy (called 'dramatism'), its own esthetics (based on the principle that works of art are symbolic actions), its logic and dialectics, its ethics (or picture of the good life) and even its metaphysics, which Burke prefers to describe as a meta-rhetoric." [156]

One cannot possibly compress the whole of Burke's thought into an article. The most that one can achieve is to signify his importance as a theorist and critic and to suggest the broad outlines of his work. Years of study and contemplation of the general idea of effectiveness in language have equipped him to deal competently with the subject of rhetoric from its beginning as a specialized discipline to the present time. To his thorough knowledge of classical tradition he has added rich insights gained from serious study of anthropology, sociology, history, psychology, philosophy, and the whole body of humane letters. With such equipment, he has become the most profound student of rhetoric now writing in America.

THE SEMANTICS OF RHETORIC   Elwood Murray

Persons of the Dialogue

DR. S. X. DECKER—*Chairman of the Committee, Professor of Public Speaking, University of Pennfornia. Especially known for his articles on the theory and criticism of present day rhetorics. Has not studied General Semantics intensely. Is interested but undecided as to its utility.*

From *Quarterly Journal of Speech*, February, 1944. Reprinted with the permission of the Speech Association of America, and of the author.

[156] Malcolm Cowley, "Prolegomena to Kenneth Burke," *The New Republic,* CXXII (June 5, 1950), 18, 19.

MR. J. DIRKS BROWN—*Head of the Speech Department, Director of Debate, Maintownia North High School. Has studied General Semantics and applies it widely in his teaching.*

DR. OSCAR WILLIAMS—*Professor of Public Speaking and Director of Research Studies, Hornelling University. A leading authority on the classical rhetoricians, especially Aristotle, Cicero, and Quintilian. Skeptical of General Semantics.*

DR. RICHTON MOORE—*Professor and Chairman, Department of Speech and Dramatic Arts, Plateau University. Although he has some publications in discussion, the personality aspects of speech, and General Semantics he does not consider himself a semanticist.*

Scene of the Dialogue

Meeting of the Committee on Problems in Public Speaking on the evening previous to a national convention of teachers of speech.

The Dialogue

DECKER: Is there anything new to consider for our report to the general session tomorrow?

BROWN: The Editor of the QUARTERLY JOURNAL OF SPEECH at the tea this afternoon suggested that we give consideration to the relations of General Semantics to rhetoric. Explicitly, he said he was interested in our exploring what he called the Semantics of Rhetoric.

WILLIAMS: He must have had something in his tea! Haven't we exhausted the profession with these endless word studies?

BROWN: He said *General* Semantics, which is vastly broader than what we usually think of as semantics. *General Semantics has to do with improving our evaluative reactions to symbols and symbol situations; it provides new methods to remove blockages to proper evaluation and interferences to adequate adjustments; it helps us better to face "reality" and handle "facts,"* it involves far more than the sense and meanings of words.

WILLIAMS: Very well, if we must discuss it, wouldn't it be better to start at some more tangible point? Perhaps we should define rhetoric and view its methodology in a nutshell. I will risk being "Aristotelian" around these "non-Aristotelians" by suggesting that we use Aristotle's definition; that rhetoric is a method for discovering the available means of persuasion in a particular situation.[1]

[1] Lane Cooper, *The Rhetoric of Aristotle* (1932), p. 7.

DECKER: The classical rhetoricians commonly spoke of three kinds of rhetoric—deliberative, judicial, and demonstrative. Speechmaking was based on *inventio, dispositio, elocutio, memoria, and pronuntiatio.* There were three sorts of proof, commonly designated as *ethos* (that which existed in the character of the speaker), *pathos* (that which had to do with arousing the feelings), and *logos* (that based upon reasoning). The modern rhetorics follow these precedents in many respects: the general ends, the central idea, gathering and assimilating of materials, methods of defining, limiting, analysis and partitioning, the methods of support, organizing and arranging materials, adapting the materials, wording the speech, and delivery.

MOORE: I suppose that a semanticist would say that rhetoric (or persuasive methods) aims at the changing of evaluations in line with the speaker's evaluations. To this extent rhetoric may be said to have a semantics—whether the speaker is aiming to improve evaluations, even though he might not be aware of the methods of General Semantics to improve evaluations.

BROWN: I would like to support the thesis that with an awareness of these mechanisms of evaluation from General Semantics what we call the "honest" speaker would probably be much more effective.

DECKER: Would you also support the corollary of that—namely, the "dishonest" speaker or "demagogue" would reform?

MOORE: I would say that he would automatically reevaluate his behavior; he would at least be far more "thoughtful," discriminating, and discrete in his statements; he would quit being intoxicated by his own words, because he would be aware of his mechanisms in doing this; at least, he would drastically improve, because the "facts" or the "truth" would loom up so much more emphatically.

WILLIAMS: That would be a boon indeed! But let us see you establish that thesis.

MOORE: Let us analyze several of the chief formulations of rhetoric by comparing what happens with and without the methods of evaluation from General Semantics. In each case I suspect that we will demonstrate that failure to use these methods makes us less able to "adjust to reality" efficiently.

II

WILLIAMS: To start at the beginning suppose you take up the semantics of the interrelationships of speaker, subject, and audience. Since the whole methodology of rhetoric takes its departure from these bases might not you thus systematically be able to develop your thesis? At the same time we will be able to criticize your point of view.

MOORE: If we apply the extensional [2] view to these relationships we find a four-way relationship in place of a three-way relationship which is assumed in our textbooks.

DECKER: If *proper evaluation* is to be better promoted, instead of only speaker, subject, and audience interrelationships, "subject-matter" would have two aspects—words and what words cover; *there would be a treatment of rhetoric which would permit a very much greater emphasis upon the relationships of words to facts;* new methods of checking statements to the "facts" they purport to represent would be made a part of the *discipline* of speakers. "Subject," as a speaker actually must deal with "it," includes both the "facts" and the words which represent "them."

MOORE: In expanding our treatment of "subject" into a treatment of the "relationships of words to facts" (a central methodology from General Semantics) we will be able to be more precise and efficient to helping speakers better represent "truth and reality" and avoid naïveté and unconscious demagoguery. Heretofore, our most intense efforts at some thing like this seemed clumsy and rule-of-thumb at their best.

WILLIAMS: What was this "extensional" business you mentioned?

MOORE: The speaker who is extensionally oriented *tends everlastingly to put his main effort, concentration, and attention upon the detailed examples and specific facts of what he is talking about and upon the reaction of those to whom he is speaking.* His concentration on words is secondary, and upon himself almost negligible. He is exceptionally apt and proficient in relating his "word-maps" to his "fact-territory." He is unusually proficient in explicitly noting discrepancies between words and "facts" *in accordance with the importance of these discrepancies.* I have attempted to illustrate this "ordering" of reactions in Chart I as applied to the making of an outline.

BROWN: A gamut of misevaluations, maladjustments, and other ineptitudes of vocal and bodily behavior and difficulties in speech composition may be expected when the speaker approaches his task from an *intensional* orientation. *Here he reverses the natural order* [3] *of*

---

[2] For the original treatment of "extension," "order," and other formulations from General Semantics see Alfred Korzybski, *Science and Sanity: an Introduction to Non-Aristotelian Systems and General Semantics* (Lancaster, Pennsylvania, second edition, 1941).

[3] See "intention," "extension," and "identification" in index of Korzybski, *ibid.*

evaluation and puts his attention chiefly upon words as such and upon himself. He confuses reactions-within-his-skin with the "realities" that he is trying to represent in his speaking. These inner reactions (includes feelings and tensions) are closely associated with and frequently inseparable from both his inner and implicit (unspoken) verbalizings and his overt speech.

THE ORDERING OF SPEECH REACTIONS

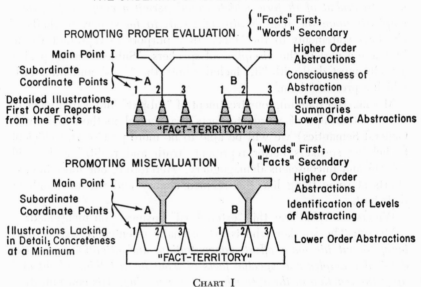

CHART I

° In the upper graph the speaker kept his main *effort and concentration* (as shown by the dark areas) upon the underlying "fact-territories" as he assembled his "materials." Also, he discriminated among his descriptions, summaries and inferences. In the lower graph this *ordering* of reactions was reversed. Although his "research" was as thorough his emphasis and concentration was upon words instead of upon "facts." Also, there was a confusing of descriptions, summaries and inferences.

MOORE: The speaker who evaluates properly doesn't confuse (identify) these inner reactions with the objective reality or "fact-territory" which he represents by his "word-maps."

BROWN: I can understand wherein the "demagogues" who play with "truth" don't always see these subtleties and this tends to keep them "demagogues." Perhaps, these persons frequently have quite fully convinced themselves that what they are saying is the "truth." They adjust to their own rhetoric as if it were "fact-territory" instead of a means of representation which was originally a deliberate slanting and distortion of the facts.

WILLIAMS: You say that a speaker with the more extensional orientation takes a vastly different attitude toward his speech materials?

BROWN: When there is this added absorption in the "territory-facts" (which is induced by the extension orientation) there are two effects upon the speaker: first, his attitude toward his facts becomes far more discrete and cautious, he is aware that he cannot know all about "them," that at the most his "knowledge" is only partial—the result of abstracting; second, his statements become more qualified and circumspect. He knows that his statements do not say *all*—that, at best, very frequently, his verbal maps only correspond roughly to his "fact-territory."

MOORE: That is what the teacher does when he insists on clear definitions; to facilitate this would make the speaker constantly aware of his word-fact mechanisms; this would require a new circumspection and exactitude of statement and it would make for effective awareness of the limitations of statement.

BROWN: In keeping a heavy emphasis upon specific cases, examples, and "meanings," the speaker would tend to avoid in his statements the "is" of identification and predication. He would not be so prone to make such statements as "persuasion *is* inducement," "orators *are* rhetoricians," "Negroes *are* inferior," "man *is* an animal," etc.; instead he would have many cases in mind, he would be aware of his mechanism of projection; he would keep this clear in his statements; he would be more extensional as he presented examples to stand for what he "meant" by "persuasion," "inducement," "orators," "rhetoricians," "Negroes," "inferior," "man," "animal," etc. His statements would thus stand qualified; at most he would indicate that his "definitions" were only statements "about" the object defined: "We *call* (*or name, or classify, or refer to*) methods of persuading as methods for inducing persons," "the name for this behavior is designated as animalistic," "our view of what Joe Smith did on that occasion was unfavorable," etc.

DECKER: What we have said about extension here seems to me to justify the suggestion that Moore advanced. Since rhetoric actually involves four-way relationships of speaker, "*meanings*" or "*fact-territory*," *words* or "*word-maps*" and auditors, it would better fit these realities than by using the present treatment which is largely by speaker, *subject*, audience. "Subject" is viewed as the relating of words to "fact."

III

WILLIAMS: How about other aspects of rhetoric? Suppose we take up the general ends or purposes of speech that we find variously stated in our textbooks?

DECKER: For example, in such a textbook as that of A. E. Phillips.[4] His general ends are to entertain, to impress, to inform, to obtain belief, to obtain action.

WILLIAMS: And these ends, of course have their equivalents in the rhetorics back through the ages including those of Quintilian, Cicero, and Aristotle. For this reason you are taking up something fundamental in rhetoric.

MOORE: While these so-called "ends" have a certain usefulness, their use also interferes with the development of mature speakers.

BROWN: I have been thinking in that direction also. What are these interferences as you see them?

MOORE: First, as we generally use and look upon these "ends" and emphasize them, we waste tremendous effort on teaching persons to speak for artificial situations. Second, we are giving them false information when we emphasize them. Third, we are making speech and rhetoric an *end* in itself, instead of a *means*. And, fourth, in thus verbally splitting the speaker's behavior, we are neglecting to have the speaker make the improvements of his inner mechanisms which is our most important point of focus if our work is to be genuinely effective.

WILLIAMS: Surely, you wouldn't attempt to convince very many of us that what we have all been doing here is all wrong.

BROWN: Actually in speechmaking the speaker merely sets up sound and light stimuli (what enable the auditors to hear and see him) from which they abstract and infer. You can't split these stimuli into separate entities, which "inform," or "impress," etc.

MOORE: These general ends also split the speaker's reactions verbally into entities that cannot actually be split; there is no such thing as a speech to inform that doesn't also obtain a certain amount of belief, that does not arouse interest at least slightly, and doesn't obtain action at least implicitly or at unobserved levels. In fact, very rarely are there speeches in "real" life which are strictly just one or the other. An effective speaker is doing all of these things more or less at once and simultaneously.

[4] Arthur Edward Phillips, *Effective Speaking* (Chicago: 1915), pp. 20–24.

BROWN: Furthermore, these ends seem to imply an unduly static picture of audiences and speech situations. Responses must be obtained in *individuals'* nervous systems, not in some vague entity of an "audience"; no two individuals will respond exactly the same and no individual will respond the same twice. Doesn't our attempt to have speakers organize their compositions according to one of these ends tend to keep them from adjusting precisely to differing and changing individuals? In trying to do this the tendency of the speaker is to put his concentration on his words and himself instead of upon his "facts" and his auditors.

WILLIAMS: But these are useful divisions for the sake of analysis and criticism.

DECKER: Why can we not appropriately abstract from the speaking something that we call general ends or purposes?

BROWN: Aside from the false information which these "general ends" represent to our speakers about speaking they block us as teachers in helping our speakers develop. And how can we expect our speakers to rise beyond the potentialities of what they are taught!

MOORE: Note they are called "general *ends.*" That is, an end of speech is to obtain *conviction,* or to obtain *action,* or to *entertain,* or to *stimulate,* or to *actuate* according to the particular textbook writer. The central emphasis in this rhetorical theory is such as to make speech an *end.* I emphatically believe that this is a basis of many of our present problems in speech education; it seems imperative that we should look on these so-called *ends* as *means,* not as *ends.*

DECKER: Then what is your notion of the *ends* of rhetoric?

MOORE: The ends of speaking generally might be designated as proper evaluation, or social integration, based upon "truth." Speeches to inform, or to convince, or to entertain, or to impress may serve as *means* to proper evaluation and social integration.[5] This must occur at the level of specific dated reactions.

WILLIAMS: I can't see a great deal of harm in continuing to do as we have been doing for quite some time in this field.

MOORE: When we put our chief concentration upon these verbalisms which convey false "facts" we frustrate our own instruction. We forget that speaking is a product of the nervous system and that to improve it in any genuine way we must improve the functioning of our speakers' nervous systems. When we make the speaker's words more important

[5] See Elwood Murray, "Speech Standards and Social Integration," QUARTERLY JOURNAL OF SPEECH, XXVI (February, 1940), 75–83.

than his nervous system which produced the words we can't expect to improve his habitual speaking greatly.

DECKER: All down through the ages, then, Moore, I understand that you view the conventional rhetorics, organized around their general ends and purposes, as making speaking an *end* instead of a *means,* and that various speech difficulties arise from this distorted thinking of rhetoricians about rhetoric.

MOORE: Not only have our "authorities" been splitting speech behavior verbally into fictitious "ends," but they have been splitting these same auditory and visual stimuli into other fictions of "content" and "delivery," "substance" and "form," "subject matter" and "presentation," etc.

WILLIAMS: What harm can this possibly have? I don't see how we could dispense with these concepts.

MOORE: Aside from misleading our students by these verbal splitting of realities that cannot be split, these practices provide the basis for at least three persistent and rather grave problems that we face in our profession. As long as we split speaking into "content" and "delivery" or colleagues in other teaching fields tend to say that we have no "content" that we don't borrow from them such as "logic," "history," "English," "psychology," "philosophy," etc.

BROWN: Although our colleagues are taking advantage of our verbal splittings, they are likewise vulnerable in their own fields. But that doesn't help or justify objectifying our own verbal fictions.

MOORE: We have a similar difficulty with many "lay" persons. When speech making is split into "content" and "delivery" they tend to think of it only as "delivery." To them speech *is* delivery! And this viewpoint is further fostered by the "charlatan" teachers of speech in our midst who still teach speech primarily as "elocution." Both the "laymen" and "quacks" are too much concerned with how a speaker "sounds" and "looks." This all too prevalent view of our work by much of the "public" is a high price to pay for retaining our own static ideas, it seems to me.

IV

BROWN: There is still another verbal splitting of speech behavior that may block or distort the speaker's thinking about his speaking and our own thinking about rhetoric. There appears to me to be a three-way splitting in Aristotle's "artistic" proofs.

WILLIAMS: We understand that you refer to the three modes of persuasion; namely, those that reside in the character of the speaker (*ethos*); and the emotional (*pathos*), and logical (*logos*) proofs? [6] These so-called ethical, pathetic, and logical proofs permeate the thinking of many of our scholars and textbooks today. I don't see how General Semantics would have any bearing upon these foundations of our work.

MOORE: This division of speaking into appeals to the "intellect" and appeals to the "emotions" is no more valid and accurate than the division of the living human organism into a "body" and a "mind," or the three-way split of "body," "mind," and "soul." Scientific psychologists have long ceased to do this. Why shouldn't we be as sensitive to the validity of our assumptions as the psychologists?

DECKER: You imply, then, that in reality there is no such thing as an appeal to the "emotions" that has not also at least a slight appeal to the "intellect" and represents likewise a certain amount of persuasiveness inherent in the prestige and personality of the speaker? And likewise with appeals to the "intellect"; they convey at least a slight appeal to the "emotions."

MOORE: Yes, every statement a speaker makes is made up of all three indivisible aspects, no one of which can ever be separated from the other.

WILLIAMS: But many of the most important studies in our field are based upon this approach. Much of our rhetorical criticism and the work upon the lives of orators give almost their main consideration to these modes of "proof."

BROWN: And, I believe, more or less to our detriment. As long as we base our work on false-to-fact assumptions, speech-making can never become a "true" science with the advantages which would thereby accrue. In other words these faulty assumptions inherited from the Aristotelian era hold up the development of more valid and effective methods of evaluation in our field.

MOORE: The psychologists had a similar problem in their verbal splitting which separated "mind" from "body," something which was false to fact. As long as they held to the old assumptions based on this verbal splitting their field remained far too philosophical and theoretical and hence could not be of much use in the work-a-day world. These habits of thinking about their work greatly hindered the use of more objective methods in psychology similar as our verbal

[6] Cooper, *op. cit.*, 1. 2, 1355^b–1356^a.

splittings in rhetoric seem to me to hinder the development and use of more valid and precise methods in our work. This is aside from the hindrances to proper evaluations of our speakers which occur.

BROWN: Let us note also what our emotion-intellect split in rhetoric does to the evaluations in the invention phase of the speechmaking process.

WILLIAMS: By invention you refer to that part of rhetoric which deals with gathering "facts," analyzing them, and "working up the case," the use of the means of support such as detailed and general illustrations, analogies, specific instances, statistics, testimony, reasoning, and re-statement.

MOORE: To use these methods to "arouse the emotions" is to block the *ability adequately to predict the consequences to personal and human welfare;* to use these methods primarily as "reasoning" devices and for the sake of their logical consistency is to dissipate the "thinking" energy to less important considerations, to remove the drive to make predictions and obtain perspectives, and results in the speaker *weighing the social and human consequences too lightly.* I need not point out the dangers of rampant emotionalism or dead impersonal intellectualism upon speaking. Present rhetorical "machinery" lends itself exceedingly well to the "mountebank," "charlatan," and "demagogue" in these respects without giving the "honest" speaker adequate devices for exposing the abuses they promulgate.

BROWN: Proper evaluation seems impossible without a balance of these two factors wherever decisions are made. Evaluation can be adequate only where it is based upon both an awareness of outcomes (predictability) and a *weighing* of the relative importance to personal and social welfare in the different outcomes inherent in the situation being adjusted to and spoken about. Proper evaluation employs the necessary balance of "feeling" and "intellect"—it does not split the reaction into fictitious divisions. The result is a tendency toward a greater wisdom of discussion and action since the *more important factors* obtain a more intense focus of attention.

DECKER: Would you say that we have a mixture of sheer "emotionalism" and indifferent "intellectualism" (that is, "feeling" without "intellect," or vice versa) at the basis of the present mess the world is in? I can see that if speakers habitually kept the two working together in their assumptions that there would be a new and continuous attention upon the really important, and a lessening of concern with the unimportant.

WILLIAMS: This discussion certainly adds fuel to that long-standing controversy initiated by Mary Yost,[7] Gladys Murphy Graham,[8] and Charles Henry Woolbert,[9] and others, who maintained a monism in these matters. But the controversy has apparently lain dormant after the series of articles by E. Z. Rowell.[10] You remember that Woolbert maintained that the "intellectual" response was merely a less observable and more implicit response than the "emotional" response which he pointed out as being more observable and explicit. Rowell maintained that the duality was an "obvious and useful one for us to maintain." It seems to me that Rowell would not accept Woolbert's explanation here merely because he wouldn't accept it. General Semantics would emphatically support Woolbert, Murphy, and Yost, since it makes clear there is a verbal splitting of the unsplittable speech reaction in our time-honored rhetorics. This is definitely what is implied in the fictitious dualities of intellect and emotion and conviction and persuasion of our rhetorics.

V

DECKER: We have been discussing the conventional methods of invention; that is, without the methods of evaluating from General Semantics. I'd like to know what differences would come into the speech-composing process if consciousness of abstracting [11] were present in the speaker?

MOORE: A speaker conscious of his abstractings, in viewing a situation either directly or through the media of other persons' spoken words, is aware that the situation he is evaluating is in constant change, *that his facts are-in-process,* that he can only become *acquainted partially with these facts* (that he cannot know *all* about them), that the verbal representations made about the situation *are not* the situation, that there are tremendous differences in the validity of these representations according to the level of abstraction, slantings, and

[7] "Argument from the Point of View of Sociology," QUARTERLY JOURNAL OF SPEECH EDUCATION, III (1917), 109–124.

[8] "The Natural Procedure of Argument," QUARTERLY JOURNAL OF SPEECH, XI (1925), 319–337.

[9] "Conviction and Persuasion: Some Considerations of Theory," QUARTERLY JOURNAL OF SPEECH EDUCATION, III (1917), 249–264.

[10] See Edward Z. Rowell, "Prolegomena to Argumentation," QUARTERLY JOURNAL OF SPEECH, XVIII (1932), 1–13, 224–248, 381–405, 585–606.

[11] Korzybski, *op. cit.,* Chapter XXVI.

inferences in the materials with which he is dealing when he listens, reads, or when he responds to his own symbolizings.

BROWN: Doesn't he have a definitely different viewpoint concerning his "facts," his descriptions, illustrations, testimony, summaries, and other "materials"?

MOORE: He *weighs* these materials with much greater discrimination. He carefully inspects and *orders* these materials according to their relationships and correspondence to the "fact-territory-in-process" which they represent. He gives first attention and weight to detailed first-order descriptions and reports which refer to specific dates and circumstances; he gives secondary, though careful, attention and weight to these statements which are most highly abstract and general. (See Chart I.)

BROWN: In this *ordering* [12] of his reactions most of his effort finds its focus in an attempt to ascertain the "fact-territory-in-process" beneath the words; the new and changing factors determining outcomes. These factors are more important than even the most detailed descriptions of them; descriptions and reports are in turn more important than summaries (which are abstractions of descriptions); descriptions and summaries are more important than low order inferences and interpretations; low order inferences are basically more important than inferences about inferences or summaries of summaries (higher order abstractions of high order abstractions).

MOORE: *In thus not confusing the different levels of abstracting the speaker becomes unceasing in his observing of his "facts";* he is aware that statements about these "facts" never represent *all*, never exactly coincide point to point with the "facts"; he looks hard at the changes and differences which are occurring; alhough he observes similarities he also sees the differences within the similarities.

BROWN: Automatically his statements take on a new discretion and exactness; he sees the "white" in the "black," the "black" in the "white," the "true" in the "false," the "false" in the "true," the "good" in the "evil," the "evil" in the "good," the *is not* and the *although* in the *is* [13] statements; he looks for what is said *between the lines* as well as what is explicitly stated; he is aware that no statement can correspond *exactly* and *completely* to its "fact-territory." His research and his

---

[12] Korzybski, *op. cit.*, Chapter XII.

[13] See Elwood Murray, "Speaking about Speaking—and General Semantics: Prologue to a Play," *Proceedings of Second American Congress on General Semantics* (Chicago, 1943).

reflection upon his materials become incomparably more thorough and deliberate. The whole speech composition process becomes better geared to the "truth."

DECKER: Would you imply that a knowledge of these mechanisms of abstracting would tend to help our "unconscious demagogue," whom we have previously mentioned, become more discrete and to qualify his statements.

MOORE: Probably he would become almost completely silent for awhile; at least his impulsiveness and his tendency toward dogmatism would be almost automatically curbed. In maintaining an orientation to specific cases he would tend to be silent when there were no cases for reference—he would literally have nothing to say.

BROWN: In habitually *ordering* [14] his reactions with much greater emphasis upon materials at the bottom of the abstraction ladder the speaking would tend to be more concrete, specific, and less general. It seems to me that this would be a boon for humanity.

MOORE: The fine art of presenting illustrations would receive a much greater emphasis. In fact detailed illustrations are probably viewed by most teachers of speech as the most important speech materials. The adequate use of specific material has always seemed to me to be about the most difficult thing we have to teach.

VI

WILLIAMS: This brings us to organization of materials, the *dispositio* or arrangement stage of speechmaking; the deciding what to put first, second, third, last, etc. I can't see wherein semantics has anything to do with this.

MOORE: You will agree that the arrangement of materials must aim at clarity and acceptability to the auditors?

BROWN: Until recent years there appears to have been no attempt to make arrangement of materials depend upon the point-of-view of the audience. The conventional introduction-discussion-conclusion arrangement of Aristotle and the expanded versions in the rhetorics of Cicero and Quintilian seem to promote a subjectivity in the speaker—to make him almost ignore his audience altogether in putting his speech together. These writers tend to make the speaker assume that distinctions among auditors rest almost wholly on age groups, wealth and other static categories.

[14] Korzybski, *op. cit.*, see "order" in index.

DECKER: Examples of the trend today are seen in the treatment of arrangement by W. N. Brigance and R. K. Immel.[15] They give much emphasis in arranging topics to fit the specific audience. Alan H. Monroe's [16] "motivated sequence," namely, his order of *attention, problem, satisfaction, visualization, action* appears to be an arrangement favorable to helping the speaker to think about his audience as he formulates the "content" of his speech. The treatments of audience analysis in other present day textbooks also indicates this trend to have the attitudes, culture-levels, and backgrounds of the auditors determine both what goes into a speech and its arrangement.

MOORE: General Semantics would greatly accentuate this trend, I believe, and especially in the arranging of materials. There are several ways in which arrangement might be more effective.

WILLIAMS: I would like to hear these.

MOORE: If the improvement of evaluations is to become a chief function of rhetoric the arrangement would be determined, first, by whatever state of blockage and prejudice to proper evaluation might exist in the auditors. The first aim of the speaker would therefore be to eliminate these blockages. He would have his first points focused on the blockages and resistances to consideration and understanding of the problem. His chief technique for doing this involves making the auditors aware of their mechanisms of blockage; that is, of their biases, dogmatism, prejudices, confusions. By one means or another, directly or indirectly, he must help them to face "reality"; he must help them achieve an objectivity.

VII

DECKER: Gentlemen, the hour is late and we have business tomorrow. I fear we must adjourn discussion.

WILLIAMS: But we have not completed this exploration of *dispositio* and haven't even come to "style" or Cicero's *elocutio*. I'm curious to hear what semanticists have to say on that.

BROWN: And remember, too, Mr. Chairman, that we have not touched what semanticists have to say about delivery, aside from our mention of the verbal splitting of "delivery" from "content."

DECKER: True, gentlemen, we have not covered either of those important topics but no discussion can exhaust the subject. Something must be left for future reflection, and enough has been said tonight

[15] *Speechmaking* (1938), Chapter XV.
[16] *Principles and Types of Speech* (1939), Chapter 12.

to occupy our reflective capacity for some time hence. Meanwhile, I assume that you wish me to report the gist of this conference to the convention tomorrow.

MOORE: If it includes the statement that the game was called on account of darkness.

DECKER: Fair enough. As to the report, I will say, in a nutshell, that rhetoric without General Semantics in all of its aspects may promote misevaluation almost as freely as proper evaluation; that rhetoric with General Semantics at its base becomes a more potent instrument in helping men adjust themselves to the realities of a rapidly changing world of 1944. That a merger of the methods of evaluation from General Semantics with rhetoric would help rhetoric function to accelerate wisdom and unity of belief and action in a world that is permeated with confusion and dissension.

SECTION IV

THE USES OF RHETORIC

A. Some Advice

B. Some Samples

A. Some Advice

THE FUNCTIONS OF RHETORICAL CRITICISM

Albert J. Croft

I

Research in rhetoric and oratory, as in any other art, ought to proceed from some clearly conceived set of relations between rhetorical theory, rhetorical criticism, and the history of public address. The statement of just what rhetorical research ought to produce can best be formulated by a re-examination of these relations. With that goal in mind, this article will pursue three main lines of inquiry: (1) that of describing or defining the aims, materials, and methods of the "standard" approach to rhetorical criticism; (2) that of analyzing some of the major inadequacies in the methods and objectives of this standard form; (3) that of proposing a revision of the aims of speech criticism. In discussing these three topics, a point of view will be presented as to the interrelations which ought to hold between theory, criticism, and history in rhetoric and public address.[1]

II

Any brief survey of what has been done in "rhetorical criticism" is bound to be controversial; so many different things go by this name. Still, there is no need for semantic controversy as to whether the term "criticism" can properly be applied to all of this research, for the only real issue is whether the research provides valuable conclusions. Among recent studies of speakers and speeches, however, there have been certain relatively common elements. The rhetorical critic selects for study either a single speaker and speech or groups of speeches and speakers representing periods, movements, regions, organizations, or

From *Quarterly Journal of Speech*, October, 1956. Reprinted with the permission of the Speech Association of America, and of the author.
[1] Although the approach of this article is very different from theirs, I am indebted to René Wellek and Austin Warren, *Theory of Literature* (New York: Harcourt, Brace and Co., 1949), for their treatment of theory, criticism, and history in literature.

ideas. His primary limitation is that he must focus on public speaking, per se. He then proceeds to analyze, report, interpret, and evaluate the speeches he has chosen for study.

The materials of these critical studies fall into three groups: (1) facts and opinions dealing with the biography of the speaker, the historical background of the speech, and the nature of the listening and reading audience; (2) the speaker's propositions as they occur in representative speeches (these propositions are derived by a wide variety of analytic devices); (3) illustrations of the speaker's use of Aristotle's three modes of proof and of various doctrines on style, arrangement, and delivery.

What, then, has the rhetorical critic done with this material? What has been his intention in assembling and examining all these data? Of what value are his conclusions, or what use can be made of them? What are the functions of this sort of rhetorical criticism? Being stylized, at least in format, nearly every graduate thesis based on these methods includes some formal statement of objective or purpose. Still, most of these statements somehow fail to provide satisfying answers to the questions being raised here. One is forced finally to examine these theses and then simply to infer what their objectives and their contributions to knowledge seem to have been. Using that highly subjective method, I believe that the following four objectives are commonly implied in the "standard" critical studies completed in the last ten or twenty years.[2]

The first objective is to present a balanced and interesting picture of the life and speaking career of a famous speaker. In this way, scholars in speech have made several real contributions to British and American biography. It may be true, however, that such contributions are not inherently rhetorical.

A second objective is to present a synopsis of propositions asserted to be important in the speeches studied—to report, that is, what the speaker said in his speeches. These synopses contribute largely to political history. One might question what kind of summary will accurately represent the full content of a speech. How does one know when he has synopsized the right thing? Still, contributions to history have clearly been made by this means.

A third objective, less common in recent years, is to present a structure of causal relations between speeches or speaking careers and

---

[2] These conclusions are based on the examination of a number of complete theses, but an examination of the thesis abstracts prepared annually for *SM* by Clyde Dow also corroborates these conclusions.

subsequent historical events. The critic asks, what part did these speakers or speeches play in determining the course of human affairs? What subsequent effects did the speeches have? Here his aim might be to explain historical developments, but there is some reason to question this sort of single-cause analysis. In terms of historical method, most events are obviously multi-causal, and the relative importance of one major cause as compared with another is very difficult to assess. Further, following Aristotle's definition of rhetoric, evaluation of speeches in terms of subsequent effect is usually unfair to the speeches.

A fourth objective is to describe the manner in which the speaking illustrates various doctrines of rhetoric. Some emphasis is usually placed on the classical rhetorical devices which the speaker used most often. The data sometimes allow quantitative generalizations about his techniques. Such conclusions are intended, one must assume, to contribute to our knowledge of rhetoric as a body of techniques.

These four objectives illustrate what can be inferred about the functions of contemporary rhetorical criticism by looking at "typical" graduate theses. Several excellent "non-typical" studies have of course made unique and meaningful contributions by working virtually outside the framework of the method described above.

III

Perhaps the chief problem of research in public address is that we have thought of it all as "criticism" when some is really theory, some is history, and some is criticism which has not evaluated the speeches studied. The argument of this article is that the methods and objectives of our research can be improved only as we clarify the relations between theory, criticism, and history. As these relations are explored, it will be possible to describe three major inadequacies in the standard forms of rhetorical research.

The relationship between theory and criticism involves an apparent paradox. In order to criticize a speech, the standards or criteria against which it is to be measured must first be established. These criteria are obviously drawn from established rhetorical theory and must remain constant if we are to examine the speeches in terms of these criteria. But if we are to improve theory, then the standards and criteria by which we judge a speech cannot remain constant. We have resolved this paradox by deciding that criticism cannot alter theory; it can only use the existing forms.

Here is the contemporary situation: a researcher takes the old theory, finds illustrations of it, piles these up, and concludes, for example, that a given man's speaking exhibits characteristics which may be said to fall properly within the categories of traditional rhetoric. This sort of criticism works upon the presumption that rhetoric is rhetoric, and, beyond deciding which traditional doctrine he prefers, the critic shall not fancy himself a creative theorist. And so we have made rhetorical criticism a dead-end street. In this view, our first need is to create a dynamic interaction between theory and criticism; we must encourage creative theorizing as a part of criticism.

For a long time now much of the really interesting literature on rhetoric has been written by scholars outside the field of Speech. Examples of what I call creative theorizing and criticism can be found in Kenneth Burke's *Rhetoric of Motives*, Richard M. Weaver's *Ethics of Rhetoric*, or in the works of I. A. Richards. Such writers certainly do not scorn traditional theory; they use it as a solid base on which to stand while they experiment. They reinterpret older theory and then apply it in criticism. The standard forms of criticism within our field, however, treat traditional theory as a closed, fixed system. This is the first major inadequacy to be noted in our typical research, and it exists because of a naive notion of the relation between theory and criticism.

A second inadequacy is related to the hoary argument concerning form versus content, technique versus idea, in rhetoric and oratory. The important question here is not whether the "form" can be separated from the "content." Of course the two are separable; we can "see" a given form or technique in several different contexts by a process of simple abstraction. The question is how these abstracted forms can be most profitably used in criticism.

As noted above, a common device in graduate theses is to illustrate traditional theory, to find examples of a speaker's use of a particular rhetorical "form." Very little effort, if any, is made to evaluate these examples, to assert that an example is good or bad, better or worse. Often no critical conclusions are drawn, or only those which suggest that, because a speaker's techniques are amenable to description in traditional terms, the speaker's rhetoric is admirable. This approach cannot be called criticism in the sense of evaluation. Nor is it evaluation to assert that some instances of the speaker's reasoning satisfy the requirements of the Aristotelian syllogism, or that his modes of narrative and descriptive support seem to be especially vivid, or that his delivery was well received by audiences. There is a subtle but unmistakable implication in all these studies that the "critical" process is not even intended to produce judgments on the merit of the speech.

To a critic, the forms or techniques of an art are of no value in themselves, but are only tools with which to pry into a specimen of the art, the means that critics have found most useful in examining the specimen. Theory, or forms, ought to be used by the rhetorical critic so as to answer at least two major questions: (1) what are the various levels of meaning implied by the form-content units in a speech—that is, what is the larger implicative meaning of the speech? (2) what are the unique and relatively artistic ways in which a particular speaker manipulates rhetorical forms in order to imply these meanings? Thus, one does not "criticize" by finding illustrations of standard, preconceived forms. He uses the framework of standard techniques as norms to help him discover and evaluate the ways in which a speaker's use of techniques is distinctive.

It does not seem to have occurred to many thesis writers that they are doing anything beyond simply looking for the traditional techniques of rhetoric in a group of speeches. After a while, the strictly rhetorical conclusions of one thesis tend to become remarkably similar to those of another using the same rhetorical categories, no matter how different the speaker or speeches may have been. This situation may have acted to drive many of these writers out of criticism and into history. This, in itself, would not be objectionable, but there are also problems in the rhetorical approach to history.

The third major area of inadequacy in rhetorical criticism involves the relation of theory and criticism to history. The concept of the "history" of an art has two clearly different aspects. First, there is the history of the art, per se, the record of the major changes in its organized theory. Thus we note the origins and development of rhetoric in Greek and Roman times and trace its theory through a series of variously conceived changes up to the present day. Or we trace the history of special doctrines of rhetoric. Or we deal with one or another of the philosophic issues on which the course of rhetorical theory has turned. By all these approaches our understanding of the total history of rhetoric has been broadened.

A second kind of history is concerned, not with theory, but with the practice of rhetoric; it is a history of oratory or of public address. Ideas in speeches, as a reflection of human society, become the center of this kind of historical study.[3]

---

[3] It may be that in some types of "art" the history of theory and the history of practice tend to duplicate each other. But in rhetoric the whole function of the art is to affect the shape of society in practical ways. The history of what has been done by speakers must deal with substantive matters, not forms or general theories.

The distinction between these two types of historical approach has been formalized and widely recognized by nearly every graduate department of Speech; still, confusion exists between these two historical functions in our teaching and our research.

In asking what the historian of public address is trying to do, we simply pose the age-long question of the function of rhetoric itself. But no matter what answer is given, the center of this kind of study is audience adaptation, or, as Donald Bryant puts it, the accommodation of ideas to men and men to ideas. Even though this adaptive process is admittedly the *sine qua non* of rhetoric, studies in rhetorical criticism and in the history of public address have not been able to deal directly with it. It is not enough to talk separately about the make-up of an audience at one point, about the main propositions of the speaker at another point, and about the speaker's use of traditional rhetorical techniques at still another point. The main function of history and criticism is to show how propositions and audiences are *connected;* how a speaker uses techniques to adapt his ideas to the ideas of his audiences.

The fault of some modern criticism has not been in wholly ignoring this necessity, but rather in devising inadequate tools to deal with it.[4] Here again an unfortunate distinction between form and content appears. Adaptation aims at the modification of certain ideas in the audience by relating them to other ideas. Here "ideas" must be taken to mean either groups of didactic propositions or, at the other extreme, mere sentiments or predispositions. As long as they are statable, they are ideas. Rhetorical adaptation can be dealt with usefully only at the level of ideas, and not at the level of techniques abstracted from their ideational context. If the rhetorical critic were to analyze, report, and interpret *ideas,* using rhetorical forms as instruments, then valuable historical understandings might be contributed. But the aim of the critic is often simply to point out the rhetorical devices of a speech as forms, not as "idea-adaptation." We argue that adequate speech criticism requires a knowledge of the historical background of the speech; yet this kind of discussion of a speaker's rhetoric ignores the historical and biographical data. The *historical* contribution of such a study is in no way different from that of any historian, untrained and uninterested in rhetoric. The fundamental point, I repeat, is that

[4] In the average thesis, audience adaptation is illustrated by such matters as whether the speaker used examples drawn from the local community or recognized the immediate audience in his introduction. These matters are wholly peripheral to the real process of audience adaptation—to the job of fitting the speaker's basic social values to those of the listeners.

research in public address by those trained in both rhetoric and history could be focused on audience adaptation to produce unique and interesting historical insights. Most theses following the standard method of rhetorical criticism have done little beyond the writing of political history. Rhetorical theory and criticism ought to have a special relation to the history of public address which graduate research has not yet fully recognized.

IV

Questionable aspects of contemporary rhetorical criticism have been pointed out by various writers. My real purpose here is not to do the same thing, but to reformulate the objectives toward which future rhetorical criticism should be directed. There is no need for all research in rhetoric to follow a single pattern. Indeed, a pluralistic approach to research is the only intellectually defensible position. Still, if the foregoing analysis of existing inadequacies in rhetorical research is accepted, then the objectives which ought to operate are somewhat as follows: (1) to report and interpret the manner in which a speaker's social values have been related to the social values of his audiences in the course of his rhetorical adaptation—this is the historical function of criticism; (2) to evaluate particular speeches and speakers by estimating the appropriateness and evaluating the uniqueness of the idea-adaptation in them—this is the evaluative function of criticism; (3) to re-examine, re-evaluate, and if possible to modify contemporary rhetorical theory through the examination of the adaptive processes in speeches—this is the creative function of criticism.

The acceptance of these objectives of historical interpretation, critical evaluation, and creative theorizing would clearly require us to devise certain new methods. I have space to indicate only a few of these methodological implications.

Historical interpretation requires that the central propositions of a speech be approached in terms of the receptivity of the audience to the ideas the speaker intended to convey. The basic materials of such an analysis are the popular ethical or social values involved in the subject. The speech will assert and compare, deprecate or heighten, and finally unite these values to imply social action. The propositions of a speech become acceptable to listeners only as they are made to derive from the listeners' values or as some attempt to modify or redirect the listeners' values is made. Consider the differences between "socialized industry" and "socialized secondary school education." An attempt to deal with the conflicting popular values implied in these terms would involve much more than semantic acuity; it would also demand an understanding of the ways in which specific groups of people have developed different attitudes toward these ideas. This kind of interpretation will produce something quite different from the usual political history; a kind of sociology of ideas is involved, or a history of public philosophies.[5]

However, a single, static concept of these popular values is neither possible nor valuable. Human values can be talked about only as constellations of attitudes moving through qualitative changes in historical continuity. The effort to comprehend this "history of ideas" is at the center of speech criticism, for rhetorical adaptation can be understood only on the basis of an adequate historical perspective on these germinal values. Not only must a study in rhetorical criticism (as historical interpretation) proceed on the basis of some such perspective, but, in turn, each additional study should expand and deepen the available perspective. In this manner, a meaningful history of public address can be created.[6]

My view of research in rhetoric derives directly from classical concepts of the function of rhetoric. The ethos, pathos, and argument of a speech can be investigated only in terms of specific patterns of value operating in specific listeners and speakers at specific places and times. Thus, historical interpretation may be thought of as the examination of speeches by reaching back in time and place to estimate ethos, pathos, or argument.

Yet even those who agree with this objective quail at the prospect of digging out these imbedded values. Anyone who has searched for such values among the bare printed words of an unfamiliar speech can testify to its difficulties. Still, this is one of the main directions which history itself has taken, from W. E. H. Lecky and James Harvey Robinson through Henry Steele Commager, Merle Curti, and Crane Brinton. A good biography, like Perry's study of William James, involves philosophy and literature as well as history.[7] Rhetorical

---

[5] Note that this historical approach to criticism is not concerned with demonstrating that speeches *caused* subsequent events; its intention is to reveal the pattern of popular ideas which *accompanied* events in history.

[6] See E. J. Wrage, "Public Address: A Study in Social and Intellectual History," *QJS*, XXXIII (1947), 451–457.

[7] Several recent publications in history are of great value to this sort of historical interpretation of speeches. One which should become "must reading" for all graduate students in rhetoric and public address is *Harvard Guide to American History* by Oscar Handlin et al. (Cambridge, Massachusetts: Harvard University Press, 1954), especially the articles on historical method. An interesting back-

criticism, however, has somehow felt that this sort of nondepartmental approach does violence to its real function. If the criticism of public address continues to turn inward on itself, and remains content with duplicative studies which pile up artificial samples of rhetorical techniques (apart from the ideas they contain), then rhetorical criticism will have passed up its most significant scholarly function.

Beyond historical interpretation lies the second objective of rhetorical criticism, the evaluation of instances of public address—the passing of judgment on the relative worth of speeches. Much "historical interpretation" has been attempted, but one searches the pages of research studies in vain for deliberate judgments of comparative merit. Perhaps such evaluation is not deemed important, but the only extended treatment of rhetorical criticism now in print argues that evaluation is the central objective of critical research.[8] The question is, what sort of comparative judgments can and should be passed on speeches?

The principal difficulty of speech criticism is that we are not really able to evaluate a man's skill as a speaker apart from his ideas (his beliefs, attitudes, etc.). The usual course, as noted above, is to abstract the speaker's techniques from the idea-content and to discuss their similarity to the norms of classical theory. Like historical interpretation, this evaluation of technique ought to be centered on idea adaptation, but the difficulty lies in the stubborn complexity and opaqueness of adaptation.

Improvement in methods for evaluating adaptation should probably begin with the presumption that technique cannot be evaluated apart from its content. The next presumption should be that adaptation can only be analyzed as an over attempt by a speaker to connect certain larger ethical-social values with specific proposals for social action, either immediate or delayed. That is to say, the speaker's aim is to secure audience acceptance of certain end-values, and then to demonstrate that the actions being urged are more consistent with those values than are any others.

Based on these presumptions, rhetorical evaluation will attempt to discover the following things: (1) the basic values on which the speaker rests his specific proposals; (2) the specific proposals themselves; (3) the manner in which the speaker attempts to connect values

---

ground of this problem of method is provided in Edward N. Saveth's *Understanding the American Past* (Boston: Little, Brown and Company, 1954). Perhaps the best brief philosophy of history now in print is contained in H. J. Muller, *The Uses of the Past* (New York: Oxford University Press, 1952); see especially p. 69.

[8] See Lester Thonssen and A. Craig Baird, *Speech Criticism* (New York: Ronald Press Company, 1948).

with proposals in the minds of his audience; (4) the extent to which these connections were appropriate to the audience being addressed. These various "connections" are not simply "logical appeals"; the connections will be established in the listener's mind by virtue of all kinds of appeal in the speech. The form of these connections, when abstracted from their idea-content, will be classifiable in terms of traditional rhetorical devices. But the important point is that the rhetorical form is only an aid in evaluating the success with which a speaker selected and established the most appropriate idea relationships in the speech.[9]

Like a critic in any field, the rhetorical critic must discover the *uniqueness* of a given speaker's efforts at adaptation. Every speaker's adaptation will be relatively unique in terms of content, and it is not simply the bizarre or extraordinary form of adaptation which we seek. Still, a speaker's uniqueness remains a function of the appropriateness of his adaptation to all the discoverable factors in the situation as that speaker faced it. To repeat, the great need in criticism is for specific methods by which to pursue this aim.

Some critics have attempted to avoid the necessity of this sort of subjective judgment by experimenting with quasi-scientific devices for measuring the elements of the speaking situation, or for correlating a rhetorical technique with an audience response. Experimental research can undoubtedly test, and may even change, much of rhetorical theory, but the way to critical evaluation will not be thus supplied. The final choice involved in any evaluative judgment is by definition subjective. Ultimately, the evaluation of greater or less rhetorical effectiveness must rest on the construction of careful historical hypotheses. The critic must be willing to immerse himself in the available data on the speech in its time, and then to make a straightforward judgment on the manner in which the speaker used the "best available means of persuasion" in terms of the specific ideas of the speaker and his audience. Such judgments will involve personal estimates of the objective "rightness" of the speaker's system of values, as well as of the potential effectiveness of these values as persuasion. No experimental or scientific device can be substituted for these processes, nor should it be. This situation is not an evil; on the contrary, it may yet

[9] The lists of "reaction tendencies," "psychological appeals," "basic human motives," etc., which appear in most rhetoric textbooks are of no great value to the critic of speeches. It is the particular value and the specific action proposition connected with it which supply the basic data by which a speech may be evaluated, not the generalized category or the abstract form.

force us to produce the greatest contribution which criticism can make.[10]

There is, however, a major objection to the type of criticism being urged here: it is difficult. This "difficulty" comes down to a matter of how long it takes to do it, for no one would have the temerity to argue the superiority of a method simply because it is easier than others. The time-consuming aspect of this sort of research is undeniable, but that very fact introduces the larger problem of limiting the scope of research in public address.

It would seem wholly appropriate for a doctoral thesis, pursuing the method I have suggested here, to be devoted to a study of the two inaugural addresses of Lincoln, or to Clay's lengthy address on the compromise of 1850, or to three or four selected sermons by Theodore Parker. What about some representative selections from the Scopes trial speeches, or the McCarthy hearings, or the political conventions of 1896 or 1912, or the Harvard Phi Beta Kappa addresses, or the meetings of the 1954 Ecumenical group at Evanston, Illinois? Some of these topics have been previously treated, in one way or another, but could anyone argue that the substance of one of these topics is no longer adequate to support intensive study by other doctoral candidates? The point is that interpretative or evaluative studies following the line suggested in this article can be managed only on subjects of limited scope. The time is overdue when doctoral theses in Speech should be less compendious and more thorough, and the presumption that every graduate student must have a whole new speaker of his own is preposterous.

The third function of research in rhetoric, in addition to historical interpretation and critical evaluation, is to modify or add to rhetorical theory itself. This function has been referred to throughout the above remarks, and only one further point need be added. The central issue in modern Speech education lies in the area of the ethics of rhetoric. The conception of rhetoric as simply a bag of tricks has been denied all the way from Plato's distrust of the Sophists to the modern distrust of Dale Carnegie. Yet the answer lies not in arguing that we must teach Speech as an "art," but in recognizing that the real difference between a defensible rhetoric and a modern sophistry can be delineated only through a fundamentally ethical criticism of the value-action connections which make up the real persuasion of a

[10] On this point, see the function of criticism as outlined by Lionel Trilling in *The Liberal Imagination* (New York: Doubleday and Company, 1950).

speech. Like the creative theorist in economics or political science, we can no longer leave ethics to the philosophy department.

From this point of view, rhetorical criticism takes on special importance for the future of Speech education, and ultimately for the future of a society dominated by mass communication. As Speech courses grow more and more "gimmicky," the need to reformulate theory through "ethical criticism" is very great. "Principles" of speech there must be, but training in Speech from Isocrates and Quintilian to our time has always been responsible for producing something more than "pitch men." As criticism in the graduate school goes, so goes rhetorical theory and teaching.

The view on research in rhetoric as expressed in this article rests on the viewpoint taken toward the relationships of theory, criticism, and history in our field. These relationships may be summarized as follows: (1) Rhetorical theory, as a basis for criticism, should consist of a series of formal techniques drawn from the history of rhetorical theory and unified into a general sytem. (2) A dynamic interaction should be maintained between this body of theory and current criticism; criticism should slowly but continuously remold theory. (3) Criticism should go beyond concern with purely formal rhetorical concepts; it must enter the field of making specific value judgments of the appropriateness and rightness of the idea adaptation to be found in speeches; criticism must *evaluate* speeches. (4) Criticism should provide the much needed monographs from which to construct an "idea-centered" history of public address. (5) Historical interpretation, critical evalaution, and creative theorizing must all become directly concerned with the ethics of rhetoric.

THE CRITERION OF RHETORICAL EFFICACY
Rosemond Tuve

Constant adjustment to some hypothetical reader is responsible for much advice in Renaissance poetic, and poets' practice shows the advice willingly taken. This meant that the poetic image was almost universally expected to meet a criterion of 'efficacy.'

The final determination of efficacy—efficacy upon the affections, as generally understood—depended upon many factors which did not

From *Elizabethan and Metaphysical Imagery*, by Rosemond Tuve, Chicago, University of Chicago Press, 1947. Reprinted by permission.

reside in the poem at all but in the mind which was to read it. The nature of that mind, its approachability, its needs—these are constant concerns of the Renaissance theorist and poet. The latter does not appear to have rebelled against this aspect of his problem; grumbles are scarce. Diatribes against particular audiences are legion; there are plenty of home thrusts at stupid critics, and complaints against ladies who do not respond to a good sonnet when they are sent one, but the poets simply declare for another audience or for silence, and no one seems to hit on the solution of thinking of poems independently of readers.

The inclusion of poets among persons who have out-and-out plans to affect readers causes discomfort, again, to a modern mind. It brings up suggestions of dogmatism or immature arrogance and seems to open the way to a confusion between perfection of technical skill and shrewd employment of neat trickery, or, worse still, to a confusion between poet and preacher. I push aside these difficulties for the moment, though they are far from chimerical, to distinguish certain emphases which this criterion brought into criticism and certain qualities which it underlined in images.

Images are often brought forward in the critical writings to demonstrate and fortify the accepted tenet that poetry should, or rather necessarily will, move the affections of a reader and hence persuade him. Among other kinds of form-determining ornament, they exemplify the poet's power to do what Puttenham calls 'inveigle and appassionate the mind,' like 'a pleader' rather than a judge.[1] The 'moving' power of poetry is everywhere noted, often in comments which stress the middle term in the commonplace *docendi, movendi, delectandi*, which (though dependent on Cicero and Quintilian) was applied to both poetry and rhetoric. The notion is implicit or stated in dozens of writers [2] and in chance comment on poems or poets; and acceptance of it clearly shows through discussions of 'delight' or 'teaching,' or of the nature and power of figures.

---

[1] III, vii, p. 154. For more emphasis on 'persuading copiously and vehemently,' see, e.g., p. 196, entreating the poet to 'play also the Orator . . . . , to pleade, or to praise, or to advise.' See above, chap. v, n. 14, n.9, or see references cited in W. Ringler's note to Rainolds' statement of the idea (*op. cit.*, in chap. vii, n.13, above). Relations between the disciplines are more carefully examined in Part II below. Obviously, no criterion for imagery can ignore poetry's *capacity* to move the affections, but this one makes specific demands.

[2] This tenet is so universally propounded that I make no attempt to cite the passages concerning it which everyone familiar with Renaissance poetic will recall—in Sidney, Minturno, Boccaccio, Tasso, Pontano, Mazzoni, Du Bellay, Scaliger, Daniel, Jonson, Carew, and others.

The criterion of efficacy was interpreted in close relation to the poet's special problems, yet statements of it show, too, how close his problems were to those of the *rhetor*. These typical passages, from Du Bellay and Peacham, point to an oratorical power in the poet and yet especially recall notions earlier examined of imagery's power to 'amplify,' to endow matters with importance or with 'evident' immediacy:

> . . . saiches, Lecteur, que celuy sera varitablement le poëte que je cherche en nostre langue, qui me fera indigner, apayser, ejouyr, douloir, aymer, hayr, admirer, etonner, bref, qui me tiendra la bride de mes affections, me tournant ça et la à son plaisir [ii, chap. 11 (1549)].
>
> [The author, especially through amplification] may prevaile much in drawing the mindes of his hearers to his owne will and affection: he may winde them from their former opinions, ... may move them to be of his side, ... to mourne or to marvel, to love or to hate, to be pleased or . . . . angry, ... to desire or to be satisfied . . . . to envy, to abhorre . . . . to be subiect to the power of his speech whither soever it tendeth [p. 121 (1593)].

It was as obvious to the Renaissance as to us that such powers as these in a poet find their parallel in powers ascribed to the orator by Cicero, Quintilian, and many others. This relation was accepted without cavil. The element that was seen as rhetorical in poetry was this conscious *penetration* into men's faculties with such power that they could not choose but be moved. 'How wonderfully shall . . . . his wordes pearce into their inward partes,' says Peacham (sig. A iii [1577]). It would be easy to annotate this understanding by quoting from the poets themselves—Drayton, King, Daniel.[3] This power which critics and poets pluck out as the distinguishing characteristic of rhetoric is a power to which poetry would be unwilling to relinquish its claim. These persuasions felt in the heart and felt along the blood are not to be confined to the sister-discipline.

However, conceptions like these involve certain differences between Renaissance and modern ways of thinking about poetry. In earlier thinking the unity of the process *moving:persuading* is not disturbed. Even a modern reader, if not forewarned, is likely to testify that both together are 'what actually happens' in reading a poem (in however small a degree). So, too, early theorists do not share the uneasiness of the modern poet who is unwilling to do the second and yet aware

---

[3] See the Appendix, Note K, for typical characterizations of 'rhetoric' by poets; the idea furnishes the basis for a favorite image.

that poetry is bound to do the first. Moreover, until long after the Elizabethans, the reader is thought of as not merely the spectator of the great 'motion of mind' of the poet. Although it is accepted that a vehement 'inward stir' will characterize the poet's sensibilities as well, discussions are little preoccupied with his feelings, greatly preoccupied with those he will evoke. The critical question of 'sincerity' is neglected in favor of the poetic problem of efficacy through credibility.[4] The truth of the affections was a serious matter, but it stood to be answered less in terms of the question 'did the poet feel it?' than 'will the reader feel it and why should he?' Nor do men of the Renaissance expect poetry to achieve this moving power simply as a by-product of the excited state of the author's sensibilities. The line the earlier period ignores is the line nervously drawn by modern poetic between *a poet himself moved* and a poet *persuading or convincing*. If the Renaissance had tried to stay to one side of this line, we should probably have lost Donne, who explodes the meaning straight out of Yeats's famous distinction: 'We make out of the quarrel with others, rhetoric, but of the quarrel with ourselves, poetry.'"

All this does not convict Elizabethans of thinking up ways to work on readers' 'emotions.' I have used various Elizabethan circumlocutions rather than the word 'emotions,' since the true meaning of their tenets would be belied by introducing terms that carry our sharper distinction between feelings and thoughts. Several of the faculties are concerned, in both parties to the communication. Images have efficacy to move a reader's affections, to quite properly affect his judgments; they move him to feel intensely, to will, to act, to understand, to believe, to change his mind.

Though poetry and rhetoric share the power of moving readers, and although to a Renaissance man this included persuading them to certain mental acts, methods of doing so may, of course, differ.[5] Yet many methods are shared, and these touch imagery nearly. Though Sidney says he deserves 'to be pounded for straying' from

[4] Sincerity is sometimes commented on, by both theorists and poets, as a prerequisite for writing credibly; Sidney's 'look in thy heart and write' is a statement on method and is so presented.

[5] Tasso, Castelvetro, Mazzoni, Sidney, and others, of course, have well-known passages in which distinctions between the disciplines are stated or implied. The important ones may be conveniently turned up through the index in A. H. Gilbert (see Bibliography). They are usually very general, and most points which affect imagery have already been drawn into this discussion (like Mazzoni's 'the credible as credible is the subject of rhetoric and the credible as marvelous is the subject of poetry,' in Gilbert, p. 370; the relation to discussions of amplification, hyperbole, and trope is clear).

Poetry to Oratory, he thinks nevertheless that 'both have such an affinity in this wordish consideration' that his digression but assists his meaning. Moreover, one of the few actual statements on imagery as such, in Sidney, is his comment here on the similitude—one of the devices of rhetorical persuasion of which poetry makes most use.[6] But special cases need not be adduced; a large amount of common ground is accepted by poets of every stripe throughout the period. Especially the tropes and figured patterns of language which rhetoric had set down as bound to move the affections of men were regarded as common property. This is not so extraordinary, and is still true; all poetry, like other impassioned speech, makes use of the methods which the rhetorician lists. But the Renaissance poet did so consciously, very willingly, and with keener realization of purposes shared with other disciplines.

His willingness to move readers by these means has already been demonstrated time and again. With clear intent to persuade readers to share their ideas of the value of something, the poets use figure after figure chiefly praised by rhetoricians for this special power. I exemplify with a handful only: *aetiologia* or the *tellcause*, to 'fortifie our allegations' (Puttenham, p. 228; this is the form of some of the most beautiful images in Elizabethan poetry and is a favorite with the Metaphysicals); similitudes;[7] *ironia*, to reprove by derision and illusion; *sarcasmus*, like bitter corrections in physic; proverbs, strong to confirm and piercing to imprint; *congeries* or the heaping figure, like the violent strokes of battle; *micterismus* (Puttenham's *fleering frumpe*, p. 191), to reprove and jest subtly, like a black frost that will nip a man's nose before he sees it.

[6] Sidney is reminding writers that the 'force' of a similitude is not 'to proove anything to a contrary Disputer but onely to explane to a willing hearer,' so that *a surfeit* of them is absurd, no 'whit informing the judgment, already eyther satisfied, or by similitudes not to be satisfied' (in Gregory Smith, I, 203; he is criticizing euphuistic writing). This antipathy to overuse of the similitude is based not on a distinction between poetry and rhetoric but on the new Ramistic definitions of the dialectic proper to all three disciplines (see below, chap. xii). The point to be noticed here is that Sidney is not concerned to make any such distinction as Yeats makes, though he, too, sees contentious 'proving' as out of place. What Yeats really objects to is what sixteenth and sevententh century alike condemned—false or sophistical rhetoric. His remark is from 'Anima Hominis,' dated 1917; that he uses the word with its usual (and uninformed) nineteenth-century connotations is clear from the closely related poem which precedes these meditations in prose ('Ego Dominus Tuus,' dated 1915; see *Essays*, Vol. IV of the *Complete Works* [New York, 1924], pp. 492, 482).

[7] Which, of course, 'confirm'—and 'to the short form of similitude pertains the metaphor' (Milton, *Art of Logic*, I, xxi). The unattributed characterizations following are from Peacham.

I have overweighted this list with satirical figures partly because they grew in favor as poets later in the period grew fonder of satire's backhanded form of persuasion and partly because much admirably subtle modern use of these same figures has somewhat extended or changed them. *Ironia* is the most important of these. The figure has no trace of the modern meaning frequently termed romantic irony; and this fact is symptomatic of the earlier period's extreme concern with the reader and his understanding of the subject, and small concern with the author save as artist. *Ironia* is praised as one of the most moving and subtle of 'dark' tropes; by it one says more forcefully what one means by saying what one does not mean. It has no tinge of self-protectiveness; it is not thought of (and so far as I can see is not used in the poetry) as a device by which the poet may forestall the objections of those who might suggest he had not seen all around his subject. He may through it forestall objections which he does not share; but I find no sure cases of what Eliot, for example, can do with such uncanny deftness—suggest sometimes what he dares not mean, sometimes what he hopes is not true. The Renaissance expectation is that the reader is more likely to be *moved* if, with delight at an added logical subtlety, he apprehends the author's true evaluation under a mask. Whether some darling conventionality is being 'derided' or only some bizarre unconventionality, the reader's assent is equally the poet's concern, and it is understood that the reader will give it on grounds of some subtlety in the argument, not some sophistication in the arguer. *Ironia* is used generally when the poet is also to some degree persuader; it is used not as a shield to ward off accusations of semi-blindness or sentimentality, but to help wind him better into the heart of his subject.

Concern with moving the affections had other immediate effects upon imagery besides a very conscious use of figures, but many of them have already been mentioned. A chief effect is increased emphasis upon imagery as functional. Given the general principle that ornament functions to move the affections, poets had yet to solve problems of choice—through processes which probably have not changed much, though sterner and more settled requisites gave more help. Donne chose patternings of repetition in the first of the two images below, intellectually pleasing subtleties in the second. Such of his reasons as we may follow lie in differences of genre, 'cause,' mood (inseparable from subject), affections and faculties addressed in the reader—all the considerations regulated by that decorum which must become second nature to a poet.

When thou sigh'st, thou sigh'st not winde,
　　But sigh'st my soule away,
When thou weep'st, unkindly kinde,
　　My lifes blood doth decay.

('Song,' p. 19)

. . . . Preachers which are
Seas of Wit and Arts, you can, then dare,
Drowne the sinnes of this place, for, for mee
Which am but a scarce brooke, it enough shall bee
To wash the staines away . . . . .

('Satyre IIII,' 237, p. 167)

Both kinds of ornament 'pierce into man's inward parts,' either the *copie* that makes the first ebb and flow and breathe itself away, or the brevity of the ironic challenge in the second, enforced by the harsh wrenching of the rhythm and the homely mocking contrast in the double similitude. The criterion of efficacy does not determine what kind of ornament a poet must use; it merely reminds him that an image powerful perhaps to him but powerless to move another fails in one of its purposes.

Such reminders strengthened the element of sensuousness in images, for 'the minde is not assailable unlesse it be by sensible approches' (Puttenham, III, xix, p. 197). Delighting the ear received the most attention, so that poetic elements especially affected are those of tone and of music—not melodiousness alone, but everything in which verse resembles music: phrasing, pauses, repetitive structures, pitch variations, accelerated and retarded tempo, etc. Such considerations modified the nature of images so greatly (as, of course, they still do) that it is generally very misleading to judge any image without reference to the *design* of sounds of which it forms a part.

Vividness and concreteness in the image are also affected—not always, however, increased. The sensuousness is likely to be truly an 'approach,' to be perceived and as quickly dropped by the reader. Marston's first image below would be the opposite of efficacious if the *gulf* remained long enough to swallow up the *cormorant:*

To everlasting *Oblivion*
Thou mighty gulfe, insatiat cormorant,
　Deride me not, though I seeme petulant
　To fall into thy chops . . . . .
But as for mee, hungry *Oblivion*
Devoure me quick, accept my orizon:
　My earnest prayers, which doe importune thee,

> With gloomy shade of thy still Emperie,
> To vaile both me and my rude poesie . . . . .
> (*Scourge of Villanie*, ed. Harrison, p. 119;
> in HH, p. 368) (Author's italics)

The vaguely sensuous epithet for *gulf* allows it, too, to have *chops*. Similarly *gloomy shade*, etc., needs the modulation through three general phrases before *hungry* Oblivion can come to possess the motionless silent power of a still empery that can veil (vail?) one. A poet's skill in muting his images must equal his skill in producing them, if the appeal to a reader's affections is to be at all a controlled one. Donne has so marvelous a power in this respect that one all but resents his dominion over one's eyes and ears. But, of course, there is scarce a poem without an example of it. It could not but receive special attention in an era when the tenets of poetic constantly reminded poets that the kind and amount of sensuousness in an image must be fitted to the way the receiving mind would work.

These conscious designs upon a reader may seem to us to give the 'art' of poetry a disreputable slot-machine quality: press a button, and a spark will ignite the reader's affections. The safeguard lay in unrelaxed attention to the principle of decorum (for one aspect or another of this principle safeguards each criterion for imagery). The poet was a trumpet to make manifest the perfection of the subject; he was in part creator of that subject, but, nevertheless, its manifested perfection was what exerted its legitimate power over the reader. The poet's responsibility not to abuse this trust is not forgotten even in speaking of the humblest kind of rhetorical figure. Images must be *both* efficacious and proportionate to the nature of what they help to express.

Comments on single figures ring all manner of changes on this double tune of fitness and efficacy (no wonder, since the two are assumed to be casually connected). *Epizeuxis* (as in 'O Absalom, my son, my son') suits the vehement expression of any affection—for pleasant ones, it is like a quaver in music; for sorrow, like a double sigh of the heart; for anger, like a double stab (Peacham, p. 47); it is not to be used but in passion, says Hoskins (p. 12). *Articulus* (*cutted comma*), if used in causes of perturbation and haste, can be a thick and thundering peal of ordnance (Peacham, p. 57). *Traductio* (like Donne's *unkindly kinde* above) may be used with or without passion, 'but so as the use of it come from some choice and not from barrenness' (Hoskins, p. 17). Puttenham rejects some examples of repetitive figures, saying they are 'not figurative but phantastical, for a figure is ever used to a purpose'; one he disdains because it neither urges affection, nor beautifies or enforces the sense, nor has any other subtlety in it, 'and therefore is a very foolish impertinency of speech, and not a figure' (III, xix, p. 202).

Figures of larger scope, and more likely to produce as well as to modify images, receive similar comment. *Congeries,* a multiplication of words 'beatyng in all one thing' (Sherry, fol. 50^v) will be used especially in summing up, being earnest and hasty, and good to enforce the cause and renew the hearer's memory (Puttenham, p. 237). *Incrementum,* the scaling ladder, which climbs to the top of high comparison, requires worthy matter; like fire it can go as high as the matter can carry it.[8] *Exclamation* is not lawful but in extremity of 'motion'; *interrogation* 'is but a warm proposition' and serves where bare affirmation would be too gentle and harmless a speech (Hoskins, pp. 33, 32). One might continue this for some hours. All such advices concern the responsibility which the writer has toward his subject. All these means of expressing subjects are treated with strict attention to suitability as well as to power.

Concepts to which I have called attention in this chapter show, naturally, differences in emphasis rather than absolute differences from modern ideas of poetry. Earlier theory reads as if poetry were conceived of as a relation established between a subject and a reader, though only establishable by a poet. The emphasis on poetry as interesting evidence of the relation between a subject and a particular poet is an emphasis we have learned since, and one which seems the least helpful of any to the understanding of earlier poetry. The earlier kind of polarity, with 'a reader to be affected' as one of the poles, did mean that poets are likely to plead, or complain, or exhort, or argue, much too openly for modern taste, and that we can often easily detect that they intend to 'breede no little alteration in man.' 'For to say truely,' says Puttenham, in discussing the sententious or rhetorical figures, 'what els is man but his minde? . . . . He therefore that hath vanquished the minde of man, hath made the greatest and most glorious conquest' (III, xix, p. 197). Modern thinking finds such emphasis upon a poet's power over readers both arrogant and aesthetically improper.

However, the oscillations toward the pole of 'affecting a reader' were counteracted by the equal strength of the other pole, 'the poem's

---

[8] Peacham, p. 169; cf. also *auxesis,* Puttenham's *avancer,* p. 218. A particular kind of *copie* is commended by Hoskins—dividing and making instances—but commended *when* the subject, if 'generally spoken,' would seem but a flourish, and when one must give more especial note of that which 'universally' could not be conceived without confusion and dulness (p. 24).

true vision of the subject.' This latter responsibility, which earlier writers felt themselves able to meet as we do not, kept serious poets from self-righteous preaching, and honest poets from technically shrewd trickery. We will style their writings exalted propaganda if we think of all ideas as postulates and all defense of the validity of any idea as hawking for one's own postulates. But the Elizabethan and seventeenth-century poet did not think thus. Consequently, he did not take ironically the responsibility of 'truth to the subject'— though he took it very gaily, and the notion that he should gain credence only for what is true did not prevent him from piling Pelion on Ossa to demonstrate the real shape of a molehill.

This tension maintained between the requirements of subject and of reader is often neglected in modern discussions of the relevance of poetic ornament to a core of conceptual meaning. Quite aside from the Renaissance poet's sterner idea of the logical control which a whole should exhibit in all its parts, he would, I think, have seen even seemingly irrelevant richness of texture as having the relevance of instrument—it is instrumental to the establishing of a right relation between reader and subject, and the medium (language) through which he must establish this relation does inescapably thus function. The modern has difficulty answering the question, 'Why add the ornament characteristic of poetic discourse, when the idea can be more clearly and economically stated otherwise?' The Elizabethan, I think, would have simply answered 'Because it would not be heard.' His answer *would have included* the other important assumption, that to 'hear it' without the strength and delicacy of poetry's form of statement was to give not that subject, but some other, a hearing.

Despite this last, there is nothing gained by denying the fact that the Elizabethan thought of the poet's function as close to that of any other thinker—philosophers, preachers, and orators included. He did see the world as a world in which the ideas of human beings were paramount realities [9]—and images convey a man's ideas movingly to others. Yet in the world of 1580 or 1630 this rhetorical aim for imagery did not so much arrogantly place man in the center of the universe, as admit sensibly that, since men were going to read the poetry, it would have to be written to men's eyes, ears, and minds, and written to the scale of human importances. Elizabethan poetry is centered in man's moral, intellectual, and affective impulses and needs, but in much the same way that a modern scholar has remarked that even Copernican astronomy is geocentric: the observations can

[9] See Appendix, Note L, for a fuller admission of the unmodern character of Renaissance poetry in this respect.

be made only from where the observer himself is located, and are stated in terms relative to the earth.[10] Like medieval poets, Elizabethan and seventeenth-century poets frequently suggested the insufficiency of his world-view. But meanwhile, however willingly the insignificancy of man is admitted, there is willing acceptance of the nature of man's mind as a condition for poetry. Even the hard conditions imposed by the nature of a reader's mind are accepted, and images take their form in obedience to the necessity of speaking to the affections, the understanding, the powers of evaluation of the only readers a poet has—other men.

Appendix

Note K

Poets' notions of the fundamental achievement of 'rhetoric' appear to be much the same, at whatever date we choose to alight. Drayton says of Mortimer's letter to the Queen, in which every character wounded like a dart (*Mortimeriados,* 2797; I, 389):

'And every one would *pierce her to the hart,*
    Rethoricall in woe, and using Art:
Reasons of greefe, each sentence doth infer,
    And evere lyne, a true remembrancer.'
King says in his 'Elegy upon Prince Henry's death' (p. 66):
'O killing Rhetorick of Death! two words
Breathe stronger terrours then Plague, Fire, or Swords
Ere conquer'd.'

Note L

'Henry's dead'—this 'were Epitaph and Verse/Worthy to be prefixt in Natures herse.' King liked the conceit; he speaks in a sermon published in 1627 of the 'rhetoric' of thunder persuading the Jews (see Bibliography; p. 13), and in another published in 1662 of the tomb as orator, the rhetoric of sorrow, eyes more 'fluent' than the tongue (pp. 2, 33). For a long Crashaw example see chap. xi, n. 48; and, of course, the famous Donne blood-speaking-in-her-cheeks image has the same base. Daniel uses it in a passage on Rosamond's beauty which I quote in full both for its explanation of that poetic power which poets thought of as 'rhetorical' and for the charming tumbled hurry of its close. The last image in it happens to be a 'Metaphysical conceit' from an unjustly neglected 'conventional' and 'prosaic' poet:

'Sweet silent rethorique of perswading eyes:
Dombe eloquence, whose powre doth move the blood,
More then the words, or wisedome of the wise:
Still harmonie, whose diapason lyes
    Within a brow, the key which passions move,
    To ravish sence, and play a world in love.'
('Complaint of Rosamond,' 121; in HH, p. 251)

[10] See Francis R. Johnson, *Astronomical Thought in Renaissance England* (Baltimore, 1937), p. 117.

I am afraid that both earlier Elizabethans and Metaphysical poets were all the things J. C. Ransom castigates in 'Poetry: A Note in Ontology,' *The World's Body* (New York, 1938); see also Allen Tate's related series of articles on 'Three Types of Poetry,' appearing in the *New Republic*, Vol. LXXVIII (1934), and with some changes in *Reactionary Essays* (New York, 1936).

These poets relate things to the human soul as a center of action; they can, I fear, be called sciencing, devouring idealists expecting to take a return from anything whatsoever, writing discourses on things on the understanding that they are translatable at every point into ideas (pp. 124, 130, 118, 122). If 'the poetic impulse' is defined by its struggle against the rational and practical impulses gratified by other modes of knowing, then quite possibly they did not have it; they are not even aware that image is *versus* idea (pp. 130, 114). I make these bold statements not through entire lack of sympathy with these critics' subtly persuasive arguments against 'Platonic poetry' but because these arguments serve admirably to help us distinguish what is 'bogus' in much poetry written during and since the Romantic period, whereas the oppositions they pose are not really pertinent to the interpretation of poems like Marvell's, or Herbert's, or Donne's, to say nothing of Spenser's or Ralegh's. The antitheses upon which these arguments are erected simply do not characterize the thought of these poets, or of their period.

The poet's world of 'stubborn and contingent objects,' rich in their *Dinglichkeit;* leaving us 'revelling in the thick *dinglich* substance'; with a sign up 'This road does not go through to action; fictitious'—Renaissance poets cannot be got whole into such a poet's world (pp. 123, 142, 131). Too much of what they insistently put into their poems is left unexplained by such a view of their world. To escape the slipperiness of generalizations, I illustrate with a much-used example; any would do, and none would bring in all the necessary points. The poem exhibits the typical and traditional relation of image to idea and of both to 'cause' or subject-and-intention.

One cannot even approach 'accounting for' Herbert's 'The Windows' (in HH, p. 743) in terms of 'reconstituting the world of perceptions,' 'holding out stubbornly against science for the enjoyment of its images,' having the courage of its metaphors (rather daring ones) for the sake of 'increasing the volume of the percipienda or sensibilia' (p. 130). Even the force of Herbert's sensuous diction is dependent on our interest in the relation of the *Dinge* to the idea. We enjoy somewhat the perception that a window uncolored produces a kind of flaring light, waterish, bleak, and thin; we enjoy more the pleasure of perceiving the aptness of the comparison between that sensuous percept and the preacher who has only speech, contrasted with the preacher that has God's life shining annealed in color, even in his brittle crazy glass, so that the light of doctrine comes through in glory, not vanishing like a flaring thing. More than this, verses like 1 and 3–5, and the tone deliberately given to the whole, are simply left on our hands as pointless or hypocritical, if we think Herbert was interested just to point out all the kinds of preachers a world thick with preachers could provide; we have to do the best we can, temporarily at least, to care whether it provides the first kind or the second, and to pursue not the fact of the difference but the idea which made Herbert bother to note it. We may not enjoy the value of the idea as 'truth,' although I think Herbert and his readers expected to, in poetry. But unless we enjoy relations to ideas, and the *possible* validity of ideas, more than *Dinge* or *Dinglichkeit,* the poet has used a technique very ill fitted to our enjoyment.

MOULDING BELIEFS IN FICTION *Wayne C. Booth*

As a rhetorician, an author finds that some of the beliefs on which a full appreciation of his work depends come ready-made, fully accepted by the postulated reader as he comes to the book, and some must be implanted or reinforced. We might expect to find that whatever space is devoted to overt rhetoric will be spent on the questionable areas. Yet there is a surprising amount of commentary directed to reinforcing values which most readers, one would think, already take for granted. "There are two sorts of people, who, I am afraid, have already conceived some contempt for my hero on account of his behaviour to Sophia," says "Fielding" in *Tom Jones* (Book IV, chap. vi), and he then attempts, through ridicule, to persuade all of his readers to feel what most of them really must have felt in some degree before the passage began—that they are "the sort" who feel contempt only when it is really justified. But Fielding knows that mere agreement is not enough. Every reader knows, or thinks he knows, "the value of true love." But the author cannot count on such general agreement to be lively enough for his purposes. By making us laugh at those imaginary fools who do not know love's true worth, he at the same time makes us value it actively, in the precise form to be encountered in his book.

> Examine your heart, my good reader, and resolve whether you do believe these matters with me. If you do, you may now proceed to their exemplification in the following pages: if you do not, you have, I assure you, already read more than you have understood; and it would be wiser to pursue your business, or your pleasures (such as they are), than to throw away any more of your time in reading what you can neither taste nor comprehend. To treat of the effects of love to you, must be as absurd as to discourse on colours to a man born blind; . . . love probably may, in your opinion, very greatly resemble a dish of soup or a sirloin of roastbeef [Book VI, chap. i].

In this way he often defines for us the precise ordering of values on which our judgment should depend. Tom's admirable "goodness of heart, and openness of temper," for example, are carefully balanced against his lack of prudence. Indispensable as they are, they are not

From *The Rhetoric of Fiction*, by Wayne C. Booth, Chicago, University of Chicago Press, 1961. Reprinted by permission.

enough. "Prudence and circumspection are necessary even to the best of men. They are indeed as it were a guard to Virtue, without which she can never be safe. It is not enough that your designs, nay that your actions are intrinsically good, you must take care they shall appear so. If your inside be never so beautiful, you must preserve a fair outside also" (Book III, chap. vii). Since in real life we do not agree about the precise ordering of "goodness of heart" and "prudence," we need such guidance—not for our own lives, but for our judgment on Tom Jones.[1]

Similar overt efforts to reinforce norms can be found in most fiction. In *Billy Budd* there is danger that the readers' admiration for Billy's integrity may be submerged beneath their contempt for his simplicity. So Melville tries to do something about it. "But shrewd ones may opine that it was hardly possible for Billy to refrain from going up to the afterguardsman and bluntly demanding to know his purpose . . . . . Shrewd ones may also think it but natural in Billy to set about sounding some of the other impressed men of the ship in order to discover what basis, if any, there was for the emissary's obscure suggestions." The shrewd may question, but "something more, or rather, something else than mere shrewdness is perhaps needful for the due understanding of such a character as Billy Budd's."[2] Similarly, in *Thomas the Imposter* readers may confuse the values by which the various "heroes" are to be judged, and Cocteau intrudes unashamedly to set us straight: "Heroism gathered together a mixed group under the same palm. Many embryonic murderers found in war the opportunity, the excuse, and the reward of their vice, side by side with the martyrs." On the one hand, there were the "criminals," the *Joyeux*, and on the other, the Zouaves and the marines, whose officers were "charming heroes. These young men, the bravest in the world and of whom not one remains alive, played at fighting without the least hatred. Alas, such games end badly."[3]

Finally, when Graham Greene senses, in *Brighton Rock* (1938), that we may apply the conventional standards of right and wrong rather than the required standards of Good and Evil, he does not hesitate

---

[1] For the best discussion of the role of Tom's imprudence, and his resulting vulnerability, see R. S. Crane, "The Concept of Plot and the Plot of *Tom Jones*," *Critics and Criticism*, ed. R. S. Crane (Chicago, 1952), pp. 616–47. Crane's discussion of the narrator is also very helpful.

[2] "Billy Budd, Foretopman," in *Melville's Billy Budd*, ed. F. Barron Freeman (Cambridge, Mass., 1948), pp. 210–11.

[3] Jean Cocteau, *Thomas the Impostor*, trans. Lewis Galantiere (London, 1925), p. 99.

to set us straight, distinguishing carefully between the pitiable but blessed "hole" where Rose lives, knowing "murder, copulation, extreme poverty, fidelity, and the love and fear of God," and the glaring, "open world outside" where people make a false claim to "experience." [4]

Though we find such reinforcing rhetoric even in works based on generally accepted norms, the need naturally increases whenever there is the likelihood of crippling disagreement with the reader. The skilful author will, of course, make his rhetoric in itself a pleasure to read; it is thus often difficult to tell whether a passage about values is present for its own sake, as ornament, or for a larger cause. "And so they fell to it," says the narrator of Balzac's "The High Constable's Wife" (*Droll Tales* [1832–37]), "in the time-honoured fashion, and in the delicious throes of that wild fever which you know of—at least, I hope you do—they became totally indifferent . . . ." And in the "Virgin of Thilhouse" he makes the point even more explicit by intruding to say that his "Droll Stories are designed rather to impart the morality of pleasure than to preach the pleasure of morality." The pleasure we take in such passages depends on their comic attack on conventional morality, and they are in this aspect self-justifying. Yet the attack is itself needed to insure the success of the dramatic portions of the stories. If the reader for a moment judges the characters by everyday standards of chastity and fidelity, the stories will be ruined. We might easily fall into the error of thinking that in this respect Balzac's readers came ready-made, but we can be sure that his work would not contain so much rhetoric in favor of licentiousness if he felt that he could count on his readers to accept licentiousness as a matter of course.

It is commonly believed that readers in the twentieth century have become tolerant about sexual matters. If we accepted this belief, we might expect that Balzac's kind of rhetoric about love or sexual behavior would disappear from our novels—especially since overt rhetoric of any kind has been in disfavor on technical grounds. But in fact we find great quantities of such rhetoric. Since the precise relationship of love to sex can never be taken for granted, each novelist is left to establish the world in which the loves of his characters take place. One of the most interesting and successful examples of this effort is the novel *La jument verte* by Marcel Aymé (1933). In this story there are two narrators, the unspecified author, suave, ironic, but reliable in his basic opinions, the other a painted portrait of a green mare, a kind of lustful goddess of love who blesses by her presence anyone who

[4] Part IV, chap. ii, conclusion (Penguin ed., 1943), p. 124.

really understands the message of her fecundity. For proper enjoyment of this story of the comic battle between two very different brothers and their contrasting families, we must grant the superiority of the peasant-brother's open and loving sexuality over the "respectable" brother's secret pleasures. In Honoré's house, the narrator tells us again and again, love was something shared; though each member of the family drank the wine of love from his own glass, he found in it an intoxication which "brother recognized in brother, father in son, and which broke out everywhere in silent song." In Ferdinand's house this "unity of pleasure" was missing. "Each member of the family followed his own road of love in a direction which he alone knew." In the whole family, only the father "bothered himself with the secrets of the others, but that was only to persecute them." [5] Whatever the real beliefs of Aymé's readers, however free or constrained they may be in their private behavior, he re-creates them temporarily in his own image—or rather, in the image of the "author" who has his existence only in the book. We cannot infer Aymé's beliefs or behavior with any certainty from the book, but we can infer with some confidence what Aymé expects his postulated readers' beliefs to be. And again it is clear that they do not come ready-made. Even the most emancipated reader will not fall unaided into the precise code of the Maison d'Honoré.

One would predict even more elaborate rhetoric when, instead of elevating one recognized code over another, an author tries to effect a transvaluation of all values, to go beyond this or that code to entirely new territory, or to hold all values in abeyance. But intrusions used for these ends are not easy to find. Such radical transformations have generally been attempted only by the very authors who were most strongly opposed to reliable narration. Gide, for example, pretending to neutrality toward his characters and the conflicts of values they face, rebukes his readers for their unfairness in asking him to pass judgment.

> I intended to make this book as little an indictment as an apology and took care to pass no judgment. The public nowadays will not

[5] "Dans la maison d'Honoré, l'amour était comme le vin d'un clos familial; on le buvait chacun dans son verre, mais il procurait une ivresse que le frère pouvait reconnaître chez son frère, le père chez son fils, et qui se répandait en chansons du silence. . . . A Saint-Margelon, dans la maison de Ferdinand, cette solidarité dans le plaisir n'existait pas. Chacun cherchait son chemin d'amour dans une direction qu'il était seul à connaître. De toute la famille, il n'y avait que le vétérinaire à se préoccuper des secrets des autres, mais c'était pour les persécuter" (Paris, 1933), pp. 152–53.

forgive an author who, after relating an action, does not declare himself either for or against it; more than this, during the very course
of the drama they want him to take sides, pronounce in favor either of
Alceste or Philinte, of Hamlet or Ophelia . . . . I do not indeed claim
that neutrality (I was going to say "indecision") is the certain mark of
a great mind; but I believe that many great minds have been very
loath to . . . conclude—and that to state a problem clearly is not to
suppose it solved in advance.[6]

If Gide really requires neutrality of his readers, then such a statement
is helpful indeed. But for good or ill, nothing like it appears within
the book itself.

Intrusions about values and beliefs offer a special temptation to
the novelist, and we can all name works in which the philosopher-
manqué indulges in irrelevant pontification. But as we have seen [7]
the quality of such passages depends far more on the quality of the
author's mind than upon whether he chooses to push his profundities
back into the mind of a dramatized character. One's attitude toward
the much debated theorizing of Gavin Stevens at the end of Faulkner's
Intruder in the Dust is not affected markedly by the fact that the
ideas are not given directly by Faulkner. The question is whether
Gavin's elaborate commentary is essentially related to the nephew's
experience of a near-lynching and his consequent growth toward
maturity. In any "truth-discovery" novel, and especially in novels
which try to lead young people to the hard truths of adulthood, the
problem is to make the discovery a convincing outcome of the experience. In *Intruder*, as in many such works, the attitude toward
which Faulkner wants his young hero to grow is so complex that
neither the boy nor the reader is likely to infer it from the experience
itself. They both must therefore be preached at by the wise uncle,
sometimes with little direct relevance to the drama. "The American
really loves nothing but his automobile: not his wife his child nor his
country nor even his bank-account first (in fact he doesn't really love
that bank-account nearly as much as foreigners like to think because
he will spend almost any or all of it for almost anything provided it is
valueless enough) but his motorcar. Because the automobile has

---

[6] Commenting on *The Immoralist*, originally published in 1921. My quotation
is from the Introduction to the Knopf Vintage edition, 1954. On Gide's general
rhetorical program, see Kenneth Burke, "Thomas Mann and André Gide," *Counter-
Statement* (New York, 1931; 2d ed.; Los Altos, Calif., 1953), pp. 92–106, as
reprinted in Zabel, *Literary Opinion in America* (rev. ed.; New York, 1951).
[7] *The Rhetoric of Fiction*, p. 77.

become our national sex symbol . . . ." And this goes on for page
after page.

If we choose to join the chorus of protests against these pages, we
must be very clear that we are not objecting to authorial commentary
but rather to a particular kind of disharmony between idea and
dramatized object. Even if Stevens' views could be shown to differ
from Faulkner's, the discovery of irony would not save the work; the
disharmony would remain. What is more, our objections would not
be stronger if these opinions had been given in Faulkner's own name.

THE MODERN USES OF PERSUASION
Richard E. Hughes and P. Albert Duhamel

Rhetoric has always been concerned with the ways in which an
appeal to the emotions can persuade an audience, because, although
Socrates claimed that when people know the right they do the right,
there is an impressive accumulation of evidence to the contrary. No
matter how compelling the logic may be on one side of the argument,
no matter how carefully and correctly a case may be presented, the
writer who intends to persuade must take into account the irrational
in human behavior.

Some rhetoricians distinguish between two states of mind that can
be engendered in an audience by a writer or speaker: conviction and
persuasion. An audience can be considered convinced when it agrees
with all that a writer has said, but it is persuaded when it is stirred to
some kind of action. Audiences can be convinced, but not persuaded.
They may also be persuaded without first having been convinced.
Unfortunately it also is possible to arouse the emotions of certain
audiences without presenting any logical reasons for the urged action.
Here the fault is with the audience for allowing itself to be persuaded
without first being convinced.

Conviction and Persuasion

The differences between writing primarily intended to convince and
writing primarily intended to persuade are illustrated by *The Federal-*

From Richard E. Hughes and P. Albert Duhamel, *RHETORIC: Principles and
Usage*, © 1962 by Prentice-Hall, Inc., Englewood Cliffs, N.J. By permission.

ist, Paper No. 10, by James Madison (see Chapter 5) and "The American Crisis," Paper No. 1, by Tom Paine (in the selections at the end of this chapter). James Madison wrote to convince readers whom he considered mature, informed, and reflective that the recently proposed Constitution should be adopted as the law of the land. According to Madison, one of the greatest reasons for adopting the proposed Constitution was its promise of controlling those factions which are bound to arise in popular governments as the result of clashes in self interest among various groups of citizens. The calm tone of *The Federalist* No. 10, and its carefully constructed logical progressions, are a proof that Madison believed in the need to convince his audience. The content of the paper indicates that he also believed some audiences could be too easily persuaded. *The Federalist* papers, taken as a whole, are perhaps the longest protracted single appeal ever directed towards convincing, not persuading, the electorate in this country. Although the series is not without some appeal to the emotions of the citizens of the State of New York, it seems to have been written on the assumption that all men can be moved by calm, detached, logical argument.

Tom Paine wanted to persuade his readers to action. The *Crisis* paper, assumed that the time had passed for rational arguments; that it was important now to act, and that the best way was to frighten and shame men into action. The audience which Tom Paine addressed was not likely to respond to a detached evaluation of their situation. This paper is dated December 23, 1776. During the preceding summer the Colonists had lost the battles of Long Island and White Plains. In November, General Washington had retreated across New Jersey into Pennsylvania with General Howe in close pursuit. Repeating the arguments which had led the Colonists to declare their independence earlier that same year would not have helped revive the spirits of a people which had experienced one reverse after another. So Paine tried another approach, and addressed himself not so much to the American reason as to the American sense of pride, courage, and fear of disgrace: He pointed out how those who adhered to a cause in this time of adversity would be admired, and how deserters would be recognized for the cowards they were. The Almighty would extend his support to those who followed their consciences and righteously did their duties.

These two documents—both are models of effectiveness of their kind —reveal the interesting contrast between Madison trying to convince a popular audience in dispassionate terms, and Tom Paine, known for his defense of the rights of reason and of man, addressing himself to the emotions of his readers. Their view of man is almost identical, but their rhetoric is adapted to circumstances of time, place and purpose.

Adapting to Audience and Circumstances

Such adaptation is far more difficult in this age of mass communication. Network radio, nationwide television, magazines with circulations in the millions represent every educational, social, and economic level. It is practically impossible to frame an argument which would appeal to the prejudices of one group without, by that same argument, alienating another part of the audience. The mass media of communication have fostered the development of a language free of local or dialect characteristics, and they have also fostered the development of neutrality of presentation. No writer is going to adapt his argument to appeal to one half of the audience, if he is thereby sure to lose the other half.

The crowds which gathered to hear Lincoln and Douglas debate in 1858 could not have numbered above the hundreds, and the groups in one section of the country shared ideas and prejudices which set them apart from the rest of the country. Both Lincoln and Douglas appealed to these prejudices to win their support. By contrast, more than 14,000,-000 people were estimated to have heard and seen the candidates of the two major parties debate on television during the 1960 presidential campaign. Many of these listeners were disappointed at the seeming agreement, on almost all issues, of the two campaigners, and at the very small number of issues which seemed to generate a real discussion. The reason for this agreement may have been that both candidates were sharply aware of how few issues there were which were "safe" for national discussion. With so large an audience a stand on almost any controversial subject was as sure to lose as many votes as it won. Mass media audiences contain representatives of every special interest group. It it impossible to appeal to one of the groups without alienating another. The speaker or writer should address himself to the group as a whole, take an honest stand with the best arguments he can muster, and leave the use of appeals to special groups with special prejudices to the few occasions where such appeals are still possible.

Such classical rhetoricians as Aristotle and Cicero never foresaw the problems which would be created by mass audiences when they discussed means of adapting written or oral compositions to the predispositions of an audience. They thought of groups which could be gathered within the range of the unassisted human voice. The rhetoricians conceived of the emotions which stood behind their prejudices in rather simple terms. Emotions, for Aristotle, were "all those affections which cause men to change their opinions in regard to their judgments, and are accompanied by pleasure and pain. Such are anger, pity, fear and all similar emotions and their contraries." The second book of Aristotle's *Rhetoric* also contains a lengthy catalog of the emotions to which the orator might appeal. These included love, anger, shame, pity, and envy. The analysis of these emotions was followed by an analysis of the various groups which were particularly subject to these various emotions. Here is Aristotle's analysis of the emotions to which old men were particularly prone.

> Older men and those who have passed their prime have in most cases characters opposite to those of the young. For, owing to their having lived many years and having been more often deceived by others or made more mistakes themselves, and since most human things turn out badly, they are positive about nothing, and in everything they show an excessive lack of energy. They always "think," but "know" nothing; and in their hesitation they always add "perhaps," or "maybe"; all their statements are of this kind, never unqualified. They are malicious; for malice consists in looking upon the worse side of everything. Further, they are always suspicious owing to mistrust, and mistrustful owing to experience. And neither their love nor their hatred is strong for the same reasons; but they love as if they would one day hate, and hate as if they would one day love. And they are little-minded, because they have been humbled by life; for they desire nothing great or uncommon, but only the necessaries of life. They are not generous, for property is one of those necessaries, and, at the same time, they know from experience how hard it is to get and how easy to lose. And they are cowardly and inclined to anticipate evil, for their state of mind is the opposite of that of the young; they are chilled, whereas the young are hot, so that old age paves the way for cowardice, for fear is a kind of chill. And they are fond of life, especially in their last days, because desire is directed towards that which is absent and men especially desire what they lack. And they are unduly selfish, for this also is littleness of mind. And they live not for the noble, but for the useful, more than they ought, because they are selfish; for the useful is good for the individual, whereas the noble is a good absolutely.
>
> And they are rather shameless than modest; for since they do not care for the noble so much as for the useful, they pay little attention to what people think. And they are little given to hope owing to their experience, for things that happen are mostly bad and at all events generally turn out for the worse, and also owing to their cowardice. They live in memory rather than in hope; for the life that remains to them is short,

but that which is past is long, and hope belongs to the future, memory to the past." [1]

A skilled orator, familiar with Aristotle's analysis of the characters of old men, would present any case he was placing before such a group in terms of its practicality and its protection of property. He would not try to present it in terms of its possible future benefits. These principles are still as effective today as they were when Aristotle pointed them out. A politician seeking office in a state with a large group of voters in the over-sixty classification might find himself addressing a group of people whose characteristics would still be fairly reflected in Aristotle's analysis.

The following selection is from an essay originally submitted by a teen-age girl as an entry in a contest conducted by a manufacturing company on the subject, "What Democracy Means to Me." When this essay was read over a nationwide television program there were more requests for copies than the network had ever received for any kind of material ever before. The proposition of the essay seems to be "I am proud and happy to be an American." The writer chose to appeal directly to the emotions, and since the audience was composed of Americans, the emotions are pride in being an American; love, or sentimental attachment, to scenes commonly associated with America; respect, perhaps even awe or reverence, for ideas and symbols commonly identified as the bases of national well being.

> I am an American. Listen to my words, Fascist, Communist. Listen well, for my country is a strong country, and my message is a strong message. I am an American, and I speak for democracy. My ancestors have left their blood on the green at Lexington and the snow at Valley Forge . . . on the walls of Fort Sumter and the fields at Gettysburg . . . on the waters of the River Marne and in the shadows of the Argonne Forest . . . on the beachheads of Salerno and Normandy and the sands of Okinawa . . . on the bare, bleak hills called Pork Chop and Old Baldy and Heartbreak Ridge. A million and more of my countrymen have died for freedom.
>
> My country is their eternal monument. They live on in the laughter of a small boy as he watches a circus clown's antics . . . and in the sweet, delicious, coldness of the first bite of peppermint ice cream on the Fourth of July . . . in the little tenseness of a baseball crowd as the umpire calls "Batter up!" . . . and in the high school band's rendition

[1] Reprinted by permission of the publishers and the Loeb Classical Library. Translated by John Henry Freeze, *Aristotle, The "Art" of Rhetoric* (Cambridge, Mass.: Harvard University Press).

of "Stars and Stripes Forever" in the Memorial Day parade . . . in the clear, sharp ring of a school bell on a fall morning . . . and in the triumph of a six-year-old as he reads aloud for the first time.

They live on in the eyes of an Ohio farmer surveying his acres of corn and potatoes and pasture . . . and in the brilliant gold of hundreds of acres of wheat stretching across the flat miles of Kansas . . . in the milling of cattle in the stockyards of Chicago . . . the precision of an assembly line in an automobile factory in Detroit . . . and the perpetual red glow of the nocturnal skylines of Pittsburgh and Birmingham and Gary.

They live on in the voice of a young Jewish boy saying the sacred words from the Torah: "Hear O Israel: the Lord our God, the Lord is One. Thou shalt love the Lord thy God with all thy heart and with all thy soul and with all thy might." . . . and in the voice of a Catholic girl praying: "Hail, Mary, full of grace, the Lord is with thee . . ." . . . and in the voice of a Protestant boy singing: "A mighty Fortress is our God, a Bulwark never failing . . ."

An American named Carl Sandburg wrote these words: I know a Jew fishcrier down on Maxwell Street with a voice like a north wind blowing over corn stubble in January. He dangles herring before prospective customers evincing a joy identical with that of Pavlova dancing. His face is that of a man terribly glad to be selling fish, terribly glad that God made fish, and customers to whom he may call his wares from a pushcart.

There is a voice in the soul of every human being that cries out to be free. America has answered that voice. America has offered freedom and opportunity such as no land before her has ever known, to a Jew fishcrier down on Maxwell Street with the face of a man terribly glad to be selling fish. She has given him the right to own his pushcart, to sell his herring on Maxwell Street . . she has given him an education for his children, and a tremendous faith in the nation that has made these things his.

Multiply that fishcrier by 160,000,000—160,000,000 mechanics and farmers and housewives and coal miners and truck drivers and chemists and lawyers and plumbers and priests—all glad, terribly glad to be what they are, terribly glad to be free to work and eat and sleep and speak and love and pray and live as they desire, as they believe! . . .

This is my answer, Fascist, Communist! Show me a country greater than our country, show me a people more energetic, creative, progressive, bigger-hearted and happier than our people, not until then will I consider your way of life. For I am an American, and I speak for democracy." [2]

[2] From "I Speak for Democracy," Elizabeth Ellen Evans. Reprinted by permission of the United States Junior Chamber of Commerce.

This essay suggests certain practices which seem to appeal to the entire contemporary audience. First, the contemporary audience— readers, viewers, and hearers—prefer quick, condensed presentations to leisurely, fully developed treatments of ideas. The modern audience, when contrasted with its eighteenth-century counterpart addressed by Tom Paine and James Madison, seems to have suffered a decline in attention span. Condensations of books sell better than their originals; public addresses, even by the highest public officials on the most important subjects, are rarely allowed to exceed twenty to thirty minutes; and dramatic presentations have to be chopped up to fit into the half-hour segments of television. Magazines with circulations in the millions preface items, already short by standards of a century ago, with capsule summaries. Newspapers have mastered a technique of compressing into a lead paragraph all of the essential details of a story so that few readers ever persist in their reading to the end of the account where the background details have been safely tucked away.

Not only must the over-all essay be brief, but its parts, its paragraphs and sentences, must also be brief, if they are to keep the attention of those already conditioned by contemporary reading and listening. The long paragraph, of five or more long sentences, is now too congested to hold the attention, and the long sentence, with its many qualifying clauses and modifiers requiring close attention of its readers, has become a rarity.

Since the contemporary writer or speaker must be brief, he must labor to make every word and sentence count. The result is a kind of writing wherein every sentence tries to summarize an idea in a pithy way, almost approaching the phrasing of a proverb, and every phrase tries to become memorable through the use of some forceful figure of speech. Such vividness is the second noticeable characteristic of expression which is effective with contemporary audiences. It is a vividness which is sometimes achieved at the expense of coherence. The connection between ideas and grammatical units is not felt to be as important as the need to make every unit of utterance strike the reader like a verbal fire-cracker. There is none of this unrelenting urgency to strike a vigorous phrase in every sentence to be found in the writings of Madison or Paine, yet some of their phrases stand out all the more strongly because of the rambling background with which they are provided.

A third characteristic of effective contemporary writing which is reflected in the preceding selection is a tendency towards reiteration. Madison and Paine develop an idea, relate it to their over-all argument, and then go on to another. The tendency exhibited in this essay seems to be to find several striking ways of saying the same thing, instead of expanding upon or clarifying an idea. There seems to be a tacit assumption that the contemporary audience has a high tolerance for repetition and a low tolerance for extended developments of involved ideas.

On the basis of this brief examination of one popular and effective essay it seems reasonable to conclude that writing which is to be adapted to the circumstances created by the mass media of communication should be brief, terse, vivid, and tend towards the reiteration of a simple message rather than attempt to develop a complex argument. Such a general statement would have to be modified before it could be said to apply to some of the literary magazines or to speeches intended for smaller, more select audiences. But no matter what segment of the modern audience a writer is hoping to reach and persuade, he should bear in mind that much of this audience has been conditioned to accept material which will engage the mind without exciting the critical faculties. There are magazines which realize that not every subject can be treated in a two-page essay, and there are readers who will sincerely pursue a subject on which they hope to be informed. But these magazines and these readers are fewer in number than the readers of the magazines with national circulations. These readers whose numbers are seemingly legion and who cannot be separated into groups on the basis of age, income, education, for they are of all ages, education, and income, seem to be persuaded best by short, scatter-gun bursts of vivid, if enervating, prose.

Motivation Research

Aristotle believed that an intelligent audience would not be moved to action until it had been first convinced of the rightness of that action. But actions are taken to fill a need, and it is not unusual to find that a need has been acted upon without being fully evaluated. More often than not human actions result from the need to satisfy some emotional drive, and these drives are usually more insistent than the demands of the reason.

Within the last decade a new study called "Motivation Research," has developed. Motivation Research uses many of the techniques of modern psychology to investigate what has always been of interest to the rhetorician: why men act the way they do, why they decide to favor one side instead of the other in a debate, why they buy one product instead of another. The distinctive aspect of Motivation Research has been to search for the hidden motives instead of accepting the reasons which people commonly give to explain their behavior. The reasons people offer are usually fairly rational, or common sense reasons; their real motives are frequently irrational.

Some of the theories and discoveries of Motivation Researchers are illustrated by the selection taken from Vance Packard's *Hidden Persuaders*. Any one of his many illustrations can serve as a proof that men are not always influenced by rational considerations, that, frequently, they are hardly aware of the motives which brought them to act.

When some of the insights into human behavior obtained by Motivation Research were made public, considerable discussion ensued, much of which revolved about the question of the moral responsibility of people who could wield this new knowledge. Advertisers and psychologists who had been conducting Motivation Research were quick to point out that the individual was still free to resist persuasion if, before assenting to a proposition or allowing himself to be persuaded to action, he examines the reasons he has been presented. The writer who hopes to persuade an audience should learn to adapt the new knowledge about motivation to his purposes; but he should also make sure that his argument is able to withstand the careful scrutiny of even the most rational audience.

Aristotle assumed that people knew what they wanted and would be moved to act if they could be shown that they would get what they wanted. Motivation Research has disproven this classical assumption and revealed, through the use of various techniques, that people frequently do not know what they really want, will not admit it even to themselves, deceive themselves, and, when questioned about their motives, will give the answer they think is "expected" of them.

One technique designed to discover the motives that will really influence buyers is the depth interview, wherein a trained psychologist encourages a consumer to talk at length about his reactions to a particular product, or a voter to ramble on about why he responded to a political candidate in the way he did. Also used are questionnaires which require a respondent to complete statements so composed as to give psychological insight into his true feelings. Thematic apperception tests require that the consumer interpret the significance of a situation represented in a series of carefully selected pictures. Word association tests, hidden cameras, and concealed microphones have all been used to arrive at an understanding of why people are motivated to do one thing instead of another.

It is interesting to speculate on the hidden motives which might have led millions to react as favorably as they did to the "I Speak for Democracy" essay reprinted above. Did the people who wrote in for copies of the essay do so because they thought the author had really succeeded in defining democracy in a new and effective way? Was it a sincere admiration for the eloquence of the message which prompted the response or a desire to be thought loyal, patriotic and correct? Were the hearers affected by references to Fourth of July ball games, Ohio cornfields, and a Chicago fishcrier because of any inherent force residing in these symbols or was their response dictated by a secret desire to win the approval of the right sort of people?

Some of the best sources of help in coming to an understanding of the true motivations of people are the writings of contemporary sociologists and psychologists. In a brilliant study on the *Small Town in Mass Society*, Arthur Vidich and Joseph Bensman explored some of the stereotypes which the small town dweller believed, or at least professed to believe, about small town life. These illusions are supposedly shared by the apartment dweller.

Vidich and Bensman found that the small-town resident "assumed the role of the warm, friendly, sociable, helpful, good neighbor and friend," which is just the way the city-dweller, who likes to preserve the illusion that the small town is a refuge from the jungle competition of the city, pictures the small-town citizen. The truth of the situation is that the small-town resident is always competing with his neighbor, just as much so as the city-dweller, and that he always estimates his success in terms of whether or not he has done better than his neighbor.

It is also part of the American mythology about the small town that every farmer and business man who lives there has an excellent chance of succeeding if he will only work hard and play fair. The researchers discovered that "the institutional means to achieving success are limited and are not equally available to all groups." The belief that politics in a small town are controlled by the people themselves also proved to be another illusion, for "in reality, local politics are controlled by external agencies." The small-town resident who persists in these illusions has to develop various techniques to conceal from himself what he knows is the truth. He throws himself completely into his work, almost to the point of self-exhaustion, thereby perpetuating the illusion that small-towners work hard, but really to take his mind off the realization that he cannot really succeed. He may join any number of local civic and religious organizations, serve on any number of committees, thereby contributing to the illusion that the citizen controls the political and social life of the small town, but actually to keep himself from thinking about his predicament. The result is a ritualization of life, wherein "the individual adheres to a fixed and repetitive daily, weekly, and seasonal routine in which no one day, week, or year exhibits any significant deviation from any other." [3]

No small town audience would respond favorably to a speaker or writer who addressed himself directly to their condition as it really exists. They would not applaud a reminder that they were, in the words of Henry Thoreau, "living lives of quiet desperation." A national audience would also react unfavorably to any attempt to tamper with its illusions about the small town as a sure refuge from a competitive, mercenary culture. So the writer had better address himself to the illusions, preserving them as far as he can, praising the people of Springdale for their good fortune in living in Springdale, and, then, if he can, appeal subtly to the hidden motives of envy, anxiety, and frustration which he knows are there. According to Vidich and Bensman's analysis no Springdaler would ever admit that he bought a car to outdo his neighbor, that he would be delighted if he could really find some way of getting ahead of everyone else, but that these would be the very strong motives which would influence a Springdaler at the moment of decision. Though a writer may know that he is pitching his appeal at motives which the audience either does not recognize or want to recognize, he must never let his audience know.

In addition to insisting upon being treated as a rational person, the modern listener also wants to be treated as an individual. There is a great tendency to purchase a product or subscribe to an idea which is believed to be in some way personalized. Sociologists interpret this as a reaction against the pressures of a society which tries to make an individual conform more and more, and abandon more and more of his individuality. Many manufacturers are doing their best to create the illusion of catering to the individual even though the availability of many products at modest prices depends upon their being mass produced. Thomas Griffith, a senior editor of *Time* magazine, summed up this desire of the individual to be treated as an individual in this fashion.

[3] Arthur J. Vidich and Joseph Bensman, *Small Town in Mass Society* (Garden City, N.Y.: Doubleday & Co., Inc., 1960) pp. 291, 292, 311, 318.

He (the average American) is told that everything is done for his listening, smoking or dining pleasure. He is the end man of all production, the object of every politician's affection. And yet, if he subconsciously feels that there is something wrong in American life today, something for which he may be partly at fault, he feels helpless to correct it. No wonder that critics find significance in the fact that his favorite character in fiction is the lone cowhand who goes his own gait and is in control of his circumstances. The legendary cowhand is a man of common sense and good heart, shy with girls but attractive to them, slow to wrath but quick on the draw, fond of solitude but capable of leading, minding his own business except when justice requires his intervention to put things right. He is the unfulfilled American dream.[4]

The writer must try to find some way of making his audience believe that he is conscious of individual differences in that group. Effective writing today depends upon an ability to convey the impression that it is trying to overcome the limitations imposed by the mass media and reaching out towards each individual as a personalized message.

Closely related to this desire on the part of the consumer to feel that he is being treated as an individual is his desire to feel that he has also had a part in the design of a product or program. Manufacturers go to great lengths to suggest in their national advertising that consumer panels were consulted in the design of their product. By the same token, some of the most effective and persuasive speeches are those which give the impression that the speaker is not lecturing at his audience but sharing his thoughts with them. Audiences made to feel that a speaker has come to discuss not to dictate are much more prone to agree with the speaker, because, after all, they have had a share in the discussion. Writers and speakers are adopting the technique used by manufacturers who advertise that their current product has been much modified in response to consumer suggestions. Audiences are now told that the speaker has recently changed his attitude on a certain point as a result of addressing audiences similar to the one he is now addressing. Aristotle would have interpreted this as an appeal to the vanity of the group; the contemporary sociologist sees it as an appeal to the group's desire to be taken into partnership in the development of a program.

The approach which made last year's advertising campaign a success cannot be used the following year because its wide discussion

---

[4] Thomas Griffith, *The Waist-High Culture*. Reprinted by permission of Harper & Row, Publishers, Inc. Copyright 1959.

in the mass media of communication has alerted the audience to its techniques and it must now assert its rationality by refusing to be taken in. Contemporary audiences are also very sensitive to some of the more obvious rhetorical appeals of a generation ago. They will react very strongly and negatively to any exaggerated, florid, theatrical appeal to their emotions. Consequently such appeals, must be skillfully implied rather than boldly announced.

The Image

In the very first chapter of his *Rhetoric*, Aristotle distinguishes between the three kinds of proof which a writer or speaker can use: "The first depends upon the moral character of the speaker, the second upon putting the hearer into a certain frame of mind, the third upon the speech itself, in so far as it proves or seems to prove."

At one time, and it is certainly still true with many contemporary audiences, the third kind of proofs was considered the most effective. The writers of *The Federalist* certainly thought of their audiences as being most responsive and most influenced by arguments which proved, or seemed to prove, their propositions. With audiences which are willing to take, and capable of taking, an objective view of a problem, the discovery of logical arguments and the clear disposition of these arguments through an essay are the best means of securing persuasion.

The second kind of proofs—those which put an audience in the right frame of mind—were for Aristotle the appeals to the various emotions and prejudices of the hearers. Such proofs, as has been noted, have increased enormously in importance.

It is only in recent times that the full significance of Aristotle's first kind of proofs, those which depend upon the moral character of the speaker or writer, has been fully appreciated. The greatest single argument in favor of a proposition is the personality of the speaker or writer as it is interpreted or understood by his audience. Contemporary advertising men, psychologists, and public relations men would be in complete agreement with Aristotle, but they would use a different terminology.

Advertisers, public relations men, and psychologists are all interested in what they call "the Image" which potential consumers have of products, persons and programs, because they have come to realize that this image, more than anything else, is responsible for the audience's reaction. People will vote for a candidate who communicates to his constituents an image of what they really want of a candidate for that office. The man who buys a car much too large for his garage, much too expensive for his bank account, and completely at odds with his need for transportation in a traffic-congested city did not buy a car but an image. The large, overpowered car he bought represented to him a means of escape from a hum-drum life.

The writer who hopes to persuade an audience should begin where the manufacturer begins, by determining what particular image product he wants to create. What Aristotle knew as the "ethical argument," the argument based upon the impression the audience had of the moral integrity of the speaker or writer, and what the modern advertiser thinks of as "the image" of a particular product or spokesman, is, indeed, the strongest argument for or against a proposition. The writer should try to create an image of himself which would be favorably received by his audiences. He should try to present his material in such a fashion as to convey an impression of himself as a calm, dispassionate, objective analyst of the situation. No matter what the subject, an audience is more likely to agree with someone it feels is impartial than with someone it senses is biased or opinionated.

Modern consumers frequently want contradictory things. They want to live in a suburb which reflects their rising social status, but, at the same time, they want to continue living in a place where they feel they have sunk their roots, where they have a sense of belonging. This is an invitation to real estate salesmen to sell—not a house, but a sense of belonging. Bakeries sell not good-tasting bakery products, but bakery products "like Mother used to make." In similar fashion, a writer might try to persuade his audience that his argument is not something new but something which preserves traditional values.

The number of variations possible in the use of appeals to the illusions of the audience cannot be enumerated, they can only be suggested. If advertisers are right in claiming that consumers are really buying "emotional security" in buying a refrigerator and not an efficient means of preserving food, then the advertiser must concentrate on selling the image of security and not the efficiency of the refrigerator. The ingenuity of the advertiser has to be expended on discovering just what it is that people are buying when they are purchasing a particular object. The writer or speaker who wants to face up to the implications of these new approaches must decide for himself what it is that people would really be "buying" when they were assenting to his proposition.

These techniques of appealing to hidden motives or of selling an image instead of a product have been particularly effective in selling products where the difference between competing brands has been marginal. Where the difference between the tobacco in one brand of cigarettes and that in another brand is practically non-existent, the consumer must be sold something else—a different image. So it turns out that some cigarettes are for "he-men," others for elegant women, still others for those "who can afford the extra luxury." A speaker or writer who is conscious that there is a real difference between his ideas and program and that of his opponent should concentrate on demonstrating that difference. The writer who feels that there is not much difference between what he proposes and what someone else proposes may feel that the best means of securing an adherence to his plan is to sell himself and not his plan.

In the 1960 political campaigns it became increasingly obvious that more and more of the effort to persuade voters toward one candidate and away from another was being channelled according to the recommendations of the Motivation Researchers. Whether as a result of pressures toward uniformity or the world situation, the two major parties kept edging closer and closer to one another, so that the differences between them seemed to be marginal. Under these circumstances the techniques used to sell marginally different products were brought into play and efforts were concentrated upon building up an image of which seemed to have the widest appeal to the undecided voters. The voter's "yes" was being engineered, just as the consumer's purchase of cigarettes.

Summary

The effectiveness of rhetorical devices is subject to change. Patterns of organization or argumentation which were effective with one audience may not be effective with another. Shakespeare's audience admired puns and complicated plays on words. Arguments based on the similarities in sound of words (breeches were called breeches because they *bore riches*) were considered very effective. Nineteenth century audiences responded very favorably to ideas which could be considered noble and traditional. Contemporary audiences are suspicious of arguments based on word play as well as arguments which are unrelated to practical situations or factual bases. The reader who knows what was considered effective in Shakespeare's day or during the Victorian period can read the literature of those periods more sympathetically, but it is much more important to know what is effective today.

To know what is currently effective, the writer or speaker must be sensitive to the reasons which are influencing the actions of people. In the middle of the twentieth century it seemed to many psychologists and sociologists that some of the strongest reasons impelling people to act were the so-called "hidden motives." Nobody was saying that an appeal to these motives ought to take the place of logical arguments, but there were many who insisted that an appeal to these motives was sometimes necessary to secure a hearing for the logical arguments. The logic of a position continued to be considered as important as ever, but it was felt that it sometimes had to be supplemented by extra-logical or emotional appeals.

One of the most influential of these extra-logical appeals is the image of himself which the writer or speaker succeeds in projecting. This image is not something wholly dependent upon the clothes he wears, the smile he flashes, or the punctuation he uses. These obvious, external appeals may always influence some, but the image with which we are concerned is something which goes deeper. It is the result of a combination of factors which include what the author has to say and how he says it. The kinds of arguments which he uses, whether they are chiefly logical or extra-logical, the tone in which he expresses them, the emphasis he places upon them—all these contribute to the image projected by writer or speaker. If these elements add up to an image of an unbiased and authoritative spokesman, they will have contributed greatly to his success in proving his case. Since the manner of expression is an important element in the image projected by a writer, it is to the study of this matter of expression—style—that we shall turn next.

B. Some Samples

"ADMINISTRATIVE" RHETORIC IN MACHIAVELLI
Kenneth Burke

Machiavelli's *The Prince* can be treated as a rhetoric insofar as it deals with the *producing of effects upon an audience.* Sometimes the prince's subjects are his audience, sometimes the rulers or inhabitants of foreign states are the audience, sometimes particular factions within the State. If you have a political public in mind, Machiavelli says in effect, here is the sort of thing you must do to move them for your purposes. And he considers such principles of persuasion as these: either treat well or crush; defend weak neighbors and weaken the

From *A Rhetoric of Motives* by Kenneth Burke, © 1950 by Prentice-Hall, Inc., Englewood Cliffs, N.J.

strong; where you foresee trouble, provoke war; don't make others powerful; be like the prince who appointed a harsh governor to establish order (after this governor had become an object of public hatred in carrying out the prince's wishes, the prince got popular acclaim by putting him to death for his cruelties); do necessary evils at one stroke, pay out benefits little by little; sometimes assure the citizens that the evil days will soon be over, at other times goad them to fear the cruelties of the enemy; be sparing of your own and your subjects' wealth, but be liberal with the wealth of others; be a combination of strength and stealth (lion and fox); *appear* merciful, dependable, humane, devout, upright, but be the opposite in actuality, whenever the circumstances require it; yet always do lip-service to the virtues, since most people judge by appearances; provoke resistance, to make an impression by crushing it; use religion as a pretext for conquest, since it permits of "pious cruelty"; leave "affairs of reproach" to the management of others, but keep those "of grace" in your own hands; be the patron of all talent, proclaim festivals, give spectacles, show deference to local organizations; but always retain the distance of your rank (he could have called this the "mystery" of rule); in order that you may get the advantage of good advice without losing people's respect, give experts permission to speak frankly, but only when asked to speak; have a few intimates who are encouraged to be completely frank, and who are well plied with rewards.

Correspondingly, there are accounts of the human susceptibilities one can play upon, and the resistances one must expect. Thus: new benefits won't make great personages forget old injuries; it is easy to persuade people, but you need force to keep them persuaded; acquisitiveness being natural, those who acquire will be praised, not blamed; the nobles would oppress the people, the people would avoid oppression by the nobles; one can satisfy the people, but not the nobles, by fair dealing; men are bound to you as much by the benefits they give as by the benefits they receive; mercenaries are to be feared for their dastardy, auxiliaries for their valor; the unarmed are despised; often what we call virtue would ruin the State, and what we call vice can save it; cruelty may reconcile and unify; men in general are *ungrateful, fickle, false, cowardly, greedy;* since all men are evil, the prince can always find a good pretext for breaking faith; it is safer to be feared than loved, since people are more likely to offend those they love than those they fear; yet though the prince should be feared, he should not be hated; the worst offense is an offense against property, for a man more quickly forgets the death of his father than the loss of his patrimony; people want to be deceived; if the prince leaves his subjects' property and women untouched, he "has only to contend with the ambitions of a few"; a ruler's best fortress is not to be hated by his own people; any faction within the State can always expect to find allies abroad.

The difference between the two lists is mainly grammatical. For instance, if we use a gerundive, "valor in auxiliaries is to be feared," the statement belongs in the second set. But we can transfer it to the first merely by changing the expression to an imperative: "Fear valor in auxiliaries." Both lists are reducible to "topics" in the Aristotelian sense.

We think of another "Machiavellian" work, written many centuries earlier. It is in praise of "eloquence," the eloquence, it says, that serves in the conquest of the public, of the senate, and of women. But it would concentrate on the third use, for it is Ovid's *Ars Amatoria*. It deals not with political power, but with another order of potency; and where Machiavelli is presumably telling how to get and hold a principality, Ovid is telling how to get and hold a woman.

Grounded in figures of soldiery, of gladiators, of the hunt, of animals enraged or ruttish, it is in form a manual of instructions, like *The Prince*. But it is really a poetic display, an epideictic exercise, the sort of literary ostentation that De Quincey had in mind when selecting Ovid as prime example of rhetoric. For one does not usually read it as he would read instructions for opening a package (though a yearning adolescent might); one reads it rather for the delight he may take in the imagery and ideas themselves, the topics or "places" of love.

But to consider some of the poet's picturesque advice is to see how close it is to the thinking of Machiavelli, except of course for the tonalities, since the Italian is solemn, the Latin playful. Having begun scenically, with a survey of locations where the hunting is good, he proceeds thus:

On deceiving in the name of friendship; feigning just enough drunkenness to be winsome; of feigned passion that may become genuine; on astute use of praise and promises; inducement value of belief in the gods; deceiving deceivers; the utility of tears; the need to guard against the risk that entreaties may merely feed the woman's vanity; inducement value of pallor, which is the proper color of love; advisability of shift in methods, as she who resisted the well-bred may yield to the crude; ways to subdue by yielding; how to be her servant, but as a freeman; risks that gain favor; on operating with the help of the servants; need for caution in gifts; get your slaves to ask her to ask you to be kind to them; the controlled use of compliments; become a habit with her; enjoy others too, but in stealth, and deny if you are found out; rekindle her love by jealousy; make her grieve over you, but not too much, lest she muster enough strength to become angry (as she might, since she always wants to be shut of you); if she has deceived you, let her think you don't know it; give each of her faults the name of the good quality most like it.

And to women he offers advice on dress, cosmetics, the use of pretty faults in speech, gait, poetry, dance, posture, cadence, games, on being seen in public (you may find a husband at the funeral of your husband), deceit to match deceit, on being late at banquets, on table manners, on drinking to excess but only as much as can be deftly controlled.

Machiavelli says of war: "This is the solé art proper to rulers." And similarly Ovid's epideictic manual of love-making is founded on the principle that "love is a kind of war" (*militiae species amor est*). "I can love only when hurt," the poet confesses (*non nisi laesus amo*). And Machiavelli rounds out his politics by saying that it is better to be adventurous than cautious with Fortune, since Fortune is a woman, "and if you wish to keep her subdued, you must beat her and ill-use her."

True, though both books are concerned with the rhetoric of advantage, principles of amative persuasion rely rather on fraud than force. But the point to note for our purposes is that in both cases the rhetoric includes a strongly "administrative" ingredient. The persuasion cannot be confined to the strictly verbal; it is a mixture of symbolism and definite empirical operations. The basic conception in Stendhal's book on love, for instance, is not rhetorical at all. For the rhetoric of love in Stendhal, we should go rather to his *The Red and the Black*. There, as in Ovid, the work is developed on the principle that love is a species of war. But the basic principle underlying Stendhal's *De l'Amour* is that of "crystallization," a concept so purely "internal," so little "addressed," that it belongs completely under the heading of "symbolic" in these volumes, naming but a kind of accretion (both unconscious and consciously sentimental) that grows about the idea of the beloved, and for all its contagiousness is rather a flowering within the mind of the lover than a ruse shaped for persuasive purposes.

We might put it thus: the nonverbal, or nonsymbolic conditions with which both lover and ruler must operate can themselves be viewed as a kind of symbolism having persuasive effects. For instance, military force can persuade by its sheer "meaning" as well as by its use in actual combat. In this sense, nonverbal acts and material instruments themselves have a symbolic ingredient. The point is particularly necessary when we turn to the rhetoric of bureaucracy, as when a political party bids for favor by passing measures popular with large blocs of voters. In such a case, administrative acts themselves are not merely "scientific" or "operational," but are designed also with an eye for their *appeal*. Popular jokes that refer to policemen's clubs and sex organs as "persuaders" operate on the same principle. For non-verbal conditions or objects can be considered as signs by reason of persuasive ingredients inherent in the "meaning" they have for the audience to which they are "addressed."

It is usual now to treat Machiavelli as a founder of modern political "science," particularly because he uses so naturalistic a terminology of motives, in contrast with notions of justification that go with super-naturalism. But this simple antithesis can prevent accurate placement of *The Prince*. For one thing, as in the case of La Rochefoucauld, you need but adopt the theological device of saying that Machiavelli is dealing with the motives typical of man after the "fall," and there is nothing about his naturalism to put it out of line with supernaturalism. But most of all, the approach to *The Prince* in terms of naturalism *vs.* supernaturalism prevents one from discerning the rhetorical elements that are of its very essence. Here again we come upon the fact that our contemporary views of science are dislocated by the failure to consider it methodically with relation to rhetoric (a failure that leads to a blunt opposing of science to either religion or "magic"). For if the rhetorical motive is not scientific, neither is it in its everyday application religious or magical. The use of symbols to induce action in beings that normally communicate by symbols is essentially realistic in the most practical and pragmatic sense of the term. It is neither "magical" nor "scientific" (neither ritualistic nor informational) for one person to ask help of another. Hence, in approaching the question through a flat antithesis between magic and science, one automatically vows himself to a faulty statement of the case.

Above all, we believe that an approach to the book in terms of rhetoric is necessary if one would give an adequate account of its *form* (and the ability to treat of form is always the major test of a critical method). Thus, though the late Ernst Cassirer gives a very good account of Machiavelli in his *Myth of the State*, his oversimplified treatment in terms of science alone, without the modifications and insights supplied by the principles of rhetoric, completely baffles an attempt to account for the book's structure. Not only does he end by treating the last chapter as a misfit; having likened the earlier chapters to Galileo's writings on the laws of motion, and thereby having offered a description that could not possibly apply to the last chapter, he concludes that the burden of proof rests with those who would consider the last chapter as a fit with the rest. By the rhetorical approach, you can meet his challenge, thus:

The first twenty-four chapters discuss typical situations that have to do with the seizing and wielding of political power. They are analytic accounts of such situations, and of the strategies best suited to the conditions. Thus they are all variants of what, in the *Grammar*, we called the scene-act ratio; and they say, in effect: "Here is the kind of act proper to such-and-such a scene" (the ruler's desire for political mastery being taken as the unchanging purpose that prevails throughout all changes of scene).

However, in the next-to-the-last chapter, Machiavelli modifies his thesis. Whereas he has been pointing out what act of the ruler would, in his opinion, have the most persuasive effect upon the ruled in a given situation, he now observes that people do not always act in accordance with the requirements set them by the scenic conditions. People also act in accordance with their own natures, or temperaments. Thus, a man may act cautiously, not because the scene calls for caution, but merely because he is by nature a cautious man. Conversely, if a man is adventurous by nature, he may act with adventurous boldness, characteristically, even though the situation itself may call for caution. In the *Grammar* we listed such motivations under the heading of the agent-act ratio, since they say, in effect: "Here is the kind of act proper to such-and-such a person."

But there may be fortunate moments in history when both kinds of motives work together, Machiavelli is saying. The scenic conditions require a certain kind of act; and the ruler may happen to have exactly the kind of temperament and character that leads him into this same kind of act. Given such a lucky coincidence, the perfect manifestation of the scene-act ratio is one with the perfect manifestation of the agent-act ratio.

Far from there being any formal break in the book, this concern in the next-to-the-last chapter forms a perfect transition to the final "Exhortation to Liberate Italy from the Barbarians." For this chapter rounds things out in a "Now is the time . . ." manner, by calling for the agent to arise whose acts will simultaneously be in tune with the times and with himself. This man will be the ruler able to redeem

Italy from its captivity. And given such a combination, there will be grounds too for the ultimate *identification* of ruler and ruled, since all will benefit, each in his way, by the liberation of their country.

True, in the last chapter there is a certain prayerlike lift not present in the others. Whereas the earlier chapters are a kind of *rhetorica docens*, the peroration becomes a kind of *rhetorica utens*. But that is a standard aspect of rhetorical form, traditional to the wind-up. Far from being added on bluntly, it is very deftly *led into* by the motivational shift in the preceding chapter.

When the ruler happens to be of such a nature that the act characteristic of his nature would also be the act best suited to the situation, we could attribute the happy combination to chance, or fortune. Here again the stress upon science *vs.* magic can somewhat mislead. True, references to a fatal confluence of factors will almost inevitably bring up connotations of "design." Hence, the "fortune" that makes the ruler temperamentally a fit for his times may take on fatelike connotations alien to science. One may find such metaphors of cosmic purpose flitting through Machiavelli's discussion. But they are not the central matter. The central matter is this fortuitous congruity of temperament and external conditions, whereas an "unlucky" combination can prevent the ruler from adopting the proper mode of action (somewhat as Cicero said that the ideal orator should be accomplished in all styles, but human limitations would restrict his range in actuality).

Machiavelli's concern is brought out clearly by La Rochefoucauld, in his comments *Des Modèles de la Nature et de la Fortune.* "It seems," he says, "that Fortune, changing and capricious as she is, renounces change and caprice to act in concert with nature, and that the two concur at times to produce singular and unusual men who become models for posterity. Nature serves to furnish the qualities; Fortune serves to put them into operation." By "nature" he is obviously referring to human nature, capacities of human agents; "fortune" is his word for scenic conditions, which impose themselves independently of human will. He calls the congruence of agent and scene an "*accord de la nature et de la fortune.*"

Concerns with the "lucky" or "unlucky" accident that may make a man temperamentally fit or unfit to employ the strategy best suited to the situation may eventually involve one in assumptions about fatal cosmic design along the lines of Carlyle's "mystifications" about heroes in history. And too great a concern with science as antithetical to magic may get one to thinking that the important point lies there. But by treating the book as a manual of "administrative rhetoric," we can place the stress where it belongs: on the problem of the orator's ability to choose the act best suited to the situation, rather than choosing the act best suited to the expression of his own nature.

Likewise, the proper approach to Machiavelli's *choice of vocabulary* is not exclusively in terms of science, but through considerations of rhetoric. (We have in mind his paradoxical distinctions between the virtues of princes and the virtues of private citizens, or his proposal to base political action on the assumption that all men are "ungrateful, fickle, false, cowardly, and greedy.") Is not Machiavelli here but giving a new application to a topic in Aristotle's *Rhetoric?* Aristotle had said in effect that privately we admit to acquisitive motives, but publicly we account for the same act in sacrificial terms. In the Christian terminology that had intervened between Aristotle and Machiavelli, however, the public, sacrificial motives were attributed to the state of *grace,* and the private, acquisitive motives were due to the state of *original sin* after the fall. In the Christian persuasion, the rhetorical distinction noted by Aristotle had thus become written dialectically into the very nature of things. And insofar as a man was genuinely imbued with Christian motives, his *private* virtues would be the traits of character which, if cultivated in the individual, would be most beneficial to mankind *as a whole.*

But Machiavelli is concerned with a different kind of universality. He starts from the principle that men are *universally at odds with one another.* For this is what his stress upon predatory or warlike motives amounts to. He is concerned with motives which will protect *special* interests. *The Prince* is leading towards the period when the interests of a feudal ruler will be *nationalistically* identified, thought to represent one state *as opposed to* other states.

Now, national motives can be placed in a hierarchy of motives, graded from personal and familial, to regional, to national, to international and universal. As so arranged, they might conceivably, in their different orders, complement or perfect one another rather than being in conflict. But where the princes, or the national states identified with them, are conceived antithetically to the interests of other princes and states, or antithetically to factions within the realm, the "virtues" of the ruler could not be the "virtues" which are thought most beneficial to mankind as a whole (in an ideal state of universal cooperation). Similarly, if we carry the Machiavelli pattern down from political to personal relations, the individual may become related to

other individuals as ruler to ruled (or at least as would-be ruler to
would-not-be ruled)—for here again the divisive motives treated by
Machiavelli apply.

Once a national identity is built up, it can be treated as an individual; hence like an individual its condition can be presented in sacrificial terms. Thus, in the case of *The Prince*, the early chapters are
stated in acquisitive terms. They have to do with the ways of getting
and keeping political power. But the last chapter, looking towards the
redemption of Italy as a nation, is presented in sacrificial tonalities; the
"virtue of an Italian spirit" is oppressed, enslaved, and scattered, "without head, without order, beaten, despoiled, torn, overrun," and endur-
ing "every kind of desolation." So Italy "entreats God to send some
one who shall deliver her from these wrongs and barbarous insolen-
cies." And "she is ready and willing to follow a banner if only some
one will raise it." This is the shift in tone that led Ernst Cassirer to
treat the last chapter as incongruous with the earlier portions.

In this last chapter, the universal, sacrificial motives are adapted to
a competitive end. The Christian vision of mankind's oneness in the
suffering Christ becomes the vision of Italians' oneness in the suffering
Italy. Since Italy actually is invaded, the analogy is not forced as it is
in the vocabulary of imperialist unction. (Contrast it, for instance, with
the building of empire under slogans like "the acceptance of grave
world responsibility," or "the solemn fulfillment of international commitments," when the support of reactionary regimes was meant.) But
whether the nationalist exaltation be for conquest or for uprising
against conquerors, in either case there is the possibility of identification between ruler and ruled. Hence the new prince, in bringing about
the new order, "would do honor to himself and good to the people of his
country." And by such identification of ruler and ruled, Machiavelli
offers the ruler precisely the rhetorical opportunity to present privately
acquisitive motives publicly in sacrificial terms.

Machiavelli is concerned with political cooperation under conditions
which make such cooperation in part a union of conspirators. Where
conspiracy is the fact, universality must often be the fiction. The ambiguity in Machiavelli is thus the ambiguity of nationalism itself, which
to some extent does fit with the ends of universal cooperation, and to
some extent is conspiratorial. The proportions vary, with the Hitlerite
State probably containing as high a percentage of the conspiratorial
as will be attained in our time, though the conspiratorial motive is now
usually strong in all international dealings. Sovereignty itself is conspiracy. And the pattern is carried into every political or social body,

however small. Each office, each fraternal order, each college faculty has its tiny conspiratorial clique. Conspiracy is as natural as breathing. And since the struggles for advantage nearly always have a rhetorical strain, we believe that the systematic contemplation of them forces itself upon the student of rhetoric. Indeed, of all the motives in Machiavelli, is not the most usable for us his attempt to transcend the disorders of his times, not by either total acquiescence or total avoidance, but by seeking to scrutinize them as accurately and calmly as he could?

SWIFT'S RHETORIC IN "A MODEST PROPOSAL"
Charles A. Beaumont

Swift's best and most popular ironical essay, "A Modest Proposal," reveals Swift at once as master ironist and master classical rhetorician. In investigating the various elements of classical rhetoric employed in this essay and indicating how each functions either within the irony or to build the irony, I will explore the following major topics: the classical form of the essay; the ethical proof; the use of the two major rhetorical devices, diminution and refining; and the less frequently used devices.

The Classical Form

The essay is organized in the manner of a classical oration, as follows:

Exordium	Paragraphs	1	through	7
Narration	Paragraphs	8	through	16
Digression	Paragraphs	17	through	19
Proof	Paragraphs	20	through	28
Refutation	Paragraphs	29	through	30
Peroration	Paragraphs	31	through	33

The exordium includes three kinds of material, all of which are acceptable in a classical exordium: a pitiful description of the state of Ireland, intended to appeal to the emotions of the reader; statements which reflect the benevolence of the author, designed to establish the ethical proof; and hints and preparatory statements for the proof to follow.

From *Swift's Classical Rhetoric*, by Charles A. Beaumont. Athens, Georgia, University of Georgia Press, 1961. Reprinted by permission.

The narration contains the statement of the proposal, with some further preparation for the proof.

Instead of going immediately into the proof, the projector inserts, in good classical form, a digression. Its subject matter parallels the subject matter of the essay by relating the custom of the Formosan court in eating the flesh of young girls whose bodies have just been cut down by the public hangman.

Following this digression containing the historical parallel is the proof, which contains six major reasons why the proposal should be accepted, plus the several summarized reasons.

In the refutation the projector brushes aside the single objection which he feels can reasonably be urged against him, that the population would be greatly decreased. He incorporates this argument into his own, claiming that it was one of his chief motives. He also sweeps aside the vain, visionary, and foolish "expedients" which have been offered in the past.

The peroration is made up of further statements which reflect favourably on the character of the projector and of a reiteration of the major topics of the essay. The appeal to the emotions stops one paragraph short of the end of the peroration. Just as Swift regularly undercuts a sentence with a fine irony at the end of the sentence, so he concludes the whole essay with a subdued minor point which is almost an ironic aside: in this case, his personal reference to the fact that his wife is past child-bearing.

The classical form of the essay is itself an important constituent of Swift's irony, for the projector's addressing his readers through an ancient and learned form helps to allay any suspicion of radical newness. A revolutionary new proposal is insinuated in a traditional, respected form.

The Ethical Proof

The moral and ethical character of the pleader is one of the three major proofs designated by Aristotle.[1] This kind of proof is one of the

---

[1] Aristotle divides all proof into two areas: inartificial (the facts which exist) and artificial (the use made of the facts through the art of rhetoric). He divides artificial proof into three kinds: ethical, emotional, and logical. The ethical proof stems from the moral character of the pleader himself (*Rhet.* I.ii.3). Quintilian agrees: although the pleader "may be modest and say little about himself, yet if he is believed to be a good man, this consideration will exercise the strongest influence at every point in the case. For thus he will have the good fortune to give the impression not so much that he is a zealous advocate as that he is an absolutely reliable witness. It is therefore pre-eminently desirable that he should

main kinds employed by Swift in most of his satires and much of his other writing (especially in his role as Examiner). In varying degrees, every essay by him which has an "author" makes use of this kind of classical proof. The sources of this proof in any oration are two: the implicit indications of the moral character of the pleader and the explicit ones. The implicit ones are made up of the whole tone of the essay and are not to be isolated. The explicit ones are the overt indications throughout the speech. Swift has made use of his exordium to begin the explicit characterization by showing the projector's concern, compassion, and high motive in modestly suggesting this beneficial solution to the state of Ireland. This establishing the character and motives of the pleader is a standard use of the classical exordium.

The specific details by which Swift builds up the ethical proof fall into four categories descriptive of the projector: his humanity, his self-confidence, his competence in the immediate subject of the proposal, and his reasonableness.

The humanity of the projector is immediately revealed in the opening words of the address. While the projector is moving his audience to pity with his description of the "melancholy Object of those, who walk through the streets of this great Town," he is also indicating the humane inclinations of the speaker, who is also capable of being moved to such pity.

In the proof the projector reflects his compassion for the "poorer Tenants" who "will have something valuable of their own" if the proposal is put into effect. Later in the same section (paragraph 26) he cites as a reason for his proposal the kind and humane treatment it would assure expectant mothers, as well as its tendency to increase "the Care and Tenderness of Mothers toward their Children."

In the digression (paragraph 17) the projector objects to the proffered "Refinement" on his proposal (that young lads and maidens be used in place of venison) because "some scrupulous People might be apt to censure such a Practice (although indeed very unjustly) as a little bordering upon Cruelty; which, I confess, hath always been with me the strongest Objection against any Project, how well soever intended." In the litotes "a little bordering upon Cruelty" the projector accomplishes several purposes. He indicates his own humane-

---

be believed to have undertaken the case out of a sense of duty, by a sense of patriotism or at any rate some serious moral consideration" (*Instit.* IV.i.7.). The texts I have used are those of the Loeb Classical Library. *The Art of Rhetoric,* Tr. John Henry Freeze (London: William Heinemann, Ltd., 1947) and *Institutio Oratoria*, Tr. H. E. Butler (London, 1953).

ness in rejecting this refinement partially on grounds of cruelty. He gains an argumentative point by branding all other proposals as cruel also. Notice that he does not explicitly exclude his own proposal when he says, "which, I confess hath always been wth me the strongest Objection against *any* Project." (Italics mine.) However, he recoups this hint of concession by observing that such an objection stems from too nice a scrupulosity.

In the last paragraph he assures the reader of his great sincerity and unselfish motives: "I PROFESS, in the Sincerity of my Heart, that I have not the least personal Interest, in endeavouring to promote this necessary Work . . . . I have no Children, by which I can propose to get a single Penny; the youngest being nine Years old, and my Wife past Child-bearing." This last sentence gives two more pieces of information which are important to the character of the pleader. He is not a childless man who can propose such a solution in ignorance of a father's feelings, and he will not gain personally from the adoption of the proposal.

Because the projector of this proposal is sometimes thought of as the *ingénu* type, a somewhat diffident, inexperienced person who has come upon the scene without being in complete touch with the whole situation, it has not been sufficiently noticed that he is at the same time a bit cocksure.[2] In creating his projector, Swift faced a rhetorical problem that required the careful balancing of these rather contrasting characteristics in one person. He had to make the projector humble enough to gain the reader's approval and sympathy and confident enough to gain the reader's confidence in his ability and qualifications with the subject.[3] Added to this double problem is the fact that, while both of these ends were being accomplished, the projector had to be kept sufficiently dense to sustain the irony.

The self-confidence of the projector is first indicated in the second paragraph, in which, a bit presumptuously, he looks forward to seeing himself commemorated with a statue for being "a Preserver of the Nation." His sureness of himself and of the efficacy of his proposal is stated in a qualified form in the opening sentence of the narration: "I SHALL NOW therefore humbly propose my own Thoughts; which

[2] A pleader must reflect self-confidence in himself and in his own proposals if he expects his audience to be convinced. The classical rhetoricians agree that the best delivery is that in which the pleader either participates in or seems to participate in the emotions and convictions which he is displayng.

[3] Quintilian *Instit.* VI.ii.26.: "The prime essential for stirring the emotions of others is, in my opinion, first to feel these emotions oneself." See also Cicero *De Oratore* II.xlv.189.

I hope will not be liable to the least Objection." and is echoed in the first sentence of the refutation: "I CAN think of no one Objection, that will possibly be raised against this Proposal; unless it should be urged, that the Number of People will be thereby much lessened in the Kingdom." This last, concessive clause is quickly done away with by the author's turning this single objection into an advantage for his cause.[4]

A pleader in the act of refuting naturally shows self-confidence. So does the projector when he tells us of his friend's suggesting that the lack of venison could be supplied by the youth of Ireland.

In paragraph nineteen the projector stands in contrast to "SOME Persons of desponding Spirit" who are in as great a concern for the aged as he is for the youth. He asserts that he is "not in the least Pain upon that matter": one could not reasonably expect the aged to be taken care of any more rapidly than they are by death, famine, and the like.

The projector speaks out boldly in introducing his proof: "I think the Advantages by the Proposal which I have made are obvious, and many, as well as of the highest Importance." And he proceeds to list and describe six of these advantages, but finally (implying that there are too many advantages to list) he summarizes the rest. Argument from a wealth of reasons indicates the firmness of the projector's position, since he can afford to waste them.

Closely related to the self-confidence of the pleader is his competence in dealing with the subject at hand. The projector gives abundant evidence that he is capable of dealing with the problem. First, he has not burst into print without first giving much thought and research to this problem: "As to my own Part, having turned my Thoughts for many Years, upon this important Subject, and maturely weighed the several *Schemes of other Projectors*, I have always found

---

[4] Decreasing the population of Ireland would, as the projector views the problem, improve the situation by lessening the number of people to be fed and otherwise maintained. But, the projector continues, this proposal is calculated *"for this one individual Kingdom of* IRELAND, *and for no other that ever was, is, or I think ever can be upon Earth."* Landa points out that an argument which recurs in Swift's Irish tracts is that, because the situation in Ireland is so pitifully unique, the best maxims on government and economics cannot operate there. Swift seems to have accepted the mercantile concept that the people are the wealth of a nation and that prosperity is dependent upon a constantly increasing population. (See Louis A. Landa, "A *Modest Proposal* and Populousness," *MP*, XL (Nov., 1942), pp. 161–70). The projector's statement is an ironical inversion of the maxim. Also, of course, Swift is making use of the maxim by rendering it literal: in "A Modest Proposal" the infants are literally to be the wealth of the nation.

them grosly mistaken in their Computation." He then plunges into a barrage of mathematical calculations, which of course indicate his painstaking work and thought on the subject. In paragraph six he begins with the figure of 200,000 couples, from which he subtracts 30,000 who can maintain their own children. He subtracts 50,000 more couples whose children will not live. This leaves 120,000 couples to be provided for. In the next two sentences he states

> I again subtract Fifty Thousand, for those Women who miscarry, or whose Children die by Accident, or Disease, within the Year. There only remain an Hundred and Twenty Thousand Children of poor Parents, annually born . . . .

The projector returns to the idea in paragraph ten: "the Hundred and Twenty Thousand Children, already computed. . . ." He subtracts 20,000 more children who are to be preserved for breeding, only one-fourth of these to be males.[5] It is this solid core of mathematics which makes the proposal so real and so practical—such a "fair, cheap, and easy Method."

This competence in calculations is reinforced by the vocabulary of the essay: "I HAVE reckoned upon a Medium. . . ." "As to our City of *Dublin;* Shambles may be appointed for this Purpose . . . ." "SUPPOSING that one Thousand Families in this City, . . . I compute . . . ."

In addition to such verbal indicants of competence, the whole movement of the proof reflects the strong debater arguing from a wealth of material. Six carefully thought out advantages are brought forward in such a way as to imply that he could continue listing advantages indefinitely, but finally he stops, being (as he says) "studious of Brevity." His two large rhetorical questions in paragraph thirty-two which he poses to his would-be answerers complement this listing by indicating movingly and thoroughly the consequence which will obtain if the proposal is not accepted. Thus, both through the careful attention to the smallest detail and through the marshalling of the whole movement of the essay, Swift has succeeded in creating an aura of rightness in the carefully thought out and convincingly presented proposal.

The reasonableness of the pleader, the fourth heading under which the character of the projector is established, is amply provided for by Swift. A reference already cited in another connection is also to the

---

[5] Swift seems here to be satirizing the economic projectors, whose pamphlets abound in mazes of mathematics. See George Wittkowsky, "Swift's 'Modest Proposal'; the Biography of an Early Georgian Pamphlet,' *Journal of the History of Ideas,* IV (Jan., 1943), pp. 75–104.

point here: "as to my own Part, having turned my Thoughts for many years, upon this important Subject . . . ." This careful deliberation suggests a reasonable rather than a rash pleader. "AFTER all, I am not so violently bent upon my own Opinion, as to reject any Offer proposed by wise Men, which shall be found equally cheap, easy, and effectual."

The projector reflects his reasonableness by the conservative nature of his calculations. In establishing 30,000 as the number of couples who can maintain their own children, he says, "although I apprehend there cannot be so many, *under the present Distresses of the Kingdom* . . . ."

Concession occurs again in the same paragraph.[6] The projector states that children under six are seldom good thieves, "although, I must confess, they learn the Rudiments [of stealing] much earlier."

In allowing that of the 20,000 reserved for breeders, only one-fourth will be males, the projector through concession emphasizes the generosity of his calculation, for this proportion "is more than we allow to *Sheep, black Cattle,* or *Swine.*'

The projector, in declining the "worthy Persons" refinement on his scheme (that the bodies of young lads and maidens between the ages of twelve and fourteen could be used for venison), concedes that here would be a slight chance for cruelty, "which, I confess, hath always been with me the strongest Objection against any Project, how well soever intended."

In describing the Formosan practice of court ministers' buying the bodies of young girls fresh from the gibbet, the projector concedes, "Neither indeed can I deny, that if the same Use were made of several plump young girls of this Town" the kingdom might be better off.

Most of these concessions are of little importance to the projector's central argument, but their use, where they cannot damage the proposition, tends to create an impression in the reader of the projector's reasonableness and lack of dogmatism.

Closely associated with this device of concession is that of deference to superiors (a device greatly needed in the Roman courts of the Empire, especially when an important or powerful personage had to be attacked but attacked politely). The projector graciously defers to the "worthy Person" who had offered a refinement on his scheme. "But

[6] I have here used the name *concession* for this device. Quintilian discusses concession, confession, and agreement as allied figures "which have a strong family resemblance." All three are used to concede points "that can do our case no harm." The act of concession implies a strong, confident position. (*Instit.* IX.ii.51–52.).

with due Deference to so excellent a Friend, and so deserving a Patriot, I cannot be altogether in his Sentiments." Such use of the young girls would be wasteful because they soon would become producers of this new food: "Then, as to the Females, it would, I think, with humble Submission, *be a Loss to the Public,* because they soon would become Breeders themselves . . . ."

Actually, of course, the projector concedes nothing; neither does he really defer to anyone. However, a tone of concession and of deference is present and contributes to the ethical proof.

I have said that the projector is a bit cocksure. He is also manifestly humble and modest. The proposal is a "modest" one. It is introduced in generally modest terms: "I SHALL NOW therefore humbly propose my own Thoughts . . ."; "I do humbly offer to *publick Considera-tion* . . . ." Swift has blended these two qualities of his projector in such a way that both are convincing and that neither quality overshadows the other. The result is a pleader whose humility is justifiably tempered by the sure knowledge that he has something to offer Ireland, to her everlasting benefit.

These are the explicit indicants of the moral character of the pleader; they are reinforced and dramatized by the whole tone of the essay. From this stable personality Swift allows only one outburst of real anger and pathos. It occurs at the climax of the essay, when the patient but exhausted old projector, "having been wearied out for many Years with offering vain, idle, visionary Thoughts," turns in righteous indignation to insist: "THEREFORE I repeat, let no Man talk to me of these and the like Expedients; till he hath, at least, a Glimpse of Hope, that there will ever be some hearty and sincere Attempt to put *them in Practice.*"

Diminution

The principle of diminution is the informing device of the entire essay; it underlies the whole animal motif. This diminution of man to animal Quintana sees in its perfected form in Book IV of *Gulliver's Travels* and in "A Modest Proposal," It is, he says, perhaps "the most devastating weapon ever used by a satirist." [7]

Swift's use of the device of diminution will be found to take three general directions, the first being the most pervasive: the creation of

[7] Ricardo Quintana, *The Mind and Art of Jonathan Swift* (Oxford: The University Press, 1936), p. 43. Several of the examples of diminution partake also of comparison; but, since diminution is the broader term for this particular context, all those examples of comparison will be considered in this section.

the illusion of animality, the substitution of the lesser word, and the imputation of the lesser motive.

The most obvious form of diminution is the use of the lesser noun to refer to people—especially to mothers and fathers. Strolling mothers are "*Beggars* of the female Sex." As if speaking of any mammal, the projector comments that "It is true a Child, *just dropped from its Dam*, may be supported by her Milk for a solar Year with little other Nourishment . . . ." In the mathematical working out of how many babies to save, the projector refers to the couples merely as "Breeders:" [8] Only a fourth part of these "breeders" are to be male "which is more than we allow to *Sheep, black Cattle*, or *Swine* . . . ." Like other animals, the mother will be able to work "until she produceth another Child."

As there are certain seasons when most animals foal, the projector with the help of a grave author finds that the human animals will produce most in December and January. He reckons that the markets will be most glutted a year after Lent.[9]

There will be no lack of people willing to set up butchery shambles in Dublin; however, "I rather recommend buying the Children alive, and dressing them hot from the Knife, as we do *roasting Pigs*." The "*true Lover of his Country*" has suggested that, "many fine Gentlemen of this Kingdom, having of late destroyed their Deer," "the Want of Venison might well be supplied by the Bodies of young Lads and Maidens, not exceeding fourteen Years of Age or under Twelve."

As if referring to cattle, the projector calculates that since the cost of maintaining 100,000 children after the age of two can be estimated at not less than ten shillings *per annum*, "the nation's Stock will be thereby increased Fifty Thousand Pounds *per annum* . . . ." (There is here a pun upon stock as livestock, as financial stock, and as pantry stock.)

"Men would become as *fond* of their Wives, during the time of their Pregnancy, as they are now of their *Mares* in Foal, their *Cows* in *Calf*, or *Sows* when they are ready to farrow . . . ." Beyond the equating

[8] In addition to this terminology's function in the animal diminution, it also satirizes the economic projector who is wont to deal with people as if they were only statistics, or as if they were cattle.

[9] The projector states, "I have reckoned upon a Medium, that a Child just born will weigh Twelve Pounds . . . ." The very grossness of the figure 12 suggests that it is a part of the animal diminution and is to be taken as an inhuman size for an *average* child at birth (for an average of 12 pounds requires some weights to be at least as high as 16 pounds). We should not, however, be too quick to apply mid-twentieth-century obstetrical standards to this figure. Only unavailable medical case histories of early 18th-century Ireland could prove the point. It is always possible that Swift simply did not know about such things, but if this be the case, it is the only instance in the whole essay which he has not investigated to the minutest detail.

the expectant mothers to animals, there is here the implication that men are humane to their animals and not to their wives.

Not only will a "well-known fat yearling Child" well grace a Lord Mayor's feast, but also the projector can depend upon the pride of the women as to "*which of them could bring the fattest Child to the Market.*" The "Customers of Infants Flesh" would in Dublin alone "take off, annually, about Twenty Thousand Carcasses; and the rest of the Kingdom (where probably they will be sold somewhat cheaper) the remaining Eighty Thousand."

At the beginning of the mathematical calculations the people were referred to as "souls," but at the end they have become "Creatures in human Figure," "Mouths and Backs."

It is easy to get the impression from reading the essay casually that Swift creates the animal transfer by avoiding the use of terms appropriate to human beings. But this is not quite true. *Mother, father, child, children, babe, youth, lad, maiden, infant* are liberally sprinkled throughout the essay. With the exception of the word *carcass* (used in reference to children in paragraphs 15, 27, and 28) all of the other nouns applied to children are terms for food (see the next paragraph, below). In addition to the use of a lower term, Swift effects the animal diminution by juxtaposition of modifier and noun, as in "yearling Child." Rhetorically, the projector's constantly varying the normal term with the animal term serves to keep the reader off guard, with the result that if the reader begins to expect the animal term, he is fooled. The resulting effect is that one term is just as normal as the other. The animal terms are slipped in unobtrusively, and they are never insisted upon.

As if the diminution of human beings to animals were not strong enough, the irony is intensified by a species of redoubled diminution: the animal becomes food. The progression of diminution thus becomes man to animal to food (with the obvious implication that man is an animal to eat such food, or even worse than an animal, their being relatively few animals which are cannibalistic). Notice the final step in the diminution to food in the following statements. A "young healthy Child, well nursed, is, at a Year old, a most delicious, nourishing, and wholesome Food; whether *stewed, roasted, baked* or *boiled;* and I make no doubt, that it will equally serve in a *Fricasie, or Ragoust.*" They will be "plump and fat for a good Table. A Child will make two Dishes at an Entertainment for Friends; and when the family dines alone, the fore or hind Quarter will make a reasonable Dish; and seasoned with a little Pepper or Salt, will be very good Boiled on the fourth Day, especially in *Winter*." One of Swift's most devastating techniques of word order is the final twist or insinuation with which he can charge the last phrase of a sentence. Witness the last phrase of the preceding sentence.

This new food will be "somewhat dear" and therefore "very *proper for Landlords;* who, as they have already *devoured* [italics mine] most of the Parents, seem to have the best Title to the Children."

If such man-to-animal diminution stood alone in the essay, it would no doubt be so offensive that it would defeat its intended purpose of persuading the reader. However, as Swift has blended the operation of this device with the functioning of the several other devices, the whole resultant fabric of the irony is made so tight-knit that this particular use of diminution is one highly successful and basic to the whole essay. The steady reiteration of this diminution tends to establish it in the reader's consciousness as a norm, and thus the rhetorical device becomes one of the means of establishing the ironic norm of the essay. Obviously care had to be exercised not to overplay the device lest it boomerang. Swift so manipulates its use that by slipping in a word here and a phrase there, the impression of normalness (and the resultant acceptance) is gradually achieved.

All of the uses of diminution in this essay are not concerned directly with the animal figure, although, since the other uses of the device contribute to the dehumanizing tone of the whole essay, they can be said to contribute indirectly. The remaining uses are of two kinds: the use of the worse word to name a thing and the assumption of the worse motive in the performance of an act.

In paragraph two the "Children" in Ireland become "a very great additional Grievance." And in paragraph nineteen the old people are "a grievous . . . . Incumbrance." A mother can nourish her child for a solar year on as little as two shillings, "which the Mother may certainly get, or the Value in Scraps, by her lawful Occupation of *Begging.*"

The proposal will prevent "those *voluntary Abortions,* and that horrid Practice of *Women murdering their Bastard Children;* alas! too frequent among us; sacrificing the *poor innocent Babes,* I doubt, more to avoid the Expence than the Shame; which would move Tears and Pity in the most Savage and inhuman Breast." There are two kinds of diminution in this sentence. The lesser motive is imputed when the projector states that the mothers will so act in order to avoid the expense rather than the shame, and animality is implied when the projector observes that such an act would move a savage or an inhuman breast to tears. The few casual references to savages, Laplanders, and the inhabitants of Topinamboo combine to suggest to the reader that here are some people who might well be emulated. These references also provide a further standard by which the ironic norm can through contrast be brought into even sharper focus.

Swift's extensive use of diminution can be studied advantageously in tabular form. The following table presents a graphic summary of all of the nouns and a few of the verbs and modifiers which Swift has used in the diminution from man to animal, indicating the extent, the incidence, and the gradations of diminution.

PARENTS

Paragraph Number	Best Name	Impersonal or Less Name	Animal or Food Term
1	mothers	female sex	
2	mothers fathers	beggars	
3	parents		
4	parents		dam
5		women	
6	wives	souls women	breeders
	poor parents parents		
10	mother		
12	parents		
14	mother	beggars cottagers labourers farmers tenants	produceth another child
17	parents	nearest relations	breeders
19		females aged, diseased, maimed poor people young labourers	
21		papists dangerous enemies good protestants	breeders
22		poor tenants	
24			constant breeders
26	mothers wives	men married women	
29		women shop-keepers	
32	parents wives	beggars beggars cottagers labourers	breed
33		the poor	

CHILDREN

Paragraph Number	Best Name	Impersonal or Less Name	Animal or Food Term
1	children helpless infants		
2	children children	grievance	
3	children infants		
4	child		just dropped from dam
5	innocent babes	bastard children	
6	children children children		number probationary thieves
7	boy girl		
9	child		wholesome food
10	children children child	males male females	for breed two dishes
11	child		
12	children		
13		Papist infants	infant's flesh
14	child	beggar's child	carcass of a good fat child 4 dishes of nutritive meat
15			carcass
16	children		bought alive & dressed hot, as we do pigs
17		bodies of lads and maidens both sexes males	for venison flesh
18		young person body of plump girl plump young girls	carcass a prime dainty
23	children		new dish goods
24	children		
25			food
26	children babes		fattest child at the market
27			carcasses fat well-grown yearling
28			child
29			infant's flesh
31			carcasses commodity
32	children	mouths backs mortals	flesh
33	infants children		

Swift refers to the parents by the best name sixteen times, by the impersonal name twenty-eight times, and by the animal name eight times. Naming them most frequently by the impersonal middle term is consistent with his purpose of neutralizing these human beings so that, on the eight occasions of referring to them in animal terms, easy acceptance of the animal terms results. By firmly establishing the middle term, Swift has not had to make the broad jump from human being to animal; he moves only from the middle or neutral term to the animal term.

The acceptance of the parents as breeders of animals makes the acceptance of babies as animals much easier. Thus, by natural sequence, the parent-as-animal diminution serves as preparation for the babies-as-animals diminution. It further allows for the larger number of references to the children as animals and as food. Swift refers to the children by the best name twenty-nine times, by the impersonal name sixteen times, and by the animal name twenty-four times. The low incidence of the middle term in naming children results from the foundation laid by its high incidence in naming parents. (This balance results not from a chronological sequence in the essay but from the sequence in nature, that the offspring will naturally be like the parents.) Building the diminution carefully in this manner, Swift was free then to push the terrible juxtaposition of the two extremes, the best name coupled with the animal or food name for children.

It is through observing and understanding each such careful handling by Swift of a particular device of rhetoric that one comes better to comprehend the full implications of Swift's rhetorical art and its contribution to his irony. Only thus can we begin to explain most readers' amazement reflected in the question, "How does he get away with rendering human beings as animals in a few brief paragraphs?" His painstaking manipulation of rhetoric supplies the answer.

Refining

Refining "consists in dwelling on the same topic and yet seeming to say something new." [10] It can be accomplished by a variation in words, in delivery, or in treatment (e.g., by a change in the form—to dialogue, to characterization, etc.). The device appears in Swift's essay; however, it is put to a much subtler use than the author of *Ad Herennium* had in mind. Swift's use of refining is akin to what Martin Price has called

[10] *Rhetorica ad Herennium*, tr. Harry Caplan (Loeb Classical Library; London: William Heinemann, Ltd., 1954), IV.xlii.54.

"redefinition": [11] in referring to something, Swift varies the word until finally the word or phrase has a new meaning, a meaning which Swift intended it to have all along but which he carefully avoided expressing.

For example, the proposal is ostensibly designed for the children of professional beggars, who hardly make up a majority of the population. Swift must redefine "professional Beggar" so as to include all of the poor within this term. The pride of the poor is as great as the pride of the rich; therefore Swift eases the redefinition in by "refining" it, by varying the terms without seeming to dwell on them. This is accomplished in three steps and reinforced in a fourth (paragraphs 2, 3, 14, and 32, in that order). The pitiful strollers in paragraph one are said to be beggars (whether technically professional beggars is not made clear). In paragraph three the projector states, "BUT my Intention is very far from being confined to provide only for the Children of *professed Beggars:* It is of a much greater Extent, and shall take in the whole Number of Infants at a certain Age, who are born of Parents, in effect as little able to support them, as those who demand our Charity in the Streets." The two groups (the beggars and the poor) are put on one footing, but they remain two groups. In the next several paragraphs all of the mathematical calculations are concerned with "the Children of the Poor," beggars not being mentioned. Swift waits until paragraph fourteen to push the identification: "I HAVE already computed the Charge of nursing a Beggar's Child (in which List I reckon all *Cottagers, Labourers,* and Four fifths of the *Farmers*) . . . ." The identification is complete, and it has been accomplished by a quite casual parenthesis. The word *beggar* is used only once again in the essay: in the peroration, where the projector states "adding those who are Beggars by profession, to the Bulk of Farmers, Cottagers, and labourers, with their Wives and Children, who are Beggars in Effect." Through such refining Swift has steered a precarious course: he has made the identification of the poor and the beggars and at the same time he has refined so subtly that he has not impugned the dignity of the group in whose behalf he is writing.

But all of Swift's refining is not so gentle; neither is it aimed at redefinition. The landlords fare far worse. The word *landlord* (or its equivalent "Gentleman of Fortune") occurs eleven times. The refining is merely verbal, and these words occur with iterative force to drive home the idea that the landlords will be the main eaters of this new food. This accusation against the landlords is prepared for in para-

[11] Martin Price, *Swift's Rhetorical Art: A Study in Structure and Meaning* (New Haven: Yale University Press, 1953), pp. 27–31.

graphs six through ten, in which this new food is discussed. Who will
eat it is only implied, until finally, late in paragraph ten, the projector
states that these babies are to be "offered in Sale to *Persons of Quality
and Fortune* through the Kingdom . . . ." The verb *offered* does not
yet explicitly mean that these persons will accept the offer. Then in
paragraph twelve the projector concedes that the food "will be somewhat dear, and therefore very *proper for Landlords;* who, as they have
already devoured most of the Parents, seem to have the best Title to
the Children." From this bold statement forward, the idea is not
allowed to rest. In paragraph fourteen, it is repeated twice: "no
Gentleman would repine to give Ten Shillings for the *Carcase of a good
fat Child* . . . . thus the Squire will learn to be a good Landlord, and
grow popular with his Tenants.. . . . " In the next paragraph (15)
we are told that the flayed carcasses will "make admirable *Gloves for
Ladies,* and *Summer Boots for fine Gentlemen.*"

In the very next paragraph (16) the idea is implied in the discussion of the butchering of new food. And in the paragraph following
(17), we meet the "VERY worthy person, *a true Lover of his Country,*"
"so excellent a Friend, and so deserving a Patriot" who sees a way to
refine this modest proposal. This is followed in the next paragraph by
the story of the usage of the Formosan court (with the parallel implied).

The refining continues in paragraph twenty-two: "SECONDLY, the
poorer Tenants will have something valuable of their very own, which,
by Law, may be made liable to Distress, and help to pay their Landlord's Rent; their Corn and Cattle being already seized, and *Money a
Thing Unknown.*"

The third reason given in favor of the proposal is that a new dish
will be introduced to the tables of "all *Gentlemen of Fortune* in the
Kingdom, who have any Refinement of Taste . . . ." The fifth reason
is that the trade of "Houses frequented by all the *fine Gentlemen,* who
justly value themselves upon their Knowledge in good Eating" will be
greatly increased, especially in houses where there is a "skilful Cook,
who understands how to oblige his Guests" and who "will contrive to
make it as expensive as they please."

Omitting it in the next paragraph, Swift returns to the idea in the
following one (27), as he visualizes the new food at all fine tables, at
the Lord Mayor's feast, and (in paragraph 28) at all "*merry Meetings*"
such as "*Weddings and Christenings.*" (It is appropriate to the subject
matter that he should single out these two occasions as examples of
merry meetings.)

In the next paragraph (29) come the "Expedients" which the projector rejects. The landlords are implied in several of them, and near the end of the series are singled out: "*Of teaching Landlords to have, at least, one Degree of Mercy towards their Tenants.*" In the peroration the landlords are hit two more times. They are blamed for much of the "perpetual Scene of Misfortunes," since tenants are borne down upon by "the *Oppression of Landlords* . . . . " And in the final paragraph in the recapitulation the landlords are given the strong final position in that series: "*and giving some pleasure to the Rich.*"

Isolating all of these examples tends to give the impression that Swift's amazingly frequent repetition of this idea is not "refining" but merely gross pounding at a theme. However, as each instance appears in full context, Swift's subtlety is fully appreciated. Swift's refining is a rhetorical device contributing to the reader's acceptance of the irony, because its operation is pervasive, it works by indirection and by implication, it is manipulated through a careful handling of the language of each sentence, and because, when it appears, the reader's attention is frequently fixed elsewhere (on the idea of the sentence rather than on the method of the sentence).

Less Frequently Used Devices

Among less frequently used, but no less important, rhetorical devices of the "Modest Proposal" is appeal to authority. In the exordium the projector assumes that all agree as to the state of the kingdom: "I THINK that it is agreed by all Parties, that this prodigious Number of Children in the Arms, or on the Backs, or at the *Heels* of their *Mothers,* and frequently their *Fathers,* is *in the present deplorable State of the Kingdom,* a very great additional Grievance . . . . " This appeal is of particular importance to Swift's English readers, for (as indicated in his "A Short View of the State of Ireland") many Englishmen, who were well entertained in fine houses during brief visits to Ireland, actually thought that Ireland was a prosperous kingdom and reported so back home.

"A principal Gentleman in the County of *Cavan*" has informed the projector that even in that county, which is famous for its thieves, there were not known to that gentleman over one or two instances in which children under the age of six were very skillful at stealing.

The projector has consulted the merchants, men who really should know about market prices, etc., in order to confirm his calculations, and he has been "assured by our Merchants" that children around the age of twelve are "no saleable Commodity."

Probably the most impressive single authority which the projector calls upon is that "grave" French author and physician, Rabelais, who has proved that a fish diet greatly contributes to potency in engendering this new commodity.

In addition to these explicit appeals to authority there are several implicit appeals. Each time that the projector says that certain gentlemen would pay this or that for various parts *of* this animal, or that such and such can be done to this commodity to please the gentlemen of fashion, he is presupposing the approval of these gentlemen. In fact one such gentleman—"a VERY worthy person, *a true Lover of his Country*" becomes so enthusiastic about the projector's plan that he "was pleased . . . to offer a Refinement on my Scheme." The older youths could be used as a substitute for venison. But the moderation of Swift's projector finds this suggestion excessive. Besides, "a very knowing American" has assured the projector that such meat is tough.

The implicit approval of authority is reflected in the following remarks which are scattered at random through the essay. "No Gentleman would repine to give Ten Shillings for the *Carcase of a good fat Child.*" The flayed carcass would make admirable gloves and summer boots. The landlords will have excellent nutritive meat "when he hath some particular Friend, or his own Family, to dine with him." Such meat would make a "considerable Figure" at a Lord Mayor's feast. These and the several other food passages in the essay completely presuppose participation in and approval of the scheme by the people of quality.

The explicit appeals to authority, especially to experts and grave authors, are standard in classical rhetoric. The indirect and implied approvals just enumerated, however, contribute more to the ironic trap than do the explicit ones, for the former imply a general acceptation among society. Appeal to the authority of the whole society is what Aristotle calls the appeal to "previous judgment," to a "necessary truth." If the truth is not necessary, then it can be an appeal to "the opinion held by the majority, or the wise, or all or most of the good." [12]

The device of interrogation is employed once in the essay. It is in the powerful thirty-second paragraph. This paragraph opens with the quite mild concession that the projector is "not so violently bent" upon his own opinion that he will not entertain other proposals. He merely makes one reservation: that any such projectors answer two questions:

[12] Aristotle *Rhet.* II.xxiii.12. See also Quintilian *Inst.* V.xi.36–37.

First, As Things now stand, how they will find Food and Raiment, for a Hundred Thousand useless Mouths and Backs? And *secondly,* There being a round Million of Creatures in human Figure, throughout this Kingdom; whose whole subsistence, put into a common Stock, would leave them in Debt two Millions of Pounds *Sterling;* adding those, who are Beggars by Profession, to the Bulk of Farmers, Cottagers, and Labourers, with their Wives and Children, who are Beggars in Effect; I desire those Politicians, who dislike my Overture, and may perhaps be so bold to attempt an Answer, that they first ask the Parents of these Mortals, Whether they would not, at this Day, think it a great Happiness to have been sold for Food at a Year old, in the Manner I prescribe; and thereby have avoided such a perpetual Scene of Misfortunes, as they have gone through; by the *Oppression of Landlords;* the Impossibility of paying Rent, without Money or Trade; the Want of common Sustenance, with neither House nor Cloaths, to cover them from the Inclemencies of Weather; and the most inevitable Prospect of entailing the like, or greater Miseries upon their Breed forever.

The final phrase "upon their Breed forever" has the inverted ring of the finality of a prayer "world without end, amen." This rhetorical question serves several purposes. It summarizes the complaints which have been scattered throughout the essay (the quotation is from the peroration); it is so couched that what has been given in mass would have to be refuted separately (a device which Quintilian recommends when a pleader has massed together what cannot be strong separately); and of course it gives the projector occasion to voice his most stinging indictment without seeming to propound, since he is merely posing a question as the basis for a possible concession on his part.

Argument by elimination is scarcely used in this essay, and in the passages in which it appears it does not occur in its full syllogistic form. It is a telling means of persuasion because it narrows the argument by excluding any consideration except the one being urged.

The passage just quoted from paragraph thirty-two is a good example of elimination, for if either question can reasonably be answered, the projector has already promised that he is ready to concede and entertain other proposals. And in paragraph nineteen in reference to the problem of old people, the projector eliminates all other problems except the one of his proposal, thus sharpening the focus on his own proposal and making the audience more ready to attack this problem with this solution, since this proposal will relieve the whole economic situation and all members of the society.

Swift uses the device of accumulation to good effect in two instances, one of which has just been quoted from paragraph thirty-two.

The second question posed there is a long series which accurately and adequately summarizes the whole situation of Ireland and the modest proposal being made.

The other use of accumulation is the brief description in the final paragraph: "having no other motive than the *Publick Good of my Country, by advancing our Trade, providing for Infants, relieving the Poor, and giving some Pleasure to the Rich.*" This series concisely echoes each of the major groups of reasons which have been set forth (except the antipapist reasons, which might, from the point of view of the projector, be included "in the public Good"). It is natural that both instances of accumulation in this essay should occur in the peroration, for recapitulation is one of the standard uses of this section of the speech.

From the understatement of the essay's title forward, litotes has an unusually strong force, since it operates within the ironic inversion. Statements which would be quite ordinary understatement are surcharged by the ironically inverted context. In paragraph twelve the projector grants that this new "Food will be somewhat dear." In an essay which is *not* built upon irony of inversion, litotes operates merely to indicate more force by couching an idea in a less forceful manner than is appropriate. But to say that this food "will be somewhat dear" lifts the ironic veil in order to state a terrible truth. And the statement comes through in all its truth, with only the one word "somewhat" holding the thin thread of irony as the observation darts for the moment to the very edge of the fine line between irony and simple truth.

The same effect is achieved in paragraph seventeen. (The reference is to the gentleman's suggestion that young boys and girls could be used as a substitute for venison.):

> And besides it is not improbable, that some scrupulous People might be apt to censure such a Practice (although indeed very unjustly) as a little bordering upon Cruelty; which, I confess, hath always been with me the strongest Objection against any Project, how well soever intended.

The single phrase "a little bordering on" holds the ironic structure tightly together during the moment that the ironist, brushing aside all except a single thin layer of irony, allows his reader a glimpse into the heart of the matter, which is that any mere proposal is cruelly fruitless since only a thoroughly normal and healthy administration of the kingdom can give genuine well-being to Ireland.

In the list of rejected "expedients" the litotes has the same function. Two of the expedients are expressed in litotes: "*Of being a little cautious not to sell our Country and Consciences for nothing: Of teaching Landlords to have, at least, one Degree of Mercy towards their Tenants.*" The litotes is strong just in these isolated examples. But, when they are set into ironic inversion, they gain added power: Let no man talk to me of being a little cautious not to sell our country and consciences for nothing; let no man talk to me of teaching landlords to have, at least, one degree of mercy toward their tenants. The negative of "Let no man talk to me" further emphasizes the already negative litotes of the *of* phrases.

Although the passage listing the expedients is not cast as a whole into litotes, the effect of the whole is quite similar to that which I have just described in connection with litotes: the ironist momentarily holds aside all but one of the several curtains of irony so that his reader may be shown the truth.

> Therefore, let no man talk to me of other Expedients: Of taxing our Absentees at five Shillings a Pound; Of using neither Cloaths, nor Household Furniture except what is of our own Growth and Manufacture: Of utterly rejecting the Materials and Instruments that promote foreign Luxury: Of curing the Expansiveness of Pride, Vanity, Idleness, and Gaming in our Women: Of introducing a Vein of Parsimony, Prudence and Temperance: Of learning to love our Country, wherein we differ even from LAPLANDERS, and the Inhabitants of TOPINAMBOO: Of quitting our Animosities, and Factions; nor act any longer like the JEWS, who were murdering one another at the very Moment their City was taken: Of being a little cautious not to sell our Country and Consciences for nothing: Of teaching Landlords to have, at least, one Degree of Mercy towards their Tenants. Lastly, Of putting a Spirit of Honesty, Industry, and Skill into our Shopkeepers; who, if a Resolution could now be taken to buy only our native Goods, would immediately unite to cheat and exact upon us in the Price, the Measure, and the Goodness; nor could ever yet be brought to make one fair Proposal of just Dealing, though often and earnestly invited to it.

Swift has left no doubt as to his real meaning: this is the only extended passage in the essay which is italicized; it is the only extended passage built upon the principle of understatement. The use of litotes is heavily limited in this essay (occurring only in the passages which have just been discussed) because the rhetoric is geared to the irony: litotes is the device which allows the ironist the thinnest facade of pretense, and obviously Swift could not allow his ironic pose to become fragile at too many points.

The projector makes several appeals directly to the emotions of his audience. One such appeal is to his reader's prejudice against Roman Catholics. Three separate passages contain this appeal. In the first paragraph of the essay such an appeal is prepared for. The "helpless infants" of these starving parents will, when they grow up, become thieves, "or leave their *dear Native Country, to fight for the Pretender in* Spain, or sell themselves to the *Barbadoes*." The next passage is in paragraph thirteen. The projector has been assured that

> . . . *Fish being a prolifick Dyet*, there are more Children born in *Roman Catholick Countries* about Nine Months after Lent, than at any other Season: Therefore reckoning a Year after *Lent*, the Markets will be more glutted than usual; because the Number of *Popish Infants*, is, at least, three to one in this Kingdom; and therefore it will have one other Collateral Advantage, by lessening the Number of *Papists* among us.

The subject is mentioned once more; it has the lead position in the reasons of the proof:

> FOR, *First*, as I have already observed, it would greatly lessen the *Number of Papists*, with whom we are yearly over-run; being the principal Breeders of the Nation, as well as our most dangerous Enemies; and who stay at home on Purpose, with a Design to *deliver the Kingdom to the Pretender;* hoping to take their Advantage by the Absence of *so many good Protestants*, who have chosen rather to leave their Country, than stay at home, and pay Tithes against their Conscience, to an idolatrous *Episcopal Curate*.

Stigmatizing the Roman Catholics as traitors and scolding the Anglo-Irish for not staying home and for not supporting the Established Church play right to the opinion of the Anglo-Irish. Swift's making this particular appeal raises the old and unanswerable question of whether he directed his Irish tracts to the whole of Ireland or to the Anglo-Irish minority.[13] If it is to all Irishmen, this device is hardly a happy choice.

[13] Quintana suggests that Swift was strongly Anglo-Irish instead of Irish (Quintana, *op. cit.*, pp. 246–47). Murry believes that Swift's motives are too unclear or mixed for us to determine. John Middleton Murry, *Jonathan Swift: A Critical Biography* (London: Jonathan Cape, 1954), p. 359. Davis, in his Introduction to Vol. X of his edition of *The Drapier Letters* calls attention to the fact that the Drapier addressed himself to the "whole State of Ireland" (p. xxxi). Carl Van Doren suggests that Swift's strong pro-Anglo-Irish sentiment gradually

The projector, with a sure knowledge of his readers' prejudice, appeals to their prejudice against dishonest shopkeepers. His appeal has a position in the long, italicized catalogue of rejected "expedients":

> Lastly, Of putting a Spirit of Honesty, Industry, and Skill into our Shop-keepers; who, if a Resolution could now be taken to buy only our native Goods, would immediately unite to cheat and exact upon us in the Price, the Measure, and the Goodness; nor could ever yet be brought to make one fair Proposal of just Dealing, though often and earnestly invited to it.

The statement comes with all the more force and conviction, for Swift had so often and earnestly invited them to it. This appeal works equally well to the general prejudice against shop-keepers or to the Anglo-Irish prejudice against Irish shop-keepers (in the event that the essay was directed mainly to the Anglo-Irish).

A favorite device of rhetorical appeal to the emotions is that of the "vivid picture" or, as it is sometimes called, "ocular demonstration." [14] Vividness being a standard quality in the best work of Swift, it might seem a bit beside the point to single out particular instances of this quality here. The rhetorical device is, however, usually meant to name an extended set piece of description. In addition to the general quality of vividness throughout Swift's essay, there is one of these set pieces: the opening paragraph. In this first paragraph of the exordium Swift sketches in minute detail the picture of the wandering, begging mothers and children. The device becomes even more obvious when we consider that in an essay to *prove* the validity of a proposal, the essay begins, not with a statement of the proposal, not with any preliminary arguments for the proposal, but with an actual picture of what has brought about the need for the proposal. In this sense the opening paragraph is an ocular demonstration. This is the only set picture in the essay; other passages which describe a situation tend to do so in terms too abstract or in a point of view too generalized and abstracted to give such a set picture. There are little phrases which,

---

gave way to a pan-Irish sympathy by the end of the Wood campaign. Van Doren cites Swift's own comment in a letter to Pope: "I do profess without affectation, that your kind opinion of me as a patriot, since you call it so, is what I do not deserve; because what I do is owing to perfect rage and resentment, and the mortifying sight of slavery, folly, and baseness about me, among which I am forced to live." Carl Van Doren, *Swift* (New York: The Viking Press, 1930), pp. 170–71. Swift himself could probably not have determined whether his vexation against English injustice to Ireland was greater or less than his disgust at Irish apathy which accepted English policies.

[14] *Ad Herennium* LV.

however, through the sure touch of the poet, give glances at little pictures, such as the final clause in this sentence: "We should soon see an honest Emulation among the married women, *which of them could bring the fattest Child to the Market.*" The last clause gives us a scene of proud and bragging mothers elbowing and vying with each other at the market place. However, such little touches tend to be more a matter of style than of rhetorical device.

Swift's use of parenthesis in the essay functions in four ways: two are used to introduce allusions which enrich the argument by suggesting situations never stated or explained; three are used to slip in cutting asides reflecting the judgment of the projector; one is used in connection with diminution; and another is used in balance with litotes.

The two which allude to arguments not specifically raised in the essay are the following: the projector points out that there is no opportunity for the employment of laborers in handicraft and agriculture: "We neither build Houses, (I mean in the Country) nor cultivate Land." The parenthesis clarifies the point. The projector does not mean primarily that construction jobs are lacking; he means that no great plantation houses are being built and that therefore there are no agricultural jobs being created. The other parenthesis of this kind is on the same subject: Dublin alone would "take off, annually, about Twenty Thousand Carcasses; and the rest of the Kingdom (where probably they will be sold somewhat cheaper) the remaining Eighty Thousand." The parenthesis again emphasizes the unfruitful conditions in the country areas. He has told his readers of the terrible conditions in Dublin, and through these two parentheses he leaves it to the reader to imagine the situation in the country, a situation even worse than that in Dublin.[15] The wealth of argument which the projector enjoys is so vast that only through these two parentheses does he have space even to indicate some lines of proof for his proposal. This is one of the most subtle refinements Swift has given to a standard rhetorical device.

In three instances Swift uses parenthesis in its more usual function of inserting an aside to his audience: "THOSE who are more thrifty (*as I must confess the Times require*) may flay the Carcase . . . ." He accomplishes little here with the parenthesis because his use of italics emphasizes what the parenthesis is supposed to tuck in unobtru-

---

[15] See Swift's "A Short View of the State of Ireland" for a description of the plight of the agricultural worker and of the depleted condition of many of the old plantations.

sively.[16] In a similar instance, the same device has much more power because italics are used for only one word and because the remark is so cutting: this proposal will insure a more humane treatment of wives by husbands, who will no longer "offer to beat or kick them, (as is too *frequent* a Practice) for fear of a Miscarriage." "There is likewise another Advantage in my *Scheme*, that it will prevent those *voluntary Abortions*, and that horrid Practice of *Women murdering their Bastard Children;* alas! too frequent among us; sacrificing their *poor innocent Babes* . . . ."

Two occasions of Swift's use of parenthesis are crucial to the passages in which they occur. Both have been discussed above, in connection with litotes and diminution, respectively. As has been noticed above, the projector has been careful gradually to refine *beggar* so that it will include all of the poor of Ireland. At the delicate point where the identification is completely made, parenthesis is brought into play to perform this task: "I HAVE already computed the Charge of nursing a Beggar's Child (in which list I reckon all *Cottagers, Labourers,* and Four fifths of the *Farmers*) . . . ."

As we have seen, too, the passages in the essay where Swift employs litotes became thin in respect to the degree of irony present. In one such instance Swift uses parenthesis to help balance the litotes: some people "might be apt to censure such a Practice (although indeed very unjustly) as a little bordering on Cruelty . . . ." Since only the litotes keeps this statement from being a literal expression of the simple truth, the ironical negation of the parenthesis helps balance the litotes and thus helps to maintain the irony.

Conclusions

"A Modest Proposal" is a brilliant example of the use of non-argumentative devices of rhetorical persuasion. The whole essay, of course, rests broadly upon argument of cause and effect: these causes have produced this situation in Ireland, and this proposal will result in these effects in Ireland. But Swift, within the general framework of this argument, does not employ specific argumentative forms in this essay. The projector chooses rather to *assert* his reasons and then to amass

---

[16] In general in this essay italics are used for emphasis and might therefore be construed as a hint concerning that part of oratory called delivery. However, the well-known problems of Swift and his printers on such textual matters renders only dubious authenticity to any particular italics. We cannot know for sure whether some are Swift's or his printers.

them by way of proof. He does not argue his reasons, and he does not prove them with formal arguments. In introducing the proof, the projector states that "I think the Advantages by the Proposal which I have made, are obvious, and many, as well as of the highest Importance." The fact that his reasons are "obvious" indicates that they need not be proved by argument. After having listed the sixth reason, he states that many more advantages could be "enumerated." This last word indicates that he is making no effort to prove, but merely to list. This refusal to argue his reasons is of course a persuasive device in itself, for it places the whole proposal upon the plane of obvious fact, necessary truth, rather than upon the plane of argued postulates open to debate.

Although the essay is not logically complex, it is extremely complex rhetorically—as is easily seen, for example, by the number of times in the preceding pages that a single passage has been used to demonstrate several devices which are operating at once.

Swift's ironic norm is established by the pervasive tone of diminution (human beings to animals) and by the projector's sustained point of view as an economist (his mathematics, his dealing with people as only statistical abstractions, his assuming that everyone will participate in this new industry). The human flesh is so consistently regarded as just another commodity that the whole society is finally drawn into a participation in the project—the producers, the sellers, and the consumers. This complete involvement of all classes of citizens into the scheme is arrived at by the subtle use of rhetorical devices which we have been examining—especially by the processes of diminution (for the producers) and refining (for the consumers). The norm is so thoroughly established that if the reader demurs, he will find himself to be the only one out of step.

In addition to the extensive use of these two devices of classical rhetoric, there is the fundamental ethical proof which informs the whole essay. Swift has fully exploited the possibilities of this proof by his thorough development of the character of the projector, whose personality is evident either implicitly or explicitly in every paragraph of the essay. And within these elaborately employed devices are manipulated the rhetorical devices which Swift uses less often: his direct and implied authorities; his appeal to the emotions through ocular demonstration and through the prejudices of the Irish and the Anglo-Irish; his rhetorical interrogation to allow him to assert strongly while he seems only to question mildly; his use of elimination, whereby all other proposals except his are swept aside; his uncanny use of litotes to hold the ironic pose by a single fine wire while truth is allowed to peek through for a moment; his effortless use of parenthesis to indicate whole areas of reasons which have had to be crowded out of the main line of proof; his repeatedly implied refusal to argue the "obvious." By the consummate skill with which Swift has interlocked these several devices of classical rhetoric, he has created "A Modest Proposal." To appreciate how fundamental the classical rhetoric is to the very texture of the essay, one need merely ask himself what the essay would be like if Swift had not availed himself of the long tradition of such rhetoric as it reached right down to Swift's own school days. To answer that the essay simply would not exist in its present perfection would be a conservative reply.

THE ARGUMENT OF MADISON'S "FEDERALIST," NO. 10   *Mark Ashin*

In the January issue of *College English*, some members of the English staff at the College of the University of Chicago questioned the value of trying to teach argument in a writing course by concentrating exclusively on the technique of formal logic. Their contention was that, while training in the inductive and deductive forms of logic would enable a student to judge the validity of arguments already constructed, such training does little or nothing to supply the young student's greatest need, some technique for discovering the material which makes up an argument. After an analysis of this problem, they recommended the introduction into courses in argument of an up-to-date system of rhetoric based upon what the classical rhetoricians called "the Topics," a term which can be translated as "the sources from which arguments are drawn." The four sources of argument which they described in detail and which the English staff at the College has tested in practice are the ideas of Genus or Definition, Consequence, Likeness and Difference, and Authority. Readers interested in the theory underlying this point of view are referred to the article in question.[1] However, even those who may be convinced that this new attack on the problem of teaching argument sounds promising in the abstract will certainly have many questions about how this rhetorical approach operates in the classroom. It is the aim of the present article

From *College English*, October, 1953. Reprinted with the permission of the National Council of Teachers of English and Professor Ashin.

[1] Bilsky, Hazlett, Streeter, and Weaver, "Looking for an Argument," *College English*, XIV (January, 1953), 210–16.

to satisfy this curiosity, at least in part, by applying "topical" considerations to the analysis and interpretation of a classroom text, a recognized masterpiece of polemics, Madison's *Federalist,* No. 10.

This particular *Federalist* paper, on the control of faction in popular
governments, has long since achieved political immortality as a classic
defense of the theory of republicanism. Its usefulness as an instrument
in teaching has been equally well demonstrated. It has been a required reading in civics and social science courses to give students an
understanding of the theoretical bases of our Constitution. It has
served the teacher of logic and argument as a cogent example of the
controlling power of syllogistic reasoning. Practically every text in
the social and intellectual history of the United States singles it out to
illustrate the Federalist position during the political controversy surrounding the adoption of the Constitution. Even Vernon L. Parrington,
whose great book is a crusade against Federalist conservatism, paid
tribute to it as a worthy enemy by calling it "the remarkable tenth
number, which compresses within a few pages pretty much the
whole Federalist theory of political science." There is no denying that
much can be and has been done with conventional modes of logical
analysis to reveal the effectiveness of Madison's reasoning, since the
essay is practically made-to-order as a sample of the syllogism in
operation. However, I believe that to supplement a formal analysis
with a consideration of the main sources from which the author draws
the material for his arguments can immeasurably enrich the English
teacher's handling of deduction, since it can present, on a level under-
standable to all, the characteristic operation of Madison's mind as he
proceeds with his demonstrations.

As will be seen, the major sources of argument for Madison are
definitions and *consequences.* In any considered statement of political
theory, careful definitions of key terms, used both as starting points
(see the definition of "faction" in paragraph 2) and as stages in the
argument (see the implied definition of "man" in paragraph 6), are
required to clarify a position. In addition, to induce an audience to
accept a recommended course of action, no more compelling motive
can be invented than one which argues for the good consequences
which will necessarily follow the adoption of your proposal and the
evil consequences which will follow the adoption of any other.

The problem with which Madison was concerned and the direction
of his reasoning are indicated in his opening sentences:

> Among the numerous advantages promised by a well constructed
> Union, none deserves to be more accurately developed than its tendency

to break and control the violence of faction. The friend of popular governments never finds himself so much alarmed for their character and fate, as when he contemplates their propensity to this dangerous vice. He will not fail, therefore, to set a due value on any plan which, without violating the principles to which he is attached, provides a proper cure for it.

However, the explicit statement of his aim is reserved for paragraph 11, after he has disposed of the visionary thesis that the causes of faction can be removed, and has turned to the practical task of describing how to control its effects. First indicating that a majority rather than a minority faction is the main danger in popular government, he states:

To secure the public good and private rights against the danger of such a faction, and at the same time to preserve the spirit and the form of popular government, is then the great object to which our inquiries are directed.

Madison thus sets himself the task of arguing for a particular design of government which will provide a "republican remedy" for the factional disturbances fostered by popular government, while, at the same time, preserving the spirit and the form of popular government. From a point high on the ladder of abstraction, this aim seems an impossible one, since it appears to call for the elimination of an effect while preserving the cause which leads to that effect. The very nature of this aim demands the careful discrimination of causes and effects which is characteristic of Madison's argument.

The formal pattern of Madison's logic is a series of "either-or" syllogisms, which, by eliminating the rejected alternatives, progressively narrow the inquiry down to the particular conclusion that a federal republic, such as that outlined in the proposed Constitution, can best control the effects of faction. In his first paragraph he presents a convincing rhetorical justification for his concern with the dangers of faction. From what general field of consideration or source of argument could he best derive the details which would make his readers equally concerned? The experiences of six years of government under the Articles of Confederation—experiences shared intimately and grievously by most of his audience—could be generalized into a statement of the *consequences* [2] which result from the operation of factions in an environment of freedom. So the indictment begins. Popular governments reveal a propensity to "this dangerous vice," factions. Once

[2] The terms "definition," "consequences," "likeness-difference," and "testimony-authority" have been italicized to call attention to Madison's uses of the sources of argument.

in existence, factions lead directly to instability, injustice, and confusion in the public councils. These, in turn, lead ultimately to the death of popular governments, "as they continue to be the favorite and fruitful topics [3] from which the adversaries to liberty derive their most specious declamation." Even though the various state constitutions of America are an improvement over popular models of the ancient and modern world, they have neither prevented the rise, nor effectively controlled the spread, of factional conflicts in the form of rival parties.

It is important to note that, in his introductory paragraph, Madison sets up the basic dichotomy which operates throughout his entire argument. The opposing terms are "justice," "the public good," and "minority rights," on the one hand, and, on the other, "majority faction."

> Complaints are everywhere heard from our most considerate and virtuous citizens, equally the friends of public and private faith, and of public and personal liberty, that our governments are too unstable, that the public good is disregarded in the conflicts of rival parties, and that measures are too often decided, not according to the rules of justice and the rights of the minor party, but by the superior force of an interested and overbearing majority.

The same dichotomy underlies the controlling *definition* of faction in paragraph 2:

> By a faction, I understand a number of citizens, whether amounting to a majority or minority of the whole, who are united and actuated by some common impulse of passion, or of interest, adverse to the rights of other citizens, or to the permanent and aggregate interests of the community.

Having demonstrated the disastrous consequences of faction in popular government and having defined his key term, Madison can proceed, in paragraph 3, to the logical development of his argument. The alternative syllogism set up there controls the movement of thought in the rest of the essay. "There are two methods of curing the mischiefs of faction: the one, by removing its causes; the other, by controlling its effects." This gives us a syllogism with the following form:

> Either A [*we can remove causes*] or B [*we can controls effects*].

The minor premise, which is developed in the first half of Madison's argument [paragraphs 3–10], is that we cannot remove the causes of faction, since they are grounded in the nature of man:

[3] Madison's use of the term "topics" in this quotation is in the same classical tradition which motivates the present article. "Instability," "injustice," and "confusion" are simply particularized *consequences* of faction in popular governments.

Not A [*we cannot remove causes*].

It follows that we must devote our efforts to controlling the effects:

Therefore, B [*we can control effects*].

An analysis of the argument for the minor premise reveals that A, the attempt to remove the causes of faction, is composed of two alternatives:

There are again two methods of removing the causes of faction: the one, by destroying the liberty which is essential to its existence; the other, by giving to every citizen the same opinions, the same passions, and the same interests.

These alternatives can be formally symbolized as A_1 and A_2.

A_1 [*destroying liberty*] is dismissed easily and speedily by means of an analogy or, in other words, by an argument based on *likenesses and differences:*

Liberty is to faction what air is to fire, an aliment without which it instantly expires. But it could not be less folly to abolish liberty, which is essential to political life, because it nourishes faction, than it would be to wish the annihilation of air, which is essential to animal life, because it imparts to fire its destructive agency.

The first analogical proportion [Liberty:Faction::Air:Fire], which would logically lead to the inference that we ought to destroy liberty, since it causes faction, is immediately modified by changing the second and fourth terms in the proportion [Liberty:Political Life::Air:Animal Life]. The folly of abolishing liberty as a cure for faction is self-evident. Madison does not need to devote time to this argument, since part of his fundamental aim was to preserve the spirit and form of popular government. Any measure which would cure faction by abolishing liberty is, as he says, a remedy worse than the disease.[4]

The argument against A_2 [*making all citizens alike in their passions, opinions, and interests*] is much more intricate and worthier of intensive study. Madison concludes that this alternative is impracticable, and his reasons for so deciding depend upon his view of human nature or, in other words, upon propositions drawn from the source of *definition*. In paragraphs 6–10, Madison uses the principles of Lockean psychology to prove that man, by nature, possesses faculties which operate to make factional conflicts inevitable. Men have a fallible reason which, in an environment of liberty, will lead to the formation

---

[4] This analogy, simple as it seems, can open the way to a devastating refutation of the argument that the totalitarian or one-party state is better than a free government because it can eliminate factions.

of different opinions. There is a connection between reason and self-love which will direct the passions created by the latter to the support of the opinions resulting from the former. In addition to the fundamental characteristics—reason and self-love—men possess a diversity of other faculties which are the origin of different aptitudes for accumulating property. Since it is the first object of government to protect these diverse faculties and thus to protect the ensuing differences in degrees and kinds of property and since diverse property interests will inevitably influence the opinions and passions of the respective proprietors, society must always be divided into different interests and parties. As a result, "the latent causes of faction are thus sown in the nature of man."

In paragraph 7, Madison develops the *consequences* of the definition which he has established. Anything sown in the nature of man will spring up in everything he does. These latent causes reveal themselves in all aspects of civil society. Factions can result from a zeal for different opinions in religion, in government, and, indeed, in all the speculative and practical affairs of mankind; from an emotional attachment to ambitious leaders; or from conflicts over even frivolous and fanciful distinctions. However, "the most common and durable source of factions has been the various and unequal distribution of property." And here Madison expresses simply and directly a view of the economic basis of political government which derives from a tradition much older than that of Marx:

> Those who hold and those who are without property have ever formed distinct interests in society. Those who are creditors, and those who are debtors, fall under a like discrimination. A landed interest, a manufacturing interest, a mercantile interest, a moneyed interest, with many lesser interests, grow up of necessity in civilized nations, and divide them into different classes, actuated by different sentiments and views. The regulation of these various and interfering interests forms the principal task of modern legislation, and involves the spirit of party and faction in the necessary and ordinary operations of the government.

The last proposition—that the spirit of faction is involved in the ordinary operations of government—requires an extension to another sphere of the *definition* of man previously presented. It is required in order to refute a possible objection. The counterargument might be raised that, since men's natures divide them into conflicting parties, it is the task of government somehow to stand above the conflicts and reconcile them in the interests of justice and the common good. This thesis would imply that legislators are superior to ordinary men in not being influenced by their own interests. To disprove this possible point of view, Madison continues in paragraph 8 with a *definition* of the two main factors in government—acts of legislation and legislators. Acts of legislation, such as laws concerning private debts, tariffs, and property taxes, are defined by Madison as judicial determinations concerning the rights of large bodies of citizens; and legislators are defined as advocates and parties to the causes which they determine. The self-love of the lawmakers will inevitably result in decisions which represent, not the principles of abstract justice, but their own party interests. Madison thinks it vain to depend upon the influence of "enlightened statesmen" to adjust the clash of diverse interests in the light of justice and the public good. Not only will such statesmen not always be at the helm, but in many cases the legislative questions will be so complex and pressing that it will be almost impossible for statesmen to act in an enlightened fashion.

Thus the first half of the paper, consisting of two powerful arguments based upon *definitions* of man and government, has led to the conclusion that all citizens cannot be made alike in their passions, opinions, and interests. As a result, "the inference to which we are brought is, that the *causes* of faction cannot be removed, and that relief is only to be sought in the means of controlling its *effects*." If we glance again at the controlling alternative syllogism:

Either A [*we can remove causes*] or B [*we can control effects*],
Not A,
Therefore, B,

we see that the argument from *likeness and difference* (directed against A_1) and the argument from *definition* (directed against A_2) have provided support for the minor premise: we cannot remove the causes of faction. The remainder of Madison's essay is devoted to substantiating the conclusion: therefore, we can control its effects.

The argument for B is much more complex than the argument against A. It is indicative of Madison's practical orientation as a political theorist that his main concern is with the control of effects rather than with the removal of causes. Removing the causes of something is a drastic but superficially simple alternative, whereas controlling effects usually involves a range of contingent methods whose varying degrees of success depend upon a multitude of factors which require careful analysis.

Before attacking the problem of the proper means for controlling the effects of faction, Madison further clarifies his problem by distinguishing between the dangers resulting from a minority and a majority faction. This key distinction, as we have seen, was set forth in the initial definition of "faction" in paragraph 2, "a number of citizens, whether amounting to a majority or minority of the whole. . . ." In paragraph 11, Madison uses another argument from *definition* to dismiss the dangers of a minority faction:

> If a faction consists of less than a majority, relief is supplied by the republican principle, which enables the majority to defeat its sinister views by regular vote.

Should this seem too cavalier a dismissal of a serious problem, one with which every state is plagued, Madison continues by revealing both his awareness of what a fanatical minority can do in a free society and the reason for his relative lack of concern. "It may clog the administration, it may convulse the society; but it will be unable to execute and mask its violence under the forms of the Constitution." The danger from a minority faction however serious, lies in the realm of practical administration and can, at the worst, be eliminated by the police power of the state. On the other hand, when a majority of the people coalesce into a faction, the very form of popular government enables such a faction to trample on the rights of other citizens and sacrifice the public good to its ruling passion. Here, exactly, was the concern of the Federalist theoreticians. How could the majority, operating in a mood of sudden and concerted aggression, be restrained from violating the rights of minorities and the over-all interests of the community?

The crucial importance of this question for Madison is indicated by the fact that, immediately after the distinction between minority and majority faction in paragraph 11, he makes explicit the aim of his essay:

> To secure the public good and private rights against the danger of such a faction [majority], and at the same time to preserve the spirit and form of popular government, is then the great object to which our inquiries are directed.

The argument in the second half of the essay involves the answer to two questions: (1) What, in theory, are the best means of controlling the effects of majority faction? and (2) Which form of popular government is best able to put these means into effect?

In form, the second main argument resembles the first, since it also starts with a division of alternatives. There are two means for controlling the effects of majority faction:

> Either the existence of the same passion or interest in a majority at the same time must be prevented, or the majority, having such coexistent

passion or interest, must be rendered, by their number and local situation, unable to concert and carry into effect schemes of oppression.

These alternatives may be symbolized as B_1 and B_2. For a true picture of Madison's logical procedure, it is important to note that in the first argument both A_1 and A_2 were rejected, thus giving us a negative minor premise. However, the conclusion is a positive one. This means that both B_1 and B_2 are acceptable means of preventing majority oppression, with B_2 acting as an auxiliary method in case it is impossible to achieve B_1. Using these two methods as standards of judgment, Madison can turn his attention to the analysis of the two main forms of popular government—the pure democracy and the republic—to see which, by nature, can best control the effects of majority faction.

Again using the source of *definition*, Madison concludes that a pure democracy, "by which I mean a society consisting of a small number of citizens, who asemble and administer the government in person, can admit of no cure for the mischiefs of faction." Such a government, because its form permits both the creation and the immediate assertion of a majority passion or interest, will be able at will to sacrifice the rights of minorities or even of individuals obnoxious to the majority. Madison might have been thinking of the condemnation of Socrates by a majority of the Athenian citizens, since he supports his theoretical analysis at this point by a reference to history:

> Hence it is that such democracies have ever been spectacles of turbulence and contention; have ever been found incompatible with personal security or the rights of property; and have in general been as short in their lives as they have been violent in their deaths.

The general effect of this argument is similar to that in the first half of the essay, since pure democracy fails because it believes that, by making all men politically equal, it can equalize their possessions, their opinions, and their passions. Madison has already disposed of such a visionary hope.

By *definition*, a republic differs from a pure democracy in two important respects: in its form and in the magnitude of its possible operation. It is a form of popular government in which power is delegated to representatives elected by the people, and it can therefore be extended over a greater number of citizens and over a greater area than can a pure democracy. The definitions of these two forms of popular government prepare the way for the rather involved reasoning which starts at paragraph 16 and continues to the end. These paragraphs can be related to the rest of the argument by seeing them as detailed statements of the *consequences* resulting from the two main points of difference between a democracy and a republic. Paragraphs 16–19 deal with the effects of the difference in form, paragraph 20 with the difference in magnitude.

The formal difference—the principle of delegative power—does not by itself provide a guaranty that majority factions will be controlled. Acting as a cause, it may lead to opposite effects. When the opinions of the people are sifted through a body of representatives who may be influenced by patriotism and the love of justice, the process might result in refining and enlarging the public views and, probably, lead to decisions advancing the public good. However, the effect may as easily be inverted. As Madison puts it:

> Men of factious tempers, of local prejudices, or of sinister designs, may, by intrigue, by corruption, or by other means, first obtain the suffrages, and then betray the interests, of the people.

Since the delegative form of government alone provides no certainty that majority factions can be controlled, Madison then proceeds to the corollary question of whether small or large republics are best able to elect good legislators. Paragraphs 17 and 18 present two considerations which decide the question in favor of the large republic. Fundamentally, these two paragraphs present the probable *consequences* of the smaller ratio between representatives and constituents which characterizes the large republic by contrast with the small one. A hypothetical example will clarify the rather close reasoning of these paragraphs. Madison starts with the assumption that, regardless of the size of the republic, the representatives must be numerous enough to guard against the cabals of a few, and limited enough to avoid the confusion of a multitude. Let us suppose that the range for an efficient legislative body is from 100 to 500 representatives. If the smaller number, 100, is selected by the constituents of a small republic, say 10,000 voters, the ratio is 1:100. If the larger number, 500, is selected by 5,000,000 voters, the ratio is 1:10,000. Therefore, if it be granted that the proportion of good men is the same in both states, the large republic will present a much wider choice and, consequently, the greater probability of a fit choice. The second consideration in favor of a large republic is that, since each representative will be chosen by many more voters, there will be less chance for the voters to be fooled by unworthy candidates using the tricks of the demagogue. The argument in paragraph 17 depends for its force solely on numerical ratios. There will be more good men in a large republic from which to make a wise choice. Paragraph 18 adds the consideration that it will be harder to fool the many than to fool the few.

Madison then goes back to the second main difference between a democracy and a republic—the greater number of citizens and larger extent of territory which can be brought within the compass of the republican form. And here he sums up the *consequences* of his definitions in such a way as to re-emphasize the superiority of a republic over a democracy, on the one hand, and of a large republic over a small one, on the other:

> The smaller the society, the fewer probably will be the distinct parties and interests composing it; the fewer the distinct parties and interests, the more frequently will a majority be found of the same party; and the smaller the number of individuals composing a majority, and the smaller the compass within which they are placed, the more easily will they concert and execute their plans of oppression. Extend the sphere and you take in a greater variety of parties and interests; you make it less probable that a majority of the whole will have a common motive to invade the rights of other citizens; or if such a common motive exists, it will be more difficult for all who feel it to discover their own strength, and to act in unison with each other.

Thus a large republic can control the effects of faction better than any other form of popular government and "in the extent and proper structure of the Union, therefore, we behold a republican remedy for the diseases most incident to republican government." Madison concludes by identifying true republicanism with the Federalist advocacy of the proposed Constitution.

Madison's powerful plea for a federal republic can be felt most strongly when the sources of his argument are brought to light and his particular propositions are seen operating in the deductive form which moves relentlessly from assumptions and premises to conclusions. Many English teachers will be content to clarify the argumentative methods from which *The Federalist*, No. 10, derives its logical power. But others, perhaps those with an interest in political theory, will want to have their students examine the assumptions and challenge the conclusions of Madison's argument. Although possible refutations are beyond the scope of this article, an understanding of the sources can help in outlining some promising lines of attack. For instance, the fundamental dichotomy set up by Madison is that between the "public good," on the one hand, and "majority faction," on the other. Madison is careful to define what he opposes; but the term "the public good" remains an undefined ideal which controls his judgments but which is never pinned down. For those of us who, almost without thinking, identify the public good with the majority will, Madison's analysis seems shockingly undemocratic. The question could be asked: How can the public good be achieved or, for that matter, even known with certainty if majority faction is considered the main danger in a republic? Another point of possible refutation rests in Madison's cynical definition of man in paragraphs 6 and 7. Would a Jeffersonian or perhaps even a Christian definition of man lead to different conclusions? Finally, some question could be raised about whether large republics actually do produce a higher quality of legislators than small ones. Madison was arguing that national representatives would, in all probability, be better than those in a state legislature. However, we might ask whether our Congress today can compare in quality with the much smaller Constitutional Convention or, if that is unfair, even with the Congress of Madison's own day.

These questions, and others, would be directed toward awakening the student's interest not only in the vital subject matter of Madison's article but also in the intellectually exciting rigors of logical procedure. Through the step-by-step reconstruction of Madison's argument, the student can be led to see how a commanding piece of rhetoric came into being. By studying Madison's sources of argument and seeing how the forms of syllogistic reasoning are filled with material drawn from the realms of theory and experience, the student writer, faced with the challenge of supporting a proposition, can learn to use these directing ideas, the sources, to make his own arguments richer, more controlled, and, ultimately, more convincing.

MATTHEW ARNOLD: THE SUBTLETIES OF PERSUASION *   John Holloway

(i) Arnold's Doctrine and Temper

'One at last has a chance of *getting at* the English public. Such a public as it is, and such a work as one wants to do with it! . . . Partly

From *The Victorian Sage*, Chapter 7, by John Holloway. © 1962, The Shoestring Press, Inc. Reprinted by permission.

* References throughout Holloway's essay quote the volume and page of the de Luxe Edition of Arnold's Works (15 vols.), Macmillan, London, 1903. The following abbreviations are used: CA. *Culture and Anarchy* (1869); DA. *Discourses in America* (1885); EC. i *Essays in Criticism, First Series* (1865); FE. *A French Eton* (1864); FG. *Friendship's Garland* (1871); LD. *Literature and Dogma* (1873); ME. *Mixed Essays* (1879); St. P. *St. Paul and Protestantism* (1870).

nature, partly time and study have also by this time taught me thoroughly the precious truth that everything turns upon one's exercising the power of *persuasion*, of charm; that without this all fury, energy, reasoning power, acquirement are thrown away'.[1] These few words lay bare the very core of Arnold's 'criticism of life', because there was one thing that he never allowed himself to forget. This was that to be successful, the moralist must do what success requires, and that success in this field requires, above all things, patience and self-control. 'Where shall we find language innocent enough, how shall we make the spotless purity of our intentions evident enough, to enable us to say . . . that the British Constitution itself' is 'a colossal machine for the manufacture of Philistines? . . . how is Mr. Carlyle to say it and not be misunderstood, after his furious raid into this field with his *Latter-Day Pamphlets?*'[2] By the fullness and care and circumspection with which he moulds and adjusts his work to the persuasive task, Arnold sets an entirely new standard—goes further here even than Newman. Yet his work does not tempt us to acquiesce in his outlook ignorant of what we are doing; it is persuasive through being a memorable specimen of what that outlook produces, a specimen powerful in illuminating his position and helping his readers to see its attraction and strength. It is what distinguishes art in literature that Arnold directs to the necessities of persuasion: he aims to transform the reader's outlook, and he makes a call upon every part of his nature.

Arnold's polemics were less irresponsible than those of Carlyle, because his effort to persuade was much more sustained and planned; and his task was a more elusive one than Newman's, because he had no rigid doctrines to argue for, only attitudes. His work inculcates not a set of ultimate beliefs—a 'Life-Philosophy'—but simply certain habits and a certain temper of mind. He limits his ambitions; he advocates not so much any definite view, as the mental prerequisites of forming views. 'The old recipe, to think a little more and bustle a little less';[3] '. . . between all these there is indeed much necessity for methods of insight and moderation';[4] 'the free spontaneous play of consciousness with which culture tries to float our stock habits of thinking and acting . . . to *float* them, to prevent their being stiff

[1] Letter to Arnold's mother, 29th October 1863 (*Works*, xiii. 266). References in this Chapter are given to the volume and page of Arnold's collected works; and when one book or essay is quoted from several times in succession, its title is indicated only in the first of the corresponding footnotes.

[2] *The Function of Criticism:* EC.i. (iii. 28–9).

[3] *My Countrymen* (vi. 388).

[4] Letter to Arnold's mother, 9th November 1870 (xiv. 241).

and stark pieces of petrifaction any longer . . . our main business at the present moment is not so much to work away at certain crude reforms . . . as to create . . . a frame of mind out of which the schemes of really fruitful reforms may with time grow'.[5] It is the frame of mind that is crucial; to what conclusions it will lead, once adopted, is for Arnold a secondary matter. Much of his work is negative: he wants to deprecate what is crude and exaggerated, to leave questions open where they have been precipitately closed. He seldom rejects an opposing view outright; all he does is to regret its undue haste or narrowness, or see in it an excess of something by no means intrinsically bad. 'There is a catchword which, I know, will be used against me . . . cries and catchwords . . . are very apt to receive an application, or to be used with an absoluteness, which does not belong to them . . . and . . . narrow our spirit and . . . hurt our practice'.[6] In this sentence Arnold condemns his opponents' frame of mind, and suggests a better, all in one.

If he ever advances a more positive doctrine, it is usually of a kind by now familiar: the vital but essentially simple truths that seem to be the sage's peculiar province. What he says of his defence of a classical education is, 'I put this forward on the strength of some facts not at all recondite, very far from it; facts capable of being stated in the simplest possible fashion'—the facts are simply those of 'the constitution of human nature'.[7] Like other moralists, he regards his important function as that merely of bringing familiar knowledge alive. 'The larger the scale on which the violation of reason's law is practised . . . the greater must be the confusion and final trouble. Surely no laudations of free-trade . . . can tell us anything . . . which it more concerns us to know than that! and not only to know, but to have the knowledge present . . . . But we all know it already! some one will say, it is the simplest law of prudence. But how little reality must there be in our knowledge'.[8]

Clearly then, Arnold rigorously circumscribes his work. It suggests an approach; or it is deliberately negative and inconclusive, or where positive its statements are deliberately commonplace and familiar. These restrictions greatly affect that element of Arnold's work which comes nearest to the speculative or metaphysical; for although he disclaims all ability for subtle philosophizing, yet, like Carlyle, like New-

[5] CA. (vi. 212–13).
[6] FE. (xii. 49).
[7] DA. (iv. 330).
[8] CA. (vi. 208–9).

man, he too has a philosophy of history, a bedrock *credo*. He too writes of 'the natural current there is in human affairs, and . . . its continual working'; [9] and the fault of his opponents, like theirs, is that 'they cannot see the way the world is going, and the future does not belong to them'.[10] Further than this, he goes on occasionally to make success a test or sign of rightness: 'sure loss and defeat at last . . . ought to govern . . . action',[11] he writes, or even 'that providential order which forbids the final supremacy of imperfect things'.[12] But this line of thought is not prominent in his work; and moreover, its development is entirely different in Arnold and in, say, Carlyle.

That difference becomes immediately plain if we complete the last quotation but one: 'sure loss and defeat at last, *from coming into conflict with truth and nature*'; or take such a remark as 'this contravention of the natural order has produced, as such contravention always must produce, a certain confusion and false movement, of which we are beginning to feel, in almost every direction, the inconvenience'.[13] The contrast is inescapable. All the apocalyptic quality of Carlyle's historical determinism is gone; the trend of events is governed not by some everready and apocalyptic Hand, but by a gentle Platonic harmony between virtue, reason, and reality. The course of history is not grand, simple and mysterious, but neat and orderly, now one thing and now another, according to time and place. There are epochs of 'expansion' and of 'concentration'.[14] Hellenism, the urgent need in Arnold's own time, would have been in the Dark Ages 'unsound at that particular moment of man's development . . . premature'.[15] Different virtues and different measures require to be insisted on in different countries.[16] France may lack political freedom, England may rely on it to excess; England's chief need is greater amenity, France's greater purity, America's, a more elevated seriousness. Each may benefit by addition even of what is harmful elsewhere. One can now see the place in Arnold's work of how he grossly simplifies in writing of national characteristics. It helps him to modify optimistic determinism, as a philosophy of history, so that it seems reasonable and unmysterious, multiple in its aspects—as indeed every unmysterious thing

[9] vi. 37.
[10] *My Countrymen* (vi. 376).
[11] ME. (x. 127–8).
[12] FE. (xii. 76).
[13] CA. (vi. 139–40).
[14] See *e.g.* CA. (vi. 59–62) and *The Function of Criticism* (iii. 14–15).
[15] CA. (vi. 130).
[16] See *A Courteous Explanation* (vi. 398) and *Numbers* (iv. 283), *passim*.

is—yet simple to grasp, having no surprises for the calm, enlightened, unprejudiced observer.

Arnold has a doctrine of man which is the counterpart of this doctrine of history. It too contains nothing paradoxical or mysterious or not readily acceptable. Man, like the world itself and its history, is a complex of different elements which are readily brought together into a simple and natural unity. These are the 'facts not at all recondite, very far from it,' touched upon above. 'We set ourselves to enumerate the powers which go to the building of human life, and say that they are the power of conduct, the power of intellect and knowledge, the power of beauty, and the power of social life and manners . . . this scheme, though drawn in rough and plain lines enough . . . does yet give a fairly true representation . . . Human nature is built up by these powers; we have the need for them all . . . the several powers . . . are not isolated, but there is . . . a perpetual tendency to relate them one to another in divers ways'.[17] Humanity is a 'composite thing,' its elements so 'intertwined' that one can temporarily do duty for another; but ultimately there must be 'mutual understanding and balance,' there must be genuine and organic integration, if the 'true and smooth order of humanity's development' is not to be arrested.[18] The 'natural rational life'—the juxtaposition, virtual equivalence of the adjectives, has significance—is one with 'body, intelligence, and soul all taken care of'.[19] These may be commonplaces; but for the present enquiry that is their interest.

This is so, because such a view offers, as it were, a minimum target to the critic; its quality of platitude enables Arnold largely to escape the burden of proof—or rather, to use an apter word, the business of justifying or arguing for a metaphysics, which constrains the other authors we have examined to a style of rhetoric, eloquence, exaltation or mystery. And such a style would inevitably have clashed with Arnold's central concern—to advocate a gentle critical reasonableness of mind. With such essentially simple and commonplace premises, he could avoid a kind of writing which it would certainly have been hard to unite with the temper of mind he admired. Thus in Arnold there are little or no rhetorical fireworks. Metaphor and imagery are (except very occasionally for certain quite new uses) absent to a degree nothing short of extraordinary by comparison with Newman or

[17] DA. (iv. 331).
[18] CA. (vi. 143-4).
[19] *My Countrymen* (vi. 374).

Carlyle or George Eliot; and although definitions of words, in a sense at least, are not uncommon, they occur for purposes much more restricted than elsewhere, and are such that the element of prestidigitation—which would have been the alien element—is almost entirely lacking from them. Yet at the same time, Arnold's premisses are important for their substance: they offer a real justification for his method of compromise—that is, of seeing more than one side to any problem, and stressing or adding just what the given case requires, even though intrinsically this may be subordinate. But they do not dictate anything in the details of his approach. Others could start with the same premisses and probably reach any detailed conclusions they liked. What significance they had for Arnold is determined in the whole texture of his writing. If he offers anything of wisdom or sanity or mental poise, it is to be found in the whole experience of reading him, in a sense of what intellectual urbanity is that transpires rather from his handling of problems than from his answers to them. He mediates not a view of the world, but a habit of mind. Let us see how this is done.

To a degree quite unusual among polemical writers, Arnold's persuasive energy goes to build up, little by little, an intimate and a favourable impression of his own personality as an author, and an unfavourable impression, equally clear if less intimate and more generalized, of the personalities of his opponents. Over and over again one finds the discussion taking shape between these two poles; and this is natural, because Arnold's chief purpose is to recommend one temper of mind, and condemn another, and such things are more readily sensed through contact than understood through description. No author, of course, can give a favourable impression of his own temper of mind, except obliquely and discreetly. When Arnold writes of himself at length, it is usually in a depreciatory vein; but he causes us to glimpse his personality through various devices, and of these, as with Newman, perhaps the most conspicuous is tone. Indeed he adopts a tone not unlike Newman's, save that it is usually less grave and calm, more whimsical and apologetic. Newman, after all, thought he had a powerful silent ally as Arnold did not.

Thus in the first few lines of the Preface to *Essays in Criticism*, Series I, we find 'indeed, it is not in my nature—some of my critics would rather say, not in my power—to dispute on behalf of any opinion, even my own, very obstinately. To try and approach truth on one side after another, not to strive or cry, nor to persist in pressing forward, on any one side, with violence and self-will—it is only thus, it seems to me, that mortals may hope to gain any vision' of truth.[20] Here the opinion is mediated to us through becoming acquainted with the author; and the second sentence, though not the first, reveals how close is the link with Newman. 'No, we are all seekers still!' Arnold writes later in the same Preface.[21] This tone is frequent elsewhere: 'in differing from them, however, I wish to proceed with the utmost caution and diffidence . . . the tone of tentative enquiry . . . is the tone I would wish to take and not to depart from'; [22] 'at present I neither praise it nor blame it; I simply count it as one of the votes'; [23] 'I have no pet scheme to press, no crochet to gratify, no fanatical zeal . . . . All I say is . . .'; [24] 'the line I am going to follow is . . . so extremely simple, that perhaps it may be followed without failure even by one who for a more ambitious line of discussion would be quite incompetent'; [25] 'even though to a certain extent I am disposed to agree with Mr. Frederic Harrison . . . I am not sure that I do not think . . . . Therefore I propose now to try and enquire, in the simple unsystematic way which best suits both my taste and my powers. . . .' [26] Such phrases as these, running throughout the fabric of his work, create an image for us of the intelligent, modest, urbane Arnold who *is* what he advocates.

But he controls more than his own tone—he foists a contrasting tone on his opponents. He puts imaginary speeches into their mouths. 'I criticized Bishop Colenso's speculative confusion. Immediately there was a cry raised: "What is this? here is a liberal attacking a liberal. Do you not belong to the movement? Are you not a friend of truth? . . . Why make these invidious differences? both books are excellent, admirable, liberal; Bishop Colenso's perhaps the most so, because it is the boldest . . . . Be silent therefore; or rather speak, speak as loud as you can! and go into ecstasies."' And, as if the contrast were not by now sharp enough, he concludes tersely 'but criticism cannot follow this coarse and indiscriminate method'.[27] It is the tone of the expression that shows the coarseness of the method; and similarly it is the tone of his opponents he points to and condemns in such remarks

[20] iii, p. v.
[21] iii, p. xi.
[22] DA. (iv. 330).
[23] ME. (x. 55).
[24] FE. (xii. 44).
[25] DA. (iv. 321–2).
[26] CA. (vi. 4).
[27] *The Function of Criticism* (iii. 32).

as 'Surely, if they knew this, those friends of progress, who have confidently pronounced the remains of the ancient world to be so much lumber . . . might be inclined to reconsider their sentence'.[28] But the inclination to reconsider, or even much to consider, is rather what they lack. It will be necessary to return to this point in examining the very distinctive contribution made to our impression of Arnold and of his opponents by irony.

(ii) Forms of Argument

Arnold is also like Newman, and unlike Carlyle (and George Eliot in her discursive works), in developing our sense of his temper of mind, and of the kind of thinking he is doing, through the distinctive forms of his argument. Newman and Arnold both employ the *argumentum ad hominem*. In Newman this form is common, it is constantly employed on points of detail, and the effect of its frequency is to amplify our sense of the great integrated system of reality, as the author conceives it. Arnold uses the argument much less often, and then in respect only of some fundamental issue. 'I speak to an audience with a high standard of civilization. If I say that certain things . . . do not come up to a high standard . . . I need not prove how and why they do not; you will feel instinctively . . . I need not prove that a high standard of civilization is desirable; you will instinctively feel that it is.'[29] *God and the Bible* is 'meant for those who, won by the modern spirit to habits of intellectual seriousness, cannot receive what sets those habits at naught'.[30] In *Literature and Dogma* [31] he writes approvingly of how Newman relies on this form of argument. But in his own case its oblique contribution is less to give the impression of system and precision than of circumspection in argument and modesty on the part of the author.

Again, like Newman, Arnold enlists the negative evidence. Scientists are likely to have an incomplete understanding of human nature not through their limitations, but actually through their special talents and interests.[32] Frederic Harrison may be right in arguing that men of culture are just the class who cannot be trusted with power in modern society; but this confirms, not his own attack on men of culture, but

[28] ME. (x. 37).
[29] ME. (x. 58).
[30] viii, p. xxxiv.
[31] vii. 318.
[32] DA. (iv. 336–7).

Arnold's on the society that cannot use them.[33] As for the Nonconformists, 'the very example (America) that they bring forward to help
their case makes against them'; [34] their knowledge of the Bible, which
they make their infallible stay, is a typical specimen of knowledge
and ignorance muddled together; [35] and when they rely on a 'fetish or
mechanical maxim' to bring about an improvement in the state of
affairs, they only succeed in adding slightly to the 'confusion and
hostility'.[36] The administration of Athens under Eubulus, which at the
time it would have seemed 'very impertinent' to condemn, was exactly
what led to the collapse of the city.[37] Burke, bitterest enemy of the
French Revolution, can yet at the very end of his work return upon
himself to explain how a great change in human affairs might under
certain circumstances be proper and inevitable.[38] The general tendency
of these arguments is not to suggest any grand system, but a polite
irony in things that sooner or later makes cocksure people look silly.[39]

The appendage to *Friendship's Garland* called 'A Courteous Explanation' is especially interesting here. First, it is an argument that finds
support for Arnold's case where one would least expect it. 'Horace,'
siding with the complacent English journals, has attacked him for
depreciating the value of free speech in England; Arnold quietly
observes that at all events this new opponent readily follows his own
lead in criticizing compatriots. 'How "Horace" does give it to his
poor countrymen . . . ! So did Monsieur de Tocqueville, so does
Monsieur Renan. I lay up the example for my own edification, and I
commend it to the editor of the *Morning Star* for his.' [40] Second,
Arnold discredits his opponent, in the same unruffled style, by a *tu
quoque* argument. 'This brings me to the one little point of difference
(for there is just one) between "Horace" and me.' [41] 'Horace' has
accused him of giving no thought to the needs of foreign countries.

[33] CA. (vi. 3).
[34] vi, p. xxx.
[35] vi. 153–4.
[36] vi. 172–3.
[37] DA. (iv. 288–9).
[38] *The Function of Criticism* (iii. 16).
[39] The example of Burke is different. (*a*) In this respect he is an *example* of
the temper of mind Arnold wishes to recommend. (*b*) Arnold recommends his
own temper of mind by taking a virtual opponent as a praiseworthy example.
(*c*) Burke's concession shows all the same how Arnold's opponents are (if intelligent enough) constrained by the nature of events to introduce exceptions and
thereby accept Arnold's view. Burke is the opponent who is wise, and retreats;
Frederic Harrison and the Nonconformists blunder obstinately on.
[40] FG. (vi. 397).
[41] vi. 398.

But does he give any thought to it himself?—far from it: he wants the English to be told not what they, but what the French need to hear. ' "Horace" and his friends are evidently Orleanists, and I have always observed that Orleanists are rather sly.' [42] When Arnold has finished, 'Horace' looks less sly than silly—or at least, one more opponent of the abrupt, unreflecting, unsubtle kind that Arnold seems so often to be dealing with.

Perhaps the two forms of argument most distinctive of Arnold are *distinguo* arguments which keep the reader sensitized to his unrelaxing circumspection, and concessive arguments which emphasize his modesty. ' "Let us distinguish," replied the envious foreigners' (who here are speaking for Arnold himself) 'let us distinguish. We named three powers . . . which go to spread . . . rational humane life . . . . Your middle class, we agreed, has the first . . . . But this only brings us a certain way. . . .' [43] Or again, 'It is not State-action in itself which the middle and lower classes of a nation ought to deprecate; it is State-action exercised by a hostile class'.[44] 'Just as France owes her fearful troubles to other things and her civilizedness to equality, so we owe our immunity from fearful troubles to other things, and our uncivilizedness to inequality.' [45] In *A French Eton* [46] he distinguishes the quite contrasting needs of schools providing for the different classes of society: those for the aristocracy need 'the notion of a sort of republican fellowship, the practice of a plain life in common, the habit of self-help'; while those for the middle classes need training in 'largeness of soul and personal dignity,' and those for the lower, in 'feeling, gentleness, humanity'.[47] The same form of argument underlies a passage quoted earlier, Arnold's version of the attacks on him for his attack on Bishop Colenso: [48] the method of his opponents is coarse and indiscriminate just because they think that all 'differences' are 'invidious.' 'The practical man is not apt for fine distinctions, and yet in these distinctions truth and the highest culture greatly find their account'.[49] Arnold finds his account in them, because they not only lead him to the conclusions he desires, but give his thought and writing a distinctive temper in the process.

[42] *Ibid.*
[43] FG. (vi. 376–7).
[44] ME. (x. 34).
[45] ME. (x. 83).
[46] FE. (xii. 40).
[47] *I.e.* distinctions which would not confirm class distinctions, but mitigate them.
[48] See above, p. 498.
[49] *The Function of Criticism* (iii. 28).

Concession in argument necessarily does little to advance the proof for one's own case; and for Arnold (believing as he did that there were many propositions true in the abstract but not needing stress in his own times) it must necessarily have had little value, save obliquely in mitigating the tone of his work, or helping to create an impression of his personality. Its comparative frequency is thus a clear sign how these oblique functions are important. 'We ought to have no difficulty in conceding to Mr. Sidgwick that . . . fire and strength . . . has its high value as well as culture'; [50] 'Hellenism . . . has its dangers, as has been fully granted'; [51] 'there are many things to be said on behalf of this exclusive attention of ours to liberty'.[52] Sometimes the concession is 'placed' as it were, by a subsequent *distinguo* argument: 'the final aim of both Hellenism and Hebraism . . . is no doubt the same: man's perfection or salvation . . . still, they pursue this aim by very different courses . . . so long as we do not forget that both . . . are profound and admirable . . . we can hardly insist too strongly on the divergence of line and of operation by which they proceed'.[53] Sometimes, too, Arnold does something explicit to relate the concession he makes to his tone, and to our conception of himself: 'it is impossible that all these remonstrances and reproofs should not affect me, and I shall try my very best . . . to profit by the objections I have heard and read'.[54] One might say here that the substantial significance of the concession is virtually nil—Arnold gives no hint of what it is he is disposed to agree with—but just for that reason, perhaps, the oblique contribution is at its most direct and powerful. There is, of course, in that last remark, a hint also of something quite other than penitent humility.

The reader must have noticed that through the forms of his arguments Arnold does something to develop our notion of his opponents, as well as of himself. The abiding consciousness of those with whom he disagrees—it is something quite distinctive in Arnold's work—finds remarkable expression in *Friendship's Garland*. This is very largely a work discrediting the opinions of others; and in the main it proceeds by methods of irony, which will be examined below. One cannot help noticing that Arnold offers almost no objections of substance to the practical measures he most clearly condemns. But three times— coloured and half-concealed, certainly, by his satirical flashes—an argu-

[50] CA. (vi. 146).
[51] vi. 155.
[52] vi. 54.
[53] vi. 121-5.
[54] vi. 45-6.

ment does appear. This is how he takes up the case made out for the Deceased Wife's Sisters Bill: 'Let us pursue his fine regenerating idea . . . let us deal with this question as a whole . . . this is not enough . . . for my part, my resolve is formed . . . as a sop to those toothless old Cerberuses, the bishops . . . we will accord the continuance of the prohibition which forbids a man to marry his grandmother. But in other directions there shall be freedom.' [55] Then he attacks the 'gospel of liberty' in the same way. '. . . have we ever given liberty . . . a full trial? The Lord Chancellor has, indeed, provided for Mr. Beales . . . *but why is Mr. Bradlaugh not yet a Dean?* These, Sir, are the omissions, these the failures to carry into full effect our own great principles which drive earnest Liberals to despair!' [56] Finally he turns, with this same weapon, to the nostrum of publicity: it is true that the government and the courts have recently refused to have sordid divorce and other cases heard *in camera.* 'All this was as it should be; so far, so good. But was the publicity thus secured for these cases perfectly full and entire? Were there some places which the details did not reach? There were few, but there were some . . . I say, make the price of the *London Gazette* a halfpenny; change its name to the *London Gazette and Divorce Intelligencer;* . . . distribute it *gratis* to mechanics' institutes, workmen's halls, seminaries for the young . . . and then you will be giving the principle of publicity a full trial.' [57] All these arguments take the form of the *reductio ad absurdum;* and above all, what they contribute to is our sense of the personality and the intellectual temper of those with whom Arnold disagrees. Caricature of the arguments is done in a style that indicates the true nature of the authors: it is Arnold's opponents, ultimately, who are being reduced to the absurd.

(iii) The Value Frame

Arnold's preoccupation, as we have seen, is with what states of mind and what attitudes are desirable in human society, and more particularly with what is the desirable temper of mind in which to conduct and enquiry. Apart from a rationalist historical determinism, which plays a minor rôle in his thought, he had no metaphysics which might

---

[55] FG. (vi. 307–9). The quotation abridges to the point of destruction a very entertaining piece of satire, though Arnold was sailing too near the wind to give his climax its real point.

[56] vi. 336. Mr. Bradlaugh was the well-known atheist and champion of birth-control.

[57] vi. 337–8.

form apparent premises for the moral principles he wished to assert. But because a certain temper of mind—the characteristic urbanity and amenity of Arnold—is so pervasively recommended to the reader by the whole texture of his writing, he had a quite distinctive means for both making and justifying value-judgments in other fields. He could praise and justify praise, or condemn and justify condemnation, by suggesting that the topic or the belief under discussion would appeal, or fail to appeal, to the frame of mind which appears throughout his work as the fundamental good.

This distinctive method is to preface or envelop the main assertion in clauses which invite the reader to view it with favour or disfavour, and suggest grounds for the attitude he is to adopt. These *value frames*, as they might be called, serve several different purposes in Arnold's work, and are sometimes very elaborate. Although by their nature they do not obtrude on the casual reader's notice, yet their influence on the texture of argument is great. It should perhaps be said that when they are quoted, one feels at first that the mere trimmings of a sentence have been given and its substantial part omitted: but this impression rapidly fades. Consider an example first: 'The aspirations of culture, which is the study of perfection, are not satisfied unless [what men say when they may say what they like, is worth saying].' [58] Here the two elements, first praise, second the grounds for praise, are fairly clear: first, a condition such as the assertion describes would satisfy one whose concern was for *perfection,* and this is as much as to call it *good;* second, it would satisfy the *cultured, aspiring* and *studious,* and these qualities—which *Culture and Anarchy* from beginning to end has endeared to us—are here the grounds of goodness. Compare 'the flexibility which sweetness and light give, and which is one of the rewards of culture pursued in good faith, enables a man to see that . . . '.[59] Here one senses that the praise itself lies in 'rewards,' the grounds of praise in 'flexibility,' 'sweetness,' 'light,' 'culture' and 'good faith': these are the qualities of mind to which the assertion recommends itself.

Another interesting example of this device is, 'Surely, now, it is no inconsiderable boon which culture confers on us if in embarrassed times like the present it enables us to [look at the ins and outs of things in this way] without hatred and without partiality and with a

[58] CA. (vi. 15). In the following quotations the assertion itself, by contrast with the value frame for it, is put in square brackets or indicated by them.
[59] vi. 28.

disposition to see the good in everybody all round' [60]—here not only can both praise and grounds of praise be located easily, but two further features appear: the first few words, and the reference to embarrassed times like the present, distinguish the author's tone and hint his personality; and the whole sentence not only puts Arnold's key word 'culture' to use, but also enriches its meaning, so that it can be employed more compendiously elsewhere. Sometimes it proves vitally important to control the exact significance of these key-words: thus 'essential in Hellenism is [the impulse to the development of the whole man, to connecting and harmonizing all parts of him, perfecting him]' [61] recommends a certain impulse, gives grounds for the recommendation through the word 'Hellenism,' whose import is already fairly well determined, and thirdly, amplifies this import itself. And this constant amplification of the import, or rather, constantly bringing it afresh to the reader's notice, allows Arnold to take liberties. He does so with 'Hellenism' on the very next page: 'that [. . .],— this is abhorrent to the nature of Hellenism to concede'—the reader can keep in mind, though, that Hellenism even *abhors* with amenity.

It is easy to see how much these value frames do, not only to recommend assertions and offer grounds for them, but also to elucidate and recommend the temper of mind to which they seem true, and above all to show that their strength lies in their appeal to such a temper. 'Do not let us fail to see clearly that [. . .]'; [62] 'when [our religious organizations . . . land us in no better result than this], it is high time to examine carefully their idea of perfection'; [63] '[this] is so evident, that no one in Great Britain with clear and calm political judgement, or with fine perception, or with high cultivation, or with large knowledge of the world, doubts it'.[64] On the other hand, there are negative instances that show equally clearly how some false proposition is born of the mental temper which Arnold condemns: 'Well, then, what an unsound habit of mind it must be which makes us [talk of . . . as . . .].' [65] In either case it is clear that in cultivating this sense of a right 'habit of mind' throughout his argument, Arnold equipped himself with a precise and powerful instrument for giving effect to judgements of value.

[60] vi. 64.
[61] vi. 154.
[62] vi. 25.
[63] vi. 27.
[64] ME. (x. 122).
[65] CA. (vi. 16).

Some of these examples influence us less because they describe than because they exemplify the right habit of mind; that is to say, they affect the reader less through their meaning than through their tone. 'Surely culture is useful in reminding us that [. . .]' [66] illustrates this tendency. But the significant point, for a comprehensive appreciation of Arnold, is how directly and openly this control of tone develops our sense of the author himself. 'Keeping this in view, I have in my own mind often indulged myself with the fancy of [. . .]'; [67] 'to me few things are more pathetic than to see [. . .]'; [68] 'the philosophers and the prophets, whom I at any rate am disposed to believe . . . will tell us that [. . .]' [69]—above all, 'now does anyone, if he simply and naturally reads his consciousness, discover that [. . .]? For my part, the deeper I go into my own consciousness, and the more simply I abandon myself to it, the more it seems to tell me that [. . .]'; [70]—Arnold is using forms of words that recommend his assertion and that develop our sense of himself, all in one. And because the value frame serves this purpose, it is naturally adapted to serve the complementary purpose: it also, often enough, adds to our impression of his opponents.

These three functions may be performed together through simple antithesis. One example quoted above was incomplete: Arnold wrote, 'So when Mr. Carlyle, a man of genius to whom we have all at one time or another been indebted for refreshment and stimulus, says [. . .] surely culture is useful in reminding us that [. . .].' Here, words like 'refreshment' and 'stimulus,' and the blunt 'says,' give a tone to Carlyle's assertion, and the whole phrase controls our impression of Carlyle himself; but Arnold's 'culture' is *useful* in *reminding* (it does not simply say); and Arnold hopes to do something more significant than refresh and stimulate. This is very similar to 'Mr. Roebuck is never weary of reiterating . . . "May not every man in England say what he likes?"—Mr. Roebuck perpetually asks; and that, he thinks, is quite sufficient. . . . But the aspirations of culture . . . are not satisfied unless, [. . .] culture indefatigably tries . . . to draw ever nearer to a sense of [. . .].' [71] The contrast is clear; Mr. Roebuck is too satisfied too easily. In the sentence 'When Protestantism . . .

[66] vi. 59.
[67] vi. 84.
[68] vi. 22.
[69] DA. (iv. 314).
[70] CA. (vi. 181).
[71] vi. 15.

gives the law to criticism *too magisterially,* criticism *may* and *must remind* it that [its pretensions, in this respect, are illusive and do it harm]',[72] Arnold's opponents are in the end described explicitly, by the words here printed in brackets; but they, and their critic, and the quality of their respective assertions, are already distinguished plainly by the value frame, as the italics make plain. The complex manner in which 'its pretensions . . . do *it* harm' illustrates what was said above about forms of argument should not, by the way, be overlooked.

Arnold is able to endow even the simplest negative with significant and contrasting tone: for example, 'And, therefore, when Mr. White asks the same sort of question about America that he has asked about England, and wants to know whether [. . .] we answer in the same way as we did before, that [as much is not done]'.[73] Here there is a subtly suggestive difference in the sameness—White's pestering is monotonous and stupid, Arnold is urbane and patient. Almost exactly this construction comes again: 'And if statesmen, either with their tongue in their cheek or with a fine impulsiveness, tell people that [. . .], there is the more need to tell them the contrary'.[74] Sometimes the denial is fuller: 'When Mr. Gladstone invites us to call [. . .] we must surely answer that all this mystical eloquence is not in the least necessary to explain so simple a matter'.[75] And while foisting one tone on his opponents, Arnold can provide himself with quite another merely by changing the mood of his verb: 'Who, that is not manacled and hoodwinked by his Hebraism, can believe that [. . .]';[76] 'When Mr. Sidgwick says so broadly, that [. . .] is he not carried away by a turn for broad generalization? does he not forget [. . .]?'[77]—the question-form itself is all that conveys Arnold's presence, but it is enough.

This quite distinctive device bears both inwards, as it were, and outwards: it suggests an attitude (and grounds for it too) that the reader should take up towards the assertion that it introduces; and through modulations of tone, it can do much to expand and sustain our notion of the writer's personality, and of that of his adversaries. In doing so it is one of the more important techniques creating that bipolarity between himself and them which runs like an axis through Arnold's work.

[72] *The Function of Criticism* (iii. 38); my italics.
[73] CA. (vi. p. xxix).
[74] vi, p. xliii.
[75] ME. (x. 90).
[76] CA. (vi. 193).
[77] vi. 147.

(iv) Definitions

It transpired above that the value frame might not only put one of Arnold's keywords, like 'culture,' to use, but that it could also control its meaning; and this is to say that the value frame may be inverted in function (or have, as is more likely, two simultaneous functions), and serve as a kind of defining formula. Since definitions proved to be so important a persuasive device in Carlyle, George Eliot and Newman, it is high time to trace the contribution they make in Arnold. But we find that it is surprisingly small. This is not so, of course, in the works of Biblical exegesis—*Literature and Dogma, St. Paul and Protestantism* or *God and the Bible.* Here Arnold's central purpose is to reinterpret some of the essential concepts of Christianity: he is, in consequence, quite explicit in giving fresh meanings to the key terms of Scripture, and his argument is full of expressions like 'and the sense which this will give us for their words is at least solid',[78] 'a plain solid experimental sense',[79] 'what they really do at bottom mean by God is . . .',[80] He even, at one stage, thinks of using re-defining arguments based on the etymologies of words, and mentions how this method is extremely common in Ruskin's social criticism—but in the end he decides not to use 'fanciful helps'.[81] These books, however, are not really of the type that concerns our enquiry. They do not seek to convince a reader that the world-view they express is true, so much as to convince him that it is the real world-view of the Old and New Testaments. Arnold's theology is not what Carlyle would have called 'Life-Philosophy'; it is a sustained *argumentum ad hominem*, addressed to those already sure that the Bible is true if rightly interpreted. When we turn to Arnold's independent work, we find that re-defining arguments virtually disappear; and at first sight this seems a very strange thing.

They are to be found, doubtless, from time to time—it would be inconceivably odd if Arnold were never to define a term anywhere. But by comparison they are certainly few in number, and what is more important, they lack the characteristic quality of such arguments, because they are trite. The typical re-definition seems to transform the import of a word, giving it a more pointed, provocative, pregnant, influential meaning by seeming to draw on some insight of unusual

[78] LD. (vii. 58).
[79] vii. 62.
[80] vii. 327.
[81] St. P. (ix. 42).

keenness. By contrast, Arnold's definitions are often textbook definitions; they are dull; they are diaphanous. It is not merely that they cannot facilitate interesting inferences; they preclude them, and this is their job.

Three examples will be sufficient: Arnold's accounts of the *State*, of *Civilization* and of *Human Nature*. If he wishes to be tendentious anywhere, surely it will pay to be tendentious here. But all we find is (1) '*The State—but what is* the *State?* cry many . . . . The full force of the term, *the State* . . . no one will master without going a little deeply . . .' So far all is like Carlyle; not, however, for long. '. . . but it is possible to give in very plain language an account of it sufficient for all Burke called it—*the nation in its collective and corporate character.* The State is the representative acting-power of the nation . . .'.[82] (2) 'What do we mean by *civilized?* . . . we will try to answer. Civilization is the humanization of man in society. To be humanized is to comply with the true law of our human nature . . . says Lucan "to keep our measure, and to hold fast our end, and to follow Nature" . . . to make progress towards this, our true and full humanity. And to be civilized is to make progress towards this in civil society.'[83] Nothing could seem less pointed than this. (3) 'When we talk of . . . full humanity, we think of an advance, not along one line only, but several . . . . The power of intellect and science, the power of beauty, the power of social life and manners . . . the power of conduct is another great element.'[84] This may be true and useful, but it is not new.

The reason for this apparent lack of enterprise is clear. Unlike Carlyle and the rest, Arnold has no wish to draw controversial or unexpected conclusions from his definitions. On the contrary, it was partisanship or legerdemain of this kind that he was resisting. He defines the State, only to rebut the view that States cannot be active except harmfully (far from this, the state is good or bad as we make it, he argues—it all depends upon the details); he defines civilization to rebut a paradoxical conclusion about France by Erskine May; in *Literature and Science* he gives the same account of human nature in its various aspects, so as to rebut the narrow and exclusive pretensions of the scientist. Arnold is using a pattern of argument contrary to the third pattern we distinguished in Newman's work: he is arguing

[82] ME. (x. 40).
[83] x. 61.
[84] x. 62-3. These same four powers are listed in almost identical words in *Literature and Science* (DA., iv. 330–31) as 'the powers which go to the building up of human life', or 'the constitution of human nature'.

that his opponents use words in unduly narrow and tendentious senses, and demanding that we adopt unsuggestive, everyday senses instead. In short, these passages are true definitions, not re-definitions; the re-definition is a persuasive technique which it is their purpose to reject and discredit.[85]

To be sure, the more usual type of tendentious re-definition is not unknown in Arnold's work—or at least one supposes oneself to have located it from time to time—but here the position is still stranger, for Arnold appears to use the technique for only one word, or rather one pair of synonyms. These synonyms are 'culture,' and 'criticism.' It has not been clearly recognized, perhaps, that he distinguishes these two by nothing substantial; but this is surely true. Culture, in its simpler sense, is grounded on 'a desire after the things of the mind simply for their own sakes and for the pleasure of seeing them as they are'; [86] criticism's rule 'may be summed up on one word—*disinterestedness*',[87] and it works against obstacles in that 'the mass of mankind will never have any ardent zeal for seeing things as they are'.[88] True, 'there is of culture another view . . .' where, though not itself active, it is a ground of action—'. . . it is *a study of perfection*'; [89] but there is another view of criticism too, and this time 'it obeys an instinct prompting it to try to know the *best* that is known and thought in the world'.[90] Most remarkable of all, perhaps, is the fact that Arnold controls the value-implications of both words by giving a particular sense to the single word 'curiosity.' Each time he shows that this word 'in the terms of which may lie a real ambiguity' [91] has, as well as its usual bad sense, a less usual but more important good sense: and then writes, in one place, 'this is the true ground to assign for the genuine scientific passion, however manifested, and for culture, viewed simply as a fruit of this passion'; [92] and in the other, 'criticism, real criticism, is essentially the exercise of this quality'. When one remembers that, after all, each of these words is being used as what Arnold would have called 'not a term of science, but . . . a term of common speech, of poetry

---

[85] Arnold occasionally uses re-definitions of the normal type—for example, 'What is freedom but machinery? What is population but machinery? . . .' (CA., vi. 14). But for the most part (though scarcely here in respect of freedom) they are trivial or incidental.

[86] CA. (vi. 6).

[87] *The Function of Criticism* (iii. 20).

[88] iii. 27.

[89] CA. (vi. 7).

[90] *Op. cit.* (iii. 18).

[91] CA. (vi. 5).

[92] vi. 7.

and eloquence, *thrown out* at a vast object of consciousness not fully covered by it',[93] their substantial identity is apparent, and that it has not been more emphasized is remarkable.

There is no need to reproduce the argument whereby, especially in *Culture and Anarchy,* Arnold develops this concept—by whichever of the two words we think of it; like the other Victorian prophets, he has been paraphrased often enough. But the form of this development is significant. Earlier, we mentioned how Newman had a pattern of argument which gradually unfolded the full sense of a word; but his method and Arnold's are entirely different. Newman first *used* his word in an apparently non-controversial way, then strove to show that in allowing him to use it like this the reader had conceded more than he knew. But Arnold is explicit that his definitions are *analyses* of concepts. He announces [94] that he will proceed to enquire 'what culture really is'; and further, he does not confine attention to what we must call its alleged essence, and say that this is really something that usually goes by another name (and the essence of this by a third, and so on through a whole series of 'charged' expressions, which in Carlyle is frequent). Arnold's methods simply takes the reader through subordinate notions that comprise the meaning of his key term. He analyses, he does not reinterpret; and only when the analysis is complete does he claim that the key-term stands for something good—recapitulating the analysis to show why, and emphasizing that this *is* why. For example, 'If culture, then, is a study of perfection, and of harmonious perfection, general perfection, and perfection which consists in becoming something rather than having something . . . it is clear that culture . . . has a very important function to fulfil for mankind'; [95] '. . . well, then, how salutary a friend is culture . . . culture begets a satisfaction which is of the highest possible value . . .'.[96] We can see how the tone becomes gradually firmer, as a positive value is set more and more confidently on what 'culture' refers to. But Arnold makes it plain that the word carries this favourable tone explicitly because of the sense he gives it —and even admits openly that one may not necessarily be in error to give it another sense. 'I must remark . . . that whoever calls anything else culture, may, indeed, call it so if he likes, but then he talks of something quite different'.[97] And there is just such a *caveat* in the

[93] LD. (vii. 191).
[94] CA. (vi. 4).
[95] CA. (vi. 12–13).
[96] vi. 16, 17.
[97] vi. 67.

essay which defines criticism: 'But stop, someone will say . . . this criticism of yours is not what we have in our minds when we speak of criticism . . . I am sorry for it . . . I am bound by my own definition of criticism: *a disinterested endeavour to . . .*'[98]—and so on.

Arnold's way of manipulating senses is thus different in kind from that of Newman or Carlyle. His discussions do not suggest, as theirs did, that investigating senses is a kind of discovery. He is really finding a single convenient *name* for a complex of features plainly listed. And this precedes argument in Arnold, whereas the typical re-definition either *is* the crucial stage of an argument, or comes just after it, and shows that what seemed innocent was in fact crucial. Arnold is at no pains to conceal how the definition he adopts is in a sense arbitrary: for him it is an arbitrary but convenient first move. We have seen how the real argument, when it begins, may also control the sense of a key word like 'culture'—sometimes, for example, through its use in a value frame. Yet this control does less to give the word a new sense, than simply to keep the established sense clearly before the reader. It emphasizes, indeed, that Arnold defines 'culture' first and then uses it with a constant meaning. Re-definition proper depends on ambiguities.

(v) Articulating the Argument: Arnold and his Opponents

The desire to have distinctive names for whatever he is discussing is a feature of much of Arnold's work. In chapter IV of *Culture and Anarchy,* writing of the 'energy driving at practice' and the 'intelligence driving at those ideas which are . . . the basis of right practice', he says 'to give these forces names . . . we may call them . . . Hebraism and Hellenism'.[99] Elsewhere we find 'these favourite doctrines of theirs I call . . . a peculiarly British form of Atheism . . . a peculiarly British form of Quietism'; [100] or 'I may call them the ways of Jacobinism'.[101] How Arnold introduces the terms 'sweetness and light', or 'Barbarians, Philistines, Populace',[102] is perhaps too well known to need further remark. The effect of some of these is clear enough—they are what may simply be called *hangdog* names. But Arnold gives a reason for using the last three which indicates how they can contribute to the general texture of his prose. 'The same desire for

[98] *The Function of Criticism* (iii. 41–2).
[99] CA. (vi. 121).
[100] vi. 109–10.
[101] vi. 36.
[102] vi. 20, 79 ff.

clearness', he writes, '. . . prompts me also to improve my nomen-
clature . . . a little, with a view to making it thereby more manageable.' [103] This is important. To be clear and manageable are not new
concepts in Arnold's work. They were the distinctive qualities of his
tone, because he made this represent his temper of mind. By providing
convenient names for his main topics, he not only influences our attitude through the nuance of those names, but articulates his argument
with nodal points that soon become familiar, and easy to trace again.
The kind of argument that is his at his most typical, an argument that
moves gently forward with a smooth, unruffled urbanity, owes not a
little to the familiarity of these coinages, as they so constantly re-
appear. They do not affect the logic of his discussion, but they transform its quality.

The same principle of style also operates more widely. Sometimes
he organizes the whole movement of his thought round a single
concept denoted by a single constantly recurring word: an example
is the essay *Numbers*, through all the earlier part of which runs the
idea of a tiny *élite* which is gradually to leaven the whole of society,
and for which Arnold borrows the word 'remnant'. Much more
frequently, a whole essay or a whole book is permeated by certain
phrases for ideas which have an abiding place of trust in his mind.
'Choose equality', 'sweetness and light', 'our best self', 'spontaneity of
consciousness', 'a free play of the mind', 'a full and harmonious development', 'perfection at all points', 'the best that is known and thought
in the world'—these phrases return constantly, and contribute not only
through their meaning, but also by their recurrence. They bring the
argument nearer to that easy limpidity which its author wishes to
recommend. By being careful to repeat himself verbally, Arnold
brings into a bright light the essential simplicity of his thought. He
orders his argument with familiar landmarks. By this means he can
hope to attune the reader to his message, just as the rich verbal confusion of Carlyle attunes a reader to an outlook which is quite different.

And the key phrases work to Arnold's advantage not only by their
recurrence, but also by their origin. The first three in the list above
are all borrowed—from Swift, Menander and Plato respectively. That
they are borrowed in this way may add to the weight they carry, or it
may not. But quoting authorities is so common in Arnold that it adds
something quite distinctive to our impression of him as we read.
Through it we see his modesty, his circumspection, and, oddly enough,
his independence—not of mind, but of prejudice or strong emotion such

[103] vi. 82.

as might provoke personal, precipitate, passionate comment. His use of authorities is a contrast to that of Carlyle. Carlyle overwhelmingly gives the impression of willingness to form and express opinions; his 'quotations' are incidental and subordinate. The reader recognizes them as a game, an expression of the author's exuberance, his intellectual self-confidence and high spirits. Arnold really quotes, he does not invent authorities; and time and again his quotation is introduced at the crucial stage, and his authority constitutes the rock of his argument.

Consider some examples. The discourse *Literature and Science* begins by drawing entirely from Plato, and the fact that Arnold by no means expects his audience to defer to Plato's authority only emphasizes the very aspect of using an authority that we are discussing. Later, however, at a really crucial point in the argument, Arnold reverts to Plato. He has been arguing that men have in their nature four 'powers' or tendencies, intellectual, moral, aesthetic and social; and that just as they have a need to relate the points of their knowledge into a system, so they have a need to relate these four powers into a system. How is he to suggest that this need is worthy to be given free play? At this point Arnold withdraws from his argument, and makes a quite fresh start to introduce the authority of Diotima in the *Symposium*. All desire, says Diotima, is at bottom desire for the good; 'and therefore this fundamental desire it is, I suppose . . . which acts in us when we feel the impulse for relating our knowledge to our sense for conduct and our sense for beauty. At any rate, with men in general the instinct exists . . . and . . . it will be admitted, is innocent, and human nature is preserved by our following the lead of its innocent instincts.' [104] In the address on *Equality* [105] Arnold goes even further. He begins by asserting that in the Burial Service is to be found the maxim 'evil communications corrupt good manners'; but this is quite irrelevant and is never referred to again. Its only significance is to have been quoted from Menander; from whom another maxim (not already quoted anywhere) is 'choose equality and flee greed'.[106] With that the argument can begin; but as it proceeds, George Sand, Turgot, Voltaire, Burke, M. de Lavelaye, Hamerton, Bossuet, the Book of Proverbs, Pepys and Charles Sumner come one after another, if not to confirm an opinion, at least to provide one which can be discussed and examined. At every turn Arnold seems to avoid taking the initiative, or forcing on the reader something

[104] DA. (iv. 333).
[105] ME. (x. 46).
[106] x. 47.

which is merely his own. He even makes his method explicit on one issue: 'now the interesting point for us is . . . to know how far other European communities, left in the same situation with us . . . have dealt with these inequalities'.[107] All the time he is building up our sense of an author who thinks others' opinions more important than his own.

Perhaps it is also worth mentioning, as examples of some special importance, the first paragraphs of the discourse *Numbers,* deriving as they do from one of Johnson's sayings; and the authority of Burke appealed to at a crucial stage in the essay on 'The Function of Criticism'; [108] and the works of Biblical exegesis, which constitute one sustained appeal to authority. But the method is so common with Arnold that it cannot be overlooked. Nor can we overlook its significance, if only because Arnold at one point states it: 'I am grown so cowed by all the rebuke my original speculations have drawn upon me that I find myself more and more filling the part of a mere listener'.[109] Arnold quotes the views of others, rather than express his own, because this modifies our sense of his argument and our view of him. This is not simply to say that he conciliates the reader by refusing to disagree with him, or instruct him directly. Had Carlyle attempted to conciliate in this way he would have had to be at special pains to prevent its being a quite false note, thoroughly discordant with his argument. Once again, our concern is not with a superficial trick of persuasion, but with some modulation of style which is a genuine aid because, through developing our sense of the writer's personality, it genuinely mediates his point of view. That Arnold sometimes uses this method to excess is undeniable; the problem is to sense its point, where it is used aptly.

Quotation, however, is something which Arnold is fonder of inflicting on his opponents than on his models. *My Countrymen,* for example, opens with a grand review of those who have disagreed with him: the *Saturday Review,* Mr. Bazley (M.P. for Manchester), Mr. Miall, the *Daily Telegraph,* the *Daily News,* Mr. Lowe, John Bright, the *Morning Star,* they are all there, marshalled against Arnold, by himself. *Culture and Anarchy* begins similarly—with Bright, the *Daily Telegraph,* and Frederic Harrison; so does *The Function of Criticism.* In *Equality,* Arnold begins with his opponents—Disraeli, Erskine May, Gladstone, Froude, Lowe, Sir William Molesworth—the moment he has done with Menander. The modest, fair, urbane Arnold shows in

[107] ME. (x. 52).
[108] See above, p. 500.
[109] FG. (vi. 391).

what seems like an attempt to do justice to the other side. But Arnold uses his opponents further. He quotes from them, and uses these quotations over and over again; wanting his readers to notice less their meaning (which is often uncertain) than their general tenor and their tone. He thus equips himself with a set of—let us say catch-phrases rather than key phrases—that crystallize the views he is resisting in the same simple and recurrent form as his most favoured expressions crystallize his own views. Both the false and the true are presented with the same urbane simplicity; and while we see Arnold's personality behind his selection and presentation of these phrases, and behind their calm and genial reiteration, we see his opponents in the catch-phrases themselves, a little more clearly and a little more disastrously each time. His own account of these phrases was 'profligate expenditure of claptrap'.[110]

Certainly, he collected some gems. Frederic Harrison was unfortunate enough to 'seek vainly in Mr. A. a system of philosophy with principles coherent, interdependent, subordinate, and derivative'.[111] Arnold never really let him forget it subsequently. Harrison it was too who told the working class that 'theirs are the brightest powers of sympathy and the readiest powers of action'.[112] Under Arnold's reiteration, the readiness takes on a fresh colour, the brightness gets a little rubbed. Arnold also lets us savour Frederic Harrison's account of the middle classes, 'their earnest good sense which penetrates through sophisms, ignores commonplaces, and gives to conventional illusions their true value'; [113] and John Bright's 'thoughtfulness and intelligence of the people of the great towns'; [114] and *The Times'* comment on East End children, 'Now their brief spring is over. There is no one to blame for this; it is the result of Nature's simplest laws!'; [115] and Robert Buchanan's account in the same context of 'that divine philoprogenitiveness . . . . He would *swarm* the earth with beings . . .' [116] and his 'line of poetry':

'Tis the old story of the fig-leaf time

The newspaper account of why a certain Mr. Smith committed suicide, that he 'laboured under the apprehension that he would come to

[110] vi. 258.
[111] vi. 299.
[112] CA. (vi. 101).
[113] CA. (vi. 101).
[114] vi, p. xxiv.
[115] vi. 201.
[116] vi. 202–3.

poverty, and that he was eternally lost'[117] does service too; so does Roebuck's 'I look around me and ask what is the state of England? Is not every man able to say what he likes? I ask you whether the world over, or in past history, there is anything like it? Nothing. I pray that our unrivalled happiness may last'[118]—which is a recurrent theme in *The Function of Criticism*, and reappears in *Culture and Anarchy*.[119] 'The Dissidence of Dissent and the Protestantism of the Protestant religion', which began life as a motto on the *Nonconformist*, is resurrected in both *Culture and Anarchy* and the *Discourses in America*.[120] *The Times'* instruction to the British Government to speak out 'with promptitude and energy' enlivens *Friendship's Garland*,[121] where Lowe's fatuous 'the destiny of England is in the great heart of England' also rears its empty head.[122] The desire of the Bishops of Winchester and Gloucester to 'do something for the honour of the Eternal Godhead' is saluted every so often throughout *Literature and Dogma;*[123] and choicest of all perhaps, the 'great sexual insurrection of our Anglo-Teutonic race',[124] product of a disciple of Hepworth Dixon, is one of Arnold's most treasured literary possessions.

Now clearly, to introduce or reiterate so many phrases of this kind does not in itself render the texture of Arnold's argument simpler and more urbane: their straightforward effect is to make it more variegated and less urbane, and it will be necessary to see how he so 'places' them in their context that this direct tendency is overruled, and the tone of the quotation is prevented from interfering with the tone of the main text. But what these quotations simplify for us is our conception of Arnold's opponents and their shortcomings. Time and again, always in the same way, they epitomize for us the defect of temper which is what above all Arnold is condemning. In one simple, natural perception, we see what this defect is; and every time they are repeated, the flaw they reveal shows a little more clearly.

The defective temper of mind which Arnold makes plain in what his opponents say, is also plain in what they do. He has no need of rhetoric or eloquence or complex argumentation: the simple facts

[117] vi. 157.
[118] iii. 23–5.
[119] vi. 110.
[120] vi. 23, and DA. (iv. 375).
[121] FG. (vi. 322).
[122] vi. 321, 371.
[123] *E.g.* vii. 4, 6–7, 33, 162, 183, 237, 239, 273, 288, 304, 364.
[124] CA. (vi. 190 and 191); FG. (vi. 306 and 307).

are silently eloquent by themselves. For this purpose, inventions are as good as realities. *Friendship's Garland* is almost a series of fictitious anecdotes of invented revealing incidents—the Philistine Bottles giving Arnold's hero Arminius a jingoistic number of *Punch* in the train, or sitting in all the Deceased-Wife's-Sisters-Bill glory of his suburban residence; the Honourable Charles Clifford addressing the crowd from the footboard of his hansom; Dr. Russell of *The Times* vainly striving to get astride his warhorse; Cole's Truss Manufactory in Trafalgar Square—'the finest site in Europe';[125] Lord Elcho's hat— 'to my mind the mere cock of his lordship's hat is one of the most aristocratic things we have'.[126] The technique reappears in *The Function of Criticism:* trying to indicate the fault of temper in a whole series of writings, Arnold again takes a single striking case. 'Their fault is . . . one which they have in common with the British College of Health in the New Road . . . with the lion and the statue of the Goddess Hygeia . . . the grand name without the grand thing.'[127]

'The grand name without the grand thing'—Arnold is not unaware that, if he selects his opponents astutely, their names alone will be enough to expose their defects; and the method is ingenious, for although it says little explicitly, it makes one unable even to think of Arnold's victim without automatically seeing him in an unfavourable light. Beside the British College of Health we have 'Cole's Truss Manufactory',[128] and the *'British Banner':*[129] Arnold adds 'I am not quite sure it was the *British Banner,* but it was some newspaper of the same stamp', which seems to show that he knew how the name, if only he could bring it in, would argue for him. It is not, however, only the sham pomposity of names that he enlists in his argument. 'Has anyone reflected', he writes 'what a touch of grossness in our race . . . is shown by the natural growth amongst us of such hideous names—Higginbottom, Stiggins, Bugg!'[130] In *Friendship's Garland* Arnold hints at the ludicrous, and also at the ugly, in his opponents, by invented names like 'Viscount Lumpington', 'the Reverend Esau Hittall', and 'Bottles Esquire'.[131] Elsewhere, for the same purpose, he selects from the material available. The result is Mr. Bazley, Mr. Blewitt, Mr. Bradlaugh, Mr. Blowitz (perhaps Arnold saw something

[125] vi. 249.
[126] vi. 262.
[127] *The Function of Criticism* (iii. 36).
[128] *Loc cit.*
[129] CA. (vi. 96).
[130] *The Function of Criticism* (iii. 26).
[131] FG. (vi. 286).

banausic in the initial B), Miss Cobbes and Mr. Murphy. There are
other names, too, which might be added to this list; and if any doubt
remains whether the method genuinely colours Arnold's argument,
a passage in *Culture and Anarchy* shows him somersaulting an opponent's argument of an exactly opposite kind: ' "Well, but," says
Mr. Hepworth Dixon, "a theory which has been accepted by men like
Judge Edmonds, Dr. Hare, Elder Frederick and Professor Bush!" . . .
Such are, in brief, the bases of what Newman Weeks, Sarah Horton,
Deborah Butler, and the associated brethren, proclaimed in Rolt's Hall
as the New Covenant!' Evidently, Arnold hints, 'Mr. Hepworth Dixon'
is taken in by *not* the grand name without the grand thing. He goes
on, 'If he was summing up an account of the doctrine of Plato, or of
St. Paul . . . Mr. Hepworth Dixon could not be more earnestly
reverential'. And now Arnold replies with his own selection of names:
'But the question is, Have personages like Judge Edmonds, and
Newman Weeks, and Elderess Polly and Elderess Antoniette, and the
rest of Mr. Hepworth Dixon's heroes and heroines, anything of the
weight and significance . . . that Plato and St. Paul have?' [132] Here
the first parade of names is enough to reveal the intellectual defects
of Arnold's opponent, and the second is enough to conclude the discussion.

Arnold's comment on the ugliness of English names occurs in a
passage when he is more serious, and is using a judiciously chosen
example in another way, less to epitomize an outlook, than to reveal
what it omits. It is of particular interest, not only because Arnold is
using quotation, authority, the value frame, and example in a single
integrated argument, but also because the contrast between the tone
of the text itself and that of the inserted passages is particularly vivid.
First, he quotes Sir Charles Adderley, 'the old Anglo-Saxon race . . .
the best breed in the world', and Mr. Roebuck, 'the world over or in
past history, is there anything like it? Nothing.' Against this comes
a simple quotation from Goethe, framed or 'placed' by the phrase
'clearly this is a better line of reflection'—we see at once how the
counter-move is directed against a certain mental temper, and recommends its opposite. Then Arnold returns to his opponents. They
would not contradict Goethe, it is simply that they 'lose sight' of
what he saw: they are carried away by controversy, they 'go a little
beyond the point and say stoutly—'; so long as they are countered in
the same spirit, 'so long will the strain swell louder and louder'.
Instead of this, Arnold proposes another spirit, which he sees in

[132] CA. (vi. 97–9).

simply giving, without comment, one example, one simple fact. 'Let criticism . . . *in the most candid spirit* . . . confront with our dithyramb *this* . . .' (my italics):

> A shocking child murder has just been committed at Nottingham. A girl named Wragg left the workhouse there on Saturday morning with her young illegitimate child. The child was soon afterwards found dead on Mapperly Hills, having been strangled. Wragg is in custody.

'Nothing but that,' he goes on, 'but in juxtaposition with the absolute eulogies . . . how eloquent, how suggestive are those few lines . . . there is profit for the spirit in such contrasts . . . . Mr. Roebuck will have a poor opinion of an adversary who replies to his defiant songs of triumph only by murmuring under his breath, *Wragg is in custody;* but in no other way will these songs of triumph be induced gradually to moderate themselves, to get rid of what in them is excessive and offensive, and to fall into a softer and truer key.' [133]

(vi) Irony

In that passage the sustained contrast between two tempers of mind, one which Arnold seeks to recommend or maintain, and one which he detects in his opponents, is so clear that the problem of how he maintains this duality is now inescapable; and his chief method, beyond question, is irony. It is widely agreed that by irony an author can seem to the casual or uninformed reader to say one thing, but really say something quite different, clear only to the reader who is initiated or more attentive. But why should such a roundabout method of communication ever be employed? Usually it is hard enough, one would suppose, to convey one's meaning straightforwardly—why, not content with one difficulty, does an author invent another? Sometimes, perhaps, because irony can be like a sophisticated intellectual game, which writer and reader alike may enjoy for its own sake. But there may be a more substantial reason. Irony is a powerful and genuine instrument of persuasion. The meaning of a statement—especially one praising or blaming what is being spoken of, or doing anything of a similar kind—usually determines a characteristic tone in which it is reasonable to write or utter that statement. Outright condemnation of essentials tends to sound indignant, partial condemnation of details to sound mildly disapproving, plain description to sound detached, praise to sound admiring. These are no more than tendencies,

[133] *The Function of Criticism* (iii. 25–7).

but they are tendencies strong enough to be inconvenient to writers who, for example, particularly desire not to sound indignant or benignant; and irony is a means whereby a writer may say something in a tone that normally would be inappropriate to it. How easily that will influence the impression he gives the reader of himself, need not be laboured.

Quintilian says that to write ironically is to praise by blaming, or to blame by praising; of which two the last, of course, is the commoner. This is a method which Arnold uses fairly often. But, more than Quintilian's formula suggests, Arnold adapts the nuance of his blame, and of his praise too, so that it serves the general impression he wishes to give. The blame behind his seeming-innocent praise is relatively constant in kind; the praise itself is such that the uncomprehending complacence with which one fancies his opponents would receive it is enough to condemn them; there is no random hitting, because Arnold's irony is adapted so as to be exactly right for the general tenor of his work. Mr. Gladstone is

> that attractive and ever-victorious rhetorician [134]

who

> concludes in his copious and eloquent way.[135]

Other examples of this lethal innocence are

> the ingenious and inexhaustaible Mr. Blowitz, of our great London *Times* [136]
> a hundred vigorous and influential writers [137]
> the newspapers . . . who have that trenchant authoritative style [138]
> this brisk and flourishing movement [139]
> our great orator, Mr. Bright . . . never weary of telling us [140]
> my nostrums of State Schools for those much too wise to want them, and of an Academy for people who have an inimitable style already [141]
> before I called Dixon's style lithe and sinewy [142]
> Mr. Lowe's powerful and much admired speech against Reform.[143]

There is no mistaking the trend of these passages. At first glance, they constitute just that genial, deferential praise which we might expect

[134] DA. (iv. 280).
[135] ME. (x. 49).
[136] DA. (iv. 311).
[137] FG. (vi. 368–9).
[138] vi. 353.
[139] DA. (iv. 321).
[140] iv. 285.
[141] FG. (vi. 353–4).
[142] vi. 306.
[143] vi. 369.

the urbane Arnold genuinely to give to his more forceful colleagues; but when the second meaning comes home, they are seen to diagnose just the smug, busy over-confidence that Arnold has made his inveterate enemy.

In this way Arnold makes his irony show both what he is like, and what his opponents are like. Images can do this as well as descriptions. In *A Courteous Explanation* he finds occasion to write: '(Horace) and his friends have lost their tails, and want to get them back'.[144] The tail here is a symbol of political liberty. But it is not long before Arnold is utilizing its ironic possibilities:

> I think our 'true political Liberty' a beautiful bushy object . . . it struck me there was a danger of our trading too extensively upon our tails, and, in fact, running to tail altogether . . . . Our highest class, besides having of course true political liberty,—that regulation tail that every Briton of us is blessed with,—is altogether so beautiful and splendid (and above all, as Mr. Carlyle says, polite) that for my part I hardly presume to enquire what it has or has not in the way of heads [145]

Clearly, this beautiful bushy tail is—may one say it?—a two-edged weapon. There is a very similar passage at the end of *Friendship's Garland*, in the letter alleged to have been written by 'A Young Lion' from Paris; the hand is the hand of a lithe disciple of Hepworth Dixon, but of course the voice is the voice of Arnold:

> While Sala was speaking, a group had formed before the hotel near us, and our attention was drawn to its central figure. Dr. Russell, of the *Times*, was preparing to mount his war-horse. You know the sort of thing,—he has described it himself over and over again. Bismarck at his horse's head, the Crown Prince holding his stirrup, and the old King of Prussia hoisting Russell into the saddle. When he was there, the distinguished public servant waved his hand in acknowledgement, and rode slowly down the street, accompanied by the *gamins* of Versailles, who even in their present dejection could not forbear a few involuntary cries of 'Quel homme!' [146]

—by now the exact nuance of the blame behind the praise is beginning to be apparent, the warhorse has become a hobby-horse, and Arnold, once more, is depicting in his opponents the perennial source of his dislike.

[144] vi. 400.
[145] vi. 400–401.
[146] vi. 345.

The ambivalency between praise and blame that makes this passage ironical depends very much upon Arnold's giving it to an alleged author doing duty for the real author whom we sense in the background. It is one of his favourite devices to invent figures to speak his opinions for him. In part its contribution is like that suggested above for quotations and authorities; but in part too it sustains that divorce of tone and statement which is the office of irony. Thus, in *My Countrymen*, it is 'certain foreigners' who deliver the attack on English life—and a most forceful and outspoken attack it is. But Arnold appears only as their interlocutor in defence of England—an anxious, embarrassed, excessively reasonable defender perhaps (as Arnold was likely to be for any cause) but a defender all the same.

> I used often to think what a short and ready way one of our hard-hitting English newspapers would take with these scorners . . . but being myself a mere seeker after truth, with nothing trenchant or authoritative about me, I could do no more than look shocked and begin to ask questions. 'What!' I said, 'you hold the England of today cheap . . .?' . . . Though I could not bear without a shudder this insult to the earnest good sense which, as the *Morning Star* says, may be fairly set down as the general characteristic of England and Englishmen everywhere . . . . I begged my acquaintances to explain a little more fully . . . .
> '. . . and intelligence [they said] . . . your middle class has absolutely none.' I was aghast. I thought of this great class, every morning and evening extolled for its clear manly intelligence by a hundred vigorous and influential writers . . . .[147]

But he has just been sent a copy of a speech by Mr. Lowe, telling how the English middle class has been performing unrivalled exploits:

> I took it out of my pocket. 'Now,' said I to my envious, carping foreigners, 'just listen to me . . . Mr. Lowe shall answer you . . . .' What I had urged, or rather what I had borrowed from Mr. Lowe, seemed to me exceedingly forcible, and I looked anxiously for its effect on my hearers. They did not appear so much disconcerted as I had hoped.[148]

In *Friendship's Garland* Arnold uses the same device to escape the awkward tone implied by what he wants to say. Here it is the mythical Prussian, Arminius von Thunder-den-Tronkh, who delivers Arnold's attack direct. And Arnold, speaking in his own person, writes:

[147] FG. (vi. 363–9).
[148] vi. 369–71.

In confidence I will own to you that he makes himself intensely disagreeable. He has the harsh, arrogant Prussian way of turning up his nose at things and laying down the law about them; and though, as a lover of intellect, I admire him, and, as a seeker of truth, I value his frankness, yet, as an Englishman, and a member of what the *Daily Telegraph* calls 'the Imperial race', I feel so uncomfortable under it, that I want, through your kindness, to call to my aid the great British public, which never loses heart and has always a bold front and a rough word ready for its assailants.[149]

Arminius himself is a likeable figure, with his pink face and blue eyes, his shaggy blond hair, his ancient blue pilot-coat, and pipe belching interminable smoke. But although his personality may be likeable, it is very different from Arnold's, and he can do what would be disastrous for Arnold himself. Arminius and his creator go down to Reigate by rail, and in the carriage is, as Arnold calls him, 'one of our representative industrial men (something in the bottle way)'. When the manufacturer begins to talk politics, Arnold tries to soothe the conversation with 'a few sentences taken from Mr. Gladstone's advice to the Roumanians'. But—'The dolt! The dunderhead! His ignorance of the situation, his ignorance of Germany, his ignorance of what makes nations great, his ignorance of what makes life worth living, his ignorance of everything except bottles—those infernal bottles!'—that is Arminius's comment.[150] On another occasion, Arnold 'runs' to appease him with a 'powerful letter' by Mr. Goldwin Smith, published in the *Daily News*, and 'pronouncing in favour of the Prussian alliance . . . "At last I have got what will please you"', cries he. But Arminius only gives a sardonic smile, and puts it all down ungraciously to the Prussian needle-gun.[151] 'Your precious *Telegraph*',[152] he says bluntly; and of *The Times*, 'that astonishing paper'.[153] Arnold contrasts Arminius and himself directly: '"You make me look rather a fool, Arminius," I began, "by what you primed me with . . . ." "I dare say you looked a fool," says my Prussian boor, "but what did I tell you?"'[154] Even Arminius himself is made to emphasize just the contrast Arnold wishes us to see. 'I have a regard for this Mr. Matthew Arnold, but I have taken his measure. . . . Again and again I have seen him anxiously ruminating over what his adversary has happened to say against his

[149] vi. 243–4.
[150] vi. 245.
[151] vi. 246.
[152] vi. 235.
[153] vi. 275.
[154] vi. 274.

ideas; and when I tell him (if the idea were mine) that his adversary is a *dummkopf,* and that he must stand up to him firm and square, he begins to smile, and tells me that what is probably passing through his adversary's mind is so and so.' [155]

This example introduces one of Arnold's most characteristic manœuvres. Having introduced imaginary characters to speak for him, he recommends himself to the reader by interruptions that deny their excesses. Here he adds to Arminius's comment the footnote, 'A very ill-natured and exaggerated description of my (I hope) not unamiable candour'. In the Dedicatory Letter to *Friendship's Garland* he reports Arminius *verbatim* at length and then appears in his own person to retract: 'I doubt whether this is sound, Leo, and, at any rate, the D.T. [*Daily Telegraph*] should have been more respectfully mentioned'.[156] Arminius asserts dogmatically that Mr. Lowe is descended from Voltaire's insufferable optimist Pangloss: Arnold says that he believes there is no more than 'a kinship in the spirit'—Arminius, he fears, was suffering from a fixed idea.[157] Later, Arminius records an unbelievable interview with Lowe. Arnold observes gravely that since everything he makes Lowe say actually appeared in Lowe's printed speeches, there is reason to fear that the interview was only imaginary.[158] When Arminius tirades against the style of the *Daily Telegraph,* Arnold writes, 'though I do certainly think its prose a little full-bodied, yet I cannot bear to hear Arminius apply such a term to it as "incorrigibly lewd"; and I always remonstrate with him. "No, Arminius," I always say, "I hope not *incorrigibly*." '[159] And Arnold has a delightful footnote to 'Young Lion's' account of Dr. Russell mounting on horseback, in which he confesses sadly to not having found, in Russell's correspondence, quite the confirmatory descriptions that 'Leo' spoke of. 'Repeatedly I have seemed to be on the trace of what my friend meant, but the particular description he alludes to I have never been lucky enough to light upon'.[160] Sometimes the retraction by Arnold is implicit in one word, as when, pretending to report Arminius's own words about his inventor, he writes 'the newspapers which you are stupid [*sic*] enough to quote with admiration'.[161]

[155] vi. 252–3.
[156] FG. (vi. 237).
[157] vi. 260.
[158] vi. 272 n.
[159] vi. 284.
[160] vi. 347 n.
[161] vi. 235.

The general effect of this device, however, might possibly be misunderstood. Only a child would see Arnold in these disclaimers
alone. To a reader acquainted with the methods of irony the first rough
impression of his personality, coming perhaps from these by themselves,
is immediately corrected by a sense that he is author of the whole tissue
of assertion dramatized in character and disclaimer with an edge to it.
The undercurrent of meaning establishes that he is fully in earnest,
has something he thinks it important to say. But concern for his
message has not carried him away, and we see him still able to select
exactly the most telling mode in which to express it; we are made
to feel that there is no self-importance in a man who can so depreciate
himself, even in play. Arnold develops both that first rough impression
of himself, and the more complete impression, by explicit means: 'for
posterity's sake, I keep out of harm's way as much as I can I
sit shivering in my garret, listening nervously to the voices of indignant
Philistines asking the way to Grub Street . . . . I write with a bit
of coal on the lining of my hat.' [162] Here the reference to posterity
reminds the reader that it is all a game, though one, perhaps, that
serves a serious end. So it is when in *Culture and Anarchy*, he, after
some hovering, offers himself as an example of the Aristotelian extreme of *defect* in possessing the virtues of his own class. 'Perhaps
there might be a want of urbanity in singling out this or that personage
as the representative of defect . . . but with oneself one may always,
without impropriety, deal quite freely; and, indeed, this sort of plain
dealing with oneself has in it, as all the moralists tells us, something
very wholesome. So I will venture to humbly offer myself as an illustration of defect in those forces and qualities which make our middle
class what it is.' [163] He has done nothing, he confesses, to help uproot
the evils of church-rates, for example. He quite lacks the 'perfect
self-satisfaction' current among the Philistines. 'But these confessions',
he concludes, 'though salutary, are bitter and unpleasant.' Here again
the effect is two-fold: first, simply, of Arnold offering himself humbly
as an example of defect; and second, less simply, of Arnold being
sufficiently at ease and in command of himself (despite the unmistakable note of seriousness) to play a nice, an elaborate game of
self-apology that is also in a way self-praise. But these impressions
converge to make a single effect: that if Arnold ever had, like Dr.

[162] vi. 395–6.
[163] CA. (vi. 80–81). Cf. vi. 90, 'I again take myself as a sort of *corpus vile*
to serve for illustration in a matter where serving for illustration may not by
everyone be thought agreeable'.

Russell, a warhorse, it had the same history as the Cheshire cat, and there is nothing left of it but the grin.

This double sense in the reader of Arnold first as simply a man in the situation he describes, and second as a writer forming that situation, arises also when he contrasts himself and his opponents. The *Saturday Review*, he says,[164] maintains that we have 'found our philosophy'; but when obliged to travel almost daily on a branch line close to the scene of a railway murder, Arnold found his fellow-travellers so demoralized by fear that to begin with he thought they disproved this. 'Myself a transcendentalist' (the *Saturday Review* has accused him of it) 'I escaped the infection; and day after day, I used to ply my fellow-travellers with . . . consolations . . . "suppose the worst to happen", I said, addressing a portly jeweller from Cheapside; "suppose even yourself to be the victim; *il n'y a pas d'homme necessaire*" . . . All was of no avail. Nothing could moderate . . . their passionate, absorbing, almost bloodthirsty clinging to life . . . but the *Saturday Review* suggests a touching explanation . . . the ardent longing of a faithful Benthamite . . . to see his religion in the full and final blaze of its triumph.' Here our impression is in part of Arnold living through the experience, and in part of him as its gleeful inventor; and of his opponents, partly in their fictitious guise of Arnold's jeweller, partly in their real form, the *Saturday Review* that can write as it does in a world of branch lines, railway murders, and fat poltroons. Nor is it impossible for Arnold to modify his effect by giving us a sense of himself as writer, even when he is most serious. The passage from *The Times*, quoted above,[165] about conditions in the East End, is fitted by Arnold into a personal experience. 'This firm philosophy', he writes, 'I seek to call to mind when I am in the East of London . . . and indeed, to fortify myself against the depressing sights . . . I have transcribed from the *Times* one strain . . . full of the finest economical doctrine, and always carry it about with me . . . .'[166] Then he continues by quoting Buchanan on the Divine Philoprogenitiveness, observes that this must be a *penchant* he shares with 'the poorer class of Irish' and continues 'and these beautiful words, too, I carry about with me in the East of London, and often read them there'. Buchanan's 'fine line' of poetry, too, 'naturally connects itself, when one is in the East of London, with God's desire to *swarm* the earth with beings'. There is no mistaking the bitterness, but our sense of Arnold himself

---

[164] EC. i (iii, pp. ix–x).
[165] See p. 516.
[166] CA. (vi. 201).

is largely a sense of the control and the grim humour that give to that bitterness this expression.

These more elaborate examples, then, confirm the view that Arnold uses irony to widen his range of assertion, while still remaining within the range of tone that his outlook demands. It is one further method whereby he conveys a certain temper of mind by example rather than description, and it emphasizes once more than this temper is essentially what his work strives to express. This explains, too, why he is so prominent himself in his writings, why his personality is progressively revealed in a favourable light that the hostile reader, revolting from Arnold's whole attempt to persuade, labels complacency. Nothing will rigorously prove this label mistaken; but we tend less, perhaps, to call Arnold's method complacent, once we have equipped ourselves with a proper knowledge of its detail, and its function.

A RHETORICAL ANALYSIS OF JOHN DONNE'S
"THE PROHIBITION"*   Thomas O. Sloan

Take heed of loving mee,

At least remember, I forbade it thee;
Not that I shall repaire my' unthrifty wast
Of Breath and Blood, upon thy sighes, and teares,
By being to thee then what to me thou wast;
But, so great Joy, our life at once outweares,
Then, least thy love, by my death, frustrate bee,
If thou love mee, take heed of loving mee.

Take heed of hating mee,

Or too much triumph in the Victorie.
Not that I shall be mine owne officer,
And hate with hate againe retailiate;
But thou wilt lose the stile of conquerour,
If I, thy conquest, perish by thy hate.
Then, least my being nothing lessen thee,
If thou hate mee, take heed of hating mee.

---

* "The Prohibition" was written in the closing decade of the sixteenth century. This text was collated from a number of MSS by Herbert J. C. Grierson and appears in his *The Poems of John Donne* (London, 1912), I, 67–68.

From *Quarterly Journal of Speech*, February, 1962. Reprinted with the permission of the Speech Association of America, and of the author.

Yet, love and hate mee too,

So, these extreames shall neithers office doe;
Love mee, that I may die the gentler way;
Hate mee, because thy love is too great for mee;
Or let these two, themselves, not me decay;
So shall I, live, thy Stage, not triumph bee;
Lest thou thy love and hate and mee undoe,
To let mee live, O love and hate mee too.

Though readers have been intrigued by the poetry of John Donne for over three hundred years, critical interest in his poetry has reached its highest peak in our time. Since the turn of the century few poets have been the subject of such wide and varied critical attention—particularly during the last three decades, when the viability of a critical method appeared to depend upon its usefulness in analyzing a poem by Donne. However, regardless of their type of analysis, modern critics frequently indicate that the uniqueness of Donne's poetry lies in its modes of persuasion. "Disputatious," "argumentative," "having the look of logic"—these are typical of the terms critics use to characterize the special qualties of Donne's poetry. Perhaps it was inevitable, then, that our time should see the publication of a major scholarly work devoted in part to exploring certain possible connections between Donne's poetry and Renaissance rhetoric.[1] And, considering the nature of modern criticism, perhaps it was also inevitable that a major modern critic should respond by warning readers against viewing Donne's complex, many-sided poetry through the unavoidable narrowness of rhetoric.[2] Yet in the midst of these positions a basic question remains to be answered: of what value, if any, is a specific Renaissance rhetorical theory in examining a specific poem by Donne? Though the question is limited, its answer should have relevance for larger theoretical questions concerning the use of rhetorical theory in exploring the province of poetry.

For a rhetorical analysis of Donne's poetry the Ramist system of "logic" and "rhetoric" is most serviceable, not only because Ramism has received extensive treatment in recent scholarship but also because it is representative of intellectual developments of Donne's day. Recent scholarship in the history of Renaissance rhetoric[3] and in the

[1] Rosemond Tuve, *Elizabethan and Metaphysical Imagery* (Chicago, 1947). See esp. ch. xii.

[2] William Empson, "Donne and the Rhetorical Tradition," *Kenyon Review*, XI (1949), 571–587.

[3] For example, Wilbur Samuel Howell, *Logic and Rhetoric in England, 1500–1700* (Princeton, 1956); and Walter J. Ong, S.J., *Ramus, Method, and the Decay of Dialogue* (Cambridge, Mass., 1958).

relation of rhetoric to Renaissance poetry [4] has underscored the importance of Ramism and increased modern understanding of Ramist theories. One of the most striking aspects of these theories is that they were in many ways a natural outgrowth of the Renaissance intellectual heritage. For example, at the same time that Peter Ramus began his educational reforms in France in the middle of the sixteenth century, the precepts of *inventio* and *indicium* in "logic" (actually, dialectic) virtually duplicated the precepts of *inventio* and *dispositio* in rhetoric. As part of his reform, Ramus resolved the confusion by depriving rhetoric of its first two processes and telling poets and orators that henceforth they were to seek invention and disposition in logic and only *elocutio* (style), plus *pronuntiatio* (delivery) for orators, in "rhetoric." When Ramus's treatise on logic is coupled with the rhetoric written by his disciple Omar Talon, the two works can be seen as clever reorganizations of four of the traditional five parts of rhetoric. Ramus's Protestantism and his "martyrdom" in the St. Bartholomew's Day Massacre (1572—the year in which, according to many scholars, Donne was born) served to increase the popularity of his theories in England. By the time Donne entered Cambridge, Ramism had already become a strong influence at that university, and Ramist logic and rhetoric remained the single most important rhetorical system throughout Donne's lifetime.[5]

But analyzing Donne's poetry by means of Ramist invention, disposition, and elocution need not necessarily assign Ramism any singularly influential role in the creation of that poetry. In the first place, Ramism certainly mirrored its own time, but in the complexities and turbulence of that time there were countless aspects which could have conspired to produce the special qualities of Donne's poetry. For that matter, in those few characteristics which distinguish Ramism from other rhetorical systems of its time, Donne is distinctly non-Ramist: e.g., his involute, paradoxical, ambiguous statements are unlike the "plain style" the Ramists favored. Secondly, like most rhetorical systems in the Renaissance, Ramism emphasized the similarities between oratory and poetry, but it was peculiarly indifferent to the unique powers of poetry. So far as the Ramists were concerned, the characteristic which distinguished poetry from the rest of rhetoric was merely rhythm.[6] Thus, any attempt to characterize Ramism as a

[4] For example, Tuve; and Sister Miriam Joseph, *Shakespeare's Use of the Arts of Language* (New York, 1947).

[5] All of the Ramist textbooks examined for this discussion, and cited in the footnotes, were published during Donne's youth.

[6] Ong, pp. 281–283.

complete theory of poetry is useless. However, once these facts are recognized, Ramist theory remains the most useable one for a *rhetorical* analysis of Donne's poetry.

"The Prohibition" is a good example of Donne's poetic manner. It was probably written during Donne's prodigal youth, and perhaps belongs to that group of poems Ben Jonson had in mind when he remarked to Drummond that Donne had written his best poetry before the age of twenty-five. All of these early poems employ the conventions of a persuasion-situation in which Donne speaks in monologue to convince another person or in soliloquy to convince himself. Also, "The Prohibition" contains Donne's characteristic, striking images. Finally, the arrangement of material in "The Prohibition" is conspicuous, as it is in many of Donne's poems.

Except for the obvious fact that the poem is a monologue addressed to a loved one, the full persuasion-situation of the poem is only implied. In realizing these implications, certain assumptions can be made on the basis of the careful wording Donne employs, and these assumptions in turn are strengthened by correspondences and contrasts in form. In a general way all three stanzas correspond: each has eight lines; each has the same rhyme scheme; and each has the same statement-proof-conclusion movement with the statement and conclusion expressed in couplets and the proof in the enclosed four lines. But certain differences serve to segregate the third stanza from the other two, differences more subtle than the variation in the couplet rhymes. Ramist disposition provides terminology that indicates these subtle differences, and Ramist invention gives their rationale. But, having named the tools, we are still left with the problem of meaning, and to complete our search we have no recourse but verbal analysis. To anticipate this discussion somewhat, the rest of the persuasion-situation appears to be this: first, though now the woman addressed appears indifferent toward him, he loves her so intensely that she cannot remain indifferent (how like Donne to confront this indifference with "Take heed of loving mee"); second, her present attitude toward him is so vague that she may yet choose to love him or to hate him, or both to love and to hate him, while he has no choice but to love her; third, her capacity for emotion is less than his.

He begins the statement of his argument in the first stanza by warning her not to love him, but in order to exonerate himself of the consequences should her emotions turn to love for him, he begs her to "remember" that he has warned her. The proof (lines 3–6) contains an interesting quality comparison which sharply indicates the difference in their capacities for emotion. Sighs and tears, as Elizabethan psychology believed, were "the two most immediate and natural ways" whereby the heart found relief from the dangers of excessive passion.[7] But so far greater is Donne's passion that he could find relief only through the expenditure of breath and blood, which being made of the same elements as "sighes" (air) and "teares" (water) heighten the directness of the quality comparison. This was an "unthrifty wast" on his part, for the returns of his investment were less than profitable, so much so that the loss could be repaired only by causing a like waste on her part. But if she loves him, or when she loves him, he could repair this waste not upon her breath and blood, but merely upon her sighs and tears—her capacity for emotion is that much less than his. The proof is expressed in the "not this, but that" form which the Ramists call the discretive axiom.[8] Donne tells her to beware of loving him, not because he plans to repair his loss by showing her that indifference which she has shown him, but because great passion—both of them in love—can cause death. Probably not her death, however. The concluding couplet indicates that it is he, with his always greater intensity of passion, whose life would be suddenly, "at once," outworn by an excess of joy. He concludes persuasively, his concern apparently only for her, that her love could be frustrated by his death. The conclusion is expressed conditionally: if you love me (and I don't really know that you do), beware.

It is the denial of this condition which leads Donne to the point of his second stanza, if you do not love me . . . . Perhaps because of his own intensely emotional state, he cannot conceive a passionate alternative any less extreme than the direct opposite of love. Another reason why hate is the subject of the second stanza (and why the negation of both love and hate naturally follows in the third) lies in a rhetorical principle of arrangement. For this principle we must turn not to disposition but to the one place in invention that is most important to questions of arrangement, distribution, "when the whole is distributed into his partes." According to Fraunce, "the more that the partes doo disagree among themselues, the better is the diuision.

---

[7] J. B. Bamborough, The Little World of Man (London, 1952), p. 128.

[8] See Abraham Fraunce, The Lawiers Logike (London, 1588), fol. 96v; Dudley Fenner, The Artes of Logike and Rhethorike (Middelburg, 1584), sig, Cir; and Roland MacIlmaine, The Logike of the Most Excellent Philosopher P. Ramus Martyr (London, 1581), p. 79. Although all three writers exemplify this axiom with an "although . . . yet" construction, Fenner, and Fraunce state that the axiom is fittest to dispose arguments from the place divers, and all three state that among the signs of the divers argument are the "not this, but that" constructions.

By which it appeereth that the best diuision must be of partes that be most repugnant, which can bee but two, therefore *Dichotomia* is most excellent, a diuision consisting onely of two partes." [9] Though the Ramists cannot claim to be the sole exponents or defenders of the persuasive force of argument by dichotomy, the dichotomizing arrangement was associated with the Ramist movement,[10] which could have brought fresh attention to this ancient device. In any case, the dichotomy is the basic principle of arrangement in this poem. Donne moves from one extreme in the first stanza to its opposite in the second; these two extremes in turn become half of a dichotomy which is completed in the third stanza. As noted below, this dichotomozing arrangement both accounts for and is enhanced by subtle structural characteristics.

Donne warns her not to hate him, but the hate of which he speaks is the hate that would arise from her exulting in the fact that she has brought him to his knees. He is completely at her mercy, and once she takes "too much triumph in the Victorie," her emotion becomes hatred. Again, the proof (11–14) of the statement is expressed in a discretive axiom. But while in the first stanza he employed images from commerce and psychology, in this stanza (both statement and proof) he speaks in terms of organized hate, war. The imagery of these two stanzas aids their contrast, and their structure aids their correspondence. Particularly in his psychological concepts in the first stanza, Donne gives the signs and terms of passionate intensity ("Breath," "Blood," "sighes," teares," "outweares," "frustrate"), but the imagery of war produces the opposite effect; it makes the hate formal and cold. He tells her that he would not return her hate (he gives himself no alternative to his present state), but her day as conqueror would be shortened by the death of her conquest. The conclusion, too, is expressed in exactly the same syntactical form as that used for the conclusion of the first stanza, conditionally; *if* you hate me (and I don't really know that you do), beware, for my death, caused by your hate, would make you less than that conqueror you had become.

The function of "Yet," which begins the third stanza, is best described with the Ramist phrase "segregative conjunction," for this stanza completes the argument of the entire poem by forming the

[9] Fraunce, fol. 57[r].

[10] According to Howell, Ramus's "followers tended to construe the natural method and the law of justice to mean the severest kind of dichotomizing, as if any given idea had only two members, one completely insulated from the other" (p. 163); see also p. 186.

argument into a dichotomy. As in the first two stanzas, the proof is expressed in a sentence of two parts (19–22); but whereas in the first two stanzas these two parts began with "Not that" and "But" to form discretive axioms, in this stanza the two parts are segregated by "Or" to form a disjunctive axiom—the best form for disposing a distribution of two opposites, a form which accords with the increasingly strict dichotomizing movement of the poem. Moreover, since the discretive and the disjunctive are the two types of segregative axioms,[11] there are both correspondence and contrast between the proof in the third stanza and that in the other two stanzas. In proving his opening statement, Donne asks her to love him that he "may die the gentler way"; the comparison is between his actual death, which would be caused by the absence of her love, and the "gentler" death of sexual intercourse (the last three words in the line cause "die" to lose some of its dimension as an Elizabethan trope and to become more of a literal statement than a pun). And he asks her at the same time to hate him because her love alone could cause his (literal) death. Or, as he explains, there is the other sense in which "these extreames shall neithers office doe." Having first considered the effect of her love-and-hate emotions on himself, each serving to counteract the effects of the other, he now considers a possible effect within her. The two emotions may destroy themselves, so that she may become incapable of feeling either emotion toward him; he may therefore be saved, beyond the dangers of death, to serve as a live demonstration of her powers and not as a dead "triumph," as temporary as a funeral procession. The conclusion of the stanza accords with the conclusions of the first two stanzas; it begins with a "lest" clause and ends with a command. In the "lest" clause, he is logically the last member of the list, for throughout the poem he has maintained a position secondary to her, to her love, and to her hate, and in every instance he has heightened the persuasiveness of his appeals by showing that the worst effect of his destruction is that it would undo her love and her hate. "To let me live," which begins the final line of the stanza, is a dramatic change from the conditional clauses that began the last lines of the first two stanzas; furthermore, having mentioned himself last in the preceding line, he comes first in this, thereby achieving added emphasis.

The whole poem eventually creates one dichotomy: she may (1) either love or hate him, or (2) both love and hate him. It is proper

[11] See Fraunce, fol. 95ᵛ; Fenner, *loc. cit.;* MacIlmaine, *loc. cit.*

that the two parts of the first alternative be disposed in stanzas which closely correspond in structure, because such an arrangement helps the reader to see that these two parts form the first alternative of a dichotomy, and because such an arrangement enhances the argument that although the nature of love may differ from the nature of hate, the two as causes produce the same fatal effect. It is precisely because these two produce the same effect—his death and the consequent frustration of her love or lessening of her victory—that the first alternative is ruled out. The second alternative would not undo her love, her hate, and him, and the contrasting structure of the third stanza enhances the difference. But the third stanza also needs *some* correspondence to the others, not only because of the prosodic requirements of songs and sonnets, but also because of the unvarying grammatical-logical-rhetorical insistence on parallelism in the construction of alternatives in a proposition. Therefore, the proof in the first two stanzas is disposed in discretive axioms and the proof in the third stanza is disposed in a disjunctive axiom, but both types belong to the category of segregative axioms. Furthermore, although there is a correspondence in the couplet form of the statement and conclusion of each stanza, the couplets of the last stanza employ rhymes which differ from those of the couplets in the first two stanzas. Or we may note this last correspondence and contrast in another way: each stanza is a kind of figure the Ramists call *epanalepsis,* "when the same sound is iterated in the beginning and ending." [12] The epanalepses of the first two stanzas ("Take heed of loving mee . . . take heed of loving mee," "Take heed of hating mee . . . take heed of hating mee") correspond to each other but contrast with the epanalepsis of the last stanza ("love and hate mee too . . . love and hate mee too").

Finally, no Ramist analysis—not even a partial one such as this—would be typical without the use of a bracketed, dichotomized diagram to represent arrangement.[13] Whereas the Ramists would cast a paraphrase of the entire poem in diagrammatic form, the following dia-

[12] Abraham Fraunce, *The Arcadian Rhetorike* (London, 1588); reprint ed. Ethel Seaton (Oxford, 1950), p. 45. Unlike Henry Peacham (*The Garden of Eloquence* [London, 1593], who in discussing the figures of repetition makes neat distinctions between "members," "clauses," and "sentences," both Fenner and Fraunce use the word "sentence" loosely. Fraunce's examples indicate that repetitions may be made at the beginning, middle, or end of some unit that may properly be thought to have a beginning, middle, or end—be that unit a phrase, a clause, a sentence, or a line, or even a stanza of poetry.

[13] An excellent example of the use of the dichotomized diagram in literary analysis is given by Fraunce, *The Lawiers Logike,* foll. 120ʳ.

gram is a simplification. The statement and development (proof and conclusion) of each stanza is represented; the brackets indicate the dichotomized arrangement of the poem.

"Take heed of loving mee"

discretive
axiom

"Then, least . . .
take heed of loving mee"

"Take heed of hating mee"

discretive
axiom

Yet

"Then, least . . .
take heed of hating mee"

"love and hate mee too"

disjunctive
axiom

"Lest . . .
love and hate mee too"

It would appear that a rhetorical analysis of this poem is useful in exploring the connection between structure and meaning. This analysis of arrangement and the observations concerning style encompass a large part of what is meant by *form*, which in poetry helps to communicate meaning. Although this analysis may not suggest that the form is extraneous or obtrusive or even absurd (qualities of form often denoted by our modern pejorative *rhetorical*), this analysis does suggest that the form is isolable, that it somehow has its own purposes to serve, or that it can even be enjoyed for itself without a full realization of meaning. The proportions of arrangement and the contrasts of imagery satisfy, perhaps even cloy, the mind's desire for order; at the same time these qualities help the reader to a partial understanding. For example, the conditional conclusions of the first two stanzas indicate the vagueness of her present attitude, and the correspondence in stanzaic structures helps indicate the formation of dichotomies. Form communicates poetic meaning, but does not contain it. Although a fuller realization of meaning than that so far arrived at will be indicated in terms of a trope, the whole poem, with all its variations, shades, and ambiguities, will not stop at the boundaries of rhetoric.

What does the poem finally come to? Donne is deeply vexed by the fact that the woman he is passionately in love with is treating him with indifference. He shows first that neither love nor hate is preferable to this indifference. Then he shows in the last stanza that the best, the safest, attitude for her to take toward him is compounded of love and hate, in which the two emotions cancel one another—leaving her with an attitude of indifference! With no choice but to love her, he actually protests her indifference (which in the past has caused his waste of breath and blood) by begging for her indifference so that he may serve as a living pageant of the extreme devotion she can inspire in one man. What the poem finally comes to is best characterized by that overused term of modern Donne criticism, a term well known to the Ramists: *irony*. The poem is a carefully stated plea for her love. Perhaps she loves him now. If she does, the intensity of her love is so much less than his that it is difficult for him to tell whether she loves him or not. In fact, she may even hate him. In either case, however, his death is certain. Her emotions, vague though they may be, are too great for him! Therefore, it is best that her emotions be compounded of love and hate—so that he may know the joys of love with the opposite emotion as a safeguard against its fatal effects, or so that she becomes totally indifferent toward him and he lives on as her conquest, not dies as her captive. It is not a large logical jump, and no emotional jump at all, to see that Donne is begging for the return of his love, in kind. Nor must one make a much larger jump to state that in light of the quality comparisons of her capacities for emotion and his, Donne is virtually defying her to return his love.

Irony is a term not confined merely to formal considerations, such as the development of the argument from protesting indifference to begging for indifference. It could also describe the voice of the speaker, as Fraunce realized when he stated that irony is "perceiued by the contrarietie of the matter it selfe, or by the manner of vtterance quite differing from the sense of the wordes, for then it is apparent that wee speake but iestinglie, and not as wee thinke." [14] However, there is more to the quality of Donne's voice than ironic jesting, just as there is more to the poem than ironic pleading for her love. Donne presents his indifferent loved one with a brilliantly conceived and cogent argument for continuing her indifference, and at the same time he interfuses

[14] *The Arcadian Rhetorike*, p. 10.

the argument with his desire for her love; for example, the drama enacted on this "Stage" could only be an "unthrifty wast" of his "Breath and Blood."

In short, the poem has both cogent argument and irony. Because it is a poem, we are not forced to choose between the two. We can have the poem both ways: in terms of its organization (*dispositio*) and in terms of its tone (*elocutio*). Or these two ways can be regrouped by employing a strategy honored by at least two decades of New Criticism, to speak of a poem as possessing both "structure" and "texture." The "structure" is the formal means of establishing the argument; essentially it involves the procedures of reasoning in a poem. In this analysis, "structure" would be virtually synonymous with *dispositio*. By making us aware of the dichotomy convention, the "structure" of this poem shows us the validity of Donne's plea for her indifference as the safest course for her emotions to take. Although the poem has the look of reason, it has the manner of irony. "Texture" involves everything not included under "structure": situation, meter, rhyme, imagery. In this analysis it would be virtually synonymous with *elocutio*. It is the "texture" which gives the poem its irony—for example, the force given the quality comparison in the first stanza by "Breath," "Blood," "sighes," and "teares," or that in the last stanza by "Stage" and "triumph," or the persuasion-situation in which a man in love protests his loved one's indifference. "Structure" and "texture" are two not necessarily discrete views of the same phenomenon; after all, both "structure" and "texture" are *in* the poem; the voice that presents the poem is not just ironic, it is also pleading a rigorously established case. At the very least, a rhetorical analysis provides local habitations and names for these constituents of poetic meaning.

AIDS TO ANALYSIS

In general, in these "Aids to Analysis," we have sought to question each selection in a way that will first of all test the student's meaningful understanding of the essay he is reading, and of the issues raised by a careful reading. We have attempted secondly to integrate the questions as much as possible: thus, a student reading the questions for Natanson's essay in the first section, will have his attention directed to Weaver's later essay on the *Phaedrus*. Nor have we integrated essays only; we have integrated ideas as well. Thus, quite early in the volume, in the questions accompanying the essays by Bryant and Wimsatt and Brooks, the students are asked to view the concept of "dialectic" in differing ways; nor is this key idea dropped after the book's opening section; later sets of questions compel the student to re-consider the concept in other contexts. Finally, we have included questions whose complete answer will demand that the student turn in an outside paper; frequently such questions include also references to other useful works on rhetoric.

Each instructor will, of course, use the questions according to the needs of his class; we emphasize only that the questions are a closely-integrated, functional part of the text as we have designed it.

Bryant: "Rhetoric: Its Function and Scope," p. 3

1. After finishing the entire essay, do you think that the following statement by Bryant, made early in the essay, is justified? "I shall not try to to present a digest of rhetoric or even an explanation of the main principles of rhetorical method . . . . I intend to discuss no particular system of rhetoric, but the functions and scope which any system will embrace."
2. What finally is the definition of rhetoric that Bryant accepts? Of what value is his exposition of various other meanings?
3. Explain what is meant by the assertion that the limitations of the theory of Aristotle are "historical rather than philosophical."
4. Distinguish between artistic and non-artistic means of persuasion.
5. What is meant by "Rhetoric is method, not subject"?
6. Distinguish between the meanings of dialectic and rhetoric.

Duhamel: "The Function of Rhetoric as Effective Expression," p. 36

1. What is the fundamental purpose of the essay? Is Duhamel attempting to write a brief sketch of the early development of rhetoric? Is he proposing a new "philosophy" for rhetoric? Is he providing a basis for rhetorical criticism? Is he attempting to provide a basis for a new history of rhetoric?
2. In discussing the rhetorical systems of Aristotle and Plato, Duhamel seems, initially, to be concerned about the differences between the

systems of the two men. Near the end of his essay, however, he writes: "The rhetoric of Plato, Aristotle, Cicero, and Quintilian may be said to be founded upon a belief in the perfectability of man, the existence of truth, and the possibility of its acquisition by the individual." This statement would seem to be one identifying the systems of Aristotle and Plato. Is there a contradiction here, or has Duhamel provided some larger framework within which the two systems are compatible or at least comparable?

3. Explain each of the statements given below in relation to Duhamel's general thesis:
   (a) "Rhetoric is better thought of as an idea, the concept of effective expression, than as a set or collection of principles with an abiding purpose."
   (b) "The rhetorical is determined by the epistemological."
   (c) "If histories of rhetoric are to be written after first postulating a definition of the concept and then reexamining the history of the assumed concept, the resulting inquiry would be the history not of rhetoric but of one concept of rhetoric."
   (d) "A re-evaluation of the conception of rhetoric, therefore, requires a recognition of the relation of effective speech to truth and to style."

4. Explain briefly the development of rhetoric in a society dominated by the Stoical philosophy.

Ong: "The Province of Rhetoric and Poetic," p. 48

1. Why does Ong say that his discussion of the differences between rhetoric and poetic will be philosophical?
2. Why are both rhetoric and poetic "logical arts"?
3. How finally is rhetoric distinguished from poetic? And how are both distinguished from logic?

Natanson: "The Limits of Rhetoric," p. 56

1. What historical data does Natanson employ in arguing the inadequacy of rhetoric conceived of as functional or dynamic?
2. The term "dialectic" is central to Natanson's analysis. Prepare an extended definition of this term.
3. Natanson admits a fundamental debt to the insights contained in Richard Weaver's "The *Phaedrus* and the Nature of Rhetoric" (reprinted in the present volume, pp. 311–329). From your careful reading of Natanson's essay, do you think he would agree with this generalization from Weaver: "All of the terms in a rhetorical vocabulary are like links in a chain stretching up to some master link which transmits its influence down through the linkages. It is impossible to talk about rhetoric as effective expression without having as a term giving intelligibility to the whole discourse, the Good." (cf. p. 327).

Hunt: "On the Sophists," p. 69

1. Summarize the traditional picture of the sophists (inspired by Plato) that Hunt modifies and, in part, corrects. Why has Plato's opinion so often been accepted so uncritically?

2. Hunt studies four figures: Prodicus, Hippias, Protagoras, and Gorgias. In what way is each a representative sophist? Can each be said to have made a unique contribution, as well, to the tradition of rhetoric?
3. In what ways does Hunt modify and correct the traditional notion of the sophist?

Jaeger: "The Rhetoric of Isocrates and Its Cultural Ideal," p. 84

1. What is the significance of the "savage scorn" with which Plato attacks the Sophists and their beliefs?
2. What strictly biographical factors aid us in understanding the career of Isocrates and his general cultural ideal?
3. Discuss the character and method of the arguments which Isocrates directs against the Socratics.
4. What, for Isocrates, were to be the most fruitful, practical results of rhetorical training according to his system?
5. As Jaeger points out, besides his opposition to the Socratic ideal, Isocrates opposed two other groups within Greek society. Identify these two other groups and explain briefly the arguments that Isocrates directed against them.
6. What is the relationship between Isocrates' insistence upon the creative character of oratory, and his general educational program?
7. Comment at length upon this statement: "There is in his [Isocrates'] system none of the inward tension that exists in the mind of Plato between the urgent will to action and the long philosophical preparation for action."

Wimsatt and Brooks: "The Verbal Medium: Plato and Aristotle," p. 111

1. Compare this interpretation of the *Phaedrus* with that by Richard Weaver (pp. 311–329).
2. Why does Plato conclude that rhetoric *is* philosophy?
3. What is meant by the distinction between *what* is to be said and *to whom* it is to be said?
4. Compare this interpretation of Isocrates with that of Werner Jaeger (pp. 84–111).
5. What is the essential difference between Aristotle and Isocrates? In what very important way are they alike?
6. What does Aristotle mean by the term *dialectia*?
7. Explain: "The function of rhetoric is not so much to persuade as to find out the existing means of persuasion."
8. Compare this interpretation of Aristotle with that of Friedrich Solmsen (pp. 128–137).

Solmsen: "Notes on Aristotle's *Rhetoric*," p. 128

1. Restate the argument against regarding Aristotle's *Poetics* and *Rhetoric* as complementary, or as moving along parallel lines. What is the value, for the student of rhetoric, in making clear the distinct and differing character of the two works?
2. Discuss the ways in which Aristotle brought philosophic weight and respectability to the practice of rhetoric.

3. In what kinds of rhetorical contexts is Aristotle most likely to abandon or dilute the philosophic manner?
4. On pp. 130–131 Professor Solmsen discusses briefly Plato's attempt in the *Phaedrus* to provide the "blueprint of a truly philosophical rhetoric." In what essential way does Solmsen's analysis differ from that provided by Weaver in his essay, "The *Phaedrus* and the Nature of Rhetoric" (pp. 311–329)?

Thonssen and Baird: "Cicero and Quintilian on Rhetoric," p. 137

1. Which of the five standard divisions of rhetoric treated by Cicero and Quintilian does not receive treatment in Aristotle? From your reading of Aristotle, what reasons can you suggest for such an omission?
2. Cicero accords to *delivery* the "sole and supreme power" in rhetoric. Explain his reasons for doing so. Would a modern rhetorician be likely to accord *delivery*—taken in the classical sense—a position of such importance?
3. Judging from the excerpts given from his *Orator*, which of the three kinds of style did Cicero himself probably regard as most important? Most effective? What is the probable argument behind the remark quoted from Baldwin, that the concept of the three styles "has been vicious as pedagogy"?
4. Cicero is sometimes summed up as practical; Quintilian as ethical or philosophical. Discuss the leading elements in the systems of each man that might give substance to such a summation.
5. What is the general meaning of the term "status"? Do Cicero and Quintilian agree as to the meaning of the term?
6. In what sense is Quintilian's insistence upon the great value of extemporary speaking a reflection of his general approach to rhetoric?
7. Which one of Quintilian's specific tenets illustrates what Colson has called "the age-long antithesis between rhetoric and philosophy"?
8. Keeping in mind the general pattern of Aristotelian or Greek rhetorical theory, what are the general differences in spirit that mark the contributions of Cicero and Quintilian?
9. If both Cicero and Quintilian contribute to rhetoric relatively little of an original character, as Thonssen and Baird repeatedly point out, why are they such important and significant figures in the history of rhetoric?

Baldwin: "St. Augustine on Preaching," p. 158

1. Why should "the very character of Christian preaching seem necessarily to reject sophistic"?
2. What is the significance for homiletic and for rhetoric in St. Augustine's repeated recommendation of imitation?
3. Explain in detail how St. Augustine utilizes and modifies these Ciceronian formulas or doctrines: (a) "inform, please, move," (b) the three styles—plain, medium, grand.

McKeon: "Rhetoric in the Middle Ages," p. 172

1. In what ways did the rhetoricians of the Middle Ages seem to follow Cicero?

2. Describe the contributions of St. Augustine to the rhetorical tradition. Compare McKeon's interpretation of St. Augustine with that of C. S. Baldwin (pp. 158–172).
3. Why was rhetoric made subordinate to logic?
4. What was the relationship between rhetoric and theology?
5. Define the three main lines in which rhetoric developed during the Middle Ages.
6. What is McKeon's summary of the contributions of rhetoric from the fourth to the fourteenth century?

Crane: "English Rhetorics of the 16th Century," p. 212

1. What sort of reaction might a twentieth century writer or critic have to the terms "amplification" and "ornamentation"? What terms might he use in their stead? Why would he probably prefer other terms?
2. Outline and comment upon the contributions of the six "rhetoricians" treated by Crane, viz.: Leonard Cox, Richard Sherry, Thomas Wilson, Henry Peacham, Abraham Fraunce, and George Puttenham. Which of these figures is most important and why?
3. Discuss the significance of the continued use of classical sources by Renaissance rhetoricians. Were there any signs that this domination was beginning to weaken?
4. From the point of view of literary history, what is the value of a knowledge of Renaissance rhetorics?

Ong: "Ramist Rhetoric," p. 226

1. What are the implications of the fact that Ramist rhetoric reserves to itself only *elocution* and *pronunciation* and surrenders *invention* and *disposition* to dialectic?
2. How is Ramist rhetoric organized?
3. How would a Ramist define *trope, figure,* and *natural dialectic*?
4. In what ways is medieval education in rhetoric different from classical education?
5. What is the significant change that the "ornamentation theory" undergoes in Ramism?
6. Explain the place of Solon's Law in the Ramist system of rhetoric.
7. What is the distinction between rhetoric and poetry in the Ramist system? Why was it felt necessary to make a distinction?
8. Describe the "plain style" that the implications of Ramist rhetoric made inevitable.
9. What kind of poetry does the "Ramist mentality" produce? Why?
10. Explaining the full implications of the following sentences will provide a working summary of Ramist rhetoric:
    (a) "The deepest meaning of Ramist rhetoric is to be found in the general framework of man's changing attitudes toward communication, with which rhetoric is so inextricably involved."
    (b) ". . . it [Ramist rhetoric] is a rhetoric which has renounced any possibility of invention within this speaker-auditor framework . . ."
    (c) ". . . Ramist rhetoric is a rhetoric which has not only no invention but also no judgment or arrangement of its own."

Guthrie: "The Elocution Movement—England," p. 255

1. Eighteenth century England was notable for its veneration of classical models. In the light of such veneration, what reasons might be advanced to explain the rise of a "rhetorical" practice—elocution—which seems not to be indebted to classical models or practices?
2. In your own experience, does the study of elocution seem, today, to be given much attention? Cite examples of contemporary speakers who might be said to be elocutionists.
3. In the other essays in this section of the present volume, is there any data to suggest that an elocutionary movement was to be part of the "expected" development of rhetoric?

Weaver: "The Spaciousness of Old Rhetoric," p. 275

1. "Spaciousness" is the key to understanding this essay. How finally does Weaver define it?
2. What does Weaver mean by each of the following terms: the uncontested term, *ad hoc* definitions, enthymeme, aesthetic distance, impertinences, illustration, polite style?
3. ". . . the will was not present." Why is this the "most significant fact" in Weaver's explanation of the way the *uncontested term* was used by the orator of the old-fashioned mold?
4. Why is it necessary to look at "the diction of the old school"?
5. What is Weaver's answer to the question: "How was the orator able to use them [large and unexamined phrases] with full public consent when he cannot do so today?"
6. What conclusions can we come to about a civilization if we know that its debates and controversies are over extremely elementary matters?
7. What is the "aesthetic of the generalization" used by the nineteenth century speaker ("the old orator")?

Howell: "Renaissance Rhetoric and Modern Rhetoric: A Study in Change," p. 292

1. Why is the Renaissance a convenient point in time from which to measure changes in rhetoric down to our own day?
2. Using Ong's essay in the present volume (pp. 226–255), as well as Howell's exposition, discuss the differences between classical rhetoric and the Ramist rhetoric.
3. Howell explains very clearly the five changes observable between Renaissance and modern rhetoric. Is there any element or feature which seems to be common to each of these changes? Comment.
4. Why is the first change that Howell discusses—the separation of logic from the communication arts and its alignment with the theory of scientific investigation—perhaps the most significant change?
5. Read the essay by Hughes and Duhamel, "The Modern Uses of Persuasion," in the present volume (pp. 431–446), and discuss the "rhetoric" there described as a sixth "change" in rhetoric. What relationships does this sixth "change" have to the five described by Howell?
6. Why does Howell seem hopeful for future rhetoric only if "she en-

deavors always to see her present problems in the light of her long and illustrious history"?

Weaver: "The *Phaedrus* and the Nature of Rhetoric," p. 311

1. What are the three ways in which language can affect men? Why is this concept basic to an understanding of Weaver's reading of the *Phaedrus?*
2. What are the qualifications and characteristics of the "non-lover," the "evil lover," and the "noble lover"? How does Weaver relate each of these to the uses of language and rhetoric?
3. What is Plato's answer to the question: "If truth alone is not sufficient to persuade men, what else remains that can be legitimately added?"
4. Since ". . . there is no honest rhetoric without a preceding dialectic," what should be the specific relationship between dialectic and rhetoric?
5. Explain: ". . . this soul is aware of axiological systems which have ontic status."
6. How has Plato himself used dialectic and rhetoric in the composition of the *Phaedrus?*
7. After studying his quotation from Kenneth Burke, define the concept of language that Weaver is attacking.

Eubanks and Baker: "Toward an Axiology of Rhetoric," p. 329

1. Since the ultimate base of this essay appears in the following sentence, it is vital that you should be able to paraphrase it adequately: "One of the most poignant truths of the present human situation is its axiological impotence." Is "axiological" used here in the same way that Weaver used it in his interpretation of the *Phaedrus?*
2. What is a "rhetoric of non-commitment"?
3. What is the relevance of rhetoric to what Eubanks and Baker call the "value illness of twentieth-century man"?
4. What are the three steps in sketching the outline for an axiological approach to rhetoric?
5. What is achieved by proving that the classical rhetoricians had a keen sense of the relationship between rhetoric and values?
6. What is the "logical function" of rhetoric? How is this related to an axiology of rhetoric?
7. How is it that values themselves have suasive force?
8. Of what importance is the Lasswell list in the development of the authors' point in this essay?

Fogarty: "I. A. Richards' Theory," p. 345

1. Discuss the methodology or manner of procedure that Richards' "dialectical" bias leads him to adopt. In what fundamental way does such a methodology differ from the Aristotelian approach?
2. What is the function of metaphor in Richards' system? Discuss the possible significance for rhetoric and for rhetorical theory in the fact that Richards' concept of metaphor differs fundamentally from that apparently held by Aristotle.
3. What, for Richards, is "the most important single concern in an improved rhetoric or communication?"

4. Discuss the implications for Richards' entire system of this sentence taken from his *Speculative Instruments:* "The exploration of comprehension is the task of devising a system of instruments for comparing meanings."
5. Prepare concise definitions of the following key terms in Richards' thought:
   (a) reason
   (b) context
   (c) abstraction
   (d) tenor-vehicle-ground
   (e) reference-symbol-referent
   (f) protocols
   (g) instruments
6. In his article, "The Limits of Rhetoric," (reprinted in this book, pp. 156–65), Maurice Natanson asserts that I. A. Richards "fails to carry out a sustained inquiry into the philosophy of rhetoric." On the basis of your close reading of Fogarty's essay, support or refute Natanson's assertion.

Marie Hochmuth Nichols: "Kenneth Burke and the 'New Rhetoric' ", p. 367

1. Why is it necessary for Mrs. Nichols to make clear to the reader Burke's ideas with respect to the nature of literature?
2. What finally is Burke's concept of rhetoric? Why is freedom of the will so important to his concept?
3. One of the best ways of comprehending the sophisticated rhetorical ideas of Burke is by making a genuine effort to understand the meanings of some of his key terms: identification, communication, division, substance, form, attitude, pure persuasion, motive. Prepare extended definitions of these terms.
4. How does Burke link dialectic with rhetoric?
5. In the operation (or use) of Burke's rhetorical system, of what value is the "pentad"?

Elwood Murray: "The Semantics of Rhetoric," p. 384

1. What does Murray probably hope to gain rhetorically by adopting the dialogue form for his essay? What famous classical precedent may he have in mind?
2. Why does Murray consistently introduce semantic terminology and technique within the framework of traditional, Aristotelian rhetoric? Give at least two possible reasons.
3. This essay's subtitle is: "A Dialogue on Public Speaking." Does this mean that the subject matter would have little relevance to problems encountered in written discourse?
4. Would you characterize Murray's essay as an argument, a polemic, or simply an exposition? What is the importance of classifying it accurately?
5. Point out several passages which, taken together, provide a compact summary of some of the important principles of General Semantics.
6. In the same issue of the *Quarterly Journal of Speech,* in which Professor Murray's essay originally appeared, there is an article by Bower Aly entitled "The Rhetoric of Semantics," which is critical of the General

Semantics approach. Read Bower's essay and discuss the differences between his attitudes toward General Semantics and those of Professor Murray.

7. A recent study by Mother Margaret Gorman, *General Semantics and Contemporary Thomism* (Lincoln, Nebraska, 1962), is critical of the philosophic foundations of General Semantics. After a reading of Gorman's book, decide whether or not the supposed philosophic shortcomings of General Semantics would materially affect its use as a system for practical help in the practice of rhetoric. (The introduction to Mother Gorman's book was written by S. I. Hayakawa, a leading semanticist. His comments should also be taken into account in answering this question.)

Croft: "The Functions of Rhetorical Criticism," p. 403

1. Does Croft disdain or derogate contributions to history or biography made by conventionally-oriented rhetorical critics? Explain the basis of his objection, if any, to such contributions.
2. Why has the traditional rhetorical critic failed in, or hesitated at, the *evaluation* of speeches?
3. Discuss the question of the "difficulty" of Croft's methods.
4. What significance is there, for rhetoric generally, and for Croft's own position, in his assertion that "much of the really interesting literature on rhetoric has been written by scholars outside the field of Speech"?
5. Croft writes near the conclusion of his essay: "Like the creative theorist in economics or political science, we can no longer leave ethics to the philosophy department." Discuss this statement. (Such essays as those in the present volume by Natanson and Eubanks and Baker may be helpful in answering this question.)
6. After a careful reading of Croft's essay, does it seem to you that he is pointing out some single, pre-eminent flaw in the conventional system of rhetorical criticism? Does he, on the other hand, seem to be offering some central argument or method aimed at the "reformation" of rhetorical criticism?

Tuve: "The Criterion of Rhetorical Efficacy," p. 414

1. What does the author wish us to understand by the term "efficacy"?
2. In what ways is the criterion of efficacy a problem common to the poet and to the *rhetor?*
3. What significant conceptions between Renaissance and modern ways of thinking about poetry must Miss Tuve take into account?
4. Why is *ironia* the most important of the rhetorical figures?
5. In what way does the poet's "conscious designs upon the reader" have an effect upon imagery?
6. What is meant by the "tension maintained between the requirements of subject and of reader"? Why is it so important to understand this idea?

Booth: "Moulding Beliefs in Fiction," p. 426

1. It is advisable to read the whole of Booth's important work on the rhetorical criticism of fiction; but you can get a very good insight into

his principal ideas if you are able to understand and explain the following sentences and phrases:

(a) "He [the novelist] often defines for us the precise ordering of values on which our judgment should depend."

(b) "Overt effects to reinforce norms"

(c) "The skillful author will . . . make his rhetoric in itself a pleasure to read . . . ."

2. From the point of view of influencing the reader, the novelist must take into account (a) those beliefs which he is reasonably sure that the audience shares with him, and (b) those beliefs which the audience may not share or may even disagree with. Are the novelist's rhetorical problems (hence, his techniques) the same in both cases?

Hughes and Duhamel: "The Modern Uses of Persuasion," p. 431

1. Although their textbook is generally Aristotelian in approach, Professors Hughes and Duhamel are keenly aware of the new possibilities for persuasion created by the mass audience and mass-media techniques. The quotations given below summarize some of the main methods of this "new" rhetoric. After a careful study of the quotations, discuss the ethical questions which might arise from the use of such methods.

(a) "The mass media of communication have fostered the development of a language free of local or dialect chaarcteristics, and they have also fostered the development of neutrality of presentation."

(b) ". . . writing which is to be adapted to the circumstances created by the mass media of communication should be brief, terse, vivid, and tend towards the reiteration of a simple message rather than attempt to develop a complex argument."

(c) "The distinctive aspect of Motivation Research has been to search for the hidden motives instead of accepting the reasons which people commonly give to explain their behavior. The reasons people offer are usually fairly rational, or common sense reasons; their real motives are frequently irrational."

(d) "No small town audience would respond favorably to a speaker or writer who addressed himself directly to their condition as it really exists. They would not applaud a reminder that they were, in the words of Henry Thoreau, 'living lives of quiet desperation.' "

(e) "The writer must try to find some way of making his audience believe that he is conscious of individual differences in that group. Effective writing today depends upon an ability to convey the impression that it is trying to overcome the limitations imposed by the mass media and reaching out towards each individual as a personalized message."

(f) "The writer who hopes to persuade an audience should begin where the manufacturer begins, by determining what particular image product he wants to create."

2. Since the two quotations given below are surrounded by material which demonstrates how effective *non-rational* appeals can be, is it justifiable to say that Duhamel and Hughes are giving lip-service only to the tradition-hallowed notion of the primacy of the rational in rhetorical practice?

(a) "The speaker or writer should address himself to the group as a whole, take an honest stand with the best arguments he can muster, and leave the use of special appeals to special groups with special prejudices to the few occasions where such appeals are still possible."

(b) "[the modern listener insists] upon being treated as a rational person . . . ."

Burke: " 'Administrative' Rhetoric in Machiavelli," p. 446

1. Burke begins his essay with two long lists which treat, respectively, of the rhetorician's (or the prince's) "principles of persuasion"; and the audience's (or the subjects') "susceptibilities" and "resistances" to attempts at persuasion. What does Burke mean when he says that the difference between the two lists is "mainly grammatical"?

2. What is the value of comparing Ovid's *Ars Amatoria* to Machiavelli's *The Prince?* Could some other "book of instructions" from a different area of knowledge have served as well for Burke's purposes?

3. Restate the argument used by Burke in asserting that *The Prince* cannot be judged accurately if considered solely as a "scientific" work.

4. Kenneth Burke is one of the most important rhetorical thinkers of our time. Thus, he cannot be studied adequately in terms of a single essay. As a means, therefore, of deepening your appreciation of Burke's contribution to the field of rhetoric, seek an answer to these three fundamental questions:

(a) What, for Burke, is the "general" or normal function of rhetoric?

(b) What is the place, in Burke's whole system, of the rhetorical dimension?

(c) In what significant way or ways has Burke added to or extended classical rhetoric?

To answer these questions, you will need the aid of your instructor, who will suggest further reading in Burke and critics of Burke. As a beginning, the following sources will be helpful: Marie Hochmuth Nichols' essay on Burke, reprinted in the present volume, pp. 367–384; Daniel Fogarty, "Kenneth Burke's Theory," in *Roots for a New Rhetoric* (New York, 1959), pp. 56–87; the section in Burke's *A Rhetoric of Motives* (New York, 1955), pp. 3–46, entitled "The Range of Rhetoric"; and finally Burke's essay, "Curriculum Criticum," in the *second edition* of his *Counter-Statement* (Chicago, 1957), pp. 213–219.

Beaumont: "Swift's Rhetoric in 'A Modest Proposal'," p. 455

1. While Beaumont admits the central importance of Swift's use of "ethical proof," he asserts that the "implicit" elements involved "are made up of the whole tone of the essay and are not to be isolated." Does such an assertion unjustly debar the critic from analyzing a major component of a writer's method? Or is Swift's *Modest Proposal* a special, unique case?

2. Read Book IV of *Gulliver's Travels* and compare the "diminution" of man to animal there with what Beaumont has observed of the same process in the *Modest Proposal*.

3. Is "diminution" one of the classical methods of rhetoric? Is it an extension of some classical rhetorical principle? Explain.

4. Is the device of "refinement" most effectively used in oral or in written discourse?
5. Define and illustrate the following minor rhetorical devices used by Swift: appeal to authority; appeal to the emotions by ocular demonstration; rhetorical interrogation; litotes; parenthesis; implied refusal to argue the "obvious."
6. Using Beaumont's essay as a guide, read a representative satirical piece by some other eighteenth-century essayist such as Addison, Steele, Goldsmith, Johnson, and discuss the use of rhetorical devices present.

Ashin: "The Argument of Madison's 'Federalist, No. 10'," p. 481

1. Can the reader infer that the terms *definitions* and *consequences* are being used by Ashin in their *traditional senses?*
2. How has the first half of "Federalist, No. 10" led to the conclusion that "all citizens cannot be made alike in their passions, opinions, and interests"
3. How does a republic differ from a pure democracy? Why is this distinction by definition so important to Madison's argument?
4. Since Ashin's analysis of Madison's essay is reprinted here as a sample of rhetorical analysis, you might try his method on any of the other *Federalist Papers,* Abraham Lincoln's "Cooper Union Address," any of the discourses from Newman's *Idea of a University,* or one of Edmund Burke's orations.

Holloway: "Matthew Arnold: The Subtleties of Persuasion," p. 492

1. What sort of "positive doctrine" (if any) does Arnold advance?
2. Explain Arnold's "philosophy of history" and his "bedrock *credo.*"
3. Which of Aristotle's three sorts of proof is most clearly exemplified in Arnold? Note that while Holloway is clear in his explanation of Arnold's argumentative methods, he in no place refers to classical or Aristotelian rhetoric. Would Holloway's own exposition have possessed more force had he utilized the Aristotelian modes in discussing Arnold as a polemicist?
4. Holloway asserts that Arnold controls tone in *two* ways. What are these two ways, and how do they relate to Arnold's general argumentative pattern?
5. Identify and discuss briefly the four forms of argument that Holloway finds in Arnold's works.
6. Define the term "value frame" as Holloway uses it, and explain its threefold function as an argumentative device.
7. Why is Arnold, in comparison with such other "sages" as Carlyle and Newman, less original and forthright in his use of definition?
8. Even the most casual reader of Arnold's prose is struck by his ability to "coin" and to utilize such memorable phrases as "sweetness and light," 'Hebraism and Hellenism," and "the best that is known and thought in the world." What argumentative or persuasive function is served by Arnold's repeated use of such terms?
9. Explain the use, in Arnold, of a double range of quotation—first of all from such distinguished writers as Plato and Edmund Burke, and

secondly from Arnold's own opponents such as Bishop Colenso, Mr. Roebuck, and Hepworth Dixon.

10. Holloway maintains that Arnold's chief method is irony. In what way does Arnold use irony in suggesting and maintaining that tone which is so central and crucial a part of his total argumentative posture?

11. Holloway's essay is a remarkable instance of perceptive analysis; his whole book is worthy of the closest, critical attention. He maintains, however, in an introductory passage that: "A very important point is that we are not studying techniques of *persuasion* . . . ." That is, Holloway goes on, we are not embarking upon any traditional sort of "rhetorical criticism." Do you agree with him? Comment.

Sloan: "A Rhetorical Analysis of John Donne's "The Prohibition,'" p. 528

1. Is there any connection between Miss Tuve's discussion of the criterion of rhetorical efficacy in poetry and the method used by Sloan in his analysis of Donne's poem?

2. Consult the article by Empson referred to in footnote 2 and compare the views in it with those of Miss Tuve.

3. Is there a contradiction inherent in the two following quotations:
   (a) "For a rhetorical analysis of Donne's poetry the Ramist system of 'logic' and 'rhetoric' is most serviceable . . . because it is representative of intellectual developments of Donne's day."
   (b) ". . . in those few characteristics which distinguish Ramism from other rhetorical systems of its time, Donne is distinctly non-Ramist: e.g. his involute, paradoxical, ambiguous statements are unlike the 'plain style' the Ramists favored."

4. Does Sloan's brief account of Ramist rhetoric concur with that of Ong?

5. Define each of the following terms used by Sloan in his analysis of Donne's poem: discretive axiom, distribution, segregative axiom, disjunctive axiom, epanalepsis, and irony.

6. Explain: "In short, the poem has both cogent argument and irony. Because it is a poem, we are not forced to choose between the two. We can have the poem both ways . . . ."

FURTHER READING

When one considers the central position of rhetoric in the tradition of Western thought, and the relationship of rhetoric to such disciplines as philosophy, psychology, education, etc., it becomes apparent that the bibliography for rhetoric is an immense one. No effort will be made in this book to provide a bibliography that pretends to completeness. However, every effort has been made to provide a practical, working bibliography that will enable the user of the book to easily find his way into whatever aspect of rhetoric he wishes. The bibliography has, thus, been divided into two distinct sections. The first section is in the nature of a bibliographical essay whose main purpose is to direct the student to other bibliographical and reference tools in the field. The second section is an alphabetical listing compiled in the interests of broad, catholic coverage of the field of rhetoric and its relations. For most projects, the student should begin with the first section. After consulting the bibliography in the books and articles given therein, he may turn to the second section to find titles which seem to provide particular aid for his problem, or titles of interest which he has not been able to find in the reference tools to which he has already been directed. The second section will also serve as a convenient "finding list" for articles and books which the student wishes to read for his own interest or in pursuit of an assignment which has been given to him.

Part I

Any consideration of rhetoric should begin with its history. The latest listing of books and articles relating to the classical rhetoricians may be found, *passim*, in George Kennedy's *The Art of Persuasion in Greece* (Princeton, N.J., 1963). This can be supplemented, particularly for the Roman rhetoricians, by the bibliographies given in *Fifty Years of Classical Scholarship* (Oxford, 1954), edited by M. Platnauer. The bibliography in Donald L. Clark's *Rhetoric in Greco-Roman Education* (New York, 1957), pp. 267–276, is especially helpful also in that Clark gives an extensive list of "Greek and Roman primary sources in available editions and translations," as well as a selection of valuable secondary sources. The student seeking materials for a study of later developments in rhetorical theory and history might first turn to the extensive bibliographical notes that are an essential part of Richard McKeon's article, "Rhetoric in the Middle Ages," reprinted in this book, pp. 172–212. References to Renaissance rhetoric are given in these three books: William G. Crane, *Wit and Rhetoric in the Renaissance* (New York, 1937), pp. 253–76 (a very complete listing); Sr. Miriam Joseph, *Shakespeare's Use of the Arts of Language* (New York, 1947), pp.

401–7; and Rosemond Tuve, *Elizabethan and Metaphysical Imagery* (Chicago, 1947), pp. 429–34. The lists given by Professors Crane and Tuve provide the reader with a bibliography of primary sources for Renaissance rhetoric, as well as selected secondary sources.

No attempt has been made in this book to provide lists of translations of the classical rhetoricians; the student is referred for such listings to the works cited above. Since these works cover the period only through the Renaissance and its aftermath, we have provided in our bibliography a few listings for rhetoricians of the eighteenth century and beyond.

General references for the entire field of rhetoric will be found in the annual bibliography compiled in *Speech Monographs* by James W. Cleary and others. For the years prior to 1950, the student should consult the similar bibliography, edited by Frederick W. Haberman in the *Quarterly Journal of Speech*. A useful tool both in the bibliographical and the expository sense is *Speech Criticism* (New York, 1948), by Lester Thonssen and A. Craig Baird. This book might well serve as a starting point for most projects in rhetoric. A general listing of sources, including those which relate rhetoric to modern movements in literary and philosophical criticism is contained in Daniel Fogarty's *Roots for A New Rhetoric* (New York, 1959), pp. 141–158.

Part II

(Two abbreviations are used in the following list: *QJS* designates the *Quarterly Journal of Speech*; *SM* designates *Speech Monographs*.)

ADAMS, JOHN QUINCY. *Lectures on Rhetoric and Oratory*. 2 vols. Cambridge, Massachusetts, 1810.

ALY, BOWER. *The Rhetoric of Alexander Hamilton*. New York, 1941.

———. "The Rhetoric of Semantics," *QJS*, XXX (1944), 23–30.

ATKINS, J. W. *Literary Criticism in Antiquity*. 2 vols. Cambridge, England, 1934.

BAIRD, A. CRAIG. *Rhetoric: A Philosophical Inquiry*. New York, 1965.

BALDWIN, CHARLES S. *Ancient Rhetoric and Poetic*. New York, 1924.

———. *Medieval Rhetoric and Poetic*. New York, 1928.

———. *Renaissance Literary Theory and Practice*. New York, 1939.

BARRY, SR. M. INVIOLATA. *St. Augustine the Orator*. Washington, D.C., 1924.

BEAUMONT, CHARLES A. *Swift's Classical Rhetoric*. Athens, Georgia, 1961.

BLACK, EDWIN. "Plato's View of Rhetoric," *QJS*, XLIV (1958), 363–374.

BLAIR, HUGH. *Lectures on Rhetoric and Belle Lettres*. 2 vols. London, 1783.

BOOTH, WAYNE. *The Rhetoric of Fiction*. Chicago, 1961.

BRANDENBURG, EARNEST. "Quintilian and the Good Orator," *QJS*, XXXIV (1948), 23–29.

BRIGANCE, WILLIAM NORWOOD, and MARIE E. HOCHMUTH, eds. *A History and Criticism of American Public Address*. 3 vols. New York and London, 1943, 1955.

BROOKS, CLEANTH, and ROBERT PENN WARREN. *Modern Rhetoric*. 2nd ed. New York, 1958.

BRYANT, DONALD C. "Aspects of Rhetorical Tradition: The Intellectual Foundation," *QJS*, XXXVI (1950), 169–176, 326–332.

———, ed. *Papers in Rhetoric*. St. Louis, 1940.

———, ed. *The Rhetorical Idiom*. Ithaca, New York, 1958.

BURKE, KENNETH. *Counter-Statement*. 2nd ed. Los Altos, California, 1953.

———. *A Grammar of Motives*. Englewood Cliffs, New Jersey, 1945.

———. *The Philosophy of Literary Form*. Baton Rouge, Louisiana, 1941.

———. *A Rhetoric of Motives*. New York, 1950.

———. *The Rhetoric of Religion*. Boston, 1961.

———. "Rhetoric Old and New," *Journal of General Education*, V (1951), 203–205.

CAMPBELL, GEORGE. *The Philosophy of Rhetoric*. 2 vols. London, 1776.

CAPLAN, C. H. "Classical Rhetoric and the Medieval Theory of Preaching," *Classical Philology*, XXVIII (1933), 73–96.

CLARK, ROBERT D. "Biography and Rhetorical Criticism," *QJS*, XLIV (1958), 182–186.

CLARKE, MARTIN L. *Rhetoric At Rome: A Historical Survey*. London, 1935.

CONGLETON, J. E. "Historical Development of the Concept of Rhetorical Properties," *College Composition and Communication*, V (1954), 140–145.

COOPER, LANE. "The Rhetoric of Aristotle," *QJS*, XXI (1933), 10–19.

COPE, E. M. *An Introduction to Aristotle's Rhetoric*. London, 1867.

CORBETT, EDWARD P. *Classical Rhetoric for the Modern Student*. New York, 1965.

CRANE, R. S., ed. *Critics and Criticism*. Chicago, 1952.

D'ALTON, JOHN F. *Roman Literary Theory and Practice*. London, 1931.

DIETER, OTTO A. L. "Stasis," *SM*, XVII (1950), 344–369.

DRUMMOND, A. M., ed. *Studies in Rhetoric and Public Speaking in Honor of James Albert Winans*. New York, 1925; rptd., 1962.

FEDER, LILLIAN, "John Dryden's Use of Classical Rhetoric," *PMLA*, LXIX (1954), 117–130.

FLYNN, LAWRENCE J., S.J. "Aristotle: Art and Faculty of Rhetoric," *Southern Speech Journal*, XXI (1956), 244–254.

FRANCIS, W. NELSON. "Modern Rhetorical Doctrine and Recent Developments in Linguistics," *College Composition and Communication*, V (1954), 155–161.

FRITZ, CHARLES A. "From Sheridan to Rush: The Beginnings of English Elocution," *QJS*, XVI (1930), 75–88.

GENUNG, J. F. *The Practical Elements of Rhetoric*. Boston, 1888.

GILMAN, WILBUR. *Milton's Rhetoric on the Tyranny of Kings*. Columbia, Missouri, 1939.

GOODRICH, CHAUNCEY. *Select British Eloquence*. New York, 1852.

GORMAN, MOTHER MARGARET, R.S.C.J. *General Semantics and Contemporary Thomism*. Lincoln, Nebraska, 1962.

GRIMALDI, WILLIAM, S. J. "Rhetoric and the Philosophy of Aristotle," *The Classical Journal*, LIII (1958), 371–375.

GUTHRIE, WARREN. "The Development of Rhetorical Theory in America," *SM*, XIII–XVIII (1946–1950).

HARRINGTON, ELBERT W. *Rhetoric and the Scientific Method of Inquiry: A Study of Invention.* Boulder, Colorado, 1948.

HAYAKAWA, S. I. *Language in Thought and Action.* New York, 1949.

HERRICK, MARVIN T. "The Place of Rhetoric in Poetic Theory," *QJS*, XXXI (1948), 1–22.

HOLLAND, L. VIRGINIA. *Counterpoint: Kenneth Burke and Aristotle's Theories of Rhetoric.* New York, 1959.

HOLLINGWORTH, H. L. *The Psychology of the Audience.* New York, 1935.

HOWELL, WILBUR S. *The Rhetoric of Alcuin and Charlemagne.* Princeton, New Jersey, 1941.

HOWES, RAYMOND F., ed. *Historical Studies of Rhetoric and Rhetoricians.* Ithaca, New York, 1961.

HUGHES, RICHARD, and P. ALBERT DUHAMEL. *Rhetoric: Principles and Usage.* Englewood Cliffs, New Jersey, 1962.

HUNT, EVERETT L. "Dialectic: A Neglected Method of Argument," *QJS*, VII (1921), 221–232.

———. "Rhetoric As A Humane Study," *QJS*, XLI (1955), 114–117.

JAEGER, WERNER. *Paideia.* 3 vols. Gilbert Highet, trans. New York, 1943–1945.

JEBB, RICHARD. *The Attic Orators.* 2 vols. London, 1893.

———. "Rhetoric," in *Encyclopaedia Britannica*, XIX (1954), 247–248.

JONES, R. F. *The Triumph of the English Language.* Stanford, California, 1953.

KENNEDY, GEORGE. "The Earliest Rhetorical Handbooks," *American Journal of Philology*, LXXX (1959), 169–178.

KITZHABER, ALBERT R. *A Bibliography on Rhetoric in American Colleges: 1850–1900.* Denver, Colorado, 1954.

———. *Themes, Theories, and Therapy: The Teaching of Writing in College.* New York, 1963.

LA DRIÈRE, CRAIG. "Rhetoric and 'Merely Verbal' Art," in *English Institute Essays: 1948.* D. A. Robertson, Jr., ed. New York, 1949.

LEE, IRVING J. "Some Conceptions of Emotional Appeal in Rhetorical Theory," *SM*, VI (1939), 66–86.

McBURNEY, JAMES H. "The Place of the Enthymeme in Rhetorical Theory," *SM*, III (1936), 49–74.

McKEON, RICHARD. "Communication—Making Men of One Mind in Truth," in *Problems of Communication in A Pluralistic Society.* Milwaukee, Wisconsin, 1956.

MALONEY, MARTIN J. "The Use of Semantics," in *Problems of Communication in A Pluralistic Society.* Milwaukee, Wisconsin, 1956.

MARROU, H. I. *A History of Education in Antiquity.* G. Lamb, trans. London, 1956.

MINNICK, WAYNE C. *The Art of Persuasion.* Boston, 1957.

MORRIS, CHARLES. *Signs, Language, and Behavior.* New York, 1955.

MYERS, L. M. "Linguistics and the Teaching of Rhetoric," *College Composition and Communication*, V (1954), 166–171.

NATANSON, MAURICE. "The Privileged Moment: A Study in the Rhetoric of Thomas Wolfe," *QJS*, XLIII (1957), 143–150.

NEBERGALL, ROGER E., ed. *Dimensions of Rhetorical Scholarship.* Norman Oklahoma, 1963.

NICHOLS, MARIE HOCHMUTH. "I. A. Richards and the 'New Rhetoric,'" *QJS*, XLIV (1958), 1–16.

——. *Rhetoric and Criticism.* Baton Rouge, La., 1963.

NORTH, HELEN. "Rhetoric and Historiography," *QJS*, XLII (1956), 234–242.

OGDEN, C. K., and I. A. RICHARDS. *The Meaning of Meaning.* London, 1923.

OLSON, ELDER. "Rhetoric and the Appreciation of Pope," *Modern Philology,* XXXVII (1939), 13–35.

ONG, WALTER J. *Ramus and Talon Inventory.* Cambridge, Mass., 1958.

——. *Ramus: Method, and the Decay of Dialogue.* Cambridge, Mass., 1958.

PACKARD, VANCE. *The Hidden Persuaders.* New York, 1957.

PARRISH, W. M. "The Tradition of Rhetoric," *QJS*, XXXIII (1947), 465–467.

PERRIN, PORTER G. "Freshman Composition and the Tradition of Rhetoric," in *Perspectives on English,* ed. Robert C. Pooley. New York, 1960.

PETERSSON, TORSTEN. *Cicero: A Biography.* Berkeley, California, 1919.

PRICE, MARTIN. *Swift's Rhetorical Art.* New Haven, Conn., 1953.

RAHSKOPF, HORACE G. "John Quincy Adams: Speaker and Rhetorician," *QJS*, XXXII (1946), 435–441.

REID, LOREN. "The Perils of Rhetorical Criticism," *QJS*, XXX (1944), 416–422.

RICHARDS, I. A. *The Philosophy of Rhetoric.* New York, 1936.

——. *Speculative Instruments.* Chicago, 1955.

ROBERTS, W. RHYS. *Greek Rhetoric and Literary Criticism.* New York, 1928.

ROCKAS, LEO. *Modes of Rhetoric.* New York, 1964.

SAMS, HENRY W. "Fields of Research in Rhetoric," *College Composition and Communication,* V (1954), 60–65.

SANDFORD, WILLIAM P. *English Theories of Public Address: 1530–1828.* Columbus, Ohio, 1931.

SATTLER, WILLIAM M. "Conceptions of *Ethos* in Ancient Rhetoric," *SM,* XIV (1947), 55–65.

SCANLAN, ROSS. "The Nazi Rhetorician," *QJS*, XXXVII (1951), 430–440.

SCHMITZ, R. M. *Hugh Blair.* New York, 1949.

THOMPSON, WAYNE M. "A Conservative View of A Progressive Rhetoric," *QJS*, XLIX (1963), 1–7.

THONSSEN, LESTER, ed. *Selected Readings in Rhetoric and Public Speaking.* New York, 1942.

UNTERSTEINER, MARIO. *The Sophists.* Kathleen Freeman, trans. Oxford, 1954.

VOEGELIN, ERIC. "Necessary Moral Bases for Communication in A Democracy," in *Problems of Communication in A Pluralistic Society.* Milwaukee, Wisconsin, 1956.

WAGNER, RUSSELL H. "The Rhetorical Theory of Isocrates," *QJS*, VIII (1922), 322–337.

WALLACE, KARL R. *Francis Bacon on Communication and Rhetoric.* Chapel Hill, North Carolina, 1943.

WALLERSTEIN, RUTH C. "Rhetoric in the English Renaissance: Two Elegies," in *English Institute Essays: 1948*, D. A. ROBERTSON, JR., ed. New York, 1949.

WEAVER, RICHARD. *The Ethics of Rhetoric*. Chicago, 1953.

———. *Ideas Have Consequences*. Chicago, 1948.

WHATELY, RICHARD. *Elements of Rhetoric*. London, 1828.

WHITTEMORE, REED. "Literature As Persuasion," in *The Fascination of the Abomination*. New York, 1963.

WICHELNS, HERBERT A., ed. *Studies in Speech and Drama in Honor of Alexander Drummond*. Ithaca, New York, 1944.

WILLIAMSON, GEORGE. "The Rhetorical Pattern of Neo-Classical Wit," *Modern Philology*, XXXIII (1935), 55–81.

WIMSATT, W. K., JR. "Rhetoric and Poems: The Example of Pope," in *English Institute Essays: 1948*, D. A. ROBERTSON, JR., ed. New York, 1949.

WIMSATT, W. K., JR., and CLEANTH BROOKS. *Literary Criticism: A Short History*. New York, 1957.